1989-1990
HOCKEY
Scouting Report

1989-90
HOCKEY
Scouting Report

Michael A. Berger
Jiggs McDonald

Summerhill Press
Toronto

Published by Summerhill Press Ltd.
52 Shafesbury Avenue
Toronto, Ontario M4T 1A2

Cover photography: Bruce Bennett
Cover design: Andrew Smith

Printed and bound in the United States.

**The National Library of Canada has catalogued
this annual as follows:**

Berger, Michael, 1960-

                    Hockey scouting report

Annual.
1986/1987-
ISSN 0836-5148
ISBN 0-920197-89-2 (1989-1990)

1. Hockey - Scouting - Periodicals. 2. Hockey
players—Periodicals. 3. National Hockey League—
Periodicals. I. Davidson, John, 1953-.
II. McDonald, Jiggs. III. Title.

GV847.8.N3B4   796.96'26
C88-039002-6

DEDICATION

To the crew of Hockey Night at Skyrink
(a Monday night tradition dating back
to the late 1950s) for teaching
me how to actually play
this game.

ACKNOWLEDGEMENTS

You might think that the authors could do this book on their own after four years. Not so. We owe nods of thanks:

To Barry Watkins of the New York Rangers public relations office, and to Greg Bouris — Barry's counterpart for the New York Islanders. And thanks to the rest of the Ranger P.R. staff — Art Friedman, Ginger Killian, Matt Loughran and P.R. Director John Halligan — and those of the Islanders as well — Chris Botta, Steve Blinn, Cathy Schutte and Jim Johnson.

As always to our sources: the coaches, general managers, chief scouts, scouts and players who help us compile these reports. And thanks to the NHL personnel who ask for copies — so they can see what the competition is saying.

To Steve Casano, public relations intern for the National Hockey League, who provided much-needed team scoring and roster report information.

To Mike Lysko, for his unending help in promoting this book

And finally to my publishers, Jim Williamson and Gordon Montador at Summerhill Press, for their continued belief in this project.

Ladies and gentlemen, take a bow; I'm still picking up the first one.

Mike Berger NYC June 1989

Contents

The Authors   8
Introduction   9
We Told You So   10

Boston Bruins   12
Buffalo Sabres   33
Calgary Flames   56
Chicago Blackhawks   77
Detroit Red Wings   99
Edmonton Oilers   123
Hartford Whalers   146
Los Angeles Kings   169
Minnesota North Stars   191
Montreal Canadiens   212
New Jersey Devils   232
New York Islanders   252
New York Rangers   274
Philadelphia Flyers   295
Pittsburgh Penguins   317
Quebec Nordiques   342
St. Louis Blues   363
Toronto Maple Leafs   385
Vancouver Canucks   406
Washington Capitals   429
Winnipeg Jets   448

Index   469

The Authors

Michael A. Berger

The editor of GOAL Magazine, the NHL's official program, Mike has frequently written about hockey in international publications like SPORT Magazine and THE HOCKEY NEWS, and for television on DODGE HOCKEY WEEK. He has been heard as a featured commentator on the NHL Radio Network and for WFAN Radio in New York City, and has also served as a special color commentator for the Toronto Maple Leaf Radio Network.

Jiggs McDonald

A founder of the NHL Broadcaster's Association, Jiggs has been broadcasting hockey since 1967. He has been the play-by-play voice of the New York Islanders since 1980, and was first introduced to national audiences in February 1988 as part of the ABC Network's Calgary Olympic Games announcing crew. McDonald is also the first-string play-by-play man for SportsChannel America, the television network of the National Hockey League. He makes his home year-round in Dix Hills, N.Y., with his wife and two daughters.

Introduction

Welcome back to Year Four of the Hockey Scouting Report, the *only* hockey book that discusses players the way the hockey professionals do — by looking at what a player can and can't do, and why he can or can't do it.

What you're holding is the number one reference book on NHL player performance available today. Chances are, anything you see, hear or read about an NHL player's ability came from this book. Your team's radio and television broadcasters use it, the writers covering your team use it — and your team uses it.

Between these covers you get over 400 scouting reports presented in the same way hockey coaches, general managers, players and scouts all over the world present their views to their colleagues. And, in many instances, you're getting this info from those self-same coaches, general managers, players and scouts.

And you get all this with no-holds-barred — that's why our top-level sources have to stay anonymous. The truth, the whole truth and nothing but the truth — that's our motto.

And we can swear to that because of the thousands of hours we've spent researching during hundreds of games. We can swear to that because of the input we've gotten from NHL executives who share their expertise with us, and then read Hockey Scouting Report to see what the *other* big-wigs are saying.

And we can swear to that because we're the *only* hockey publication that analyzes players the way the pros do. Here's how the book works:

Each player's game is broken down into three parts, categories which consolidate the factors used by the pros to evaluate talent at all hockey levels. We discuss a player's skating, stickhandling, scoring, pass-ing, play-making, checking and defensive abilities in The Finesse Game. How he uses his body, whether he takes advantage of his size and strength, his balance, his ability — and willingness — to play physically and to fight in The Physical Game. How he relates to his teammates, whether he's frequently injured, if he works hard to improve his game and if he's dedicated to his profession in The Intangibles.

Each player report is augmented by a graphic that instantly illustrates where a shooter is most dangerous from. For goaltenders that graphic shows areas of weakness.

Each team section leads off with a team report, where we've listed players by either line combinations and defense pairing, or by position. Following that is a scouting report on team power play and penalty killing. A list of a club's best faceoff men closes the team review.

Some of those reports are highly arbitrary: sometimes we omit traded players, sometimes we don't. Sometimes blank spaces have been left in either the Line Combination or Defense Pairing section of the team reports. Two examples would be different left wings rotating onto different lines, or a defenseman whose partner has retired.

We even take ourselves to task for incorrect information. But — fair warning — you're going to have to wade through the list of what we got right first.

Once again, the Hockey Scouting Report brings the game to you in an intelligent, articulate and concise discussion of the players behind the headlines.

We hope you enjoy reading it as much as we enjoyed creating it.

We Told You So

Yeah, here we go — mouthing off again. By now, you know that we're proud of the information in this book; we get a lot of satisfaction in knowing we gave you solid information. But we also know that we made some mistakes, yet admit those freely — that way, you'll always know where we stand. And you'll be able to believe us when we say we're right, because we come right out and tell you when we've screwed up.

Here are last year's beauties. Among other things, readers of this book last year learned months ahead of time:

That Mark Johnson can't stay healthy. Ditto Bruce Driver. That Alain Chevrier was history in New Jersey — and that Bob Sauve would back up Sean Burke. That Jack O'Callahan isn't a full-time NHLer. That Murray Craven would have trouble holding a spot in the Flyer lineup. That Doug Crossman was outta here in Philly. Same with Mark LaForest. That Rick Tocchet was a 40-goal scorer — easy.

That Mike Bullard's production would fall off. That Ken Linseman, Gord Kluzak and Michael Thelven should invest in Blue Cross. That Rick Middleton would retire and that Tom McCarthy would be retired. Ditto Willi Plett.

That Pete Peeters is good enough to lose. That Mike Ridley was better than 30 goals. That Clint Malarchuk shouldn't consider himself at home in Washington. That Tom Fergus can't backcheck to save his life (he had the NHL's worst plus/minus rating last season). That Sean McKenna was a marginal NHLer. That Adam Oates could improve his playmaking at the NHL level, and that teammate Bob Probert was no better than questionable to remain in the NHL.

That Don Maloney (broken collarbone) was brittle, and that Norm Maciver wouldn't play regularly for the Rangers. That Gino Cavallini would score 20 goals, and that Minnesota's Craig Hartsburg and Dennis Maruk would retire. That Minnesota would dump Moe Manthta and that Ville Siren was injury-prone.

We said Perry Berezan was a goner from Calgary, and that Gilles Meloche, Perry Ganchar and Frank Pietrangelo were just as done in Pittsburgh. That Mario Lemieux would score more points that he ever did before, and that Paul Coffey would rediscover the 100 point mark.

That Darren Pang might not stay number one for the Hawks. That Steve Ludzik was eminently replaceable and that teammate Mike Stapleton was no better than marginal in the NHL.

We waved Adam Creighton and Doug Smith goodbye from Buffalo, and Pierre Larouche from New York City. We said Jari Kurri had tons to prove — *before* Wayne Gretzky was traded. We said Craig Muni would improve — he had the NHL's fourth best plus/minus last season.

If you read us last year, you knew that Jimmy Carson wanted out of Los Angeles (one not-so-small reason the Gretzky trade came off). That Ken Priestlay wasn't ready for full-time NHL duty, and that Ray Sheppard would have a much tougher time scoring this season. That Marcel Dionne would be sitting — not playing — last season. That Luc Robitaille could suffer a scoring let-down.

That John Tonelli's tenure with the Flames was finished; so was Paul Reinhart's. That Hakan Loob wasn't a 50-goal, 100-point scorer. That Calgary's Stanley Cup hopes rested on Mike Vernon's shoulders, and that Stephane Richer might have a problem with his new coach.

We said Chris Chelios would be a Norris Trophy contender (so he won, so sue us). That Mario Brunetta, Lane Lambert, Mike Eagles, Norm Rochefort and Jason Lafreniere would all bid adieu to Quebec. Same thing for Al Leiter of the Islanders and Marc Bergevin of the Blackhawks.

And finally, we mentioned that Vancouver's David Bruce had an injury problem, that Steve Weeks would split the goaltending evenly with Kirk McLean, and that Doug Wickenheiser would be leaving the Canucks.

Those were last season's beauties. Here are the beasts:

Andy Moog would back up Reggie Lemelin (he played more games than Lemelin); Borje Salming would play somewhere other than Toronto in 1988-89 (we were off by a season); Steve Chiasson is a defensive defenseman (that's why he led Wing blue liners in scoring); Joe Murphy would see more ice-time (honest — we meant the AHL). Richard Brodeur would benefit from a defensive-oriented team (maybe he did — in some senior league).

We happened to mention that Jocelyn Lemieux could help turn the Blues around (but we didn't mean by leaving them) and that the Penguins would count heavily on Steve Guenette (to open the door to the players' bench). Oh yeah —Dave (All Star) Manson can't handle the puck — 18 goals worth (and counting). We thought Buffalo had plenty of confidence in Calle Johansson, and that Mario Marois was an important part of the Jets (Obviously, Buffalo didn't have enough confidence in Johansson, and Marois wasn't *that* important to Winnipeg).

That John Tonelli would score very often (30 goals is often enough). That Dale Hawerchuk was a character player (yeesh!). We said Steve Rooney would stay in Winnipeg and that Steve Konroyd was the Islanders' defensive linchpin.

What's ahead this season? Just turn the page to find out.

Team Reports

BOSTON
BRUINS

LINE COMBINATIONS
BOB JOYCE-BOB CARPENTER-BOB SWEENEY
RANDY BURRIDGE-CRAIG JANNEY-CAM NEELY
KEITH CROWDER-KEN LINSEMAN-ANDY BRICKLEY

DEFENSE PAIRINGS
ALLEN PEDERSEN-RAY BOURQUE
GLEN WESLEY-GREG HAWGOOD
GARRY GALLEY

GOALTENDERS
REGGIE LEMELIN
ANDY MOOG

OTHER PLAYERS
LYNDON BYERS— Right wing
GREG JOHNSTON — Right wing
RAY NEUFELD — Right wing
MICHAEL THELVEN — Defenseman

POWER PLAY

FIRST UNIT:
KEITH CROWDER-KEN LINSEMAN-ANDY BRICKLEY
RAY BOURQUE-GARRY GALLEY

SECOND UNIT:
CAM NEELY-CRAIG JANNEY-BOB JOYCE

On the first unit, LINSEMAN sets up at right wing circle, with CROWDER in front and BRICKLEY on left side. BOURQUE will play catch with BRICKLEY and GALLEY to open up LINSEMAN for the cross-ice pass and shot. If BOURQUE shoots, forwards converge on net.

JANNEY takes LINSEMAN's spot on second unit, but both JOYCE and NEELY post up in slot. BOURQUE will play all two minutes if possible, with GLEN WESLEY, MICHAEL THELVEN and GREG HAWGOOD getting point time. The object for this unit is to get the puck in front for NEELY or JOYCE to bang home.

Last season Boston's power play was POOR, scoring 85 goals in 429 opportunities (19.8 percent, 16th overall)

PENALTY KILLING

FIRST UNIT:
GREG JOHNSTON-BOB SWEENEY
GLEN WESLEY-ALLEN PEDERSEN

SECOND UNIT:
RANDY BURRIDGE-ANDY BRICKLEY
GARRY GALLEY-GREG HAWGOOD

Boston sends a forward deep into the offensive zone for the puck, with the other sitting high to pick up the breaking wing. BURRIDGE is the most aggressive of the forwards, but all the forwards will pressure the puck at the points and along the boards. The defense will do the same, with only PEDERSEN staying fairly stationary in front of the net.

Last season Boston's penalty killing was EX-CELLENT, allowing 67 goals in 374 shorthanded situations (82.1 percent, fourth overall).

CRUCIAL FACEOFFS
LINSEMAN gets the call for these, but CARPENTER isn't bad.

RAY BOURQUE

Yrs. of NHL service: 10
Born: Montreal, Quebec, Canada; December 28, 1960
Position: Defenseman
Height: 5-11
Weight: 210
Uniform No.: 77
Shoots: left

Career statistics:

GP	G	A	TP	PIM
718	211	545	756	578

1988-89 statistics:

GP	G	A	TP	+/-	PIM	PP	SH	GW	GT	S	PCT
60	18	43	61	20	52	6	0	0	1	243	7.4

LAST SEASON

Games played total was career low (knee injury), with point total second-lowest of career. He finished fourth in team scoring (first among defensemen), second in plus/minus and first in shots on goal.

THE FINESSE GAME

We've said it before, but we'll say it again: Ray Bourque is one of the world's best skaters. Both agility and strength mark his skating and he possesses both explosive acceleration for rink-length speed and the balance and foot speed to change direction — any direction — within one step. He's never predictable in his skating, and he makes his rushing ability more valuable by showing excellent discretion in his runs up-ice.

Second — barely — in Bourque's weapons arsenal is his shot, also of the world-class variety. He has an excellent selection of shots, from a howitzer slap shot to a laser-like wrist shot, and any of his shots can beat any goaltender in the world. He switches to the right side on the power play and loves to sneak toward the net to fire an almost unstoppable wrist shot.

Third — again, barely — of Ray's skills are his hockey sense and ice vision. Offensively and defensively, Bourque can break down a rush better than any other defenseman in the League. His reading ability combines with his excellent hand skills to deliver the puck to a teammate anywhere, any time — making his transition game one of (if not the) game's best.

THE PHYSICAL GAME

Yet *another* reason why Bourque is the player he is, is his physical ability. He's tremendously strong and can handle all of the League's bigger players; credit his upper body strength and balance here. Those two attributes also make him almost unbeatable in any confrontation in the corners.

His great strength also powers his great shot.

THE INTANGIBLES

Undoubtedly the best overall defenseman in the NHL, Bourque would also rank in the top 10 of *all* the League's best players. He is the Bruins' on-ice leader, and their most important player.

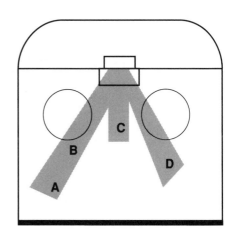

ANDY BRICKLEY

Yrs. of NHL service: 5
Born: Melrose, Mass., USA; August 9, 1961
Position: Left wing
Height: 6-0
Weight: 195
Uniform No.: 25
Shoots: left

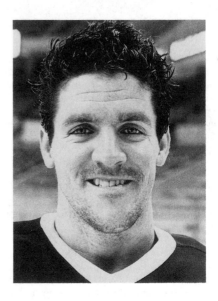

Career statistics:

GP	G	A	TP	PIM
265	58	110	168	61

1988-89 statistics:

GP	G	A	TP	+/-	PIM	PP	SH	GW	GT	S	PCT
71	13	22	35	4	20	2	0	3	1	98	13.3

LAST SEASON

Games played total was a career high. Point totals were second highest of Brickley's career. He was acquired by Boston on waivers from New Jersey.

THE FINESSE GAME

Brickley is a good skater and the Bruins put that skill to work on a checking line and the penalty killing unit. Andy has good lateral movement and quickness, and he reads the play well; that accounts for his checking success. He is also a strong skater and has good endurance, making him almost tireless on his feet.

He is not a gifted puck handler, but his anticipation will carry him to the openings in the ice, where he can put a good wrist shot to work to the tune of 15-20 goals per season.

He sees the ice well but has difficulty moving the puck to an open teammate should he gain it through checking. Brickley brings his skating and anticipation to bear in his penalty killing role, and he does well there.

THE PHYSICAL GAME

Brickley is willing to use his body against the opposition, but he is not a thunderous hitter. He plays smartly and gets himself in his opponent's way, and is effective without hurting his club through penalties.

THE INTANGIBLES

Andy is a role player and he filled that defensive role with the Bruins. His night in, night out work ethic — though not rewarded in point totals — makes him a role model for the Bruins, and a valuable player besides.

RANDY BURRIDGE

Yrs. of NHL service: 3
Born: Fort Erie, Ontario, Canada; January 7, 1966
Position: Left wing
Height: 5-9
Weight: 180
Uniform No.: 12
Shoots: left

Career statistics:

GP	G	A	TP	PIM
234	76	87	163	188

1988-89 statistics:

GP	G	A	TP	+/-	PIM	PP	SH	GW	GT	S	PCT
80	31	30	61	19	39	6	2	6	1	189	16. 4

LAST SEASON

Burridge was the only Bruins to play all 80 games. He set career highs in all point categories, finishing second on the team in goals and fourth in points. He led the team in shorthanded goals, tied for first in game-winners, and finished third in SOG total. His plus/minus was the club's fourth best.

THE FINESSE GAME

Quickness and agility mark Burridge as a skater. His good mobility and lateral movement (because of balance and foot speed) lets him beat people to loose pucks — credit his one-step quickness here. Despite his good jump, however, Burridge isn't a rink-length speedster.

His good hockey sense works both offensively and defensively. His play-reading ability and anticipation help Randy check well, and then he adds this quickness to the recipe to close opposing openings. Those same abilities let him hit the openings himself, and his outstanding quickness makes him particularly dangerous when there are loose pucks around the net.

Burridge can handle the puck fairly well when he's moving, and his one-step quickness makes him a threat to stutter-step past the defense. He takes advantage of his teammates, moving the puck to them when they are in better scoring positions.

He gets his shot away fairly quickly (as befits his style around the net), but he still hasn't demonstrated the ability to score from distances; that makes him fairly predictable. He has also taken to shooting the puck more; that makes him more dangerous.

THE PHYSICAL GAME

Burridge could be said to play bigger than his size. He's got good strength and is willing to put it to work in any area of the ice, but he's going to get outmuscled because of his size.

He's a willing physical player who gives up his body in order to make a play, but his best work is done from outside the heavy traffic.

THE INTANGIBLES

Burridge has filled in the offense that used to be provided by Keith Crowder, and Randy has the talent to score 30 goals consistently. His play within a season bears examination, as he scored just eight goals in his first 31 games and just one in his last six.

His work ethic is good, and because we consider last season essentially just Randy's second full NHL campaign we think he has the ability to improve still further.

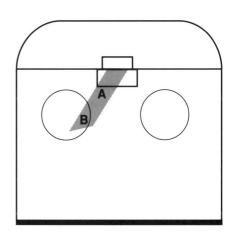

LYNDON BYERS

Yrs. of NHL service: 3
Born: Nipawin, Sask., Canada; February 29, 1964
Position: Right wing
Height: 6-1
Weight: 190
Uniform No.: 33
Shoots: right

Career statistics:

GP	G	A	TP	PIM
168	17	35	52	589

1988-89 statistics:

GP	G	A	TP	+/-	PIM	PP	SH	GW	GT	S	PCT
49	0	4	4	-8	218	0	0	0	0	25	0.0

LAST SEASON

Byers was sidelined late in the season with a separated shoulder. He led the club in PIM total, and his plus/minus was the team's fourth worSt.

THE FINESSE GAME

As befits his game, strength is the key to Byers' skating. He doesn't have a great deal of speed, but Lyndon's good balance and strength greatly aid him in his physical style.

His play reading isn't bad, but it is his desire more than his brains that can make him a serviceable checking forward. He needs time and space to make his plays when he has the puck, and the plays he makes will be simple ones at best.

His hands aren't good enough to fool NHL goaltending, so he'll have to score from near the net on rebounds and broken plays.

THE PHYSICAL GAME

If a guy averages 34.65 PIM for each goal he scores, what kind of game do you think he plays? Byers plays the game physically, using his size well in checking and putting his strength to use along the boards and in the corners.

He also fights. A lot.

THE INTANGIBLES

As we mentioned last year, Byers' physical style betrays him with injury. With Jay Miller gone to Los Angeles, the bulk of Boston's police work will fall to Byers — who will perform willingly and ably.

He remains, however, a role player.

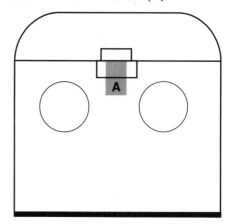

BOBBY CARPENTER

Yrs. of NHL service: 8
Born: Beverly, Mass., USA; July 13, 1963
Position: Center
Height: 6-0
Weight: 190
Uniform No.: 11
Shoots: left

Career statistics:

GP	G	A	TP	PIM
588	216	258	474	533

1988-89 statistics:

GP	G	A	TP	+/-	PIM	PP	SH	GW	GT	S	PCT
57	16	24	40	7	26	4	0	3	0	137	11.7

LAST SEASON

Games played total was career low. He was traded from Los Angeles to Boston near mid-season. Point totals were second lowest of his career. He missed several late season games with a thumb injury.

THE FINESSE GAME

Carpenter is an excellent skater, with superb strength and balance. He is almost impossible to push off the puck and can carry it very well in traffic, and because of his balance, you'll almost never see him thrown to the ice. He has great speed with and without the puck, is an agile skater, has good lateral movement for change of direction and has good quickness.

Bob anticipates and passes the puck well because of his good hands that are soft with the puck. He has a terrific slap shot and an accurate wrist shot, and is a good faceoff man because of his eye/hand coordination and speed.

THE PHYSICAL GAME

The key to Carpenter's success is his physical game, but he's not consistently successful because he's not consistently physical. When he is up for the game and ready to battle for the puck, then he is a top player. When he's not mentally ready to play, his physical play and aggressiveness are questionable.

When he plays physically you know it, because he can be a punishing hitter. He'll take the pounding in front of the enemy net and dish it out the same way. He's strong in the upper body, especially in the arms and wrists, and can pull the puck out of a tangle because of that.

THE INTANGIBLES

He was supposed to be Wayne Gretzky's reclamation project, but even the Great One got tired of him.

Carpenter has the skills to play a solid two-way game and earn 60-70 points a season. When he plays the way he can, he can provide those points and that two-way game; he just has to want to.

He doesn't have great self-motivating qualities and, in fact, Carpenter most readily responds to negative reinforcement. He's the kind of guy who, when blasted by the coach that morning, goes on to have a great game that night.

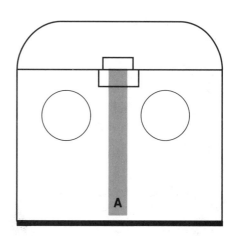

KEITH CROWDER

Yrs. of NHL service: 9
Born: Windsor, Ontario, Canada; January 6, 1959
Position: Right wing
Height: 6-0
Weight: 190
Uniform No.: 18
Shoots: right

Career statistics:

GP	G	A	TP	PIM
607	219	258	477	1,261

1988-89 statistics:

GP	G	A	TP	+/-	PIM	PP	SH	GW	GT	S	PCT
69	15	18	33	6	147	5	0	2	0	121	12.4

LAST SEASON

All point totals were full-season lows (lowest since Crowder's abbreviated rookie season). A charley horse sidelined Crowder early in the season. He finished fourth on the club in PIM.

THE FINESSE GAME

Not a greatly skilled finesse player to begin with, Crowder's game is showing the signs of age and NHL wear and tear. While he has great strength on his skates (making him relentless in his pursuit of the puck), Keith has little speed or agility — and he's losing a step or two of what he does have. He does have great balance, and that trait is what makes his physical game work, keeping upright and in the play after collisions.

Keith can make use of his teammates because he keeps his head up, looking for that play from the corner instead of blindly flinging the puck goal-ward.

Using his physical style to open ice for his teammates is a great strength of Crowder's game, and he complements that style by effectively moving the puck to his now-open teammates. However, when he gets near the net he just barges through.

Most of Keith's goals are of the second effort variety, with him shooting from the bottom of the faceoff circle and chasing the puck. But, he also likes to work his way around the back of the net and tuck the puck in.

THE PHYSICAL GAME

Crowder is fearless in the corners and works them excellently. He sacrifices his body, shift after shift. His strength and willingness to take physical abuse makes Crowder successful when he charges the net and, because of his strength, his shot is a powerful one.

Keith plays the same way at both ends of the ice and will rub out the opposition in the defensive zone as well as the offensive zone. Physical though he is, Crowder isn't a real fighter. He won't back down, but he won't fight unless heavily provoked.

THE INTANGIBLES

Durability remains a big question for Keith Crowder, considering that he has never played a full NHL season. His style is the reason for that (though his all-out willingness makes him a true team leader).

Still, his 30-year-old body is probably closer to 40 years old because of the pounding Crowder has subjected himself to in nine NHL seasons.

This prototypical Bruin would keep himself in the lineup until his heart gives out, but his 30-goal days are behind him. That makes him, essentially, a role playing forward — and role playing forwards are (after all) expendable.

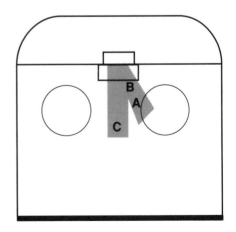

GARRY GALLEY

Yrs. of NHL service: 5
Born: Montreal, Quebec, Canada; April 16, 1963
Position: Defenseman
Height: 5-11
Weight: 190
Uniform No.: 28
Shoots: left

Career statistics:

GP	G	A	TP	PIM
311	38	108	146	319

1988-89 statistics:

GP	G	A	TP	+/-	PIM	PP	SH	GW	GT	S	PCT
78	8	21	29	-7	80	2	1	0	0	145	5.5

LAST SEASON

Games played total tied career high. PIM total was second highest of career. He had the lowest plus/minus among defensive regulars.

THE FINESSE GAME

Galley is a good skater, and his ability helps make the Bruins' defense corps one of the more mobile groups in the League.

He has good speed forward and back and is also agile. He handles the puck well and likes to rush it from the defensive zone, and has learned to tone down his defensive gambles. He still gambles by carrying the puck when he is the last man back, or going too far into the offensive zone (note the plus/minus rating), but his thought processes and positional play have improved.

Garry plays his position fairly well, and has learned to concentrate on the man rather than the puck. That has helped him to improve his angle play at forcing the opposition wide of the net. He does think well on the ice and has good anticipation skills, making him valuable on the power play. He can find the open man and get the puck to him.

THE PHYSICAL GAME

Galley has good size and takes the body fairly well, but because he's often looking to start the play up ice, the opposition will sneak back into the play. He is effective if not spectacular along the boards and in front of the net, but he will never really be a hitter.

His conditioning has improved since he entered the League, and he will also sacrifice his body to block shots; several times in his career he's taken pucks off the head to prevent goals.

THE INTANGIBLES

Garry is willing to learn and brings a good attitude and work ethic to the rink. If we follow the rule that a defenseman needs five years to hit his NHL maturity, than Galley fits right here. He's never going to be a defensive stalwart — he may never get to be better than a fourth or fifth defenseman — but Galley wants to be, and desire can make up for a lot of deficiencies.

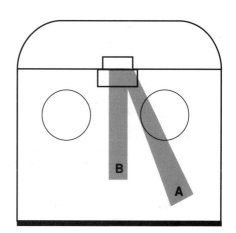

GREG HAWGOOD

Yrs. of NHL service: 1
Born: Edmonton, Alta., Canada; August 10, 1968
Position: Defenseman
Height: 5-8
Weight: 175
Uniform No.: 38
Shoots: left

Career statistics:

GP	G	A	TP	PIM
57	16	24	40	84

1988-89 statistics:

GP	G	A	TP	+/-	PIM	PP	SH	GW	GT	S	PCT
56	16	24	40	4	84	5	0	0	1	132	12. 1

LAST SEASON

First full NHL season.

THE FINESSE GAME

Hawgood is a skilled finesse player in a number of ways. First, he' a very mobile skater, possessing good rink-length speed as well as fine agility and lateral movement. He moves well in confined areas because of his one-step quickness and balance, and skates equally well forward or backward.

Greg handles the puck well when skating and he likes to rush from the zone with it. He'll carry it into the offensive zone and become a fourth attacker; he isn't satisfied with gaining the blue line and dumpimg the puck. He has pretty good smarts, so he does know when to challenge the opposition in this way and when to play a more conservative game.

He passes the puck well because of his good hands and his good hockey sense and vision, and all of his finesse abilities work equally well offensively and defensively. They also make him perfect for specialty team play.

He plays a skating game defensively and will challenge the puck carrier as soon as possible, looking to step up and turn the play around. His skating allows him to force plays wide of the net, and to forecheck offensively.

Greg has a good shot from the point and he'll move in when given the room. He shoots frequently, and his shot is good for tips and deflections.

THE PHYSICAL GAME

Size is always going to be a concern with Hawgood, but he plays bigger than his diminutive stature would indicate — he has to. Greg has deceptively good strength on his feet, and that strength combines with his fine balance to allow him to strip the puck from bigger players while in the traffic areas.

Hawgood also uses the size he has very aggres-sively, and he'll fight with anyone to prove that he won't be intimidated.

THE INTANGIBLES

Hawgood's an excellent playmaking defenseman, the kind of player any team would like to have. His continued development (and there will be plenty of players who will test his courage over this season and the next) may put players like Michael Thelven and Garry Galley on the shelf, because Hawgood does what they do offensively — but better — without sacrificing defense.

Had he played a full season last year (he was bounced back and forth from Maine), he might have contested for the rookie defenseman goal-scoring record now held by New York's Brian Leetch.

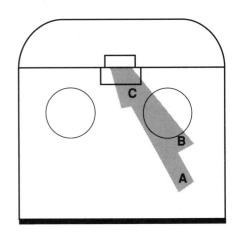

CRAIG JANNEY

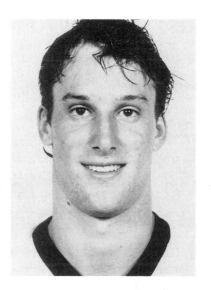

Yrs. of NHL service: 2
Born: Hartford, Conn., USA; September 26, 1968
Position: Center
Height: 6-0
Weight: 190
Uniform No.: 23
Shoots: left

Career statistics:

GP	G	A	TP	PIM
77	23	55	78	12

1988-89 statistics:

GP	G	A	TP	+/-	PIM	PP	SH	GW	GT	S	PCT
62	16	46	62	20	12	2	0	2	0	95	16.8

LAST SEASON

Janney's first full NHL season. He led the club in assists and finished tied for second in plus/minus. He was sidelined throughout the season with a recurring groin injury.

THE FINESSE GAME

A full year's look at Janney reveals that he is, indeed, a superbly talented finesse player, but that he has a stretch to go before he becomes the NHL's next superstar.

His skating is excellent, equipped with speed, agility, quickness, balance and acceleration. He has explosive, rink-length speed as well as dynamic shiftiness and one-step quickness. He can scuttle anywhere within a step, making openings deadly opportunities for Janney to practice his second-best skill: playmaking.

His excellent anticipation, understanding and play reading abilities keep him one or two plays ahead of the game. He complements that non-physical finesse ability with hand skills that are as superior as his foot skills.

He passes equally well to both the forehand and backhand sides, using his vision to lead his teammates into the openings he's detected. Craig can muscle a pass just as easily as he can float one, and he handles the puck with equal ability. He had a tendency last season to over-pass, especially when he was in shooting position in the slot.

His hockey sense carries him to scoring position, and his hand skills and balance allow him to succeed in traffic. He'll get most of his goals in tight, because when he's farther out he looks to pass, but he doesn't shoot anywhere near often enough. In fact, Janney must become more selfish in exploiting opportunities himself.

THE PHYSICAL GAME

Janney is not built to be a physical player, and he generally doesn't play like one. There isn't a lot of bulk on his six-foot frame, but that doesn't mean Craig avoids the rough going.

Rather, he will succeed in those areas because of his hand and foot skills and not because of his ability to knock the opposition on its butt. Janney is unafraid of traffic and unintimidated around the opposition goal.

He also has excellent reach that he puts to work when he bursts to an opening, using this asset to his advantage to snare loose pucks or to poke them from the opposition.

THE INTANGIBLES

Janney faced a lot of pressure last season, and he led off the year in good form. But his recurring groin injury slowed him throughout the season, so he wasn't always in the shape necessary to play his best hockey.

We said last season that his potential is excellent, but we also said he had to prove he could succeed in the NHL grind. This is a season for Janney to say, "Okay, I saw what the NHL could dole out last season, now I'm going to pull my game up a notch to exploit the experience I've gained and make the rest of the League try to stop me again. "

We think he can do that. He'd be helped in that ambition by adding some physical strength to his frame (to help him take the pounding — and maybe even surprise some people by doing some muscle work of his own on the ice) and by playing more selfishly (and therefore less predictably).

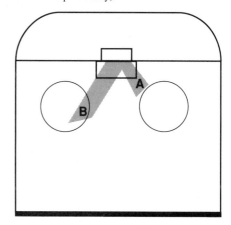

GREG JOHNSTON

Yrs. of NHL service: 2
Born: Barrie, Ontario, Canada; January 14. 1965
Position: Right wing
Height: 6-1
Weight: 190
Uniform No.: 39
Shoots: right

Career statistics:

GP	G	A	TP	PIM
174	25	28	53	113

1988-89 statistics:

GP	G	A	TP	+/-	PIM	PP	SH	GW	GT	S	PCT
57	11	10	21	7	32	0	1	5	0	89	12. 4

LAST SEASON

Games played total was second highest of career.

THE FINESSE GAME

Johnston is a a good-to-very-good skater: nice touch of speed, good agility, good balance. Those assets served him well in his capacity as a checking forward and as a penalty killer.

Teamed with his good sense of anticipation, Johnston's skating becomes more valuable. He has not yet developed his puck handling skills to the NHL level, an area that must improve.

What also must improve is Johnston's shooting and goal scoring. He has not yet adapted to the quicker NHL pace, thus openings close on him before he gets his shots off. Also, he does not yet get himself into good scoring position, thus rendering him virtually unable to take advantage of any pucks the opposition might turn over due to his checking.

THE PHYSICAL GAME

Johnston will put his size to fairly effective use when checking, but he is not a punishing hitter. He does a good job of taking the body cleanly, thus making his checking effective by keeping himself out of the penalty box.

He has good strength along the boards and is 50/50 to win the puck in any contest there and make a play from the corner if he can.

THE INTANGIBLES

Johnston has an excellent attitude and is a good worker, and must put those two assets to work to improve his other skills and thus increase his NHL longevity.

He's been up and down with Boston five times since being drafted in 1983 and, at 24, must finally make the move to the big club. Without improving his finesse skills (particularly his scoring, which improved at the junior and minor league levels), Johnston will remain a utility forward.

As such, his job will always be in jeopardy.

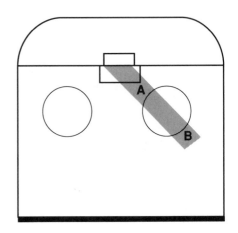

BOB JOYCE

Yrs. of NHL service: 2
Born: St. John, N.B., Canada; July 11, 1966
Position: Left wing
Height: 6-1
Weight: 190
Uniform No.: 27
Shoots: left

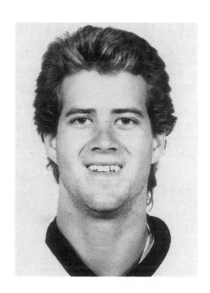

Career statistics:

GP	G	A	TP	PIM
92	25	36	61	56

1988-89 statistics:

GP	G	A	TP	+/-	PIM	PP	SH	GW	GT	S	PCT
77	18	31	49	8	46	7	0	3	0	142	12.7

LAST SEASON

Joyce's first full NHL season.

THE FINESSE GAME

The strengths of Joyce's game rest more in the physical categories than the finesse ones, but he does have some very good finesse skills.

He's got an excellent shot that's quickly released and fairly accurate, so that makes Joyce a threat from near the net — say, 15-20 feet away. His hand skills go beyond just shooting the puck, as Joyce operates well with the puck in traffic; that's good, because he does his best work from the slot and along the boards. He also has good hand strength, so he'll get his shot off when being checked, hooked or leaned on.

Joyce is a strong skater equipped with powerful strides, good balance (giving him a degree of agility unexpected in a player of his size) and speed. His acceleration skill is good and should get better as he plays and practices more and more against NHL competition.

Unlike linemate Cam Neely, Joyce doesn't grab attention when he's on the ice because he isn't scattering bodies with jarring checks. He plays his wing without flair, using his hockey sense to get into position to score.

THE PHYSICAL GAME

Joyce's size, balance and strength key his game — particularly as he likes to hang around in the slot for his opportunities. He's not a big thumper, but Joyce has good strength and uses it well in his contests in the corners for the puck. His size and strength are made more valuable by his ability to make a play coming out of the corner, especially because his balance keeps him vertical after hits.

He's very strong on the puck along the boards, and Joyce also makes sure to finish his checks.

THE INTANGIBLES

Joyce's rookie season must be looked at as a disappointment. Though in good muscular shape, Joyce must adapt better to the rigors of the NHL; he had just six goals in his final 36 games and only three of those came at even strength.

He must show the determination to work through NHL checking, and he must shoot the puck more frequently in order to fulfill his good NHL potential.

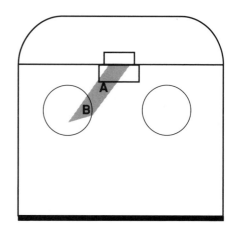

REGGIE LEMELIN

Yrs. of NHL service: 10
Born: Sherbrooke, Quebec, Canada;
November 19, 1954
Position: Goaltender
Height: 5-11
Weight: 160
Uniform No.: 1
Catches: left

Career statistics:

GP	MINS	G	SO	AVG	A	PIM
413	22,918	1,340	9	3. 51	15	61

1988-89 statistics:

GP	MINS	AVG	W	L	T	SO	GA	SA	SAPCT	PIM
40	2,392	3. 01	19	15	6	0	120	1,061	. 887	6

LAST SEASON

Lemelin didn't record a shutout for the first time in five seasons. Goals allowed was third-fewest of career.

THE PHYSICAL GAME

Unspectacular is the way Reggie plays the game. Though he's incorporated more of a reflex style into his game then ever before, Lemelin remains a strong stand-up goaltender. He squares himself to the puck excellently, so that all he has to do is let the shot hit him. He controls his rebounds well after the initial shot, and he clears them to safety alertly.

Lemelin is a good skater laterally, covering his posts well, and he also moves in and out of the net with ease. He chooses to not chase the puck, and when he does leave his net he only flags the puck down and deposits it for the defense — nothing more.

Reggie has good balance, so he'll readily regain his stance should he leave his feet. He quickly re-establishes his position for the next save, or regains his feet after one of his infrequent flops to the ice. He has good — not great — hand speed (better on the glove side) and sees the puck well.

His feet remain his consistent weakness, in that he is vulnerable after he opens up and has his feet moving.

THE MENTAL GAME

Lemelin anticipates and reads the play in front of him very well. His concentration is good, in terms of both individual shots from odd angles or scrambles around the net and throughout a game. Bad goals don't generally affect him.

He also has the ability (because he plays with such coolness) to come into a game and immediately play his best. He certainly has big save capability.

THE INTANGIBLES

Lemelin puts forth his best effort at all times, and is always prepared to play. Though capable of becoming white-hot over a period of time, Reggie's greatest attribute is his consistency. Though climbing upward in years (he'll be 35 in November) Lemelin should have several good seasons left in him.

KEN LINSEMAN

Yrs. of NHL service: 11
Born: Kingston, Ontario, Canada; August 11, 1958
Position: Center
Height: 5-11
Weight: 175
Uniform No.: 13
Shoots: left

Career statistics:

GP	G	A	TP	PIM
741	238	497	735	1,533

1988-89 statistics:

GP	G	A	TP	+/-	PIM	PP	SH	GW	GT	S	PCT
78	27	45	72	15	164	13	1	2	1	159	17.0

LAST SEASON

Games played total was highest in seven years. Linseman finished second on the club in scoring, assists and power play goals, third in PIM total. Torn knee ligaments sidelined late in the year and through the playoffs.

THE FINESSE GAME

Linseman (prior to his knee injury, at any rate) is an excellent skater. He has great speed, and his one-step skills (lateral movement, agility and quickness) are among the League's best. He can turn, change direction, stop and start within a single stride, and that waterbug shiftiness is what makes him so effective.

His skating is made more effective by his puck-handling ability, which is also superior. Linseman can perform excellently with the puck at any speed, and he combines that skill with ice vision anticipation to lead a teammate into an opening. His skills also allow him to exploit those openings himself. Those skills manifest themselves particularly on the power play, where his vision and one-step quickness keep the passing lanes open.

His goal scoring comes from anticipation and quickness, not from great shot selection. Linseman usually get his goals from in close — deflections and the like — and he could increase that total if he would take advantage of the opportunities he creates and shoot more.

His checking and defensive game are as solid as his offensive output, and Linseman's play without the puck is strong in all three zones. He is one of the NHL's best faceoff men and will take many of the important defensive zone faceoffs.

THE PHYSICAL GAME

Ken is a very physical player — certainly playing bigger than his size — and is unafraid to hit in the corners. He is also mean with his stick and elbows, doing whatever is necessary to stop an opponent — like pitchforking the defenseman after he gets rid of the puck. He is also one of the NHL's best holders, making him a frustrating player to play against. Linseman is not, however, a fighter.

His physical game is made better by the fact that Linseman certainly has the hand skills to make plays from the corners.

THE INTANGIBLES

We told you that Linseman would perform well for the Bruins if he could stay away from injury, something he did for all but two games last season. Now he must recover from a fairly severe knee injury.

His work ethic says he should recover well (barring complications), and it is that work ethic and will to succeed that makes him a leader for the Bruins.

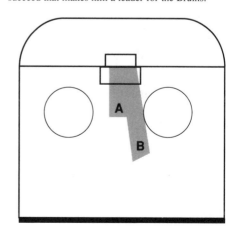

ANDY MOOG

Yrs. of NHL service: 8
Born: Penticton, B.C., Canada; February 18, 1960
Position: Goaltender
Height: 5-8
Weight: 165
Uniform No.: 35
Catches: left

Career statistics:

GP	MINS	G	SO	AVG	A	PIM
282	15,743	927	6	3.53	12	52

1988-89 statistics:

GP	MINS	AVG	W	L	T	SO	GA	SA	SAPCT	PIM
41	2,482	3.22	18	14	8	1	133	1,079	.877	6

LAST SEASON

Minutes played total was third highest of career.

THE PHYSICAL GAME

Where his goaltending partner relies on positioning and simplicity, Moog is more flamboyant. Unlike Reggie Lemelin, Moog primarily plays a reflex game — though Andy has toned down his scrambling and flopping.

Moog's learned that, quick as he is, he can't grow. In other words, if he doesn't cut his angles properly, smart shooters will just put the puck over his shoulders all night long. When playing well, Moog will be challenging the shooter from the top of the goal crease. You'll know he's in trouble when he's deep in his net (though his reflexes are good enough to bail him out even when he's struggling).

He's strong to both hands, and Moog sees the puck very well (making him effective on screen shots, despite the inequalities in height between him and the League's forwards).

Though he skates well and is proficient in using his stick to clear rebounds, Moog doesn't go that second step and handle the puck when he's out of the net. Instead, he prefers to leave it for his defense.

He regains his stance very quickly and is very balanced, always in position to make the second save.

THE MENTAL GAME

Though he does suffer the occasional mental lapse (the weakness between his legs, for example, is an error of commission — not omission — because he has very fast feet and should be able to close the five-hole), Moog has good concentration. Additionally, he raises his concentration depending on the importance of the contest.

He anticipates plays well, particularly around the net, and that allows him to put his spectacular reflexes to work. He is mentally tough and will recover from bad goals or games. Moog can also come in cold and perform well, and he does have the ability to make big saves.

THE INTANGIBLES

Moog is a fine complement to Lemelin in a number of ways, of which the reflex versus stand-up style is just one point. More importantly, he's only 28 years old, young enough to give Boston excellent goaltending for many more seasons.

CAM NEELY

Yrs. of NHL service: 6
Born: Comox, B.C., Canada; June 6, 1965
Position: Right wing
Height: 6-1
Weight: 205
Uniform No.: 8
Shoots: right

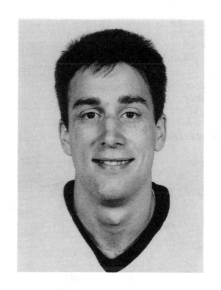

Career statistics:

GP	G	A	TP	PIM
419	166	154	320	828

1988-89 statistics:

GP	G	A	TP	+/-	PIM	PP	SH	GW	GT	S	PCT
74	37	38	75	14	190	18	0	6	1	235	15.7

LAST SEASON

Neely led the club in points, goals and power play goals. He finished second in shots on goal (first among forwards) and PIM total, despite missing games with thumb and knee injuries.

THE FINESSE GAME

Skating is probably the best of Neely's finesse skills, with his still-improving shot and hockey sense following behind. Cam is an excellent skater in terms of strength and balance, both of which make him undeterrable in his pursuit of the puck. Both of those elements also power his physical game, with his stride adding strength to drive checks and his balance keeping him vertical after those collisions.

Neely has also developed some agility and foot speed, but last year those assets worked against him rather than for him (more later).

Cam can carry the puck well, and his growing understanding of the ice and a play's possibilities helps him in his playmaking. But, again, those assets worked against him last season. Overall, though, he still needs some time and space to make a play.

When playing well, Neely is a scorer and shooter. He's best at charging the net and pounding the puck at the goalie. Neely usually aims low and for the five-hole, and he has improved the release of his shot to make it quicker and more accurate.

THE PHYSICAL GAME

Neely is a titan in the physical game, fearless and ferocious. He is very physical and he puts his size and strength to work exceedingly well in the cramped confines of the Garden. He can muscle anyone with the puck in the corners and is almost impossible to knock down himself (courtesy of his balance).

Neely hits punishingly hard in the corners and the open ice and he is afraid of no one. He may take his lumps, but he'll give out a few too, as he is a good fighter.

The physical game does have its side effects in game-missing injuries.

THE INTANGIBLES

Like many physical players who gain scoring success, Neely began last season thinking of himself as an artist and not a plumber; that's what we meant about his improving finesse skills working against him. He attempted plays when he should have shot the puck, stickhandled too frequently and generally did his game more harm than good. The proof? Just 9 goals in his first 29 games — and just three of those at even strength.

But he recaptured his game in the season's second half to re-establish himself as one of the game's premier power forwards. When he's on his game (and we think that Neely's great character and heart will keep him there all this season), he's a guaranteed 40-goal scorer with potential for 50.

We maintain that the future for this 24-year-old is a brilliant one.

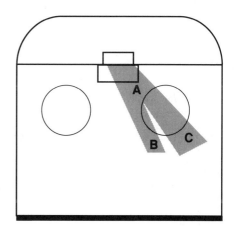

RAY NEUFELD

Yrs. of NHL service: 9
Born: St. Boniface, Man., Canada; April 15, 1959
Position: Right wing
Height: 6-2
Weight: 215
Uniform No.: 19
Shoots: right

Career statistics:

GP	G	A	TP	PIM
594	157	200	357	816

1988-89 statistics:

GP	G	A	TP	+/-	PIM	PP	SH	GW	GT	S	PCT
45	6	5	11	-11	80	0	0	0	0	63	9.5

LAST SEASON

Neufeld was acquired from Winnipeg in exchange for Moe Lemay. Games played total was a seven-year low (he missed 27 games with a knee injury); ditto point totals. He had the team's second worst plus/minus rating.

THE FINESSE GAME

Strength is the key to Neufeld's game, so it's only fitting that strength would be the highlight of his skating. Ray has a lot of power in his stride, giving him a degree of speed and acceleration (age and wear and tear have slowed him in this regard). He has good balance and that serves him well in his physical game, keeping him upright after collisions so he can continue his plays.

He is poised and confident enough to handle the puck while skating, or to move it patiently to a teammate, but Neufeld will not turn anyone inside put with his puckhandling. His big move is going to be the swoop behind the defenseman after using his outside speed — and that's if he makes a move at all.

He can get the puck to his teammates after he grinds around in the corners, but he needs time and space to do so. Neufeld is an opportunistic scorer, banging in goals from around the crease, where he takes advantage of his size and strength.

That plus/minus largely reflects his status as a checking, banging forward — though he's not above a costly positional lapse or two.

THE PHYSICAL GAME

Neufeld is a very physical player, very tough but generally clean, and his skating strength allows him to drive through his checks along the boards. When his feet stop moving he uses his good upper-body strength and balance to out-muscle the opposition along the boards.

Ray can also take the abuse, demonstrated most notably on the power play when he positions himself in front of the enemy net. He is difficult to control in front of the net because of his strength and he is also fairly strong on his skates, making him difficult to knock down.

Neufeld plays his style consistently — home or away, winning or losing — and does so in all three zones.

THE INTANGIBLES

Missing from Ray's repertoire are the finer — as in less coarse or powerful — skills of agility and quickness. He has never been a fancy player in any of his skills, so Neufeld smartly sticks with what he can do.

He is a smart and capable player, and he knows who to hit how and when, and his are the kind of hits that pick up a team. He's an honest hockey player, consistent and dependable, but his age and decreasing offensive skills will now begin to work against him — so much so that Boston may not be his last professional (notice we didn't say last NHL) team.

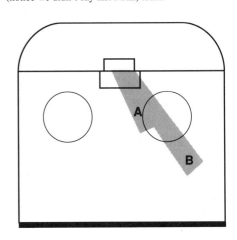

ALLEN PEDERSEN

Yrs. of NHL service: 3
Born: Edmonton, Alberta, Canada; January 13, 1965
Position: Defenseman
Height: 6-3
Weight: 210
Uniform No.: 41
Shoots: left

Career statistics:

GP	G	A	TP	PIM
208	1	23	24	230

1988-89 statistics:

GP	G	A	TP	+/-	PIM	PP	SH	GW	GT	S	PCT
51	0	6	6	-3	69	0	0	0	0	24	0.0

LAST SEASON

Abdominal and shoulder injuries kept Pedersen sidelined throughout the season. Games played total was career low.

THE FINESSE GAME

Pedersen continues to improve in his NHL skills, most notably in his skating. While he still has improvements to make, his agility and foot speed have improved, thus making him more mobile.

Not as improved is his play-reading ability. Pedersen still follows the puck as the rush comes toward him, and he still reacts to the opposition instead of acting upon it (improved skating would also help here). As such, he hasn't developed beyond forcing the play wide. He'll be a better player when he's able to step up on the opposition. His understanding and reading of plays around the net could also improve.

He can make the correct pass from his own end quickly, and Pedersen generally makes correct decisions when moving the puck. Again, though, better ice vision would allow him to make better decisions.

He doesn't carry the puck and rarely joins the attack. He costs Boston some offensive pressure by not pinching in, and he doesn't add any offense from the point when he does station himself there.

THE PHYSICAL GAME

Intelligence makes Pedersen's physical game a valuable one; he applies his good size and strength to contain the opposition without taking penalties. He has the strength to win corner and crease battles, though in his attempts to play physically he's re-discovered his penchant for cross-ice wandering.

Allen sacrifices his body as a good shot blocker but, though physical, is not a fighter.

THE INTANGIBLES

Pedersen's development was put into a holding pattern last season because of his injuries. If he can regain his footing along the path toward NHL defensive maturity, he can be an important part of Boston's success because the Bruins don't have a strictly defensive force.

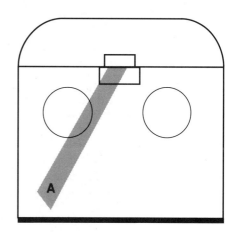

BOB SWEENEY

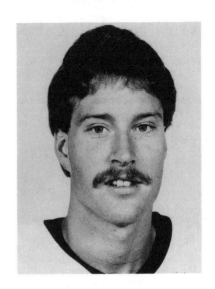

Yrs. of NHL service: 3
Born: Concord, Mass., USA; January 25, 1964
Position: Center
Height: 6-3
Weight: 210
Uniform No.: 42
Shoots: left

Career statistics:

GP	G	A	TP	PIM
169	38	41	79	193

1988-89 statistics:

GP	G	A	TP	+/-	PIM	PP	SH	GW	GT	S	PCT
75	14	14	28	-19	99	2	1	3	0	117	12.0

LAST SEASON

Sweeney missed three games with a back injury. His plus/minus was the team's worst.

THE FINESSE GAME

After a fairly solid rookie year, Sweeney seems to have gone backwards rather than forwards. Some — maybe much — of the blame for that can be laid at Coach Terry O'Reilly's doorpstep (more later), but Sweeney hasn't necessarily improved as he should.

He remains slower than he should be to be a consistent player at the NHL level, and that's reflected in his lack of agility or lateral movement. His lack of quickness isn't off-set by outstanding rink length speed and strength, so Bob's charges to the net aren't always going to produce positive results. Frequently, in fact, his skating will create negative results when Sweeney is trapped as the puck turns over; note his plus/minus.

He does handle the puck fairly well, and he can put his hands to work as a passer, but he remains primarily a 1-on-1 player. His stickhandling and reach help him keep the puck from the defenders as he heads goalward.

Bob has a degree of anticipation and vision, but he must learn to react quicker — more at the NHL pace. Sweeney's shot isn't bad, and the best thing about it is his quick release. He would be helped if he shot more frequently.

THE PHYSICAL GAME

Sweeney uses his size well in several ways. First, he'll take the body along the boards (though he's not a punishing hitter) and he can make plays from there when he gets the puck. Second, his reach aids his puckhandling (and he uses his body well to protect the puck when he carries it), and third, he plugs the front of the net well.

He is not outstandingly strong, so he can be out-muscled by some forwards approaching his size.

THE INTANGIBLES

Sweeney never settled into one spot last season, as coach O'Reilly bounced him all over the lineup. It's difficult to play well when always playing with new linemates, yet Sweeney didn't show enough progress in the time he did play. If he is to get off the fourth line, he must work harder at distinguishing himself when he does play, and he must also shore up last season's defensive weaknesses.

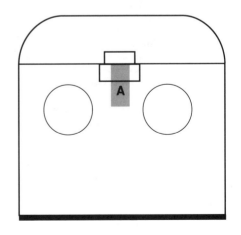

MICHAEL THELVEN

Yrs. of NHL service: 4
Born: Stockholm, Sweden; January 7, 1961
Position: Defenseman
Height: 5-11
Weight: 180
Uniform No.: 22
Shoots: left

Career statistics:

GP	G	A	TP	PIM
201	20	78	98	194

1988-89 statistics:

GP	G	A	TP	+/-	PIM	PP	SH	GW	GT	S	PCT
40	3	18	21	10	71	1	1	0	0	68	4. 4

LAST SEASON

Games played total was second-lowest of four NHL seasons (recurring knee injury).

THE FINESSE GAME

Skating and puck handling are the hallmarks of Thelven's game. Though not possessing great speed, Thelven can take advantage of the openings he sees and exploit them.

Michael handles the puck well in traffic, and likes to rush the puck and become a fourth attacker in the offensive zone. Once there, he's likely to run a give-and-go with the trailing forward and head for the slot. Most of his goals, however, will come not from the slot but from the point.

His defensive game is unexceptional, but Thelven will hold his own as the play comes down his side. He's more apt to use his skating skill to thwart the opposition (by stepping up to force a play) than he is to back in and try to take an opponent wide. That's because taking an opponent wide means Thelven would have to use his body, something he doesn't generally do.

THE PHYSICAL GAME

Michael will get his hits in when he can, on his terms. He is not an aggressive individual and won't really take the hits to make his plays, generally throwing snow instead of getting into the corner for the puck.

His front of the net coverage is going to be more tactical than physical, in that Thelven will attempt to block passes to the slot instead of bodying the opposing forward camped there.

THE INTANGIBLES

As we've said, durability remains a major question mark for Thelven. Also of note is the fact that the Bruins have a host of defensemen who can play his kind of game, but will add greater degrees of physical involvement (Don Sweeney, Stephane Quintal, Greg Hawgood, Garry Galley).

All of this makes Thelven's continued presence with a Bruins a questionable circumstance.

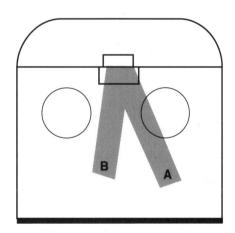

GLEN WESLEY

Yrs. of NHL service: 2
Born: Red Deer, Alta., Canada; October 2, 1968
Position: Defenseman
Height: 6-1
Weight: 190
Uniform No.: 26
Shoots: left

Career statistics:

GP	G	A	TP	PIM
156	26	65	91	130

1988-89 statistics:

GP	G	A	TP	+/-	PIM	PP	SH	GW	GT	S	PCT
77	19	35	54	23	61	8	1	1	1	181	10. 5

LAST SEASON

Wesley finished second in the club in defensive scoring, first in overall plus/minus. He finished fourth in shots on goal.

THE FINESSE GAME

Strength and balance are the hallmarks of Wesley's skating, and he has the potential to be among the NHL's best skaters. His strength powers his good-to-very-good speed, but Glen also possesses the foot speed and balance to be an agile skater with good one-step performance (both quickness and lateral movement). He changes direction well, and he skates with equal skill both forward and backward; he is, however, just a little weak in his turns to the left, and he'll take penalties on forwards who beat him that way.

His hockey sense is excellent, and it meshes well with his skating to make him a potent offensive threat as well as an effective defender. He sees the ice and anticipates plays — both offensively and defensively — very well, and he uses all of his finesse skills to exploit his mental abilities.

His hand skills are as well developed as his foot skills, so Wesley will lead a teammate into the clear with an accurate pass that will be as strong as the situation demands. Glen controls and carries the puck excellently, and because he can move with the puck at any speed Glen's puckhandling is that much more effective,

He contains the point excellently and is already a power play regular because of his play making. Wesley also has excellent shot selection, and he delivers both his slap and wrist shots quickly and accurately.

Defensively, he reads the play excellently and steps up well to thwart it. His breakout passes are smooth and most always the correct decisions, and Wesley will rush the puck when necessary.

THE PHYSICAL GAME

Wesley is still in a boy's body, but that doesn't stop him from playing like a man. He takes the body well along the boards and in front of the net, but he lacks the strength that would make his hitting punishing. That will come as his body matures and fills out.

His physical play is made more valuable by Wesley's ability to make plays after contact.

THE INTANGIBLES

Continued improvement is on the agenda for this already impressive young man. He plays with a poise and confidence that belies his youth, and that poise will help him grow into one of the NHL's very best defenders. His physical skills will continue to blossom, and it's certainly not out of the question for Wesley to chalk up 25-30 goals and 80 points in a season.

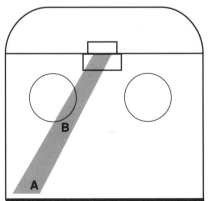

BUFFALO
SABRES

LINE COMBINATIONS
SCOTT ARNIEL-CHRISTIAN RUUTTU-RICK VAIVE
DAVE ANDREYCHUK-BENOIT HOGUE-JOHN TUCKER
MIKE HARTMAN-JEFF PARKER-KEVIN MAGUIRE
MARK NAPIER-PIERRE TURGEON-MIKE FOLIGNO

DEFENSE PAIRINGS
DOUG BODGER-PHIL HOUSLEY
MIKE RAMSEY-GRANT LEDYARD
UWE KRUPP

GOALTENDERS
CLINT MALARCHUK
JACQUES CLOUTIER
DAREN PUPPA

OTHER PLAYERS
LARRY PLAYFAIR— Defenseman
RAY SHEPPARD — Right wing

POWER PLAY

FIRST UNIT:
DAVE ANDREYCHUK-PIERRE TURGEON
RICK VAIVE
PHIL HOUSLEY-DOUG BODGER

SECOND UNIT:
JOHN TUCKER-MIKE FOLIGNO
RAY SHEPPARD
GRANT LEDYARD

On the first unit, TURGEON controls from the right wing corner, VAIVE is in the right faceoff circle and ANDREYCHUK is at the base of the left faceoff circle. BODGER completes the overload on the right point, and the puck works its way up and down the right wing until either VAIVE or BODGER is open for the shot. The forwards go to the net, and ANDREYCHUK is the primary rebound man.

On the second unit, TUCKER controls behind the net, FOLIGNO jams the crease and SHEPPARD is stationed in the left wing faceoff circle. SHEPPARD is the primary offensive weapon here, with FOLIGNO picking up rebounds. CHRISTIAN RUUTTU will sub for the centers.

Last season Buffalo's power play was FAIR, scoring 78 goals in 380 opportunities (20.5 percent, 13th overall).

PENALTY KILLING

FIRST UNIT:
SCOTT ARNIEL-CHRISTIAN RUUTTU
PHIL HOUSLEY-GRANT LEDYARD

SECOND UNIT:
JEFF PARKER-MIKE FOLIGNO
MIKE RAMSEY-UWE KRUPP

The first forward pair is aggressive on the puck in all three zones, the second set less so. All units pressure the puck in the offensive zone, though RAMSEY and KRUPP least of all. Buffalo keeps LEDYARD on for as long as possible, trying to maximize his quickness and skating.

Last season Buffalo's penalty killing was FAIR, allowing 86 goals in 410 shorthanded situations (79.0 percent, 12th overall).

CRUCIAL FACEOFFS
JEFF PARKER takes these, particularly because of his ability to tie up the opposing center.

DAVE ANDREYCHUK

Yrs. of NHL service: 7
Born: Hamilton, Ontario, Canada; September 29, 1963
Position: Left wing
Height: 6-3
Weight: 214
Uniform no.: 25
Shoots: right

Career statistics:

GP	G	A	TP	PIM
478	202	266	468	371

1988-89 statistics:

GP	G	A	TP	+/-	PIM	PP	SH	GW	GT	S	PCT
56	28	24	52	1	40	7	0	3	0	145	19.3

LAST SEASON

Games played total was full-season low (knee injury). Andreychuk finished fifth in team scoring, third in goals. Goal total was second lowest of career, assist and point totals full-season lows.

THE FINESSE GAME

Andreychuk's best finesse skills are concentrated in his head and his hands, not his feet. He's got a real good wrist shot that forces the goaltender to make saves, and Dave's hands are soft enough for him to release the puck quickly and while in traffic. He smartly makes use of his shot by shooting often, and he makes his shooting in tight more effective by using his backhand when necessary (instead of circling to his forehand).

While primarily a finisher, Dave does look for his teammates. Because he handles the puck well and has excellent anticipation, Andreychuk is a good passer. He sees openings for his teammates and gets the puck to them well, but his anticipation is more likely to put him in scoring position (where he wants the puck).

As a skater, Andreychuk has little foot speed or quickness above the NHL average. While he has good balance (which helps him maintain body position in front of the net), Andreychuk lacks the foot speed that — when working in tandem with balance — creates agility.

He is a good defensive player and pays attention to that aspect of the game, backchecking deeply in his own zone.

THE PHYSICAL GAME

His balance and strength on his skates are what make Andreychuk a slot scorer. He drives the net and is almost impossible to move once he's planted himself there. Andreychuk also uses his great size to gain position either along the boards or in front of the net. Because he's practically impossible to move legally, he'll draw a lot of penalties.

He won't clobber people, but Dave will use his size while checking and will rub out the opposition along the boards. He uses his hand and arm strength to get the puck away while people are draped all over him; he'll also draw some faceoff duty because of that strength.

Andreychuk also puts his big wingspan to use around the net, first to gather in pucks (good hand and wrist strength helps here) and then to muscle a shot away despite checking.

THE INTANGIBLES

Andreychuk is one of the few Sabre youngsters who entered the League to big expectations who has actually come anywhere near fulfilling his notices. Though essentially a non-contributor in this season's playoffs (three assists in five games), Dave has shown that he can contribute in key situations. On a team as enigmatic as Buffalo, that's an important characteristic.

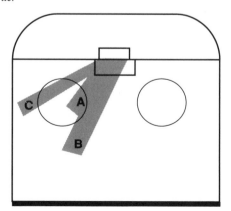

SCOTT ARNIEL

Yrs. of NHL service: 8
Born: Kingston, Ontario, Canada; September 17, 1962
Position: Left wing/right wing
Height: 6-1
Weight: 188
Uniform no.: 9
Shoots: left

Career statistics:

GP	G	A	TP	PIM
547	121	155	276	415

1988-89 statistics:

GP	G	A	TP	+/-	PIM	PP	SH	GW	GT	S	PCT
80	18	23	41	10	46	0	2	3	1	122	14.8

LAST SEASON

Played 80 games for the third time in career, one of just two Sabres to play all 80 games last season. Goal and point totals were three season highs. His plus/minus was third best, second among forwards.

THE FINESSE GAME

Arniel is an average player in terms of finesse skills and their application. He has some speed in his skating, along with good balance, but lacks the quickness that would create true agility. He combines his skating with a modicum of hockey sense to forecheck fairly well. Those traits also make him an effective checker or penalty killer.

His anticipation does not, however, translate into the ability to get into scoring position — to find the openings. Nor does he have the ability to translate that modicum of anticipation into even above-average playmaking. Scott's thinking is essentially one-dimensional — "This is the play I have to make now," — without consideration of a second step.

His shot is less than outstanding, so Arniel will have to use his speed to crash the net and score opportunistically. He may also convert a handful of shorthanded opportunities.

Arniel is a conscientious defensive player, succeeding by playing his position well.

THE PHYSICAL GAME

Scott has decent strength and size, but is wildly inconsistent in his use of those assets. Some nights he'll hit, others he'll push and shove. Some nights he won't go into the high density areas, others he does nothing except get trapped along the boards.

Not surprisingly, Arniel gets his best results when playing a sound physical game, probably because he is more aware of what is going on around him as he hits and grinds away and attempts to avoid checks so he can make his plays.

In other words, when he keeps his head up, he can make plays. He will also sacrifice his body to block shots.

THE INTANGIBLES

Arniel is succeeding in Buffalo because the coaching staff hasn't set a too-high standard that Arniel won't reach. He is a very hard worker and a very coachable player, but he is not a great player — so what you see with Arniel is what you get.

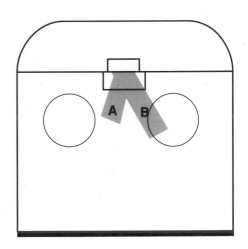

DOUG BODGER

Yrs. of NHL service: 5
Born: Chemainus, B.C., Canada; June 18, 1966
Position: Defenseman
Height: 6-2
Weight: 200
Uniform no.: 8
Shoots: left

Career statistics:

GP	G	A	TP	PIM
360	421	72	214	344

1988-89 statistics:

GP	G	A	TP	+/-	PIM	PP	SH	GW	GT	S	PCT
71	8	44	52	15	59	6	0	1	0	156	5.1

LAST SEASON

Acquired by Buffalo from Pittsburgh (along with Darrin Shannon) in exchange for Tom Barrasso. Games played total was second highest of career, assist and point totals career highs. He missed five games with an abdominal injury, one game with a back injury. He was third on the club in SOG total, first in plus/minus.

THE FINESSE GAME

Bodger's skating powers his finesse game. He is a good skater with a strong stride and good agility. He has good lateral movement and one-step quickness (surprisingly so for a man with his size and bulk) and those skills allow him to implement his other finesse skills. He carries the puck confidently from the defensive zone, and will join the attack when he can. Bodger is also smart enough — and poised enough — to know when to fall back to defense.

Doug sees the ice very well from the blue line, so he's able to get the puck to his teammates with good result. He makes good passes to both sides. Defensively, he consistently makes the safe, smart plays to get the puck out of the zone, and he forces the play wide when it is coming at him. He will, however, make the occasional blind pass around the boards that gives the puck to the opposition.

Bodger brings those vision and puck-handling skills to bear on the power play, exploiting openings for his teammates with his passing skills. He'll lead his teammates into those openings, but Doug's hands are good enough to get passes through traffic.

Bodger's shot is probably the weakest of his finesse skills, in that it is only average in terms of speed and power. He has learned to shoot more frequently, though, and that will help his offense improve. He must also contribute more at even strength, as he scored just twice in even strength situations.

THE PHYSICAL GAME

Basically, Bodger is a finesse player with size. Doug uses his body fairly effectively and efficiently around the net and on the boards, but he could use his size and develop his strength so that he becomes a punishing hitter, making opposing forwards think twice before venturing near him. That would also give him some more room for his finesse plays.

THE INTANGIBLES

Bodger and Phil Housley should feed well off each other, as the presence of each now means that neither can be checked exclusively — that would leave the other free.

In the meantime, Doug's continuing to improve. He works hard and takes coaching well, and continued improvement could make Bodger an All Star defender.

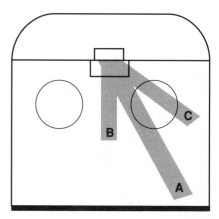

36

JACQUES CLOUTIER

Yrs. of NHL service: 5
Born: Noranda, Quebec, Canada; January 3, 1960
Position: Goaltender
Height: 5-7
Weight: 167
Uniform no.: 1
Catches: left

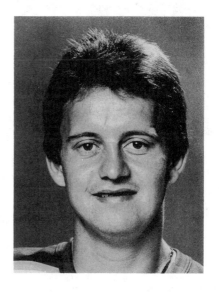

Career statistics:

GP	MINS	G	SO	AVG	A	PIM
144	7,442	459	1	3.70	7	29

1988-89 statistics:

GP	MINS	AVG	W	L	T	SO	GA	SA	SAPCT	PIM
36	1,786	3.63	15	14	0	0	108	857	.874	6

LAST SEASON

Games played total was second highest of career.

THE PHYSICAL GAME

Cloutier is a little guy and as such must be able to play his angles very well or else the league's better shooters will put the puck over his shoulder before he can blink. He is at his best when he stays on his feet.

But that doesn't mean he does that often. He scrambles, he flops, he's very helter-skelter. To play angles and challenge the shooters requires confidence, something that is not always in long supply for Cloutier.

He handles the puck fairly well and will come out of his net to stop the puck from rolling around the boards. He is not a terrific skater, moving in and out of his net a little sluggishly, and that leaves him susceptible on rebound shots and two-on-ones where he must regain his position quickly. His balance problems are another reason why he's always flopping around.

He is very quick with his hands and feet, so he is successful in scrambles around the net, but Cloutier has difficulty with shots low to the glove and short sides, classic indications of failure to cut down the angle properly.

THE MENTAL GAME

Cloutier folds his tent if reached early and a bad goal destroys his confidence. He doesn't carry bad games with him, but — because he is more a backup than a first-stringer — Jacques will be rusty in his next start and the process is likely to start all over again.

THE INTANGIBLES

Cloutier is a tremendously hard worker in practice, always giving his best effort. He's a very quick goaltender but he can't sustain his performances because he's just not good enough at the NHL level.

MIKE FOLIGNO

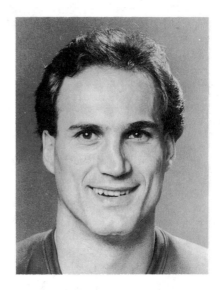

Yrs. of NHL service: 11
Born: Sudbury, Ontario, Canada; January 29, 1959
Position: Right wing
Height: 6-2
Weight: 195
Uniform no.: 17
Shoots: right

Career statistics:

GP	G	A	TP	PIM
758	305	317	622	1,656

1988-89 statistics:

GP	G	A	TP	+/-	PIM	PP	SH	GW	GT	S	PCT
75	27	22	49	-7	156	11	0	5	1	144	18.8

LAST SEASON

Assist total was career low, point total second lowest of career. Finished fourth on the club in goals, third in power play goals and tied for first in game winners. He was third in PIM total, and his plus/minus was the worst among the club's regulars.

THE FINESSE GAME

The strength of Foligno's game — other than strength — is Mike's hockey sense and anticipation. Both rank as very good, and he uses those traits as an excellent checker, determined and successful (so forget that plus/minus). Foligno sees the play well both offensively and defensively, and he is then aided in his checking or playmaking by his skating.

He's not a fancy skater by any means; his strength gives him a relentless pace. He's a hard skater, very strong and sturdy on his skates and with good acceleration up-ice. Because he doesn't really have the foot speed to transform sturdiness and balance into agility, there isn't a lot of weaving or swirling in Foligno's skating.

While he is able to recognize the play before it happens offensively, Mike's hands don't quite match the level of his hockey sense. Foligno is a little tough with the puck and sometimes too strong with his passes. He does have the stick skills to defend the puck well when he has it and can carry it at top speed for big slap shots off the wing. His best scoring weapon, however, is his wrist shot: strong, heavy and very accurate — and also way under-used. He can put that shot wherever he likes.

THE PHYSICAL GAME

Before the term came into vogue, Foligno was a power forward. His strength and the application of that strength is the basis for his success, and it sets up his finesse ability.

Foligno is a very aggressive forward and extremely effective against the boards, using his bigger frame to hit hard and to jar the puck loose. Part of Mike's sense manifests itself here, when he positions himself to make plays — he doesn't just hit for the sake of hitting, there's purpose.

He backs down from nothing and is an excellent fighter. His upper body strength, especially in his hands, wrists and forearms, power his shot and it is that strength that makes him so effective along the boards.

THE INTANGIBLES

Foligno is a team leader because of his attitude and his work habits. The fact that he's always in tremendous physical shape and always ready to play attest to that, and that's why it's so interesting to see the friction that has developed between Foligno and Coach Ted Sator.

That rift bears watching.

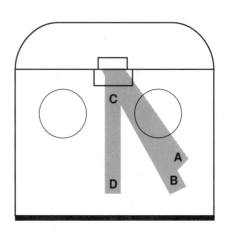

MIKE HARTMAN

Yrs. of NHL service: 2
Born: Detroit, Mich., USA; February 7, 1967
Position: Left wing
Height: 6-0
Weight: 183
Uniform no.: 20
Shoots: left

Career statistics:

GP	G	A	TP	PIM
105	14	13	27	475

1988-89 statistics:

GP	G	A	TP	+/-	PIM	PP	SH	GW	GT	S	PCT
70	8	9	17	8	316	1	0	0	0	91	8.8

LAST SEASON

Hartman's first full NHL campaign after two previous attempts. He led the club in PIM total. He was sidelined mid-season with a back injury.

THE FINESSE GAME

Hartman is a strong skater, and his stride gives him some decent NHL speed. He doesn't have a lot of agility, but — in his role as a checking forward — Mike can stay with the competition because of the modest speed he possesses.

His other finesse skills are about in line with his skating, probably below the skating level. He has no real sense of the ice offensively, nor does he have the hand skills necessary for puck work anyway. He'll have to be opportunistic for his goals, shovelling loose pucks into empty nets.

He succeeds in his checking and defensive work through diligence and effort, and not through exceptional hockey sense or play-reading ability.

THE PHYSICAL GAME

Hartman beats people up. That, essentially, is his game. He uses his strong skating stride to track down the opposition and will hit them when he can, but Mike is in the lineup for his fistic willingness and prowess.

THE INTANGIBLES

Unlike linemate Kevin Maguire, Hartman is young enough to have some future ahead of him — despite the limited role he plays. It's interesting to note, however, that despite the time he spends in the box (almost five and quarter *games* worth), Hartman is a plus-hockey player. Clearly, when he stays on the ice, he doesn't hurt the Sabres defensively.

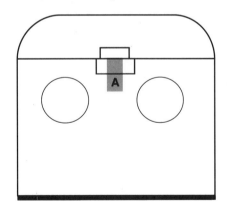

BENOIT HOGUE

Yrs. of NHL service: 1
Born: Repentigny, Quebec, Canada; October 28, 1966
Position: Center
Height: 5-10
Weight: 177
Uniform no.: 33
Shoots: left

Career statistics:

GP	G	A	TP	PIM
72	15	31	46	120

1988-89 statistics:

GP	G	A	TP	+/-	PIM	PP	SH	GW	GT	S	PCT
69	14	30	44	-4	120	1	2	0	0	114	12.3

LAST SEASON

First full NHL campaign. Finished third among rookies for shorthanded goals, first among rookies in first goals. He missed three games with a back injury.

THE FINESSE GAME

Hogue demonstrated some good skills last season, especially in his skating. He has NHL speed along the straightaways, and his strong stride provides him with acceleration so he can pull away from the defense and go to the net. He doesn't yet have NHL-level agility or lateral movement because he lacks the requisite quickness, but he's shown the balance necessary so the agility can't be too far behind.

Benoit has fairly good hand skills. He takes the puck off the boards well, and he handles the puck well in tight situations. He doesn't yet have the ability to carry the puck and skate with speed at the same time, but he can get the puck to his teammates.

He's shown a fairly good understanding of the game at the NHL level, and he knows how to get into position to score; greater foot speed will get him into that position consistently.

Because of his good hands, Hogue will score from in close. He'll get his shot away in traffic, and he's also got the eye/hand coordination to tip and deflect the puck. He shoots the puck with strength and accuracy, and he makes his shot better by getting it off quickly.

THE PHYSICAL GAME

He doesn't have great size, but Hogue plays well in the traffic areas — his balance helps here. He uses his body to gain position in front of the net and along the boards, and that willingness makes his finesse ability more valuable.

Hogue also uses his body to maintain position after he has the puck, protecting it well from opposition checking.

THE INTANGIBLES

Hogue showed well in his rookie season, carving out some power play and penalty-killing time along with his regular shift. That's a lot of responsibility for a rookie, and Hogue will see more of that time as his career progresses.

He has a good attitude and great desire, and that should power his continued NHL improvement.

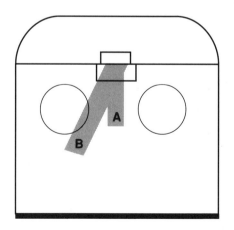

40

PHIL HOUSLEY

Yrs. of NHL service: 7
Born: St. Paul, Minn., USA; March 9, 1964
Position: Defenseman
Height: 5-10
Weight: 179
Uniform no.: 6
Shoots: left

Career statistics:

GP	G	A	TP	PIM
528	157	320	477	354

1988-89 statistics:

GP	G	A	TP	+/-	PIM	PP	SH	GW	GT	S	PCT
72	26	44	70	6	47	5	0	3	0	178	14.6

LAST SEASON

Games played total was career low, but point total was second highest of career. He missed four games with a back injury. He finished second on the club in scoring (sixth among NHL defenders — second in goals).

THE FINESSE GAME

Housley is an excellent skater, fluid in his stride and with great agility. He has tremendous acceleration, superb balance and quickness and excellent lateral movement, and he uses all these assets to drive the defense off the blue line to create room for his teammates.

He handles the puck extremely well (though less so at full speed), but his 1-on-1 play against the defense is sometimes rendered less than effective because of Housley's inability to consistently find his teammates and take advantage of them. Not that Phil is selfish; rather, he simply doesn't see the play from alongside or at its head as well as he does when he's behind it.

Defensively, Housley forces many plays at the Buffalo blue line, and he can do that because he closes the gap on the puck carrier excellently. He has developed a better understanding of his defensive angles, and when he fails to play positionally his skating will bail him out.

Housley does well on the power-play unit, where he can put his speed and puckhandling ability to use, and he can score. He has a good wrist shot that he likes to deliver from the high slot and he can slap the puck well (quick, not heavy) from the point.

THE PHYSICAL GAME

Housley's finesse skills and improved physical game have given him an excellent transitional game. His ability to make plays along the boards or from the corners is amplified by his willingness to take the body to free the puck. He also covers the front of his net with better effectiveness, though he still won't belt anyone into next week.

THE INTANGIBLES

Despite seven NHL seasons, Housley still hasn't corrected his 1-on-1 flaws. Though he possesses skills that would be classified as world-class, Housley's consistent inability to bring those skills to bear (43 points at home last season, 27 on the road), and his inability to correct — after seven NHL seasons — his 1-on-1 flaws, turn his world-class skills into those of an underachiever.

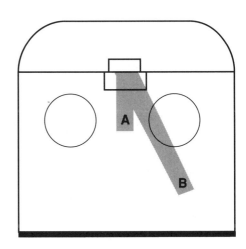

UWE KRUPP

Yrs. of NHL service: 3
Born: Cologne, West Germany; June 24, 1965
Position: Defenseman
Height: 6-6
Weight: 230
Uniform no.: 4
Shoots: right

Career statistics:

GP	G	A	TP	PIM
171	8	26	34	229

1988-89 statistics:

GP	G	A	TP	+/-	PIM	PP	SH	GW	GT	S	PCT
70	5	13	18	0	55	0	1	0	0	51	9.8

LAST SEASON

Second season games played total fell from first year, but all point totals were career highs. He missed time with a rib injury.

THE FINESSE GAME

Krupp has demonstrated quiet efficiency in his first two NHL seasons. While he'll never be confused with teammate Phil Housley, Krupp has good vision and anticipation and he uses those skills to move the puck and make correct defensive decisions.

His skating is good but not great, and Krupp would benefit from increased foot speed for quickness and agility. He's going to play defense positionally and force the play wide of the net, rather than challenge the puck carrier at his blue line.

He's making good decisions to turn the play around by getting the puck to the forwards quickly. One reason he does well here is because he keeps his head up to make plays — of course, Krupp is already head and shoulders above most other players just through his size. That ability to keep his head up evidences itself at the offensive blue line, where Krupp knows to lift his shot over a sliding forward.

He will otherwise not make many contributions offensively, nor will he regularly lug the puck from the Sabres zone.

THE PHYSICAL GAME

Krupp is very similar in style to Philadelphia's under-rated Kjell Samuelsson, in that they both play efficiently and unspectacularly. Krupp takes the body well and then moves the puck up-ice, but many people are going to see his 6-foot-6 body and expect board-breaking checks. They aren't going to get them. Krupp's physical game — and he's not afraid to play one — is based on efficiency, not spectacular crunches.

THE INTANGIBLES

As he gains experience, Krupp's NHL ability improves. He's never going to be an outstanding player in any regard. Rather, he has the potential — and has shown progress along this path — to be a solid and dependable defenseman. And there's nothing wrong with that.

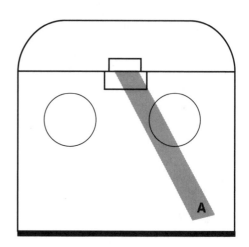

GRANT LEDYARD

Yrs. of NHL service: 5
Born: Winnipeg, Manitoba, Canada;
November 19, 1961
Position: Defenseman
Height: 6-2
Weight: 190
Uniform no.: 3
Shoots: left

Career statistics:

GP	G	A	TP	PIM
306	40	88	128	361

1988-89 statistics:

GP	G	A	TP	+/-	PIM	PP	SH	GW	GT	S	PCT
74	4	16	20	2	51	1	0	2	0	106	3.8

LAST SEASON

Acquired from Washington (along with Clint Malarchuk) in exchange for Calle Johansson. Games played total was second highest of career.

THE FINESSE GAME

Grant is a very skilled finesse player. He's a very good skater vertically as well as horizontally (up and down the ice and laterally, that is) and he has good quickness and agility for a big man.

He reads the play offensively very well, but fails to do the same thing defensively. He still gets hypnotized by the puck as he backskates, and because of that he begins his turns to angle off the opposition too late. That means passes that shouldn't even get released get completed, and it also means that Ledyard can be left grabbing at air despite his skating skill. He also has a tendency to wander, thus leaving openings.

He handles the puck well and can rush it from his zone, and he has learned to be less predictable with it once he crosses the opposing blue line. He no longer boxes himself into bad ice by carrying the puck too deeply, and he looks for his teammates to make a play. He knows how to move the puck quickly on both offense and defense, and thus does a fair job of getting it to the open man.

His best talent is unquestionably his shot, which is one of the League's hardest — hard, accurate and fast from the blue line.

THE PHYSICAL GAME

Ledyard is a very strong player, but he doesn't use his strength in front of his net or along the boards, where he could combine it with his hand skills to great advantage (making a play out of the corner after taking the puck from the opposition). Because he just pushes and shoves, the enemy will occasionally get away from him and reenter the play, so Ledyard must improve his takeouts.

In short, he's a finesse player with size — and he doesn't play up to that size.

He has a long reach and uses it well to contain the offensive point and to pokecheck the puck.

THE INTANGIBLES

Ledyard's a hard worker and an enthusiastic player, and his presence lends an offensive talent, and some more depth, to the Buffalo blue line corps. But what we see is essentially what the Sabres are going to get.

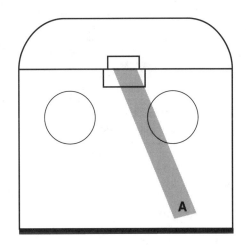

KEVIN MAGUIRE

Yrs. of NHL service: 2
Born: Trenton, Ontario, Canada; January 5, 1963
Position: Right wing
Height: 6-2
Weight: 200
Uniform no.: 19
Shoots: right

Career statistics:

GP	G	A	TP	PIM
123	12	16	28	477

1988-89 statistics:

GP	G	A	TP	+/-	PIM	PP	SH	GW	GT	S	PCT
60	8	10	18	9	241	0	0	2	0	35	22.9

LAST SEASON

Games played, all point totals and PIM mark were career high, despite missing time with an ankle injury. PIM total was second on team, plus/minus rating the team's fourth best.

THE FINESSE GAME

Not much of one. Maguire is a strong skater, but not a particularly graceful one. He has neither rink-length speed nor one-step quickness, and his lack of agility is attributable to that missing foot speed.

He doesn't handle the puck particularly well, and he has no real vision or sense of the ice and the offensive game. He succeeds as a checking forward because of his desire (his strong stride helps him close gaps and stay with his man) and physical play.

Any goals he scores will have to come on loose pucks near the net, as Maguire doesn't have a shot that will fool NHL goaltending.

THE PHYSICAL GAME

This is why Maguire is here. He'll bang whatever bodies he can catch, and his skating stride helps him drive through his checks. He can punish the opposing defensemen — if he can catch them — and that serves to make him a decent forechecker.

He also fights. A lot.

THE INTANGIBLES

Not much to say. Maguire fills a role for Buffalo and will continue to do so until a younger player with a drop more talent shows up. Then, it's goodbye to Kevin.

It is, however, worth noting that Maguire more than held his own defensively (note the plus/minus). That means that at least the Sabres can play him in most any situation — unless of course they need a goal with less than a minute remaining.

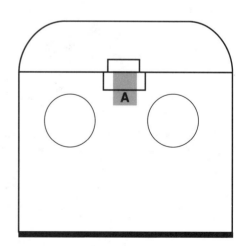

CLINT MALARCHUK

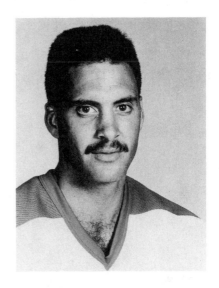

Yrs. of NHL service: 6
Born: Grand Prairie, Alta., Canada; May 1, 1961
Position: Goaltender
Height: 6-0
Weight: 190
Uniform no.: 30
Catches: left

Career statistics:

GP	MINS	G	SO	AVG	A	PIM
243	13,664	790	11	3.47	8	95

1988-89 statistics:

GP	MINS	AVG	W	L	T	SO	GA	SA	SAPCT	PIM
49	2,754	3.36	19	19	8	2	154	1,287	.880	18

LAST SEASON

Acquired from Washington (along with Grant Ledyard) in exchange for Calle Johansson. Games played total was three-season low. He missed four games with a neck injury.

THE PHYSICAL GAME

Malarchuk is a good angle goaltender, but he is strong on the reflex side as well. He has very fast hands and feet and his improved angle play has helped him to subdue his stickside weakness, though he is still weak there.

Top-of-the-net glove shots will elude him, and he generally does not control pucks he stops with his glove. He'll get a piece of a shot but he fails to hold the puck much of the time, so a shot to his glove will often result in rebounds.

On the whole he does not control any rebounds well, and that is where his reflexes serve him best, allowing him to quickly get into position to get a piece of the second shot. When he is playing his best he is square to the puck and doesn't need to scramble after a rebound.

Clint is a good skater and he likes to leave the net to handle the puck, but is not a great puck handler. He has good foot speed and so he regains his stance quickly, and also moves well from post to post.

His fast hands and feet make him very effective in scrambles near the net, but he does not always see the puck well, so he'll stay deep in the net on screens to get a longer look.

THE MENTAL GAME

Malarchuk is mentally tough and will fight you for the next goal after giving up a bad one — most of the time. He does have a tendency to give up goals in bunches, but he is able to pull himself together and forget a bad outing.

Clint has good anticipation and concentration, another reason why he is so effective around the net.

THE INTANGIBLES

We won't question whether or not Malarchuk has completely recovered from his neck injury; just getting back in the barrel indicates great courage, which should answer any questions about his ability to function in the NHL.

But that question will persist, especially if Clint falters during the season. Perhaps of greater importance — if his recovery is a given — is the fact that, despite his regular season successes, Malarchuk still has yet to win his first playoff game.

That's quite a monkey to carry, and it's one reason why we told you last year that Malarchuk might get moved from Washington.

MARK NAPIER

Yrs. of NHL service: 11
Born: Toronto, Ontario, Canada;
January 28, 1957
Position: Right wing
Height: 5-10
Weight: 183
Uniform no.: 65
Shoots: left

Career statistics:

GP	G	A	TP	PIM
767	235	306	541	157

1988-89 statistics:

GP	G	A	TP	+/-	PIM	PP	SH	GW	GT	S	PCT
66	11	17	28	-4	33	0	2	1	0	92	12.0

LAST SEASON

Point totals were all second lowest of career. Tied for team lead in shorthanded goals.

THE FINESSE GAME

Skating speed is the key to Napier's game, and it's what he puts to work as a checking forward. He remains an excellent skater, equipped with a good burst of speed, excellent acceleration ability and good agility. His balance combines well with his quickness to give him outstanding lateral movement, and that helps him greatly in his forechecking and puck pursuit.

His hands haven't stood the test of time nearly as well as his feet, so Mark's big scoring days are behind him. Where previously his hands could operate in time with his foot speed, Napier no longer handles the puck well when at full throttle. He won't, therefore, waste his opportunities, and Napier puts a hard and accurate shot on net. He will score most of his goals from wihin the slot area, using his speed and quickness in opportunistic fashion.

THE PHYSICAL GAME

During the days of his goal scoring, Napier's hand and wrist strength powered his shot and keyed his finesse game. It allowed him to reach into the pileups from the outside and come away with the puck. No more. The opposition is too big and too strong.

Mark will play a physical game when he can, but his best work has always been in open ice. Since he's used for his speed, it's unlikely he'll be found along the boards with any regularity.

THE INTANGIBLES

Napier has an excellent attitude and work ethic, but his skills are such that he has become a role player. And old role players are vulnerable to replacement. Don't be surprised if he finishes the season with a team other than the one on which he started the year.

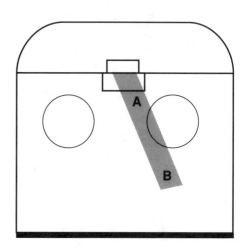

JEFF PARKER

Yrs. of NHL service: 1
Born: St. Paul, Minn., USA; September 7, 1964
Position: Center
Height: 6-3
Weight: 194
Uniform no.: 29
Shoots: right

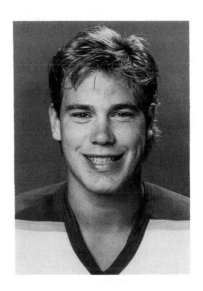

Career statistics:

GP	G	A	TP	PIM
76	12	14	26	91

1988-89 statistics:

GP	G	A	TP	+/-	PIM	PP	SH	GW	GT	S	PCT
57	9	9	18	3	82	0	0	2	0	78	11.5

LAST SEASON

First full NHL season. Began season in American Hockey League, then missed time with knee and finger injuries.

THE FINESSE GAME

Parker is primarily a grinder, and that's because his skating isn't particularly exceptional and his offensive mindset is not especially creative.

He has a big stride that takes him where he's going, and there's some speed and quickness to be brought to bear, but Jeff succeeds more on desire than skating talent.

While he reads the play in front of him fairly well, and combines that read with his modicum of skating talent to be a good forechecker and defensive player, Parker doesn't translate that read into offense; the game is still a little too fast for him. And since he thinks in straight lines, his offense is going to be straight forward: opportunistic and direct — he'll have to score on loose pucks that his checking has created.

His defensive game is very sound, and Parker covers his man way back into the Buffalo zone. He understands and executes his defensive responsibilities, and he'll see penalty killing time because of that.

THE PHYSICAL GAME

Jeff has great size, but he doesn't really do anything with it. He's not timid, but neither does he impose himself on the opposition. Right now, teamed with tough guys Mike Hartman and Kevin Maguire, Parker doesn't have to be a bruiser, but the question is, how well will he cover the NHL's big, strong centers?

His reach helps him snare loose pucks and tie up the opposition, and his eye/hand coordination and arm strength make him a good faceoff man.

THE INTANGIBLES

Not a bad rookie year, especially considering that Parker was a right winger switched to center. But it's worth noting that his main contributions come in the defensive areas, in the role player realm of checking forward. At age 25, Parker's going to need to improve on that role if he intends to spend any significant time in the NHL.

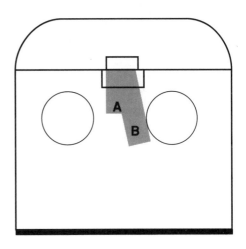

47

LARRY PLAYFAIR

Yrs. of NHL service: 11
Born: Fort St. James, B.C., Canada; June 23, 1958
Position: Defenseman
Height: 6-4
Weight: 200
Uniform no.: 27
Shoots: left

Career statistics:

GP	G	A	TP	PIM
684	26	93	119	1,810

1988-89 statistics:

GP	G	A	TP	+/-	PIM	PP	SH	GW	GT	S	PCT
48	0	6	6	-7	126	0	0	0	0	10	0.0

LAST SEASON

Acquired from Los Angeles for Bob Logan and a draft choice. Games played total was second lowest of career.

THE FINESSE GAME

Finesse has never been Playfair's game and most of his skills reflect that, but he does have a couple of finesse assets. He is not a good skater and has trouble with any kind of speed attack because of his lack of mobility. Playfair has a great deal of trouble stopping and starting, which means he won't be able to make the evasive maneuvers necessary to lose a forechecker when he goes back for the puck.

A defenseman without speed needs positional smarts, something Playfair does not have a great deal of. He is just average at playing his defensive angles, relying more on his imposing size to prevent the opposition from setting up camp in his zone than he does correct defensive positioning.

Larry does have some offensive ability that has been overshadowed by his physical play. While he won't join the rush as a fourth attacker, he can make a fairly positive offensive move at the blue line and he is an exceptionally good passer.

He can play a role on left wing as well as defense, functioning as the forward staying back to cover defensively or down low to plug the net. He'll get a goal or two a year from the front of the net, and another couple from the point.

THE PHYSICAL GAME

Playfair is a big tough guy, strong in his own end of the ice when he can catch the opposition. He is tough in the corners and in front of the net because of his good strength and he likes to hit — a lot. He is a punishing hitter and can also muscle the puck away from the opposition.

But he suffers from over-aggressiveness, charging at people, elbowing, obviously rubbing his gloves in their faces. Then the referee has no choice but to send him to the box.

He can contribute in a limited defensive role if he curbs his temper and will sacrifice his body to block a shot or two. He is also an accomplished fighter.

THE INTANGIBLES

Playfair is a quality team individual, a very positive guy and hard worker. However, his ice skills are limited.

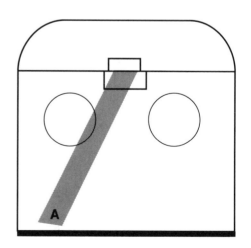

DAREN PUPPA

Yrs. of NHL service: 2
Born: Kirkland Lake, Ontario, Canada;
March 23, 1965
Position: Goaltender
Height: 6-3
Weight: 191
Uniform no.: 31
Catches: right

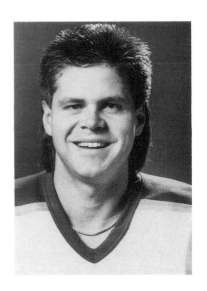

Career statistics:

GP	MINS	G	SO	AVG	A	PIM
64	3,368	202	2	3.60	5	18

1988-89 statistics:

GP	MINS	AVG	W	L	T	SO	GA	SA	SAPCT	PIM
37	1,908	3.36	17	10	6	1	107	961	.889	12

LAST SEASON

First full NHL campaign. He suffered a broken arm on January 31 that sidelined him for the season.

THE PHYSICAL GAME

Puppa's game is easily divisible into two separate entities. When the puck is above the faceoff circles, Puppa uses his size to advantage by standing up and challenging the shooter. Once the puck moves nearer the net, Puppa's going to be flopping around the net.

The result is that, with play nearer the net, Puppa is going to be on his knees handing out rebounds. And instead of being on his feet forcing the opposition to make good shots from the slot for goals, they've got their choice of corners — especially the high ones — to shoot for.

He's not a bad skater, and Puppa comes out of his net to help himself by gathering loose pucks and moving them to the defense. He doesn't have great lateral movement, so criss-cross, bang-bang plays across the crease will have a high degree of success.

His reflexes do help him here, as does his size in covering a lot of net, but should he make the save a loose puck is going to be on the doorstep.

THE MENTAL GAME

Puppa's concentration goes through peaks and valleys from contest to contest. He's generally ready to play, and though he can give up goals in bunches those seem to be more an effect of his style than any indication of his caving in mentally.

His history shows that he's won big games, but he has yet to demonstrate that at the NHL level.

THE INTANGIBLES

Right now, health is a big question mark. Puppa has to recuperate from the broken arm that sidelined him from mid-season on. He was ready to accept the challenge and responsibility of being the Sabres' number one goalie (which was a big reason Tom Barrasso was traded), and his history shows that he's been a winner at many levels.

But to this point, Puppa has yet to show that he's anything out of the ordinary in the NHL. This season, in which he must wrest the top spot from Clint Malarchuk, will go a long way toward determining Puppa's NHL future.

MIKE RAMSEY

Yrs. of NHL service: 9
Born: Minneapolis, Minn., USA; December 3, 1960
Position: Defenseman
Height: 6-3
Weight: 187
Uniform no.: 5
Shoots: left

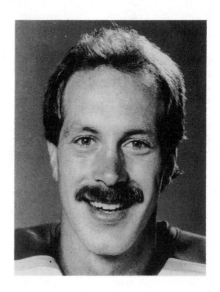

Career statistics:

GP	G	A	TP	PIM
668	58	199	257	744

1988-89 statistics:

GP	G	A	TP	+/-	PIM	PP	SH	GW	GT	S	PCT
56	2	14	16	5	84	0	0	1	0	63	3.2

LAST SEASON

Games played, goal and point totals were all career lows; assist total tied career low. He missed 14 games with a hand injury, eight with a groin injury.

THE FINESSE GAME

First glance says that Ramsey's talents are unexceptional — until his excellent smarts are factored into the equation. Simply, he almost never makes a bad defensive decision. He is an excellent positional player who understands his defensive angles and plays them almost to perfection. He reads the play exceptionally well, and his anticipation and sense tell him what to do after he has the puck or after he has made a takeout. He's anything but a one-dimensional defenseman; Mike can handle any defensive zone responsibility.

Don't get us wrong — Mike is not an unskilled player. Rather, his smarts make his less-than-superstar level skills *defensive* superstar skills. He skates forward or back equally well, and has fairly good agility. He can close the gap on the puck carrier, and his challenging at the blue line is textbook.

Mike passes the puck from his zone very well, but he can carry the puck to take pressure off his forwards. He'll never overhandle the puck. He's not an offensive force, so his 7-10 goals a year will come on a good low shot (with nore than a little power) from the right point.

THE PHYSICAL GAME

Like his finesse play, Ramsey's physical play is anything but spectacular. He plays a physical style and is very tough in front of his own net, where he'll tie up most every forward. Mike takes the body very well along the boards, always positioning himself to make a play after a takeout.

He checks well in open ice, so the opposing forwards can't make plays with their heads down. Mike is also willing to sacrifice his body to block shots, and is one of the league's best in that category. The only downside to his shot-blocking is the fact he takes himself out of the play by going down to block the puck.

THE INTANGIBLES

He's smart, he works hard, he plays in pain. Ramsey's a leader, arguably Buffalo's most important player, possibly — even with Phil Housley — Buffalo's best defenseman.

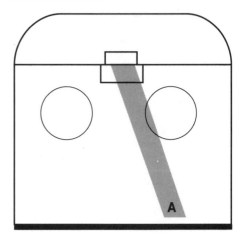

CHRISTIAN RUUTTU

Yrs. of NHL service: 3
Born: Lappeenranta, Finland; February 20, 1964
Position: Center
Height: 5-11
Weight: 194
Uniform no.: 21
Shoots: left

Career statistics:

GP	G	A	TP	PIM
216	62	134	196	245

1988-89 statistics:

GP	G	A	TP	+/-	PIM	PP	SH	GW	GT	S	PCT
67	14	46	60	13	98	5	0	1	0	149	9.4

LAST SEASON

Games played, goal and point totals were all career lows (he missed eight games with a chest injury). PIM total was career high, and he finished third on the club in scoring, second in assists and plus/minus (first among forwards in the last category).

THE FINESSE GAME

Ruuttu is an excellent finesse player, particularly outstanding in his skating skill. Christian's excellent speed, quickness and acceleration (plus a great change of pace) drives the defensemen off the blue line and creates room for his teammates. Since he comes back deeply into his own zone, his skating also allows him to move up-ice with the puck. There aren't many centers who have to be checked in their own zones, but Ruuttu's speed makes that imperative. His balance and quickness combine to give him exceptional lateral movement, and Ruuttu uses those skills in traffic exceedingly well.

Christian's excellent hockey sense makes his skating more effective, showing him how to exploit the openings his skating has created. He is a very creative player without the puck, and he knows how to get into playmaking and scoring position.

Ruuttu's stick skills match his skating skills and that means he can carry the puck *and* make his plays at top speed, always an asset. He sees the ice well and makes excellent use of his teammates, making his plays with his head up in order to take advantage of the open man.

He drives a quick and accurate wrist/snap shot at the goalie and, because he rarely shoots from outside the slot area, his shots are usually high percentage plays. He also has soft hands, so Ruuttu can and will score from in tight while being checked.

His skills make him a sound defensive player, as well as a specialty teams natural.

THE PHYSICAL GAME

He doesn't have great size, but Ruuttu is a pretty feisty player. Not only is he completely unafraid of the corners or of accepting physical play, Ruuttu also likes to initiate contact. That physical willingness makes his finesse game better, because it opens up more ice for his use.

His excellent balance comes into play in the physical game, keeping him upright and in the play after collisions. He sacrifices his body to make plays.

THE INTANGIBLES

Though his scoring went south last season (don't worry, it'll come back), Ruuttu didn't have a bad season (as his plus/minus and assist totals indicate). He's quality goods, a player with a good work ethic, and Ruuttu's mental toughness ensures that he'll continue his NHL development.

We repeat: The best is still to come with this young man.

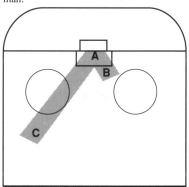

RAY SHEPPARD

Yrs. of NHL service: 2
Born: Pembroke, Ontario, Canada; May 27, 1966
Position: Right wing
Height: 6-1
Weight: 182
Uniform no.: 23
Shoots: right

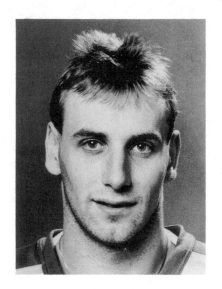

Career statistics:

GP	G	A	TP	PIM
141	60	48	108	29

1988-89 statistics:

GP	G	A	TP	+/-	PIM	PP	SH	GW	GT	S	PCT
67	22	21	43	-7	15	7	0	4	1	147	15.0

LAST SEASON

All totals fell in second NHL season, except PIM total. He missed time with a foot injury.

THE FINESSE GAME

Two particular traits of Sheppard's are standout finesse skills: his nose for the net, and his hands for shooting the puck. Sheppard knows how to get into scoring position and he always knows where the net is.

His shot is a superior one, courtesy of Ray's soft hands. His release of the puck is exceptional, very quick, and he shoots off the pass excellently: that's a quick release, and that's why Ray gets so many shots during a game.

At the other end of the spectrum, his skating is very questionable. He needs greater foot speed in order to consistently function at the NHL level. That foot speed would also aid his playmaking ability, by giving Sheppard more time to move the puck because — strangely — Sheppard doesn't read the ice as well (and therefore doesn't move the puck quickly enough) as he reads a scoring opening.

His defensive skills would also improve with better skating, but even given that Sheppard could apply himself better to that aspect of the game.

THE PHYSICAL GAME

There really isn't one. Sheppard doesn't have a great deal of strength, and he doesn't challenge the opposition with what he does have. When he goes to the net, Ray needs to bump the defense to earn more space. Instead, he just takes his lumps.

THE INTANGIBLES

We told you last year that his second year was going to be much tougher for Sheppard, and he was a big disappointment for the Sabres last season. One reason for his decreased output was his failure to work hard enough to get into scoring position.

Ray was often content to get screened off or checked and thus prevented from getting to the openings, so much so that he was beyond ineffective in certain games — he was invisible.

This was especially so on the road, where he scored just three goals and 10 points in 30 games. That says something about his work ethic and intensity, and those things must change if he is to regain his rookie year success.

Frankly, we're unsure that he will.

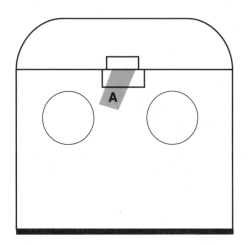

JOHN TUCKER

Yrs. of NHL service: 6
Born: Windsor, Ontario, Canada; September 29, 1964
Position: Center
Height: 6-0
Weight: 197
Uniform no.: 7
Shoots: right

Career statistics:

GP	G	A	TP	PIM
319	114	149	263	136

1988-89 statistics:

GP	G	A	TP	+/-	PIM	PP	SH	GW	GT	S	PCT
60	13	31	44	-4	31	3	0	1	0	94	13.8

LAST SEASON

Games played total was three-season high, but goal total was career low; point total second lowest of career. Missed time with back and hand injuries. Plus/minus was tied for third worst among regulars.

THE FINESSE GAME

Tucker's greatest finesse skill, the one that really powers the rest of his game, is his outstanding anticipation. He sees the openings excellently and he combines his anticipation and excellent vision with his superior hand skills to exploit those openings in a number of ways.

John is an exceptional passer; his sense is one reason and his hand skill is another. He passes well to both sides and has great touch, so his passes are always easy to handle. He uses his passing to either hit a breaking teammate, or to lead a teammate into an opening.

His hand skills extend to his puckhandling ability, and they dovetail well with his skating. Not seemingly spectacular, Tucker nevertheless has excellent agility and lateral movement. His balance and foot speed are the keys here — especially his excellent one-step quickness. His skating and hand skills allow him to make plays while moving, and he's able to slip away from his man quickly to get clear.

John combines his hand, foot and sense skills to great success in the tight quarters around the enemy net. He needs just the slightest opening to get free and then finesse the puck home, but he also has the strength to score from farther out.

He's a regular on both specialty teams.

THE PHYSICAL GAME

He's got better size than he seems to have; John's a solid six feet, 190 pounds, but his style has him playing smaller. Tucker doesn't impose himself on the opposition, but he's not intimidated by it. He willingly goes to the traffic areas and takes whatever abuse is necessary for him to make his plays.

And considering his propensity toward injury, it might not be a bad idea for him to stay away from contact.

THE INTANGIBLES

Tucker is a hard-working center with some outstanding finesse skills, yet he has never fully brought those skills to bear consistently at the NHL level. He can come through in big games — as he showed in the playoffs two springs back — but he hasn't done that in the regular season.

Since becoming a full-time NHLer (and he's still only 25 years old), Tucker has played only 298 of a possible 400 games — he's missed over 20 percent of the contests. A full season would demonstrate Tucker's talent.

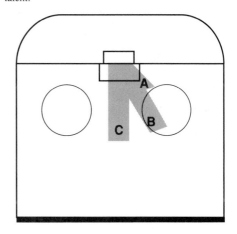

PIERRE TURGEON

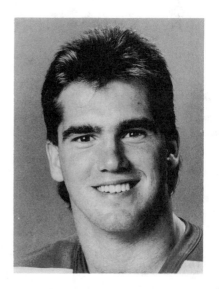

Yrs. of NHL service: 2
Born: Rouyn, Quebec, Canada; August 29, 1969
Position: Center
Height: 6-1
Weight: 203
Uniform no.: 77
Shoots: left

Career statistics:

GP	G	A	TP	PIM
156	48	82	130	60

1988-89 statistics:

GP	G	A	TP	+/-	PIM	PP	SH	GW	GT	S	PCT
80	34	54	88	-3	26	19	0	5	0	182	18.7

LAST SEASON

Led the club in scoring with career highs in all categories. He was one of just two Sabres to play all 80 games. Finished first in goals, assists, power play goals, game winners and shots on goal.

THE FINESSE GAME

The strength of Pierre's game is in the hockey sense and playmaking categories. He has great vision and anticipation, and Turgeon recognizes — and is beginning to exploit — the openings he's seeing.

He has excellent hands in all categories (passing, puckhandling and shooting), and he'll excel at getting the puck to his teammates anywhere, any time. Pierre will use his puckhandling ability in conjunction with his skating to be very creative with the puck — to open up space that his teammates can skate into, or that he can pass to.

Turgeon shoots the puck extremely well, and because his sense gets him into scoring position his scoring opportunities are many. He has quick release necessary to score from in close, the ability to put the puck anywhere he wants, and the strength to score from a distance. Better even-strength scoring is a must, however, as just 15 of his goals came at full strength.

Skating is currently the least of Turgeon's skills, but his very strong stride provides him with speed and acceleration ability. He also has exceptional balance, and that allows him to maintain body position while being checked.

His skills make him a specialty teams natural. Defensively, he tends to coast back to the Sabres zone instead of keeping his feet moving.

THE PHYSICAL GAME

If Pierre ever gets the urge to really impose himself on the opposition (and he must if he is to achieve his full potential), watch out. He's already got good size and strength, despite the fact that he's only 20 years old and still several years away from physical maturity.

Right now, Turgeon's neither a banger nor a power forward, but he goes to the traffic areas to score. He takes checks to make his plays and he uses his body very well to protect the puck. His balance is the key here.

Pierre controls the puck well with his feet, and his good hand and arm strength make him a good faceoff man.

THE INTANGIBLES

He led the club in scoring both in the regular season and the playoffs. That means a lot — and his potential is still largely untapped. We're talking here about 45-50 goals and 100-120 points — maybe not this season, but certainly consistently throughout his burgeoning career.

Turgeon could grow into one of the NHL's dominant players, but he's going to see more determined checking this year than ever before. How he responds to that will go a long way toward determining just how high he'll go.

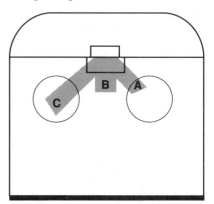

RICK VAIVE

Yrs. of NHL service: 10
Born: Ottawa, Ontario, Canada; May 14, 1959
Position: Right wing
Height: 6-1
Weight: 190
Uniform no.: 22
Shoots: right

Career statistics:

GP	G	A	TP	PIM
715	386	298	684	1,283

1988-89 statistics:

GP	G	A	TP	+/-	PIM	PP	SH	GW	GT	S	PCT
58	31	26	57	2	124	16	0	4	0	138	22.5

LAST SEASON

Acquired by Buffalo from Chicago in exchange for Adam Creighton. Games played, goal and point totals were full-season career lows; he missed 11 games with a neck injury. He finished fourth in scoring, second in goals and power play goals.

THE FINESSE GAME

Vaive is an excellent skater, and that skill is marked by his strength and ability to drive through checks. That strength also gives him good acceleration ability and rink-length speed. He'll pull away from checking within several strides.

Though his skating often forces the opposition to take penalties to slow him, Vaive helps the referee by executing some of the League's best dives. His favorite diving tactic is to grab the opponent's stick — on the ref's blind side, naturally — to make it look like he's being hooked, and then fling himself to the ice and flop like a fish out of water.

Excellent instincts around the net serve as the complement to his physical finesse skills, because he knows where to be to score. His skating gets him to that opening but so does his stickhandling, which helps him get tight to the net.

He has a good wrist shot and an excellent slap shot, and Vaive is a threat to score from anywhere inside the offensive zone because his strength drives the puck through the traffic and to the net. All his finesse talents manifest themselves especially well on the power play. He's a goal scorer and he'll look to the net before he looks to his teammates.

THE PHYSICAL GAME

Vaive is a very physical hockey player, excellent at muscling the opposition off the puck with strong hits and good upper body strength along the boards or in the corners.

Vaive hits hard and those hits jar the puck free, and he has the talent to make plays after he gains the puck. He is very difficult to control in front of the net because of his strength, and he most always gets his shots away despite being checked.

Vaive's entire game is based on playing in traffic. He gets hammered every shift because he's always going to the front of the net.

THE INTANGIBLES

Bloodied, perhaps, but unbowed — that's Rick Vaive. He was practically thrown away by the Hawks, but he showed (during the regular season, at least) that he can still score goals. Still of concern would be the inequity between his power play and even strength goal scoring, with half of his goals coming with the man-advantage.

He has yet, by the way, to play a full NHL season — a result of his physical style, no doubt.

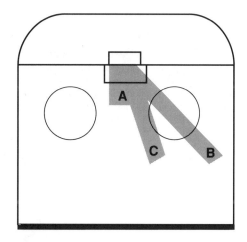

CALGARY
FLAMES

LINE COMBINATIONS
COLIN PATTERSON-DOUG GILMOUR-JOE MULLEN
GARY ROBERTS-JOE NIEUWENDYK-
JIM PEPLINSKI-JOEL OTTO-MARK HUNTER

DEFENSE PAIRINGS
GARY SUTER-BRAD MCCRIMMON
JAMIE MACOUN-AL MACINNIS
DANA MURZYN-ROB RAMAGE

GOALTENDERS
RICK WAMSLEY
MIKE VERNON

OTHER PLAYERS
THEO FLEURY — Center
TIM HUNTER — Defenseman
BRIAN MACLELLAN — Left wing
LANNY MCDONALD — Right wing
RIC NATTRESS — Defenseman

POWER PLAY

FIRST UNIT:
JOE MULLEN-JOEL OTTO-DOUG GILMOUR
GARY SUTER-AL MACINNIS

OTTO plugs the front of the net, MULLEN works in the left wing corner and GILMOUR is at the side of the right faceoff circle. He and SUTER distribute the puck, with the the objective of getting MACINNIS open for a shot. On the shot, MULLEN comes to the front of the net for the rebound.

As second unit would include the now-departed HAKAN LOOB and JOE NIEUWENDYK. LOOB worked off the right wing side, and NIEUEWNDYK is in the slot. BRAD MCCRIMMON and ROB RAMAGE are the second set of defense, even if the first unit forwards stay on.

Last season Calgary's power play was EXCELLENT, scoring 101 goals in 405 opportunities (24.9 percent, second overall).

PENALTY KILLING

FIRST UNIT:
JOEL OTTO-COLIN PATTERSON
JAMIE MACOUN-BRAD MCCRIMMON

SECOND UNIT:
JOE NIEUWENDYK-JOE MULLEN
DANA MURZYN-AL MACINNIS

OTTO and PATTERSON are very aggressive when the puck is on the point, and MACOUN is aggressive down low. MCCRIMMON stays in front of the net.

NIEUWENDYK and MULLEN are less agressive, but they too force the puck at the points and along the boards.

Last season Calgary's penalty killing was EXCELLENT, allowing 78 goals in 457 shorthanded situations (82.9 percent, first overall).

CRUCIAL FACEOFFS
DOUG GILMOUR

THEOREN FLEURY

Born: Oxbow, Sask., Canada; June 29, 1968
Position: Center
Height: 5-6
Weight: 155
Uniform no.: 14
Shoots: right

Career statistics:

GP	G	A	TP	+/-	PIM	PP	SH	GW	GT	S	PCT
36	14	20	34	5	46	5	0	3	0	89	15.7

LAST SEASON

An eighth round choice in the 1987 Entry Draft, Fleury joined the Flames in mid-season.

THE FINESSE GAME

Fleury is a whole package of finesse skills. He's an excellent skater with speed, acceleration, strength, quickness and agility, and he should have no trouble elevating those skills to the superior level in the NHL.

He makes his skating better by being able to handle the puck well at all speeds. He can scoot around a defender for a shot on goal, but Theoren can just as easily find the open man and move the puck to him.

He sees the ice and anticipates fairly well at the NHL level, despite his short major league tenure, and that skill should improve with additional experience.

Fleury will score from around the net because of his quickness in getting to loose pucks, but he'll also convert from farther out — using a quick wrist shot after driving a defenseman backward and then stepping around the defender after gaining an opening.

THE PHYSICAL GAME

Fleury might as well be 6-4 and 220 pounds for the way he applies himself to his physical game. There is no area to which Theoren won't go, no opponent he won't check, no opposing player he won't fight. His willingness and persistence will gain him more loose pucks than he'll lose, especially because Fleury has the skills and smarts to make plays after contact.

He will inevitably, however, be overpowered when matched against bigger and stronger opponents. The key for Fleury's success is not that he has to avoid traffic, but rather that he has to hit-and-run.

THE INTANGIBLES

We'll avoid the "good things in small packages," routine, but the fact is, Fleury is a gutsy, intense player, and he brings an excellent work ethic and spirit to his game. He has tremendous desire, and he should (no pun intended) grow into a fine NHLer.

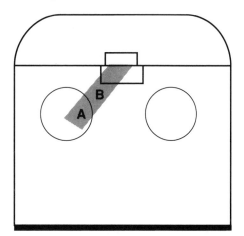

DOUG GILMOUR

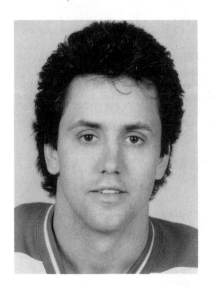

Yrs. of NHL service: 6
Born: Kingston, Ontario, Canada; June 25, 1963
Position: Center
Height: 5-11
Weight: 165
Uniform no.: 39
Shoots: left

Career statistics:

GP	G	A	TP	PIM
456	175	264	439	308

1988-89 statistics:

GP	G	A	TP	+/-	PIM	PP	SH	GW	GT	S	PCT
72	26	59	85	45	44	11	0	5	1	161	16.1

LAST SEASON

Acquired from St. Louis along with Mark Hunter, Michael Dark and Steve Bozek in exchange for Mike Bullard, Craig Coxe and Tim Corkery. Games played total tied career low (jaw injury), but assist total was second highest of career. Finished third on the club in points, tied for first in assists, was second in plus/minus rating (second in NHL).

THE FINESSE GAME

Gilmour is an extraordinarily talented player. In the offensive zone he not only sees openings but uses his sense to create them — he is excellent without the puck. In the defensive zone he uses that anticipation and vision to understand the opposition's plays and to break them up.

Gilmour looks unspectacular but he's a very good skater, not overly fast but equipped with a one-step quickness that lets him dart in and out of traffic and change direction quickly. He is very nimble on his feet — even though he won't out-race anyone — and is exceptionally dangerous within 10 feet of any loose puck. He applies that skill offensively *and* defensively. He uses his skating defensively to close passing lanes, cut off skating lanes and intercept passes.

His one-step quickness gets him to the openings his hockey sense reveals (because he shoots lefty he likes to work from the left wing) so he'll attack from there and do damage with opportunistic goals, hence his power play success.

He also uses that skill to get into the clear to make and receive passes. He is a good stick handler and can handle the puck at all speeds. He uses his teammates very well, and shows excellent creativity on the ice.

THE PHYSICAL GAME

Gilmour plays aggressively, doing whatever is necessary to make his plays — offensively or defensively. He'll go to the corner to hit or to the front of the net and get batted around when necessary.

He should learn to avoid some of that traffic because his stature can't handle it, and he'll become fatigued or injured. As he gets older it will be more difficult for him to come back from those aches and pains.

His eye/hand coordination and arm and wrist strength make him a good faceoff man.

THE INTANGIBLES

We proved ourselves remarkably — and unknowingly — prophetic last year when we wrote — *before* Gilmour's off-ice problems became known that "For this year Gilmour has to clear his mind and just do what he does best — which is play hockey better than 90 percent of the other NHLers."

Well, Doug did that — and he especially proved himself in the Stanley Cup playoffs. He's a tremendous talent, one of the very best in the NHL, and he gets better as the games become more important.

Since the Flames figure to be playing some important games for the next few springs, we should be seeing just how good Gilmour is. He's a leader with a burning desire to win.

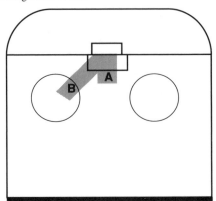

MARK HUNTER

Yrs. of NHL service: 8
Born: Petrolia, Ontario, Canada; November 12, 1962
Position: Right wing
Height: 6-0
Weight: 200
Uniform no.: 22
Shoots: right

Career statistics:

GP	G	A	TP	PIM
480	187	137	324	1,049

1988-89 statistics:

GP	G	A	TP	+/-	PIM	PP	SH	GW	GT	S	PCT
66	22	8	30	4	194	12	0	2	1	116	19.0

LAST SEASON

Acquired from St. Louis along with Doug Gilmour, Michael Dark and Steve Bozek in exchange for Mike Bullard, Craig Coxe and Tim Corkery. All point totals were three-season lows. He was sidelined with a shoulder injury.

THE FINESSE GAME

Though he can make an impact in the finesse aspects of the game, Hunter is not a finesse player. He is a strong skater with good acceleration, but he's not very agile and could do better in the area of balance.

He has to have a center get him the puck because Mark isn't going to razzle-dazzle his way to the net from his own zone, nor is he going to make plays coming out the corners. Because of his goal scoring success, Hunter doesn't use his teammates well, often shooting instead of passing to a more open teammate. Since he neither handles the puck well nor sees the ice well (which is why he needs that unselfish center in the first place), perhaps it's not a bad thing that Hunter shoots first and asks questions later.

His shot is the best of his finesse skills. Hunter gets great strength behind it and it will get to the net through traffic, but he'll need time to get it off. He'll chase his own rebounds and will get many goals on second effort. The best he'll do is 35 goals — maybe an honest 40, *maybe* — but no more than that. He works best from the faceoff circle for the original shot.

He's improved the level of his defensive game by backchecking more conscientiously, making better transitions from offense to defense, but he'll never be confused with Bob Gainey.

THE PHYSICAL GAME

The strength of Hunter's game is his strength. He's a hardnosed player and has to play that way to be successful. He has the strength and the size to play a dominant physical game, but could apply those assets more consistently. Mark can be very good in the cor-

ners at creating havoc because of his toughness, yet sometimes he does and sometimes he doesn't.

One area where he has improved his physical play is in the defensive zone, where he is taking the body better than ever.

THE INTANGIBLES

His health is a big question; Hunter has never played a full season. Secondly, he's not the hardest worker to ever put on skates. And considering the fact that he played less than half of last spring's Stanley Cup playoff games (so that essentially the Flames won without him), perhaps Mark shouldn't get too comfortable in Calgary.

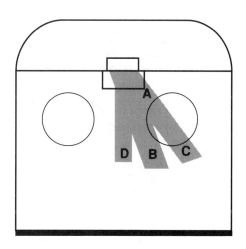

TIM HUNTER

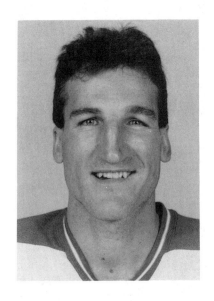

Yrs. of NHL service: 7
Born: Calgary, Alta., Canada; September 10, 1960
Position: Right wing
Height: 6-2
Weight: 202
Uniform no.: 19
Shoots: right

Career statistics:

GP	G	A	TP	PIM
414	41	51	92	1,816

1988-89 statistics:

GP	G	A	TP	+/-	PIM	PP	SH	GW	GT	S	PCT
75	3	9	12	22	375	0	0	1	0	67	4.5

LAST SEASON

Games played and PIM totals were career highs. He led the NHL in PIM total.

THE FINESSE GAME

Hunter is an average skater at best, with no real speed or agility in his stride. He does have good balance and strength on his skates and that serves him in his physical game. He has a slow driving stride that carries him from one end of the rink to the other.

Otherwise, Hunter is not gifted offensively. He does not have good hands with which to move or carry the puck, nor does he see the ice well. He is not a goal scorer, but maybe the pucks will bounce off him enough for 10 goals a year.

THE PHYSICAL GAME

Hunter is a one-man hammer-show, and his success is in his physical game. He is big, tough and strong, willing not only to mix it up but to provoke the battles. Hunter is also tough when he stations himself in front of the opposition net, where his strength and size make him a practically immovable object.

Because of his size and strength, Hunter is very difficult to out-muscle along the boards, but he will wander out of position because he's looking to belt someone. Hunter is also mean with his stick, and will use it with abandon. After all, something has to provoke his fights.

He is always in great condition.

THE INTANGIBLES

He's filled a well-defined role for the Flames for six seasons, and the Flames think so much of his leadership ability that they made him an alternate captain.

But ... Hunter didn't dress for games five and six of the Cup Final against Montreal. That makes us wonder how much longer he'll be with the Flames.

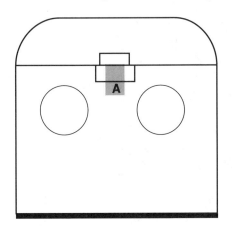

AL MACINNIS

Yrs. of NHL service: 6
Born: Inverness, N.S., Canada; July 11, 1963
Position: Defenseman
Height: 6-2
Weight: 195
Uniform no.: 2
Shoots: right

Career statistics:

GP	G	A	TP	PIM
449	98	318	416	541

1988-89 statistics:

GP	G	A	TP	+/-	PIM	PP	SH	GW	GT	S	PCT
79	16	58	74	38	126	8	0	3	0	277	5.8

LAST SEASON

Goal and point totals were three-season lows, assist total tied career high. PIM total was career high. He led Flames defenders in scoring (third overall in NHL), and he led the club in SOG total.

THE FINESSE GAME

Any hockey fan, unless he's been living on Mars, knows that Al MacInnis has the hardest shot in the NHL. It's clearly his best finesse skill and it is the kind of slap shot that goaltenders fear, for it will either blow right past them or hurt them as they stop it. Al knows a good thing when he sees it, and he puts his shot to use many times during a game by shooting as often as possible. If he finishes a game with 4-5 official SOG, you know he shot the puck 10-12 times.

MacInnis uses his slap shot to great effect on the power play, unloading from the blue line and collecting assists as teammates bang home an uncontrolled rebound — a major difference in the styles between MacInnis and teammate Gary Suter.

But Al brings more than just a big shot to the Flames. He sees the ice well, and he uses his good anticipation to lead teammates into the open with his passes. Unlike Suter, MacInnis doesn't generally rush the puck, but chooses instead to move up with the attack to become a fourth attacker in the enemy zone. He's improved at playmaking within the offensive zone because of his improved skating.

Al has improved his foot speed, long the weakest of his skills, — making him a much more agile defender. That allows him to come off the point to forecheck or charge the net in the offensive zone, and it also allows him to step up and challenge the puck carrier at the Flames blue line. He's doing both of those things better now than at any time in his career.

THE PHYSICAL GAME

Al has very good size, and the strength to match. For one thing, his size helps him see the ice — he's just taller than a lot of players. He also has very good upper body strength, which manifests itself in his shot. MacInnis also uses his strength fairly well at clearing the slot and at holding the opposition away from the play, but he's really not a banger in front of the net. He is, actually, a finesse player who has added a solid physical element to his game.

He willingly goes to the corners for the puck, suffering whatever abuse he gets, yet he still makes his plays. He uses his outstanding reach to pokecheck and deflect pucks.

THE INTANGIBLES

Al has really become a superior all-around defenseman, and that accomplishment shouldn't disguise the effort that he put into it. He's worked very hard to improve, and his improvement is a consequence of his dedication.

We thought he needed to redeem himself this May for his lackluster performance in 1988, and MacInnis did that and more. He was a fine choice as playoff MVP, and he deserves to be recognized as one of the NHL's best players.

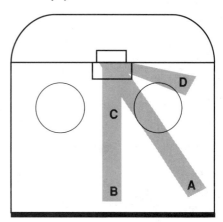

BRIAN MACLELLAN

Yrs. of NHL service: 5
Born: Guelph, Ontario, Canada; October 27, 1958
Position: Left wing
Height: 6-3
Weight: 215
Uniform no.: 27
Shoots: left

Career statistics:

GP	G	A	TP	PIM
461	138	204	342	432

1988-89 statistics:

GP	G	A	TP	+/-	PIM	PP	SH	GW	GT	S	PCT
72	18	26	44	3	118	7	0	0	0	137	13.1

LAST SEASON

Acquired from Minnesota in exchange for Perry Berezan. Games played total tied full-season career low. Point total was career low, PIM total career high.

THE FINESSE GAME

MacLellan has one excellent and some very average finesse skills, all punctuated with a big IF — which will be explained later. He doesn't have great skating skill in terms of speed or agility, but he does have great strength and balance in his stride.

He is a straight-ahead player and his puckhandling reflects that. He does not carry the puck well around the opposition, doesn't even carry it well as he heads up-ice unchecked. Nor does he have outstanding passing ability. Brian doesn't have good anticipation or hockey sense and therefore doesn't use his teammates well.

What he does have is an excellent shot. MacLellan releases his shot very quickly, and both his slap shot and wrist shot are heavy and accurate. His shots will carry into the net unless the goaltender is firmly in front of them.

Defensively he's a disaster, and his skating is why. Factor in laziness and the result is, while he is in his lane, MacLellan is usually far behind his check.

THE PHYSICAL GAME

This guy looks like Arnold Schwarzenegger. MacLellan has outstanding size and strength and uses neither of those skills regularly. To say he is inconsistent in the use of his size is an understatement. He is willing to be acted upon — to take hits and knocks and so on — but will not initiate anything that would put his strength and size advantage to use.

He will score from in front of the net with defensemen draped all over him, and that's a testament to MacLellan's strength, but he won't put that strength to consistent use in his battles along the boards or in front of the net.

He is not a fighter, though he can fight when he feels compelled, but MacLellan's size forces him into the role of policeman, a role he does not particularly relish.

THE INTANGIBLES

Every Stanley Cup team has unlikely ring-wearers on its roster. Players like Rick Chartraw, Hector Marini — and Brian MacLellan.

MacLellan has much better skills than his numbers indicate, but the bottom line with him is that if you expect anything above these numbers you're just fooling yourself. When he gets fired up he's a great player, but Brian gets fired up as often as Halley's Comet comes along.

Because of that lack of intensity, MacLellan is no better than a third line left wing. His stay in Calgary may be a short one.

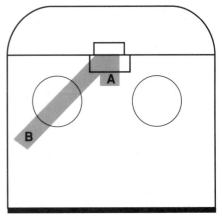

JAMIE MACOUN

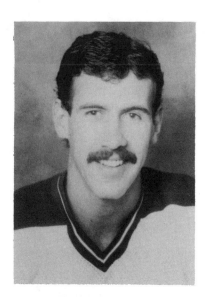

Yrs. of NHL service: 6
Born: Newmarket, Ontario, Canada; August 17, 1961
Position: Defenseman
Height: 6-2
Weight: 197
Uniform no.: 34
Shoots: left

Career statistics:

GP	G	A	TP	PIM
392	45	130	175	457

1988-89 statistics:

GP	G	A	TP	+/-	PIM	PP	SH	GW	GT	S	PCT
72	8	19	27	40	76	0	0	2	0	89	9.0

LAST SEASON

Macoun returned to the Flames lineup after missing all of 1987-88 because of injuries suffered in a car accident. His plus/minus rating was the club's fifth highest, second among defensemen. He missed time with a concussion.

THE FINESSE GAME

Skating is the best of Macoun's finesse skills, and he uses his skating exceptionally well. He's an exceptionally mobile skater, and his quickness, agility and lateral movement allow him to challenge the puck at both blue lines. Macoun has an explosive start and excellent one-step quickness; he'll use his speed to join the attack and to penetrate all the way to the opposition's net. He also uses one-step quickness to get to loose pucks. He's a free spirit because of his talent, wandering all over the ice, but his ability gets him out of any trouble he gets into.

While he's a fine passer, his puckhandling ability doesn't mesh well with his foot speed. So Jamie makes the most of his puckhandling by getting rid of the puck as quickly as possible. He finds the open man in both zones and gets the puck smartly to him.

Despite his talents, Macoun is not an overwhelming offensive threat. He'll get his goals on a low slap shot from the point.

Macoun sees the ice well and anticipates well too, and he combines those skills with his skating to be an outstanding penalty killing defenseman.

THE PHYSICAL GAME

Macoun combines his skating power with his size and upper body strength to become a tough and aggressive defenseman who hits well, often and punishingly — when he hits, it hurts. Macoun easily clears the front of the net (and he'll apply his stick liberally for help), and he's a dominating player in the corners. He'll outmuscle most any forward to gain the puck.

He uses his size to gain position and shield the puck along the boards, and he also uses his reach to pokecheck or deflect pucks. He has excellent eye/hand coordination and will occasionally be used for faceoffs.

THE INTANGIBLES

He's frequently ignored because of his unspectacular style, but Macoun is a very important player for Calgary. He's a defensive stalwart and — though he'll never match the numbers of a Suter or MacInnis — a proficient offensive player: he gets the puck into scoring position. Forget about under-rated — he's one of the NHL's most unknown players. And undeservedly so.

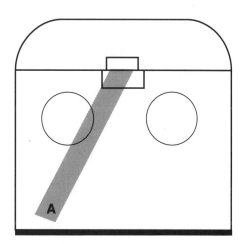

BRAD MCCRIMMON

Yrs. of NHL service: 10
Born: Dodsland, Sask., Canada; March 29, 1959
Position: Defenseman
Height: 5-11
Weight: 197
Uniform no.: 4
Shoots: left

Career statistics:

GP	G	A	TP	PIM
747	64	241	305	876

1988-89 statistics:

GP	G	A	TP	+/-	PIM	PP	SH	GW	GT	S	PCT
72	5	17	22	43	96	2	1	2	0	78	6.4

LAST SEASON

Missed six games with a foot injury. Plus minus was club's fourth best (fifth overall in the NHL), best among defensemen. Assist and point totals were third lowest of career.

THE FINESSE GAME

Powerful skating and defensive smarts make Brad one of the NHL's finest defensive defensemen. He's got a very strong stride and he uses it to close the gaps between himself and the opposition. He doesn't have a lot of rink-length speed, but in the confines of the defensive zone McCrimmon moves well. He's not a very agile skater, and his pivots and turns are not exceptional, but Brad counters that flaw with superior positioning.

He has excellent understanding of his defensive angles and almost always succeeds in forcing the play wide of the net. His positioning is also good in the offensive zone, where Brad knows when to challenge and when to fall back.

He's not much of a weapon in the offensive zone. He makes the simple play in his end and can rush the puck if necessary. He'll find the open forward when he's stationed at the offensive blue line.

THE PHYSICAL GAME

McCrimmon is good at keeping the front of the net clear and he does it physically and meanly. He's strong in the upper body and he'll muscle the opposition off the puck either in front of the net or along the boards.

His short reach betrays him when larger forwards are camped in the crease, but Brad makes them pay for every shot they get off.

THE INTANGIBLES

McCrimmon's begun to get some well-deserved recognition for his efforts. He may very well be the NHL's best defensive defenseman, but he fills another role for the Flames; when one of their defensemen is struggling, the Flames just team him with McCrimmon — whose own stability and dependability straightens out the struggling player.

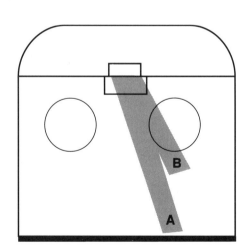

LANNY MCDONALD

Yrs. of NHL service: 16
Born: Hanna, Alta., Canada; February 16, 1953
Position: Right wing
Height: 6-0
Weight: 194
Uniform no.: 9
Shoots: right

Career statistics:

GP	G	A	TP	PIM
1,111	500	506	1,006	899

1988-89 statistics:

GP	G	A	TP	+/-	PIM	PP	SH	GW	GT	S	PCT
51	11	7	18	-1	26	0	0	3	0	72	15.3

LAST SEASON

Games played and all point totals were second lowest of career. He was the only Flame regular to be a minus player.

THE FINESSE GAME

Age and wear have taken their physical tolls on McDonald, once a blazing skater and shooter. He is less than a shadow of his former finesse self.

His explosive speed is almost all gone, and McDonald has never been exceptionally agile. He has always preferred to drive to the net from around the outside of the defense, but he won't beat many NHL defensemen any more. He retains the balance he's always had, and he still uses that attribute in his physical game.

McDonald's howitzer slapshot is no longer as effective as it has been, in part because he can't get into the open ice to use it. His release with it is also slower now, so goaltenders have time to set for it. He still has his anticipation and hockey sense, but his body can't follow his brain's orders quickly enough for him to consistently get into scoring position.

His passing and playmaking skills have also suffered because of his decreased skating quickness. Again, the brain far outraces the body's ability to perform.

THE PHYSICAL GAME

McDonald has always been a complete hockey player, and that meant attention to the physical side of the game. He's paid for that diligence with injuries, but Lanny still takes the body and dishes out checks whenever he can.

His balance and strength on his feet have always served him in this regard, and they continue to do so now. McDonald will take the abuse when he goes to the front of the net and will certainly give it back.

THE INTANGIBLES

We said last year that Lanny deserved a better end than the one his diminished skills had in mind for him, and he got that last season when he scored his 500th goal and won the Stanley Cup. Always a fine individual and a character player, he now deserves to leave hockey as a winner.

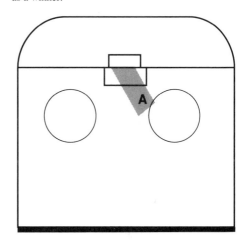

JOE MULLEN

Yrs. of NHL service: 8
Born: New York City, N.Y., USA; February 26, 1957
Position: Right wing
Height: 5-9
Weight: 180
Uniform no.: 7
Shoots: right

Career statistics:

GP	G	A	TP	PIM
568	305	350	655	116

1988-89 statistics:

GP	G	A	TP	+/-	PIM	PP	SH	GW	GT	S	PCT
80	50	59	109	51	16	13	1	7	0	270	18.9

LAST SEASON

Led club in goals (sixth in NHL), assists, points (seventh in NHL) and plus/minus totals (first in NHL). All point totals were career highs. Was second on the club in SOG total (first among forwards), power play goals and game winners.

THE FINESSE GAME

There are two keys to Mullen's finesse game, one physical — his balance — and one mental — his anticipation.

First, Mullen's superior balance powers his total finesse game by allowing him to maintain body position and retain the puck despite checking. That's important, because Mullen plays in the game's high-density areas. Joe also possesses outstanding acceleration ability (which he uses to break into the clear), *and* he has tremendous one-step quickness (which he uses to dart into openings after loose pucks). He moderates his speed excellently, never allowing the opposition to predict what he will do.

His goal scorer's anticipation and great hockey sense show him those openings, and then he uses his vision and hand skills to get the puck to his teammates. Joe is unselfish and makes the best play at all times. If that means a good pass to a teammate in better position, then that's the play Mullen makes. His hand skills also allow him to carry the puck well, and they combine with his skating skills to make Mullen very shifty should he gain an opening himself.

He is very dangerous when he has the puck, but more so around the slot or just inside the faceoff circle. His shot selection is excellent: forehand or backhand, wrist, slap or snap. Mullen's shot is keyed by his quick wrists and release. He is good at one-timing his shots and can score from anywhere in the zone.

THE PHYSICAL GAME

Because of — and not in spite of — his size, Mullen is one of the toughest players in the NHL. He's completely unafraid of traffic, and will do his own mucking in the corners by consistently initiating contact.

As such, he takes more abuse per pound than almost any other NHLer; only Montreal's Mats Naslund comes to mind as an equal, and Mullen's a better scorer. His balance is, once again, the key, and his skating strength makes it difficult to dislodge him from the puck.

THE INTANGIBLES

We took some issue with Mullen's performance in the 1988 Division Final, where Joe scored just three assists and the Flames were swept in four games. Mullen responded this year by leading the playoffs in goal scoring.

Which is not surprising, considering his character and work ethic — both of which are superb. He's an excellent team man, and he deserves all the attention he earned last season.

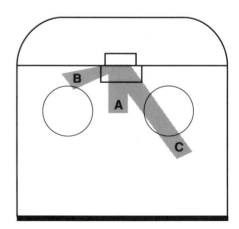

DANA MURZYN

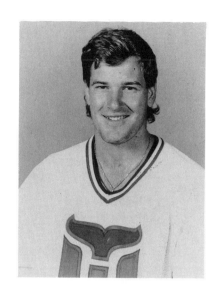

Yrs. of NHL service: 4
Born: Calgary, Alberta, Canada; December 9, 1966
Position: Defenseman
Height: 6-2
Weight: 200
Uniform no.: 5
Shoots: left

Career statistics:

GP	G	A	TP	PIM
289	21	78	99	499

1988-89 statistics:

GP	G	A	TP	+/-	PIM	PP	SH	GW	GT	S	PCT
63	3	19	22	26	142	0	1	1	0	91	3.3

LAST SEASON

Games played and point totals were career lows. PIM total was career high. He missed six games with a knee injury.

THE FINESSE GAME

Murzyn is a relatively limited finesse player, most likely because of his skating. He does fine on the straightaways both forward and back (his long stride covers a lot of ground so he isn't frequently left in the dust), but even after four seasons Dana lacks the agility and lateral movement that would elevate from a *re-active* to an active defenseman.

His foot speed and turns to his left are still weak, but the Flames have minimized that flaw by moving him from right defense (where his weakness left the middle open) to the left side (where the opposition is against the boards). Murzyn does have good balance and strength on his skates, so he'll hold his own during goal mouth collisions, but his lack of foot speed forces him to concede the blue line too quickly.

Dana handles the puck well and likes to carry it to center ice. He's improved his understanding of the pace of the NHL game and so he makes his passes quickly and efficiently when he chooses not to carry the puck.

He's shown little potential for scoring at the NHL level, though he has improved his playreading ability and will consistently get the puck to the open man. Murzyn shoots infrequently but well from the point, either a slap shot or a wrist shot, and both are low, hard and accurate.

THE PHYSICAL GAME

Dana is an aggressive player, and he puts his good size and strength to work often by hitting and taking the body. He uses his strength to his advantage in holding the man out along the boards, and he can clear the crease as well.

Murzyn sacrifices his body by blocking shots, and he puts his good reach to use by pokechecking effectively. Though aggressive, he is not a fighter.

THE INTANGIBLES

Rather than ask for things he cannot readily produce, the Flames are taking from Murzyn what he can give — a strong and relatively steady defensive presence. But when you combine Calgary's plethora of defensemen with Murzyn's still unrectified flaws, you get the idea that he could be vulnerable to replacement a season or two down the road.

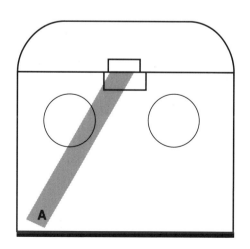

RIC NATTRESS

Yrs. of NHL service: 7
Born: Hamilton, Ontario, Canada; May 25, 1962
Position: Defenseman
Height: 6-2
Weight: 210
Uniform no.: 6
Shoots: right

Career statistics:

GP	G	A	TP	PIM
331	14	79	93	196

1988-89 statistics:

GP	G	A	TP	+/-	PIM	PP	SH	GW	GT	S	PCT
38	1	8	9	12	47	0	0	0	0	28	3.6

LAST SEASON

Games played total was four-season low (he missed time with a hamstring injury).

THE FINESSE GAME

Nattress is no better than an average skater in terms of speed or agility. While his improved backskating has helped Nattress more consistently force the opposition wide of the net, his backskating remains far from fluid and his pivots are still weak.

He's playing his defensive angles better, but Nattress still has a tendency to wander from his position. That creates breakdowns all through the defensive zone and creates openings for the opposition.

Ric does not handle the puck well and is subject to giveaways if pressured. He doesn't clear the zone well at all, either by skating the puck or moving it to a forward, so he's going to have to be paired with a more skilled partner.

He is not a goal scorer and any goals he gets will come on shots from the point.

THE PHYSICAL GAME

While willing to wrestle with the opposition in front of the net (and to liberally apply his stick), Nattress still doesn't get all he can from his size and strength. Because he lacks the skating ability to power him through checks, he pushes and shoves instead of hits. That means the opposition can easily out-muscle or skate him from the corner or the crease.

He'll likely give the puck up when hit because he doesn't use his body well to shield the puck.

THE INTANGIBLES

Calgary has a plethora of defensemen, and Nattress would have to be ranked as no better than a fifth or sixth defenseman. The Flames may want to keep him around as insurance, but Ric stands a good chance of finishing the season in a uniform other than the one in which he starts the year.

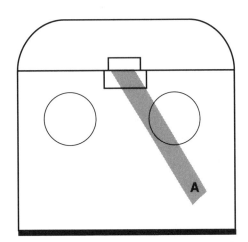

JOE NIEUWENDYK

Yrs. of NHL service: 2
Born: Oshawa, Ontario, Canada; September 10, 1966
Position: Center
Height: 6-1
Weight: 175
Uniform no.: 25
Shoots: left

Career statistics:

GP	G	A	TP	PIM
161	107	73	180	63

1988-89 statistics:

GP	G	A	TP	+/-	PIM	PP	SH	GW	GT	S	PCT
77	51	31	82	26	40	19	3	11	2	215	23.7

LAST SEASON

Finished first overall in NHL in game winners, fifth among all goal scorers. Finished fourth on club in scoring, but assist and point totals fell in second season. Finished tied for first on club in goals, first outright in power play, shorthanded, game winning and game tying goals, as well as shooting percentage. Finished third in SOG total among forwards.

THE FINESSE GAME

Nieuwendyk uses his exceptional hockey sense, hand skills and balance to key a superior finesse game. Joe uses his sense of the game's flow and his ice vision to get into scoring position; once there, his hands and balance take over.

Joe has great touch with the puck, and he combines that sensitivity in his hands with his balance to extend himself for seemingly unreachable pucks — or to squeeze into seemingly unenterable spaces. His excellent balance allows him to maintain control of both his body and the puck while being checked — and, more importantly, to shoot the puck while being banged around. He can make any move with the puck in traffic and still control the puck.

Nieuwendyk uses those skills to great advantage along the boards and out of the corners, where he gains the puck and moves it to an open teammate, but while he'll find the open man (again, vision and anticipation) Joe is a scoring center. Joe has an excellent selection of shots, though he's most likely to score from somewhere in close proximity to the net. He loves to shoot and will do so from all angles.

His skating is nondescript but, while lacking tremendous speed, Nieuwendyk can accelerate past the opposition.

THE PHYSICAL GAME

Joe has a wiry strength that he uses in conjunction with his balance to take opponents off the puck and to succeed in front of the net. He plays an extremely physical game by working the corners in both zones and charging the net with impunity. He's completely unintimidated by the rough going and he can't be brutalized — and believe us, he takes some beating.

THE INTANGIBLES

Tireless work ethic, fantastic determination, great heart and character — these are the assets Nieuwendyk brings to his game. He still needs to better pace himself throughout the season for consistent scoring (just 20 goals and 31 points in his first 30 games), but even we have to admit that this is reaching for a negative.

Because with Nieuwendyk, there really aren't any negatives. Sure. he could achieve a better balance between goals and assists — but he will as he continues to grow in the NHL.

He has exceptional potential, and there are many 50-goal and 100-point seasons in his future. The only real question facing Nieuwendyk is how he'll respond to the absence of Hakan Loob (he's returned to Sweden), who has been Nieuwendyk's right wing through the youngster's NHL career.

For some reason, we're not all that worried.

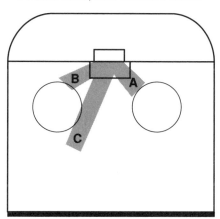

JOEL OTTO

Yrs. of NHL service: 4
Born: St. Cloud, Minn., USA; October 29, 1961
Position: Center
Height: 6-4
Weight: 220
Uniform no.: 29
Shoots: right

Career statistics:

GP	G	A	TP	PIM
298	84	143	227	808

1988-89 statistics:

GP	G	A	TP	+/-	PIM	PP	SH	GW	GT	S	PCT
72	23	30	53	12	213	10	2	2	1	123	18.7

LAST SEASON

Games played and goal totals were second highest of career, point total tied for second highest and assist total career low. Finished fourth on the club in PIM total, also a career high.

THE FINESSE GAME

Power is Otto's game, and his finesse skills reflect that. He is a strong skater but not a fluid or exceptionally agile one. His long, strong stride will either pull him away from the opposition when he is on offense, or bring him closer to the opposition defensively.

Joel covers a lot of ground, and that asset combines with his vision and anticipation to help his forechecking and defensive center work. He'll get many offensive opportunities because of the loose pucks his checking creates but, because his shot is the weakest of his finesse skills, Otto will have to be an opportunistic scorer on pucks near the net.

Otto also makes his offense suffer by overpassing the puck, perhaps because he doesn't have great confidence in his shot (though he doesn't really have the hand skills to finesse the puck in traffic). At any rate, he certainly doesn't shoot enough for the loose pucks he gains.

THE PHYSICAL GAME

Big, strong and tough — that's Otto's game. He hits punishingly in all three zones, and any center smaller than he is going to get worn down by the pounding. When he can't line up the opposition, Otto still takes the body well and moves the opposition off the puck.

Because he has great strength on his feet, Otto gives the defense all kinds of trouble once he's stationed himself in front of the enemy net (his overtime goal against the Canucks in game seven of the Smythe Division semifinal in April came just this way).

Because he plays an outstandingly physical game, Otto will tire over the course of a season. Therefore, on nights when there is no big, strong center to neutralize, Otto will coast.

THE INTANGIBLES

A dedicated athlete and a tireless worker, Otto skates all through the summer to stay in shape. Quiet off the ice, he is an on-ice leader. And his talent is such that every NHL team now wants a player like Otto. Because clubs covet his combination of size, strength and talent, he's almost become the League's most sought-after player.

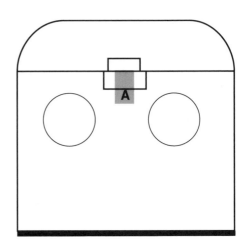

COLIN PATTERSON

Yrs. of NHL service: 6
Born: Rexdale, Ontario, Canada; May 11, 1960
Position: Left wing
Height: 6-2
Weight: 195
Uniform no.: 11
Shoots: left

Career statistics:

GP	G	A	TP	PIM
355	83	96	179	170

1988-89 statistics:

GP	G	A	TP	+/-	PIM	PP	SH	GW	GT	S	PCT
74	14	24	38	44	56	0	0	1	0	103	13.6

LAST SEASON

Games played, PIM and assist totals were career highs, point total second highest and goal total tied for second highest of career. His plus/minus was both NHL's and club's third best.

THE FINESSE GAME

Speed and smarts combine to make Patterson one of the NHL's best defensive forwards. While not outstandingly agile, Patterson has good acceleration and strength in his skating — and he does have just enough quickness to close holes and angle off the opposition. His skating strength makes him almost relentless in his pursuit of the puck.

These skills combine with his good hockey sense and anticipation to make him a good forechecker, and because he sees the ice well, reads the plays and contains the puck, Patterson gets many offensive opportunities.

But his hand skills — especially his shot — are not at the level of his skating and play reading abilities. So while his checking creates opportunities that might result in 25 goals a season, Colin's merely-average release and shot strength will usually limit his goal scoring to the teens.

He is skilled enough to move the puck fairly well (again, credit his vision and sense), but Patterson will always primarily be a defensive forward.

THE PHYSICAL GAME

Patterson makes his decent size and strength better by playing like a kamikaze. He sacrifices his body whenever necessary, and that style goes a long way toward explaining why he's injured more often than not.

THE INTANGIBLES

Patterson is a character individual. He's a very hard worker and a very dedicated athlete. In the locker room he's the kind of guy to crack jokes and keep the team loose, and on the ice he gives 100 percent of himself and is very coachable.

As a 29-year-old role player, his continued NHL success is predicated upon healthy seasons. He must stay in the lineup to stay valuable to the Flames.

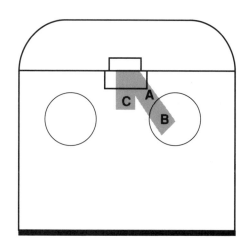

JIM PEPLINSKI

Yrs. of NHL service: 9
Born: Renfrew, Ontario, Canada; October 24, 1960
Position: Left wing/center
Height: 6-3
Weight: 209
Uniform no.: 24
Shoots: right

Career statistics:

GP	G	A	TP	PIM
699	160	262	422	1,452

1988-89 statistics:

GP	G	A	TP	+/-	PIM	PP	SH	GW	GT	S	PCT
79	13	25	38	6	241	0	0	2	1	103	12.6

LAST SEASON

Goal and point totals tied second lowest of career. PIM total was career high, third highest on club.

THE FINESSE GAME

Since strength is the name of Peplinski's overall game, it should come as no surprise that strength is what gives Jim his finesse abilities. Surprisingly fast for a man with his size and bulk, Peplinski's powerful skating stride gives him good acceleration ability and speed. He's fast enough to beat defenders to the outside and then drive the goal.

Though his speed and strength present him with scoring opportunities by taking him to the front of the net, Peplinski will have difficulty finishing those plays because his hands lack the softness necessary to finesse the puck from in close. He'll score in the 20-goal range by sweeping home rebounds and other junk, but don't expect him to turn the goaltender inside out.

And by extension, Peplinski's not much of a fancy playmaker (lacking both the hands and the anticipation). Instead, he'll get his assists because the opposition leaves him a lot of room to operate in, and Peplinski needs that time and space to make his plays. He enjoys playing the left wing because he is a right-handed shot.

While he can't project a play offensively, Peplinski does get a fairly good read of the ice and combines that with good positional play to be a good checker and defensive player.

THE PHYSICAL GAME

Physical is the name of Peplinski's game. He is tough and strong and hits hard along the boards and in the corners. Peplinski can't do much after he makes the hits, but he is strong enough to out-muscle the opposition along the boards.

Jim is very hard to knock off his skates because of his balance and strength and that means he can recover from collisions and be in position to make some kind of play. That steadiness on his skates also serves him when he plugs the front of the opposition net and has to withstand the defense's abuse.

He can fight, and he's pretty good at it.

THE INTANGIBLES

Here's an interesting case: Peplinski is a leader for Calgary, an excellent and upbeat team man whose enthusiasm and attitude add a spark to the Flames.

He's their captain, but consider this: He was scratched during the Cup Finals, including the Cup winning game. We wonder what that means for his continuing in a Flames uniform.

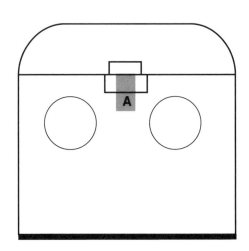

GARY ROBERTS

Yrs. of NHL service: 3
Born: North York, Ontario, Canada; May 23, 1966
Position: Left wing
Height: 6-1
Weight: 190
Uniform no.: 10
Shoots: left

Career statistics:

GP	G	A	TP	PIM
177	40	41	81	617

1988-89 statistics:

GP	G	A	TP	+/-	PIM	PP	SH	GW	GT	S	PCT
71	22	16	38	32	250	0	1	2	0	123	17.9

LAST SEASON

All point totals were career highs. He finished second on the club in PIM total.

THE FINESSE GAME

The temptation is to look at Gary's physical game and his PIM total and see a player who bashes his way to points — and that's true, to a degree. But Roberts has more than a modicum of finesse skill he can bring to bear.

His skating is marked by good speed and acceleration capability, and Roberts has improved his foot speed so that his new dash of quickness blends with his balance to give him some agility and lateral ability.

He combines that improved skating with his improved hand skills and greater understanding of the NHL game to possess good — and improving — puckhandling ability. Roberts can carry the puck around a player or two, and what helps him is ability to keep his head up.

Roberts uses these skills to find open teammates (though he still needs plenty of time to move the puck), and to open space. He'll look up at the blue line to find his teammates, and then try to carry the defenseman wide in order to create space.

He also could improve the release of his shot and the frequency with which he shoots. Right now his goals will have to come from near the net.

THE PHYSICAL GAME

Roberts is a very aggressive player. He hits and takes the body with abandon, gaining the puck and excellent position along the boards. His improving finesse skills also serve to make his physical play that much more effective.

Gary is also a willing and ready fighter, though he couldn't be considered an NHL heavyweight.

THE INTANGIBLES

Roberts will continue his improvement (which is only natural when you play and practice against players like Joe Mullen, Joe Nieuwendyk and Gary Suter), and that improvement alone will help his point totals. Toss in the fact that he's usually to the left of Nieuwendyk, and it's easy to anticipate Roberts' offensive game blossoming.

As long as he remembers to do the dirty work, Gary will be okay.

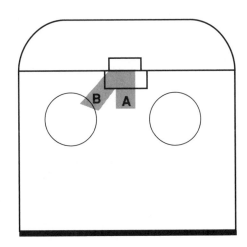

GARY SUTER

Yrs. of NHL service: 4
Born: Madison, Wisc., USA; June 24, 1964
Position: Defenseman
Height: 6-0
Weight: 190
Uniform no.: 20
Shoots: left

Career statistics:

GP	G	A	TP	PIM
286	61	209	270	375

1988-89 statistics:

GP	G	A	TP	+/-	PIM	PP	SH	GW	GT	S	PCT
63	13	49	62	26	78	8	0	1	0	216	6.0

LAST SEASON

Games played total was career low (missed 16 games with an appendectomy, and was also sidelined through the playoffs with a broken jaw). Finished 12th in scoring among League defensemen.

THE FINESSE GAME

Suter is an exceptional skater, and that talent is the springboard for his other considerable finesse skills. He has superior speed and power, but it is the combination of his one-step quickness and superior balance that makes Gary almost unsurpassed in terms of agility and lateral movement. He changes speed and direction within a stride.

Gary uses his skating exceptionally well at both blue lines. He steps up defensively to close the gap and force the puck carrier at the Flames blue line, and also uses his quickness to contain the point and open passing lanes at the offensive blue line.

His hand skills match his foot skills, and Suter rushes the puck excellently. He is not a rink-length rusher, however, and alertly looks for a breaking forward once in center or across the opposing blue line. He finds the open man excellently in all zones, leading his teammates into the clear with efficient passes.

Suter delivers a low, hard slap shot to the net (good for tips and deflections), and he will cheat into the zone a few strides if the opportunity exists.

THE PHYSICAL GAME

An enigma. Suter has excellent strength in both his upper and lower body, and he uses this strength to power his slapshot and help in his checking (his lower body strength obviously helps in his battles with the opposition, by helping him drive through checks). He can withstand hits and still make his plays, or he can muscle the opposition off the puck. Suter also does a good job of shielding the puck with his body when he is in the corners.

But four seasons have shown us that Suter is injury prone. No one can fault him for last season's appendectomy, but the fact remains that he has played only 206 of a possible 240 games over the last three seasons.

THE INTANGIBLES

Health is obviously the big factor here, and — considering the Flames essentially won the Stanley Cup without him — the idea that Suter is expendable is an interesting one.

Not that we'd trade him — we're just introducing a hypothetical (but just think what Calgary could get for him!). He's a tremendous talent, one who has probably not yet reached his complete NHL potential.

And all he has to do to reach that potential is stay in the lineup.

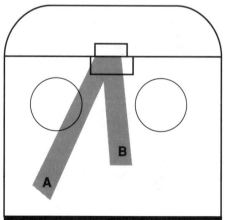

MIKE VERNON

Yrs. of NHL service: 4
Born: Calgary, Alta., Canada; February 24, 1963
Position: Goaltender
Height: 5-9
Weight: 155
Uniform no.: 30
Catches: left

Career statistics:

GP	MINS	G	SO	AVG	A	PIM
191	10,492	585	3	3.35	14	83

1988-89 statistics:

GP	MINS	AVG	W	L	T	SO	GA	SA	SAPCT	PIM
52	2,938	2.65	37	6	5	0	130	1,263	.897	18

LAST SEASON

Games played total was three-season low, but Vernon led NHL in wins, was second in goals-against-average and fourth in save percentage.

THE PHYSICAL GAME

Vernon is an outstanding standup goaltender who complements that angle cutting style with exceptional reflexes. At the root of his challenging style is his skating ability, which is very good. Vernon has excellent balance and lateral movement, so not only is he tough to beat on crossing plays near the net but he's also going to quickly regain his stance if he's left his feet. He moves well in and out of the net, but Vernon doesn't usually leave the net to handle the puck.

He likes to use the butterfly style on point and screen shots, so that's the time to beat him — if he's going to be beaten — because Mike won't make the mistakes that result in long shot goals. But because he regains his feet so quickly, those openings won't be open for long. He holds his feet very well on breakaways and wraparounds, forcing the opposition to make the first move nine times out of ten.

Mike complements his compact, standup game with excellent reflexes. Vernon is very quick with his hands and feet, and he's going to get a piece of most every goal that beats him — and few of those are going to come on direct rush attacks. Because of his abilities, extreme corner shots are the opposition's only chance. He clears rebounds effectively — especially of his stick side.

THE MENTAL GAME

Mike has exceptional poise and concentration regardless of circumstance. He'll fight for every goal, yet he easily dismisses bad goals and games. He's always had big save capability (despite the critics' carping), and he certainly proved that during last spring's Stanley Cup run.

His anticipation greatly enhances his quickness, especially on plays around the net and in the slot. He has very good vision of the puck, and he's shown the ability to play at a consistently high level — to win games himself — from one game to the next.

THE INTANGIBLES

We told you last year that any hope Calgary had of collecting the Stanley Cup rested squarely on Vernon's shoulders, and we're happy to see this much-underrated player finally get his due. His consistent performances through several playoff years indicate that his success is no fluke. He'll continue to prosper as one of the NHL's best goalies.

RICK WAMSLEY

Yrs. of NHL service: 9
Born: Simcoe, Ontario, Canada; May 25, 1959
Position: Goaltender
Height: 5-11
Weight: 185
Uniform no.: 31
Catches: left

Career statistics:

GP	MINS	G	SO	AVG	A	PIM
322	18,439	1,019	10	3.32	8	46

1988-89 statistics:

GP	MINS	AVG	W	L	T	SO	GA	SA	SAPCT	PIM
35	1,927	2.96	17	11	4	1	95	796	.881	8

LAST SEASON

Games played total was second-lowest in career (for full season). Goals-against-average was second-best of career and eight-season best; he finished fifth in the NHL in GAA.

THE PHYSICAL GAME

The stand-up, angle-cutting style is Wamsley's game. By playing that style (rarely leaving his feet), Rick maximizes his good size and minimizes his skating flaws.

He's no better than average as a skater,; he'll move fairly well out of the net, less well back into it. His balance is no better than average, so when he does go to the ice he needs time recovering his feet. Rick keeps his feet in motion forward and back constantly, which inhibits his ability to move laterally. Because of that he's going to be vulnerable to shots on the ice toward the corners, and on bang-bang crossing plays in front. That's why Wamsley is smart to stand up and challenge as best he can.

For the most part, he handles rebounds well by directing them away from traffic. His hands are not especially fast so Rick benefits from cutting down the angles so the puck just hits him. He sees the puck fairly well and has good anticipation.

THE MENTAL GAME

Rick maintains a level-headed approach to the game mentally, neither getting too high after a win nor too low after a loss. He prepares well for each game and is ready to play, so he's largely unaffected by a bad performance the night before or a bad goal at any time.

His concentration is good, but it does tend to wander when he has nothing to do for stretches of time, and he looks unsteady on shots following that "empty" period.

THE INTANGIBLES

We wondered last season how Wamsley would react to his first season as a backup, and he showed us this year. He's a dependable goaltender, and he gives the Flames a solid (if unspectacular) presence in net when Mike Vernon gets the night off.

CHICAGO
BLACKHAWKS .

LINE COMBINATIONS
DAN VINCELETTE-TROY MURRAY-DUANE
SUTTER
DIRK GRAHAM-DENIS SAVARD-STEVE
LARMER
STEVE THOMAS-ADAM CREIGHTON-WAYNE
PRESLEY

DEFENSE PAIRINGS
DOUG WILSON-DAVE MANSON
STEVE KONROYD-KEITH BROWN
TRENT YAWNEY-BOB MURRAY

GOALTENDERS
ALAIN CHEVRIER
DARREN PANG

OTHER PLAYERS
GREG GILBERT — Left wing
BOB BASSEN — Center
JEREMY ROENICK — Center
BOB MCGILL — Defenseman

POWER PLAY

FIRST UNIT:
DIRK GRAHAM-DENIS SAVARD-STEVE
LARMER
TRENT YAWNEY-DAVE MANSON

SECOND UNIT:
WAYNE PRESLEY-ADAM CREIGHTON-STEVE
THOMAS

Chicago overloads the left side, with GRAHAM down low, SAVARD near the boards by the faceoff circle and YAWNEY at the point. LARMER is perched at the right faceoff circle. SAVARD distributes the puck and will look for LARMER on a cross-ice feed, and shots from the point (with GRAHAM getting to the front of the net) are the other option.

On the second unit, THOMAS sets up in LARMER's spot, CREIGHTON plugs the front of the net and PRESLEY is at the left faceoff circle. Shots from PRESLEY or THOMAS are preferred, with blue line shots and the forwards crashing the other alternative. On both units, the Hawks like MANSON to load up and fire. TROY MURRAY and DOUG WILSON will also see power play time, with MURRAY in front and WILSON shooting from the point.

Last season Chicago's power play was GOOD, scoring 91 goals in 434 opportunities (21.0 percent, ninth overall).

PENALTY KILLING

FIRST UNIT:
DIRK GRAHAM-STEVE LARMER
DOUG WILSON-DAVE MANSON

SECOND UNIT:
DENIS SAVARD-
TRENT YAWNEY-KEITH BROWN

The Hawks will send both forwards at the puck in the offensive and neutral zones, but within the defensive zone the units play a fairly disciplined box with the puck forced by the nearest player.
Last season Chicago's penalty killing was POOR, allowing 122 goals in 481 shorthanded situations (74.6 percent, 19th overall).

CRUCIAL FACEOFFS
TROY MURRAY, even though he's far less dependable than he used to be.

BOB BASSEN

Yrs. of NHL service: 3
Born: Calgary, Alta., Canada; May 6, 1965
Position: Center
Height: 5-10
Weight: 180
Uniform no.: 15
Shoots: left

Career statistics:

GP	G	A	TP	PIM
233	20	43	63	277

1988-89 statistics:

GP	G	A	TP	+/-	PIM	PP	SH	GW	GT	S	PCT
68	5	16	21	5	83	0	0	1	0	51	9.8

LAST SEASON

Acquired along with Steve Konroyd (from the Islanders) in exchange for Marc Bergevin and Gary Nylund. Games played was career low, but point total was second highest.

THE FINESSE GAME

Bassen is a very good skater with excellent speed and quickness. He gets to the openings and closes them before the opposition can exploit them, and he pursues the puck relentlessly. His checking also forces turnovers by the opposition, and Bob's quickness gets him to those loose pucks. He puts that speed to use as a good checking forward and a penalty killing regular.

Unfortunately his transition game after that turnover is faulty, and that's because Bassen doesn't handle the puck well. His hands are not the greatest, and patience isn't high in his list of assets either. If he took more time and looked for his temmates, he'd be better able to cash in on those loose pucks.

For himself, he'll do his scoring from in close as he pounces on errant pucks.

THE PHYSICAL GAME

Though not a predominantly physical player, Bassen has no distaste for the physical game. He'll take the body when he can and that's usually enough to break up a play, but Bassen is not an overly strong player.

He can be out-matched along the boards, so he's at his best closing the passing lanes rather than trying to physically restrain an opponent.

THE INTANGIBLES

Bassen plays with enthusiasm and determination, but hasn't shown that he can succeed in anything beyond a role playing situation.

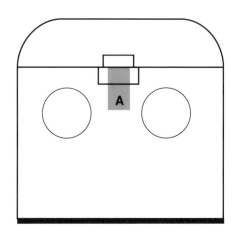

KEITH BROWN

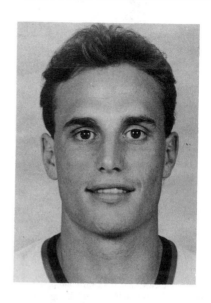

Yrs. of NHL service: 10
Born: Corner Brook, Nfld., Canada; May 6, 1960
Position: Defenseman
Height: 6-1
Weight: 192
Uniform no.: 4
Shoots: right

Career statistics:

GP	G	A	TP	PIM
610	50	220	270	604

1988-89 statistics:

GP	G	A	TP	+/-	PIM	PP	SH	GW	GT	S	PCT
74	2	16	18	-5	84	1	0	0	0	105	1.9

LAST SEASON

Games played total was five-season high, but point total was second lowest of career.

THE FINESSE GAME

Keith's skating is the best of his finesse skills, and he's above average in that skill. Brown has excellent balance and foot speed, and that translates into rink-length speed, quickness and agility. He has very good lateral movement, and his skating allows him to challenge the play at the Hawk blue line — to step up on the puck carrier — instead of just forcing the play wide.

But — and this is a big but — Brown lacks the playreading and anticipation skills that would allow him to make best use of his skating. He doesn't exercise good judgment in challenging because he reads the rush no better than fairly, despite a decade in the NHL.

Offensively, Brown has obvious mechanical skills — but his less-than-good instincts prevent his application of those skills. He'd be greatly aided if he kept his head up all the time, but Brown just puts his head down and charges when he has the puck. He has, however, cut down his wild forays up-ice, in order to better concentrate on defense.

He brings an above average shot from the blue line, and Keith will use his speed to cut to the right faceoff spot if the opening exists. Otherwise, his offensive contributions will be minimal.

THE PHYSICAL GAME

Brown is very strong in both the upper and lower body (courtesy of his dedication to training). His hip and leg strength power his speed, and his upper body strength stands him in good stead in the battle zones in the corners and the front of the net.

He plays a fairly aggressive but smart game, though Keith could be more determined in following through on his checks so as to forbid the opposition from getting back into the play. His balance is a little high, however, so Brown can be tipped off the puck by better balanced, but not necessarily stronger, opponents.

THE INTANGIBLES

He's not the most driven player to ever put on skates, but Brown made legitimate attempts last season to taper his style toward the type of game Mike Keenan wants to play. At this stage of his career, however, what you see is what you get. And what you see with Keith Brown is a guy who will be in great condition (when he can stay away from injury) but will make mistakes he should have stopped making after two seasons in the NHL.

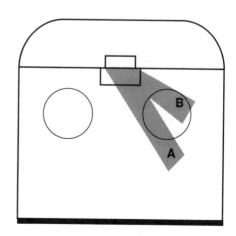

ALAIN CHEVRIER

Yrs. of NHL service: 3
Born: Cornwall, Ontario, Canada; April 23, 1961
Position: Goaltender
Height: 5-8
Weight: 170
Uniform no.: 30
Catches: left

Career statistics:

GP	MINS	G	SO	AVG	A	PIM
189	10,034	688	2	4.11	8	27

1988-89 statistics:

GP	MINS	AVG	W	L	T	SO	GA	SA	SAPCT
49	2,665	3.83	21	19	4	1	170	1,294	.870

LAST SEASON

Chevrier was traded first to Winnipeg (by New Jersey) and then Chicago. Games and minutes played totals were second highest of his career, and he was over .500 for the first time ever. He missed six games with a knee injury.

THE PHYSICAL GAME

Chevrier is an angle goaltender, though he doesn't challenge shooters as well as he could. One reason for that is because of his skating. Since he is only an average skater, Alain can't be overly aggressive when challenging because he won't get back into the net in time for rebounds or the second save. He does have good balance on his feet and can regain his stance quickly after sprawling.

His reflexes are good and his glove hand is fairly solid, but he'll have trouble with low shots just inside the posts and high to the stick side (again, because these space are open due to his not cutting the angle well enough).

He's not afraid to go behind the net and cut the puck off as it rips around the boards and he can handle the puck fairly well in getting it to his defensemen.

He stays in the net too deep and too long on screen shots, hoping for an extra second of time for the reflex save and to get a better view. He would do better to square himself to the puck.

THE MENTAL GAME

Chevrier suffers concentration lapses that result in successive goals, or goals from bad angles. He can give a good 15-20 minutes and then his concentration starts to slip and his confidence begins to go. Additionally, he's not mentally strong enough to play for long stretches — say, four or more games consecutively. He does not do well when he comes into a game cold.

He anticipates the play well and is especially sharp that way in action around his net. By and large, Alain will come back strongly from a poor outing, but his inability to hold his concentration is bound to affect him again.

THE INTANGIBLES

As we said last year, Chevrier proved two things: One, that he'd be moved by the Devils, and two, that he's definitely a major league goalie (as his playoff performance indicates).

He gives the Hawks stability in goal, but he may very well face a battle for the number one job from rookie Jimmy Waite.

ADAM CREIGHTON

Yrs. of NHL service: 4
Born: Burlington, Ontario, Canada; June 2, 1965
Position: Center
Height: 6-5
Weight: 216
Uniform no.: 22
Shoots: left

Career statistics:

GP	G	A	TP	PIM
215	55	74	129	288

1988-89 statistics:

GP	G	A	TP	+/-	PIM	PP	SH	GW	GT	S	PCT
67	22	24	46	-9	136	11	0	4	0	155	14.2

LAST SEASON

Acquired in trade from Buffalo, games played, points and PIM totals were all career highs. He finished second on the club in power play goals. His PIM total was third highest among forwards.

THE FINESSE GAME

While his agility and balance are almost remarkable for a guy with his size and weight, Adam lacks speed and quickness. He gets where he's going because of a long stride, but don't confuse the way he covers ground with speed. He's a decent skater at best.

Where he shows best is in his hand skills. Creighton handles the puck well in traffic and at his feet, and that's where his agility helps him; no one expects such shiftiness in a bigger man. He controls the puck well when he skates and makes his moves.

His anticipation and sense reveal the exploitable openings, but Adam's lack of speed leaves him hamstrung because he can't get to those holes or those loose pucks. He'll score his 20-25 goals a year from within 10 feet of the net, for while he has good hands for puck control his shot is not at the NHL level in terms of speed or release. That's why he performs well on the power play — he has extra time and space to shoot the puck.

He tries to take advantage of his teammates, but that's difficult when he can't keep away from the opposition. His lack of speed makes Creighton no better than average defensively.

THE PHYSICAL GAME

Don't be deceived by his great size; Creighton is not a power forward. He is big and gangly, and would do well to beef himself up, because he is easily removed from the puck despite his balance; he's simply outmuscled. He is, however, playing a more aggressive game than before, and Adam doesn't hesitate to bring his elbows up when he goes at the opposition.

He has a good reach and he puts it to work well in snaring loose pucks along the boards or in traffic.

THE INTANGIBLES

Creighton seems to have found his stride under Coach Mike Keenan, so the change of scenery must be helping him. He's still only 24 years old, so he has plenty of time left, and his fairly successful playoff performance speaks well about his development.

This year, essentially his second full NHL season, should give us a better idea of just where he is in that development.

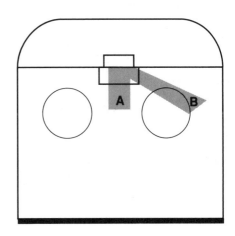

GREG GILBERT

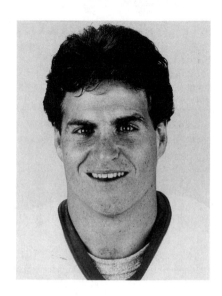

Yrs of NHL service: 7
Born: Mississauga, Ontario, Canada; January 22, 1962
Position: Left wing
Height: 6-0
Weight: 190
Uniform no.: 14
Shoots: left

Career statistics:

GP	G	A	TP	PIM
429	93	138	231	324

1988-89 statistics:

GP	G	A	TP	+/-	PIM	PP	SH	GW	GT	S	PCT
59	8	13	21	2	45	0	0	1	0	75	10.7

LAST SEASON

Traded to Chicago by the Islanders late in the season. He missed time with a shoulder injury.

THE FINESSE GAME

Gilbert is an average skater at the NHL level, possessing neither great speed nor agility on his skates. He is strong in his stride and does have good balance, so when he plays his physical style he remains upright and ready to resume play after collisions. Improved foot speed would make him a better skater, as it would combine with his balance to make him more agile — to say nothing of quicker.

He doesn't have a great understanding of the NHL offensive game, and when he overhandles the puck he goes to bad ice. That means he's trapped in a corner at an oblique angle or on his backhand or in need of a fancy pass in order to make an ordinary play. Keeping the game simple — and keeping his head up to see openings — is how Gilbert will succeed offensively. He must move the puck quickly and early.

Greg shoots well and gets the puck away quickly and fairly accurately. He has both the wrist shot and the slap shot and can score from the mid-distances — 25 feet or so.

Gilbert backchecks well, stopping numerous opposing scoring chances through his defensive play.

THE PHYSICAL GAME

Greg is a big, strong man and likes to hit, displaying a mean streak at times that allows him to cross-check opposing forwards into the boards after a play is whistled dead. His size best serves him in the corners, where he digs the puck out well, and in front of the net, where he can and will take the requisite pounding.

His game is the same in the defensive zone, where he will sacrifice his body to block shots or take out opposing forwards. Gilbert, though not a fighter per se, can more than handle his own because of his upper body strength.

THE INTANGIBLES

Gilbert is a building block player, a dependable sort a coach doesn't often need to worry about, a role player. He is an enthusiastic and willing player, though he also tends to worry about his own performances, but his work ethic and dedication make him a character player.

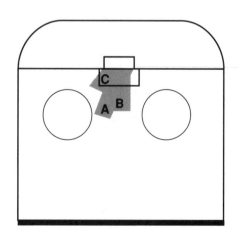

DIRK GRAHAM

Yrs. of NHL service: 5
Born: Regina, Sask., Canada; July 29, 1959
Position: Right wing
Height: 5-11
Weight: 190
Uniform no.: 33
Shoots: right

Career statistics:

GP	G	A	TP	PIM
348	117	143	257	407

1988-89 statistics:

GP	G	A	TP	+/-	PIM	PP	SH	GW	GT	S	PCT
80	33	45	78	8	89	5	10	5	1	217	15.2

LAST SEASON

Games played total tied career high; point totals were career highs. He finished third in team scoring and goals, fourth in SOG total, first in shorthanded goals (second overall in NHL and a team record) and tied for second in plus/minus.

THE FINESSE GAME

Graham is an average skater, not equipped with a lot of speed but strong and sturdy on his skates and tireless as well, making him well suited for his checking role. He is not very agile on his skates, but he has sufficient foot speed to get a jump on an opposing defenseman controlling the point in the Hawks' zone. Dirk would be best described — at least skating wise — as a power forward.

He combines skating with good anticipation and vision. Dirk reads the play well and is able to spot the opening and jump into it even though he is not tremendously quick. That quickness makes him particularly effective killing penalties, because his persistent skating efforts result in turnovers that he can convert into shorthanded goals.

Dirk has some talent with his hands and can use his teammates, able to get a pass to them with good touch. He can fake and deke, and likes especially to go to his right. He has shown a degree of goal scoring talent at the NHL level, but is not a natural goal scorer; the puck doesn't follow him around, he has to go get it.

THE PHYSICAL GAME

Graham is very tough, under-rated tough. He stands up for his teammates and is a mucker and a grinder. Dirk plays a very physical style, using his body well along the boards to take the opposition off the puck. He can take care of himself when the going gets rough and is a fairly good fighter.

He is difficult to take off the puck because of his sturdiness on his skates, one reason why he can work the boards well. Because he goes into traffic to get the puck and to score, Graham gets punished a lot.

THE INTANGIBLES

Graham works so hard that his spirit becomes infectious. He garners tremendous respect from teammate and foe alike because of his work habits, and those work habits are the embodiment of his character. He developed his skills in three minor leagues before making the jump to the NHL, and he deserves a ton of credit for his accomplishments.

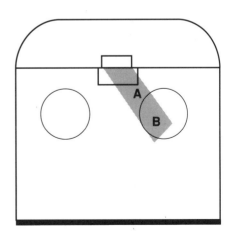

STEVE KONROYD

Yrs. of NHL service: 8
Born: Scarborough, Ontario, Canada;
February 10, 1961
Position: Defenseman
Height: 6-1
Weight: 195
Uniform no.: 5
Shoots: left

Career statistics:

GP	G	A	TP	PIM
575	31	131	162	613

1988-89 statistics:

GP	G	A	TP	+/-	PIM	PP	SH	GW	GT	S	PCT
78	6	12	18	-16	42	0	0	1	0	132	4.5

LAST SEASON

Traded to Chicago from the Islanders (along with Bob Bassen) in exchange for Marc Bergevin and Gary Nylund. Goal total was second highest of career. Plus/minus was the club's worst.

THE FINESSE GAME

Quietly effective are the words that best describe Konroyd's finesse skills. He's a very mobile skater both forward and back and he pivots excellently. He has a fair degree of agility he can put to use in sliding around a forechecker and some acceleration skill for use when going back for the puck. He uses his skating to play his position in just that way — positionally.

Konroyd excellently and consistently forces the play wide of the net by angling off the incoming forward. Then he takes the forward to the boards, wrests the puck free and sends the play up-ice with a crisp pass. Nothing fancy, just quietly effective.

Steve is very good at moving the puck from his own end. He sees the whole ice surface, finds the open man and gets the puck to him quickly and easily. If a passing option is unavailable, he'll skate the puck from the zone. He handles the puck well, though he does not make himself part of the attack, and Konroyd won't rush the offensive zone.

When play is established in the opposition end, Konroyd will sit back at the point and fire away with a slap shot that is average in power. He can find the open man in the offensive zone (that's why he'll see some power play time) and Steve will more than likely get the puck to him.

THE PHYSICAL GAME

Konroyd is big and strong and he can take players off the puck with his size and strength. He is aggressive in the corners and the front of the net, and knows how to play physically without taking penalties that hurt his team. He uses his reach to contain play at the offensive blue line (especially his reach in getting to loose pucks).

Though strong and aggressive, Konroyd is not a fighter.

THE INTANGIBLES

Konroyd is a smart, confident player with excellent hockey sense. Steve plays a dependable game, and will almost always turn in a 100 percent effort. He's a good team man and will probably function as the defensive linchpin for the Blackhawks.

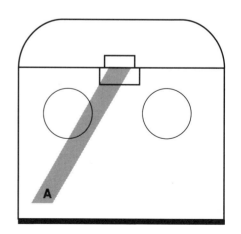

STEVE LARMER

Yrs. of NHL service: 7
Born: Peterborough, Ontario, Canada; June 16, 1961
Position: Right wing
Height: 5-10
Weight: 185
Uniform no.: 28
Shoots: left

Career statistics:

GP	G	A	TP	PIM
567	267	321	588	243

1988-89 statistics:

GP	G	A	TP	+/-	PIM	PP	SH	GW	GT	S	PCT
80	43	44	87	2	54	19	1	2	0	269	16.0

LAST SEASON

Goal total matched second highest of career; point total was third highest. Led team in goals and points (fourth in assists), power play goals and shots on goal. Played all 80 games (for seventh consecutive season), one of just two Hawks to do so. His plus/minus tied for fourth best among forwards.

THE FINESSE GAME

What Larmer knows how to do — better than 99 percent of the NHL population — is get into scoring position. Steve's not a great skater. He has neither blazing speed nor exceptional agility, though he does have great strength and balance on his skates; he has to, because he's always operating in the traffic areas near the net.

And its is near the net that Larmer's tremendous sense of the game puts him into position to shoot the puck before the puck gets to him. Then, his excellent shot does the rest.

He obviously accepts a pass excellently, and he prefers to shoot from the base of the right faceoff circle, but will move to the goal-crease if opportunity demands. Though his quick and soft hands would allow him to handle the puck well, Larmer leaves that part of his game (smartly — Steve's skating also mitigates against it) to his center — Denis Savard.

When he does have the puck, Larmer passes extremely well, using his sense to find the openings. And his skating is good enough, combined with his brains, to make him a very solid defensive performer; that's why he'll kill penalties.

THE PHYSICAL GAME

Larmer doesn't impose himself on the opposition. He won't initiate a lot of contact, doesn't bang in the corners. But he's always working in traffic to score his goals, willingly taking punishment when he flits around the net.

THE INTANGIBLES

His games-played streak (Larmer is the NHL's iron man) is one sign of his consistency. The other is his scoring ability: he averages 38 goals a season. That's dependable.

His quiet and unspectacular play — often overshadowed by that of Savard — makes Larmer one of the NHL's most-unknown (forget about under-rated) players.

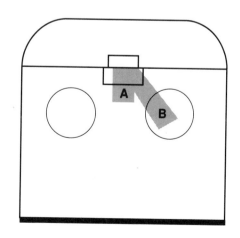

DAVE MANSON

Yrs. of NHL service: 3
Born: Prince Albert, Sask., Canada; January 27, 1967
Position: Defenseman
Height: 6-2
Weight: 190
Uniform no.: 3
Shoots: left

Career statistics:

GP	G	A	TP	PIM
196	20	50	70	683

1988-89 statistics:

GP	G	A	TP	+/-	PIM	PP	SH	GW	GT	S	PCT
79	18	36	54	5	352	8	1	0	1	224	8.0

LAST SEASON

All totals were career highs. Finished fifth in team scoring (second among defensemen, though first in goals among defenders), third in SOG total and plus/minus, and first in PIM total (third in the NHL).

THE FINESSE GAME

Skating is the key to Manson's success, and he's a surprisingly agile skater for a man with his size and strength. His good balance and foot speed provide him with good agility and lateral movement (and he'll improve), as well as speed both forward and backward. Dave skates well both forward and backward, certainly well enough that he can step up to close the gap on the puck carrier. That makes him an active — rather than re-active — defenseman.

His skating allows him to move fairly well in traffic, and his hands have developed to the point where he can move confidently with the puck. Because he has good vision of the play, Dave moves the puck from his end well (and will improve here too). He's also joining the play as it moves up ice, jumping into the holes on the give-and-goes.

Though defense is his first priority, Manson is containing the point well. He doesn't do a lot of pinching in, but he does challenge at the offensive blue line to keep the play alive. He finds the open man from the blue line, and his strong, quickly released shot is low and accurate to the net.

All his skills make him a natural for special teams play.

THE PHYSICAL GAME

Balance plays a big part in Manson's physical game, because it is his balance that makes him so effective as a hitter. He remains vertical after collisions, and that means he's able to re-join the play immediately.

And a hitter he is. Dave is an excellent bodychecker — and mean besides. He really punishes the opposition along the walls or in front of the net (sometimes too vigorously, as his PIM total indicates). He uses his body and his strength to great advantage in gaining position, and he completes all his checks.

Manson also doesn't have to be told what his job is. No coach has to tap him on the shoulder and say, "You see that guy on the other team? He's running our guys; why don't you do something about it?" Manson sees what has to be done on the ice, and then he goes and does it.

He drops the gloves willingly, and he's a pretty good fighter. He also sacrifices his body to block shots.

THE INTANGIBLES

Manson is tremendously gifted. His combination of strength and finesse skill is greatly similar to that of Washington's Scott Stevens, and Manson can grow to be one of the NHL's most dominating defensemen.

He certainly has the right attitude. Though Dave is apt to put pressure on himself, he comes to play each night and is a very intense player. His growing confidence should mirror his growing on-ice ability.

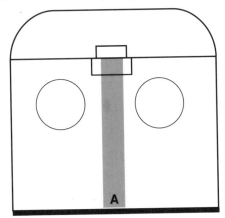

BOB MCGILL

Yrs. of NHL service: 8
Born: Edmonton, Alta., Canada; April 27, 1962
Position: Defenseman
Height: 6-1
Weight: 190
Uniform no.: 25
Shoots: right

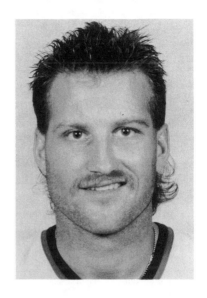

Career statistics:

GP	G	A	TP	PIM
431	7	36	43	1,243

1988-89 statistics:

GP	G	A	TP	+/-	PIM	PP	SH	GW	GT	S	PCT
68	0	4	4	9	155	0	0	0	0	38	0.0

LAST SEASON

Games played total tied second highest of his career. PIM total was four-season high (fourth highest on team, second among defensemen).

THE FINESSE GAME

The only way for McGill to succeed in this area is to play an uncomplicated game. He has improved his defensive ability by concentrating on simple tasks (and less wandering around the defensive zone), but the opposition's eyes are still going to light up when McGill's on-ice.

His skating is — at *best* — average, probably less so backward and laterally. He's going to have to play his position positionally, because he lacks the skating abiliy to challenge the play.

His puck handling skill is almost non-existent, so look for McGill to tie up the opposition when possible and wait for a teammate to pick up the puck. Bob's scoring is also almost nil, aided by the fact that — for all his size and strength — his slap shot is soft.

THE PHYSICAL GAME

This is McGill's game, and he has made it somewhat more effective by limiting his seek-and-destroy missions. McGill is a very physical player and will hit hard and often when he can. He can clear the front of the net or take the opposition off the puck along the boards, and McGill must play tough to play at all.

He benefits from playing in Chicago Stadium because of the smaller ice surface, which makes his skating better and his hitting more insistent.

THE INTANGIBLES

Though working at correcting his deficiencies, McGill exists to take on the McRaes, Ewens and Kocurs that exist in the Norris Division. He'll continue to get spotted in and out of the lineup and — because of his limited skills — will also continue to be eminently replaceable.

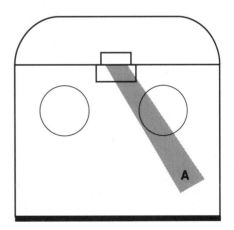

BOB MURRAY

Yrs. of NHL service: 14
Born: Kingston, Ontario, Canada; November 26, 1954
Position: Defenseman
Height: 5-10
Weight: 185
Uniform no.: 6
Shoots: right

Career statistics:

GP	G	A	TP	PIM
959	127	363	490	826

1988-89 statistics:

GP	G	A	TP	+/-	PIM	PP	SH	GW	GT	S	PCT
15	2	4	6	-4	27	2	0	0	0	19	10.5

LAST SEASON

Games played total was career low (demotions, benchings), all point totals second lowest.

THE FINESSE GAME

Solid, dependable, consistent and unknown: that's Bob Murray. He doesn't do anything fancy, he just gets the puck and moves it out of the Hawks zone quickly, efficiently and correctly. Murray plays his defensive angles as if he were writing a textbook, and he has to do that because of his size. He reads the offensive rush and anticipates its ramifications very well. He's an above average defenseman, so forget that plus/minus rating.

Bob remains an outstanding skater, but he doesn't have the quickness he once had, so he doesn't rush the puck as he used to. His offensive instincts are very good and that's why he'll see time on the power play.

He sees the play well in both zones and gets the puck to his teammates in the openings. He'll pinch in prudently at the blue line and he uses a good slap shot from the point as a scoring weapon.

THE PHYSICAL GAME

Murray is a direct contradiction to Darwinian principle of only the strong surviving. Rather, he embodies the theory regarding the inheritance of acquired characteristics: He learned how to be smart, how to play the body when the situation is in his favor, how to make the most of what he has.

He can't make the play in the corner on strength alone if he runs into a strong, hard-working forward. Vision and ability to move the puck quickly to teammates once it's won are Murray's assets here.

Because of his strength (or lack thereof) the opposition would like to get Murray isolated in front of the net, where he'll be unable to hold off big forwards. Murray counters that by holding and interfering smartly.

THE INTANGIBLES

Time is running out for Murray in Chicago — or may already have, considering how Coach Mike Keenan spotted him in and out of the lineup. At 35 years old, there may not be much of an NHL career left for Bob, and he may finish that career in a city other than Chicago.

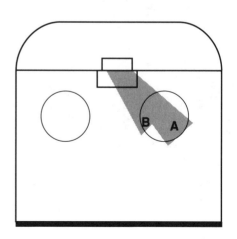

TROY MURRAY

Yrs. of NHL service: 7
Born: Winnipeg, Manitoba, Canada; July 31, 1962
Position: Center
Height: 6-1
Weight: 195
Uniform no.: 19
Shoots: right

Career statistics:

GP	G	A	TP	PIM
511	165	226	391	516

1988-89 statistics:

GP	G	A	TP	+/-	PIM	PP	SH	GW	GT	S	PCT
79	21	30	51	0	113	5	2	2	1	156	13.5

LAST SEASON

Point totals fell for fourth straight season. PIM total was career high.

THE FINESSE GAME

Anticipation and strong skating are the hallmarks of Murray's game, and he uses those assets as one of the NHL's better checking forwards. He is very strong on the puck, using his leg strength and superb balance to pursue it relentlessly — and through traffic when necessary. He is very difficult to knock down and that strength meshes perfectly with his robust style of play, allowing him to come away with the puck more often than not.

Anticipation is the second asset that makes Murray's game go, and he applies it defensively and offensively. Defensively, he sees the openings the opposition will try to exploit, and thus thwarts the opposing center in his attempts to exploit them.

Offensively, Troy's vision and anticipation allow him to use his teammates. In this way, he takes advantage of the loose pucks that his checking creates to be a well-rounded player (and not just a defensive role player).

Murray chooses not to handle the puck when he gains it, far too frequently dumping it deeper and chasing it only seconds after gaining it — despite the fact that his skating strength would allow him to barrel over the defense, or that his agility might get him closer to the net.

Murray is in the wrist and snapshot range and is very dangerous if he can penetrate the area inside the faceoff circles, where he will unleash a quick and accurate shot. He'll score from 20-25 goals a season.

THE PHYSICAL GAME

Troy is an excellent player away from the puck, and this is where his fine physical game comes into play. Unlike many checking forwards, Murray's relentless hitting and good strength wear down the opposition; it is his nearly tireless skating that makes him so difficult to avoid and then — bang! — another hit.

He is an excellent forechecker because he really bruises the opposing defensemen.

While his leg strength and balance carry him to the heart of the traffic areas, it is Murray's arm and hand strength that pull the puck from the opposition. That means he can take the puck away without having to use the strength of his whole body; very convenient in traffic when he can only get his hands near the puck. Because of that strength, Murray is a good — and can be dominating — faceoff man.

THE INTANGIBLES

Considering that Chicago — team-wise — was minus-38, the idea that Murray (the Hawks' best checker) was an even player gives you an idea of just how good Troy can be.

He is very much a Mike Keenan-type of player in demeanor and talent, and Troy should continue as one of the NHL's foremost defensive players — made more valuable by the fact that he can pot a goal or two as well.

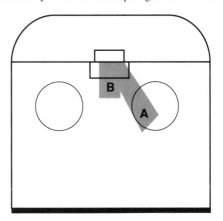

DARREN PANG

Yrs. of NHL service: 2
Born: Medford, Ontario, Canada; February 17, 1964
Position: Goaltender
Height: 5-5
Weight: 155
Uniform no.: 40
Catches: left

Career statistics:

GP	MINS	G	SO	AVG	A	PIM
81	4,252	287	0	4.05	9	6

1988-89 statistics:

GP	MINS	AVG	W	L	T	SO	GA	SA	SAPCT
35	1,644	4.38	10	11	6	0	120	915	.869

LAST SEASON

Pang led five Hawk goalies in games played. Games and minutes played totals fell in second NHL season.

THE PHYSICAL GAME

Pang squeezes every bit of his size he can get from his (by NHL standards) undersized body, and he does that by standing up in the net and challenging the shooters — most of the time.

But in certain circumstances, Pang is his own worst enemy. He doesn't challenge well screen shots, and he also hangs back in the goal when his concentration flags. His excellent reflexes, however, can often counter those flaws. He has an excellent glove hand, certainly in the League's top five and maybe better than that. He also has excellent foot speed.

Darren is a good skater and is greatly aided by his balance. That allows him to move well both forward and back and laterally (from post to post). He uses his skating when retrieving loose pucks for his defense. His balance also helps him regain not only his feet, but his stance quickly.

Pang will move the puck to his defense, but he can't handle the puck backhanded; he has to reverse his hands on the stick. He uses his stick to clear rebounds well except for shots off his pads; those rebounds squirt back toward the opposition.

Because of his size, most opponents tend to go high on him, and that's where his challenging style helps. He has special pads for his shoulders because of all the shots that hit him there.

THE MENTAL GAME

Pang has incredible poise, because he is essentially nerveless. Neither bad goals nor bad games get to him. He'll give up four goals in the first period and come back for the second as if nothing has happened. His concentration is fairly solid; he maintains it well from game to game and within the contest. One indication of just how into the game he is, is the fact — because of his size — Pang gets hit in the head a lot. But he remains unafraid, and just picks himself up and gets back to work.

He has big save capability and plays on quiet emotion — the type of goalie whose spectacular saves inspire the team.

THE INTANGIBLES

He's funny and outgoing, and his teammates love him, but we questioned last year if Pang could maintain his number one status. Since the arrival of Alain Chevrier, it's obvious Pang has been relegated to backup status. And, with the imminent arrival of Jimmy Waite, Pang may not even fill that role this season.

WAYNE PRESLEY

Yrs. of NHL service: 4
Born: Dearborn, Mich., USA; March 23, 1965
Position: Right wing
Height: 5-11
Weight: 175
Uniform no.: 17
Shoots: right

Career statistics:

GP	G	A	TP	PIM
235	72	67	139	304

1988-89 statistics:

GP	G	A	TP	+/-	PIM	PP	SH	GW	GT	S	PCT
72	21	19	40	-3	100	4	3	4	1	132	15.9

LAST SEASON

Games played, PIM and all point totals were second highest of his career. He was demoted to the International League briefly early in the season. He suffered a dislocated shoulder in the playoffs.

THE FINESSE GAME

Presley continues to develop as an NHLer, in all of his finesse categories. His skating has improved because his foot speed has improved, and that development dovetails well with Wayne's hockey sense. He has intelligence, patience and good instincts, and each of those is improving at the NHL level as well. Those instincts serve him well in penalty killing situations, where he forces the play at the point and creates shorthanded opportunities.

He's becoming very creative without the puck, looking for openings and opportunities, and he's learned to do this without sacrificing his defensive game. Where previously he failed to apply himself defensively the way he does offensively, Wayne has worked at improving his positional play; now the Hawks don't have to worry about him in the defensive zone.

His patience and poise is gradually making itself evident in his offensive game, though Wayne is still primarily a run-and-gunner. He's going to boom 'em from the right faceoff circle when he gets the opening.

THE PHYSICAL GAME

As with his finesse game, Presley has stepped up his physical contributions. However, the smarts that are beginning to categorize his finesse game are not always present when he checks; he can take some pretty stupid penalties in his over-anxiousness to hit somebody.

That added element of physicality should help him carve out some space to put his finesse skills to better use.

THE INTANGIBLES

Presley responded tremendously to the pressure put on him by Coach Mike Keenan, and Keenan responded by giving Presley more and more responsibility.

Wayne has the ability to be an above average finesse player in the NHL, certainly a 30-35 goal scorer. In many ways, he's really just approaching his third full NHL season — despite being in the League during five calendar years. We think this is the year that Presley shows where he stands as an NHLer.

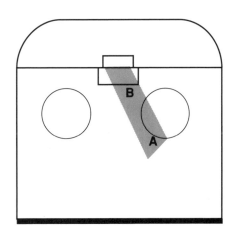

JEREMY ROENICK

Yrs. of NHL service: 1
Born: Boston, Mass., USA; January 17, 1970
Position: Center
Height: 5-11
Weight: 170
Uniform no.: 27
Shoots: right

Career statistics:

GP	G	A	TP	+/-	PIM	PP	SH	GW	GT	S	PCT
20	9	9	18	4	4	2	0	0	0	52	17.3

LAST SEASON

He was the Hawks' first round pick in the 1988 draft.

THE FINESSE GAME

Roenick is a supremely talented player with great NHL potential, especially characterized by his skating. He already has excellent speed and acceleration, so he can drive the defense off the blue line (and will, because his hockey sense tells him to keep moving — and not just stop — once he's gained the blue line). Roenick also has good balance and quickness, which combine with his speed to make him an agile skater.

As for his sense, he reads the play very well (and will improve as he becomes better accustomed to NHL speed) and uses that sense to lead his teammates into the clear, to forecheck and to exploit openings.

Jeremy has good hand skills, and he uses them in his passing, puckhandling and shooting. He has good strength in his passes and he distributes the puck well to both sides. He carries the puck well at high speed (and fairly well in traffic), and his shots are hard, accurate and quickly released.

His sense helps him in his defensive game, where Roenick is fairly conscientious positionally.

THE PHYSICAL GAME

Jeremy doesn't have great size, but he uses what he has well. He goes to the boards for the puck and throws checks there, and he's not above bullying players smaller than himself.

His balance helps him here, as does the fact that he can make plays after gaining the puck.

THE INTANGIBLES

Roenick showed well during his brief stint in Chicago, especially in the Hawks' playoff run. He's willing to take the rough going and he's got a good attitude. But now that he's no longer a secret, let's see how he responds — both physically and mentally — to the assortment of pressures he'll face (tighter checking, full NHL grind, etc.) this season.

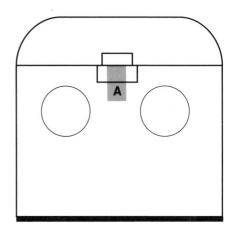

DENIS SAVARD

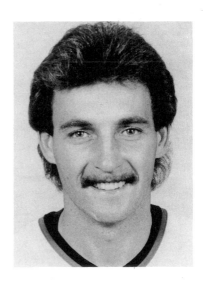

Yrs. of NHL service: 9
Born: Pointe Gatineau, Quebec, Canada;
February 4, 1961
Position: Center
Height: 5-10
Weight: 170
Uniform no.: 18
Shoots: right

Career statistics:

GP	G	A	TP	PIM
676	324	609	933	772

1988-89 statistics:

GP	G	A	TP	+/-	PIM	PP	SH	GW	GT	S	PCT
58	23	59	82	-5	110	7	5	1	1	182	12.6

LAST SEASON

Games played and goal totals were career lows (ankle injury), point total second lowest, assist total third lowest. Finished second on club in scoring, first in assists.

THE FINESSE GAME

Savard's skating is the best of his spectacular finesse repertoire. His incredible balance and foot speed are the main components of that skill, and they combine to make him almost unbelievably agile. Denis executes directional changes forward, backward or laterally within a single stride, and he also has the incomparable one-step acceleration that gives him breakaway speed.

His combination of soft hands and amazing ice vision and anticipation make Savard an excellent playmaker. He can either exploit an opening for a teammate (by sending a pass anywhere at any time) or use his fantastic puckhandling skill to maneuver through traffic at will. He is one of the best one-on-one players in the League, though sometimes too much so.

Savard can score from anywhere within the offensive zone because of his excellent wrist shot (accurate, quickly released, heavy), but he's equally dangerous in traffic around the net; he can finesse the puck home with just half an inch of room.

THE PHYSICAL GAME

By no stretch of the imagination could Savard be considered a physical hockey player. In fact, he's the only player who comes to mind who belies the theory that a physical game helps a finesse one. Savard likes to stay out of the fray in front of the opposition net because of his size, but his small stature does him no harm because he is quick and difficult to hit. He will put his stick into people on occasion.

THE INTANGIBLES

Not known for being a great character player (his run-ins with officials and his disdain for playing in pain are examples), Savard had some difficulty making the adjustment to Mike Keenan last season.

But, though Savard did try to skate off the ice in mid-practice (Denis didn't like the drills; Doug Wilson forced him to remain), Denis did make attempts to get along with his new coach. Nevertheless, the cloud of trade rumor followed him all season, and Savard will probably be the subject of those rumors again this season.

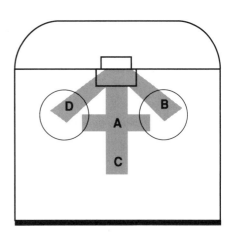

DUANE SUTTER

Yrs of NHL service: 10
Born: Viking, Alberta, Canada; March 16, 1960
Position: Right wing
Height: 6-1
Weight: 185
Uniform no.: 12
Shoots: right

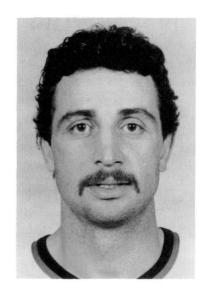

Career statistics:

GP	G	A	TP	PIM
659	135	189	324	1,177

1988-89 statistics:

GP	G	A	TP	+/-	PIM	PP	SH	GW	GT	S	PCT
75	7	9	16	-11	214	0	0	1	0	83	8.4

LAST SEASON

Goal, assist and point totals were career lows. PIM total was career high and second highest on club (first among forwards). Plus/minus was club's third worst, second worst among forwards.

THE FINESSE GAME

More than anything else, determination marks a Sutter game — and that's especially so in the finesse aspects. Duane gets where he is going on work, not fleet feet. He doesn't have great agility or lateral movement, but his strong skating stride moves him up the ice and — more importantly — allows him to play his physical game.

Sutter can carry the puck, but his lack of hand skill combines with his lack of foot skill to make him below average in the puckhandling and puck movement categories. He's more effective on the right side, because his stick is open to the center of the ice and he's on his forehand. His understanding of the creative game is limited too, as demonstrated by his tendency to go to his backhand when carrying the puck. Nor does he anticipate well; he won't lead teammates into openings — they're going to have to already be there.

THE PHYSICAL GAME

Sutter's skating strength powers his physical game. It allows him to drive through his checks, thus helping him take the opposition off the puck. He's a persistent checker who works 100 percent of the time, and he's good in the corners because he works so hard and is fearless. He will throw his body to make plays, or take hits as well, and that corner work ties up defensemen to allow openings for the pure goal scorers. For that reason, he just may be on the ice in a crucial situation.

He also uses his physical ability in his scoring, because he is tough in front of the net.

THE INTANGIBLES

What you get in Sutter is a leader by example. He stands up for the team, he's a character individual and plays his heart out. What more could you ask for?

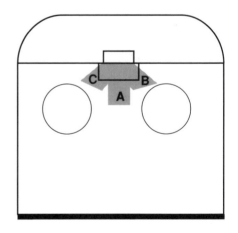

STEVE THOMAS

Yrs. of NHL service: 4
Born: Stockport, England; July 15, 1963
Position: Left wing
Height: 5-10
Weight: 185
Uniform no.: 32
Shoots: left

Career statistics:

GP	G	A	TP	PIM
236	90	98	188	261

1988-89 statistics:

GP	G	A	TP	+/-	PIM	PP	SH	GW	GT	S	PCT
45	21	19	40	-2	69	8	0	0	0	124	16.9

LAST SEASON

Games played was second lowest full season total (knee surgery). Goal total was second highest of career.

THE FINESSE GAME

Before knee surgery, excellent speed, balance and strength afoot marked Thomas's skating game. Those assets provided him with good lateral movement and the ability to make quick directional changes — like when he pulls his favorite move: gain the blue line, pull up short, and then shoot.

His shot is his best weapon, particularly his big slap shot from the wing; he can beat any goaltender with it. It is not, however, exceptionally accurate — maybe only three or four of 10 attempts are actually on net; the rest rattle the glass. The slap shot is not his only weapon, as he uses a good snap shot too. For as often as he shoots, Thomas doesn't pull the trigger fast enough. Improvement in accuracy and release would bolster Thomas's scoring marks.

Steve has good sense in the offensive zone and he uses that ability to get into scoring position. Thomas also uses that sense for passing. He has nice hands and can pass well, but because he's a scorer he looks to the net first.

THE PHYSICAL GAME

Thomas is a mucker and a grinder. He works the corners well and is fearless, banging bodies with any of the opposition. He has good upper body strength and can get the puck free, while his balance and sturdiness on skates keep him vertical to make his plays.

THE INTANGIBLES

Like 1987-88, last season was a wash because of injury — which more and more seems a clear and present danger to Thomas. How he comes back from his knee surgery (he did play five playoff games) is the big question.

He will be counted on greatly by the Hawks, because they could use his scoring from the left side. He's even lucked out center-wise, because Denis Savard, Troy Murray and Jeremy Roenick are all right-handed shots, which means Thomas will be on their forehands as a left wing.

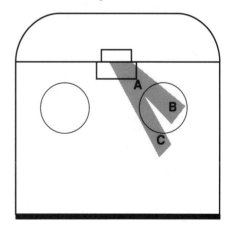

DAN VINCELETTE

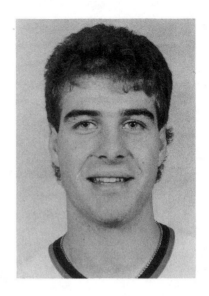

Yrs. of NHL service: 2
Born: Verdun, Quebec, Canada; August 1, 1967
Position: Left wing
Height: 6-1
Weight: 202
Uniform no.: 11
Shoots: left

Career statistics:

GP	G	A	TP	PIM
135	17	15	32	226

1988-89 statistics:

GP	G	A	TP	+/-	PIM	PP	SH	GW	GT	S	PCT
66	11	4	15	-9	119	1	0	0	0	76	14.5

LAST SEASON

Goal and PIM total rose in second season, games played and point total fell. His plus/minus was the club's fourth worst. He missed five games with a groin injury.

THE FINESSE GAME

The heart of Vincelette's game is rooted in the strength aspects of his finesse game. Dan is a strong skater with a powerful stride, and that stride aids him tremendously in his checking game and his mucking in the corners. He hasn't developed NHL-level agility or quickness (lacking the foot speed necessary for those skills), but greater NHL experience (play with the best and become the best) may help in that area.

Because he lacks that speed, Dan also lacks the time to make plays: his mind doesn't read the ice fast enough to communicate a play to Vincelette's body in the time his skating provides before the opposition shows up. Right now, Dan has to play a very simple finesse game — like throw the puck in front and skate back like hell on defense if (when?) the puck turns over.

He has a hard slap shot but won't fool anyone with it consistently, so his scoring right now will have to come from close to the net.

In other words, Dan is going to have to succeed as a checker until his skills improve.

THE PHYSICAL GAME

Dan's an aggressive winger and enjoys playing that game. Vincelette has good size and strength, and he uses them to advantage in his grinding game. He doesn't just bump into the opposition, he hits them, and his strength carries him through his checks.

His balance keeps him upright and in the play after collisions, and his hitting could become more effective if he were to develop better foot speed. Then he could better close gaps, and depart from the corner quicker.

THE INTANGIBLES

His strength and aggressiveness are what the Hawks like best about Vincelette — and the fact that he knew how to put the puck in the net in junior. In the meantime, he'll do well because of the increasing physical tenor of the Norris Division.

He does have to show, however, that he's better conditioned for the season, as injury — in just two NHL seasons — has already set him back twice.

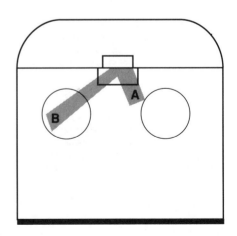

DOUG WILSON

Yrs. of NHL service: 12
Born: Ottawa, Ontario, Canada; July 5, 1957
Position: Defenseman
Height: 6-1
Weight: 187
Uniform no.: 24
Shoots: left

Career statistics:

GP	G	A	TP	PIM
817	191	475	666	692

1988-89 statistics:

GP	G	A	TP	+/-	PIM	PP	SH	GW	GT	S	PCT
66	15	47	62	8	69	4	1	3	0	248	6.0

LAST SEASON

Led club's defense in scoring (10th among NHL), finishing fourth overall. Plus/minus tied for second best. He was second in assists and shots on goal. Assist and point totals were three-season highs, despite being sidelined with hand injury.

THE FINESSE GAME

Wilson's superb skating makes him not just one of the NHL best defensemen, but one of the NHL's best players. He's got speed, quickness, agility, superb lateral movement and a change of pace that makes his skating twice as effective.

He makes his skating work by complementing it with excellent hockey sense and playreading ability; his understanding of the play — both offensively and defensively — is truly world class. His vision meshes with his excellent hand skills, allowing him to use his teammates excellently. Doug can put a pass anywhere, finessing or firing the puck when necessary. He is an exceptional puckhandler, and is always a threat to not only rush from the Hawks zone but to spearhead a Chicago attack.

His skating and hand skills make him one of the NHL's best at containing the point, and he takes the puck off the boards and makes a play within a stride better than almost anyone.

His excellent slap shot — again, one of the NHL's best — is famous for its quickness and strength, delivered low to the ice and always on net. Doug charges the slot whenever possible, and his only flaw is that he doesn't shoot to score enough.

His skills make him a specialty teams natural.

THE PHYSICAL GAME

Doug's physical game is just as impressive as his finesse game. He's an excellent bodychecker, separating his man from the puck — and then making a play with the loose puck — exceptionally well. He stands the man up well and follows through on his checks so that give-and-gos are impossible. He succeeds in those confrontations because of his strength and balance.

THE INTANGIBLES

As always, the number one intangible with Wilson is his health. When healthy, Wilson is one of the top five defenders in the game — maybe better. His attitude and dedication are excellent, and he is a tremendous leader — only a Doug Wilson could convince Denis Savard not to walk out of a Mike Keenan workout.

He is the one player the Hawks can't afford to lose, because their defense is by and large clueless without him.

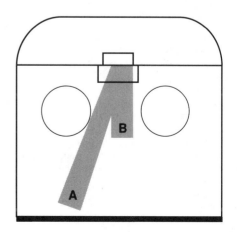

TRENT YAWNEY

Yrs. of NHL service: 2
Born: Hudson Bay, Sask., Canada;
September 29, 1965
Position: Defenseman
Height: 6-3
Weight: 185
Uniform no.: 8
Shoots: left

Career statistics:

GP	G	A	TP	PIM
84	7	27	34	131

1988-89 statistics:

GP	G	A	TP	+/-	PIM	PP	SH	GW	GT	S	PCT
69	5	19	24	-5	116	3	1	0	0	75	6.7

LAST SEASON
Yawney's first full NHL season.

THE FINESSE GAME
As mentioned last year, Yawney has solid fundamental that portend NHL success. What he must do to achieve that success is improve his NHL speed in the finesse categories — something he showed signs of last season.

His skating is strong, favoring the strength part of the game but with improving agility. Better foot speed would help his quickness and lateral movement, and thus allow him to use his good hockey sense to step up and challenge the play at both blue lines.

Yawney also has to improve the speed of his puck movement. He's very smart and has great sense for the game but his hands don't react at NHL speed. That results in missed passes and possible turnovers. Again, that's expected; Yawney will learn and improve. He does control the point fairly well, but his decision making could improve (he's taking chances his skating is not yet ready to justify).

His hockey sense and anticipation allow Yawney to move to the openings himself when he can (better quickness will help here), and Trent also knows how to lead a teammate into the clear. He's got a good shot from the blue line and will cheat into the zone for shots if he can.

THE PHYSICAL GAME
Yawney has good size and he uses it to his advantage by playing an efficient, take-the-body style. He won't knock anyone senseless, and greater upper body strength would help his duels with opposing forwards camped in the crease, but his skating strength and balance will help him win more than his share of these battles.

Of course, his physical willingness is amplified by his ability to make plays after checks. He uses his reach effectively when snaring loose pucks or deflecting shots with his stick.

THE INTANGIBLES
Fine progress was made by Yawney last season, and he'll continue to improve as time goes by. He has tremendous drive and a super attitude, and both will help him become a superior player.

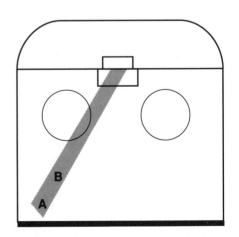

DETROIT
RED WINGS

LINE COMBINATIONS
GERARD GALLANT-STEVE YZERMAN-PAUL MACLEAN
TIM HIGGINS-SHAWN BURR-KRIS KING
PETR KLIMA-ADAM OATES-DAVE BARR

DEFENSE PAIRINGS
LEE NORWOOD-MIKE O'CONNELL
STEVE CHIASSON-RICK ZOMBO
JEFF SHARPLES-

GOALTENDERS
GLEN HANLON
GREG STEFAN

OTHER PLAYERS
JOHN CHABOT — Center
ADAM GRAVES — Center
MARC HABSCHEID — Left wing
DOUG HOUDA — Defenseman
JOE KOCUR — Right wing
CHRIS KOTSOPOULOS — Defenseman
JIM NILL — Right wing
TORRIE ROBERTSON — Right wing
BORJE SALMING — Defenseman

POWER PLAY

FIRST UNIT:
GERARD GALLANT-STEVE YZERMAN-PAUL MACLEAN
LEE NORWOOD-STEVE CHIASSON (JEFF SHARPLES)

SECOND UNIT:
ADAM OATES-DAVE BARR
MIKE O'CONNELL

On the first unit, GALLANT takes the left faceoff circle, MACLEAN the right and YZERMAN the slot and the back of the net. NORWOOD and CHIASSON (or SHARPLES) play catch at the point, with YZERMAN the preferred pass recipient if he can split the seams of the penalty-killing unit. The other forwards are next, but all three forwards crash the net on shots from the point.

On the second unit (if YZERMAN doesn't go all two minutes), OATES controls from the boards on an overloaded left side. BARR will plug the net, and a variety of left wings takes the left faceoff circle.

Last season Detroit's power play was FAIR, scoring 73 times in 352 opportunities (20.7 percent, 12th overall).

PENALTY KILLING

FIRST UNIT:
SHAWN BURR-STEVE YZERMAN
RICK ZOMBO-STEVE CHIASSON

SECOND UNIT:
TIM HIGGINS-SHAWN BURR
LEE NORWOOD-MIKE O'CONNELL

The forwards on both units are very aggressive on the puck, especially in the offensive and neutral zones. BURR and YZERMAN are excellent shorthanded threats and will pressure the puck from tat the points and down the boards, leaving the defense to prevent the cross-ice pass through the slot.

Last season Detroit's penalty killing was GOOD, allowing 79 goals in 426 shorthanded situations (81.5 percent, sixth overall).

CRUCIAL FACEOFFS
BURR and YZERMAN are the guys, with BURR getting a slight edge in defensive zone draws.

DAVE BARR

Yrs. of NHL service: 6
Born: Edmonton, Alta., Canada; November 30, 1960
Position: Center/right wing
Height: 6-1
Weight: 195
Uniform no.: 22
Shoots: right

Career statistics:

GP	G	A	TP	PIM
359	86	132	218	306

1988-89 statistics:

GP	G	A	TP	+/-	PIM	PP	SH	GW	GT	S	PCT
73	27	32	59	12	69	5	2	3	1	140	19.3

LAST SEASON

A hand injury didn't stop Barr from ringing up his second-highest games played total and career highs in goals and points. He finished third on the club in plus/minus, second among forwards.

THE FINESSE GAME

Barr is a case of the whole being greater than the sum of its parts. Taken individually, Barr's finesse talents are average — no better, no worse.

His skating is unremarkable, with no appreciable speed or agility. He'll get from Point A to Point B fairly well, but Barr's footspeed won't blow anyone's doors off. He skates well enough to serve as a good defensive forward, determined and persistent.

Dave has good hockey sense and is smart with the puck, knowing when to get rid of it on the offensive end and then move into a scoring position, and when to hound it defensively.

Barr will score from around the crease through his persistence and forechecking, again because his shooting is not exceptional. Rather, Dave knows that he's in the right place through his sense, and his checking pays off with created offensive opportunities. He doesn't handle the puck particularly well, so don't expect any rink-length rushes or dynamic passing plays.

THE PHYSICAL GAME

Dave is a strong winger with good size, and he uses his strength enthusiastically along the boards and in the traffic areas. He hits willingly and his checking will (more often than not) jar the opposition off the puck, and he accepts hits in order to make his plays.

THE INTANGIBLES

Dave experienced good offensive success last season (in part because he played with the talented Adam Oates), but that is several shades out of character for him. Rather, Barr succeeds because of his work ethic and determination to make the most of his ability. He's extremely coachable and is the kind of player who can carry out an assignment.

He's dependable and consistent, and that is his greatest strength.

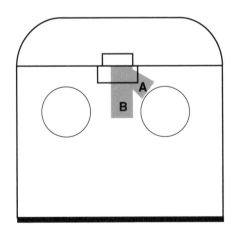

BERNIE FEDERKO

Yrs. of NHL service: 13
Born: Foam Lake, Sask., Canada; May 12, 1956
Position: Center
Height: 6-0
Weight: 185
Uniform no.: 24
Shoots: left

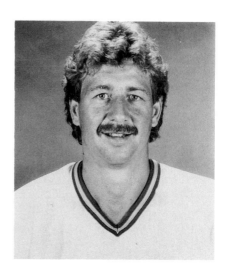

Career statistics:

GP	G	A	TP	PIM
927	352	721	1,073	463

1988-89 statistics:

GP	G	A	TP	+/-	PIM	PP	SH	GW	GT	S	PCT
66	22	45	67	-20	54	9	0	6		2	115	19.1

LAST SEASON

Games played total was second lowest full season mark of career. He finished third in scoring (second in assists) and tied for first in game winners. His plus/minus was the team's third worst, worst among forwards. He missed time with a late season elbow injury.

THE FINESSE GAME

Federko has outstanding hockey sense and anticipation, and those abilities have long been his hallmarks as an NHLer. He sees the ice excellently and immediately looks to make plays once he gains the offensive blue line. Bernie has excellent hands and passes the puck with the League's elite, and he does so without hesitation.

He's not a great skater, never has been (and that makes his playmaking accomplishments even more remarkable), but his balance allows him to work well in the traffic areas — where he can let his hand skills work to their best advantage. He can make plays almost regardless of body position.

Bernie's 35-goal days are past, especially since he is so unselfish a player. If he has a choice, Bernie's going to pass the puck. He'll pick up loose pucks around the net for his goals, and his sensitive hands are ideal for slot scoring. All his skills make him a natural for the power play.

THE PHYSICAL GAME

Federko takes his hits to make his plays and, as mentioned, works willingly in traffic — but he has never been a physical player. His excellent balance allows him to bump along the boards and gain control of the puck there, but he's never going to knock anyone into the cheap seats.

THE INTANGIBLES

He suffered through a less-than-spectacular season, but then Federko came on to lead his team in playoff scoring — that's an indication of his ability and intensity. He's a professional, and he carries a lot of weight in the Blues organization. He's also amazingly consistent — he's averaged more than a point-per-game for the last 10 seasons.

He's aging nicely, and his continued contributions will ease the development of players like rookie Rod Brind'Amour.

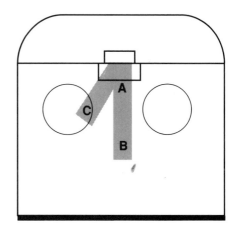

SHAWN BURR

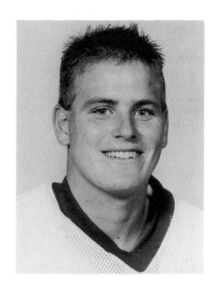

Yrs. of NHL service: 3
Born: Sarnia, Ontario, Canada; July 1, 1966
Position: Center
Height: 6-1
Weight: 180
Uniform no.: 11
Shoots: left

Career statistics:

GP	G	A	TP	PIM
237	59	75	134	288

1988-89 statistics:

GP	G	A	TP	+/-	PIM	PP	SH	GW	GT	S	PCT
79	19	27	46	5	78	1	4	2	0	149	12.8

LAST SEASON

He led the club in shorthanded goals. Assist total was career high.

THE FINESSE GAME

Excellent balance and strength are the keys to Burr's skating game, a game that melds with his excellent hockey sense to become an excellent penalty killer and forechecker.

Burr's strength afoot gives him acceleration and overall speed. He continues to improve in his mobility, largely because of his excellent balance. That balance is also a key to his outstanding physical game. His hockey sense (ice vision plus anticipation) lets him read plays extremely well.

His goal scoring and playmaking abilities are offshoots of his skating and checking. His sense tells him when a play will develop and his checking will turn over a lot of pucks because of that. His hand skills, however (even after three NHL seasons), could still use improvement.

Burr hasn't yet adapted his hand speed to the NHL level, and is reluctant to attempt offense. He must learn to not be satisfied at just forcing turnovers and must work on cashing them in, because Burr's shot and puckhandling abilities are good and show potential for improvement.

THE PHYSICAL GAME

Burr is a strong player and he welcomes physical confrontations. He initiates a lot of contact and succeeds in body checking because of his foot strength and balance. He stays vertical after collisions to make plays, and his persistent hitting will wear down the opposition.

Shawn's hand and wrist strength make him a good faceoff man, possibly the team's best.

THE INTANGIBLES

We said last year that the 1988-89 season was one in which Burr had to turn the corner, one where he had to show he was better than a role player *par excellence*.

That didn't happen. Shawn is a solid, dependable two-way player, one who works very hard at his game and brings a good attitude to the rink. But his potential says he should be scoring 25-30 goals a season — that would take him out of the role player class. He'll give the Wings a lot of good years, but we maintain there is more to his game and he should be showing it.

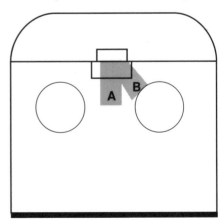

JOHN CHABOT

Yrs. of NHL service: 6
Born: Summerside, P.E.I., Canada; May 18, 1962
Position: Center
Height: 6-2
Weight: 200
Uniform no.: 16
Shoots: left

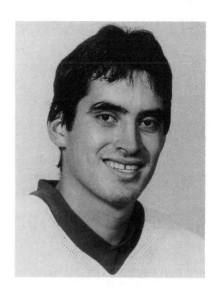

Career statistics:

GP	G	A	TP	PIM
412	70	183	253	57

1988-89 statistics:

GP	G	A	TP	+/-	PIM	PP	SH	GW	GT	S	PCT
52	2	10	12	-18	6	0	2	0	0	49	4.1

LAST SEASON

Games played total was career low (demotion to AHL). Plus/minus was the club's worst.

THE FINESSE GAME

John is a very good skater with a fluid, rather than strong, style. Because he doesn't have terrific leg strength John has neither explosive acceleration nor rink-length speed. Instead, his quickness and balance give him a high degree of agility and excellent lateral movement; that's how he gets where he's supposed to be.

He handles the puck well, putting his long reach to work very effectively. That reach also helps him carry the puck, especially in traffic.

When John combines his anticipation and hockey sense with his skating, he can be a proficient defensive forward. They also power his offensive game, showing him the openings. Chabot takes advantage of those chances by leading his teammates into the clear with good passes.

His checking opens up plenty of offensive opportunities, but John is largely unable to take advantage of them because he doesn't get his shot away quickly enough.

THE PHYSICAL GAME

Chabot is not physically tough at all. He does not hit, preferring to poke check the puck away from the opposition (there's that reach again) so he can remain free to skate with it. He does his defensive work by staying between the puck and his check, rather than by wearing his check down with hits.

In turn, he is difficult to hit because he is willowy on his skates, bending and swaying away from contact in order to keep working on the puck.

THE INTANGIBLES

We said last year that Chabot — like the other members of Detroit's curfew breaking crew of the 1988 playoffs — had much to answer for. No doubt, his term in the minors was one way of answering for that episode.

His next challenge will be regaining a permanent roster spot. He's got Steve Yzerman and Shawn Burr ahead of him, Adam Oates coming on and Adam Graves in the wings. A season split among Detroit, the bench and the AHL doesn't seem out of the question for Chabot.

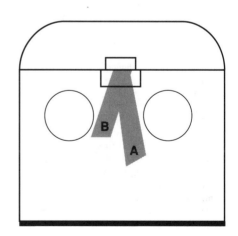

STEVE CHIASSON

Yrs. of NHL service: 3
Born: Barrie, Ontario, Canada; April 14, 1967
Position: Defenseman
Height: 6-0
Weight: 202
Uniform no.: 3
Shoots: left

Career statistics:

GP	G	A	TP	PIM
139	15	48	63	279

1988-1989 statistics:

GP	G	A	TP	+/-	PIM	PP	SH	GW	GT	S	PCT
65	12	35	47	-6	149	5	2	0	0	187	6.4

LAST SEASON

Chiasson missed time with a late-season back injury, but he nevertheless posted career highs in games played and all point categories. He led all Wing defensemen in scoring and PIM total, and he finished third on the club in SOG total.

THE FINESSE GAME

Play with the big boys and you'll play like the big boys. That's what happened to Chiasson last season. His skating has developed tremendously, so that he is demonstrating strength (and the balance and speed that follows) and a fair degree of agility. His improved skating is a boon to his offensive game, especially since he likes to rush the puck. He does, however, need to exercise better judgment in this area.

Chiasson's playmaking talents are developing as well. He passes well and knows how to lead a teammate into an opening. Chiasson also recognizes those openings himself, and he'll charge the net if he can. Steve has a very good slap shot, heavy, low and on net.

His defensive game has also improved, in terms of his positional play without the puck. Steve forces the play wide by playing his defensive angles well, doesn't wander around the ice and doesn't try to do things that are beyond his abilities.

THE PHYSICAL GAME

Steve has good size and better strength, and he likes to use both. He plays a physical game and can be a punishing hitter in both open ice and along the boards. He'll handle most anyone in the corners, and Chiasson has the strength to battle — and succeed — against most of the League's bigger forwards in front of his net.

He uses his body smartly to protect the puck when he carries it.

THE INTANGIBLES

We said Chiasson could succeed as a defensive defenseman, but we had him mis-cast. He has developeable offensive tendencies and greater NHL experience should showcase those. He's mentally tough and wants to succeed, and Steve brings a good attitude to the rink — he's a real leader, maybe even captain material if not for Steve Yzerman.

His best days are ahead of him.

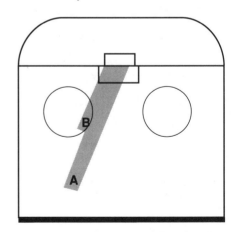

GERARD GALLANT

Yrs. of NHL service: 5
Born: Summerside, P.E.I., Canada; September 2, 1963
Position: Left wing
Height: 5-10
Weight: 185
Uniform no.: 17
Shoots: left

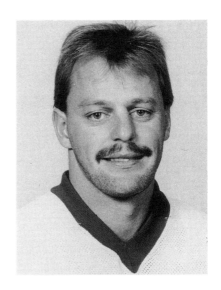

Career statistics:

GP	G	A	TP	PIM
313	137	158	295	860

1988-89 statistics:

GP	G	A	TP	+/-	PIM	PP	SH	GW	GT	S	PCT
76	39	54	93	7	230	13	0	7	0	221	17.6

LAST SEASON

All point totals were career highs. Gallant second on the club in goals, points and SOG totals, first in PIM total and third in power play goals. His plus-7 was third best among forwards.

THE FINESSE GAME

As with the League's other power forwards, strength is the key to Gallant's finesse game. Most noticeably, he isn't a graceful skater by any means: his agility, quickness and speed are not exceptional. But he has good balance and strength on his skates, and that makes his physical game more effective by allowing him to remain vertical after checks. Essentially, Gallant gets where he's going by running over people — not by dancing around them.

His vision and anticipation — both offensively and defensively — are above average. He recognizes openings and can lead a teammate to them, and he also closes those openings while checking. He's a solid defensive player and will be on the ice in any crucial situation because he has the smarts and the skills to make the right play.

His success as a goal scorer comes — again — from his strength. He's not a virtuoso with the puck when handling or carrying it, so he has to put his excellent wrist shot (very heavy in its delivery) to work from near the net. Shooting more frequently has also helped his offense. He's successful when he remembers not to overhandle the puck.

THE PHYSICAL GAME

Gallant demonstrates his strength in several ways. First, he gets his shot off while in traffic and being checked. His upper body strength also allows him to out-muscle the opposition for the puck along the boards, and Gallant makes his physical play more valuable by being able to make plays coming out of the corner.

His leg and skating strength allow him to drive through his checks and bounce the opposition off the puck. He loves to hit and initiates much contact, and Gallant also takes hits to make plays. He is also a willing and able fighter.

THE INTANGIBLES

Gallant is a character player, and his on-ice performance last season is only partly attributable to Steve Yzerman being his center. Gerard's combination of skill and strength make him a much desired commodity (as does his excellent attitude and work ethic; he's a leader for the Wings), and if the Wings ever developed a second scoring line to absorb some of the opposition's checking, Gallant just might score 45 or 50 goals.

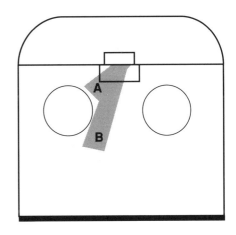

ADAM GRAVES

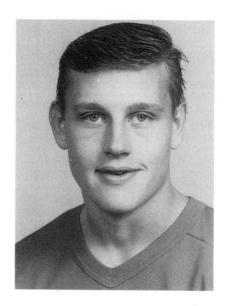

Yrs. of NHL service: 1
Born: Toronto, Ontario, Canada; April 12, 1968
Position: Center
Height: 5-11
Weight: 185
Uniform no.: 12
Shoots: left

Career statistics:

GP	G	A	TP	PIM
75	7	6	13	68

1988-89 statistics:

GP	G	A	TP	+/-	PIM	PP	SH	GW	GT	S	PCT
56	7	5	12	-5	60	0	0	1	0	60	11.7

LAST SEASON

Detroit's second pick in the 1986 draft, this was his first "full" NHL season (though he did spend time in Adirondack of the AHL).

THE FINESSE GAME

Graves is a very talented finesse player. He's an excellent skater with balance, strength and agility. He has good-to-very-good quickness, and that trait combines with his balance to give him good change of direction and lateral movements skills.

Adam's stick skills match his foot skills. He controls the puck very well (especially when he plays in traffic), and he also shoots the puck well. His shot is hard and accurate, forcing the goaltender to make saves.

His physical finesse skills are amplified by his hockey sense. Graves has a great sense of where the puck will be and what is the best way for him to get there. He also plays an aware and disciplined defensive game, and his skills make him a good transitional player — he'll get the play started from the Wings' zone skillfully.

THE PHYSICAL GAME

Though he doesn't have great size, Graves has great strength and he plays a very physical game. He works very well against the boards and in traffic because of his strength and balance, and he likes to play a hitting game.

He's an aggressive player but a smart one, so he won't hurt his team with penalties. His strength powers his shot and also makes him a good faceoff man.

THE INTANGIBLES

The Wings thought they got a first-rounder in Graves, though they drafted him in the second round. He seems ready to make the transition from the AHL to fulltime NHL duty, and that's bad news for players like John Chabot and Adam Oates.

Graves is a dedicated and determined player, one who works hard in practice and games. He can be a leader because of these traits.

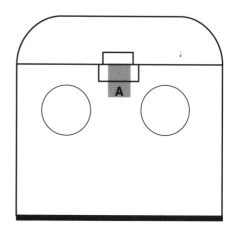

MARC HABSCHEID

Yrs. of NHL service: 4
Born: Swift Current, Sask., Canada; March 1, 1963
Position: Center
Height: 5-10
Weight: 170
Uniform no.: 10
Shoots: right

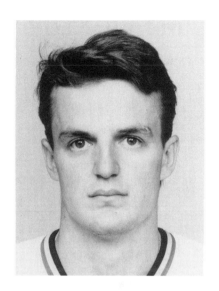

Career statistics:

GP	G	A	TP	PIM
187	41	61	102	74

1988-89 statistics:

GP	G	A	TP	+/-	PIM	PP	SH	GW	GT	S	PCT
76	23	31	54	2	40	7	3	3	0	182	12.6

LAST SEASON

Games played and all point totals were career highs. Finished tied for third in goals and power play goals, fourth in shots on goal.

THE FINESSE GAME

Habscheid is an excellent skater, with agility and lateral movement his best assets. Marc has extremely quick feet, and they combine with his exceptional balance to make him very shifty. He likes to combine that agility with his good quickness to drive the defense off the blue line, then pull up short and wheel 360-degrees to open ice.

His hand skills complement his skating skill well, because Marc handles the puck well at top speed. He's got a good shot, not a great one, but he makes the most of his opportunities because of his ability to dart to lose pucks around the net.

His anticipation and smarts are such that he can play in all situations, and Habscheid is also a conscientious and attentive defensive player — an acquired trait.

THE PHYSICAL GAME

Habscheid plays an involved physical game — he's willing to get his nose dirty — and that willingness amplifies his finesse game. But he doesn't have a lot of strength, and doesn't have great size, so his best work is going to be done in the open ice.

His eye/hand coordination is very good, and he does well at faceoffs because of that. He'll take most of Minnesota's defensive zone draws.

THE INTANGIBLES

Marc can stick with the Stars because — right now — they need as many skilled players as they can get, regardless of those players' negatives. Habscheid is talented enough to be one of Minnestoa's top six forwards, but he'd rank less high on a better club. Still, he's playing a good all-around game and giving the Stars some spark while doing so.

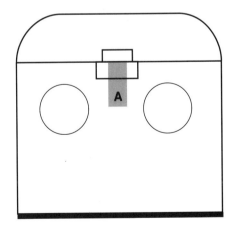

GLEN HANLON

Yrs. of NHL service: 11
Born: Brandon, Man., Canada; February 20, 1957
Position: Goaltender
Height: 6-0
Weight: 185
Uniform no.: 1
Catches: right

Career statistics:

GP	MINS	G	SO	AVG	A	PIM
413	22,885	1,361	12	3.57	8	209

1988-89 statistics:

GP	MINS	AVG	W	L	T	SO	GA	SA	SAPCT	PIM
39	2,092	3.56	13	14	8	1	124	1,055	.882	12

LAST SEASON

Goals-against-average was four-season high. He missed two late-season games with a back injury.

THE PHYSICAL GAME

Where once he relied solely on his reflexes, Hanlon has made the transition to stand-up style. He succeeds now by squaring himself to the puck and letting his body stop the shot, as opposed to his previous limbs-in-every-direction style.

Once he gets his feet moving, though, it's another story. Glen's balance is not exceptional (he'll lose it once he moves his feet), so once he opens up he's going to be on the ice. His innate quickness, however, allows him to somehow recover and get his body in front of that second shot. He could cut down on this flaw if he cut down his angles better; Hanlon squares to the puck from deep in his net.

Hanlon leaves handles the puck fairly well, and he likes to get involved in play by moving it to his defense. He clears rebounds fairly well, but retains the habit of turning his back to the play when he skates back to his net after challenging a shooter. He loses sight of the play developing in front of his net, and can get burned by an incoming winger because of that.

He is weak on his glove side on any shot below the waist, but is good above it. He flops immediately on screen shots, but doesn't butterfly his pads, and that makes it difficult for him to move around once he is on the ice.

THE MENTAL GAME

Glen has the ability to charge up his game for a big contest, and he does well at maintaining his concentration within a game, but he could still improve between games.

Hanlon has always been a tough competitor, but he used to punish himself for bad games or goals and carry those in his consciousness. But he developed a looser attitude during his last season in New York, so that the goals — good or bad — no longer distract him from doing his job.

THE INTANGIBLES

Funny, upbeat and positive, Glen Hanlon is a super team guy. His teammates enjoy being around him because of his attitude, and it is his attitude and mental outlook that has made him successful in Detroit.

However, like battery-mate Greg Stefan, Hanlon has reached the peak of his ability. Whether or not the Wings can get to a Stanley Cup with Hanlon behind them is a highly debatable subject.

TIM HIGGINS

Yrs. of NHL service: 11
Born: Ottawa, Ontario, Canada; February 7, 1958
Position: Right wing
Height: 6-1
Weight: 185
Uniform no.: 20
Shoots: right

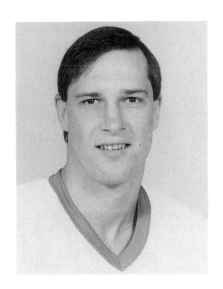

Career statistics:

GP	G	A	TP	PIM
706	154	198	352	719

1988-89 statistics:

GP	G	A	TP	+/-	PIM	PP	SH	GW	GT	S	PCT
42	5	9	14	0	62	0	0	0	0	45	11.1

LAST SEASON

Games played total was career low; ditto point totals. He spent time at Adirondack of the American Hockey League during mid-season.

THE FINESSE GAME

Higgins is a strong skater with a powerful stride and that stride gives him good speed. He translates that speed and almost tireless skating ability into checking and defensive work, and that's how he makes his best contributions to the Wings.

On the offensive end, Tim gets his chances because his speed and checking create loose pucks. His problem in those situations is that he has hands of stone. Because Tim can't handle the puck well in the high traffic area of the slot, his scoring totals will be unspectacular. Higgins hesitates when handling the puck and that flaw — along with his tough hands — means he doesn't use his teammates particularly well.

He also brings pretty good hockey sense to his game, and that greatly complements his checking ability.

THE PHYSICAL GAME

Higgins is a bull in a china shop. He's not afraid to be aggressive along the boards or in the corners, and he uses his size and strength well in those areas. His hitting also serves to wear down the opposition over the course of the game, taking the enemy out of the contest.

THE INTANGIBLES

Higgins is a great team man, a tremendous leader off the ice for the Wings through his attitude; that makes his dearth of scoring less difficult to accept.

He is otherwise a role player, who will be shuttled in and out of the lineup.

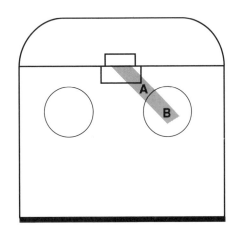

DOUG HOUDA

Yrs. of NHL service: 1
Born: Blairmore, Alta., Canada; June 3, 1966
Position: Defenseman
Height: 6-2
Weight: 190
Uniform no.: 27
Shoots: right

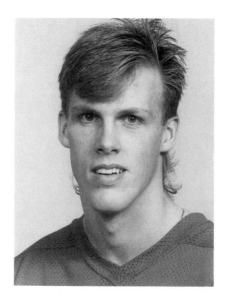

Career statistics:

GP	G	A	TP	PIM
74	3	12	15	81

1988-89 statistics:

GP	G	A	TP	+/-	PIM	PP	SH	GW	GT	S	PCT
57	2	11	13	17	67	0	0	0	0	38	5.3

LAST SEASON

Houda's first full NHL season. Plus/minus was tied for second best.

THE FINESSE GAME

Houda's a quietly skilled player, more efficient than spectacular. He covers a lot of ground when he skates because of his stride, but he's also balanced and quick enough to have good mobility in both directions.

That agility allows him to do more than just back in on his goaltender; it allows him to challenge at the blue line by stepping up on the incoming forward — to be *active*, not just *re*-active.

Doug plays his position smartly, and he makes the correct decisions to get the puck from his zone. He doesn't overhandle the puck or try to do things he's not capable of. He contributes rarely from the blue line, acting more as the fall-back defender than as the fourth attacker.

THE PHYSICAL GAME

Houda has very good size and strength. He cleans out the front of the net well, again in efficient and unspectacular fashion (as reflected by his relatively low PIM total). He's not a big banger.

Doug will win the battles in the high traffic areas, and because he makes simple and effective plays his physical play is that much more effective.

THE INTANGIBLES

Houda is another of the Red Wing youngsters (he's just 23 years old) who will be counted on more and more and will find his ice-time growing. That's bad news for players like Gilbert Delorme and Mike O'Connell.

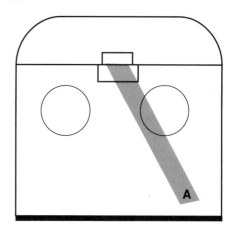

PETR KLIMA

Yrs. of NHL service: 4
Born: Chaomutov, Czechoslovakia;
December 23, 1964
Position: Left wing
Height: 6-0
Weight: 190
Uniform no.: 85
Shoots: left

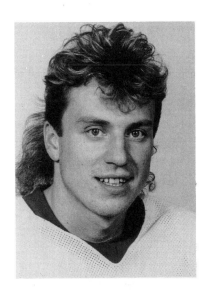

Career statistics:

GP	G	A	TP	PIM
280	124	88	212	148

1988-89 statistics:

GP	G	A	TP	+/-	PIM	PP	SH	GW	GT	S	PCT
51	25	16	41	5	44	1	0	3	0	145	17.2

LAST SEASON

Games played total was a career low (club suspensions, ankle and back injuries). All point totals were career lows.

THE FINESSE GAME

Klima is an excellent skater in all skating areas: quickness, speed, balance, power and agility. He will out-race most any checker, or cut inside most any defenseman. He stops on a dime, has tremendous one-step quickness, and his explosive acceleration puts him in the clear within two strides.

Petr's hand skills are as superior as his foot skills. He plays with the defense when he carries the puck, and he's got the hands to work with the puck in tight situations. That skill extends to his shot. His shot selection is excellent, and his slap shot from the wing will beat any goaltender in the League — if it gets on net; Klima will shoot 10-15 times a game and have just 2-3 shots on goal. He must make goaltenders work to stop his shot.

His abilities to anticipate and get into position to score are very high. He has excellent hockey sense in the offensive zone, and he uses his finesse skills to drive for the openings. All of his skills make him a natural for specialty teams duty.

His defense has improved from peremptory to something-better-than-casual, but he remains inconsistent in his defensive play from shift to shift and game to game.

THE PHYSICAL GAME

While primarily an open ice player, Klima has gradually edged closer and closer to the boards and corners. He's getting his body in the way of the opposition. There is still room for improvement in this area,

as Klima still prefers the outside of the scrum, But Klima even tosses the occasional check here and there.

THE INTANGIBLES

Thousands of words have been written about Petr Klima and his off-ice problems. Suffice to say that he is top 10 in the League in talent.

If he ever finds the emotional maturity necessary to dedicate himself to hockey, he'd become one of the NHL's elite players. We don't knows if he'll ever find that maturity, but we do know that this is his most important NHL season — if he's ever going to get anywhere, 1989-90 is the time.

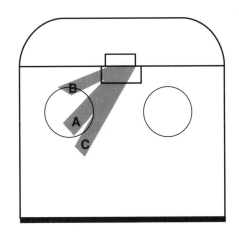

JOE KOCUR

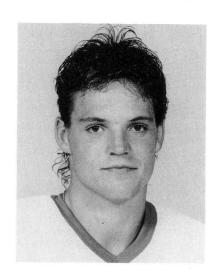

Yrs. of NHL service: 4
Born: Calgary, Alta., Canada; December 21, 1964
Position: Right wing
Height: 6-0
Weight: 195
Uniform no.: 26
Shoots: right

Career statistics:

GP	G	A	TP	PIM
277	35	31	66	1,193

1988-89 statistics:

GP	G	A	TP	+/-	PIM	PP	SH	GW	GT	S	PCT
60	9	9	18	-4	213	1	0	1	0	76	11.8

LAST SEASON

Games played total was three-season low (recurring back injury), but point totals tied career highs. PIM total was career low, but second-highest on the club.

THE FINESSE GAME

In terms of balance and speed, Kocur is a pretty good skater. He uses those abilities in his physical game so that when he hits he remains vertical. His balance gives him solid footing for fighting. His speed is an indication of his skating strength, and that strength allows him to drive through his checks. He lacks, however, the agility and lateral movement that would make his search and destroy missions more succesful. His turning is also weak and Kocur needs room to change direction.

Kocur has some puckhandling ability, so he's not afraid to carry the puck and challenge the defense. He sees passing openings and he can get the puck there (he also takes a pass fairly well), but he generally succeeds in these skills because of the room he gets from the opposition.

Joe has a great shot which he doesn't use enough. He doesn't drive for openings and doesn't think offensively, so it could be said that he could improve all aspects of his play without the puck.

THE PHYSICAL GAME

Kocur hits hard and he hits to hurt people — and that goes for his body-checking (which, because of his deficient agility isn't as good as it could be) and especially his fighting.

He is an exceptional fighter, generating knockout power in his punches. Kocur enjoys that reputation, and he'll take however many shots he has to in order to get in one or two punches. His play in this regard doesn't generally cross over to stickwork.

Kocur also keeps himself in excellent physical shape.

THE INTANGIBLES

Joe is a highly prized commodity; opposing clubs always ask about his availability. That's not to say he can't improve. Kocur could make himself a better player by working harder on the ice, remembering — for example — to always keep his feet moving, a simple thing, but one that he hasn't grasped in four NHL seasons. His work ethic and dedication are questionable.

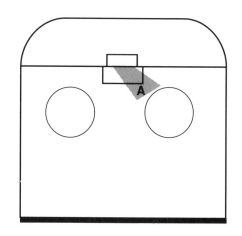

TONY MCKEGNEY

Yrs. of NHL service: 11
Born: Montreal, Quebec, Canada; February 15, 1958
Position: Left wing
Height: 6-1
Weight: 215
Uniform No.: 10
Shoots: left

Career statistics:

GP	G	A	TP	PIM
791	285	290	575	416

1988-89 statistics:

GP	G	A	TP	+/-	PIM	PP	SH	GW	GT	S	PCT
71	25	17	42	-1	58	7	0	2	0	154	16.2

LAST SEASON

Games played total was three-season low. Finished third in goals and shots on goal.

THE FINESSE GAME

McKegney's a good skater, whose strength gives him speed and acceleration down the wing. Tony does have a degree of agility (and some lateral movement), but his is mostly a straight ahead speed. It is that speed that puts him in the clear and allows him to use his tremenendous shot. He can also be a good checker because of his speed, making quick transitions up and down the ice.

His shot is excellent, laser-like and quickly released, but for some reason McKegney didn't use it as often as he could have last season (his SOG total fell from 241 — and 40 goals — in 1987-88 to 154 last year). It is hard and accurate, and McKegney uses it whenever possible; he wants the puck when he's in shooting position.

His offensive diligence makes him a solid bet for an annual 25 goals, and that diligence extends to the defensive zone where he plays well positionally. His anticipation and vision — his hockey sense — help him at both ends of the ice.

THE PHYSICAL GAME

Tony has good physical abilities — and excellent strength — but he doesn't always use those abilities the best he can. He can be very effective along the boards and especially in front of the net, because — once he plants himself — Tony's balance makes him very difficult to move. But there are times when he could be using those assets to muscle the puck in the corners or along the boards, but he's found instead outside the scrum and waiting for the loose puck to come to him.

He'll take the rough going and return it, but he is not a dirty player.

THE INTANGIBLES

We talked last year about McKegney's "second year in a franchise and down the tubes," reputation, suggesting instead that his rep should be amended to an "alternate year," theory. At any rate, his production plummeted last season.

Tony knows about the rep and wants to prove it wrong, but his streakiness as a scorer works against him. He had a poor start last season (seven goals in the first 20 games), followed by a poor finish (four goals in his last 19 games) with no fire in between.

He likes St. Louis and wants to stay there, but he'll have to do better than this if he wants to continue as a Blue.

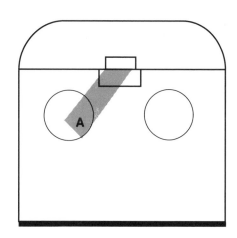

JIM NILL

Yrs. of NHL service: 9
Born: Hanna, Alta., Canada; April 11, 1958
Position: Right wing
Height: 6-0
Weight: 185
Uniform no.: 8
Shoots: right

Career statistics:

GP	G	A	TP	PIM
509	58	85	143	836

1988-89 statistics:

GP	G	A	TP	+/-	PIM	PP	SH	GW	GT	S	PCT
71	8	7	15	-1	83	0	1	2	0	39	20.5

LAST SEASON

Games played was second highest of career. He had the fewest shots on goal among Wing regulars.

THE FINESSE GAME

Nill is an average skater. He's not equipped with much speed or agility, nor is he exceptionally quick either in terms of acceleration or changing direction. He's an up-and-down winger without much imagination.

He's a good checker and plays his position well and that reflects in his defensive game as well. He patrols his wing in the offensive zone and doesn't wander, and he picks up his man and comes back deeply wth him on the backcheck. Don't hold his minus-1 mark against him; considering the players he must play opposite, that's a respectable total.

Jim has good anticipation and vision skills, abilities that make him good as a checking forward but, since he doesn't handle the puck or skate all that well, those mental qualities don't translate into offensive production.

THE PHYSICAL GAME

Nill is a banger, taking the body fairly well, getting in the way of his check and holding him out of the play. He has good strength and size and both serve him when he works along the boards, allowing him to out-muscle the opposition.

That ability is somewhat minimized because Nill doesn't have the skills to take full advantage of the pucks he wins in those battles. He does play the same way all the time and is consistent in the use of his body home or away, winning or losing.

THE INTANGIBLES

What you see with Jim Nill is what you get, a dedicated player and a hard worker, a character player and an individual who'll play when hurt. He's a role player, but his dependability guarantees him ice time.

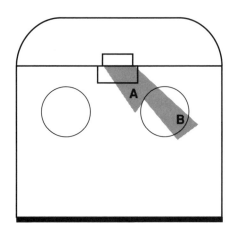

LEE NORWOOD

Yrs. of NHL service: 6
Born: Oakland, Calif, USA; February 2, 1960
Position: Defenseman
Height: 6-1
Weight: 198
Uniform no.: 23
Shoots: left

Career statistics:

GP	G	A	TP	PIM
292	38	111	149	678

1988-89 statistics:

GP	G	A	TP	+/-	PIM	PP	SH	GW	GT	S	PCT
66	10	32	42	6	100	4	1	0	0	97	10.3

LAST SEASON

Games played total was three-season high depsite missing time with a knee injury. All point totals were career highs.

THE FINESSE GAME

Norwood is one of those players who makes his limited skills better by playing within his abilities. He is no better than average as a skater, with little speed and mobility, but Lee maximizes this talent by playing defense positionally. Norwood uses his defensive angles well to force the play wide of the net.

Though his point totals last season were career highs, Norwood isn't essentially an offensive threat. Rather, he succeeds by moving the puck quickly and efficiently to the forwards in breakouts.

Lee is a power play mainstay, however, where he is used primarily as the safety valve. But since he's on the ice he's going to get chances to pick up points, and Norwood does just that from the left point. He sees the ice fairly well and makes good passes, but will not rush the puck or become a true fourth attacker in non-power play situations.

THE PHYSICAL GAME

Norwood is a fearless player, very rugged and completely without regard for his body. He blocks shots, he mixes it up in front of the net, he muscles with forwards against the boards. He enjoys the physical game and makes the most of his size.

THE INTANGIBLES

Norwood has emerged as Detroit's steadiest defenseman, and because of that he receives a tremendous amount of responsibility. His presence has allowed the Wings to break their young defensemen in slowly, gradually acclimatizing them to the NHL. He's a hard worker and a coachable athlete, and he leads by example on and off the ice.

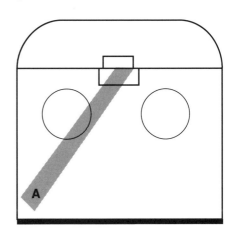

MIKE O'CONNELL

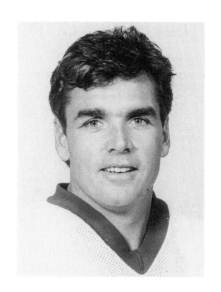

Yrs. of NHL service: 11
Born: Chicago, Ill., USA; November 25, 1955
Position: Defenseman
Height: 5-9
Weight: 180
Uniform no.: 2
Shoots: right

Career statistics:

GP	G	A	TP	PIM
794	101	320	421	583

1988-89 statistics:

GP	G	A	TP	+/-	PIM	PP	SH	GW	GT	S	PCT
66	1	15	16	-8	41	0	0	0	0	49	2.0

LAST SEASON

Games played total was second lowest full season total of career. His plus/minus was the lowest among full-time Wing defenders. Goal and point totals were career lows.

THE FINESSE GAME

At this late stage in his career, smarts are the key to O'Connell's NHL success. No longer the gifted skater he once was, Mike counters the opposition with his brains by anticipating and reading the play well. He uses his defensive angles to play sound positional defense; that's important, because O'Connell more and more has difficulty keeping up with the opposing forwards.

He's always been an agile skater with good mobility and quickness, but age has taken a lot of snap from his legs. Still, he's not often beaten one-on-one (though more and more frequently he's forced into giving ground) and he does retain enough quickness to intercept a pass and start the play up-ice.

His puck movement has been affected by the fact that he no longer has as much time to pass as he once did (decreasing skating speed), O'Connell can still make correct decisions. He's also less like likely to carry the puck than he was earlier in his career.

His ice vision is good both offensively and defensively, and he'll follow the play up-ice and join in the attack in the offensive zone when he can chance it.

THE PHYSICAL GAME

Because of his size or lack thereof, O'Connell must play a smart physical game. He can't go running at people because he isn't going to be effective that way. But Mike takes the body along the boards well, understanding that sometimes the best check is just getting in someone's way.

Because he does have strength he can tie up wingers in the corners or the front of the net, but he'll be overpowered by the League's bigger forwards. He's willing to hit, but he'll never plant anyone into the cheap seats.

THE INTANGIBLES

O'Connell's just the kind of player a young defense corps needs, a veteran with an upbeat attitude who takes coaching well (setting a good example for the youngsters), and he can also impart his knowledge — how to succeed in the NHL. He's probably the Wings' smartest defenseman.

Of course, the Wings have assistant coach Dave Lewis to do that. And considering the youngsters the Wings' want to move into the lineup, O'Connell's NHL days may be numbered.

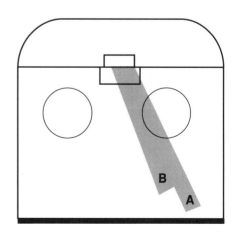

TORRIE ROBERTSON

Yrs. of NHL service: 7
Born: Victoria, B.C., Canada; August 1, 1959
Position: Left wing
Height: 5-11
Weight: 200
Uniform no.: 14
Shoots: left

Career statistics:

GP	G	A	TP	PIM
400	48	94	142	1,639

1988-89 statistics:

GP	G	A	TP	+/-	PIM	PP	SH	GW	GT	S	PCT
39	4	6	10	-4	147	0	0	1	0	26	15.4

LAST SEASON

Robertson missed 29 games with a broken ankle. He was acquired from Hartford late in the season.

THE FINESSE GAME

Torrie is not a good skater. He mucks along his wing with neither speed nor agility and with no idea where he is going and what he's going to do when he gets there — except bash the nearest opponent as soon as possible.

He'll get a lot of room to operate but he won't do anything with that room because he doesn't have the stick skills or vision necessary to do anything but make the most rudimentary NHL play. If given enough time and space he'll eventually find an open teammate and get the puck to him. Robertson will score a literal handul of goals during a year, but he exists otherwise in a finesse vacuum.

THE PHYSICAL GAME

Should he actually catch anyone during his seek-and-destroy missions, Robertson will jar the puck loose with a good hit. He likes to check and will attempt to connect every time he's on the ice.

But Robertson is mainly a fighter and a rough guy. He keeps you honest and you don't make too many plays around Robertson with your head down.

THE INTANGIBLES

Someone has to fight the McRaes and the Ewens and the Kordics, and that's what Robertson does. He is an enforcer and nothing else.

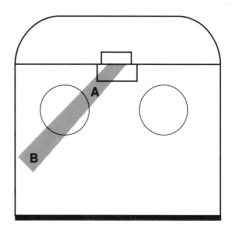

BORJE SALMING

Yrs. of NHL service: 16
Born: Kiruna, Sweden; April 17, 1951
Position: Defenseman
Height: 6-1
Weight: 195
Uniform no.: 21
Shoots: left

Career statistics:

GP	G	A	TP	PIM
1,099	148	620	768	1,292

1988-89 statistics:

GP	G	A	TP	+/-	PIM	PP	SH	GW	GT	S	PCT
63	3	17	20	7	86	1	0	0	0	58	5.2

LAST SEASON

Goal total was second lowest of career; point total tied career low. He led club in plus/minus for the second straight year.

THE FINESSE GAME

Where once smarts and skill competed for top billing with Salming, his deteriorating skills make his smarts his primary asset.

That's not to say Salming is now devoid of skill. In fact, considering his length of service, he's still a great skater. His stride retains its fluidity, and Borje still has NHL quality speed and agility — just not in the quantities he once had. His balance is more affected than any other aspect of his skating, so that he will end up on the ice after checks, even ones he initiates. Still, he recovers to make a play somehow, some way. He also has some difficulty going to his left.

He no longer rushes the puck, instead squiring the Leafs' offensive-minded defensemen. He's the safety valve now, reading the defensive play and moving the puck from the defensive zone. Salming plays his angles very well to steer the opposition wide of the net, but he also anticipates very well and can stand up at the blue line, close the gap on the puck carrier and turn the puck up-ice.

That puck movement skill is also evident in his play in the offensive zone, where he easily finds the open man.

THE PHYSICAL GAME

Age and the NHL's wear and tear have clearly taken their toll on Salming; he's only played one full 80-game season. He remains a very well conditioned athlete, but he's going to be in and out of the lineup; that's just the fact.

Borje still has good strength, and can tie the opposition up in front of the net or along the boards. He's not much of a hitter now, more of a pusher and shover, but Salming can be effective in muscling opposing forwards off the puck.

THE INTANGIBLES

To say that Salming is a shadow of what he once was is to do him a disservice. Rather, let us say that he is aging gracefully — and he certainly isn't occupying a roster spot better spent on a youngster. In fact, on many nights Salming is Toronto's best player — skating, taking the man, moving the puck.

He works extremely hard at all times, and — coming from a future Hall of Famer — that's an important signal to a team that too frequently coasts.

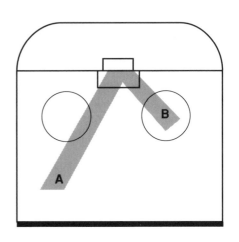

JEFF SHARPLES

Yrs. of NHL service: 2
Born: Terrace, B.C., Canada; July 28, 1967
Position: Defenseman
Height: 6-1
Weight: 195
Uniform no.: 34
Shoots: left

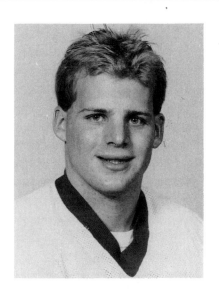

Career statistics:

GP	G	A	TP	PIM
102	14	35	49	70

1988-89 statistics:

GP	G	A	TP	+/-	PIM	PP	SH	GW	GT	S	PCT
46	4	9	13	5	26	3	0	0	0	48	8.3

LAST SEASON

Sharples played fewer games in his second season than he did his first (foot injury and demotion to AHL).

THE FINESSE GAME

One step forward and two steps back would describe Sharples in 1988-89. He's a solid package of finesse skills, but too often last season Jeff was tentative and hesitant in his application of those skills.

He packs a lot of power in his long stride and he can make his skating more effective by carrying the puck well. Sharples likes to rush the puck from the Detroit zone and set up as fourth attacker in the offensive end, but he hesitated all too frequently last season as if afraid to make mistakes or take chances.

He uses his skating ability to get back into defensive position, and Sharples likes to try to force the play at his own blue line. He plays a fairly good positional defensive game from his blue line in, and he's certainly mobile enough to force most players wide of the net.

He handles the puck well at all speeds, passing and receiving it at top speed. Jeff's good hockey sense helps him as a playmaker, and he'll make the correct pass most of the time. His vision shows him the openings and he leads his teammates into position. Sharples has a hard and accurate shot from the blue line, and he'll sneak to the top of the faceoff circle if he can. Still, he doesn't shoot enough.

THE PHYSICAL GAME

A thumping game is not Sharples's style. He plays a modest and fairly efficient game by taking the body along the boards. He won't knock anyone through the glass with his hitting, and Jeff has good strength in front of the net.

He also sacrifices his body to block shots.

THE INTANGIBLES

He's just 22 years old so there's no reason to panic, but Sharples has to show better than he did last season. The one thing the Wings lack is a rushing defenseman to run the power play, and that's a role they envision Sharples fulfilling.

He has the talent to be a successful offensive defenseman (without sacrificing defense) and he must develop enough confidence in his ability to accept that role. He has the potential, but must be called disappointing to date.

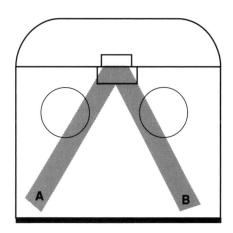

GREG STEFAN

Yrs. of NHL service: 7
Born: Brantford, Ontario, Canada; February 11, 1961
Position: Goaltender
Height: 5-11
Weight: 180
Uniform no.: 30
Catches: left

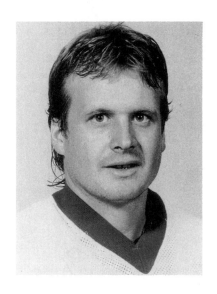

Career statistics:

GP	MINS	G	SO	AVG	A	PIM
292	15,974	1,044	5	3.92	14	206

1988-89 statistics:

GP	MINS	AVG	W	L	T	SO	GA	SA	SAPCT	PIM
46	2,499	4.01	21	17	3	0	167	1,290	.870	41

LAST SEASON

Games played total tied second highest of career, despite missing nine games with a back injury. Posted third consecutive winning season, but GAA was three-seasons high.

THE PHYSICAL GAME

Stefan's skating, particularly his exceptional balance, are the keys to his reflex style of goaltending. His balance allows him to regain his stance very quickly after making a save or flopping to the ice, and that balance also allows him to lunge in one direction to get a piece of the puck, even after leaning the other way.

Greg frequently goes to the ice because he doesn't cut his angles as well as he should. Since he isn't squared with the puck, Greg will make phantom saves and has to regain his stance quickly after flashing out a skate toward the puck. Greg's quickness means he'll usually get a piece of any puck, even the ones that get past him for goals. He uses his quickness to its best advantage in goal-mouth scrambles and on deflections, whipping an arm or leg into the path of a seemingly inevitable goal.

Stefan sees the puck well and tracks the play alertly. He will not generally leave his net to handle the puck, and is content to allow it to skitter behind the goal instead of stopping it for his defense. His hands are fast (like his feet), but Stefan is not particularly adept at handling the puck.

THE MENTAL GAME

Greg is one of those hot-and-cold goalies. When he's on he's super, but Stefan is erratic in his performances because he plays so emotionally. One apsect of that emotional game has been his temper and his PIM totals (and, we might add, League-mandated suspensions), but the positive side of that is mental toughness.

He has the ability to come back from bad goals or games, and he can lift his game to fit the circumstances.

THE INTANGIBLES

By this time in his career, what you see with Stefan is what you get. He has the ability to reach great heights when his concentration is on, but he also has the ability to plummet when his emotions get the better of him.

He thrives on competition, even within the team, so a goaltending partner who can be a number one goalie makes Greg work harder. A pressure situation such as the playoffs makes Greg work harder. His competitiveness makes him a leader for the Wings.

Altogether, however, he has gone as far as he can as an NHL goaltender. Despite the fact that he can carry the team when hot, Stefan isn't good enough often enough to be placed with the NHL's best goalies.

STEVE YZERMAN

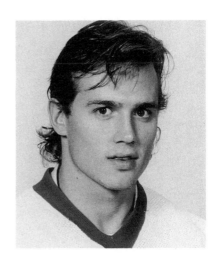

Yrs. of NHL service: 6
Born: Cranbrook, B.C., Canada; May 9, 1965
Position: Center
Height: 5-11
Weight: 185
Uniform no.: 19
Shoots: right

Career statistics:

GP	G	A	TP	PIM
435	229	336	565	255

1988-89 statistics:

GP	G	A	TP	+/-	PIM	PP	SH	GW	GT	S	PCT
80	65	90	155	17	61	17	3	7	2	388	16.8

LAST SEASON

Yzerman finished third in NHL scoring, as well as in goals and assists. He led the NHL in shots on goal. He was first in his club in goals, assists, points, power play goals and games played (he was the only Wing to play all 80 games). He finished second in plus/minus and shorthanded goals. All point totals were career highs and team records.

THE FINESSE GAME

Excellence in every department.

Steve is a superior skater with explosive acceleration, breakaway speed, and exceptional balance and quickness. He changes direction within a stride and does the same thing with his speed — both up and down the speedometer.

His hand skills are no less intimidating, whether he's carrying the puck himself, moving it to a teammate or scoring goals. Yzerman does it all at all speeds and in every circumstance — open ice or traffic, even-strength or specialty team. Defenders *must* play the body with Yzerman (if they can catch him), because he'll turn them inside out if they don't.

Yzerman can score as well as he sets up a teammate. His quick wrist shot is excellently released, and he'll score from varying depths around the slot, both because of his shot and because he has the hands to work in traffic. He needs only the slightest opening to slide the puck home, and he puts a lot of shots on goal.

Hockey sense? Excellent, superior—what else? He sees the opening before anyone and either leads a teammate there or gets there himself.

His defense is exemplary, and Yzerman doesn't sacrifice any of his defense for offense — or vice versa.

THE PHYSICAL GAME

Yzerman squeezes more from his body than players six inches taller and 30 pounds heavier. He's constantly improving his strength, so that he can operate in the heavily trafficked areas of the ice. While he won't knock anyone unconscious with his hits, Yzerman is fearless about going to the corners and the front of the net, and he'll fight to protect himself too. He's also not above the retaliatory elbow or slash.

He uses his body well in all three zones, initiating contact in all areas. The result? He gets more respect on the ice, and more open space in which to work.

THE INTANGIBLES

If this were golf, if there were a way to handicap such things, Yzerman might not be the third best player in the game: he'd be the second-best — right behind Wayne Gretzky.

Nobody but Wayne gets more from the talent and tools he possesses, and Steve is in this category because of his fanatical work ethic, tremendous heart and dedication. It's because of his size and the difficulty it should present to NHL success that we say Steve is the NHL's second-best player.

And no, we haven't forgotten Mario Lemieux. But if Mario worked as hard and squeezed as much from his talent as Yzerman does, Lemieux would have 300 points. But he doesn't, and that's why Yzerman's the NHL's second-best player.

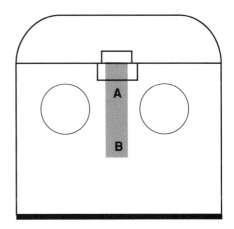

RICK ZOMBO

Yrs. of NHL service: 3
Born: Des Plaines, Illinois, USA; May 8, 1963
Position: Defenseman
Height: 6-1
Weight: 195
Uniform no.: 4
Shoots: right

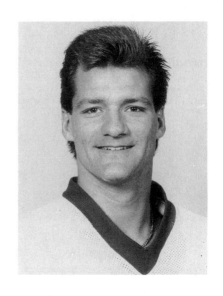

Career statistics:

GP	G	A	TP	PIM
196	5	39	44	277

1988-89 statistics:

GP	G	A	TP	+/-	PIM	PP	SH	GW	GT	S	PCT
75	1	20	21	23	106	1	0	0	0	64	1.6

LAST SEASON

Games played, assist and point totals were career highs. He led the club in plus/minus. He missed time with a knee injury.

THE FINESSE GAME

Zombo has become a solid if unspectacular NHL skater. While he doesn't possess explosive acceleration or dynamic quickness, Zombo has developed dependable speed and agility for his defensive work. He moves well in all directions, enough that he can challenge the incoming forward instead of just backing in. He understands his defensive angles and plays them well, so he is sound positionally.

That improved skating has gained him additional time to make his plays, and Rick is making not only correct decisions but good ones as well. He handles the puck well in his defensive zone and is patient in his passing, making sure to execute the right play.

His play reading ability aids him in gaining the correct position, and it's that same trait that helps him make good breakout plays. But Zombo plays it safe at the opposing blue line, refusing to venture into unsafe positions. As such, he'll make almost no contribution at the offensive blue line.

THE PHYSICAL GAME

Rick enjoys a physical game and, while he doesn't play a dominating one, willingly brings his good size and strength to bear. His improved skating ability (particularly in the area of balance) helps him handle the front of the net well, and he more than holds his own along the boards.

THE INTANGIBLES

The best thing Zombo could do for himself he did: improve as a player. The Wings have a plethora of young defensive talent they want to introduce to the NHL, but Zombo's steadiness is something the Wings won't want to sacrifice.

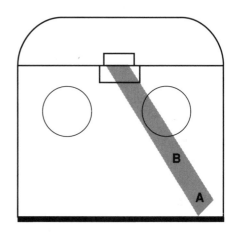

EDMONTON OILERS

LINE COMBINATIONS
KELLY BUCHBERGER-CRAIG MACTAVISH-
DAVE HUNTER-CRAIG SIMPSON
MARK MESSIER-GLENN ANDERSON
KEVIN MCCLELLAND-DAVE BROWN
ESA TIKKANEN-JIMMY CARSON-JARI KURRI

DEFENSE PAIRINGS
CHARLIE HUDDY-JEFF BEUKEBOOM
STEVE SMITH-CRAIG MUNI
KEVIN LOWE

GOALTENDERS
GRANT FUHR
BILL RANFORD

OTHER PLAYERS
MIROSLAV FRYCER — Left wing
RANDY GREGG — Defenseman
TOMAS JONSSON — Defenseman
NORM LACOMBE — Right wing

POWER PLAY

FIRST UNIT:
CRAIG SIMPSON-JIMMY CARSON-JARI KURRI
CHARLIE HUDDY-TOMAS JONSSON

SIMPSON is in front of the net, CARSON controls along the left boards and KURRI is in the right circle. One plan is to isolate KURRI for a shot, but all plans want SIMPSON in front for tips and rebounds.

MARK MESSIER, ESA TIKKANEN and GLENN ANDERSON will also see time, with TIKKANEN moving between the left circle and the slot, ANDERSON looking for shots on the right side and MESSIER midway in the slot. STEVE SMITH will see time on the point.

Last season Edmonton's power play was POOR, scoring 83 goals in 419 opportunities (19.8 percent, 17th overall).

PENALTY KILLING

FIRST UNIT:
DAVE HUNTER-CRAIG MACTAVISH
KEVIN LOWE-CHARLIE HUDDY

SECOND UNIT:
ESA TIKKANEN-GLENN ANDERSON
RANDY GREGG

The Oilers use three sets of forwards to kill penalties, with MARK MESSIER and JARI KURRI the third pair. They are the most aggressive of the forwards, pressuring the puck before it gets to the Oiler zone, and then jumping the puck carrier as soon as possible. TIKKANEN and ANDERSON mirror that attack, with HUNTER and MACTAVISH the least aggressive of the pairings.

Once in the zone all pressure the puck, except GREGG — who covers the front of the net.

Last season Edmonton's penalty killing was EXCELLENT, allowing 78 goals in 452 shorthanded situations (82.7 percent, second overall).

CRUCIAL FACEOFFS
MARK MESSIER.

GLENN ANDERSON

Yrs. of NHL service: 9
Born: Vancouver, B.C., Canada; October 2, 1960
Position: Right wing
Height: 6-1
Weight: 190
Uniform no.: 9
Shoots: left

Career statistics:

GP	G	A	TP	PIM
681	355	414	769	605

1988-89 statistics:

GP	G	A	TP	+/-	PIM	PP	SH	GW	GT	S	PCT
79	16	48	64	-16	93	7	0	3	0	212	7.5

LAST SEASON

Games played total was three-season low. Goal total was career low, point total second lowest of career. PIM total was career high. Plus/minus was the club's second worst, worst among forwards. He finished third in SOG total.

THE FINESSE GAME

Anderson's ability to do more things faster than almost anyone in the League (with the possible exception of teammate Mark Messier) makes him a remarkable finesse player. Glenn is an excellent skater with tremendous speed; no one can catch him. His speed is made better because of his balance, so Glenn adds fantastic agility and quickness to his repertoire. His balance makes the opposition suffer the brunt of the physical punishment when Anderson gets hit, rather than the other way around.

Anderson's feet and hand skills are made better by each other, in that Glenn needn't slow down to make his plays. He works excellently at full throttle. His shot gains most from this ability. Because of his lightning-quick release and soft hands, Anderson can score anytime from anywhere — and into any part of the net. He's most usually on net with his shot, and he excels in the traffic around the net for tough goals too.

He's a creative player in the offensive zone without the puck (except that he likes to go to the net from the right side), and his good vision and anticipation allow him to make good use of his teammates.

THE PHYSICAL GAME

Glenn plays like a kamikaze, flinging his body into people with abandon. As mentioned, his exceptional balance makes him successful here. He initiates a good deal of contact and is unafraid of the hitting that accompanies his work in the corners, and he'll also get his stick into people.

THE INTANGIBLES

We mentioned last year that desire was the key to Anderson, and he more than any Oiler will be subject to intense scrutiny this season because of his poor performance last season. He has 50-goal and 100-point tools which are not frequently enough brought to bear.

When the Oilers won Stanley Cups that was okay, because Glenn hit his mark in the playoffs. But that's unacceptable if the Oilers aren't winning championships. He has much to prove this season, and we wouldn't be surprised if he proved it with another club.

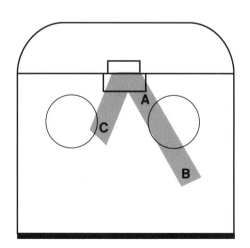

JEFF BEUKEBOOM

Yrs. of NHL service: 3
Born: Ajax, Ontario, Canada; March 28, 1965
Position: Defenseman
Height: 6-4
Weight: 215
Uniform no.: 6
Shoots: right

Career statistics:

GP	G	A	TP	PIM
153	8	33	41	419

1988-89 statistics:

GP	G	A	TP	+/-	PIM	PP	SH	GW	GT	S	PCT
36	0	5	5	2	94	0	0	0	0	26	0.0

LAST SEASON

Games played, all point totals and PIM mark were all career lows. Beukeboom missed much of the season with a knee injury.

THE FINESSE GAME

Beukeboom has made improvements in his NHL game, most notably in his skating and play-reading ability. He is a smoother skater with improved speed, quickness and agility both forward and back.

Jeff has also improved his understanding of the NHL play, including reading the play and reacting to it more quickly. He is recognizing the rush toward him earlier and combines that better read with his better skating to more consistently force the play wide and to more consistently close the gap on the puck carrier.

He can make the plays to the forwards and has improved in this aspect of his game (better skating equals more time to look and make a play), but right now is content to be the takeout defenseman, rather than the breakout defender.

THE PHYSICAL GAME

Jeff is big and likes to hit, so he can certainly be said to get the most from his size. He is an aggressive player in front of the net and in the corners and he punishes people when he hits them.

Again, his improved finesse skills — notably his skating — help him to be a better physical player. Since he moves his feet better, Jeff is better able to get to the opposition and use his strength.

THE INTANGIBLES

An intelligent player and an earnest young man, Beukeboom works hard at developing his skills. His improvement should continue, but there are a lot of bodies in the Oiler defense corps — which means Beukeboom may have some competition for ice time.

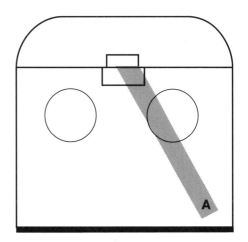

DAVE BROWN

Yrs. of NHL service: 6
Born: Saskatoon, Sask., Canada; October 12, 1962
Position: Right wing
Height: 6-5
Weight: 205
Uniform no.: 32
Shoots: right

Career statistics:

GP	G	A	TP	PIM
335	33	31	64	1,089

1988-89 statistics:

GP	G	A	TP	+/-	PIM	PP	SH	GW	GT	S	PCT
72	0	5	5	-12	156	0	0	0	0	42	0.0

LAST SEASON

Acquired from Philadelphia at the All-Star break in exchange for Keith Acton. Games played total was second highest of career, but all point totals were career lows. PIM total was club's third highest.

THE FINESSE GAME

Brown remains a below-average finesse player, though he has improved his skills. He still lumbers up and down the ice, though more smoothly and with better balance than previously. He has little speed and less agility.

He can handle the puck when going straight forward in his wing position, but is not really an accomplished puck handler. If given time and space, he can get the puck to his teammates, but he lacks the vision and anticipation (the hockey sense, really) to be a consistent offensive player.

His scoring will have to be done from directly in front of the net. He can play well defensively if matched against an equally-talented opponent.

THE PHYSICAL GAME

A physical style of game would seem to benefit Brown, but that's not so. Because he's unable to catch most everyone, and thus can't hit them, a mucking role is currently out of Brown's grasp; opponents just step out of his way and let him thunder by. Additionally, when he is able to connect he's probably going to get the worst of the bargain because his balance is bad.

He is a fighter, and that's what keeps him in the NHL. Brown's fighting clears the way for players like Esa Tikkanen to be pests on the ice, for Brown will take care of anyone who disapproves of Tikkanen's tactics. While he has a big reputation, Brown is not one of the NHL's best fighters, as he has had trouble with smaller opponents who won't be intimidated.

THE INTANGIBLES

He's certainly among the NHL's most improved players, in terms of his skill development from his first NHL game to today, but Brown is still an extremely limited player. He's shown that he can be put on the ice and not be a liability (if he can keep his temper), but don't lose sight of Brown's purpose in the NHL: to intimidate.

The difference between Brown and a Rick Tocchet or Dave Manson type of player is that, while Brown can now be sent onto the ice and not perform negatively, the Tocchets and Mansons perform positively. That's an important difference.

Because of his limited role, his position with the Oilers must be regarded as vulnerable. After all, as soon as a tough guy with more talent shows up, Brown is history.

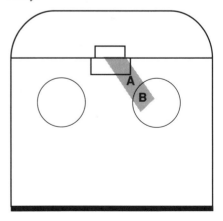

KELLY BUCHBERGER

Yrs. of NHL service: 1
Born: Langenburg, Sask., Canada; December 2, 1966
Position: Left wing
Height: 6-2
Weight: 190
Uniform no.: 16
Shoots: left

Career statistics:

GP	G	A	TP	PIM
85	6	9	15	315

1988-89 statistics:

GP	G	A	TP	+/-	PIM	PP	SH	GW	GT	S	PCT
66	5	9	14	-14	234	1	0	1	0	57	8.8

LAST SEASON

Buchberger's first full NHL season, despite missing time with a fractured ankle. He led the club in PIM total, and his plus/minus was the team's third worst — second worst among forwards.

THE FINESSE GAME

Strength more than finesse is the hallmark of Buchberger's game. He's a strong skater with some speed, but not yet consistent agility or quickness at the NHL level. He lacks an understanding of the NHL game in terms of speed, so Kelly is going to have trouble making a play or reading a rush.

He doesn't yet handle the puck well when carrying it, particularly at higher speeds. His shot is no better than average, and he'll have to be near the net to score.

THE PHYSICAL GAME

This is where Buchberger can shine. His strength gives a relentless quality to his skating, so his checking is insistent and physical. He can rap guys pretty good, *if* he can catch them — and that's where the agility bit comes into play. Kelly can be a good forechecker because of his hitting, but he must be able to reach the defensemen and backchecking opposing forwards.

Obviously too, he has no problem throwing his fists.

THE INTANGIBLES

There might — just might — be a glimmer of finesse skill under the physical game Buchberger's presented; he's managed to augment his physical game with some scoring aptitude at previous levels. Most important now, however, is increased skating skill — better balance and foot speed. Those qualities would improve all of Buchberger's game.

He may be slowed in that development because of the broken ankle he suffered late last season.

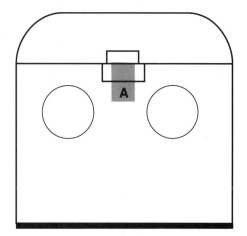

JIMMY CARSON

Yrs. of NHL service: 3
Born: Southfield, Michigan, USA; July 20, 1968
Position: Center
Height: 6-0
Weight: 185
Uniform no.: 12
Shoots: right

Career statistics:

GP	G	A	TP	PIM
240	141	145	286	103

1988-89 statistics:

GP	G	A	TP	+/-	PIM	PP	SH	GW	GT	S	PCT
80	49	51	100	3	36	19	0	5	1	240	20.4

LAST SEASON

Acquired by the Oilers from the Kings (along with Martin Gelinas and draft choices) in exchange for Wayne Gretzky and Marty McSorley. He finished second on the team in scoring (ninth in the NHL), first in goals, power play goals and shots on goal.

THE FINESSE GAME

Carson's finesse skills are excellent — and still with potential to improve. He might look like a lumbering skater, but Carson has excellent quickness, the kind that allows him to stop and start in one direction or another within a step. He's not overly fast, but he has excellent acceleration, so he will pull away from the opposition. He has a smooth stride and is well balanced and agile in all three directions: forward, back and sideways.

Good as his skating is, Jimmy's hand skills are better. He regularly makes thread-the-needle passes and he has very soft hands that control the puck well. Combined with his ice vision and anticipation, the skills make him an excellent playmaker. He anticipates very well offensively, particularly in making the transition from offense to defense.

His shot selection is also excellent and is already among the League's best, both slap shot and wrist shot. He shoots often and accurately and makes the goalie stop him, rather than firing shots wide of the net.

THE PHYSICAL GAME

Though not primarily a physical player (Carson would never be called a power forward), Jimmy has good size and uses his body very well offensively. He protects the puck with his body very well and will certainly get stronger as he matures.

He's still a little too casual in his defensive aggressiveness, often getting out-fought and out-positioned because he's not as intense as he should be.

He also needs greater strength on faceoffs, particularly in the defensive zone — where he frequently loses more than he wins. When he loses those faceoffs he's beaten to the net by the opposing center.

THE INTANGIBLES

We told you last year that Carson wanted out of Los Angeles (and that was one quiet factor in the Gretzky deal), and into a hockey enviroment. Now the buzz is, he wants out of Edmonton.

That may be, but that attitude certainly didn't affect his output. He played every game for the third straight season, breaking the 100-point plateau for the second consecutive time. And that's important, because — next to Jari Kurri — Jimmy Carson had more to prove in the Gretzky deal than anyone.

He's still a pup by NHL maturity standards, and his best seasons are ahead of him — wherever he's playing.

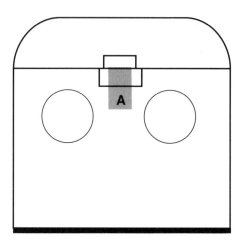

MIROSLAV FRYCER

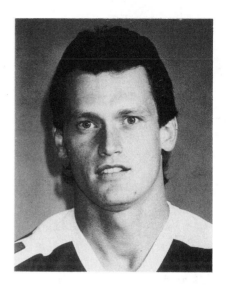

Yrs. of NHL service: 9
Born: Opava, Czechoslovakia; September 27, 1959
Position: Right wing
Height: 6-0
Weight: 200
Uniform no.: 14
Shoots: left

Career statistics:

GP	G	A	TP	PIM
414	146	183	329	486

1988-89 statistics:

GP	G	A	TP	+/-	PIM	PP	SH	GW	GT	S	PCT
37	12	13	25	-2	65	4	0	1	0	73	16.4

LAST SEASON

Traded in the off-season from Toronto to Detroit (in exchange for Darren Veitch), Frycer was later sent to Edmonton. Games played total was second lowest of career (League suspension, recurring back injury).

THE FINESSE GAME

Once upon a time, several major injuries ago, Frycer was a good skater. He had good balance (which helped him play in traffic), and he had a nice change of pace and good speed. Miro was both fast and strong enough on his skates to go barrelling right at the defense, but smart enough to know when to moderate his speed. He also had good agility and one-step quickness and changed direction well, making him good laterally as well as up and back. We use the past tense because of his injuries; time will tell if he still has those abilities.

He has excellent hands and was often used to control the power play, and that hand skill also made him a successful player in tight quarters close to the net. He carried or moved it equally well, but he did have a tendency to move to his backhand once across the opposing blue line. While moving that way is usually the kiss of death in terms of playmaking, Frycer was talented enough to make plays off his backhand.

He uses his teammates well because he has good vision on the ice, coupled with good anticipation. Miro is able to spot the openings and will cut to them himself or lead a teammate into the hole. He has good touch around the net and a good wrist shot, and will score from farther out as well, releasing the puck quickly, frequently and (generally) accurately.

He used those skills to particular success on the power play, where his quickness kept him in the clear as well as kept the passing lanes open.

THE PHYSICAL GAME

Frycer played physically up and down his wing and was quite willing to get in front of the net and take the requisite abuse. He wasn't a devastatingly hard hitter, but he took the body well and muscled the opposition off the puck.

Frycer also had the talent to make the plays after hitting and the fact that he has good balance and remains vertical most of the time after a collision is a big help here.

THE INTANGIBLES

Frycer has to prove that he's not the injury-prone player he's been for the last three seasons. The Oilers seem to want him around this season, but his injuries make his continued NHL presence doubtful.

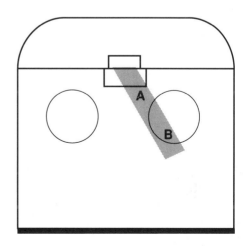

GRANT FUHR

Yrs. of NHL service: 8
Born: Spruce Grove, Alta., Canada;
September 28, 1962
Position: Goaltender
Height: 5-10
Weight: 185
Uniform no.: 31
Catches: right

Career statistics:

GP	MINS	G	SO	AVG	A	PIM
389	22,051	1,361	7	3.70	36	52

1988-89 statistics:

GP	MINS	AVG	W	L	T	SO	GA	SA	SAPCT	PIM
59	3,341	3.83	23	26	6	1	213	1,714	.875	6

LAST SEASON

Games played total was second highest of career (third in NHL last season), as was goals allowed. Losses led wins for first time in career.

THE PHYSICAL GAME

Fuhr combines his outstanding reflexes with a modified stand-up style to great succes as the NHL's best goaltender. He has the NHL's best hand and foot speed, and he maximizes those skills by squaring himself to the puck and cutting down the shooter's angle excellently.

When forced to move, Grant does so with great ease because of his excellent skating skill. Fuhr has tremendous balance, so his lateral movement is exceptional. He regains his feet (after going to the ice) or his stance (after movement) almost instantaneously. He moves in and out of the net and around the defensive zone excellently.

His one weakness is between the pads, and that's because Grant keeps his weight on his inside edges — because he likes to butterfly. That weight distribution sometimes makes it difficult for Fuhr to snap his legs closed but — really — his foot and leg speed usually closes that hole very quickly.

He handles the puck better than almost any other goaltender and often starts plays up ice by sending the puck to the forwards. Grant handles his stick well and has the fastest glove hand — just pure radar — in the world.

THE MENTAL GAME

His attitude and mental outlook are at least as large a reason for Fuhr's success as is his physical skill. He is unaffected by the circumstances of the game and is essentially nerveless. Pressure means nothing to him. Stanley Cup games, Canada Cup games, mid-December Norris Division games — they're all the same to Fuhr.

Neither bad goals nor bad performances bother him; Fuhr just shrugs them all off. His concentration is excellent and he maintains it throughout any type of game, but Fuhr also pulls his game to the level of the game being played.

Right now, he's still the NHL's best money goaltender.

THE INTANGIBLES

Should the Oilers fade from Stanley Cup contention, Fuhr is likely to be consigned to the "They're nothing without Gretzky," scrap heap. Which couldn't be further from the truth, as Fuhr's international performances have shown.

He remains the world's best goaltender.

RANDY GREGG

Yrs. of NHL service: 7
Born: Edmonton, Alta., Canada; February 19, 1956
Position: Defenseman
Height: 6-4
Weight: 215
Uniform no.: 21
Shoots: left

Career statistics:

GP	G	A	TP	PIM
405	36	128	164	267

1988-89 statistics:

GP	G	A	TP	+/-	PIM	PP	SH	GW	GT	S	PCT
57	3	15	18	-9	28	1	0	1	0	42	7.1

LAST SEASON

Games played was a three-season high, despite being sidelined with a recurring groin injury. His plus/minus was second worst among defensive regulars.

THE FINESSE GAME

Gregg is a good skater both forward and backward, with an efficient more than spectacular style. He's fairly fluid though not exceptionally agile, and he lacks real speed or quickness, but his hockey sense more than compensates for any skating deficiencies he might have.

He is a defensive style defenseman, moving the puck quickly for the forwards to carry up-ice. Though he will make a foray or two, rushing the puck is not Gregg's strong point. Rather, he quickly turns the puck up-ice.

Randy reads the rush very well and channels it wide of the net effectively. He rarely makes a defensive mistake and that's important for a scoring team like the Oilers.

Gregg will join the play up-ice and he will control the point well, but rarely pinches in. He has an average shot from the point but will find the open man for a pass.

THE PHYSICAL GAME

As with his finesse play, steady and unspectacular describes Gregg's physical game. He takes the body very well, is strong and clears the front of the net or holds the opposition out of the play well.

He puts his reach to work deflecting passes and pokechecking the puck, and he will also sacrifice his body to block shots.

THE INTANGIBLES

Gregg, one of the NHL's throwbacks in that he is a pure defensive defenseman, is a hard worker and a character player. His maturity is an important stabilizing influence for the younger Oiler defensemen.

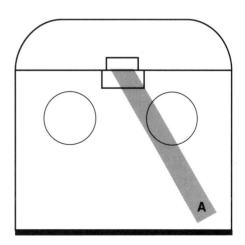

CHARLIE HUDDY

Yrs. of NHL service: 8
Born: Oshawa, Ontario, Canada; June 2, 1959
Position: Defenseman
Height: 6-0
Weight: 210
Uniform no.: 22
Shoots: left

Career statistics:

GP	G	A	TP	PIM
571	75	242	317	412

1988-89 statistics:

GP	G	A	TP	+/-	PIM	PP	SH	GW	GT	S	PCT
76	11	33	44	0	52	5	2	0	0	178	6.2

LAST SEASON

Point total was third highest of career, a four-season high. He led the defense in scoring, power-play goals and shots on goal. He missed time with a hamstring injury.

THE FINESSE GAME

Charlie's hockey sense is his outstanding finesse skill. He reads plays very well, breaks up rushes excellently by forcing the opposition wide of the net and he can step into an offensive rush up-ice if need be, moving the puck quickly and smoothly. That play-reading ability makes him one of the best pinching defensemen in the League.

Huddy combines his ice vision with his hand skills to move the puck to the open man well in both zones. He controls the point well because he is a good stickhandler, much better than he is given credit for. When shooting, Charlie delivers a hard slap shot from the point, one that is accurate and low, good for tip-ins and deflections. He'll move to the deep slot if he can.

Huddy is a good skater, probably above average but without any exceptional skill in this asset. Neither tremendously agile nor exceptionally fast, Charlie skates well both forward and backward and is smooth in his pivots.

THE PHYSICAL GAME

Huddy doesn't have great size or strength, but he'll hold his own against most players in the corner and crease battles. He'll make a play quickly because of his balance and hand skills, but Charlie will find himself outmatched against the League's bigger and stronger forwards; he'll be paired with a stronger partner because of that.

He will sacrifice his body by blocking shots.

THE INTANGIBLES

Again, Huddy's versatility — his ability to contribute at both ends of the ice — was what he added to the Oilers last season. He picked up some of the offensive slack left by the absence of Steve Smith, without really harming the Oilers defensively.

Edmonton does have a surplus of defenders, and Huddy may find himself squeezed by the numbers game (as well as any desire the Oilers have to retool after losing the Cup), but he can still play a role as a dependable defender.

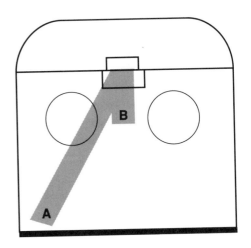

DAVE HUNTER

Yrs. of NHL service: 10
Born: Petrolia, Ontario, Canada; January 1, 1958
Position: Left wing
Height: 5-11
Weight: 195
Uniform no.: 27
Shoots: left

Career statistics:

GP	G	A	TP	PIM
746	133	190	323	918

1988-89 statistics:

GP	G	A	TP	+/-	PIM	PP	SH	GW	GT	S	PCT
66	6	6	12	-8	83	0	1	0	0	87	6.9

LAST SEASON

Acquired first by Winnipeg in the waiver draft, then traded to Edmonton. Games played total was three-season low, goal total tied and assist and point totals set career lows.

THE FINESSE GAME

Not a graceful player in the finesse sense, Hunter remains an outstanding defensive forward. He's a good skater with some speed and good balance, but is not really agile on his feet. Hunter is more of a straight-line player than a fancy swirling type forward anyway.

He has good vision on the ice and reads the play well, able to anticipate openings and get to them before his check can. Hunter stays with his check deep into the defensive zone and always plays his position. He doesn't wander, and that's a big reason for his defensive effectiveness.

Dave is not tremendously gifted offensively, so he'll need to be in tight to the net to score. His ability to handle the puck and use his teammates is no better than average.

THE PHYSICAL GAME

Dave is a mean player, extremely physical and effective along the boards, and won't hesitate to put his stick into anyone. He will hit his check in all three zones, and that hitting will wear down the opposition. He has the strength to hold the opposing forward out of the play when necessary.

THE INTANGIBLES

Hunter is a role player par excellence, an excellent road player because of his toughness and the type of player every club needs to be successful. At 31 years old, however, the NHL life expectancy for role players is a short one. He may, once again, find himself ending the season on a club different from the one on which he started.

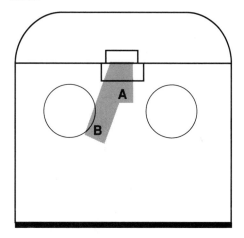

TOMAS JONSSON

Yrs. of NHL service: 8
Born: Falun, Sweden; April 12, 1960
Position: Defenseman
Height: 5-10
Weight: 185
Uniform no.: 23
Shoots: left

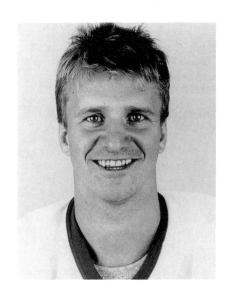

Career statistics:

GP	G	A	TP	PIM
552	85	259	344	482

1988-89 statistics:

GP	G	A	TP	+/-	PIM	PP	SH	GW	GT	S	PCT
73	10	33	43	-25	56	5	1	1	0	149	6.7

LAST SEASON

Acquired late in the season from the Islanders. Finished second in scoring among Oiler defenders, but plus/minus was the club's worst.

THE FINESSE GAME

Jonsson is a very good skater, with excellent balance and foot speed, and those two traits combine to make him very agile. He has excellent lateral movement and his outstanding one-step quickness helps him get to loose pucks. He also has good power in his stride, and that gives him good acceleration ability.

That acceleration and quickness are important to Jonsson's game because he is a puck-carrying defenseman. Those skating skills gain him the puck and then put him in the clear as he charges up ice. Jonsson doesn't forecheck as well or as often as his skating would allow, and he could certainly use that skill to better degree defensively. He handles the puck well when he carries it. His skating and hand skills make him an excellent point man, as he contains the point very well.

His slap shot from the right point is excellent, though Jonsson does have a good wrist shot that he likes to use if he can sneak into the high slot on the power play. He goes for the middle of the net and is usually best high on the glove side. Either way, he is too unselfish and should shoot more.

THE PHYSICAL GAME

Though his role is that of the breakout (and not takeout) defenseman, Jonsson is still not as strong as he should be. That lack of strength manifests itself when the opposition is able to isolate him in front of the net; Jonsson just can't handle many of the League's forwards because of their greater strength and bulk. This is where you'll see him take penalties, as interference is sometimes his only weapon.

He does take the body fairly well along the boards, and his balance should be credited for that. In the reverse, that balance keeps him from being bumped off the puck.

THE INTANGIBLES

Attitude and intelligence mark Jonsson's play. He's smart enough to know his limits and — generally — not supersede them, and he's also got an excellent attitude and works hard in each game. He is very popular with his teammates and he remains coachable.

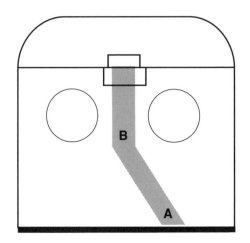

JARI KURRI

Yrs. of NHL service: 9
Born: Helsinki, Finland; May 18, 1960
Position: Right wing
Height: 6-1
Weight: 195
Uniform no.: 17
Shoots: right

Career statistics:

GP	G	A	TP	PIM
676	441	509	950	300

1988-89 statistics:

GP	G	A	TP	+/-	PIM	PP	SH	GW	GT	S	PCT
76	44	58	102	19	69	10	5	8	1	214	20.6

LAST SEASON

Games played total was four-season low (knee injury), but Kurri led the club in scoring (eighth in the NHL) and game winners. His plus/minus was tops among forwards; he finished second in SOG total and third in power-play goals. PIM total was career high.

THE FINESSE GAME

Kurri is an outstanding finesse player. He's an outstanding skater with exceptional balance, quickness and speed, and he uses those abilities to dip and duck around and behind the defense to snare passes and loose pucks. His outstanding one-step quickness translates into excellent lateral movement and direction-changing ability, and Kurri uses those to hit the openings in the offensive zone.

Jari complements that ability — in fact, makes that ability what it is — by using his great instincts and anticipation to get into scoring position. Kurri may be the NHL's most creative player without the puck, using the ice well to create openings by moving from lane to lane.

His shot is probably the best of his physical finesse skills. Jari needs just the slightest opening (and gets it with his quickness) and his quickly released, hard and accurate wrist shot is goal-bound. He excels at one-timing the puck. He is dangerous around the net because his balance and superior hand skills allow him to control the puck in traffic.

His puckhandling is excellent, he takes a pass in stride better than most NHLers, and his sense and hands combine to make him a good passer. When he chooses to carry the puck into the offensive zone, he likes to skate parallel to the blue line from the left wing to the right wing boards, and then jet around the defense.

Kurri's skills make him an exceptional specialty teams player. His scoring ability is evident on the power play, and he uses his breakaway speed and anticipation to score short handed. He is also a fine positional player defensively.

THE PHYSICAL GAME

Kurri isn't a physical player per se, in that he doesn't smash the opposition into the boards, but he excels at taking the body efficiently along the boards — thus allowing his balance and hand skills to come into play.

He is un-intimidatable, going into the corners and taking any abuse aimed his way.

THE INTANGIBLES

We told you last season — before Wayne Gretzky's departure — that Kurri had a lot to prove for 1988-89. Add the loss of the Great One, and Kurri had more to prove than any other Oiler.

Though he may never score 50 goals in a season again (and he still has the ability), Kurri demonstrated his character by leading the club in scoring. It's just his misfortune that his name will always be linked with Gretzky's, so that when Jari's production falls people will continue to say he's nothing without Wayne.

Which just ain't so.

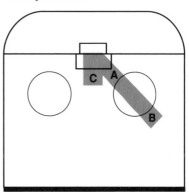

NORM LACOMBE

Yrs. of NHL service: 3
Born: Pierrefond, Quebec, Canada; October 18, 1964
Position: Right wing
Height: 6-0
Weight: 205
Uniform no.: 19
Shoots: right

Career statistics:

GP	G	A	TP	PIM
212	37	38	75	141

1988-89 statistics:

GP	G	A	TP	+/-	PIM	PP	SH	GW	GT	S	PCT
64	17	11	28	2	57	2	0	1	0	71	23.9

LAST SEASON

Games played and all point totals were career highs. He missed eight games with a shoulder injury.

THE FINESSE GAME

Lacombe is good with his stick and with the puck and is successful at making plays out of the corners. He sees the ice pretty well and has a fair idea of what to do with the puck once he gains it.

Norm has good speed, a steady tempo up and down the ice and is a little more agile than one would expect from a 200-pounder. He has an average shot and will collect his goals from around the edge of the faceoff circle, maybe a little tighter.

Lacombe also plays well defensively, coming back with his check and paying attention to his position in the defensive zone. He also sees time on the power play because he works the boards well.

THE PHYSICAL GAME

Lacombe plays a physical style, going to the corners to dig the puck out. He uses his weight well and has fairly good strength in the corners, able to bounce people off the puck and come away with it.

He grinds up and down the boards at both ends of the ice and is not afraid to stick his nose into the rough going.

THE INTANGIBLES

Age 25 is a bit old for what is essentially a first NHL season, but Lacombe showed well in his first-ever full-time role. He's a grinder and a mucker, and he can do the dirty work for more talented teammates.

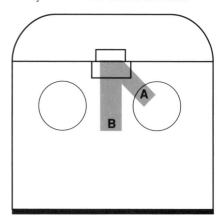

KEVIN LOWE

Yrs. of NHL service: 10
Born: Lachute, Quebec, Canada; April 15, 1959
Position: Defenseman
Height: 6-2
Weight: 195
Uniform no.: 4
Shoots: left

Career statistics:

GP	G	A	TP	PIM
760	61	249	310	804

1988-89 statistics:

GP	G	A	TP	+/-	PIM	PP	SH	GW	GT	S	PCT
76	7	18	25	26	98	0	0	1	0	85	8.2

LAST SEASON

Goal total was three-season low, PIM total four-season high. Plus/minus total was club's second best.

THE FINESSE GAME

Smarts are what make Lowe the defensive force he is. His oustanding hockey sense and vision give him superior understanding of the defensive play, and he uses that skill to make both the correct plays and the good ones.

Kevin easily forces the play wide of the net, and his sense makes his skating better — it allows him to step up and challenge the play at his blue line, but he won't force a play where one doesn't exist. He's a good skater in all directions, and he maintains good agility and lateral movement. Lowe isn't very fast, but his strength and balance help him work in traffic.

And even as he makes his move, Lowe knows what he's going to do after he gains the puck. Kevin's anticipation and vision work on the second half of the defensive play, when he relieves the enemy of the puck and starts the play up ice.

He sees the best play presented, and Lowe will make that best play eight-to-nine times out of 10. He moves the puck quickly and crisply to the forwards, using his good hand skills on breakouts and at the opposing blue line (when he follows the play up ice).

Lowe can skate the puck if necessary, but he isn't a puck carrying defender. Nor is he an offensive threat at the NHL level, so the handful of goals he scores each year will come from the point.

THE PHYSICAL GAME

Lowe plays a very efficient physical game, one marked — like his finesse game — by smarts. Instead of immediately pounding the opposition into tomorrow (which Lowe, despite his good size and strength, isn't really suited for), Kevin waits for the correct moment to start pounding. By doing so he stays physical and avoids penalties.

His crease coverage is excellent, and he takes people off the puck with authority in the corners. His good balance leaves him in position to make plays after hits, making his hitting more valuable. He uses his good reach to pokecheck or deflect pucks efficiently.

He's an excellent open-ice hitter, and Lowe is absolutely fearless in sacrificing his body to block shots.

THE INTANGIBLES

Lowe is a leader for the Oilers, a player with fire and determination who burns to win. He plays through pain and would be a number one defender on any club in the League. He's a fine, fine player.

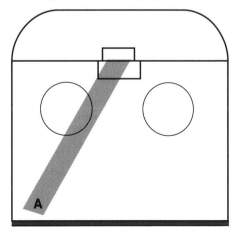

CRAIG MACTAVISH

Yrs. of NHL service: 8
Born: London, Ontario, Canada; August 15, 1958
Position: Center
Height: 6-1
Weight: 195
Uniform no.: 14
Shoots: left

Career statistics:

GP	G	A	TP	PIM
530	123	157	280	301

1988-89 statistics:

GP	G	A	TP	+/-	PIM	PP	SH	GW	GT	S	PCT
80	21	31	52	10	55	2	4	2	2	120	17.5

LAST SEASON

Played 80 games for second consecutive season. Assist and point totals were career highs, goal total second highest. Plus/minus tied for club's fourth best, second best among forwards.

THE FINESSE GAME

MacTavish has become a good skater with a lot of strength in his stride. He is neither exceptionally fast nor outstandingly quick, but he pursues the puck well at a steady pace. He has good balance — which helps his physical game — and he uses his skating skills to be a good two-way player who's able to contribute at both ends of the ice. Craig can move the puck fairly well within his class of player, and he can get it to his teammates effectively. He also demonstrated a scoring touch around the net.

Craig's anticipation, hockey sense and ice vision are his primary tools as a defensive center. He recognizes where the openings will be and uses his strong skating to thwart the opposition's intentions.

THE PHYSICAL GAME

MacTavish complements his checking by body checking. He initiates contact along the boards and in open ice, and he also absorbs his share of abuse when camped out in front of the opposition's net. He applies himself along the boards and can muscle the opposition off the puck. He's still not a belter, more of a pusher and shover, but he's become increasingly effective in the traffic areas.

One reason for that is his improved balance, for it is that skill that adds to his leg strength and helps keep him vertical in contact situations.

He is strong on faceoffs because of his eye/hand coordination.

THE INTANGIBLES

Craig is a role player, but he makes himself more valuable by successfully contributing at both ends of the ice. He's a dedicated athlete, and he works hard at his game. He is one of those unglamorous players any team must have to be successful.

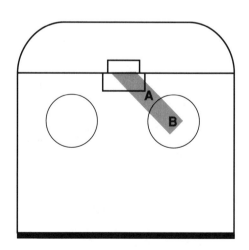

KEVIN MCCLELLAND

Yrs. of NHL service: 7
Born: Oshawa, Ontario, Canada; July 4, 1962
Position: Center
Height: 6-2
Weight: 205
Uniform no.: 24
Shoots: right

Career statistics:

GP	G	A	TP	PIM
490	63	105	168	1,424

1988-89 statistics:

GP	G	A	TP	+/-	PIM	PP	SH	GW	GT	S	PCT
79	6	14	20	-10	161	0	0	0	0	43	14.0

LAST SEASON

Games played total tied career high. Goal total was full season low; point total second lowest full-season total of career. PIM total was lowest in five seasons, but second highest on club. His plus/minus was third worst among forwards.

THE FINESSE GAME

McClelland isn't much of a finesse player; whatever he accomplishes comes from work and desire. He's a strong skater with a burst of speed keyed by his powerful stride, but he won't out race anyone over the length of the ice. He's basically a straight-ahead player, and uses his skating strength to pursue the puck relentlessly.

Because he may not have the agility to stick with the fancier forwards, Kevin must succeed in his checking by playing positionally and remaining with his check up and down the ice.

He can combine his anticipation with his skating to shut down the opposition, but he doesn't translate those skills into offensive contributions. McCelland needs time and space to get the puck to the open man, and he rarely takes advantage of an opportunity by shooting the puck himself. Kevin doesn't have a great shot, so he'll have to do his scoring from within close proximity of the net.

THE PHYSICAL GAME

The physical game is McClelland's game, and he plays it with gusto. His excellent upper-body strength and leg power make him very effective along the boards and his balance enters into play here, keeping him upright and driving after collisions.

He loves to hit and play it rough all over the ice, and he fears nothing and no one; Kevin is only too willing to back up his play with his fists.

He sacrifices his body to block shots, a rare trait among forwards, and stands up for his teammates in any situation.

THE INTANGIBLES

When there's enemy ground to be gained, McClelland is going to get the call. He's the type of player who will do anything to win, and Kevin's yeoman effort in the trenches is the type that's crucial to any team's success. McClelland works hard and has tons of heart and enthusiasm making him a leader and an important part of the Oilers.

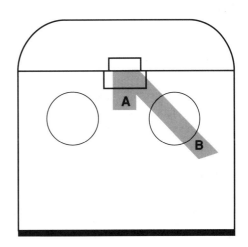

MARK MESSIER

Yrs. of NHL service: 10
Born: Edmonton, Alta., Canada; January 18, 1961
Position: Center
Height: 6-1
Weight: 210
Uniform no.: 11
Shoots: left

Career statistics:

GP	G	A	TP	PIM
719	335	506	841	1,009

1988-89 statistics:

GP	G	A	TP	+/-	PIM	PP	SH	GW	GT	S	PCT
72	33	61	94	-5	130	6	6	4	1	164	20.1

LAST SEASON

Missed time with a League suspension (six games) and knee injury (two games). Finished third on club — and thirteenth in NHL — in scoring (first in assists), fourth in PIM total. Was second in shorthanded goals. Games played and all point totals were three-season lows.

THE FINESSE GAME

Messier is the League's best combination of finesse and physical skills — the prototypical power forward. He's an excellent skater with blazing speed and superior agility and lateral movement; he literally changes direction and speed within a stride. Messier consistently does more things faster than anyone else in the League.

Mark's hand skills are the equal of his foot skills. He's an excellent puckhandler who can do anything with the puck at any speed. He can get the puck to a teammate anywhere, or he can work around an opposing defenseman just as easily.

He has superior anticipation and hockey sense, making him dangerous at both ends of the rink. Defensively he is unparalleled, simply skating over the opposing center almost without exception. He backchecks excellently and is aided by his play-reading ability and hockey sense.

His best scoring weapon is his wrist shot, made especially effective by his ability to deliver it in stride. He uses that shot almost exclusively and, though Mark is another player who can score from anywhere, the majority of his goals will come from the high traffic area near the net.

All his skills combine to make him a specialty team natural. His quickness and sense make him a shorthanded scoring threat, and his ability to either work the corners or the front of the net, or to keep the passing lanes open with his one-step quickness, give him power-play success.

THE PHYSICAL GAME

Though he is tremendously strong, it is Messier's balance that keys his physical game. It allows him to crash into the opposition yet remain vertical, and thus able to continue the play.

Mark has excellent size and strength, and he will out-muscle anyone anywhere, hit often and punishingly (thanks to leg and upper body strength) and hurt the people he hits. Mark will fight and he has a nasty temper — which helps make him mean with his stick.

His hand and wrist strength, combined with his quickness and eye/hand coordination, make him one of the best faceoff men in hockey.

THE INTANGIBLES

His leadership ability is unquestioned, his hunger and desire to win foremost in his mind. There is nothing Mark Messier cannot do when he puts his mind to it, and — despite the fact that his club is no longer the Stanley Cup champion — it is that physical skill in combination with his mental toughness that serves to make Mark the best all-around player in the world.

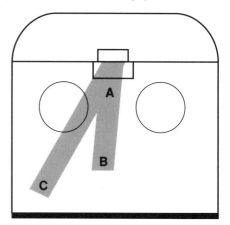

CRAIG MUNI

Yrs. of NHL service: 3
Born: Toronto, Ontario, Canada; July 19, 1962
Position: Defenseman
Height: 6-3
Weight: 200
Uniform no.: 28
Shoots: left

Career statistics:

GP	G	A	TP	PIM
236	16	52	68	239

1988-89 statistics:

GP	G	A	TP	+/-	PIM	PP	SH	GW	GT	S	PCT
69	5	13	18	43	71	0	0	1	0	40	12.5

LAST SEASON

Games played, PIM and point totals were three-season lows (missed 10 games with a shoulder injury), but plus/minus led the club (fourth in the NHL).

THE FINESSE GAME

Muni is a deceptive skater, in that he doesn't seem to possess either great speed or quickness, balance or agility. But somehow, he gets to where he has to be when he has to be there. He uses his modest speed and quickness to challenge the opposing forward, and Craig makes those plays work by not over-extending himself or challenging foolishly.

He remains essentially a conservative player, and Muni succeeds by identifying the best play and making it. He doesn't get fancy with the puck, he just gets the job done. He knows to move the puck with his head up, so he sees his options and his best opportunities.

Because he'll fall back to defend, Muni isn't an offensive threat. But when given the time, Muni can find the open man in the offensive zone. His shot is no better than average, and he'll do his scoring from the point.

THE PHYSICAL GAME

Craig has good size and strength, and he uses them smartly and efficiently. He takes men out of the play in front of the net and along the boards with little flair but great success, and the use of his strength is made better by the fact that he stays out of the penalty box.

He takes the body well along the boards, and Muni makes sure to complete his takeouts so the opposition can't sneak behind him — and back into the play.

THE INTANGIBLES

We projected Muni's improvement last season, and we laid much of the responsibility for that improvement on Steve Smith — Muni's defense partner. But with Smith sidelined throughout much of last season, Craig demonstrated that he can indeed play this game and be a valuable asset.

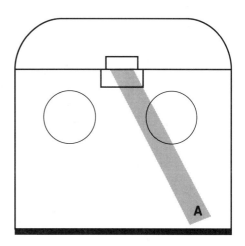

BILL RANFORD

Yrs. of NHL service: 3
Born: Brandon, Man., Canada; December 14, 1966
Position: Goaltender
Height: 5-10
Weight: 170
Uniform no.: 30
Catches: left

Career statistics:

GP	MINS	G	SO	AVG	A	PIM
80	4,308	238	4	3.31	3	10

1988-89 statistics:

GP	MINS	AVG	W	L	T	SO	GA	SA	SAPCT	PIM
29	1,509	3.50	15	8	2	1	88	718	.877	2

LAST SEASON

Games played total was career high.

THE PHYSICAL GAME

Ranford is a standup goaltender, coming out of his net to challenge the shooters because he is a strong skater. When he is on Ranford plays his angles very well, but he does have the disturbing tendency of losing his net at times. He stands up well and maintains that stance — instead of going to the ice — on screen shots and shots from the point with crowds around the net.

He has very quick reflexes and moves well in and out of the net (Ranford leaves the net to handle the puck), but his movement across the crease — his lateral movement — could improve. He has not yet learned to control a rebound after a save, so the second save is a problem for him. Of particular concern would be his tendency to leave fat rebounds off pad saves.

Because Bill frequently gets by on the speed of his hands and feet, he has a tendency to not get back into his stance — surviving, as it were, on reflex. Because of that, he is often too deep into his net when the puck is in the slot. The results are goals allowed to the corners, especially low.

THE MENTAL GAME

He's got good confidence in his ability, but Ranford's concentration can sometimes take a beating. He anticipates fairly well, but because he allows the opposition to screen him — and because he doesn't do anything to improve his vision on those screens (deeper crouch, butterfly, hack ankles) Ranford doesn't always see the puck as well as he should.

THE INTANGIBLES

There was a short period of time early last season when Grant Fuhr struggled and he and Ranford almost split the goaltending chores, instead of Ranford acting solely as backup. As he continues to develop (he is only 23 years old), Ranford will grow into NHL maturity. But playing behind Fuhr, he's going to remain the backup.

142

CRAIG SIMPSON

Yrs. of NHL service: 4
Born: London, Ontario, Canada; February 15, 1967
Position: Right wing/left wing
Height: 6-2
Weight: 192
Uniform no.: 18
Shoots: right

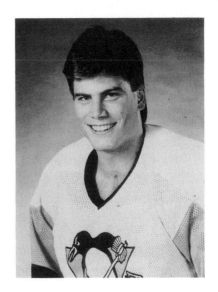

Career statistics:

GP	G	A	TP	PIM
294	128	117	245	263

1988-89 statistics:

GP	G	A	TP	+/-	PIM	PP	SH	GW	GT	S	PCT
66	35	41	76	-3	80	17	0	4	0	121	28.9

LAST SEASON

Games played total was career low (ankle injury — 11 games), but point totals were second highest of career. He was second in power play goals, third in goals and fifth in scoring. He finished second in shooting percentage in the NHL.

THE FINESSE GAME

Stick skills and smarts are the keys to Simpson's finesse game. He's an excellent passer and puckhandler, putting his reach to work for him in the rink's congested areas to pull the puck from traffic. But he also uses his hand skills to control the puck in those tight areas, and his quick release makes his shot (both forehand and backhand) an exceptional one; that's one big reason for his power-play success. He also excels on tip-ins and deflections.

Craig's fine anticipation and vision help him get into position to score. His vision is excellent and he tries to make the most of his teammates by finding the openings and getting the puck there.

He's not a bad skater, but his foot skills are definitely behind his hand skills — even after four NHL seasons. He lacks outstanding foot speed, quickness and agility (the absences of which might actually make his scoring success more remarkable). He does have a lot of strength, so he can drive the net, and that also allows him to put his balance —the one exceptional component of his skating — to work. That balance keys his ability to work in traffic by allowing him to maintain body position and control of the puck. He's almost impossible to knock down.

Simpson's defensive play remains weak, largely because he works so deep to the opposing net that his lack of foot speed prevents him from getting back into the play in time. When he can get into position, Craig plays a conscientious defensive game.

THE PHYSICAL GAME

Craig is very strong, and that's the ability that lets him drive the net. He is unafraid of traffic or the fearsome areas in front of the net and in the corners.

Most important is the fact that Craig not only takes hits to make plays, but he takes hits and makes successful plays. He could benefit by initiating more of that contact, rather than just accepting it when it occurs.

He uses his reach very well in keeping the puck from the opposition, or to snare loose pucks, and he uses his body well to protect the puck when he carries it.

THE INTANGIBLES

It would be easy to look at last season and claim it was a disappointing one for Simpson. After all, his production fell from 56 goals to 35. But, if we do some number-crunching, we find that over his 66 games last season he averaged 0.53 goals-per-game, an 80-game total of 42 goals. Obviously, Simpson has goal-scoring capacity.

A full, healthy season will prove that. More important was last season's inadequate even-strength performance: 50 percent of Craig's goals came on the power play, making him a less-than-awesome 17-goal scorer at even strength. That must improve.

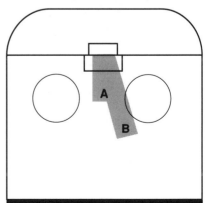

STEVE SMITH

Yrs. of NHL service: 4
Born: Glasgow, Scotland; April 30, 1963
Position: Defenseman
Height: 6-4
Weight: 215
Uniform no.: 5
Shoots: right

Career statistics:

GP	G	A	TP	PIM
233	26	97	123	716

1988-89 statistics:

GP	G	A	TP	+/-	PIM	PP	SH	GW	GT	S	PCT
35	3	19	22	5	97	0	0	0	0	47	6.4

LAST SEASON

Games played and all point totals were full season lows (shoulder surgery).

THE FINESSE GAME

Smith has become — considering his size and bulk — a very good skater at the NHL level. He moves well both forward and backward, and his improved quickness has given him deceptive agility and lateral movement. He uses his skating skill well in an active — rather than *re*-active — role at both blue lines.

He reads the rush and anticipates well, and Smith makes that talent work thrice: closing the gap on the puck carrier, taking him off the puck and starting the play up-ice.

Steve can carry the puck from the zone, but is more likely to move it to the forwards and then join the play as it heads up ice. His play reading ability extends to the offensive zone (and has been improved by his improved skating) and Steve will not only find the open forward but will find an opening and lead a forward to it with a good pass.

His hand skills have developed along with his foot skills and Smith contains the play very well at the offensive blue line, so much so that he will get good power-play time. He has a good slap shot, nothing exceptional, and Smith wil shoot from the point or the middle of the blue line.

THE PHYSICAL GAME

Steve is an excellent and aggressive physical player, especially now that his skating allows him to completely track down the opposition and consistently put his excellent size and strength to work against them.

He's very strong in front of his net and will succeed against most all NHL forwards, including those of the power variety. He's just as sure to win the battles in the corners, and his ability to make plays coming out of the corner magnifies his already superb physical play.

His size makes him very difficult to get around at the blue line and Smith will sacrifice his body to block shots.

THE INTANGIBLES

We said last year that Smith — despite an exceptional 1987-88 — remained a player of great potential. His continued improvement was sidetracked last season because of his injury, but he combines size and skill in a way that few NHL defenders can. He's already a defensive force, and we maintain that he will one day be considered for the Norris Trophy.

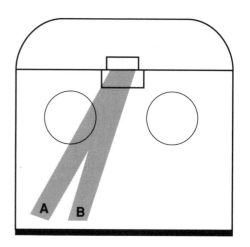

ESA TIKKANEN

Yrs. of NHL service: 4
Born: Helsinki, Finland; January 25, 1965
Position: Left wing
Height: 6-1
Weight: 200
Uniform no.: 10
Shoots: left

Career statistics:

GP	G	A	TP	PIM
258	95	148	243	393

1988-89 statistics:

GP	G	A	TP	+/-	PIM	PP	SH	GW	GT	S	PCT
67	31	47	78	10	92	6	8	4	0	151	20.5

LAST SEASON

Games played and PIM totals were full-season career lows (recurring wrist injury), but point total tied career high. He finished fourth on the club in scoring, first in shorthanded goals and tied for second in plus/minus among forwards.

THE FINESSE GAME

Tikkanen is an excellent skater with great speed, acceleration, quickness, balance and agility. His balance allows him to retain his body position (and thus control of the puck) as he's being fouled, and he was much more aggressive in using this skill last season than he was in 1987-88. Esa also moderates his speed to make it more effective, but he does perform well at high speed.

He's a smart player and uses his play-reading ability both offensively and defensively. He's very good at turning the play around by intercepting a pass or closing a hole, and his smarts combine with his skating to make him an excellent forechecker and penalty killer.

Esa's hand skills are just as advanced as his foot skills, and he makes particularly good use of his hands in traffic and around the net. His smarts amplify the ability of his hand skills by putting him in places where his hands can go to work.

Tikkanen has an excellent wrist shot, and he can put it anywhere courtesy of his soft hands. It's quickly released and accurate, and Esa would benefit by using it more often. He's most dangerous from the top of the circle and in.

He excels defensively, playing his position and checking well in all three zones.

THE PHYSICAL GAME

Tikkanen is a very tough player and loves hitting and working in the trenches. He plays bigger than his size and is fearless in the corners, a style that belies the European stereotypes. Esa's excellent balance aids him in his physical play by allowing him to remain vertical after he initiates a hit, and he more than has the skills to make the play coming out of the corner.

He's fairly liberal in the use of his stick, but overall Tikkanen would be said to play bigger than his size.

THE INTANGIBLES

He's high on everyone's list of disturbers, a player who yaps non-stop, digs in with little hooks and slashes — and generally doesn't show respect to players who — in their own minds — deserve it. He just drives the opposition nuts.

He's a flamboyant player and he plays with emotion and spark that enlivens the Oilers. Tikkanen also has the talent, by the way, to improve on his numbers — he has 50-goal potential. But the problem is, Tikkanen wants out of Edmonton. Whether he'll get his wish or not, that desire can become a factor in his play.

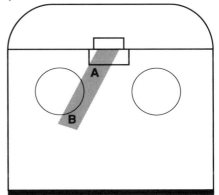

HARTFORD
WHALERS

LINE COMBINATIONS
DON MALONEY-RON FRANCIS-KEVIN
DINEEN
DAVE TIPPETT-DEAN EVASON-JODY HULL
JOHN ANDERSON-RAY FERRARO-PAUL
MACDERMID
BRIAN LAWTON-BRENT PETERSON

DEFENSE PAIRINGS
RANDY LADOCEUR-SYLVAIN COTE
GRANT JENNINGS-ULF SAMUELSSON
NORM MACIVER-DAVE BABYCH

GOALTENDERS
MIKE LIUT
PETER SIDORKIEWICZ

OTHER PLAYERS
SCOTT YOUNG — SYLVAIN TURGEON
JOEL QUENNEVILLE

POWER PLAY

FIRST UNIT:
KEVIN DINEEN-BRIAN LAWTON-RON
FRANCIS
DAVE BABYCH-NORM MACIVER

SECOND UNIT:
JOHN ANDERSON-RAY FERRARO-PAUL
MACDERMID
SCOTT YOUNG-ULF SAMUELSSON

On the first unit, DINEEN plugs the front of the net, LAWTON takes the left wing corner and FRANCIS rotates along the boards on both sides and behind the net. He'll primarily control the puck on the left side, leaving LAWTON to slide in front for a shot. Shots from the point are another option, with LAWTON again going to the slot and FRANCIS taking a position in the deep slot.

On the second unit, YOUNG works from the top of the left circle (where he'll also work if he takes LAWTON's place on the first unit. Then the first unit keeps moving the puck along the perimeter for an open shot, with DINEEN still plugging the net). MACDERMID plugs the net, ANDERSON takes the deep slot and FERRARO is in the left faceoff circle. FERRARO is the preferred shot, with ANDERSON second and YOUNG third. If YOUNG isn't on the blue line for the unit, the unit does nothing but act as decoys; shots should come from the forwards.

Last season Hartford's power play was GOOD, scoring 87 goals in 418 opportunities (20.8 percent, 10th overall).

PENALTY KILLING

FIRST UNIT:
DAVE TIPPETT-BRENT PETERSON
JOEL QUENNEVILLE-ULF SAMUELSSON

SECOND UNIT:
RON FRANCIS-DEAN EVASON
GRANT JENNINGS-SYLVAIN COTE

Neither of these units is overly aggressive. They play a standard box without forcing the puck, simply keeping the play to the outside. QUENNEVILLE will play as much of the two minutes as possible, with JENNINGS doing fill-in work to get QUENNEVILLE a rest. RANDY LADOCEUR will also see occasional time on defense.

Last season Hartford's penalty killing was GOOD, allowing 70 goals in 377 shorthanded situations (81.4 percent, seventh overall).

CRUCIAL FACEOFFS
FRANCIS and FERRARO get the nods for these.

JOHN ANDERSON

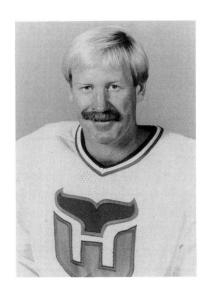

Yrs. of NHL service: 12
Born: Toronto, Ontario, Canada; March 28, 1957
Position: Left wing
Height: 5-11
Weight: 200
Uniform no.: 20
Shoots: left

Career statistics:

GP	G	A	TP	PIM
814	282	349	631	263

1988-89 statistics:

GP	G	A	TP	+/-	PIM	PP	SH	GW	GT	S	PCT
62	16	24	40	15	28	1	0	0	0	132	12.1

LAST SEASON

Games played total was full season career low. All point totals were second lowest of his career. Anderson missed time with a groin injury. He finished third in plus/minus, best among forwards.

THE FINESSE GAME

Concomitant with his advancing NHL age (Anderson is 32 years old), John's skills continue their decline. His skating is the most affected of his skills, as Anderson lacks the jump and agility that had in previous seasons made him a dangerous forward. His stride has lost much of its strength, his feet much of their speed.

His sense and anticipation remain intact, but he lacks both the foot and hand speed to consistently make his hockey sense pay off. He can find his teammates but he needs more time and space than ever, and since Anderson was a scorer (rather than a playmaker) his ability to get into position to score is questionable — his feet don't get him there in time.

His SOG total continues to drop, because Anderson can't get into position to release he puck. Since his shot was his best finesse weapon (he had slap shot power, a quick wrist shot and the hands to tuck the puck into the net from close quarters) he is that much less effective.

He has become, as he slows down, more and more a power play specialist.

THE PHYSICAL GAME

Even in his more successful days, Anderson did the grinding along the boards necessary for success. He wasn't a big thumper, but he took the body and used his hand skills to their best advantage. He does that today — when he can get to the puck in time — but he doesn't have the strength to change styles in mid-stream and still be successful.

THE INTANGIBLES

We told you prior to 1987-88 that Anderson had to prove his ability to still function as an NHL goal scorer. He didn't do that last season, and his age and diminishing effectiveness may mean the Whalers aren't the only team Anderson plays for this season.

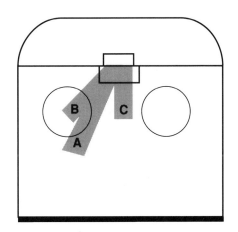

DAVE BABYCH

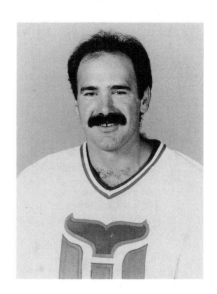

Yrs. of NHL service: 9
Born: Edmonton, Alta., Canada; May 23, 1961
Position: Defenseman
Height: 6-2
Weight: 215
Uniform no.: 44
Shoots: left

Career statistics:

GP	G	A	TP	PIM
659	111	401	512	582

1988-89 statistics:

GP	G	A	TP	+/-	PIM	PP	SH	GW	GT	S	PCT
70	6	41	47	-5	54	4	0	2	0	172	3.5

LAST SEASON

Babych led Whaler defensemen in scoring and was fourth on the club in assists. Goal total tied career low; assist total was three-year high. He finished third in SOG total. He missed six games with a hand injury.

THE FINESSE GAME

Babych is a good skater in terms of straightaway, forward movement, but he's slowing up in other areas. He retains some good speed as he rushes from the Hartford zone, but in the areas of agility he's less sure. That means the opposition may get that extra space to slide inside him, or that extra second to make a play from the corner.

Babych uses the speed he does have to create plays in the offensive zone, particularly on the power play where Dave is the general of Hartford's offense. He combines his skating with good puckhandling skills and is especially effective in traffic.

His vision and hockey sense allow Dave to use his teammates well, but again, his decreasing quickness means loose pucks once snared may now be lost — or an opening once recognized may be closed before the puck gets through it. He passes well, but Babych likes to shoot the puck when he can (though his shot total decreased last season — down from 233 in 1987-88).

His defensive game has never been better than fair, sometimes poor, and it remains so. He lacks patience in passing from the defensive zone and that leads to turnovers.

THE PHYSICAL GAME

Babych is inconsistent in his attempts at clearing the front of the net and he allows his checks to sneak back into the play, so he could improve his takeouts. Though he has the tools to play a good one, he plays a no better than fair physical contest.

THE INTANGIBLES

As we said last season, Babych has always been a pretty much one-dimensional player. Now, age and youth — someone else's — may force him to the periphery for the Whalers, especially with the presence of a Norm Maciver and the development of Scott Young (both of whom play well on the power play).

As before, injuries and durability are also questions. The Whalers have considered moving Babych for several seasons, and he may very well finish the season with another club.

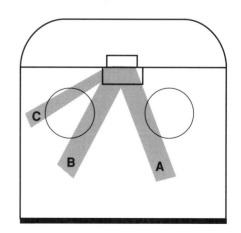

SYLVAIN COTE

Yrs. of NHL service: 4
Born: Quebec City, Quebec, Canada; January 19, 1966
Position: Defenseman
Height: 5-11
Weight: 185
Uniform no.: 21
Shoots: right

Career statistics:

GP	G	A	TP	PIM
281	20	47	67	116

1988-89 statistics:

GP	G	A	TP	+/-	PIM	PP	SH	GW	GT	S	PCT
78	8	9	17	-7	49	1	0	0	0	130	6.2

LAST SEASON

Games played and goal totals were career highs. He missed two games with a late-season hand injury.

THE FINESSE GAME

Skating is Cote's best skill both offensively and defensively. He uses his speed and quickness very effectively as the play moves up ice and those same assets counter any positional mistakes he makes. Cote uses his skating prowess instead of solid positional play to play defense (and he can get burned because of that). Still, his speed, his quickness and agility insure that he won't often be beaten 1-on-1.

He has sort of stagnated in his ability to handle the puck at NHL speed, whether that means skating it from the zone (which he does frequently) or making the breakout pass. He's got the ability to make correct decisions and just needs to exercise some patience to do so.

Sylvain does anticipate plays in both directions fairly well, and he's shown confidence in his own abilities by taking chances — things like charging the net, knowing that his skating can help him recover.

THE PHYSICAL GAME

Cote rides the fence in this area. While not necessarily averse to a physical game, Cote doesn't really have the size or strength to play an effective physical game. So what you get instead is a lot of pushing and shoving, and some out-muscling by the opposition when Cote gets caught in front of the net.

He'll try to tie up the opposition along the boards, and if Cote can get both himself and the puck free he can make a play.

THE INTANGIBLES

While still an NHL youngster (in terms of both age and experience), Cote needs to learn better positional play (he could take a cue from teammate Joel Quenneville) and should develop some strength. Last season was really just his second full NHL stint; this season will go a long way toward determining exactly what kind of player Cote will be.

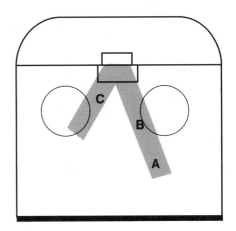

KEVIN DINEEN

Yrs. of NHL service: 5
Born: Quebec City, Quebec, Canada;
October 28, 1963
Position: Right wing
Height: 5-11
Weight: 190
Uniform no.: 11
Shoots: right

Career statistics:

GP	G	A	TP	PIM
345	168	159	327	740

1988-89 statistics:

GP	G	A	TP	+/-	PIM	PP	SH	GW	GT	S	PCT
79	45	44	89	-6	167	20	1	4	0	294	15.3

LAST SEASON

Dineen led the club in scoring with career highs in all point totals. He was second in assists and PIM total, first in power play goals (fifth in the NHL) and shots on goal. Games played total was a career high.

THE FINESSE GAME

Kevin succeeds as an NHLer because of his excellent skating. His strong stride gives him good acceleration and rink-length speed, as well as the ability to drive through checks. He combines his speed with quickness and balance to move better laterally than would be expected for a physical player. His excellent balance makes him effective physically, as he retains his upright stance despite his many collisions.

Making Dineen's skating even more effective are his hand skills. He passes and carries the puck well at full speed, but he makes better plays when he is skating slower. He has excellent anticipation and can either break for the holes or lead a teammate with a perfect pass.

Dineen has good scoring instincts and he shoots the puck a lot (his SOG total increased by almost 25 percent last season, from 223 in 1987-88 to 294 last season). He releases his shot quickly, and is less frequently looking for the artistic goal (top shelf away), concentrating instead on just getting the puck on net.

THE PHYSICAL GAME

Kevin's physical ability is very high, and made better by his ability to make a play coming out of the corner. He's a tough and fearless player, and does his best by playing that way.

THE INTANGIBLES

Dineen made good progress last season back toward being the team player he was before he scored 40 goals in 1986-87. He's lost a lot of his selfishness, and he's gone back to his down-and-dirty style. Most important, though, is his greatly reduced PIM total. In 1987-88 he had 219 PIM. In five more games last season, he had just 167.

That means he's playing smart. If Dineen can keep himself from becoming selfish again, Hartford's attempts to return to the NHL's upper levels will be greatly aided.

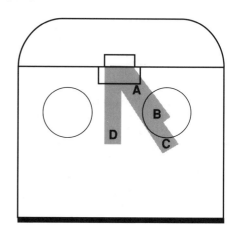

DEAN EVASON

Yrs. of NHL service: 4
Born: Flin Flon, Man., Canada; August 22, 1964
Position: Center
Height: 5-10
Weight: 180
Uniform no.: 12
Shoots: left

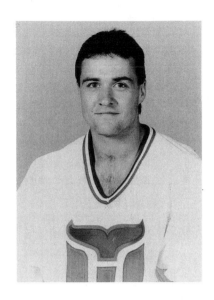

Career statistics:

GP	G	A	TP	PIM
298	66	104	170	313

1988-89 statistics:

GP	G	A	TP	+/-	PIM	PP	SH	GW	GT	S	PCT
67	11	17	28	-9	60	0	0	0	0	95	11.6

LAST SEASON

Point total tied career low; assist mark was career low. He missed time with an ankle injury.

THE FINESSE GAME

On a strictly objective evaluation of his skills, Evason is fairly gifted. He has good speed and anticipation, and can utilize that vision to make some plays. He has okay hands and controls the puck well enough to take advantage of the openings his skating can create.

His skating and anticipation make him valuable as a penalty killer, and he is also fairly successful on the power play because of the open ice (where he, again, can put his skating to work).

Dean has a little bit of a scoring touch and can score from the bottom of the faceoff circle with a quick wrist shot or from the top of the circle with a snap shot.

THE PHYSICAL GAME

Once Dean's size is factored into the equation of his skills, the answer is he's just too small for his skills to succeed at the NHL level.

Evason isn't afraid of physical play but so what? He's not going to be effective in traffic anyway because of his lack of size, and his hand and foot skills aren't good enough for him to negotiate his way among the giants he has to face.

THE INTANGIBLES

Evason is a quality player in terms of heart and character, but it's doubtful that his skills are going to develop further. That — combined with his horrendous defense — will keep him on the periphery of the NHL. He will, by the way, be playing on a new contract this season.

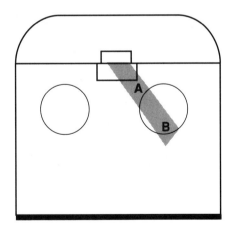

RAY FERRARO

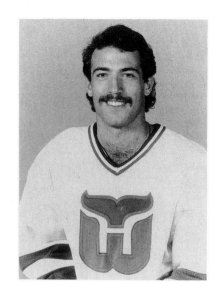

Yrs. of NHL service: 5
Born: Trail, B.C., Canada; August 23, 1964
Position: Center
Height: 5-10
Weight: 185
Uniform no.: 26
Shoots: left

Career statistics:

GP	G	A	TP	PIM
348	130	160	290	308

1988-89 statistics:

GP	G	A	TP	+/-	PIM	PP	SH	GW	GT	S	PCT
80	41	35	76	1	86	11	0	7	0	169	24.3

LAST SEASON

Ferraro played 80 games for the second time in his career (and twice in last three years). Goal total was career high (second on club), with assist and point totals second highest of career. He finished first on the team in game winners and shooting percentage, second in power play goals and third in scoring.

THE FINESSE GAME

Skating is the best of Ferraro's finesse skills, and he is way above average in that skill. Ray has both rink-length speed and one-step quickness, and he uses both to either get to the openings or to create them by driving defensemen off the blue line. He has excellent agility and lateral movement because of his balance, as well as breakaway acceleration.

His scoring ability is a direct reflection of his ability in getting to loose pucks and getting his shot off. Ray is opportunistic, and he makes the most of his opportunities by shooting often and quickly. He also has good sense and knows how to get into scoring position (as his power play ability particularly attests).

He succeeds as a playmaker by using his head. Ray has good patience, and he looks over the ice for his best play. He also has good — not great — ability to make his plays while moving. His feet, though, sometimes out-race his hands.

THE PHYSICAL GAME

Despite his size (or lack of it), Ray is willing to play a tough physical game. But willing doesn't mean able, and he can be physically overwhelmed by bigger players. He's not intimidated by play along the boards, nor afraid of the rough stuff in front of the net. His hand and wrist strength helps him pull the puck out of traffic and power his shot past the goaltender.

His balance is a big help to him in those traffic areas, especially because Ferraro does have the hand skills to make plays coming out of the corners. And he must remain opportunistic to succeed; he must get to those loose pucks before bigger, stronger opponents he'll be unable to out-muscle.

THE INTANGIBLES

Ferraro works fairly hard each night to put his assets to work, but we're not convinced he's a 40-goal scorer. His scoring last season suggests a hot streak (he had just six goals in the first 20 games), and as the NHL gets bigger *and* faster he's going to have more and more trouble repeating last season's performance.

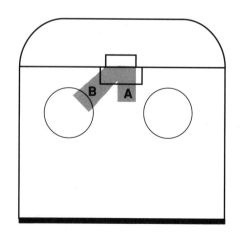

RON FRANCIS

Yrs. of NHL service: 8
Born: Sault Ste. Marie, Ontario, Canada;
March 1, 1963
Position: Center
Height: 6-2
Weight: 200
Uniform no.: 10
Shoots: left

Career statistics:

GP	G	A	TP	PIM
567	211	433	644	416

1988-89 statistics:

GP	G	A	TP	+/-	PIM	PP	SH	GW	GT	S	PCT
69	29	48	77	4	36	8	0	4	0	156	18.6

LAST SEASON

Games played total was second-lowest full season mark of career, and lowest in three years (broken finger). Assist total was full-season career low, but was team high. He finished second in team scoring. His plus/minus was the second-highest among forwards.

THE FINESSE GAME

Francis's excellent balance keys his skating and gives him speed and agility surprising for a bigger man. He's a smooth skater with better than average foot speed, and that asset combines with his balance to give him superior lateral movement and agility. He uses his foot speed and balance to lean away from checks, and he also functions well in traffic because of his balance.

His hockey sense (Ron always knows where he is on the ice) complements his skating skills by guiding him to places where he can put his soft hands to work. Once there, he can feather a pass through traffic or throw the puck into the open for a teammate to snare.

Because he is unselfish, Francis is a better playmaker than scorer. He's most effective from the slot, because his balance allows him to get his shot off while in traffic. Francis can also blast a slap shot past the goaltender from farther away.

He plays a complete game in all three zones.

THE PHYSICAL GAME

Just because we said he *can* succeed in the traffic areas doesn't mean Francis will. He has good upper body strength and can combine that strength with his superior balance to muscle the opposition off the puck, but Francis rarely puts his size to work for him in congested areas. Instead he waits outside the scrums to snare loose pucks with his good reach.

He won't shy away from contact, but Francis hasn't learned the lessons a Steve Yzerman or Pat LaFontaine (players smaller than Francis) have learned: a physical game improves a finesse one.

THE INTANGIBLES

If he used his size the way he uses his finesse skills, Francis could be a consistent 100-point scorer. Health could be a definite concern here: he's played only 508 of 560 possible games since becomming a full-time NHLer. He is an unselfish player who puts the team first, and he has learned to do the character things a captain must — like play through pain.

But while Ron is a strong two-way center, he's clearly not in the class of the NHL's best centers. And at 26, with seven NHL seasons behind him, it certainly seems he never will be.

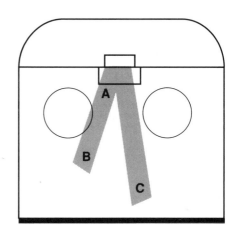

JODY HULL

Yrs. of NHL service: 1
Born: Cambridge, Ontario, Canada; February 2, 1969
Position: Right wing
Height: 6-2
Weight: 200
Uniform no.: 8
Shoots: right

Career statistics:

GP	G	A	TP	+/-	PIM	PP	SH	GW	GT	S	PCT
60	16	18	34	6	10	6	0	2	0	82	19.5

LAST SEASON

First NHL campaign. Hull was a 1987 first round draft pick. He finished fourth in the club in plus/minus, second among forwards. He missed six games with a pulled hamstring.

THE FINESSE GAME

Hull's skating and shooting strengths indicate that he has the tools to play a successful NHL game. He's a strong skater with good balance and that's important, because he drives the net for shots and works the corners for the puck. Hull's strength also means that he can pick up a step or two on a defenseman to cut to the net.

He handles the puck well in the traffic areas, making his physical play more effective, and his good hands are also demonstrated in his ability to give and accept passes in stride, and to shoot the puck. His shot is accurate, quickly released, and hard, forcing the goaltender to make saves, and he would benefit by shooting the puck more.

Jody works hard at his defense, getting into position and backchecking throughout all three zones. He is attentive in his own end, and plays with discipline (by staying in position and not wandering).

THE PHYSICAL GAME

Hull has good size and promising strength, but he doesn't use his body as well as he might. He carries a reputation for liking to hit, but that ability wasn't readily evident last season, especially in his work along the boards defensively.

He does make the most of his strength by going to the net, but he could impose himself more in the corners.

THE INTANGIBLES

A fairly solid rookie year for Hull, who will no doubt play to his own strengths (pun intended) as time goes by. He's a hard worker who should make the improvements necessary to pull his game up a notch. He is also versatile, and can play all three forward positions.

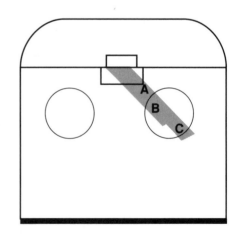

GRANT JENNINGS

Yrs. of NHL service: 1
Born: Hudson Bay, Sask., Canada; May 5, 1965
Position: Defenseman
Height: 6-3
Weight: 200
Uniform no.: 25
Shoots: left

Career statistics:

GP	G	A	TP	+/-	PIM	PP	SH	GW	GT	S	PCT
55	3	10	13	17	159	0	0	0	0	39	7.7

LAST SEASON

First full NHL campaign. He was acquired from the Capitals in July 1988 (along with Ed Kastelic in exchange for Neil Sheehy and Mike Millar). He finished third in PIM (second among defensemen) and second overall in plus/minus. He missed time with a shoulder injury.

THE FINESSE GAME

Though first glance says that Grant is obviously gifted in the physical department, he's not a bad finesse player. He takes what skills he has and makes them work by staying within his limitations.

So, while his skating is slow and sometimes ponderous at the NHL level (because he lacks foot speed), Jennings makes it work by playing a strong positional game defensively. He generally won't challenge at the offensive blue line (he demonstrates smarts by pinching in only when he knows he won't be beaten) and he won't rush the puck.

Instead, Jennings knows he has to make the simple play, and so he does. Find an open man, move the puck. He doesn't have great hand skills, so his assists are going to come on plays he's started from the Hartford zone, and his goals are going to come from the blue line — few and far between.

THE PHYSICAL GAME

This is where Jennings has the chance to shine, and if he can improve his mobility he can be a dominant force. He has great size and is very effective in front of the net, using his strength to clear the crease.

He works well in the corners when he can isolate the opposition there, and Jennings likes to use his size and strength in the traffic areas. He's not a big banger, but he gets the job done.

THE INTANGIBLES

Exactly how much Jennings can improve is questionable. While 24 isn't old for an NHLer, it is old for a rookie. But Grant played with good poise last season (example: not chasing the puck when defending 5-on-3) and made the most of his opportunity. He should continue to develop and give Hartford a much-needed physical presence behind the blue line — a second defender (after Ulf Samuelsson) to joust with the Cam Neelys of the world.

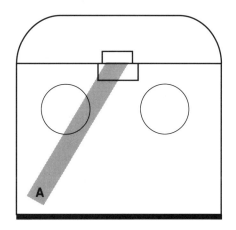

RANDY LADOCEUR

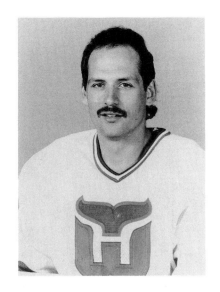

Yrs. of NHL service: 7
Born: Brockville, Ontario, Canada; June 30, 1960
Position: Defenseman
Height: 6-2
Weight: 220
Uniform no.: 29
Shoots: left

Career statistics:

GP	G	A	TP	PIM
468	19	83	102	685

1988-89 statistics:

GP	G	A	TP	+/-	PIM	PP	SH	GW	GT	S	PCT
75	2	5	7	-23	95	0	0	0	0	56	3.6

LAST SEASON

Games played total was three-season high. His plus/minus was the team's worst.

THE FINESSE GAME

Ladoceur isn't tremendously gifted finesse-wise, but he makes what he has work by staying within his modest limits. He skates well enough to keep up with the NHL play, though his agility in turning and pivoting is weak and could be improved.

Randy doesn't anticipate exceptionally well, so he finds himself reacting instead of acting defensively; you won't often find him stepping up to close the gap on the opposition. He plays his position well, keeping himself in the correct areas to force the opposition wide of the net; that's what we mean by not overstepping his limits. Ladoceur knows he needs a certain amount of time and space to make his defensive plays and he makes sure to get that space.

He does very little handling of the puck, leaving that for the backchecking forward or his defensive partner. He will not carry the puck from the defensive zone and doesn't see the openings on the ice well. He will follow the play up-ice and will shoot from the point, so any goals he gets will come from those shots.

THE PHYSICAL GAME

Randy has some good size and strength, and he's willing to use those assets — that's what makes him a successful NHL player. He uses his size fairly well in front of the net but could benefit from greater strength in his upper body, as well as better balance in his legs.

Because he is somewhat lacking in the latter two categories, Randy can be knocked off the puck. Still, he plays the body willingly and can generally tie up opposing wingers when necessary.

THE INTANGIBLES

Ladoceur is a competent but no better than average NHL player. He helps give Hartford depth on the blue line but he'll never be more than a fifth defenseman.

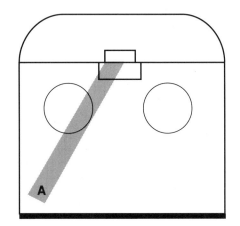

BRIAN LAWTON

Yrs. of NHL service: 6
Born: New Brunswick, N.J., USA: June 29, 1965
Position: Left wing/center
Height: 6-0
Weight: 190
Uniform no.: 7
Shoots: left

Career statistics:

GP	G	A	TP	PIM
368	88	117	205	317

1988-89 statistics:

GP	G	A	TP	+/-	PIM	PP	SH	GW	GT	S	PCT
65	17	26	43	-11	67	10	0	2	0	128	13.3

LAST SEASON

Acquired in December (along with Don Maloney and Norm MacIver) from New York in exchange for Carey Wilson. Games played total was three-season low (wrist injury). He finished third in power play goals.

THE FINESSE GAME

Lawton is no better than average as a skater, particularly lacking strength and balance on his feet — that's why he'd do better as a center, playing in the middle of the ice, than as a wing along the boards. He will get from Point A to Point B fairly effectively, and he uses his anticipation and vision to be a good checker.

While he has shown an increased ability to make plays, playmaking at the NHL level remains largely out of Lawton's reach for two reasons. One, he doesn't have great hands and tends to rush his passes to his teammates. Two, his hands and his brain don't function at NHL speed for offense. By the time Brian sees an opening, it's closed.

Lawton will do something with his opportunities but he won't finesse any plays, and his goal scoring is no exception. Because he releases his shot quickly Lawton has a degree of goal scoring talent (and that quickness is why he succeeds on the power play), but neither his skating nor his anticipation will get him to the openings so he'll have to get his goals from close to the net by taking advantage of loose pucks.

THE PHYSICAL GAME

He's gotten bigger but Lawton's size and the attendant strength remain only fair; that's another reason to take him off the boards and put him at center. Because he can't be successful here, Lawton is not much interested in the physical game. He's also very susceptible to an opposing player just lifting his stick and taking the puck.

THE INTANGIBLES

Brian is a role player, nothing more. He has some checking ability and could be used in that capacity (his plus/minus is largely a result of that use), but because his offensive zone game is less than extraordinary, he's not going to rise above that role player level.

As such, he will always be vulnerable to replacement.

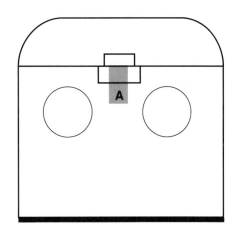

MIKE LIUT

Yrs. of NHL service: 10
Born: Weston, Ontario, Canada; January 7, 1956
Position: Goaltender
Height: 6-2
Weight: 195
Uniform no.: 1
Catches: left

Career statistics:

GP	MINS	G	SO	AVG	A	PIM
570	32,998	1,943	20	3.53	12	20

1988-89 statistics:

GP	MINS	AVG	W	L	T	SO	GA	SA	SAPCT	PIM
35	2,006	4.25	13	19	1	1	142	1,027	.861	0

LAST SEASON

Games played total was career low. Goals-against-average was highest of career. Win total was lowest of career.

THE PHYSICAL GAME

Liut is a good skater, moving in and out of his net very well. His good balance allows him to rapidly regain his stance when he leaves his feet, so as to be in position to make a second save if a rebound is given. He uses his skating to track down loose pucks and control them for his defensemen, and Liut will pass it to a defenseman or forward quickly for a breakout. He excels at poke checking the puck away from incoming forwards.

Liut generally handles his rebounds, sticking them to a corner or covering them if necessary to keep them from the opposition. He has a good glove hand and will catch anything he can (he cheats to that side), but is less sure on his stick side, where pucks bounce high in the air off his blocker. He also leaves the puck at his feet after left pad saves on shots from the right point. Liut is weak on the short stick side and can fall prey to shots low to the ice, most noticeably on the stick side again and also between the legs, as he is a little slow snapping his pads closed.

He takes advantage of his size when he does go to the ice, occupying large areas of net. However, because he goes down early on screen shots, he leaves himself vulnerable on subsequent shots.

THE MENTAL GAME

Anticipation and preparation are big parts of Liut's game. He's ready to play in each of his starts, but he can give up goals in bunches if scored on early. Then he regains his composure and buckles back down to business.

He's a very smart player — hockey sense would be the term used if he skated out. Liut understands the game and its flow very well, and he uses that sense to his advantage on cross-ice passes or re-directions.

THE INTANGIBLES

Liut will take a team to a certain level, but — and you may have noticed its omission under *The Mental Game* — he doesn't have the capacity to win that one big game. (i.e., the 1981 Canada Cup loss to the Soviet Union, Hartford's Game 7 overtime loss to the Canadiens in 1986, the six-game upset loss to the Rangers in April 1981 after the St. Louis Blues finished second in the League in points, the 1987 loss to the Nordiques in the first round).

Still, he's given Hartford a fairly high level of performance throughout his tenure. But the emergence last season of rookie Peter Sidorkiewicz (and with Kay Whitmore in the background, *and* with Emile Francis — his chief supporter — out of the picture) may spell the end of Liut's time in Hartford — if the Whalers can find takers for his two-plus years, big-ticket contract.

PAUL MACDERMID

Yrs. of NHL service: 5
Born: Chesley, Ontario, Canada; April 14, 1963
Position: Right wing
Height: 6-1
Weight: 205
Uniform no.: 23
Shoots: right

Career statistics:

GP	G	A	TP	PIM
344	62	71	133	675

1988-89 statistics:

GP	G	A	TP	+/-	PIM	PP	SH	GW	GT	S	PCT
74	17	27	44	1	141	5	0	3	2	113	15.0

LAST SEASON

Games played total ties second highest of career (sternum injury). Assist and point totals were career highs; goal total second highest. Was fourth in PIM total (second among forwards). Led team in game tying goals.

THE FINESSE GAME

MacDermid's serviceable finesse game is predicated on his skating — especially his balance. MacDermid's balance keeps him vertical after hits and ready to continue the play. That's important, since Paul is in the lineup because of his physical play. He has fairly good speed and agility (good enough so that the opposition can't just get out of his way when MacDermid lines them up) and he uses those assets as a good forechecker.

Paul has average hockey sense or anticipation ability, hence he's an average goal scorer and play maker. He'll collect most of his goals on muscle work around the crease (he's handy there on the power play). His hands are also good enough for him to finesse the occasional goal into an opening.

THE PHYSICAL GAME

Paul hits hard and often, and those hits will cough up the puck and hand it to the Whalers. He can level most players if he hits them squarely and he has a pretty good penchant for doing that. Paul goes in the corners and bangs around and he is very successful there, often forcing the puck free.

THE INTANGIBLES

MacDermid is a very hard worker and his scoring success last season made his already valuable physical play even more important to the Whalers, because guys who can hit *and* score are tough to find.

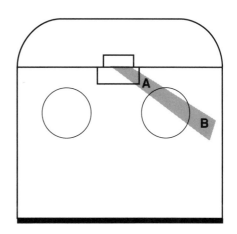

NORM MACIVER

Yrs. of NHL service: 2
Born: Thunder Bay, Ontario, Canada;
September 1, 1964
Position: Defenseman
Height: 5-11
Weight: 180
Uniform no.: 33
Shoots: left

Career statistics:

GP	G	A	TP	PIM
103	10	48	58	52

1988-89 statistics:

GP	G	A	TP	+/-	PIM	PP	SH	GW	GT	S	PCT
63	1	32	33	-3	38	1	0	0	0	87	1.1

LAST SEASON

Acquired from New York in December (along with Don Maloney and Brian Lawton) in exchange for Carey Wilson. Games played, assist and point totals were all career highs.

THE FINESSE GAME

Maciver is an excellent skater with great quickness, agility and speed. He has excellent change of pace and uses his speed to drive defenders off the opposing blue line. His one-step quickness gets him to loose pucks and, combined with his balance, allows him to change direction within a stride. That gives him great lateral movement. Norm plays his defense by speed, but he is improving his positional play (thus allowing him to thwart bigger, stronger opponents).

He is also gifted in puckhandling and will rush the puck when given the opportunity, and his judgement is improving — so he's less likely to carry the puck too deep and get trapped.

Maciver is a good playmaker in feeding his teammates in the offensive zone. He has a good shot from the point and will slide to the high slot if he can, knowing that his skating (and more-defensive minded defense partner) can rescue him when necessary.

THE PHYSICAL GAME

Maciver is willing to go into the corners and do the dirty work, but don't confuse willingness for ability. His lack of size and strength makes him ill-suited for work in traffic, and works against him when he meets a stronger opponent (his separated shoulder courtesy of a Scott Stevens check is a case in point).

Added bulk and muscular strength would help prevent such injuries, but shouldn't be added if

Maciver's speed will suffer. That added strength would help defensively too, because Norm will be over-matched in many confrontations in front of the net or along the boards.

THE INTANGIBLES

Norm must be paired with a strong, defense-minded partner to be successful — he must be allowed to create offense if he's going to be a Whaler advantage. His growing NHL experience is helping him to improve his defensive game, and his ability to contribute on the power play makes him a valuable commodity.

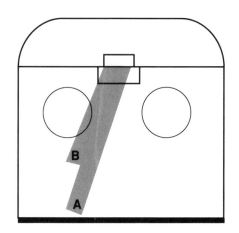

DON MALONEY

Yrs. of NHL service: 11
Born: Lindsay, Ontario, Canada; September 5, 1958
Position: Left wing
Height: 6-1
Weight: 190
Uniform no.: 14
Shoots: left

Career statistics:

GP	G	A	TP	PIM
674	198	318	516	762

1988-89 statistics:

GP	G	A	TP	+/-	PIM	PP	SH	GW	GT	S	PCT
52	7	20	27	3	39	1	0	1	0	72	9.7

LAST SEASON

Acquired by Hartford (along with Norm Maciver and Brian Lawton) from New York in December in exchange for Carey Wilson. He missed 18 games after the trade with a broken collarbone. Games played total was second-lowest of his career.

THE FINESSE GAME

Balance and a low center of gravity are the keys to Maloney's skating and to his game. Because of them, he can gain the puck in the corners and that makes him valuable as a forechecker. Otherwise, he has no real speed and is not particularly adept at carrying the puck while moving.

The extent of Maloney's playmaking prowess is throwing the puck in front after gaining it in the corners. His shot is fair and any goals he gets are going to have to come from in tight. He's sound defensively, despite his lack of speed in making the transition from offense to defense.

THE PHYSICAL GAME

Though no longer the dominating corner-man of his youth, Maloney remains a strong, physical hockey player. It is difficult to knock him down and he has a knack of pushing opponents in the direction he wants to go.

Clearly, injuries play a key part in Maloney's career at this point and he'd have to be judged as somewhat brittle. That is the consequence of his physical style.

THE INTANGIBLES

Don is finishing his career as a role player and checker, a role in which he performs extremely well. He has a fine work ethic and dedication, and he will be a quiet leader in that regard for the Whalers — a team that could use some character.

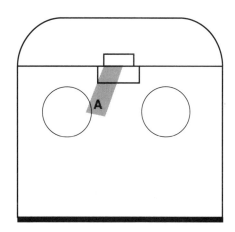

BRENT PETERSON

Yrs. of NHL service: 9
Born: Calgary, Alta., Canada; February 15, 1958
Position: Center
Height: 6-0
Weight: 190
Uniform no.: 17
Shoots: right

Career statistics:

GP	G	A	TP	PIM
620	72	141	213	484

1988-89 statistics:

GP	G	A	TP	+/-	PIM	PP	SH	GW	GT	S	PCT
66	4	13	17	2	61	0	0	2	0	56	7.1

LAST SEASON

Games played total was two-season high.

THE FINESSE GAME

Peterson is a good skater, a strong skater who can see a lot of ice time but rarely gets tired. He is not exceptionally quick or agile and cannot make the moves required to succeed in the offensive zone but Peterson will get where he's going on hustle and determination.

Brent's high degree of anticipation and hockey sense let him see the ice and read plays very well, making him an excellent checker and outstanding penalty killer (the latter almost his only ice-time during games). His anticipation makes him a threat for a short-handed goal, but his lack of speed makes that possibility a slight one. He plays smart defense and will not make checking mistakes, and his plus/minus is all the more remarkable for his limited duty.

He is an excellent faceoff man, one of the more underrated in the league in that department. Brent has good eye/hand coordination and that, along with his hand strength, gives him an edge in the circle.

Peterson is not really an offensive threat, but he can handle the puck fairly well and he does get it to his teammates because of his anticipation ability. Any scoring he does will have to be from close to the net.

THE PHYSICAL GAME

Peterson is tough and he can take the physical abuse. He is a grinder in a defensive kind of way and he uses his body well when checking to tie up the opposition. He has very strong hands and wrists and that powers his faceoff ability, as well as making him effective along the boards or in the corners.

THE INTANGIBLES

Peterson is a worker and a talk-it-up guy in the locker room. He is a character player and brings a maturity and high work ethic — to say nothing of a strong defensive performance — to a needy Whaler team.

His age and limited role (as well as the fact that his contract expired in June), may mean that he'll be playing with a different club this season.

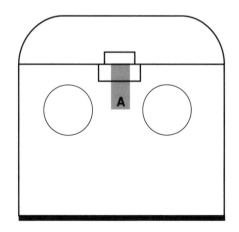

JOEL QUENNEVILLE

Yrs. of NHL service: 11
Born: Windsor, Ontario, Canada; September 15, 1958
Position: Defenseman
Height: 6-1
Weight: 200
Uniform no.: 3
Shoots: left

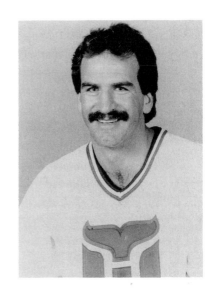

Career statistics:

GP	G	A	TP	PIM
750	52	132	184	671

1988-89 statistics:

GP	G	A	TP	+/-	PIM	PP	SH	GW	GT	S	PCT
69	4	7	11	3	32	0	0	0	0	45	8.9

LAST SEASON

He missed time with a shoulder injury. Point total was three-season high. He had lowest PIM total among defensemen.

THE FINESSE GAME

Joel doesn't have a lot of skating ability to begin with, and what he does have is showing signs of age. But Quenneville makes the most of what he does have by playing smartly and within his limits. He plays a conservative and unspectacular defensive game, simply forcing the play to the outside and moving the puck to the forwards.

Joel sees the ice well and excels at moving the puck quickly up-ice and out of the Whaler end. He doesn't carry the puck (he'll rarely take more than a handful of strides with it in any zone), preferring smartly to make the easy play up the boards instead of the risky cross-ice pass.

He demonstrates those same smarts in the offensive end, containing the point intelligently without getting trapped out of position. Quenneville shoots from the point with a low slap shot, not overly powerful, and he'll slide to the middle of the blue line for the same shot.

And sometimes — amazing! — he'll charge the net for a rebound or loose puck.

THE PHYSICAL GAME

If the criterion is dents in the boards, then Quenneville isn't a physical player. He doesn't do a lot of banging in the corners, actually pushing and shoving in the corners. But Joel keeps the front of the net clean by using his upper body strength to hold opponents out of the play — by doing a lot of clutching and grabbing.

He uses his body well to protect the puck along the boards to kill time or get a faceoff, but he doesn't otherwise sacrifice his body (he doesn't block shots).

THE INTANGIBLES

Smarts and dependability, those are the values that make Joel a meaningful contributor for the Whalers.

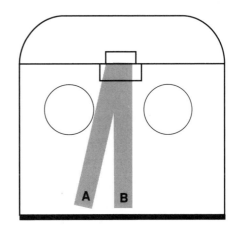

ULF SAMUELSSON

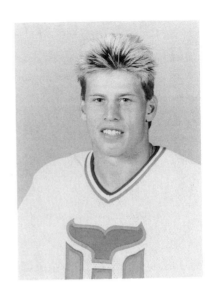

Yrs. of NHL service: 5
Born: Fagersta, Sweden; March 26, 1964
Position: Defenseman
Height: 6-1
Weight: 195
Uniform no.: 5
Shoots: left

Career statistics:

GP	G	A	TP	PIM
346	26	115	141	757

1988-89 statistics:

GP	G	A	TP	+/-	PIM	PP	SH	GW	GT	S	PCT
71	9	26	35	23	181	3	0	2	0	122	7.4

LAST SEASON

Games played total was full-season career low, but goal total was career high. He led team in both PIM and plus/minus.

THE FINESSE GAME

Samuelsson is an excellent skater with agility, quickness and speed. Ulf's excellent lateral movement and foot speed allow him to play defense actively — instead of *re*-actively — by stepping up to close the gap on the puck carrier and force him to make a play.

Once he's forced that play, Samuelsson takes the puck from the opposition and makes not just a correct decision but a good one. He gets the puck up-ice and out of the zone very well, and his foot speed allows him time to be patient and to view his play options.

Ulf carries the puck well because of his skating and his vision, and he is very effective at containing the point once he moves into the offensive zone. Samuelsson pinches in smartly and effectively, and his skating allows him to drive to the net to snare a pass. Still, most of his goals will come from the blue line.

THE PHYSICAL GAME

Samuelsson is a very physical defenseman. He bodychecks any opponent he can and isn't above adding an elbow or a stick to the process. He has great upper body strength and balance, and those assets allow him to not only succeed but dominate in the corners or front of the net.

He can be too aggressive, as his PIM indicates (particularly because Ulf doesn't fight), but he generally plays a smart physical game and makes the opposition pay when necessary.

He is also willing to sacrifice his body and is a shot-blocker supreme.

THE INTANGIBLES

Samuelsson is Hartford's best defenseman, maybe their best player over the last three years. He's a true world-class talent, a dedicated athlete and a character player.

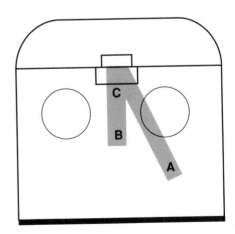

PETER SIDORKIEWICZ

Yrs. of NHL service: 1
Born: Dabrown Bialostocka, Poland; June 29, 1963
Position: Goaltender
Height: 5-9
Weight: 180
Uniform no.: 30
Catches: left

Career statistics:

GP	MINS	G	SO	AVG	A	PIM
\45	2,695	139	4	3.09	3	0

1988-89 statistics:

GP	MINS	AVG	W	L	T	SO	GA	SA	SAPCT	PIM
44	2,635	3.03	22	18	4	4	133	1,207	.890	0

LAST SEASON

He finished fourth league-wide in shutouts in his first full NHL season.

THE PHYSICAL GAME

Sidorkiewicz plays a standup style that makes the most of his less-than-great size. He stays on his feet and moves from the net to the top of the crease (and beyond when necessary) to challenge the shooter, and he also leaves the net to flag down loose pucks and set them up for the defense (though he's not a real stickhandler).

On plays around the net, Peter goes to a butterfly style. He recovers his stance fairly quickly, but overall isn't a flashy, speedy goaltender. He'll succeed more on angle play than he will reflex play, and can thus be beaten with tips and re-directed pucks.

Like many goaltenders, he tends to cheat to his stick side. That, and his tendency to not completely square himself to the puck, make him more vulnerable to his left side than his right.

THE MENTAL GAME

While he generally plays a controlled, unemotional game, Peter can have trouble with his confidence and concentration. That trouble will manifest itself in his failing to cut the angle properly, as well as in the tendency to struggle throughout a game.

He otherwise has fairly good concentration and anticipation.

THE INTANGIBLES

As with several other Whalers, Sidorkiewicz had a relatively impressive rookie year. He has a track record of success at the junior and minor league levels, but he'll still have to contend with Mike Liut and Kay Whitmore in competing for the Whalers number one goalie spot.

DAVE TIPPETT

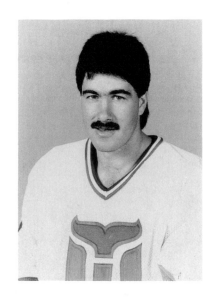

Yrs. of NHL service: 5
Born: Moosomin, Sask., Canada; August 25, 1961
Position: Left wing/center
Height: 5-10
Weight: 180
Uniform no.: 15
Shoots: left

Career statistics:

GP	G	A	TP	PIM
417	67	101	168	149

1988-89 statistics:

GP	G	A	TP	+/-	PIM	PP	SH	GW	GT	S	PCT
80	17	24	41	-6	45	1	2	1	0	165	10.3

LAST SEASON

Tippett played 80 games for the fifth straight season, recording career marks in all point totals. He led the club in shorthanded goals.

THE FINESSE GAME

Tippett's hallmarks as a player are his excellent anticipation and hockey sense. Dave sees the ice very well and he uses his vision and anticipation to stay with his check excellently. That sense also makes him an excellent penalty killer, his anticipation makes his average skating better. He doesn't have a lot of speed or agility, but Tippett has a strong and steady pace that gets him where he's going.

His offensive prowess has improved, making his defense even more valuable; Tippett is cashing in more and more on the loose pucks and opportunities his checking creates.

Still, he doesn't have exceptional stick skills. He'll have to make his plays on smarts and anticipation and not fancy skating or passing. He moves the puck well to his teammates because of his vision and he'll have to get his own goals from around the crease on rebounds and junk shots.

THE PHYSICAL GAME

Unlike some other checking forwards, Tippett isn't exceptionally physical; he won't wear down the opposition. Dave is strong enough to hold the opposition out of the play when necessary, and his arm and hand strength are good enough to wrestle the puck away from the opposition.

What Tippett does best is use his body correctly along the boards. He takes the body well against the opposition, and he does so smartly, so as not to hurt the club via penalties.

THE INTANGIBLES

Tippett doesn't do anything exceptionally well — except succeed. He's a great example of the whole being greater than the sum of its parts. He was used last season as the defensive anchor while on a line with Ray Ferraro and Jody Hull.

He has tremendous determination and work ethic, and he's a true leader for Hartford.

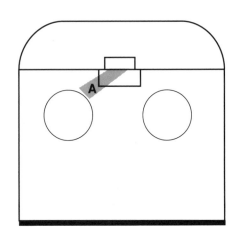

PAT VERBEEK

Yrs. of NHL service: 6
Born: Sarnia, Ontario, Canada; May 24, 1964
Position: Right wing
Height: 5-9
Weight: 195
Uniform no.: 16
Shoots: right

Career statistics:

GP	G	A	TP	PIM
463	170	151	321	943

1988-89 statistics:

GP	G	A	TP	+/-	PIM	PP	SH	GW	GT	S	PCT
77	26	21	47	-18	189	9	0	1	0	175	14.9

LAST SEASON

Goal total was three-year low; assist and point totals four-year lows. His plus/minus was the team's third-worst and his three games missed (benchings) means that Verbeek still has not played a complete NHL season.

THE FINESSE GAME

All the things that clicked for Pat Verbeek in 1987-88 to make him an offensive threat — and forced observers to say "How did he do that?" — were absent last year, forcing the question, "Where did it all go?"

Where Verbeek had previously learned to be in the right place at the right time — and thus become a goal scorer by going to where the puck was going to be — Pat last year was a stride early or late. Where he scored off scrambles in front by picking up rebounds in 87-88 (and even 86-87), now the opposing defensemen were getting to those loose pucks.

His best finesse strength now is his ability to plant himself in the crease, and he's demonstrated the hand skills for traffic work, but those abilities went for naught last year.

Verbeek skates strongly and is tough to dislodge from the puck, but he's not real good at carrying it; look for him to dish off and head to the net as his big-bang style is accurately reflected in his limited playmaking ability. His up-ice forays benefit from the law of inertia that says a body in motion tends to stay in motion, but he doesn't have breakaway speed.

THE PHYSICAL GAME

This is an area that should be a strength, given Verbeek's tools. He has great strength in his fire-hydrant body, and he can be a heavy checker along the boards — he can hurt people when he hits them. He doesn't have exceptional balance, so Pat's body-crunching style may work against him ocassionally. Still, he plants himself well enough to post-up in front of the opposing goal.

THE INTANGIBLES

Last year we admitted we were wrong in our assessment of Verbeek and his abilities, even going so far as to say he might deserve mention with the Rick Tocchets and Cam Neelys of the NHL.

But based on his uninspired performance this past season, Verbeek has proven us wrong again. A contract dispute in pre-season led to his late arrival in training camp, and Verbeek never got off the ground. He failed to use his physical skills to the best of his ability, and never seemed to reach the levels of intensity or determination he had climbed in the previous seasons.

We said last year that Verbeek and his teammates must work to keep the Devils improving. Pat's less-than-spectacular performance is one big reason the Devils failed to do so in 1988-89.

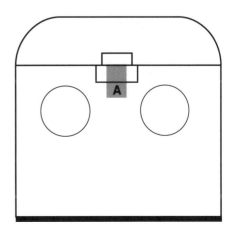

SCOTT YOUNG

Yrs. of NHL service: 1
Born: Clinton, Mass., USA; October 1, 1967
Position: Right wing/defense
Height: 6-0
Weight: 190
Uniform no.: 27
Shoots: right

Career statistics:

GP	G	A	TP	PIM
83	19	40	59	29

1988-89 statistics:

GP	G	A	TP	+/-	PIM	PP	SH	GW	GT	S	PCT
76	19	40	59	-21	27	6	0	2	0	203	9.4

LAST SEASON

Young's first full NHL campaign. He finished fourth in points, second in shots on goal and next to last in plus/minus (worst among forwards).

THE FINESSE GAME

Young is a good-to-very-good skater, strong in all skating categories. He has balance and foot speed, and those assets make him an agile skater with good lateral movement (especially important when he's shifted back to defense), and he also has strength — that gives him speed and acceleration ability (important as a forward).

Scott has pretty good hockey sense, and he knows what to do with the puck and his body. He gets into position to score fairly well, and he also moves the puck very well to his teammates. He passes well across the spectrum (feathered passes or hard ones), and his good hands extend to his ability to carry the puck while skating at top speed.

He's got a good shot that's accurate and released quickly, and he has the ability to get his shot off while checked or in motion.

His history is that of a sound and willing defensive player, and while his shifting in and out of the lineup — and from offense to defense — must bear some responsibility for his woeful plus/minus, Young must learn to better judge NHL speed (when making passes from his own zone — he can be hurried into mistakes) and to make better decisions in his passes and his challenges from the point.

THE PHYSICAL GAME

Young has good — not great — size and strength for the NHL, but while they can be improved he certainly uses what he has willingly. He's not a big banger, but Scott takes the body well and uses his body to gain position in the traffic areas (thus making his finesse abilities more valuable). He could finish his takeouts a little better when he's playing defense.

He drives the net on offense and hits when he can, and Scott will also sacrifice his body by blocking shots. Improved strength would make it more difficult for the opposition to strip him of the puck by just lifting his stick.

THE INTANGIBLES

All in all, not a bad debut. Young has a lot of talent, but the Whalers must decide how they want to use that talent. He's already a good power play player (because of his skills and smarts), and Young will work hard to improve himself in all areas. He has an excellent attitude and comes to play each night.

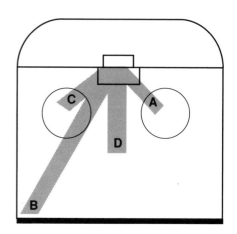

LOS ANGELES
KINGS

LINE COMBINATIONS
MIKE KRUSHELNYSKI-WAYNE GRETZKY
MIKE ALLISON
JOHN TONELLI-STEVE KASPER
LUC ROBITAILLE-BERNIE NICHOLLS
DAVE TAYLOR
JAY MILLER-RON DUGUAY
MARTY MCSORLEY

DEFENSE PAIRINGS
STEVE DUCHESNE-TOM LAIDLAW
BRUCE BAUMGARTNER-TIM WATTERS
DEAN KENNEDY

GOALTENDERS
KELLY HRUDEY
GLENN HEALY

OTHER PLAYERS
DALE DEGRAY — Defenseman
JIM FOX — Right wing

POWER PLAY

FIRST UNIT:
LUC ROBITAILLE-BERNIE NICHOLLS
DAVE TAYLOR
STEVE DUCHESNE-WAYNE GRETZKY

SECOND UNIT:
MIKE KRUSHELNYSKI-STEVE KASPER
MIKE ALLISON

TAYLOR sits in the slot, ROBITAILLE is off the right post. NICHOLLS is at the top of the left circle, GRETZKY on the side of the right circle and DUCH-ESNE at the blue line. A NICHOLLS shot is the first choice, with an open ROBITAILLE getting rebounds or tap-ins across the crease.

On the second unit KRUSHELNYSKI controls the play, KASPER is in the left wing corner and ALLISON jams the net. Now-departed DOUG CROSS-MAN would take the second half of the power play, but DUCHESNE will take as much of the two minutes as he can.

Last season Los Angeles' power play was FAIR, scoring 82 goals in 395 opportunities (20.8 percent, 11th overall).

PENALTY KILLING

FIRST UNIT:
RON DUGUAY-WAYNE GRETZKY
TIM WATTERS-DEAN KENNEDY

SECOND UNIT:
STEVE KASPER-MIKE ALLISON
TIM WATTERS-TOM LAIDLAW

Each of the penalty-killing units puts on immediate pressure when the puck is against the boards in order to force turnovers. Both sets of forwards pressure the point, and both sets of defense are less aggressive than the forwards.

Last season Los Angeles' penalty killing was GOOD, allowing 80 goals in 407 shorthanded situations (80.3 percent, 10th overall).

CRUCIAL FACEOFFS
The Kings have several very good faceoff men. KRUSHELNYSKI and KASPER are probably 1 and 1A, and DUGUAY can also win his share.

MIKE ALLISON

Yrs. of NHL service: 9
Born: Fort Frances, Ontario, Canada; March 28, 1961
Position: Right wing/center
Height: 6-1
Weight: 195
Uniform no.: 10
Shoots: right

Career statistics:

GP	G	A	TP	PIM
444	100	155	255	552

1988-89 statistics:

GP	G	A	TP	+/-	PIM	PP	SH	GW	GT	S	PCT
55	14	22	36	7	122	6	0	2	0	71	19.7

LAST SEASON

Assist and point totals were second highest of career, goal total third highest. Was sidelined with knee injury. PIM total was career high, third among forwards.

THE FINESSE GAME

Allison is a below average skater because he has too wide a stride, not much speed and even less agility. In fact, the knee and leg injuries that have hobbled him throughout his career are directly attributable to his stride.

Because it's so wide and his feet are so far apart, his weight is really planted when his feet are on the ice. When he gets hit, he is unable to shift his weight or dance away from the check, and so all the force is absorbed by one knee or the other.

Aside from skating, Mike has a good view of the ice and is a very good forechecker because of that. He pursues the puck well and gets good angles on the puck carrier to force him into a corner and into a poor play. He is also a very good penalty killer for thr same 'angle' reasons.

He is not outstanding as an offensive player but for a checking forward he gets good point production. He sees the game and makes the play necessary to score.

THE PHYSICAL GAME

Despite his injuries, Allison willingly plays a physical game. He is a grinder and a mucker, persistent in his pursuit of the puck. He works the boards and the back of the net well, taking the body to free the puck.

He wins all faceoffs very well, especially the crucial ones.

THE INTANGIBLES

We say "Despite the injuries ... " but Allison is always going to be hurt. He's going to miss 10 games here, three games there.

On and off the ice, Mike is an excellent team man. What he lacks in skill he makes up for in desire and heart, so Mike brings an excellent attitude and work ethic to the Kings.

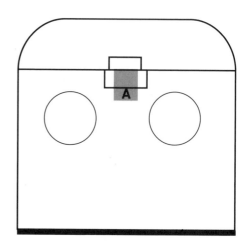

KEN BAUMGARTNER

Yrs. of NHL service: 2
Born: Flin Flon, Manitoba, Canada; March 11, 1966
Position: Defenseman
Height: 6-1
Weight: 200
Uniform no.: 22
Shoots: left

Career statistics:

GP	G	A	TP	PIM
79	3	6	9	475

1988-89 statistics:

GP	G	A	TP	+/-	PIM	PP	SH	GW	GT	S	PCT
49	1	3	4	-9	286	0	0	0	0	15	6.7

LAST SEASON

Finished third on the club in PIM total, first among defensemen. He shuttled between Los Angeles and New Haven of the American Hockey League, and was also sidelined with pneumonia.

THE FINESSE GAME

Baumgartner is below average in his finesse skills. He lacks the agility and turning ability (particularly to his right) necessary to be a consistent NHL defenseman. Because of that, any lateral movement or fake is going to put him out of position. He's going to have trouble with any kind of speed attack, and he's going to take a lot of penalties because he has to foul the opposition.

Ken does not anticipate or read the rush well. On a 3-on-1 or 4-on-2 with a late man, Baumgartner almost always commits totally to the puck carrier.

His passing and shooting skills are as marginal as his skating and vision, so his offensive contributions are going to be minimal. Defensively, he *must* make the simple up-the-boards play to be successful.

THE PHYSICAL GAME

Ken is a very tough kid, and he tries to play the enforcer role. He has good strength and will hit anyone he can lay into, and Baumgartner is a more than willing fighter; he throws his fists pretty well. He clears the front of the net fairly well, but he lacks the concentration necessary to constantly cover the opposing forward camped there.

He is, however, prone to taking the extra penalty through being ultra-aggressive.

THE INTANGIBLES

Baumgartner needs to significantly upgrade his skills, especially his skating, if he wants to be a full-time NHLer. His presence is not essential, because the Kings have Jay Miller and Marty McSorley available, but a club can always use a mean defenseman.

He's not intimidated by his surroundings, a good example of which is the following: when the Kings played the Rangers, Ken went out of his way to run Guy Lafleur at every opportunity.

That says something about Baumgartner's attitude toward the opposition.

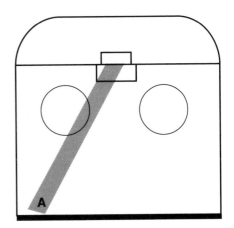

171

DALE DEGRAY

Yrs. of NHL service: 2
Born: Oshawa, Ontario, Canada; September 1, 1963
Position: Defenseman
Height: 6-0
Weight: 200
Uniform no.: 24
Shoots: right

Career statistics:

GP	G	A	TP	PIM
147	18	47	65	189

1988-89 statistics:

GP	G	A	TP	+/-	PIM	PP	SH	GW	GT	S	PCT
63	6	22	28	3	97	0	0	1	0	87	6.9

LAST SEASON

Games played, assist, point and PIM totals were career highs. He finished second in scoring among Kings' defenders.

THE FINESSE GAME

Degray is a talented skater, fairly mobile on his feet and possessing good speed and quickness. He's able to put that skating skill to work offensively by containing the point well at the blue line and by charging the net for shots.

He has good ice vision and looks to move the puck quickly from the point, and he has good hands for making passes. His quickness allows him to avoid checking at the blue line.

He has a great slap shot from the point, and Degray should use it more.

He plays a positional defensive game, reading the rush toward him and forcing it wide well. Degray is good in his transitions and rapidly turns the play around.

THE PHYSICAL GAME

Degray has good size and he's not afraid to use it. He takes the body well along the boards to force the opposition out of the play, and he has great strength to tie up the opposition in front of the net or muscle a forward off the puck in the corner.

He is also in great physical condition.

THE INTANGIBLES

Dale is a very upbeat person, and is very good in the locker room because of his positive attitude. He plays every night as hard as he can play, and playing regularly brings out his confidence. He's a hard worker and should do nothing but improve.

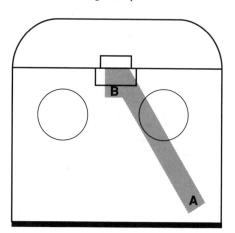

STEVE DUCHESNE

Yrs. of NHL service: 3
Born: Sept-Iles, Quebec, Canada; June 30, 1965
Position: Defenseman
Height: 5-11
Weight: 195
Uniform no.: 28
Shoots: left

Career statistics:

GP	G	A	TP	PIM
225	54	114	168	275

1988-89 statistics:

GP	G	A	TP	+/-	PIM	PP	SH	GW	GT	S	PCT
79	25	50	75	31	92	8	5	2	0	215	11.6

LAST SEASON

Games played and all point totals were career highs. Finished fourth on club in scoring (second among NHL defenders), leading defense in points, power play goals, shots on goal (fourth on the team) and games played. His plus/minus was the team's best.

THE FINESSE GAME

Duchesne is a very talented finesse player in most every finesse category. He's a good skater with very good speed, and he exploits that skating skill by joining the play as a fourth attacker whenever possible. He has the quickness to jump into holes and contain the point well or charge the slot for a shot (which he does whenever possible), and his skating also gets him back into defensive position.

He challenges the puck at the defensive blue line, and Steve combines his skating with his puck-carrying ability to be a fine rushing defenseman. He handles the puck well at top speed, making and accepting passes very well (he excels at controlling bouncing pucks).

Another key to his offensive success is his ability to keep his head up when making plays. He sees the open man very well at both ends of the ice, and he also sees challenging opponents at the offensive blue line — he'll skate around sliding shot-blockers, for example.

He has an excellent shot from the point, a strong, low slap shot that powers its way through traffic. He also shoots off the pass very well. When he comes off the point he goes high glove with his wrist shot. He knows when to shoot to score and when to shoot for rebounds and deflections.

All his skills make him a specialty teams regular.

THE PHYSICAL GAME

Where previously Duchesne was an underwhelming physical player, he's progressed to adequate. His strength has improved, so his corner and crease game is slightly better, and Steve has also improved his positional awareness in front of his goalie, but he's still going to be paired with a strong, stay-at-home defender.

THE INTANGIBLES

For a guy with his tools, and with Wayne Gretzky ahead of him, Duchesne should have done better offensively than he did last season. Mind you, we're not complaining; he's clearly the Kings' most talented defender. A second season of teaming with the Great One on the power play (combined with Duchesne's strong work ethic) should further improve Duchesne's numbers.

But for a player who went undrafted, Steve's success is just fine.

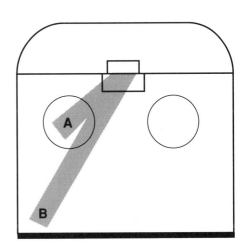

RON DUGUAY

Yrs. of NHL service: 12
Born: Sudbury, Ontario, Canada; July 6, 1957
Position: Right wing/center
Height: 6-2
Weight: 200
Uniform no.: 44
Shoots: right

Career statistics:

GP	G	A	TP	PIM
864	274	346	620	582

1988-89 statistics:

GP	G	A	TP	+/-	PIM	PP	SH	GW	GT	S	PCT
70	7	17	24	23	48	0	0	0	0	80	8.8

LAST SEASON

Missed time with a concussion. Plus/minus was second best among forwards.

THE FINESSE GAME

Even with a dozen years of NHL service, Ron remains a very good skater. He doesn't have great fluidity to his motion (never has), but he's a strong skater with good balance and a surprising amount of quickness for a bigger man. His good foot speed combines with his balance to give him the ability to change direction well, and that skill meshes with his skating strength to make him a good forechecker and penalty killer.

His puck-handling skills do not match his speed, so he's better at getting rid of the puck than he is at receiving it while at full speed. Because he sees the ice fairly well, he'll do his best to get the puck to a teammate. He doesn't, however, possess exceptional anticipation ability— so he won't use his passing to create an opening. Essentially, he needs an open teammate to call for the puck.

Duguay's big offensive weapon has been his slap shot, but his hands have lost much of their sting. He can still score with the blast off the wing occasionally, but most of his scoring is going to be done opportunistically — loose pucks in front of the net.

THE PHYSICAL GAME

Though always blessed with excellent size and strength, Ron's consistent use of those assets has been questionable throughout his career. His balance and strength on his skates would make him an excellent boards-and-corners player, but Duguay does more pushing and shoving than he does hitting.

He's generally willing to take his lumps, and he's a valuable player because he can play tough without taking penalties. He'll fight when sufficiently pro-voked (and he is a good fighter) and his upper body strength and overall balance make him a good faceoff man.

THE INTANGIBLES

What you see with Ron is what you're going to get. His 40-goal days are gone, but he still contributes as a checking forward. Additionally, his size and strength make him something of a counter against some of the Division's bigger centers and scorers. Just don't expect much offensively.

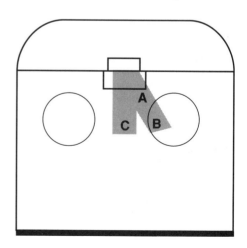

JIM FOX

Yrs. of NHL service: 8
Born: Coniston, Ontario, Canada; May 18, 1960
Position: Right wing
Height: 5-8
Weight: 183
Uniform no.: 19
Shoots: right

Career statistics:

GP	G	A	TP	PIM
567	185	291	477	143

1987-88 statistics:

GP	G	A	TP	+/-	PIM	PP	SH	GW	GT	S	PCT
68	16	35	51	-7	18	2	0	1	0	120	13.3

LAST SEASON

Missed all of the 1988-89 season with a knee injury and resulting surgery.

THE FINESSE GAME

The hallmarks of Fox's game are quickness and smarts. In a race around the rink many players would beat Jimmy to the finish line. But set Points A and B 30 feet apart and few players would beat him to the finish. His low center of gravity gives him excellent balance, so he can remain upright after taking hits and is very difficult to remove from the puck.

His quickness gets him to many loose pucks, and that's where his smarts come in. Jim is very smart and he sees the game especially well offensively. That ability (along with his selflessness) combines with his hand skill to make him a very good playmaker — regardless of the numbers. He'll get the pass to a teammate through traffic or lead him into the openings.

Jim handles the puck well himself, if a little predictably (he screeches to a halt just after he crosses the offensive blue line so the defense races past him). He is one player who definitely *could* make a play to save his life. His hand and vision skills make him a power-play regular, and he'd be a regular on that unit with any NHL team.

He has an accurate wrist shot, one released very quickly, and will beat goalies from in close. He can, on occasion, surprise them with longer drives as well, but Fox is more adept in tight.

THE PHYSICAL GAME

Fox takes his licks offensively, but he is not a tough or aggressive player. He goes to the traffic areas and willingly takes a pounding, but he initiates almost no contact. That's bad when he loses the puck.

His defense suffers too, for while he knows his defensive role Jim is not physical enough and not ready to be physical enough to complete his defensive assignment.

THE INTANGIBLES

This report is untouched from last season, just as Fox's career is on hold because of his knee injury. His recovery from that is THE intangible. He's an excellent competitor and a top team guy but his game is in a state of limbo right now.

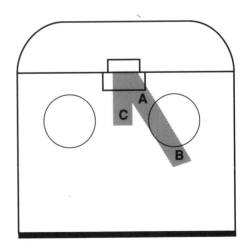

MARIO GOSSELIN

Yrs. of NHL service: 5
Born: Thetford Mines, Quebec, Canada; June 15, 1963
Position: Goaltender
Height: 5-8
Weight: 165
Uniform no.: 33
Catches: left

Career statistics:

GP	MINS	G	SO	AVG	A	PIM
192	10,525	644	6	3.67	8	40

1988-89 statistics:

GP	MINS	AVG	W	L	T	SO	GA	SA	SAPCT	PIM
39	2,064	4.24	11	19	3	0	146	1,105	.868	6

LAST SEASON

Games-played total was second highest of career. Win total was full season low, goals-against-average career worst. He spent time with Halifax of the American Hockey League.

THE PHYSICAL GAME

Gosselin lives and dies with his reflexes. Because of his fast hands and faster feet (his left foot in particular) he'll get to almost every puck he can see.

He uses his speed to great effect on scrambles in close to the net, and though he flops to the ice constantly his balance helps him regain his footing — so he can fling himself at the next shot. The problem, however, is that his butterfly style leaves the top of the net open for rebounds — of which there are plenty.

Mario is a good skater and he moves well in and out of the net to counter screens. He tracks down loose pucks, but doesn't help himself with puck movement; he just leaves the puck for his defense.

Because he doesn't conserve energy by cutting down the angle and just letting the puck hit him, Gosselin suffers fatigue both within games and throughout the season.

THE MENTAL GAME

Gosselin has good concentration skills, and he can certainly raise the level of his game to make big saves. But he's been largely unable to do that with any consistency.

His concentration within a game is good, especially as he tracks the puck near the net, and he's easygoing in that bad goals or games don't stay with him.

THE INTANGIBLES

After five seasons, Mario's goose may be cooked in Quebec. The Nordiques are whispered to be considering Ron Tugnutt as their main man, and they're looking for suitable backup to him. Additionally, bear in mind that Michel Bergeron is returning as coach and he and Gosselin have had their tiffs in the past about Gosselin's playing time.

Mario has the talent to be something more than just an average NHL goalie, but time may no longer be on his side.

176

WAYNE GRETZKY

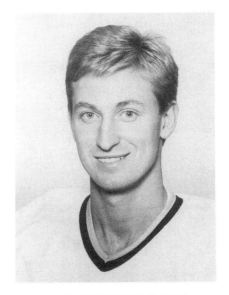

Yrs. of NHL service: 11
Born: Brantford, Ontario, Canada; January 26, 1961
Position: Center
Height: 6-0
Weight: 170
Uniform no.: 99
Shoots: left

Career statistics:

GP	G	A	TP	PIM
774	637	1,200	1,837	349

1988-89 statistics:

GP	G	A	TP	+/-	PIM	PP	SH	GW	GT	S	PCT
78	54	114	168	15	26	11	5	5	2	303	17.8

LAST SEASON

Acquired from Edmonton (along with Mike Krushelnyski and Marty McSorley) on August 9, 1988 in exchange for Jimmy Carson, Martin Gelinas, draft picks and cash. He finished second in NHL scoring for second consecutive season (fourth in goals, second in assists). He led club in assists and points, was second in goals, power play goals and SOG total (sixth in NHL in last category). Plus/minus was third best among club's forwards.

THE FINESSE GAME

Wayne is an excellent skater with good speed and quickness, and exceptional balance; that asset gives him excellent agility and lateral movement.

His anticipation and hockey sense are extraordinary, almost computer-like in his ability to see two and three plays ahead and then factor in his teammates' possible plays and the opposition's possible responses before choosing the best course of action.

His stick skills match his foot and brain skills. He uses his entire team better than anyone in the world, and his touch as a passer is remarkable: by all claim, he's never broken a stick in the NHL. He'll put the puck anywhere at anytime, regardless of circumstance.

His passing skills are obviously keyed by his hockey sense, but Gretzky's puckhandling also serves to strengthen his passing. He creates openings by hypnotizing defenders with the puck. Even after 10 years, defensemen still fall for his tricks and chase him all over the ice, leaving openings for his teammates.

Finally, his shooting is exceptional. Wayne puts the puck anywhere he wants from anywhere he wants, making the puck rise or sink depending upon how he releases it (and he exploits the top of the net like no one else in the NHL). He does, however, think too much about his options on breakaways, instead of just reacting to openings.

The great myth of the Great One's performances is that he doesn't play defense. Wrong. Critics are confusing physical play with defense. He is always around the puck in all three zones, and his presence on the ice immediately forces the opposition to think defensively. What better defense is there?

THE PHYSICAL GAME

The physical game is not Gretzky's game, and there's no need for it to be. In fact, he'd most likely be ineffective if he did play physically because he lacks the innate strength necessary.

That is not to say that Wayne won't play physically or is afraid of hits. He plays in the high traffic areas all the time, but he uses his balance and anticipation to avoid the hits that would do the damage. If someone does get a piece of him, Wayne is able to lean away from the hit to avoid much of its impact; again, balance.

THE INTANGIBLES

Only one player could have energized the Los Angeles Kings in particular — and the hockey world in general — and that's Gretzky. And, with all due respect, he may be the player most responsible for Calgary's Stanley Cup win.

Anyway, he is a leader *nonpareil* because of his heart, dedication and work ethic — second to none in the NHL. And if we have to win one game, the player we most want on our side is Wayne Gretzky.

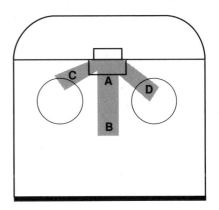

GLENN HEALY

Yrs. of NHL service: 2
Born: Pickering, Ontario, Canada; August 23, 1962
Position: Goaltender
Height: 5-10
Weight: 175
Uniform no.: 35
Catches: left

Career statistics:

GP	MINS	G	SO	AVG	A	PIM
83	4,619	333	1	4.33	3	34

1988-89 statistics:

GP	MINS	AVG	W	L	T	SO	GA	SA	SAPCT	PIM
48	2,699	4.27	25	19	2	0	192	1,509	.872	28

LAST SEASON

Games and minutes played totals were career highs. Tied for fifth in shots-against.

THE PHYSICAL GAME

Healy plays a one-dimensional game, in that he relies almost completely on his reflexes. Like the little girl with the curl, when Glenn's reflexes are on, he can be very good. When they don't work — when his lack of an effective angle game kicks in — he can be rotten.

Though good as a skater (and Healy uses his skating ability to get to many loose pucks — some as far away as the blue line), balance isn't big on Glenn's list of assets. Because of that, he has trouble regaining stance after flopping to the ice. He does move well laterally — across the net from post to post — and his quick feet help him here.

While his fast hands and feet will get him to most any gettable puck, Glenn's big problem is his failure to sufficiently and correctly cut down the shooter's angle. Because of that, he is weak on direct rush attacks — forwards breaking down the wing. He'll allow soft goals to the corners to very average shooters because of this weakness. And, because he hasn't set his angles properly to begin with, Healy has great difficulty finding the net again after one of his flopping forays.

He makes his job more difficult.

THE MENTAL GAME

Glenn has a very strong mental outlook. He's a very tough competitor; he puts bad games behind him and comes ready to play the next night. He doesn't maintain his concentration as well throughout games, and one reason is because he hasn't fully developed the ability to anticipate plays. But that's consistent with his reflex game — no need to anticipate when his hands and feet can bail him out.

Though his concentration and preparation are good in all instances, the result can sometimes be flawed because Glen is a streaky goalie, the kind who can get hot for a few games, but can get cold too. When he's hot he'll win the game regardless of how many shots he faces; when he's cold he'll lose the game regardless of how few shots he faces. And when he's cold he's got to get the hook.

THE INTANGIBLES

He spent most of the season in the number one role, and Healy showed well there, especially considering that he faced an average of more shots-on-goal per game (while finishing fifth in SOG faced) than the four goalies who faced more shots than he.

But to what effect? Despite his early-season heroics, Healy is now number two to Kelly Hrudey. And at 27 years old, with Hobey Baker winner Robb Stauber in the wings, Healy could — sooner rather than later — find himself number three. Or number one on the farm team.

KELLY HRUDEY

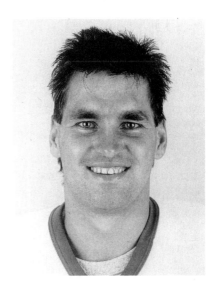

Yrs. of NHL service: 6
Born: Edmonton, Alberta, Canada; January 13, 1961
Position: Goaltender
Height: 5-10
Weight: 180
Uniform no.: 32
Catches: left

Career statistics:

GP	MINS	G	SO	AVG	A	PIM
257	14,592	834	7	3.43	10	107

1988-89 statistics:

GP	MINS	AVG	W	L	T	SO	GA	SA	SAPCT	PIM
66	3,774	3.66	28	28	5	1	230	1,948	.880	19

LAST SEASON

Acquired from the New York Islanders late in the season in exchange for Mark Fitzpatrick, Wayne McBean and Doug Crossman. Games and minutes played totals were career highs, and he led all goalies in those categories, as well as in shots-against. He finished fifth in the NHL in wins.

THE PHYSICAL GAME

Speed and brains are the keys to Kelly Hrudey's game. He is an excellent standup goaltender who backs up superb angle and positioning play with lightning-fast reflexes.

Because of his exceptionally fast hands and feet, Hrudey will not let pucks blow past him. He'll make the first save on any shot, so tip-ins or deflections are the keys to beating him. Even so, rare is the puck that Hrudey won't at least get a piece of.

He positions himself very well in the net and sees the puck better than most. He makes the spectacular save, he makes the routine save and he has tremendous ability on the scrambles in front of the net because of his vision and reflexes.

Hrudey has excellent balance on his feet and regains his stance almost instantaneously. He controls the puck well after a save, whether that means holding it for a faceoff or directing it harmlessly to the corner.

Hrudey likes to cheat a bit on the glove side, but will come back and take the opening away. He has good puck handling skills and skates well, but doesn't take many chances outside the net and will not wander astray.

THE MENTAL GAME

Superb concentration is a hallmark of Hrudey's game, as is his ability to bring that concentration to bear night after night. Kelly is mentally tough, able to bounce back from a bad goal and to make yet another game saving-save when necessary.

He rarely makes the mental mistake to beat himself, as in being unprepared to play. He knows the League's shooters and the areas where they are most dangerous and keeps a mental book of that night's opposition in order to prepare for a game.

THE INTANGIBLES

Kelly is one of the few goalies in the NHL who can win games by himself; he's demonstrated that for several seasons. That makes the Kings dangerous any time against anyone, and much of Los Angeles' future success will rest on Hrudey's shoulders — one of the League's outstanding goaltenders.

STEVE KASPER

Yrs. of NHL service: 8
Born: Montreal, Quebec, Canada; September 28, 1961
Position: Center
Height: 5-8
Weight: 170
Uniform no.: 11
Shoots: left

Career statistics:

GP	G	A	TP	PIM
593	144	235	379	464

1988-89 statistics:

GP	G	A	TP	+/-	PIM	PP	SH	GW	GT	S	PCT
78	19	31	50	-2	63	5	2	2	0	130	14.6

LAST SEASON

Acquired from Boston in mid-season in exchange for Bobby Carpenter. Games played and goal totals were three-season lows.

THE FINESSE GAME

Kasper's skills are of the quiet variety, in that nothing he does leaps out at you on first notice. He's a fine skater with average speed and quickness, but his biggest skating strength is his stamina; he can just go and go and go. That's important for him in his role as a checking forward.

The skills in Kasper's game that do demand attention are his ice vision and anticipation, both of which are excellent. He uses them in checking to keep himself between the man and the puck, and in breaking up forming plays, two reasons he is an excellent penalty killer. Kasper always know where he is on the ice in relation to his man, the puck and the net.

Offensively, Steve can put that vision and sense to work with his teammates. He is a good stickhandler and controls the puck well, moving the puck smoothly to his wingers and the point men.

Even with last year's offensive success — and including his previous 20-goal seasons — Kasper is a little difficult to figure as a scorer. He doesn't seem to take full advantage of the opportunities he gets, primarily because he is so preoccupied with his defense. He has a good, hard wrist shot from the slot, as well as an NHL-caliber slap shot.

Kasper is also a very strong faceoff man and he's one of the guys the opposition is most likely to see on the ice for those crucial draws in the Kings' zone late in the game.

THE PHYSICAL GAME

Pure effort and conditioning are the keys to Kasper's game, the physical reasons he is able to work so efficiently so often against the League's top stars.

He certainly doesn't have great size but that's okay, because Kasper plays the game with his head more than his body. He can hit but is not punishing when he does so, and rare are the times that he hits anyway.

He does have good strength that he puts to use when he takes his man out of the play, holding him for that extra second necessary to disrupt the offense's rhythm.

Kasper has the stamina and the conditioning to double-shift if need be, and trying to run him ragged won't work.

THE INTANGIBLES

Though he contributes at the offensive end, Kasper's great value is the scoring he prevents. He truly enjoys playing defensively and checking the opposition's stars, and he takes great pride in doing so.

And don't be fooled by that minus-1. For the job Kasper does against the Gilmours, Carsons, Savards and Lemieuxs of the NHL, to be *only* minus-1 is to really be *at least* plus-20.

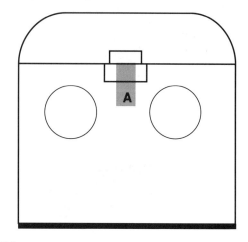

DEAN KENNEDY

Yrs. of NHL service: 6
Born: Redvers, Sask., Canada; January 18, 1963
Position: Defenseman
Height: 6-2
Weight: 203
Uniform no.: 6
Shoots: right

Career statistics:

GP	G	A	TP	PIM
361	13	63	76	631

1988-89 statistics:

GP	G	A	TP	+/-	PIM	PP	SH	GW	GT	S	PCT
67	3	11	14	17	103	0	0	1	0	45	6.7

LAST SEASON

Traded to, then reacquired from, the New York Rangers. He missed time with a concussion and was also demoted to the American Hockey League.

THE FINESSE GAME

Kennedy is not overly gifted in the finesse areas. He's no betterthan average as a skater, primarily because his agility (quickness plus balance) is very questionable. Because of his poor lateral movement, Dean is very prone to forwards faking one way and heading the other. When that happens he has no choice but to take penalties.

He could circumvent these negatives if gifted with above-average hockey sense, vision or anticipation. But Dean is not so gifted, so his play *must* be the simple one. Fortunately for him, his play is most often characterized as such. As long as Dean sticks with the up-the-boards-and-out pass and doesn't look to make the fancy glamorous passes some of his teammates make, he'll function well (note the plus/minus).

He's essentially a throw-in on offense, though Kennedy will work to contain the puck at the point. He follows the play up-ice but his role is to be the safety valve — the one man back when necessary. That fact that he hardly shoots the puck indicates how little he is concerned with offense.When he does shoot, he fires a slap shot from the point that is no better than average in strength, speed or accuracy.

THE PHYSICAL GAME

Dean is a very physical player and this is the strength of his game. He'll try to thwart the play at the Kings blue line by standing up the puck carrier, he ties up the opposition in front of the Kings net, and Kennedy will outmuscle many players because of good upper body strength. He's a good body checker who makes the opposition pay for shots on goal or chances

at the King net, and Dean has to play that way to succeed.

THE INTANGIBLES

To have come through a season like last season, where he was almost literally abandoned by two teams, requires strong character and determination. That's what Kennedy has, traits physicalized (for example) by his off-ice work ethic; Dean works hard to be in his best condition.

To be successful in the NHL, Kennedy need only play alertly and aggressively while staying within his limitations. When he loses that focus, he is a very marginal NHLer.

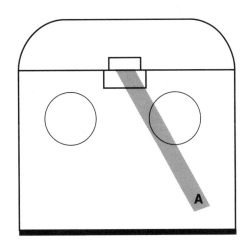

MIKE KRUSHELNYSKI

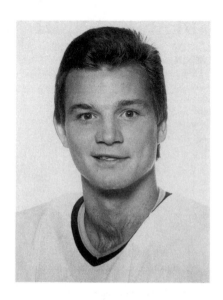

Yrs. of NHL service: 8
Born: Montreal, Quebec, Canada; April 27, 1960
Position: Left wing/center
Height: 6-2
Weight: 200
Uniform no.: 26
Shoots: left

Career statistics:

GP	G	A	TP	PIM
530	172	232	404	423

1988-89 statistics:

GP	G	A	TP	+/-	PIM	PP	SH	GW	GT	S	PCT
78	26	36	62	9	110	5	0	8	1	143	18.2

LAST SEASON

Acquired from Edmonton (along with Wayne Gretzky and Marty McSorley) in August 1988 in exchange for Jimmy Carson, Martin Gelinas, draft picks and cash. Point totals were four-season highs; PIM total career high. He led the club in game winners (seventh in the NHL).

THE FINESSE GAME

Skating is the best of Krushelnyski's skills, one where he ranks as excellent. Mike has a long stride and covers a lot of ground with it, though he doesn't have exceptional speed. He accelerates very well and he puts that asset to work as he bursts down the wing. He is also very balanced on his feet and that makes him very agile; he can take a hit and maintain his composure to make a play. Mike doesn't get the most he can from his skating though, and he can be downright lazy in the offensive zone in terms of forechecking.

Mike's good hands mean good puck control skills. He is an excellent faceoff man and stickhandler and can dance the puck past a defenseman because of his skills and reach (here too his balance helps, giving him the ability to sway out of reach). His good vision and anticipation help him to find the open man and to pass well.

Mike is a good shooter, possessing a hard and accurate wrist shot that he releases quickly and that forces the goaltender to make saves. He is an opportunist and will swoop to the net to pick up a loose puck in an attempt to shovel it home.

THE PHYSICAL GAME

The physical game has never been Krushelnyski's cup of tea, and he prefers to stay out of the high traffic areas in the corners and in front of the net. He will make his plays while being hit (an indication of good concentration) but Krushelnyski doesn't enjoy the physical part of the game.

He uses his reach very well in snaring pucks. He has good strength in his wrists and arms, and that's what powers his shot.

THE INTANGIBLES

Krushelnyski doesn't bring a lot of intensity or emotion to his game, though the added responsibilities he's acquired in Los Angeles certainly force him to be better focused during games.

He has the skills to be an above-average player, but Mike must find the desire to bring those skills to work all the time. What success he accrues, he gains solely through his skills. Otherwise, Krushelnyski could be said to play comfortable — he doesn't push himself as often as he could.

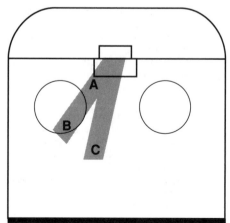

TOM LAIDLAW

Yrs. of NHL service: 9
Born: Brampton, Ontario, Canada; April 15, 1958
Position: Defenseman
Height: 6-1
Weight: 205
Uniform no.: 3
Shoots: left

Career statistics:

GP	G	A	TP	PIM
648	24	131	155	675

1988-89 statistics:

GP	G	A	TP	+/-	PIM	PP	SH	GW	GT	S	PCT
70	3	17	20	30	63	0	0	1	0	31	9.7

LAST SEASON

Assist and point totals were third highest of career. He finished tied for second in plus/minus, and he missed time with a charley horse.

THE FINESSE GAME

Smarts and the intelligence to stay within his limits have forged Laidlaw's NHL success. He's certainly the club's best and most dependable defensive defenseman, and he uses his knowledge of positional play and good play reading ability to earn that ranking.

He won't do anything spectacular; Tom will just see and meet the offensive rush, and then capably force it wide of the net. He isn't a great skater, so he won't do a lot of challenging at either blue line, but his ability to see the play will make his skating better.

He doesn't carry the puck very well, so he makes sure he hardly has to carry the puck at all by making quick and simple passes to his forwards. He will shoot from the point and has developed a tendency to sneak in a stride or two for a wrist shot, but he takes so long to deliver the shot that — considering the results — the effort seems hardly worth while.

THE PHYSICAL GAME

Laidlaw is a very strong player, and he uses his strength to great result in front of the net and in the corners. He plays a consistent physical game at all times and is an agressive (but not necessarily punishing) hitter. He uses his body well to clog up the middle of the ice or to block shots and he will take on anyone in the slot.

THE INTANGIBLES

Laidlaw is a great team guy, with a super upbeat attitude. On top of that, he's highly effective at his defensive job. To be plus-30 on the NHL's 17th-ranked defensive team is just a small indication of Laidlaw's worth.

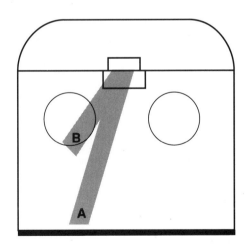

MARTY MCSORLEY

Yrs. of NHL service: 6
Born: Hamilton, Ontario, Canada; May 18, 1963
Position: Defenseman/right wing
Height: 6-2
Weight: 220
Uniform no.: 33
Shoots: right

Career statistics:

GP	G	A	TP	PIM
313	34	57	91	1,236

1988-89 statistics:

GP	G	A	TP	+/-	PIM	PP	SH	GW	GT	S	PCT
66	10	17	27	3	350	2	0	1	0	87	11.5

LAST SEASON

Acquired from Edmonton (along with Wayne Gretzky and Mike Krushelnyski) in August 1988 in exchange for Jimmy Carson, Martin Gelinas, draft picks and cash. Games played total was second highest of McSorley's career, point and PIM total career highs. He led the club in PIM total, finishing in the NHL. He missed three games with a shoulder injury, nine with a knee injury.

THE FINESSE GAME

McSorley is an average skater at the NHL level, making do more with his power and strength than with any speed, quickness or agility. McSorley's skating greatly improved through his association: by playing and practicing with and against the world's best players (when he was with the Oilers), Marty naturally became a better skater.

Marty doesn't handle the puck all that well, and he counters that weakness by not handling the puck except when necessary. When playing defense and moving the puck from the defensive end, rare is the time that he took more than three strides with it.

As a forward he reads the offensive play fairly well, though he is not heavy in the anticipation department. He holds his position fairly well in the offensive zone, but he does have a tendency to wander because he goes on search-and-destroy missions.

THE PHYSICAL GAME

McSorley hits at every opportunity and does so punishingly. He has good strength and will win the battles in the corners and the boards, as well as the front of both nets.

McSorley is a fighter and sees more than his share of action. He is one of those players with a Jekyll-and-Hyde personality, and he can 'click out' (as the vernacular goes) on the ice and go crazy.

THE INTANGIBLES

Marty plays a very emotional game, and that sometimes backfires on him because he can't control his temper. But the key to McSorley's character is that, despite the fact that he is just legitimately happy to be in the NHL, he works constantly at improving his skills. He is one of the NHL's legitimate heavyweights in terms of toughness, and that role is one he willingly embraces as he defends his teammates unfailingly.

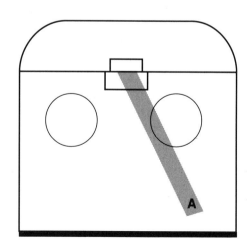

JAY MILLER

Yrs. of NHL service: 4
Born: Wellesley, Mass., USA; July 16, 1960
Position: Left wing
Height: 6-2
Weight: 210
Uniform no.: 29
Shoots: right

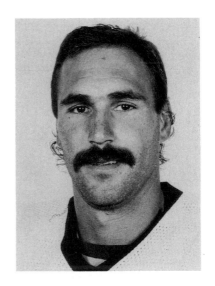

Career statistics:

GP	G	A	TP	PIM
245	18	23	41	989

1988-89 statistics:

GP	G	A	TP	+/-	PIM	PP	SH	GW	GT	S	PCT
66	7	7	14	-9	301	0	0	0	0	30	23.3

LAST SEASON

Acquired from the Bruins in mid-season. Games played and PIM totals were second highest of career. He finished second on the club in PIM total.

THE FINESSE GAME

Miller is an average skater, with no real speed or quickness. He does have good balance, and he puts that balance to work in his physical game. It allows him to generally remain vertical after collisions, and it certainly allows him to plant himself when fighting.

He demonstrates no real ability in handling the puck, whether by carrying it or passing it to teammates, and rarely — if ever — shoots when he is in position to do so. If he's going to make a play, Miller needs plenty of time and space.

Jay will occasionally find himself on a checking line and that's because he has improved his view and understanding of the game around him, a natural consequence of NHL experience. Miller is unable, however, to put that increased understanding to work offensively and probably never will.

Miller rarely, if ever, scores and as such must be in close proximity of the net to take advantage of whatever he can.

THE PHYSICAL GAME

With no pun intended, this is where Miller makes his impact. He makes fairly good use of his body when checking, and his excellent strength and size means he can hurt the opposition when checking — if he can catch them.

More consistent hitting, combined with skating instruction to further improve his balance after he hits, would gain Miller more ice time. If he could catch those enemy skaters, Miller would be more valuable, to say nothing of less one-dimensional.

Miller is also an enforcer, plain and simple with no disguise. When the going gets rough, he is used on search and destroy missions against the other team's tough guys. Miller's willingness is an asset for him and the team, keeping more talented players on the ice and out of the penalty box.

Jay's size, strength and balance make him a good fighter, one of the best and most feared in the NHL. It is also that combination of physical skills that gains him some room in which to operate on the ice.

THE INTANGIBLES

Miller plays a robust style (not dirty, because he doesn't use his stick and he doesn't bully smaller players), but his role will continue to be as a role player, unless he can improve his skills enough to merit a regular shift. Otherwise he'll remain an enforcer and a fourth-line player.

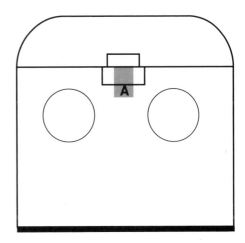

BERNIE NICHOLLS

Yrs. of NHL service: 8
Born: Haliburton, Ontario, Canada; June 24, 1961
Position: Center
Height: 6-0
Weight: 185
Uniform no.: 9
Shoots: right

Career statistics:

GP	G	A	TP	PIM
555	300	383	683	699

1988-89 statistics:

GP	G	A	TP	+/-	PIM	PP	SH	GW	GT	S	PCT
79	70	80	150	30	96	21	8	6	0	385	18.2

LAST SEASON

Finished fourth among NHL scorers with career highs in all point categories. He was second in the NHL in goals (led club), fourth in assists (second on club), power play goals (led club) and shorthanded goals (led club), and second in SOG total (led club). He was second on the club in game winners and tied for second in plus/minus. Games played total was second highest of career.

THE FINESSE GAME

For all his finesse skill, Nicholls is not an exceptional skater. If he was judged just on his touch of quickness and good balance, he wouldn't be expected to score 50 points, let alone 150. But because he has such high levels of anticipation and hockey sense — and the other physical finesse skills necessary to utilize that anticipation and sense — Nicholls leaps from ordinary to extraordinary.

Despite the fact that he doesn't pursue the puck well, Nicholls reads the offensive zone almost as well as teammate Wayne Gretzky. He picks off passes, takes the puck off the boards and gets into scoring position exceptionally well.

Now add his superior hand skills, and you begin to see how Nicholls succeeds. He's very patient with the puck along the boards, getting the puck under control before making a play, and can slip the puck through the smallest opening to a teammate.

His puckhandling is excellent. His favorite play is to fake his slap shot (a shot the defense *must* respect) and then deke to his forehand. That slap shot is an excellent one, among the League's best, and Bernie makes it better by being an excellent one-touch shooter. One reason for last season's phenomenal goal-scoring was his SOG total: in 1987-88 he took 236 SOG; last season, 385 — an increase of more than 50 percent.

All his talents make him not just a specialty teams regular, but a specialty teams star.

THE PHYSICAL GAME

Nicholls is extremely strong on the puck, so don't try the ol' stick-lifting trick; it won't work. That strength and balance combine to make him an exceptional traffic player, and he not only accepts checks and the physical game, but initiates contact as well. That hitting helps get him into the game.

His big, strong hands power his wrist shot and help him win faceoffs, and his wiry strength complements his size.

THE INTANGIBLES

We said last year that Nicholls was the team's top player — so sue us for the post-book deadline Gretzky trade. Nevertheless, though frequently overlooked (both because of the Kings' formerly mediocre performances and because of his playing on the left coast), Nicholls is among the NHL's very best players.

Now he's not necessarily a 150-point scorer, but 50-60 goals and a like number of assists is never out of the question for Nicholls. He's a great competitor who loves the pressure to perform, and that's no small reason why we think he can approach last season's success.

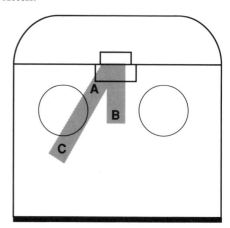

186

LUC ROBITAILLE

Yrs. of NHL service: 3
Born: Montreal, Quebec, Canada; February 17, 1966
Position: Left wing
Height: 6-1
Weight: 190
Uniform no.: 20
Shoots: left

Career statistics:

GP	G	A	TP	PIM
237	144	149	293	175

1988-89 statistics:

GP	G	A	TP	+/-	PIM	PP	SH	GW	GT	S	PCT
78	46	52	98	5	65	10	0	4	0	237	19.4

LAST SEASON

Games played total was lowest of career. He finished third on club in goals, assists, points, power play goals and SOG total.

THE FINESSE GAME

Like all great scorers, Robitaille possesses the ability to get into scoring position and the shot to make that sense count. Luc reads the ice very well, and he uses that anticipation (more so than his skating) to get into position. His ability to create openings or to slip into holes makes him very dangerous away from the puck, and he combines his sense and hand skills with good ice vision to make or receive his passes well.

Robitaille has great hands, carrying the puck well and able to make plays while at most speeds. His puckhandling ability makes him a good 1-on-1 player, but he's far better at getting into scoring position for a shot than he is at deking through an entire team. He is very strong on the puck and is not easily stripped of it; as with teammate Bernie Nicholls, the stick-lifting trick won't work on Luc.

His best finesse skill is his shot — by far. Luc has great hands in front of the net and a very quick stick, and his touch is demonstrated by his ability to score up high and between the goaltender's legs while in close. To score in front takes a bang-bang play, and for Robitaille to place his shots so well is a good barometer of his scoring skill.

At the other end of the spectrum is his skating, which isn't as bad as it's been made out to be but is certainly lacking in specific areas. He's a strong and well-balanced skater, but Luc lacks the explosive quickness present in the skating of the League's more dynamic forwards.

He pays attention to his check when backchecking, but he still creates openings for the opposition by collapsing to the puck. A 98-point scorer with just a plus-5 rating is a poor defensive player.

THE PHYSICAL GAME

Luc plays a physical game, in that he accepts contact to make his plays; his scoring from the traffic area in front of the net proves that. He initiates contact that gains him the puck (his balance keeps him vertical after collisions, and thus ready to make plays), but he's not a big banger.

He has the strength to shrug off the defense while making plays in front, but must remember to keep his feet moving when angled toward the boards, which makes him a defensive liability in his own zone.

He can be goaded into retaliatory penalties.

THE INTANGIBLES

Luc began the season well (his midway scoring pace indicated a 120-point season) but he slowed in the second half — just 12 goals in his last 28 games. He's a tremendous scorer, but across his three seasons he's been less than consistent from one half to the next.

We're not questioning his desire or work ethic (he's got tons of desire and determination). Rather, Robitaille must get his work ethic to power his game every night.

And, his poor playoff (just 2 goals and eight points in 11 games) bears some scrutiny. In a lot of ways, this season is a big test for Robitaille. We still think he can do the things necessary to play at the superstar level, but there's a big difference between 46-goal and 50-goal seasons. We want to see Robitaille prove that his 50-goal and 100-point sophomore campaign was the rule — and not the exception — to his game.

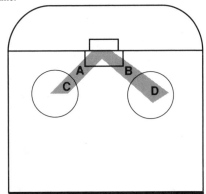

DAVE TAYLOR

Yrs. of NHL service: 11
Born: Levack, Ontario, Canada; December 4, 1955
Position: Right wing
Height: 6-0
Weight: 190
Uniform no.: 18
Shoots: right

Career statistics:

GP	G	A	TP	PIM
822	373	551	924	1,205

1988-89 statistics:

GP	G	A	TP	+/-	PIM	PP	SH	GW	GT	S	PCT
70	26	37	63	10	80	7	0	4	0	141	18.4

LAST SEASON

Games played total was three-season high, despite missing nine games with a knee injury. Assist total tied second lowest, and point total was third lowest, of career.

THE FINESSE GAME

The mark of Taylor's skating skill (and the microcosmic example of his NHL game) is his skating strength. He's a model corner-and-boards player because of his exceptional balance; Dave's very difficult to knock down, and that balance also serves to give him a surprising degree of agility. Taylor changes direction quickly, and that skill serves him in two ways: First, it allows him to gain an opening in traffic, and second, it also allows him to combine his agility with his skating strength to pursue the puck relentlessly as a very good forechecker. He also uses his strength to drive to the net.

He has good anticipation and the hands to cash in on that ice vision and hockey sense, so Taylor makes good plays coming out of the corner. He does not, however, possess an exceptional shot. But because he is opportunistic, Taylor works very well around the net (of course, his balance helps tremendously).

He positions himself well defensively and is a smart defensive player, but Dave often sacrifices himself so much along the offensive boards — and is thus too deep in the offensive zone — that he can't be used defensively.

THE PHYSICAL GAME

Dave makes the most of his physical finesse skills (balance and skating strength) by playing an intensely physical game. He's not only willing but able to drag people all over the ice to make a play. Taylor hits hard and often, and is not intimidated by anyone, regardless of size or reputation.

THE INTANGIBLES

There's no question that work ethic and determination have made Taylor the player he is, and those traits will keep him successful despite his (by athletic standards) advanced age; he'll be 34 in December. That's old for a player *without* Taylor's proclivity for physical play.

As such, his health will continue to be a question mark — especially since Dave has never played a full season. Nevertheless, the example he sets both on and off the ice make him the perfect captain for any team.

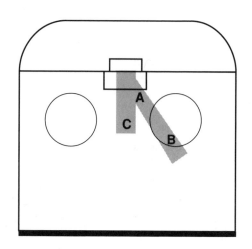

188

JOHN TONELLI

Yrs. of NHL service: 11
Born: Milton, Ontario, Canada; March 23, 1957
Position: Left wing
Height: 6-1
Weight: 200
Uniform no.: 27
Shoots: left

Career statistics:

GP	G	A	TP	PIM
755	246	414	660	639

1988-89 statistics:

GP	G	A	TP	+/-	PIM	PP	SH	GW	GT	S	PCT
77	31	33	64	9	110	1	1	3	0	156	19.9

LAST SEASON

Goal and point totals were three-season highs, PIM total career high. He was signed by the Kings as a free agent in June 1988.

THE FINESSE GAME

Strength and balance have marked Tonelli's skating throughout his career, though he lacks the acceleration he once had. He's never been especially agile, so as a straight-ahead player he's succeeded more on determination than skill. His offensive resurgence last season was not matched by a change in his defensive game, which could be called half-hearted at best. John retains his long-time laziness, coasting back to save his energy for another offensive rush, instead of working as hard toward his zone as he does the offensive zone.

His strength as a finesse player has been his drive to the net and his shooting ability. He holds the puck too long while looking to make his plays, and he tends to circle away from the play instead of facing it. He'll leave good ice to go to bad ice, and when he does that in his own end, defensive breakdowns occur. Tonelli also goes to bad ice in the offensive zone, often at an angle as wide from the net as possible.

His proclivity for working in traffic frequently leaves him in an awkward body position, but John's balance helps him maintain his feet and possession of the puck.

His best weapon remains the big slap shot from the left wing, but his decreased skating speed makes his ability to get into the clear to use that shot questionable. More and more, his goals will come from nearer the net on opportunistic play.

THE PHYSICAL GAME

John has always had a reputation for physical play, charging the corners with reckless abandon. He does less of that now, and a lot more leg grinding to look busy. He's always been mean with his stick, but has never fought after provoking an incident.

THE INTANGIBLES

We were wrong last season when we said that Tonelli's not going to score very often — 31 goals is often enough. But consider this: he had just one goal in his first 11 games, just 10 goals in his final 36 games (only 9 at even strength), just 1 goal (and only four points) in his last 15 games.

In other words, he had a mid-season hot streak. He does deserve credit, however, for scoring all but two of his goals at even strength. But to us, that's not dependable, consistent scoring — certainly not the kind of work that makes us say Tonelli's stemmed the tide of his declining career.

Of course, we're willing to be proved wrong again — but we're not sure we will be.

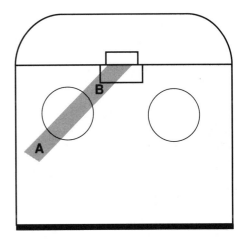

TIM WATTERS

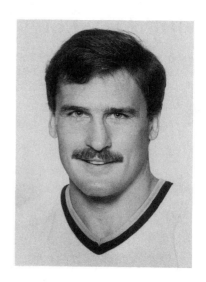

Yrs. of NHL service: 8
Born: Kamloops, B.C., Canada; July 25, 1959
Position: Defenseman
Height: 5-11
Weight: 180
Uniform no.: 5
Shoots: left

Career statistics:

GP	G	A	TP	PIM
514	24	119	143	928

1988-89 statistics:

GP	G	A	TP	+/-	PIM	PP	SH	GW	GT	S	PCT
76	3	18	21	17	168	0	0	0	0	62	4.8

LAST SEASON

Signed as a free agent in June 1988. Games played and PIM totals were second highest of career. He was second in PIM total among defensemen, fourth on club.

THE FINESSE GAME

Though his conservative style hides it, Watters has a number of finesse skills. He is a good skater, both forward and backward and he can carry the puck from the zone if need be (and he is unafraid to do so), though his game is to pass it up quickly and efficiently to the forwards.

He handles the puck well and is poised with it, not likely to give it away even under pressure. Tim doesn't carry that part of his game into the offensive zone though, and will most likely be the safety valve on a Kings' rush.

Watters reads the enemy rush well and plays his position excellently, forcing play wide of the net by using his defensive angles to cut off passing and skating lanes.

THE PHYSICAL GAME

Like two of his stylistic peers — Detroit's Mike O'Connell and Chicago's Bob Murray — Tim is not a big guy and must play a smart physical game. He is effective at tying up the forward in the crease and can do the same thing along the boards.

He is much stronger than his size and is willing to use it, hitting effectively and using his body to take out and hold out the opposition. He is also able to shield the puck well with his body, protecting it from the opposition when he is trapped along the boards or in the corners.

He sacrifices his body by blocking shots, and is one of the few players left in the NHL to use the hip check.

THE INTANGIBLES

Watters is a stabilizing force on the Kings blue line, a guy who is a defensive inspiration because he plays bigger than his size. He is a smart player who learned much from Serge Savard during the current Montreal GM's stay in Winnipeg.

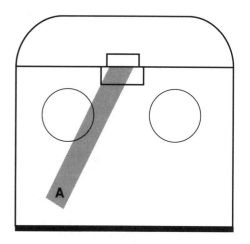

MINNESOTA
NORTH STARS

LINE COMBINATIONS
STEWART GAVIN-PERRY BEREZAN
BOB BROOKE
NEAL BROTEN-DON BARBER
DAVE ARCHIBALD-DAVE GAGNER
MIKE GARTNER

DEFENSE PAIRINGS
FRANTISEK MUSIL-CURT GILES
SHAWN CHAMBERS-REED LARSON
LARRY MURPHY

GOALTENDERS
JON CASEY
KARI TAKKO

OTHER PLAYERS
BRIAN BELLOWS — Right wing
CURT FRASER — Left wing
BASIL MCRAE — Left wing
VILLE SIREN — Defenseman

POWER PLAY

FIRST UNIT:
DAVE ARCHIBALD-DAVE GAGNER
MIKE GARTNER-LARRY MURPHY

SECOND UNIT:
NEAL BROTEN-DON BARBER
SHAWN CHAMBERS-REED LARSON

On the first unit, ARCHIBALD goes to the front, GAGNER and GARTNER take up positions at the left and right faceoff circles, respectively. Now-departed MARC HABSCHEID paired with MURPHY, playing catch at the point to free GARTNER. Second option is a MURPHY shot with GAGNER crashing the net.

On the second unit, BARBER is the focus; the Stars want loose pucks for him to put home. BROTEN distributes the puck from the inside of the left circle, moving as close as he can to the middle of the ice. He'll move deeper into the slot on point shots, and the other forward (occasionally BASIL MCRAE) will crash the net.

Last season Minnesota's power play was FAIR, scoring 78 goals in 392 opportunities (19.9 percent, 15th overall).

PENALTY KILLING

FIRST UNIT:
PERRY BEREZAN-STEWART GAVIN
FRANTISEK MUSIL-SHAWN CHAMBERS

SECOND UNIT:
NEAL BROTEN-MIKE GARTNER
CURT GILES

Both units play a fairly strict box, with each set of forwards sending one man in the offensive and neutral zones. DAVE GAGNER will also see time here.

Last season Minnesota's penalty killing was GOOD, allowing 82 goals in 441 shorthanded situations (81.4 percent, eighth overall).

CRUCIAL FACEOFFS
The North Stars lack a dominating faceoff man, but BOB BROOKE or BROTEN will get these.

DAVID ARCHIBALD

Yrs. of NHL service: 2
Born: Vancouver, B.C., Canada; April 14, 1969
Position: Center
Height: 6-1
Weight: 185
Uniform no.: 14
Shoots: left

Career statistics:

GP	G	A	TP	PIM
150	27	39	66	40

1988-89 statistics:

GP	G	A	TP	+/-	PIM	PP	SH	GW	GT	S	PCT
72	14	19	33	-11	14	7	0	2	0	105	13.3

LAST SEASON

Goal total was up one, assist total down one, from rookie year. Plus/minus was club's fourth worst. He missed time with a back injury.

THE FINESSE GAME

There's a whole lot of promise in this kid. Archibald skates very well and his balance is exceptional, which means his puckhandling in traffic situations is good and will be better. He has excellent agility, but he lacks matching speed or quickness. Greater NHL experience may provide those.

Because of his balance and hands, Dave carries the puck exceptionally well. His hand skills extend to his passing ability (though he's still not well acclimated to the speed of the NHL game), but especially to his shooting; he can really deliver the puck to the net with his wrist shot. As good as his shot is, Archibald needs to shoot it more.

He tends to be unselfish and enjoys playmaking, and he has the hockey sense to be a very good assist man. He finds openings and exploits them with his passing, but he also exploits them with his 1-on-1 skills (especially in the neutral zone). He controls the puck very well when carrying it, but he's smart enough to give it up to a teammate in better position.

All of his skills have already made him a power play regular, but he must develop his even strength play — just as he needs to succeed more defensively, so as to insure the regular shifts that will allow him to contribute offensively.

THE PHYSICAL GAME

Archibald's size is good, and he's still growing. He is not, however, a physical player; he doesn't impose himself on the opposition. He's not afraid to take hits or go to the traffic areas (and this is where his superior balance serves him), but added strength would allow him to initiate contact and thus capitalize more on his finesse skills.

THE INTANGIBLES

One aspect from which Archibald will benefit is the stability that has now settled over the Stars. He'll have one coach to please — not a rotating set — and that's important for a kid trying to compete and improve in the NHL.

He has fantastic potential and good maturity for his age. His work ethic is good, and Dave has the desire to succeed. We believe he will.

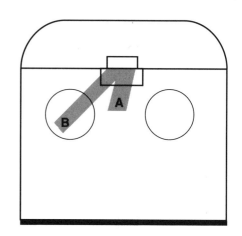

DON BARBER

Yrs. of NHL service: 1
Born: Victoria, B.C., Canada; December 2, 1964
Position: Left wing
Height: 6-1
Weight: 205
Uniform no.: 37
Shoots: left

Career statistics:

GP	G	A	TP	+/-	PIM	PP	SH	GW	GT	S	PCT
23	8	5	13	2	8	3	0	2	2	42	19.0

LAST SEASON

His first NHL exposure. He tied for the club lead in game-tying goals.

THE FINESSE GAME

Barber's best assets as a potential NHLer are in the physical game, but there are certain finesse skills that key that physical game. He succeeds by going to the net and taking his punishment, and Don has the balance and skate strength necessary to succeed in confrontation situations. He remains vertical after getting hit, and his skating strength allows him to drive through checks to the goal.

Don has fairly good hands, as one must for scoring work in close quarters. He gets his shot off quickly and on net (hard to miss from gimme-putt distance), and he's going to score most of his goals in opportunistic fashion (on the power play particularly): in other words, don't expect him to whip slappers past anyone from the blue line.

He handles the puck fairly well when carrying it, though he is still not completely acclimated to NHL speed, but his ability will show best by his gaining the puck and controlling it in traffic — not in rink-length rushes.

Barber is a fairly conscientious defensive player, with a good understanding of — and attention to — his positional play.

THE PHYSICAL GAME

Unlike some players who succeed in traffic, Barber isn't going to plow anyone over. What he will do is drive ceaselessly for the net and take the punishment once he gets there. He makes his physical play better by having good hand skills, and he'd be even more valuable if he initiated some of that contact instead of solely accepting it.

THE INTANGIBLES

Barber's a determined youngster willing to work and sacrifice himself for the team. That speaks well of his character, and that alone should keep him in the Stars lineup. But that's not to minimize his skills. Barber has good NHL potential, and could become an above average NHL player.

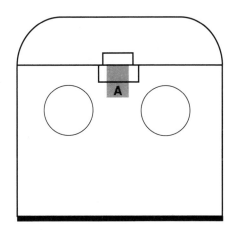

BRIAN BELLOWS

Yrs. of NHL service: 7
Born: St. Catherines, Ontario, Canada;
September 1, 1964
Position: Right wing
Height: 5-11
Weight: 195
Uniform no.: 23
Shoots: right

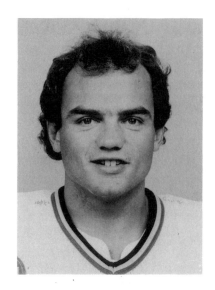

Career statistics:

GP	G	A	TP	PIM
513	222	251	473	381

1988-89 statistics:

GP	G	A	TP	+/-	PIM	PP	SH	GW	GT	S	PCT
60	23	27	50	-14	55	7	0	4	1	196	11.7

LAST SEASON

Games played total was career low (recurring abdominal/groin strain); ditto goal and point totals. Led team in game winners, was second in SOG total. His plus/minus was worst among players with at least 60 games played.

THE FINESSE GAME

Bellows' strength and balance are what power his game — both finesse-wise and physically. His skating stride is very strong and his balance is exceptional, and that combination makes him almost unbeatable along the boards, his stride driving him through checks and his balance keeping him upright to continue making plays. He doesn't have a lot of agility or rink-length speed but his strong stride gets him where he's going.

Brian's hand skills mirror those of his foot skills. He makes good plays out of the corner, skimming accurate passes through traffic or leading a teammate into the clear (his excellent hockey sense and vision help him in his playmaking). Because of his straight-ahead style, and because of the agility that he lacks, Bellows isn't an exceptional puck carrier.

He puts his good hands to work around the net by scoring in a number of ways. Brian shoots quickly from the traffic areas in front of the net, and he also has the strength to power the puck past the goaltender from a distance. He shoots a lot and chases the rebounds.

He is usually a conscientious defensive player who maintains his position up and down the ice.

THE PHYSICAL GAME

Bellows likes to play a corners and boards game, and he makes the most of the assets he has that allow him to succeed there. He's a mucker and a grinder and the main component of Brian's physical success is his leg strength, but he is also very strong in the upper body. That strength helps him out-muscle the opposition along the boards and is especially important in allow-ing him to get his shot through traffic — or to get his shot off at all while being checked.

He initiates a lot of intelligent hitting (as his PIM totals attest), but he does not carry that over into fighting.

THE INTANGIBLES

The broom that cleaned the Minnesota house could sweep two ways with Bellows. The Stars could decide to move him (he did a lot of talking himself about moving during the summer prior to last season) so as to complete their housekeeping, or Bellows could dig in and contribute.

In one way, circumstances mitigate against him, because the Stars accomplished what they they did last year with Bellows' help over the tail end of the year. That doesn't bode well for his importance to the club.

He's matured as a player, and this season will test his maturity to the utmost.

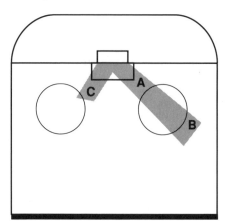

PERRY BEREZAN

Yrs. of NHL service: 4
Born: Edmonton, Alta., Canada; December 5, 1964
Position: Center
Height: 6-2
Weight: 190
Uniform no.: 21
Shoots: right

Career statistics:

GP	G	A	TP	PIM
168	32	46	78	158

1988-89 statistics:

GP	G	A	TP	+/-	PIM	PP	SH	GW	GT	S	PCT
51	5	8	13	6	25	0	1	0	0	65	7.7

LAST SEASON

Games played total was second highest of his career. Plus/minus was the club's third best. Acquired by Minnesota near the season's end — he played 16 games as a Star.

THE FINESSE GAME

Berezan is an excellent skater, with great speed, agility and quickness. He's also a strong, tireless skater and Perry combines those skating skills with superb puck smarts, anticipation and vision to be an excellent penalty killer and checker.

Berezan reads the play very well, and he can use that ability as a play maker, where he can also put his good hands to work. Berezan handles the puck well — especially when skating — and would succeed offensively as a playmaker and not a scorer, because his shot is not outstanding. He has touch around the net and the strength to score from a little farther away, but Perry's goals will usually be few and far between.

THE PHYSICAL GAME

Berezan's balance is what helps him succeed here (and, of course, it is the primary reason for his skating agility and lateral movement). He's able to use his body very well and gain position against the opposition because he remains vertical after collisions. He'll initiate contact in the high-traffic areas.

THE INTANGIBLES

We told you last year that Berezan would be moved from Calgary, but he's re-joined former Flame scout (and now Stars GM) Jack Ferreira in Minnesota. Perry is a very skilled player, probably the best on the Stars in terms of each component of the game. To be valuable for the Stars, though, he must stay in the lineup — and his history of injury doesn't bode well for him in that regard.

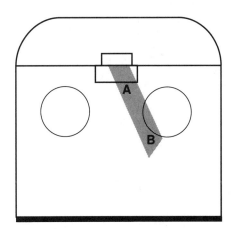

BOB BROOKE

Yrs. of NHL service: 5
Born: Melrose, Mass., USA; December 18, 1960
Position: Center/right wing
Height: 6-1
Weight: 205
Uniform no.: 13
Shoots: right

Career statistics:

GP	G	A	TP	PIM
374	57	83	140	457

1988-89 statistics:

GP	G	A	TP	+/-	PIM	PP	SH	GW	GT	S	PCT
57	7	9	16	-12	57	0	1	2	0	77	9.1

LAST SEASON

Games played total was full season career low; assist and point totals tied career lows. He missed time with a shoulder injury. His plus/minus was the club's third worst.

THE FINESSE GAME

Brooke is an excellent skater with strength, speed, and balance, and he uses those assets best as a checking forward. He plays the game at very high speed, and he can do that because his strong stride gives him the power necessary for acceleration. He doesn't have the quickness that creates one-step agility.

His hockey sense and vision are excellent and they serve him in both the offensive and defensive game. His smarts and skating ability will create many offensive opportunities for him, almost none of which he will cash in on.

As good as Bob's foot skills are, that's how bad his hands are. They betray him when giving or accepting passes, and when he is carrying the puck. He'll be able to get into scoring position because of his speed and sense, but he'll never be able to get the puck away fast enough. He'll have to get his goals, therefore, by being opportunistic around the net.

And forget that plus/minus; his defensive play is excellent. Brooke is always aware of his check and plays his position deep into the defensive zone.

THE PHYSICAL GAME

Brooke is in excellent condition, and his conditioning allows him to take full advantage of his size and strength (as well as to maximize his skating skill). He uses his strength and balance to work the corners and boards ceaselessly, and he can come away with the puck (what he does with it after gaining it — see 'hand skills' — is another matter). His balance keeps him upright after collisions, and ready to make plays.

He is an aggressive player who backs down from no one (don't interpret this to mean he's a fighter, however) and he hits well at both ends of the ice.

He has excellent eye/hand coordination, so he'll get loose pucks and win faceoffs.

THE INTANGIBLES

He's an honest, hard working player, and Bob also has the ability to play both forward and defense. That versatility is important for a role player.

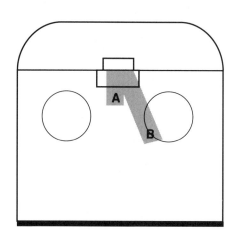

NEAL BROTEN

Yrs. of NHL service: 8
Born: Roseau, Min., USA; November 29, 1959
Position: Center
Height: 5-9
Weight: 170
Uniform no.: 7
Shoots: left

Career statistics:

GP	G	A	TP	PIM
559	193	382	575	327

1988-89 statistics:

GP	G	A	TP	+/-	PIM	PP	SH	GW	GT	S	PCT
68	18	36	56	1	57	4	5	1	1	160	11.3

LAST SEASON

Games played total was three-season high; ditto points total. He missed 11 games with a sternum injury. He finished third on the club in points (second in assists) and first in shorthanded goals.

THE FINESSE GAME

Playmaking is the best of Neal's finesse skills, and that's because of his superior hockey sense, vision and anticipation. He sees the ice very well and his anticipation tells him where the openings will be and where his teammates will be, thus laying the groundwork for his hand skills.

His hands generate the correct amount of strength or softness to get a pass to a teammate anywhere, any time. His hand skills extend to his puckhandling, and Broten creates openings with that skill because the defense must respect his ability. His shot doesn't match the capabilities of his passes, but Broten compensates by getting into scoring position — so he doesn't have to drive the puck to the net.

His skating is a key component in that puckhandling, and it's that skill that forces the opposition to retreat and thus create openings. Neal is an excellent skater with superior balance, speed and quickness. Broten has excellent acceleration and lateral movement, and he brings all his skills to bear in one stride.

His skills make him a natural specialty teams player, and he is good without the puck defensively as well, making the transition from offense to defense quickly and efficiently.

THE PHYSICAL GAME

Broten will take the requisite pounding for his points, but he doesn't initiate a lot of contact. That's fine, because he can succeed without it. Just a little bump along the boards gives him the time and space he needs to take the puck and make a play.

THE INTANGIBLES

The obvious one is Neal's health; he's played just 168 of a possible 240 in the last three seasons. And even if Neal remains healthy, a second intangible is his age; he'll be 30 years old by November's end. For sports, that's old.

Add the fact that Dave Archibald continues to develop, Dave Gagner has proven he's a full-time NHLer and Mike Modano will probably be in the lineup, and that makes for an interesting center-ice scenario for both Broten *and* the Stars.

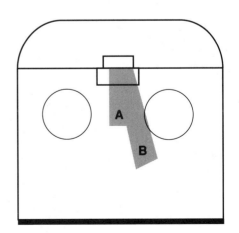

JON CASEY

Yrs. of NHL service: 3
Born: Grand Rapids, Minn., USA; March 29, 1962
Position: Goaltender
Height: 5-10
Weight: 155
Uniform no.: 30
Catches: left

Career statistics:

GP	MINS	G	SO	AVG	A	PIM
97	5,110	289	1	3.39	1	18

1988-89 statistics:

GP	MINS	AVG	W	L	T	SO	GA	SA	SAPCT
55	2,961	3.06	18	17	12	1	151	1,509	.900

LAST SEASON

Games and minutes played totals were career highs. Winning season was first of NHL career. GAA was career low. Finished second in the League in save percentage.

THE PHYSICAL GAME

Casey is an angle goaltender and is fairly adept at that style of play. He doesn't have great size (the puck isn't going to just hit him as it might for teammate Kari Takko), so Casey must play a challenging game to be successful.

Jon complements his angle game by having good speed in both his hands and feet, so that he can still make a save if he's failed to cut the angle completely. He needs that speed on his glove side, because he's flawed in his net coverage on shots from deep on the right wing side (Casey doesn't 'hinge' off the post as well as he could to cut the angle on that side).

His speed and ability to stand up help him on plays in the slot, but he could do better in lateral movement from post to post. As such, he's vulnerable to crossing-pattern type plays in the slot.

He sees the puck fairly well and moves well in and out of the net, but he has shown some difficulty in recovering his angles after moving out of his net.

THE MENTAL GAME

Casey is fairly confident and poised in the net and that's evidenced by his non-scrambly type of play. His concentration has improved to the point that he holds it well over a game, and over a stretch of games. He's anticipating plays fairly well at this level, and that helps him in his ability to stand up.

THE INTANGIBLES

Casey showed well last year, certainly benefitting as the team in front of him learned to play defense. He can be a more than adequate NHL goaltender, but it's also worth noting that he enters the season at 27 years of age; that's old for a goalie who has essentially just played his first full NHL season. That makes him vulnerable for replacement.

SHAWN CHAMBERS

Yrs. of NHL service: 1
Born: Royal Oaks, Mich., USA; October 11, 1966
Position: Defenseman
Height: 6-2
Weight: 215
Uniform no.: 26
Shoots: left

Career statistics:

GP	G	A	TP	PIM
91	6	26	32	101

1988-89 statistics:

GP	G	A	TP	+/-	PIM	PP	SH	GW	GT	S	PCT
72	5	19	24	-4	80	1	2	0	0	131	3.8

LAST SEASON

First full NHL season. Minnesota's first choice in 1987 Supplemental Draft. Led the defense in shorthanded goals.

THE FINESSE GAME

For a guy with his size and relative bulk, Chambers skates well and shows signs of definitely improvable all-around NHL skill. He has a fair degree of foot speed, and that quickness allows him to forecheck and pinch in at the offensive blue line without making an offensive move he can't recover from.

Shawn will also use his skating skill to go to the net with the puck, and all he needs is greater experience to help him make better — and less risky — decisions. But he has also shown a good degree of poise and patience. He looks for the winger at the net — and Chambers smartly takes something off his shot for possible deflections — and Shawn also stands up and challenges the breaking winger at the offensive blue line.

He plays a quiet, defensive angle style of defense and generally makes the right pass from the zone, but Chambers could improve by moving the puck quicker. Again, greater NHL experience should help there.

Chambers has a good, but not yer great, shot from the point. He could get it off a little quicker, but he uses it fairly often and it's fairly accurate.

THE PHYSICAL GAME

Chambers has good size and he's not afraid to use it. He bodychecks fairly well and covers the front of the net effectively. He's not a big banger, and he could do with some additional upper body strength for his close-quarter tussles with the League's bigger forwards, but Shawn handles himself pretty well.

THE INTANGIBLES

Chambers has youth and talent on his side, and he's joined the Stars at the right time. There's stability here now, and that will allow him to learn from a single coach, rather than the rotating staff that the Stars have had previously. He sees time on both specialty teams, and Chambers is already Minnesota's number two (and perhaps soon-to-be number one, depending on Larry Murphy) offensive defenseman.

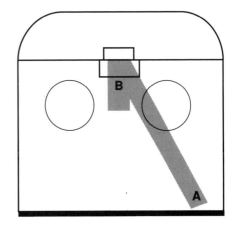

GAETAN DUCHESNE

Yrs. of NHL service: 8
Born: Les Saules, Quebec, Canada; July 11, 1962
Position: Left wing
Height: 5-11
Weight: 197
Uniform no.: 14
Shoots: left

Career statistics:

GP	G	A	TP	PIM
601	119	182	301	383

1988-89 statistics:

GP	G	A	TP	+/-	PIM	PP	SH	GW	GT	S	PCT
70	8	21	29	0	56	2	1	1	0	110	7.3

LAST SEASON

Games played, goal and point totals were second lowest of career. He was sidelined with a shoulder injury. His plus/minus was the club's second best, tops among forwards.

THE FINESSE GAME

Vision and skating strength have long been the keys to Duchesne's game. He uses his outstanding anticipation and vision skills to gain full view of the play and to understand its ramifications, so that when the holes open Duchesne can use his skating skill to close them. He also uses his hockey sense and skating to be a good forechecker and penalty killer.

His skating doesn't have an obviously outstanding trait, being marked instead by strength and balance. He's almost tireless as a skater, which makes his puck pursuit almost relentless, and his balance combines with his modicum of foot speed to make him fairly agile.

His puck pressuring will net him some offensive opportunities, but Gaetan is inconsistent in his exploitation of those chances. He really lacks the hand skills to convert on anything but the most elementary loose pucks (among other things, Duchesne takes forever in getting his shot off), but he can handle the puck and certainly has the awareness of teammates that would be expected from a player with his vision and hockey sense.

THE PHYSICAL GAME

Duchesne is a tough but clean player, but he lacks the power or strength to really wear down or punish the opposition with his checks. Instead, he'll succeed by taking the body and by using his own body to establish position along the boards or on the puck.

He willingly accepts all the abuse he gets from disgruntled opponents, but Duchesne doesn't get involved in retaliation — and he certainly won't fight.

THE INTANGIBLES

Duchesne is a dedicated athlete, a tireless worker and a character player. His actions make him a leader, but his age (27) and role playing status could leave him vulnerable to replacement.

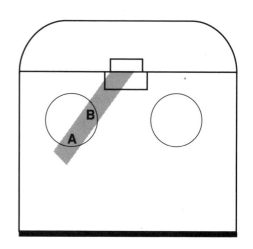

CURT FRASER

Yrs. of NHL service: 12
Born: Cincinnati, Ohio, USA; January 12, 1958
Position: Left wing
Height: 6-0
Weight: 190
Uniform no.: 18
Shoots: left

Career statistics:

GP	G	A	TP	PIM
696	192	240	432	1,284

1988-89 statistics:

GP	G	A	TP	+/-	PIM	PP	SH	GW	GT	S	PCT
35	5	5	10	-15	76	1	0	0	0	58	8.6

LAST SEASON

Games played total was second lowest of his career and lowest in four seasons. All point totals were career lows. He was sidelined by wrist surgery.

THE FINESSE GAME

Balance is the key to Fraser's skating game — and thus his entire game. His great balance (and no small level of agility) allows Fraser to play the hitting game he relishes.

Fraser drives to the spots he has to be in to make the plays. He is also excellent in traffic because of superior upper body strength and he will drive to the net for the puck.

Fraser loves to work the corners and does so with success because of the good balance he has on his skates. His defensive coverages are good and his shot is a little above average because he gets it away quickly. He scores through hard work and determination, not artistry.

THE PHYSICAL GAME

Regardless of who he skate with, Fraser's incessant physical play opens up the ice.

The good balance Curt has on his skates serves him well in the corners and along the boards, and so does the willingness to hit or be hit in order to make a play. He uses his body at both ends of the rink and will plow into anything and throw his body at everything.

Fraser's strength and persistent hitting make his checking especially telling on opposing forwards.

THE INTANGIBLES

Just like last year, this report remains virtually unchanged, given the unsure status of Fraser's health. There can be no question of his tremendous skill level and determination (or of his teammates' respect for him), just as there can be no question that his health is the biggest thing standing in the way of his continuing his NHL career. Whether he ever returns to the NHL on a consistent basis because of his proclivity toward injury is questionable.

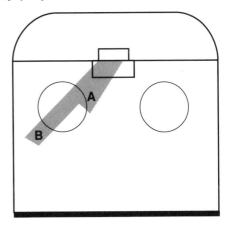

DAVE GAGNER

Yrs. of NHL service: 3
Born: Chatham, Ontario, Canada; December 11, 1964
Position: Center
Height: 5-10
Weight: 180
Uniform no.: 15
Shoots: left

Career statistics:

GP	G	A	TP	PIM
206	54	70	124	206

1988-89 statistics:

GP	G	A	TP	+/-	PIM	PP	SH	GW	GT	S	PCT
75	35	43	78	13	104	11	3	3	2	183	19.1

LAST SEASON

Games played, PIM and all point totals were career highs. Led the club in goals, assists, points, plus/minus, power play goals and game tying goals.

THE FINESSE GAME

Here's a case of the whole being better than the sum of the parts — and the parts work because Dave forces them to. He's a good skater with balance and quickness, which gives him good agility and lateral movement. Gagner uses his skating to be really tough on the puck in the offensive zone, even though he doesn't have great speed.

Dave complements those physical skills with his mental ones. Dave understands and anticipates the play well, and he uses his skating and hand skills to exploit the openings his brain shows him. He's also shown the ability to get into scoring position; that's important, because it means he's not always fighting off bigger players.

Gagner has also demonstrated patience (which comes largely from confidence). He's waiting for the openings for his shot instead of shooting wildly (that means getting into better shooting position), and he's also holding the puck for the extra second it takes for his teammates to get open.

Dave will have to be an opportunistic scorer at the NHL level, scooping up loose pucks that his quickness gets him to. His shot isn't bad, but he's going to succeed more on exploiting openings than he is in blowing the puck past opposing goalies.

His skills make him good on the specialty teams, and they also make Dave a solid defensive player.

THE PHYSICAL GAME

Gagner uses his balance in his robust physical game, where it allows him to remain vertical and ready to make plays after collisions. He's an aggressive player — willing to hit against anyone at any time, and doing so at every opportunity — but because he doesn't have good size Dave is sometimes hoist with his own petard.

His size can mitigate against him as he plays in the congested areas, so Gagner has to play smart physically. He can't stay in the crowd and mix it up, he's got to be on hit-and-run missions to take advantage of his quickness and hands. Once he gets trapped, he's apt to get over-powered (through no fault of his own).

THE INTANGIBLES

This guy is the hardest worker in the NHL, bar none. No one deserves success more than Gagner, because no one works harder for it. His success last year (though largely concentrated in the season's first half — 22 of 35 goals, 41 of 78 points by his 41st game) is the direct result of confidence — both his own in himself and the club's in him.

He'll be playing on a new contract this season, but that won't matter. Gagner will play just as hard with a new deal as he did under the old one, regardless of terms. That's his value, and he deserves to be with the North Stars to impart that work ethic, even if he doesn't score a single point.

And hey, last season was really Dave's first full NHL campaign. Not a bad rookie year, huh?

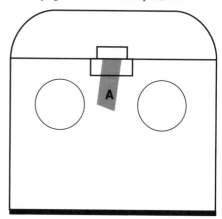

MIKE GARTNER

Yrs. of NHL service: 10
Born: Ottawa, Ontario, Canada; October 29, 1959
Position: Right wing
Height: 6-0
Weight: 185
Uniform no.: 11
Shoots: right

Career statistics:

GP	G	A	TP	PIM
771	404	399	803	772

1988-89 statistics:

GP	G	A	TP	+/-	PIM	PP	SH	GW	GT	S	PCT
69	33	36	69	11	73	9	0	1	1	223	14.8

LAST SEASON

Acquired by Minnesota at the trading deadline (along with Larry Murphy) from Washington in exchange for Bob Rouse and Dino Ciccarelli. Finished second on the club in goals, points, plus/minus and power play goals — first in shots on goal. Goal total was career low, point total second lowest of career.

THE FINESSE GAME

As a successful finesse player, Gartner has two main skills he brings to bear against the opposition: his skating and his shot. He has explosive skating speed coming down the wing, speed that he puts to use by blowing past his check and breaking wide on a defender before cutting behind him for a swoop in on goal.

Mike's acceleration is outstanding and he commands an almost instantaneous burst of speed from a stationary position. He is tremendously agile, has terrific lateral movement for his inside cuts and an outstanding change of pace to turn his speed up another notch.

Gartner's slap shot is just as lethal. It is a rocket from the edge of the right faceoff circle that drives goaltenders backward because of its speed and heavyness. If a goaltender isn't fully in front of that shot, it's going in the net, and obviously, the NHL's goaltenders see a lot of shots from Gartner. He gets into position to score and is a shooter first and a playmaker second.

Mike handles the puck well at top speed and his vision shows him the entire ice surface. He'll look for a play (and is a good passer), but Gartner expects the puck.

Gartner is also a good defensive player, making a concerted effort to play a solid defensive game.

THE PHYSICAL GAME

Gartner has long known the value of adding a physical element to a finesse game. Though not a thunderous hitter, he willingly hits and takes the body well along the boards and in all three zones. He excel-

lently protects the puck with his body, shielding it from the opposition when he swoops around the defensemen and leans away from checks.

He's also very strong on his skates and almost impossible to dislodge from the puck.

THE INTANGIBLES

The general thought regarding Mike Gartner is that he's an excellent character player, a hard worker who aims to contribute at all times. He's a leader by example. Still, there are questions. Always a streaky scorer, Gartner is at the point of his career where age and wear and tear must have an effect; no one could play 10 NHL seasons and not be affected. He may benefit some from the looser checking of the Norris Division, and — dedicated though he might be — he certainly needs to prove his value to his new team.

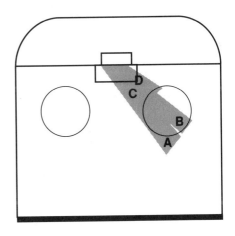

STEWART GAVIN

Yrs. of NHL service: 8
Born: Ottawa, Ontario, Canada; March 15, 1960
Position: Left wing
Height: 6-0
Weight: 185
Uniform no.: 12
Shoots: left

Career statistics:

GP	G	A	TP	PIM
552	99	126	225	386

1987-88 statistics:

GP	G	A	TP	+/-	PIM	PP	SH	GW	GT	S	PCT
73	8	18	26	3	34	0	1	0	0	129	6.2

LAST SEASON

Goal total was a full-season career low. He was acquired by the Stars from the Whalers in the waiver draft. He missed time with a facial injury.

THE FINESSE GAME

Gavin is an excellent skater, with superior speed and acceleration. He's a good two-way winger because of that, but he uses those skills best as a checking forward. He reads the defensive play very well and uses his speed to counter it, and his anticipation toward offense is good enough for him to score more than a handful of goals. When he doesn't score, chances are Gavin's forechecking has provided an opportunity for a teammate.

Stewart handles the puck fairly well as he rushes up-ice and he uses good vision to help him make good passes to his teammates. He'll score by driving for the openings (remember his speed) and does his best work from near the net by pouncing on loose pucks. He also has a big slap shot off the wing and will use it often.

He's very sound positionally, always aware of where he is on the ice, especially in the defensive zone. He comes back very deeply with his check and is tenacious when assigned a particular winger to watch. His skills also combine to make him a very good penalty killer.

THE PHYSICAL GAME

Because he has good strength and balance, Gavin is very effective at rubbing his man out along the boards. His speed helps him in his physical game by getting him to the opposition for a check, and Gavin's physical game is an underrated part of his entire performance.

THE INTANGIBLES

Hartford's loss was Minnesota's gain, on and off the ice, when the Stars picked up Gavin. He's well respected by his teammates for his excellent work ethic. He's an unsung — and generally unnoticed — player, but his ability to function at the NHL level — both offensively and defensively, physically and finesse-wise — is what makes Gavin so valuable.

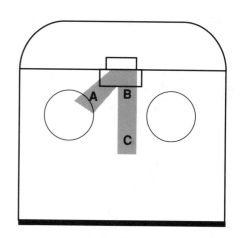

CURT GILES

Yrs. of NHL service: 10
Born: The Pas, Manitoba, Canada; Nov. 30, 1958
Position: Defense
Height: 5-8
Weight: 180
Uniform no.: 2
Shoots: left

Career statistics:

GP	G	A	TP	PIM
690	37	172	209	589

1988-89 statistics:

GP	G	A	TP	+/-	PIM	PP	SH	GW	GT	S	PCT
76	5	10	15	2	77	0	1	0	0	64	7.8

LAST SEASON

Games played total was a four-season high. He was the only Stars defenseman to post a plus rating.

THE FINESSE GAME

Curt is a solid finesse player, and his skating and playreading skills power that finesse game. He skates well in both directions, with speed and agility. He has good lateral movement, and Giles is able to step up and close the gap on the puck carrier. Defensively, he plays his angles well and is not often beaten one-on-one. Because of his positional play, he's very good at breaking up two-on-ones and three-on-twos. His skating also allows him to rush the puck when necessary.

His smarts allow him to read the rush coming at him well, and he will turn the puck up to his forwards quickly. He'll join the play up-ice and will move into the offensive zone, but Giles quickly — sometimes *too* quickly — abandons the point and falls back to defense.

Not that he'll create a lot of offense when he is at the point. While Curt will find the open man (and thus gain some power play time), he's not a tremendous offensive force. He has an average slap shot from the point and could shoot more.

THE PHYSICAL GAME

Giles's size belies his physical ability. He's a strong body checker (one of the best in the NHL), hitting as if he were a foot taller and 50 pounds heavier. He'll hit anyone. Giles is also very strong in the less spectacular skill of using his body along the boards. He plays smartly, not hurting the team through penalties.

Curt has the strength to muscle the opposition off the puck, and the skills to make a play afterward. He sacrifices his body to block shots, but it is his willingness to put himself on the line that has kept him from ever playing a complete NHL season.

While willing, however, he must keep himself away from the larger, stronger forwards whose own innate physical abilities would allow them to overwhelm Giles.

THE INTANGIBLES

Giles is a perfect kind of player for a club in transition, and a club needing experience; the North Stars fit both those bills. His professionalism makes him a quiet leader (he's a great person in the locker room, on the bus and on the ice and his upbeat personality is infectious), and his smarts make him valuable on the ice.

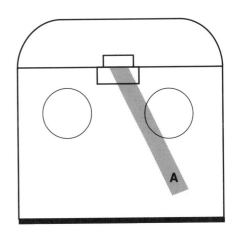

REED LARSON

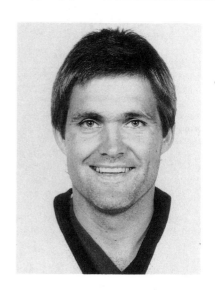

Yrs. of NHL service: 13
Born: Defenseman
Position: Minneapolis, Minn., USA; July 30, 1956
Height: 6-0
Weight: 195
Uniform no.: 28
Shoots: right

Career statistics:

GP	G	A	TP	PIM
903	222	463	685	1,391

1988-89 statistics:

GP	G	A	TP	+/-	PIM	PP	SH	GW	GT	S	PCT
54	9	29	38	-10	68	6	1	1	0	115	7.8

LAST SEASON

He began the season with Edmonton and was released, then signed a tryout with the Islanders, then was traded to Minnesota for future considerations. Games played total was a full-season career low; ditto goal total. Assist and point totals were three-season highs. His plus/minus was the defense's worst.

THE FINESSE GAME

Time and injury have taken their toll on Larson's finesse skills. Never really possessing a great change of pace or outstanding agility, Larson has also pretty much lost whatever straight ahead speed he's had. He will still join the play as a fourth attacker or start the occasional rush himself, but he doesn't do that as frequently as he once did. This, by the way, is why his plus/minus suffers. Larson can't recover defensively as well as necessary after committing himself offensively.

He uses his hand skills more than his skating when he rushes the puck or contains the point. He's very good at taking the puck off the boards in one motion, ready to shoot the puck or pass it to an open teammate. Reed sees the offensive zone well and can use his teammates effectively, but he's always thought shoot first and pass second.

His slap shot is still an effective one, that either scores or leaves rebounds, so Larson gets his assists when a teammate converts his shot. He's developed a half wrist shot-half slap that is very difficult to read, but just as fast and just as powerful. Larson likes to deliver the shots from the right point, but he'll cheat into the deep slot if he can.

THE PHYSICAL GAME

Larson has never been a thumper along the boards, in that he doesn't make the big check with a lot of flash and dash. He's generally effective along the boards and in front of the net, and just a little mean with his stick. He uses his size well to keep his defensive area clear, and his strength is the reason why his shot is so powerful.

THE INTANGIBLES

Larson is a fill-in for the Stars, someone to add a little depth and some offensive ability to a defensive corps in need of both. He'll be shuttled in and out of the lineup, and don't be surprised if he finishes the season somewhere — including retired.

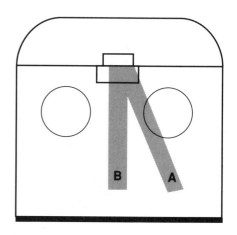

BASIL MCRAE

Yrs. of NHL service: 5
Born: Beaverton, Ontario, Canada; January 5, 1961
Position: Left wing
Height: 6-2
Weight: 205
Uniform no.: 17
Shoots: left

Career statistics:

GP	G	A	TP	PIM
277	33	41	74	1,241

1988-89 statistics:

GP	G	A	TP	+/-	PIM	PP	SH	GW	GT	S	PCT
78	12	19	31	-8	365	4	0	0	0	122	9.8

LAST SEASON

Games played total was second highest of his career; all point totals were career highs. His PIM total led the club (second in the NHL).

THE FINESSE GAME

There is more to McRae's finesse skills than readily meets the eye. Which is not to say that Basil is the next Denis Savard, but there are some skills he can bring to the game.

He's basically a straight-ahead player with limited agility and quickness, but he's a fairly strong skater. He has average balance, so he's going to be a little off-kilter after hitting or being hit.

Basil can carry the puck but won't do anything fancy; he takes advantage of the room his reputation gives him. He's showing more patience and less nervousness when he handles the puck, and that's paying off in points — he's seeing and making plays instead of just tossing the puck away. He doesn't have a great shot, so he'll have to be close to net (as when plugging it on the power play) to score.

He's also a conscientious defensive player, but his limited skills sometimes prohibit his putting those thoughts into practise.

THE PHYSICAL GAME

McRae plays a willing physical game, and he's made that game stronger and of greater importance by learning to accept being hit. He doesn't necessarily play like an idiot. If the other team is keeping its nose clean regarding McRae's teammates, Basil will behave too.

That allows him to use his good strength in confrontations along the boards. He can hurt people when he hits them, as his leg strength allows him to drive through checks.

As for fighting — well, Basil is more than willing to go with anyone. Not a heavyweight in himself (in terms of punching power or casting fear into anyone), McRae nevertheless goes willingly with the League's heavyweights. But just because people know they're going to fight him doesn't mean they're afraid of him, and the League's heavyweights aren't.

THE INTANGIBLES

McRae can play the game and he is always working hard to improve his limited skills. Is he an enforcer/policeman/goon? Yes. Is he a great team player with an excellent attitude, a relentless competitor? Yes. Does Minnesota need everyone it can get who has those desires?

Yes.

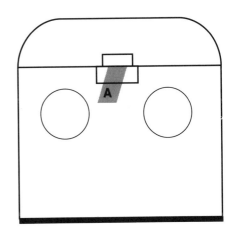

LARRY MURPHY

Yrs. of NHL service: 9
Born: Scarborough, Ontario, Canada; March 8, 1961
Position: Defenseman
Height: 6-2
Weight: 208
Uniform no.: 8
Shoots: right

Career statistics:

GP	G	A	TP	PIM
708	141	420	541	599

1988-89 statistics:

GP	G	A	TP	+/-	PIM	PP	SH	GW	GT	S	PCT
78	11	35	46	0	82	6	0	1	1	160	6.9

LAST SEASON

Murphy was acquired at the trading deadline from Washington (along with Mike Gartner) in exchange for Dino Ciccarelli and Bob Rouse. Games played total was a three-year low. Led team defense in scoring, but assist and point totals were career lows.

THE FINESSE GAME

Murphy is an excellent skater, and that ability keys whatever offensive success he garners. His strong stride means good acceleration, and he's also learned to moderate that speed to make it more effective. His gear shifts are tough to defend against, and he'll use that skating skill to rush the puck.

His defensive play has wavered in the last two seasons, but Murphy has generally learned to rush at the right times. He contains the point well offensively and forces the play wide defensively. He can, however, be beaten to his left, and Murphy needs to maintain his concentration in the defensive zone by focusing more on the man and less on the puck.

Minnesota needs Murphy's puckhandling and playmaking abilities. Those skills are good-to-excellent, and Larry uses his teammates well because of them. Primarily a playmaker from the point, Murphy's shot is low and accurate to the net, allowing for deflections, rebounds and tip-ins. Murphy also likes to let his shot go from the edge of the left faceoff circle, and he'll walk into the slot for a wrist shot if he can.

One reason his numbers decreased last season is that his SOG total fell dramatically. From 201 shots in 1987-88, Murphy's total fell to 160 — a fall off of 20 percent.

THE PHYSICAL GAME

Murphy is a finesse player with some size, but he's not a big physical player. He'll take the body along the boards more by getting in the way than by rubbing the man out, and Murphy's checks won't knock anyone into the cheap seats — if he hits at all.

He is adequate in front of the net, but his is the job of the break-out and not take-out defenseman. Whatever physical play he contributes is made more effective by his ability to make a play after a hit.

THE INTANGIBLES

Murphy struggled for his second consecutive season, and that — combined with the development of Kevin Hatcher — hastened his departure from the Caps. He can be a huge contributor for Minnesota, but he must regain the confidence he had three seasons back.

Right now, he's not playing smartly. He's taking penalties that cost the team, and he isn't moving the puck with anything near his previous alacrity.

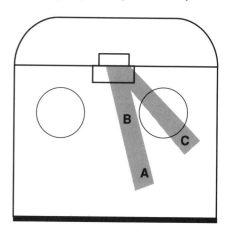

FRANTISEK MUSIL

Yrs. of NHL service: 3
Born: Pardubice, Czechoslovakia; December 17, 1964
Position: Defenseman
Height: 6-3
Weight: 205
Uniform no.: 6
Shoots: left

Career statistics:

GP	G	A	TP	PIM
207	12	36	48	415

1988-89 statistics:

GP	G	A	TP	+/-	PIM	PP	SH	GW	GT	S	PCT
55	1	19	20	4	54	0	0	1	0	78	1.3

LAST SEASON

Games played, goal and PIM totals were career lows, but assist and point totals were career highs. He missed time with a foot injury. His plus/minus led the defensemen.

THE FINESSE GAME

Everything about Musil has improved in his three NHL seasons, and should conttinue to do so. Already a skilled finesse player, Musil's skating shows more snap (speed and quickness) and agility than before; that's what happens when you practice and play against NHL competition. He's moving well in both directions, and he's developing both the skating and the smarts to close the gap on the puck carrier and challenge at the blue line. He already forces the play wide well.

His improved hand skills help him rush the puck when necessary, but that doesn't mean he does it frequently. Rather, Musil will pass the puck to the forwards to get it out of his zone, and he's making not just correct decisions but good ones as well.

Frantisek's forechecking and pinching ability is also improving, but he'll fall back to defense rather than take an iffy chance. He won't generate a whole lot of offense from the point; in fact whole games will go by without him taking a single at goal, never mind *on* goal.

THE PHYSICAL GAME

Musil has very strong physical abilities. For one thing, he can be a terror in front of his net, and he's learned how to serve that role without getting sent to the box.

Part of what helps him is his continued acclimation to the NHL. He's learning how to better take — or avoid — hits, and how to pace himself through a season. And, just as his finesse skills have improved at the NHL level, so too has his strength.

THE INTANGIBLES

Frantisek can be a dominating player because of his physical and finesse potential. That's important for the Stars, especially since the retirement of their steadiest defenseman — Craig Hartsburg — and trade of their most physical defender — Bob Rouse. Musil has a big role to fill and has the potential to fill it.

His work ethic says he'll continue to raise the level of his game.

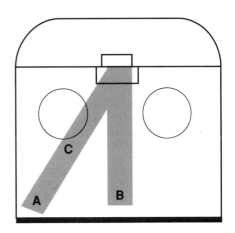

VILLE SIREN

Yrs of NHL service: 4
Born: Helsinki, Finland; November 2, 1964
Position: Defenseman
Height: 6-1
Weight: 185
Uniform no.: 5
Shoots: right

Career statistics:

GP	G	A	TP	PIM
237	13	55	68	216

1988-89 statistics:

GP	G	A	TP	+/-	PIM	PP	SH	GW	GT	S	PCT
50	3	10	13	0	72	0	0	0	0	50	6.0

LAST SEASON

Was acquired from Pittsburgh. Games played total was career low (missed 10 games with an ankle injury).

THE FINESSE GAME

Siren's skills have topped out at average at the NHL level. His skating is consistently at the NHL level now, and he skates well backward and with greater agility and lateral movement, so he's consistently able to angle the opposition to the boards.

His skating has gained him the time to read the play better, and Siren now sees the rush both ways fairly well. He is able to react to the play at the NHL level, and his improved defensive play is attributable to that. He understands the play better and moves better when necessary. He also moves the puck better now than ever before, courtesy of his improved play reading ability. Ville generally makes correct passing decisions. He'll carry the puck to center if he can, but Siren doesn't charge into the offensive zone.

Siren reads the offensive play better than before, pinching in and containing the point, but still concentrates on defense. He shoots nowhere near frequently enough, and his shot could use improvement in strength and quickness of release.

THE PHYSICAL GAME

While primarily a finesse player, Siren has increased the tempo of his physical play. He is not aggressive, but Siren quietly plays the body and takes a hit.

Additional strength would help him in his corner and crease battles, as he can be out-muscled by the competition. He probably won't ever be a punishing hitter, but Siren now plays an effective physical game, especially since he can make a play after taking the puck away.

THE INTANGIBLES

We've told you ad nauseum about Siren brittleness regarding injury. Not only does that factor remain a question, it draws his (in the short term) stay in Minnesota and (in the long term) his entire career into question. At 25 years of age, Siren is too old and too marginal a player to be shuttling in and out of the lineup because of injury.

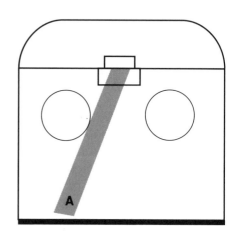

KARI TAKKO

Yrs. of NHL service: 3
Born: Uusikaupunki, Finland; June 23, 1962
Position: Goaltender
Height: 6-2
Weight: 182
Uniform no.: 1
Catches: left

Career statistics:

GP	MINS	G	SO	AVG	A	PIM
108	5,657	358	1	3.80	0	28

1988-89 statistics:

GP	MINS	AVG	W	L	T	SO	GA	SA	SAPCT	PIM
32	1,603	3.48	8	15	4	0	93	922	.899	6

LAST SEASON

Games and minutes played fell for third straight season (he was sidelined after mid-season with a virus). He finished, however, third in the NHL in save percentage.

THE PHYSICAL GAME

Takko is a standup goaltender who plays his angles well. Because of his questionable balance he's not an outstanding skater, but he will come out of the net to challenge the shooter and to handle the puck. He moves well from post to post and likes to use his quick feet in the butterfly style; his long legs help him cover a lot of net in this style.

He goes to the butterfly on screen shots and is fairly agile, but his balance slows him in regaining his stance. This makes him vulnerable on shots from the slot, where he can't use his size to cut down the angle (because he's already on the ice).

Kari will handle the puck out of the net and he also uses his stick to pokecheck very well. He does not, however, handle his rebounds well, and that's where his agility comes into play. Takko will most usually be back in some kind of position for the second save (this doesn't mean a balanced stance), and will — at the very least — get some part of himself or his equipment in the way of that second attempt.

THE MENTAL GAME

Takko concentrates fairly well during a game, and he's using his better understanding of the NHL and its speed to anticipate plays (note his pokechecking ability).

THE INTANGIBLES

Takko can play successfully in the NHL, but the improvements he has to make are directly related to the improvement of the team in front of him. Until we see if Minnesota can play a successful defensive style (they may have finished sixth in goals against, but they were fifth highest in shots allowed — that tells you about the goalies), we won't know exactly how solid Takko can be.

MONTREAL
CANADIENS

LINE COMBINATIONS
MIKE MCPHEE-BRIAN SKRUDLAND
CLAUDE LEMIEUX
RUSS COURTNALL-STEPHANE RICHER
SHAYNE CORSON
BOB GAINEY-GUY CARBONNEAU
RYAN WALTER
MATS NASLUND-BOBBY SMITH
MIKE KEANE

DEFENSE PAIRINGS
PTER SVOBODA-RICK GREEN
CRAIG LUDWIG-CHRIS CHELIOS
LARRY ROBINSON

GOALTENDERS
BRIAN HAYWARD
PATRICK ROY

POWER PLAY

FIRST UNIT:
RUSS COURTNALL-STEPHANE RICHER
SHAYNE CORSON
PTER SVOBODA-CHRIS CHELIOS

SECOND UNIT:
MATS NASLUND-BOBBY SMITH-CLAUDE
LEMIEUX

On the first forward unit, the Habs overload the left side. COURTNALL is at the base of the left faceoff circle, RICHER between the circle and the blue line and SVOBODA at the blue line between the circles.

CHELIOS is at the top of the right circle and CORSON plugs the net. A RICHER shot is the objective, with COURTNALL going to the open side for the rebound.

LEMIEUX takes the net on the second unit, with SMITH in the slot. NASLUND works out of the left wing corner, and SMITH is the primary shot-maker. CHELIOS will shoot on both units to spread out the penalty killers.

Last season Montreal's power play was GOOD, scoring 80 goals in 381 opportunities (21.0 percent, eighth overall).

PENALTY KILLING

FIRST UNIT:
BOB GAINEY-GUY CARBONNEAU
CRAIG LUDWIG-CHRIS CHELIOS
MIKE MCPHEE-BRIAN SKRUDLAND
LARRY ROBINSON-RICK GREEN

Both forward units are very aggressive, especially in forechecking in the offensive zone. They also pressure the points outstandingly, and each set of defense will force the puck in the defensive zone (GREEN is the only exception).

Last season Montreal's penalty killing was EXCELLENT, allowing 58 goals in 326 shorthanded situations (82.2 percent, third overall).

CRUCIAL FACEOFFS
GUY CARBONNEAU, with BRIAN SKRUDLAND second. RUSS COURTNALL, though on the wing, will take the faceoffs for his line.

GUY CARBONNEAU

Yrs. of NHL service: 7
Born: Sept-Iles, Quebec, Canada; March 18, 1960
Position: Center
Height: 5-11
Weight: 180
Uniform no.: 21
Shoots: right

Career statistics:

GP	G	A	TP	PIM
554	146	208	354	416

1988-89 statistics:

GP	G	A	TP	+/-	PIM	PP	SH	GW	GT	S	PCT
79	26	30	56	37	44	1	2	10	0	142	18.3

LAST SEASON

Goal total was career high, point total tied second highest mark of career. He led club in plus/minus, shorthanded goals and game winners, finishing second in the NHL in the last category.

THE FINESSE GAME

As good as Wayne Gretzky and Mario Lemieux are at anticipating the offensive play, that's how good Carbonneau is defensively. He reads plays and situations almost perfectly and thus knows where the puck is headed or how the opposition intends to operate. He blocks shots just by being in position, because Guy always knows where he is in relation to the puck, the net, the opposition and his teammates.

Factor in his exceptional skating (superior in all categories) and you've got the NHL's best forechecker, penalty killer and defensive forward — tireless in his pursuit of the puck.

And as if this isn't contribution enough, Carbonneau can also put the puck in the net. He doesn't have the 50-goal ability that many people think he has, but 25-30 goals a season is definitely in character for him.

His skating and sense get him to the loose pucks his checking creates, and Carbonneau's excellent hands can thread the puck through a crowd onto a teammate's stick or handle the puck well at full speed and in traffic.

Carbonneau has a fast wrist shot and is particularly effective from the edges of the faceoff circles, though he has the touch to score from in tight as well.

THE PHYSICAL GAME

Carbonneau uses his body excellently, despite the fact that he lacks great size. What he does, firstly, is use his skating to take the body — then his hand skills take over. But Guy also uses his body to gain good position along the boards when contesting the puck in traffic; his balance helps him remain vertical.

He willingly sacrifices his body as the NHL's best shot-blocking forward, and Carbonneau excels at faceoffs because of his hand speed, strength and balance (the latter skill gives him an excellent base of support).

THE INTANGIBLES

Guy's a tremendous worker and leader, and his all-around game has too long been hidden by his defensive prowess. Nevertheless, he's the prototypical defensive forward.

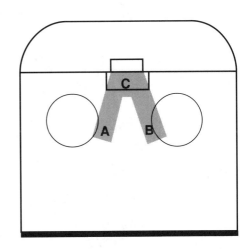

CHRIS CHELIOS

Yrs. of NHL service: 6
Born: Chicago, Ill, USA; January 25, 1962
Position: Defenseman
Height: 6-1
Weight: 187
Uniform no.: 24
Shoots: right

Career statistics:

GP	G	A	TP	PIM
349	63	215	278	647

1988-89 statistics:

GP	G	A	TP	+/-	PIM	PP	SH	GW	GT	S	PCT
80	15	58	73	35	185	8	0	6	0	206	7.3

LAST SEASON

Games played, assist, point and PIM totals were career highs; goal total second highest of career. Finished third on the club in points, second in assists, plus/minus rating and PIM, third in SOG total (first among defense in last three categories). He finished fourth in scoring among NHL defensemen.

THE FINESSE GAME

Chelios is an excellent skater with speed, quickness and balance. Those three assets combine to give him great agility and lateral movement, and he teams his skating with his puckhandling to become an excellent rushing defenseman. He has the speed and the skills to go end-to-end to score.

He's an active — rather than reactive — defenseman, using his skills to quickly turn the play around. Chris handles the puck very well and can make plays at all speeds. He'll carry the puck to the opposing blue line, and then use his passing skills to hit the open man or lead a teammate into the clear. Chris draws on the combination of his vision/hockey sense and hand skills to become a superior playmaker.

Chelios has a strong slap shot from the point and he'll sneak to the top of the circle if he can. He also drifts into the slot for a good wrist shot. Chelios can take those chances because he is fast enough to recover if necessary.

His skating and sense allow him to challenge the puck at both blue lines. He forechecks and contains the point well offensively, and just as easily steps up to close the gap on the puck carrier (and then begin the transition game) defensively.

THE PHYSICAL GAME

Chelios is very strong, certainly strong enough to control the league's big forwards. He takes the body very well and crosses the border to mean (just ask Brian Propp). He's also liberal with his stick. His combina-tion of strength and balance means he can take the puck away from anyone along the boards.

Chris can hold the opposition out of the play in the corner, and he can clear the front of his net too. He uses his body very well to shield the puck when he is rushing with it, and he will sacrifice his body by blocking shots.

THE INTANGIBLES

Chelios is a supremely talented player, the kind that can play any style of game and play it well. Attitude and desire fuel his game; when he has them, he plays a superior game. Without the desire, he's an ordinary player.

Chris put a more consistent effort on the ice last season, and he reaped the benefits: a Norris Trophy. We told you last season that a Chris Chelios in the correct frame of mind is a Norris Trophy winner. Now we say he can win the award again — as long as he wants to.

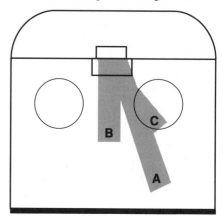

SHAYNE CORSON

Yrs. of NHL service: 3
Born: Barrie, Ontario, Canada; August 13, 1966
Position: Center
Height: 6-0
Weight: 175
Uniform no.: 27
Shoots: left

Career statistics:

GP	G	A	TP	PIM
209	50	62	112	491

1988-89 statistics:

GP	G	A	TP	+/-	PIM	PP	SH	GW	GT	S	PCT
80	26	24	50	-1	193	10	0	3	1	133	19.5

LAST SEASON

Games played, goal, point and PIM totals were career highs. He led the club in PIM total, was third in power play goals and last (among regulars) in plus/minus rating.

THE FINESSE GAME

Consistent with his overall style, strength is the hallmark of Corson's game. His above-average skating strength gives him some speed and acceleration ability. He has good foot speed and balance, but not sufficient to be labelled an agile forward. Rather, his balance and skating strength key his physical game, driving him through checks and keeping him vertical (and able to make plays) after hits.

He is a smart player in terms of ice vision and play reading, and he combines that intelligence with his skating to become a good forechecker and penalty killer.

He's not a fancy puckhandler, but since he's more inclined to skate over the defense instead of around it that's okay; Shayne can carry the puck at his top speed, but he's not likely to finesse the puck through traffic to a teammate. He is smart enough, though, to open up to the center of the rink and to keep his head up. He likes to carry the puck over the blue line — rather than dump it in — whenever possible.

Shayne will succeed as a scorer now by being around the net to force turnovers, and then by pouncing on the loose pucks he forced. He's especially effective plugging the net on the power play.

THE PHYSICAL GAME

Corson is a very aggressive player, sometimes too aggressive for his own good. His temper often gets the better of him, and he's not mature enough to take a check and keep playing — he's going to go right back at the guy that hit him. That's bad, because it distracts Corson from the game.

His skating strength makes him a hard hitter, and he plays that style consistently. He is also a willing fighter, but not one who is feared by other fighters.

THE INTANGIBLES

Temper (as mentioned) is one, but that trait reflects his on-ice intensity. He's a hard worker with a determination to succeed, but he does have something to prove this season after his disappointing playoff (four goals in 21 games, zero goals and one assist in the Finals).

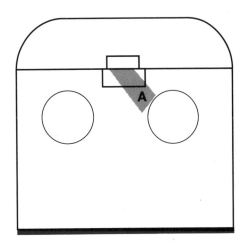

RUSS COURTNALL

Yrs. of NHL service: 5
Born: Duncan, B.C., Canada; June 2, 1965
Position: Center
Height: 5-11
Weight: 180
Uniform no.: 9
Shoots: right

Career statistics:

GP	G	A	TP	PIM
373	112	145	257	258

1988-89 statistics:

GP	G	A	TP	+/-	PIM	PP	SH	GW	GT	S	PCT
73	23	18	41	9	19	7	1	3	0	147	15.6

LAST SEASON

Acquired from Toronto early in the season in exchange for John Kordic. Assist and point totals were second-lowest full season marks of career.

THE FINESSE GAME

Skating and shooting are the hallmarks of Russ Courtnall's finesse game. He's an excellent skater, possessing breakaway speed, superior balance, excellent quickness and agility. Russ puts that speed to use by driving the defensemen off the blue line, forcing them to backpedal and open up ice for his teammates. He doesn't need to coast to make his plays, and can handle and move the puck at almost full speed. He changes direction and speeds within a step. He's a great forechecker and penalty killer.

Courtnall has good hands and vision, and he combines those abilities with anticipation to become an effective playmaker. However, he undercuts his playmaking ability by overhandling the puck (too much 1-on-1 play versus the opposition). He tries to make a play from a crowd, leading to turnovers. If he'd move the puck a little quicker and then jump into the holes he'd be twice as effective.

Russ has an excellent wrist shot, just packed with power. It is a dangerous offensive weapon, and Courtnall uses it to great effect from right in front of the net. He'll often be at a wing position on offensive zone faceoffs in order to take advantage of his shot.

THE PHYSICAL GAME

For a little guy, Courtnall plays awfully tough. He is not a physically imposing player and he isn't going to knock anyone out with his physical game, but Courtnall hits willingly, frequently and with a good bit of strength.

He plays the body well in open ice (his balance on his skates is the key to that ability), but he won't win many battles along the boards because of his stature. Courtnall is unafraid and — though much more suited to a finesse game — will fight when he has to.

THE INTANGIBLES

Courtnall has a good attitude,. He wants to win and he works hard, and can be a super player for the Habs because — unlike in Toronto — he won't have to be the whole show.

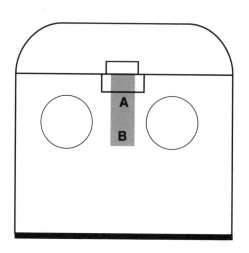

BOB GAINEY

Yrs. of NHL service: 16
Born: Peterborough, Ontario, Canada; December 13, 1953
Position: Left wing
Height: 6-2
Weight: 200
Uniform no.: 23
Shoots: left

Career statistics:

GP	G	A	TP	PIM
1,160	239	262	501	585

1988-89 statistics:

GP	G	A	TP	+/-	PIM	PP	SH	GW	GT	S	PCT
49	10	7	17	13	34	1	0	2	0	65	15.4

LAST SEASON

Games played total was second lowest, goal and point totals were third lowest of career; assist total tied career low. Foot and knee injuries sidelined him throughout the season.

THE FINESSE GAME

Gainey remains, even after a decade and a half, a strong and powerful skater. He is a straight-ahead player and his skating style reflects that no-nonsense approach. Gainey has excellent lateral movement and balance and good acceleration, though he's neither overwhelmingly fast nor exceptionally quick. His balance keys his physical game, keeping him upright and in the play after checks.

His exceptional anticipation and hockey sense always keep him around the puck (of course, his relentless skating helps) — allowing him to either forecheck or keep the puck away from the man he's guarding. His tremendous vision and hockey sense allow Gainey to understand a play and its ramifications. Between his mental and physical skills, he can track the opposition all over the rink.

He has never done much offensively, and does even less now. He won't blow you away with his shots from afar (that's why his wing shots are scoring area B) but can convert most of his opportunities around the net (area A).

THE PHYSICAL GAME

There has always been a consistent physical element to Gainey's game, and his insistent checks wear down the opposition. He is very strong along the boards and very hard to muscle off the puck, and Gainey has the strength to hold his man out of the play for as long as necessary.

He makes his physical play more efficient by hitting smartly; rarely does his defensive work draw penalties.

THE INTANGIBLES

One sign of Gainey's dedication is his conditioning: he's in phenomenal shape. A dedicated athlete and the consummate professional. Gainey is an on-and-off ice leader for the Canadiens. Now he must decide if he has anything left to accomplish in his career, but should he decide to return for the 89-90 season, rest assured Gainey will play as if he were a rookie.

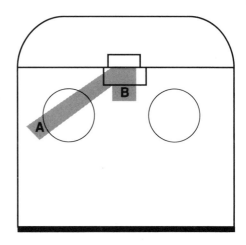

RICK GREEN

Yrs. of NHL service: 13
Born: Belleville, Ontario, Canada; February 20, 1956
Position: Defenseman
Height: 6-3
Weight: 210
Uniform no.: 5
Shoots: left

Career statistics:

GP	G	A	TP	PIM
776	41	206	247	564

1988-89 statistics:

GP	G	A	TP	+/-	PIM	PP	SH	GW	GT	S	PCT
72	1	14	15	19	25	0	0	0	0	42	2.4

LAST SEASON

Games played tied second highest total of career. Assist and point totals were four-season highs. He missed time with a virus (four games) and a wrist injury. PIM total was fourth-lowest among club regulars.

THE FINESSE GAME

Smarts and sound positional play are the keys to Rick's quiet but dependable defensive game. Rick is always aware of where he is on the ice in relation to his net, the opposition and the puck. Because of his vision and play reading skill he can cut off the attack by using his defensive angles to force the opposition to the outside.

Though no better than good as a skater (he has very little speed to speak of) Green's agility and foot speed allow him to effectively close the gap between himself and the puck carrier. Again, his smarts tell him when to make this challenging move and when to simply force the play wide of the net.

Green makes the most of his limited skills by moving the puck quickly and efficiently from his own zone. He is not a playmaker, nor is he the kind of defenseman to rush the puck in order to take pressure off the forwards; he just doesn't have the skill.

Though he's shown (over the past two seasons) a willingness to charge the net for shots, Green is not likely to join the rush as a fourth attacker. His contributions from the offensive blue line will otherwise be minimal and any goals he gets will have to come on shots from the point.

THE PHYSICAL GAME

Green is a physical player, and he takes the body at each opportunity. He uses his strength to hold the opposition out of the play or to neutralize them in front of the net, and he won't often be beaten in these areas.

He uses his reach to poke check effectively or to deflect pucks out of play, and Green also plays the percentages by being one of the League's best holders.

THE INTANGIBLES

Age and health are important considerations here, made more important by the plethora of defensemen the Canadiens want to rotate into their lineup.

He's certainly shown well in his NHL tenure and has nothing to answer for (though he's never played a full season) in terms of output, but the above factors may serve to limit Green's contributions to the Habs this season — if not end them entirely.

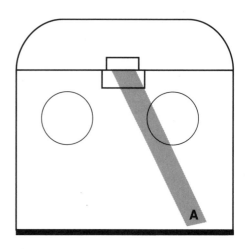

BRIAN HAYWARD

Yrs. of NHL service: 7
Born: Georgetown, Ontario, Canada; June 25, 1960
Position: Goaltender
Height: 5-10
Weight: 175
Uniform no.: 1
Catches: left

Career statistics:

GP	MINS	G	SO	AVG	A	PIM
277	15,623	960	5	3.69	12	73

1988-89 statistics:

GP	MINS	AVG	W	L	T	SO	GA	SA	SAPCT	PIM
36	2,091	2.90	20	13	3	1	101	894	.887	10

LAST SEASON

Games played total was three-season low. He and Patrick Roy shared the Jenniungs Trophy for the League's lowest goals-against-average for third consecutive season. Missed one game with the flu.

THE PHYSICAL GAME

Hayward is a cool, consistent and stand-up goaltender, adept at squaring himself to the puck and cutting down the shooters' angles. He challenges the shooters in almost all situations and lets the puck do the work by just hitting him; you won't often see Hayward flinging himself flying around the ice.

His style is based on smarts and self-knowledge, because Brian is not a great skater. While he has good foot speed and moves around the net well, he has below average balance and does not recover his stance quickly. His lateral movement reflects that, making him vulnerable in scramble situations because he is unable to get into position to stop second and third attempts.

He also fails to use his challenging style sufficiently on screen shots, where he hangs back in the net instead of coming to the top of the screen. That's when you'll see him beaten to the extreme ends of the net — beyond his feet and inside the posts on both sides.

Hayward is average at controlling the puck after a save, usually able to direct it out of danger. He does not frequently leave his net to retrieve loose pucks, and that's smart because he does not handle them well.

THE MENTAL GAME

Brian's concentration and mental toughness have grown steadily since his time in Montreal, to the point now that he applies himself mentally throughout a game. He's less affected by bad goals or games, knowing that a good outing isn't far away. He's competitive and wants to play more often than he gets a chance to, so he does his best to make the most of his opportunities.

THE INTANGIBLES

Hayward is a steady goaltender, and that consistency makes him a more dependable goaler than Patrick Roy. Hayward gives the Canadiens a solid performance most every night out, but he lacks Roy's potential (albeit Patrick's only shown it once — but it won Montreal a Stanley Cup) to raise his game to the situation, to become a hot and thus unbeatable goaltender.

MIKE KEANE

Yrs. of NHL service: 1
Born: Winnipeg, Man., Canada; May 28, 1967
Position: Right wing
Height: 5-10
Weight: 175
Uniform no.: 12
Shoots: right

Career statistics:

GP	G	A	TP	+/-	PIM	PP	SH	GW	GT	S	PCT
69	16	19	35	9	69	5	0	1	0	90	17.8

LAST SEASON

Keane's first in the NHL. He missed one game with a neck injury, seven with a shoulder injury.

THE FINESSE GAME

Keane is a player whose physical style both disguises and powers his finesse game. He's a good skater who uses his skating strength and balance to charge the net, but he also has good vision and hockey sense — so he can make a play en route to the goal.

Mike generally keeps his head up to look over the ice, but he doesn't yet move the puck at NHL speed. He has the hands to make good backhand passes, and he accepts passes well too. His hands are good enough for him to one-time the puck, and he delivers his shots to the net with a good release and some power. Right now, though, he's going to have to be more opportunistic than artistic in order to score.

THE PHYSICAL GAME

He doesn't have great size, but Keane is a tough physical forward. His skating and balance help him greatly in the traffic areas. He takes the body and rubs out his man well in all three zones, and Mike has the strength to be a good hitter.

He's not primarily a fighter, but he can go pretty well. He fights lefty, making him a more difficult opponent. He'll sacrifice his body by blocking shots.

THE INTANGIBLES

There's some solid potential here, 25 goals worth (maybe more) with sufficient NHL experience. Keane's a good worker and the kind of dependable player who can be on the ice in any situation. As a type, he is comparable to Mike McPhee or Ryan Walter.

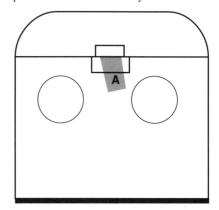

CLAUDE LEMIEUX

Yrs. of NHL service: 4
Born: Buckingham, Quebec, Canada; July 16, 1965
Position: Right wing
Height: 6-1
Weight: 205
Uniform no.: 32
Shoots: right

Career statistics:

GP	G	A	TP	PIM
242	89	82	171	470

1988-89 statistics:

GP	G	A	TP	+/-	PIM	PP	SH	GW	GT	S	PCT
69	29	22	51	14	136	7	0	3	0	220	13.2

LAST SEASON

Games played total was three-season (and full season) low; he missed time with a groin injury. Goal total was second highest of career, third best on club. He was third on the club in PIM total (second among forwards) and first in SOG total.

THE FINESSE GAME

Claude is a power forward, a combination of strength aqnd finesse. His skating is represented by strength, as his stride gives him acceleration, speed and driving ability. His balance is good enough to keep him upright after checking, but Lemieux lacks the fine edge that would make him an agile player. He just charges straight ahead with the puck.

Lemieux has good hockey sense and a solid read of the ice, and he combines those mental attributes with his skating to be a good forechecker. He does not, however, make good use of those skills when he has gained the puck.

While he does carry it well at top speed, Claude undercuts his chances by keeping his head down — he's focused on the puck and the defenseman in front of him. If he looked up, he'd make better use of his teammates. Additionally, Lemieux is a goal-scorer — so he shoots first and asks questions later.

His shot is excellent, strong and accurate, quickly released, and he certainly has the hands to nail the far corner. His release (as well as his ability to work in traffic) benefit the Habs on the power play, when Claude camps in front of the net for garbage goals. He has enough power to blow the puck past the goaltender from the top of the circle.

Lemieux has improved his defensive play, but he'll never be mistaken for teammate Guy Carbonneau.

THE PHYSICAL GAME

Lemieux has superior strength, and that asset works in tandem with his balance to make him a good traffic player. He uses his skating strength to drive the net, and Lemieux has the upper body and arm strength to get his shot off despite the checking he encounters in the slot.

Because he's so strong in his upper body — and because he has excellent balance on his feet to remain vertical after collisions — Lemieux can be a terror up and down the boards. He bangs around with reckless abandon in the corners and continues around the opposition net.

There is, however, a big but.

THE INTANGIBLES

Lemieux is an enigma. He's a big strong winger, an agitator and a chippy/dirty player who can handle most anything his play stirs up — but therein lies the contradiction: He won't always do so.

Lemieux is hugely inconsistent in his use of his physical ability; there are games that he floats through without touching a soul. He needs to consistently apply himself in his very strong physical game; he'd rather dive for penalties than muscle his way into position.

We questioned last year whether or not his new coach would appreciate Lemieux's style of game; Pat Burns did not. Lemieux needs an attitude transplant if he wants to play for Burns, but we wouldn't be surprised if a change of scenery was in his future.

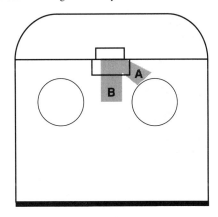

CRAIG LUDWIG

Yrs. of NHL service: 7
Born: Rhinelander, Wisconsin, USA; March 15, 1961
Position: Defenseman
Height: 6-3
Weight: 217
Uniform no.: 17
Shoots: left

Career statistics:

GP	G	A	TP	PIM
524	25	96	121	511

1988-89 statistics:

GP	G	A	TP	+/-	PIM	PP	SH	GW	GT	S	PCT
74	3	13	16	33	73	0	1	1	1	83	3.6

LAST SEASON

Assist total was four-season high. He missed six games with a League-imposed suspension. His plus/minus was the club's fourth best, second among defensemen.

THE FINESSE GAME

Finesse is not really the name of Ludwig's game, so he succeeds by smartly staying within his limitations. He's not a bad skater, though no one element in his skating leaps to the fore. Craig doesn't have exceptional speed, quickness or agility, but he can step up and close the gap on the puck carrier.

Because he sees the defensive zone fairly well, Ludwig can get away with the occasional fancy pass, the pass up the middle to the breaking forward. But he'll most often make the pass necessary to get the puck out of danger. His good vision also powers his transition game; he can make the takeout and get the play up ice quickly.

Paired as he is with Chris Chelios, Ludwig generally serves as the defensive safety valve — the last man back. As such, he doesn't usually become a fourth attacker in the offensive zone. He does, however, have a good enough read of the offensive zone that he can successfully drop the puck and charge the net.

His offense is otherwise minimal.

THE PHYSICAL GAME

Ludwig is a tough guy and a mean sonofagun, as his suspension-earning elbow to Trent Yawney proved. Craig is aggressive in the corners and the front of the net, but he will take shots as well as give them. He frequently uses his stick, so forwards won't make too many plays with their heads down.

He also sacrifices his body by blocking shots.

THE INTANGIBLES

Teams love mean defensemen, especially those who don't usually accrue many penalties. Ludwig fits into this mold, and he's pretty good defensively too. Craig's non-fancy style of just clearing the man and moving the puck perfectly complements that of his partner, offensively oriented Chris Chelios. That's Ludwig's greatest value.

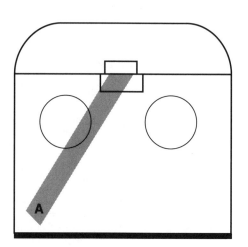

MIKE MCPHEE

Yrs. of NHL service: 6
Born: Sydney, N.S., Canada; July 14, 1960
Position: Left wing
Height: 6-2
Weight: 200
Uniform no.: 35
Shoots: left

Career statistics:

GP	G	A	TP	PIM
389	101	108	209	415

1988-89 statistics:

GP	G	A	TP	+/-	PIM	PP	SH	GW	GT	S	PCT
73	19	22	41	14	74	1	1	1		1	154	12.3

LAST SEASON

Games played total was three-season low (toe injury). Assist total tied career high, goal and point totals tied and established, respectively, second highest marks of career.

THE FINESSE GAME

Strength is the basis of McPhee's game, so it's only fitting that strength marks his skating. That power gives him speed and acceleration, as well as making him an almost tireless skater. Mike has a good helping of balance, which combines with his skating strength to allow him to drive through checks. He has a modicum of foot speed, but not so much that he could be labelled an exceptionally agile skater.

McPhee combines speed with anticipation to become a very good forechecker and penalty killer. His checking creates many loose pucks and McPhee is talented enough to convert on those opportunities around the net.

Though he lacks the sensitive hands needed to be considered a true goal scorer (McPhee isn't going to finesse three inches of puck into two inches of net), his anticipation will get him to scoring position and loose pucks.

And, because he gets a good read of the ice, McPhee can make plays because his hands are sensitive enough to give and take soft passes.

McPhee is a determined back checker and plays good, positional defense, rarely wandering from where he is supposed to be when in his defensive zone.

THE PHYSICAL GAME

McPhee is a very strong player, and he uses his strength to play a very aggressive game. He gets into the corners and bulls around, and his balance helps keep him vertical and ready to make plays after banging into the opposition. Mike can be a punishing hitter and he hits relentlessly.

He'll win more than his share of battles along the boards.

THE INTANGIBLES

His all-around skills serve to take McPhee out of the role-playing category, and he's a much-sought-after commodity. But like many of his teammates, McPhee was less than his usual self during the Cup Final last spring, and his response to that failure bears watching.

His work ethic suggests McPhee will come back better than before.

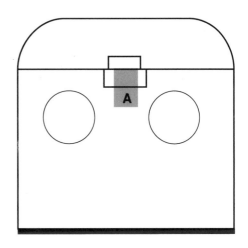

MATS NASLUND

Yrs. of NHL service: 7
Born: Timra, Sweden; October 31, 1959
Position: Left wing
Height: 5-7
Weight: 160
Uniform no.: 26
Shoots: left

Career statistics:

GP	G	A	TP	PIM
545	222	349	571	88

1988-89 statistics:

GP	G	A	TP	+/-	PIM	PP	SH	GW	GT	S	PCT
77	33	51	84	34	14	14	0	4	0	165	20.0

LAST SEASON

Led club in goals (third highest of career and three season high), points (second best of career and three season high) and power play goals. His plus/minus rating was second best among forwards, third on the club. He was sidelined with an ankle injury.

THE FINESSE GAME

Probably foremost among Naslund's considerable finesse skills is his skating — which is excellent. Mats has tremendous speed and acceleration, great change of pace ability (he'll shift gears and direction within a stride), and exceptional balance. He has excellent lateral movement and is extremely agile with and without the puck.

Naslund has excellent hands, and that asset manifests itself in his puckhandling. He handles the puck at any speed, leaning away from defenders but dangling the puck on the end of his stick and just out of their reach. He gives and takes passes excellently while in full stride.

His hand and foot skills work in combination with his superior hockey sense and vision to show him the best plays, and Naslund is talented enough to either exploit those openings himself or to lead a teammate to them.

Mats can score from anywhere in the offensive zone with his excellent wrist shot, shooting from almost impossible angles to keep the goaltender honest. Because his excellent hands need just the slightest opening to work with, Naslund is especially dangerous in the area around the net, but he doesn't shoot enough for the opportunities he gets. He likes to go to his forehand on breakaways.

All his skills make him a specialty teams regular (he'll set up at the left hashmarks to feed Bobby Smith and Claude Lemieux in the slot on the power play).

THE PHYSICAL GAME

Like Calgary's Joe Mullen, Naslund absorbs more punishment than almost any other player in the NHL. But despite the beatings, Naslund remains a tough, aggressive *and* successful physical player.

He doesn't have great size, but his balance and leg power help him dish out checks that knock the opposition off the puck. Naslund is absolutely fearless and will go to the corner with any player, even though his game is made in the open ice. He backs down from no one.

THE INTANGIBLES

Always a fine character player with a solid work ethic, Naslund was surprisingly unheard from during the Habs loss to Calgary in the Cup Final (just one goal in the finals). In fact, his whole playoff performance was a disappointment.

He's entering the option year of his contract, and rumor has it he wants to head back to Sweden. Those factors bear watching heading into 1989-90.

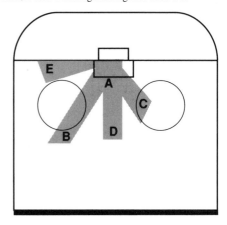

224

STEPHANE RICHER

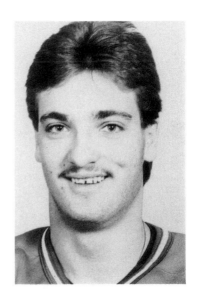

Yrs. of NHL service: 4
Born: Ripon, Quebec, Canada; June 7, 1966
Position: Center
Height: 6-2
Weight: 200
Uniform no.: 44
Shoots: right

Career statistics:

GP	G	A	TP	PIM
263	116	98	214	263

1988-89 statistics:

GP	G	A	TP	+/-	PIM	PP	SH	GW	GT	S	PCT
68	25	35	60	4	61	11	0	6	0	214	11.7

LAST SEASON

Assist total was career high, goal, games played and point totals second highest of career. He missed 10 games with a League-imposed suspension. He finished fourth on the club in scoring, third in power play goals and second in SOG total.

THE FINESSE GAME

Richer has exceptional finesse skills, primary of which is his slap shot, one of the two or three best in the League. That shot is pretty much unstoppable from the edge of the faceoff circle and in, but Stephane is more than just a one-hit wonder. His soft hands make him extremely dangerous around the net, as he can finesse the puck through the smallest opening regardless of checking.

He's an excellent skater whose powerful stride gives him explosive acceleration and rink-length speed. His speed will not only get him to the openings but will create them as well. His exceptional foot speed and balance give him one-step quickness, and they also combine to make Richer a very agile player — he has excellent lateral movement.

His excellent hockey sense works in tandem with his skating to put Richer into position where he can unleash his shot; he gets into scoring position excellently. He uses his anticipation to lead his teammates into openings with his passes.

Primarily a goal-scoring center, Richer's hand skills extend to his puckhandling and passing. He carries the puck excellently at all speeds, but he can also take and give passes at full speed because of his soft hands. He likes to work 1-on-1 against the defense, and is that rare player who could stickhandle through an entire team and score.

THE PHYSICAL GAME

Richer has excellent physical tools. He's got size, strength and balance — all of which could guarantee a successful physical game. His use of his physical skills is limited, however, to occasional forays into the corners. Still, he's bumping the opposition for the puck.

His strength can also help him in the high traffic area around the net, allowing him to hold the puck longer and withstand checks. He uses his body well to protect the puck, and Richer's reach and arm strength help him pull loose pucks from traffic.

THE INTANGIBLES

Just a huge one, as in attitude. Also, the offshoots of that: desire, work ethic, character — all the things we thought Richer had shown during his 50-goal campaign two seasons back.

But it seems we were premature in discussing Stephane's maturity. He reverted last season to his previous form, including battling with his coach (which, by the way, we mentioned as a factor in his possible success last season).

Only if Richer regains his positive attitude will he repeat his outstanding work of two years back; he'll otherwise be saddled with the tag of underachiever, and a great possibility exists that he'll find himself in a different uniform next season.

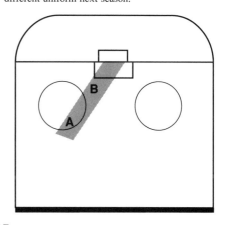

LARRY ROBINSON

Yrs. of NHL service: 16
Born: Winchester, Ontario, Canada; June 2, 1951
Position: Defenseman
Height: 6-3
Weight: 220
Uniform no.: 19
Shoots: left

Career statistics:

GP	G	A	TP	PIM
1,202	197	686	883	706

1988-89 statistics:

GP	G	A	TP	+/-	PIM	PP	SH	GW	GT	S	PCT
74	4	26	30	23	22	0	0	0	0	79	5.1

LAST SEASON

Games played total was three-season high, but goal total was third lowest and point totals second lowest (full-season) totals of career.

THE FINESSE GAME

Despite age and the requisite wear and tear, Robinson still skates well. While his rushes up-ice have generally fallen by the wayside the odd rush to relieve pressure on his forwards isn't out of the question. He is slower afoot than ever before, so he can be beaten to the corners or left a step behind by a successful fake.

Larry still moves the puck for the breakout pass extremely well, and he'll still see power play time because of his ability to find the open man. Larry does a little cheating into the zone, and he still does well in containing the play.

Smarts and almost two decades of NHL experience are the keys to Robinson's success now. He knows when to challenge and when to stay within his diminishing range of skills.

His positional play is almost textbook-like, courtesy of his anticipation and play-reading capabilities. Robinson sees the ice defensively as well as any superstar forward sees it offensively.

THE PHYSICAL GAME

Though less aggressive than earlier in his career, Robinson still plays a physical game. He does whatever is necessary to contain the play and gain the puck; if that means just taking the body, fine. If it means thumping a little harder to clear the crease, fine.

Larry is still a strong player, and he'll often shoulder the responsibility of handling the League's bigger and tougher forwards. Perhaps the most startling thing is that his physical game has remained effective without Robinson growing into larger PIM totals. In other words, his physical play doesn't hurt the team.

THE INTANGIBLES

We mean no disrespect when we say Robinson's skills have diminished. In fact, his ability to contribute in the NHL despite 17 years of combat shows just how extraordinary Robinson is.

His will to win remains unsurpassed, and he is an invaluable example to the team's younger players. He is personable, and a fun guy in the dressing room, and he should be inducted into the Hall of Fame immediately upon his retirement.

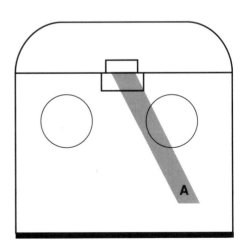

PATRICK ROY

Yrs. of NHL service: 4
Born: Quebec City, Quebec, Canada; October 5, 1965
Position: Goaltender
Height: 6-0
Weight: 175
Uniform no.: 33
Catches: left

Career statistics:

GP	MINS	G	SO	AVG	A	PIM
187	10,687	517	9	2.90	12	28

1988-89 statistics:

GP	MINS	AVG	W	L	T	SO	GA	SA	SAPCT	PIM
48	2,744	2.47	33	5	6	4	113	1,228	.908	2

LAST SEASON

Finished first in the NHL in goals-against-average and save percentage, second in wins, and fifth in shutouts — all career bests. Along with Brian Hayward, Roy won the Jennings Trophy for fewest goals against for third consecutive season. Games and minutes played totals were career highs. Missed three games with tonsillitis.

THE PHYSICAL GAME

While he's added a certain degree of stand-up play to his game. Roy lives and dies with his reflexes. He flops a lot (sometimes too early and too frequently) but that works for him because of his size; his long legs cover almost the entire bottom of the net. His fast feet cover the low corners, and serve as his version of lateral ability.

His balance is good, and Roy quickly springs from the ice to regain his stance. However, it's while he's on the ice that he's often left scrambling for loose pucks around the net. He does not generally roam from his net to handle the puck and that's good, because he's not a particularly gifted stickhandler and doesn't show great puck movement judgment anyway.

Because he doesn't cut his angles or square himself to the puck as best as he can, Patrick is weak on his short stick side. That indicates failure to properly cut down the angle. He's also stiff on his glove side with shots that are close to his body and don't allow him to extend his arm; the Flames consistently beat him over his glove during the Finals.

He also does not handle rebounds off his chest protector well, leaving the puck to bounce loose in front of him.

THE MENTAL GAME

Patrick has big save capability. He can be tough mentally and return from bad goals or games, and his confidence helps him in that.

His concentration and vision are excellent, especially on scrambles around the net. He sees the puck very well and tunnels in on it, and he keeps his concentration intact within games.

THE INTANGIBLES

While he showed well throughout the season and much of the playoffs (and deserves credit for his regular-season unbeaten streak at the Forum), Roy was certainly out-goaled by Mike Vernon during the Final. So while Patrick has made certain improvements in his game, we maintain — Vezina Trophy aside — that he hasn't reapproached his stellar status of the 1986 Stanley Cup playoffs.

BRIAN SKRUDLAND

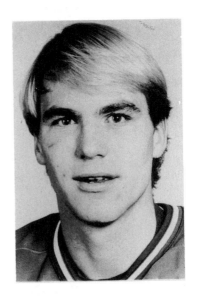

Yrs. of NHL service: 4
Born: Peace River, Alta., Canada; July 31, 1963
Position: Center
Height: 6-0
Weight: 188
Uniform no.: 39
Shoots: left

Career statistics:

GP	G	A	TP	PIM
294	44	83	127	360

1988-89 statistics:

GP	G	A	TP	+/-	PIM	PP	SH	GW	GT	S	PCT
71	12	29	41	22	84	1	1	5	0	98	12.2

LAST SEASON

Games played total was three-season low, assist and point totals career highs. He missed three games with the flu.

THE FINESSE GAME

Quickness and strength make Skrudland a good skater and very effective defensive forward. His skating is strong and almost tireless and, while Skrudland is not a tremendously agile player, his foot speed and quickness help him stay on his man all the time. That extra step helps him close the passing lanes and thus deny puck movement.

Good — and improving — anticipation and sense of the NHL game help Brian in his checking role. That means he can use his skating more efficiently when necessary by closing off areas of the ice through smarts. His offensive skills are growing apace as Skrudland takes greater and greater advantage of the loose pucks his checking creates.

His good vision serves him in those offensive moments as he looks for plays around the net instead of just slamming the puck into the goaltender. Like others on the Canadiens checking staff, his growing ability to contribute offensively makes him more valuable and moves him out of the role player category.

THE PHYSICAL GAME

Skrudland plays an aggressive and consistently physical game, with his quickness allowing him to close the gaps between himself and the puck carrier. His good strength makes him a hard checker and he bumps his man at every opportunity, though sometimes to his disadvantage. Penalties and missed checks are the result, but this aspect of Skrudland's game is also improving.

He plays that physical style home and away and at both ends of the ice. He uses his size well against the boards and can take the puck away from the opposition fairly frequently, and his improving offensive ability makes his physical play more effective.

THE INTANGIBLES

Skrudland is a character player, the kind who gives 100 percent every night. His growing offensive ability is carrying him beyond the defensive forward role, though that is clearly where his talent is. But like other members of the squad, Skrudland has something to prove this season in response to his own less-than-impressive performance against the Flames in the Finals.

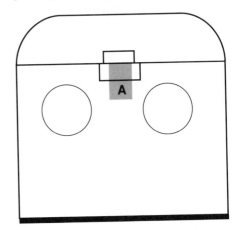

BOBBY SMITH

Yrs. of NHL service: 11
Born: North Sydney, N.S., Canada; February 12, 1958
Position: Center
Height: 6-4
Weight: 210
Uniform no.: 15
Shoots: left

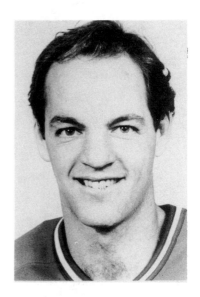

Career statistics:

GP	G	A	TP	PIM
838	316	590	906	703

1988-89 statistics:

GP	G	A	TP	+/-	PIM	PP	SH	GW	GT	S	PCT
80	32	51	83	25	69	6	0	3	0	195	16.4

LAST SEASON

One of three Habs to play all 80 games. Goal total was second highest of career and a seven-season best; he finished second in team scoring. Plus/minus was third best among forwards, SOG total fourth highest on club.

THE FINESSE GAME

Smith is a very smooth and fluid skater, with a long stride that belies his speed: that stride gets him away from the opposition quickly. He also has excellent balance and lateral movement, and he adds his skating to that agility to make plays beyond the capabilities of many NHLers.

Smith's vision and anticipation skills are also very high, and he uses those traits to recognize and exploit openings with either his own exceptional puck control, or by leading a teammate into the openings with soft and accurate passes.

Bobby's outstanding hand skills and hockey sense combine to make him a very dangerous scorer who can score in many ways, from almost anywhere in the offensive zone. Smith has an excellent selection of shots (hard and accurate wrist shot, very good slap shot), but his sneakiest weapon is the League's best backhand — it hits the upper right corner almost every time. The Canadiens set Smith up for that shot on the power play, otherwise he's more likely to score from deeper in the slot.

His transitional game down-ice is good, and he's a solid and consistent defensive player.

THE PHYSICAL GAME

Though he plays exceptionally well in traffic, Smith is not primarily a physical player. Rather, his excellent balance and reach allow him to dislodge opponents from the puck or to take it from them while he maintains body position.

He does not shy away from contact and he takes more physical punishment now than ever before. Bobby also initiates a great deal of contact, though not of the body-bashing kind.

His reach is exceptional and allows him access to the puck while on the outside of the crowd, and he certainly has the ability to make a play coming away from the boards. Hand and wrist strength help him snare those pucks, and they also make him a good faceoff man.

THE INTANGIBLES

Smith has matured into a disciplined player with upper-level finesse skill, and a solid team attitude and work ethic.

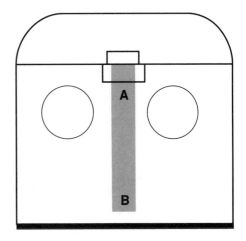

PETR SVOBODA

Yrs. of NHL service: 5
Born: Most, Czechoslovakia; February 14, 1966
Position: Defenseman
Height: 6-1
Weight: 170
Uniform no.: 25
Shoots: left

Career statistics:

GP	G	A	TP	PIM
356	25	121	146	517

1988-89 statistics:

GP	G	A	TP	+/-	PIM	PP	SH	GW	GT	S	PCT
71	8	37	45	28	147	4	0	1	0	131	6.1

LAST SEASON

All point totals were career highs. PIM total was second highest of career, and second highest among Hab defensemen. He was sidelined with a late season back injury.

THE FINESSE GAME

Skating is the key to Svoboda's total game, and he demonstrates speed, quickness, agility and balance. Petr moves forward and back with equal ease and agility, as his balance and foot speed give him outstanding mobility and lateral movement. He uses that skill to challenge the puck at both blue lines.

He complements his skating ability with good hand skills, and will rush the puck to take pressure off the Canadiens' forwards. Petr handles the puck well and has soft hands that make him a good passer. He also takes the puck off the boards extremely well in the defensive zone and starts the play away almost in one motion.

Svoboda uses his hand skills to get the puck to his teammates and to contain the point well, but his ice vision still does not completely jibe with NHL speed. He doesn't always find the open man as easily as possible, and Svoboda also has a tendency (because his head is dropped) to drive a shot into a charging opposing player. His shot is accurate but lacking in strength. He'll cruise to the top of the faceoff circle if he can.

THE PHYSICAL GAME

Petr is an aggressive player, especially in the use of his stick. He'll get nailed for his cross-checks and slashes, but one reason Svoboda has to resort to stickwork is because his strength isn't sufficient to clear the front of the net or take the opposition off the puck.

He needs more muscle on his frame, or else he'll continue to be bounced off the puck and out-muscled in front of the net.

THE INTANGIBLES

Svoboda's matured into a fairly dependable and consistent two-way defenseman. His aggressive style of play doesn't always work against him, as that style often takes the opposition out of the game — they're too busy trying to clobber him, instead of paying attention to the play.

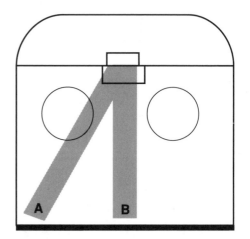

RYAN WALTER

Yrs. of NHL service: 10
Born: New Westminster, B.C., Canada; April 23, 1958
Position: Center/left wing/right wing
Height: 6-0
Weight: 195
Uniform no.: 11
Shoots: left

Career statistics:

GP	G	A	TP	PIM
816	247	354	601	816

1988-89 statistics:

GP	G	A	TP	+/-	PIM	PP	SH	GW	GT	S	PCT
78	14	17	31	23	48	1	1	0	0	104	13.5

LAST SEASON

Games played total tied second highest of career and was six-season high. Goal and assist totals were second lowest of career, point total a career low. His plus/minus total was fourth best among the club's forwards.

THE FINESSE GAME

Like many of his teammates, Walter has a finesse game that springs from his physical one. His skating is particularly marked by his strength, especially in his ability to pursue the puck as a checking forward. He has good balance and power, and those assets help him in his physical game by driving him through his checks and by making him a tenacious checker.

Walter has learned to read the ice and anticipate the play fairly well, so he's able to break up a pass or find an opening by positioning himself well.

Because of his vision, Ryan can capitalize on the opportunities his checking creates by getting the puck to his teammates. He'll need to be opportunistic for his own scoring, picking up junk near the net, because his shot lacks the quick release that will fool NHL goaltending. He'll also be used to plug the front of the goal on the power play.

THE PHYSICAL GAME

Ryan gets the most from his physical ability by playing a controlled but aggressive game. He's got a mean streak, but Walter plays aggressively in all three zones — at home or on the road, winning or losing — without taking penalties. Because of his balance, Walter comes out of most collisions vertical and ready to make a play.

He backs down from nothing and he uses his body well, showing good strength along the boards where he out-muscles the opposition.

THE INTANGIBLES

Walter is an honest player who works hard and always gives 100 percent of himself. Of all the Canadiens, he's one who can look at his play during the playoffs — especially during the Final — and be satisfied.

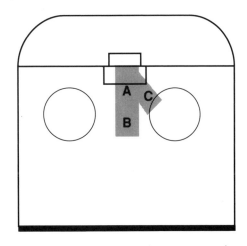

NEW JERSEY
DEVILS

LINE COMBINATIONS
PATRIK SUNDSTROM
BRENDAN SHANAHAN-JOHN MACLEAN
AARON BROTEN-KIRK MULLER
PAT VERBEEK-CLAUDE LOISELLE
DOUG BROWN

DEFENSE PAIRINGS
RANDY VELISCHEK-JOE CIRELLA
TOMMY ALBELIN-TOM KURVERS
KEN DANEYKO-CRAIG WOLANIN

GOALTENDERS
SEAN BURKE

OTHER PLAYERS
MARK JOHNSON — Center
JIM KORN — Right wing
JACK O'CALLAHAN — Defenseman
BRUCE DRIVER — Defenseman
PERRY ANDERSON — Left wing

POWER PLAY

FIRST UNIT:
PAT VERBEEK-KIRK MULLER-JIM KORN
TOM KURVERS-AARON BROTEN

KORN plugs the front of the net, VERBEEK is in the left faceoff circle and MULLER the right faceoff circle. BROTEN controls the play from the point and distributes the puck; VERBEEK isolated is the first choice, with a KURVERS shot and VERBEEK and MULLER crashing the net the second option.

A second unit typically consists of BRENDAN SHANAHAN, PATRICK SUNDSTROM AND JOHN MACLEAN. MACLEAN plays off the right wing post, SHANAHAN is at the hashmarks and SUNDSTROM controls from the left boards. TOMMY ALBELIN will see time at the blue line, as will BRUCE DRIVER when healthy.

Last season New Jersey's power play was POOR, scoring 85 goals in 466 opportunities (18.2 percent, 20th overall).

PENALTY KILLING

FIRST UNIT:
DOUG BROWN-CLAUDE LOISELLE
RANDY VELISCHEK-JOE CIRELLA

SECOND UNIT:
MARK JOHNSON-
KEN DANEYKO-CRAIG WOLANIN

The Devils send a forechecker after the puck in the offensive zone, and keep the other forward high. Both units are aggressive on the puck in the defensive zone, playing from a box formation.

Last season New Jersey's penalty killing was POOR, allowing 115 goals in 467 shorthanded opportunities (75.4 percent, 18th overall).

CRUCIAL FACEOFFS
CLAUDE LOISELLE is the key here, with MULLER following.

PERRY ANDERSON

Yrs. of NHL service: 7
Born: Barrie, Ontario, Canada; October 14, 1961
Position: Left wing
Height: 6-1
Weight: 225
Uniform no.: 25
Shoots: left

Career statistics:

GP	G	A	TP	PIM
351	48	51	99	903

1988-89 statistics:

GP	G	A	TP	+/-	PIM	PP	SH	GW	GT	S	PCT
39	3	6	9	5	128	0	0	0	0	36	8.3

LAST SEASON

Games played mark was lowest since joining New Jersey, with a late season shoulder separation contributing to that. Goal and point totals were "full-season" career lows.

THE FINESSE GAME

There really isn't one. Anderson can skate — forward at least — with tremendous speed from one end of the ice to the other, but that's about it. He has little agility and lateral movement, taking himself out of the play with wide turns and enabling the opposition to simply sidestep his bull-in-a-china-shop charges.

Perry doesn't add a whole lot of smarts to his skating, and that makes him poor positionally. His wandering in search of opposing bodies to crunch almost always leaves him out of position, and Anderson has little understanding of what to do when he is in position.

Anderson likes to unload long-distance slap shots when he does latch onto the puck, but his shot isn't going to fool NHL goaltending. He's going to have be in front of a wide-open net with the puck at his feet for him to score.

THE PHYSICAL GAME

If he can catch anybody, Anderson can be a punishing hitter. He has great upper body strength and can really lay on the muscle along the boards or in the corners, but he'd better have a teammate nearby to make a play with the loose puck because Anderson can't.

What Anderson *can* do, aside from skate fast, is fight. He throws his fists pretty well, and he's more than willing to stand up for his smaller teammates, but he also looks to fight at every instigation.

If he gets decked by a clean check, Anderson takes it as a personal affront. Aside from the finesse abilities, that's the difference between the Tocchets and Neelys and Perry Anderson; they accept checks and stay away from taking that retaliatory — and stupid — penalty. He doesn't.

THE INTANGIBLES

What's to say? Anderson is a role player whose role was severely crimped last season. He'll be shuttled in and out of the lineup again, and don't be surprised if it's a lineup other than New Jersey's.

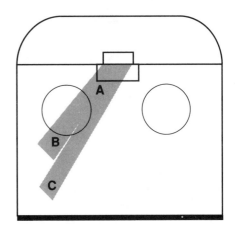

AARON BROTEN

Yrs. of NHL service: 8
Born: Roseau, Minn., USA; November 14, 1960
Position: Left wing
Height: 5-10
Weight: 168
Uniform no.: 10
Shoots: left

Career statistics:

GP	G	A	TP	PIM
599	152	299	451	331

1988-89 statistics:

GP	G	A	TP	+/-	PIM	PP	SH	GW	GT	S	PCT
80	16	43	59	-7	81	4	0	2	0	178	9.0

LAST SEASON

Finished fifth on the club in points, he was one of just four players to play all 80 games. Goal total tied second-lowest of career and was lowest in five seasons.

THE FINESSE GAME

Of the three players on what used to be New Jersey's top line (together with Kirk Muller and Pat Verbeek) Broten's finesse skills are the most subtle, and therefore the most likely to suffer when the line suffers. Skating and smarts are the keys to his game, but when his linemates can't open up the ice with their physical play, Aaron's skills are going to fall by the wayside.

He doesn't have outstanding speed, but his balance makes him agile enough to change direction in a step or hit the holes to get to open ice. That balance also allows Broten to handle the puck well in traffic, and his anticipation helps him find the openings for his teammates. Broten can pass well to both sides, and his puck skills make him indispensable on the power play.

Broten's a playmaker before he's a goal scorer (one reason for his unremarkable goal total), but his shot isn't good enough to overpower any NHL goaltender from a distance. That's why his teammates have to open up ice for him, so he can get closer to the net. He likes to go to the upper right corner with his shot.

THE PHYSICAL GAME

Broten's size mitigates against his physical play, so his strength game is a minimal one. He can — but not necessarily will — gain the puck along the boards because of his hands and balance, and he'll bump bigger forwards, but he certainly won't knock anyone into the sixth row.

THE INTANGIBLES

Like the rest of his Devil teammates, Aaron never really got himself untracked last year. And too, his 59-point season is far more typical of his NHL career (four of six seasons, he's finished with fewer than 60 points) than it is atypical.

While his play during the Devils' 1987-88 playoff season indicated he can be an on-ice leader, Broten's efforts last year paint him as an average NHL left wing.

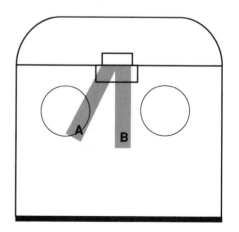

DOUG BROWN

Yrs. of NHL service: 2
Born: Southborough, Mass., USA; June 12, 1964
Position: Right wing
Height: 5-11
Weight: 180
Uniform no.: 24
Shoots: right

Career statistics:

GP	G	A	TP	PIM
137	29	22	51	35

1988-89 statistics:

GP	G	A	TP	+/-	PIM	PP	SH	GW	GT	S	PCT
63	15	10	25	-7	15	4	0	2	0	110	13.6

LAST SEASON

Goal total was career high, despite shuttling between AHL and NHL.

THE FINESSE GAME

Brown is a good skater, possessing more quickness than speed. He moves very well in contained spaces, stopping and starting and changing direction within one step very well. He has less rink length speed, but his good jump will get him ahead of the opposition winger when Doug makes the transition from defense to offense. His skating makes him an excellent checker and penalty killer.

His scoring and puckhandling abilities are less sure at the NHL level. He doesn't handle the puck well near the opposition *or* at top speed, so when he comes into the offensive zone — and in order to avoid the defenseman — Brown is always moving to the left wing and his backhand side. He takes himself to bad ice and tries to stutter-step past the defender, but the fakes don't work on NHL competition.

THE PHYSICAL GAME

Brown deserves all the credit in the world for throwing his body around recklessly, bowling into the opposition, charging the corners. Unfortunately, Doug lacks the strength to tie up the NHL's stronger forwards, willing though he may be. Worse, Brown doesn't have the strength to even slow down most NHL left wings. Of course, that makes his checking more special, because he's doing it all with brains and skating.

An improvement in upper body strength (he must be able to at least serve as a halfway effective roadblock)

is mandatory if Brown is to remain in the checking winger role.

THE INTANGIBLES

Brown's a smart player, and he shows that when he plays. He's enthusiastic and hard working, and he's shown that he can rise to the NHL's most special occasions. He brings an enthusiasm and intensity to the club, and he can be a leader in that regard.

Rudderless that they were last season, Brown should be in the Devils lineup each night; they need an example of work and intensity.

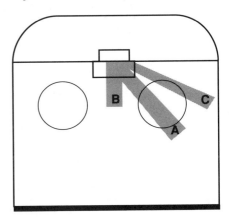

SEAN BURKE

Yrs. of NHL service: 2
Born: Windsor, Ontario, Canada; January 29, 1967
Position: Goaltender
Height: 6-3
Weight: 185
Uniform no.: 1
Catches: left

Career statistics:

GP	MINS	G	SO	AVG	A	PIM
75	4,279	265	4	3.72	3	60

1988-89 statistics

GP	MINS	AVG	W	L	T	SO	GA	SA	SAPCT	PIM
62	3,590	3.84	22	31	9	3	230	1,823	.873	54

LAST SEASON

First full NHL season, with corresponding career numbers in all categories. He missed four games with a January groin injury.

THE PHYSICAL GAME

Size and the ability to complement it with great reflexes are the hallmarks of Burke's game. He generally uses his size in a stand-up style (especially on breakaways, where he almost always forces the opposition to make the first move), but his extremely fast feet and legs belie the general wisdom about shooting to the feet of big men.

Sean demonstrates great balance in his stance and is an excellent skater. He moves well across the front of the net (laterally), and out of his net as well (he moves to the screens to take up as much space as possible and minimize deflections). His balance also helps him regain his stance quickly when he butterflies to the ice. He does, however, have the tendency to hold the ice with his inner edges, so he is vulnerable to five-hole goals.

Sean has a good glove hand and a quick stick, though his hand speed doesn't match his foot speed. He really benefits from his size on high shots. He handles the puck well in moving it to his teammates.

THE MENTAL GAME

Burke's mental game is almost as accomplished as his physical one. He has excellent anticipation and vision and is very tough mentally. His excellent concentration is unfazed by bad goals or games. He is always prepared to play and not only has the capability of making the big save, but of winning games by himself.

THE INTANGIBLES

Burke returned to earth somewhat last season, after his sky-high playoff run of 1988. But while he showed he was indeed human, he also showed that he is still one of the game's best prospects for superstardom.

Unfortunately for him (and his team), when he was less than his best, New Jersey faltered. In order for him to improve as a player, his team's play must improve as well. Otherwise, great potential exists for him to fall into bad habits while covering up the Devils' defensive mistakes.

But we stand fast when we say that what Burke can mean to the Devils — and what he has already meant — is inestimable.

KEN DANEYKO

Yrs. of NHL service: 5
Born: Windsor, Ontario, Canada; April 17, 1964
Position: Defenseman
Height: 6-0
Weight: 200
Uniform no.: 3
Shoots: left

Career statistics:

GP	G	A	TP	PIM
295	13	38	51	832

1988-89 statistics:

GP	G	A	TP	+/-	PIM	PP	SH	GW	GT	S	PCT
80	5	5	10	-22	283	1	0	0	0	108	4.6

LAST SEASON

Played 80 games for second consecutive year. Point total tied full-season career low, but PIM total was career high. He led the team in that department, and was third-worst in plus/minus (worst among defensemen).

THE FINESSE GAME

Like defense partner Craig Wolanin, Daneyko seems stalled in second gear. The improvements he'd shown in his skating and judgement seemed to have been abandoned last season.

Where his skating and improving concentration had better helped him cover the front of the net and make plays in the corners, Daneyko last year was often caught flat-footed around the cage. He is getting to the puck better when he chases it, but still shows little understanding of the depth of the plays available to him; Ken is just going to throw the puck up the boards.

After a season otherwise, Daneyko is once again allowing the opposition to come to him, rather than forcing a play by stepping up. Of course, skating ability has a lot to do with that, and thus the circle starts again. And, after three full NHL seasons, Daneyko has yet to demonstrate consistent ability in handling forechecking and making correct passing decisions.

He's no real offensive threat. Despite his upper body strength, his shot is surprisingly mild.

THE PHYSICAL GAME

This guy is strong and tough. He shows no favorites in who he pounds, and he uses his body at all opportunities. He is a punishing hitter along the boards and is very strong in front of his net. He just might be the most punishing front-of-the-net defenseman in the NHL.

But he does get carried away, and will often take needless (or retaliatory) penalties. His PIM total also reflects the fact that he will fight anyone any time. But even given that, Daneyko doesn't rank as one of the League's heavyweights; not many players are afraid to fight him.

He benefits from his low center of gravity, which makes him difficult to knock down and ready to continue play after collisions.

THE INTANGIBLES

There is potential here, not the least in the fact that Daneyko works fairly hard at his game. But he too, like Wolanin, would greatly benefit from an older defensive presence to learn from. By the way, isn't Coach Jim Schoenfeld a former NHL defenseman?

Ken is a good team man and enthusiastic, and his willingness should be put to better use.

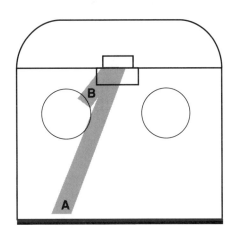

BRUCE DRIVER

Yrs. of NHL service: 5
Born: Toronto, Ontario, Canada; April 29, 1962
Position: Defenseman
Height: 6-0
Weight: 185
Uniform no.: 23
Shoots: left

Career statisitics:

GP	G	A	TP	PIM
286	34	123	157	196

1988-89 statistics:

GP	G	A	TP	+/-	PIM	PP	SH	GW	GT	S	PCT
27	1	15	16	0	24	1	0	0	1	69	1.4

LAST SEASON

A recurring leg injury forced Driver to the sidelines, limiting him to his lowest full-season NHL game total.

THE FINESSE GAME

Driver is definitely a finesse player. He's a smooth skater, not overly gifted with speed but quick enough to get a jump on the opposition. He won't often rush the puck because he lacks the speed to either force or exploit openings himself, but Driver joins the play as a fourth attacker at the opposing blue line.

He sees the play in front of him fairly well and he can get the puck to his teammates in those openings, so he's a power play natural.

He has an average shot from the point, but has taken to shooting more frequently. That leads to more opportunities and more points.

He plays positional defense and is adept at forcing the play wide of the net by using his defensive angles; his skating helps him there by allowing him to keep pace with the League's faster forwards.

THE PHYSICAL GAME

Unlike many finesse players, Driver is willing to sacrifice his body for defense. He blocks shots and will play along the boards although he is not outstanding there because he doesn't match up well strength-wise against the opposition. He is a push and shove guy, not a hitter.

THE INTANGIBLES

We told you last year that Driver's durability must be questioned, and his leg injury last season illustrates that. One hesitates to label a player as brittle, but Driver may fit that mold.

Because of his limited playing time last year, his report this year remains largely unchanged.

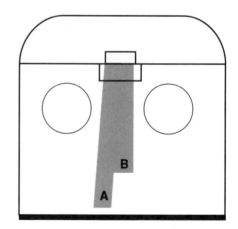

MARK JOHNSON

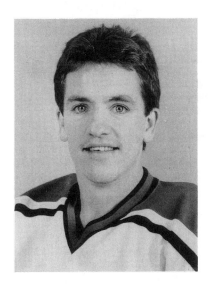

Yrs. of NHL service: 10
Born: Minneapolis, Minn., USA; September 22, 1957
Position: Center/left wing
Height: 5-9
Weight: 160
Uniform no.: 12
Shoots: left

Career statistics:

GP	G	A	TP	PIM
606	187	276	463	248

1988-89 statistics:

GP	G	A	TP	+/-	PIM	PP	SH	GW	GT	S	PCT
40	13	25	38	-1	24	4	0	2	0	95	13.7

LAST SEASON

Jaw and hamstring injuries (28 games for the latter) limited Johnson to his lowest full-season NHL game total. Goal total was a seven-season low.

THE FINESSE GAME

Hands and brain are the keys to Johnson's skills — when he can stay in the lineup. He handles the puck well when carrying it and passes with equal ease to the forehand and backhand sides. His anticipation and vision combine with his hand skills to make him a good playmaker, and he is above average at leading teammates into the clear.

Johnson's "louder" skating skills — those of speed and quickness — don't stack up to his hand abilities, but his balance gives him good lateral movement and makes him difficult to hit. He does have some one-step quickness, so he can gain an opening.

Like Aaron Broten, Johnson concentrates on playmaking and will often sacrifice better shooting positions. He'll convert on loose pucks around the crease, and he also excels at tips and deflections.

He is a valuable specialty teams member because of those skills. His passing makes him a good power play point man, and his anticipation makes him a good penalty killer.

THE PHYSICAL GAME

Mark is not a physical player, which is probably just as well given his propensity toward injury. He generally makes it a point to stay away from the high-traffic areas, and won't initiate contact.

He does have excellent eye/hand coordination, allowing him to succeed at the tip-ins and deflections we mentioned earlier.

THE INTANGIBLES

As stated in last year's edition, durability is the primary question regarding Johnson — who has yet to play a full NHL season. Though inclined to go out and do his job (but not with such intensity as to actually be a team leader), Johnson allows himself to be slowed by injury and is not particularly known for playing with pain.

Still, Johnson was one of the few New Jersey players to maintain his on-ice contributions last season, so as to keep the Devils headed in the right direction. They failed through no fault of his.

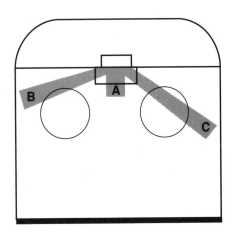

JIM KORN

Yrs. of NHL service: 8
Born: Hopkins, Minn., USA.; July 28, 1957
Position: Left wing
Height: 6-4
Weight: 220
Uniform no.: 14
Shoots: left

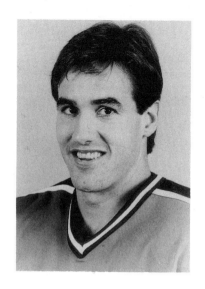

Career statistics:

GP	G	A	TP	PIM
551	64	117	181	1,676

1988-89 statistics:

GP	G	A	TP	+/-	PIM	PP	SH	GW	GT	S	PCT
65	15	16	31	-3	212	4	0	3	1	65	23.1

LAST SEASON

Games played total matched second-highest of NHL career, with goal and point totals career highs. Finished third on team in PIM.

THE FINESSE GAME

Korn is not as lumbering a skater as his size might dictate, but he is no Nureyev either. He is not overly agile on his feet — one reason he was moved from defense to left wing — and he is not exceptionally skilled with his hands — not for puck work, anyway.

He doesn't handle the puck well when he carries it, and Korn is not gifted in terms of play making skills. He does not see the ice well, does not shoot the puck well and neither gives nor takes a pass well.

Any goal scoring Jim is going to do will have to be accomplished from the front of the net.

THE PHYSICAL GAME

Look at the penalty minute total. What do you think? Korn's obviously playing a very physical type of game and the Devils obviously want that kind of presence.

Korn is big and he can use his size to advantage when he rubs out an opponent along the boards. Of course, he also gets carried away and turns that hitting into fighting.

He also carries the reputation of being *extremely* selective as to how and on whom he uses his size and strength — read, smaller and less aggressive players.

THE INTANGIBLES

What's to say? Korn is yet another in the multitude of Devils' role players. He played — for him — a useful role last season, and he did allow Coach Jim Schoenfeld the dubious luxury of alternating between Korn between forward and defense as needed.

He's not a real courageous player, as his selective phsyicality demonstrates, and he'd be an even more borderline player on a better team. What he has on his side is his connection with GM Lou Lamoriello, for whom Korn played at Providence College. Korn is otherwise a marginal NHLer.

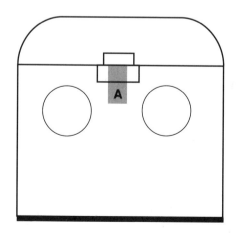

TOM KURVERS

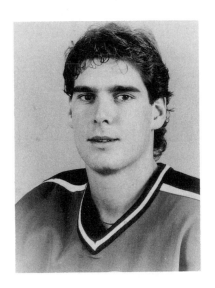

Yrs. of NHL service: 5
Born: Minneapolis, Minn., USA; October 14, 1962
Position: Defenseman
Height: 6-0
Weight: 190
Uniform no.: 5
Shoots: left

Career statistics:

GP	G	A	TP	PIM
323	44	154	198	172

1988-89 statistics:

GP	G	A	TP	+/-	PIM	PP	SH	GW	GT	S	PCT
74	16	50	66	11	38	5	0	0	1	190	8.4

LAST SEASON

Games played total was second-highest of career, but all point totals were career highs. He led club in assists and was second in shots on goal. He was the only defenseman to be plus-rated.

THE FINESSE GAME

Skating and puckhandling are the skills that make Tom Kurvers the Devils' best offensive defenseman. He complements good skating speed and quickness with balance for agility and lateral movement. Kurvers then makes his skating better by combining it with his good-to-very good puck carrying ability; he handles the puck well at all speeds.

Because of these skills, Kurvers is more apt than any Devils defender to skate the puck over center ice and to then join the attack. However, that doesn't mean Tom will lead the rush to the net. Rather, because he likes to run the offense from the offensive blue line, he'll carry it to center and then get it to a breaking winger before setting up camp at the left point.

Kurvers contains the point well with his quickness and anticipation, and he makes good passes to his teammates from there because of his vision. As such, he's a power play natural. He has a fine shot from the blue line, low and almost always on net, and Kurvers will almost always move to the center of the line to improve his shooting angle.

His defensive zone work is less outstanding, but Kurvers is nevertheless competent. He generally makes good decisions regarding outlet passes, but he can be rushed into mistakes.

THE PHYSICAL GAME

Kurvers is not much of a physical player, despite good size. He's probably going to be out-muscled should he get trapped along the boards (and that's an area of the ice best left to Kurvers' partner), but he does have the skills to make plays from the boards.

THE INTANGIBLES

We said last year that Kurvers could develop as a player, and he did so last season — he set a franchise record for points in a season by a defenseman. His acquisition by GM Lou Lamoriello was a quiet one, but one that nevertheless improved the Devils' blue line. Because of his offensive capabilities, Kurvers could be argued to be one of the Devils' three most important players.

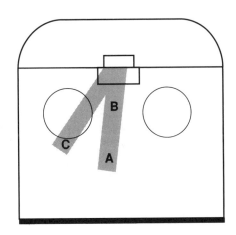

JOHN MACLEAN

Yrs. of NHL service: 6
Born: Oshawa, Ontario, Canada; November 20, 1964
Position: Right wing
Height: 6-0
Weight: 195
Uniform no.: 15
Shoots: right

Career statistics:

GP	G	A	TP	PIM
388	131	153	284	560

1988-89 statistics:

GP	G	A	TP	+/-	PIM	PP	SH	GW	GT	S	PCT
74	42	45	87	26	127	14	0	4		2	266	15.8

LAST SEASON

Led the Devils in points, goals, plus/minus, power play goals, game-tying goals and shots on goal. Set career highs in all point categories despite being sidelined six games with back and elbow injuries.

THE FINESSE GAME

MacLean's best finesse tool is his shot — and his willingness to use it (he finished 14th in the NHL last season for SOG, and increased his shot total by 25 percent last year versus 1987-88). He gets a lot of strength into his slap shot from the wing, and he can drive the puck past a goalie from the further distances, but MacLean is also good with a hard wrist shot in close. His shot is made better by the fact that it is generally accurate and forces the goaltender to make saves, instead of rattling off the glass. His shooting makes him a power play natural.

Working as he did with Patrik Sundstrom and either Brendan Shanahan or Mark Johnson, MacLean is going to get the puck as the designated shooter, but John has also opened up his offense by getting the puck to teammates in better scoring position. He's not a Gretzky, but MacLean *is* improving his playmaking.

Patience is also the key to his improved defense. Where he waits for opportunities offensively — rather than forcing a play — MacLean has also learned to be patient and attentive in the neutral and defensive zones.

As a skater, MacLean is best described as a straight-ahead — rather than artistic — performer. While he has fairly good lateral movement and quickness, MacLean is not a darting forward; he'll succeed by out-distancing the opposition up the ice and releasing his above-average shot.

THE PHYSICAL GAME

MacLean doesn't have great size, but he does use what he has effectively and aggressively. He initiates play in the trenches, and he's well aided by his balance (which keeps him vertical and ready to make a play after collisions). Still, he can get out-muscled if matched against larger forwards or defensemen.

Obviously, it is his strength that powers his shot, and that same strength allows him to deliver the puck goal-ward even while in traffic.

THE INTANGIBLES

John MacLean was the one saving grace of New Jersey's wasted 1988-89 season. We told you he needed to approach each game with intensity and to play with consistency and he did that last year, leading the club in scoring from Day One.

The key now is for him to build on that performance. What he does for an encore isn't so much the question as what he must not do in 1989-90 — and that is fall back to his former levels. We think he will continue to build on his success.

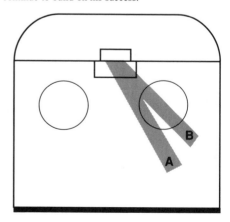

KIRK MULLER

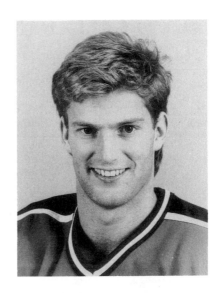

Yrs. of NHL service: 5
Born: Kingston, Ontario, Canada; February 8, 1966
Position: Center
Height: 5-11
Weight: 185
Uniform no.: 9
Shoots: left

Career statistics:

GP	G	A	TP	PIM
396	136	228	364	422

1988-89 statistics:

GP	G	A	TP	+/-	PIM	PP	SH	GW	GT	S	PCT
80	31	43	74	-23	119	12	1	4	0	182	17.0

LAST SEASON

One of four Devils to play all 80 games (third time personally), he finished second on the club in goals and points. Goal total was second highest of career, but point total was a three-year low. Set a career high in PIM, finished tied for second in power play goals, was third in shots on goal and second worst in plus/minus rating.

THE FINESSE GAME

In terms of individual finesse skills, Kirk is probably at the highest levels he is going to attain. He's no longer the completely straight-ahead player that he was when he entered the league, but his style remains a battering-ram one and that's where his skating strength benefits him. His balance also allows him to recover fairly well after imposing himself physically upon the opposition, and Kirk does have a modicum of foot speed and agility. Still, he will never be mistaken for a crafty, darting skater.

He has shown greater patience in making his plays — though that ability was not always in evidence last season — and the ability to recognize the opportunities as they develop. His developing facility at moving to the middle of the ice to create plays, rather than looking for loose pucks to squeak through to the perimeter, was also frequently absent last season.

THE PHYSICAL GAME

Muller has— as previously mentioned — a battering-ram style. He scores dirty goals (he's often prone on the ice when he scores) and his willingness — key word here — to apply himself physically against all opponents is the key to his game's success.

Kirk has good — not outstanding — size and he effectively uses his strength and body along the boards and in the corners, sacrificing his body to initiate contact. His balance and hand skills make his physical play doubly effective.

THE INTANGIBLES

Like many of the Devils, Muller played comfortable the first half of last season. He didn't demonstrate his trademark intensity until the season's second half (Kirk had just 13 goals and 31 points by Game 41), by which time the Devils were desperately trying to erase the non-playoff writing on the Patrick Division wall.

A team captain has the responsibility of making sure that both he and his team are prepared to play all out, all the time. In his own game — and in the Devils' game — Muller faltered badly last season. He has much to atone for this year.

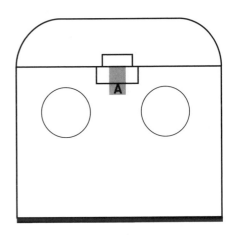

JACK O'CALLAHAN

Yrs. of NHL service: 7
Born: Charlestown, Mass., USA; July 24, 1957
Position: Defenseman
Height: 6-1
Weight: 185
Uniform no.: 7
Shoots: right

Career statistics:

GP	G	A	TP	PIM
389	27	104	131	541

1988-89 statistics:

GP	G	A	TP	+/-	PIM	PP	SH	GW	GT	S	PCT
36	5	21	26	0	51	5	0	0		1	96	5.2

LAST SEASON

Games played total was a full-season career low, but assist total was a career high. A finger injury sidelined him early in the season, with benchings responsible for the majority of his absence.

THE FINESSE GAME

About all O'Callahan brings to the game is his shot from the point, which the Devils used almost exclusively on the power play. O'Callahan delivers his shot low to the net, and with good accuracy (all of his goals came on the power play).

Otherwise, finesse skills are not the high point of O'Callahan's game. He's no better than average as a skater in both directions, but he plays fairly well positionally and is fairly sound in one-on-one confrontations. He doesn't carry the puck, but he'll generally make the right breakout pass. He is vulnerable to turnovers, however, when subjected to heavy forechecking.

THE PHYSICAL GAME

O'Callahan's strength would have to be his defensive zone play. O'Callahan keeps the zone clean, is willing to hit and can be a punishing hitter. However, he'll need assistance in the play after tying up a forward along the boards.

He will take the man out from in front of his own net, but because his anticipation and concentration are lacking (he tends to get hypnotized by the puck), opposing forwards can sneak in behind him.

THE INTANGIBLES

We told you last year that O'Callahan wouldn't be a regular in New Jersey's lineup, and that situation won't change much this year. He remains a limited player, and one who will probably play most — if not all — of this season in another uniform.

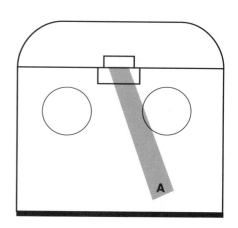

WALT PODDUBNY

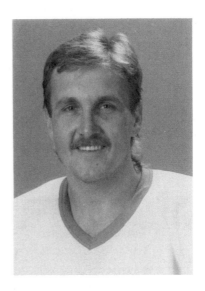

Yrs. of NHL service: 7
Born: Thunder Bay, Ontario, Canada;
February 14, 1960
Position: Center
Height: 6-1
Weight: 205
Uniform no.: 75
Shoots: left

Career statistics:

GP	G	A	TP	PIM
414	175	220	395	410

1988-89 statistics:

GP	G	A	TP	+/-	PIM	PP	SH	GW	GT	S	PCT
72	38	37	75	-18	107	14	0	2	2	197	19.3

LAST SEASON

Acquired from New York (along with Jari Gron-strand and Bruce Bell) in exchange for Norm Rochefort and Jason Lafreniere in August 1988. Games played total was three-season low. Goal and point totals were second highest of career, PIM total career high. He finished second on club in points and SOG total, first in goals, power-play goals and game-tying goals. He missed time late in the season with nose and cheekbone injuries.

THE FINESSE GAME

Balance and the attendant agility make Poddubny a good skater, and his skating and scoring skills make him a good player.

He has rink-length speed to outrace the opposition, and his balance and lateral movement make him agile and allow him to absorb checks and still make plays.

Walt combines his foot speed and puckhandling ability with his anticipation skills to get into the open, or to get the puck to his open teammates. Those passing and anticipation skills — along with an excellent wrist/snap shot — make Poddubny a power-play stalwart.

Poddubny shoots the puck well and often, using a fast (but not exceptionally hard) wrist shot to beat goaltenders from 30 feet or so. Because he has good hands, Poddubny can also operate well in the traffic around the net, and is very dangerous around the crease.

THE PHYSICAL GAME

Poddubny's balance keys his physical game and allows him to operate wuth the puck in traffic. He's willing to get involved along the boards, but he's not really a mucker. He'll go into traffic for a loose puck but won't muscle anyone out of the way for it; Walt will let his hand skills pull the puck out for him.

His balance also makes him difficult to dislodge from the puck. Though not an extraordinarily physical player, Poddubny will take his licks and can dish some out as well.

THE INTANGIBLES

After asking for a trade from Quebec, Poddubny settled in by the end of the season. Now the big question is the reappearance of Michel Bergeron, the coach with whom Walt did not see eye-to-eye while in New York. Only time can tell how the pair will react to each other in their second go-round, but expect Poddubny to be moved from center to wing.

Walt needs to develop some consistency in his scoring. He had 27 of his 38 goals by personal game 40, scoring just 11 goals (and just seven at even strength) in his last 32 games.

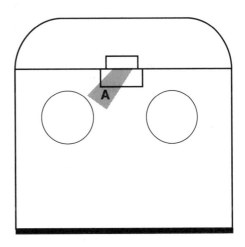

245

BRENDAN SHANAHAN

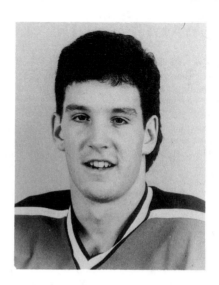

Yrs. of NHL service: 2
Born: Mimico, Ontario, Canada; January 23, 1969
Position: Center/right wing
Height: 6-3
Weight: 205
Uniform no.: 11
Shoots: right

Career statistics:

GP	G	A	TP	PIM
133	29	47	76	246

1988-89 statistics:

GP	G	A	TP	+/-	PIM	PP	SH	GW	GT	S	PCT
68	22	28	50	2	115	9	0	0	1	152	14.5

LAST SEASON

Point totals were all career highs. Was third in plus/minus among full-time forwards. Concussion, neck and back injuries served to sideline him for parts of the season.

THE FINESSE GAME

What a difference a year can make. Where a year ago Shanahan handled the puck the way a cow handles a gun (thank you, Bill Chadwick), last season Shanahan was confident and willing. He carried the puck across the blue line whenever possible, where previously he looked for his first reason to get rid of it.

And, miraculously, every time he carried the puck the defense backed up. Skating room! Playmaking room! Shooting room! And Brendan took advantage of all that space and began to make plays, and to move the puck, and work give-and-goes, and get into scoring positon. And then he scored goals.

Already possessing better than average agility for his size, Brendan's skating picked up as well. He's still no speed demon — nor is he ready for the Denis Savard Lookalike Contest — but he is improving and is already putting his improved skills to work.

Shanahan still needs to consistently respond at the NHL level in terms of playmaking decisions, but he's showing good patience in looking for plays and keeping his head up to look for open teammates.

He could — and should — also improve the release of his shot. He's strong enough to get it to the net from a distance or through traffic, but he'd benefit greatly from a quicker release.

THE PHYSICAL GAME

Strength will be the key to Shanahan's development as an NHLer. He already has a good dollop of it at the tender age of 20, and his physical potential is great. He likes to take advantage of his size by playing a hitting game, and Brendan will go into a corner against anyone. If that provokes a fight so be it; Brendan isn't intimidated and he'll drop the gloves with anyone.

But he also has a tendency to be selectively physical, playing a much bolder (dare we say bullying style?) against smaller — and non-North American — players. It is, after all, one thing to belt Pelle Eklund, and quite another to smack around Rick Tocchet.

THE INTANGIBLES

Brendan continues to show excellent potential, and his performance in the second half of the season bodes well for his continued development: he scored 15 goals and 15 assists in his final 23 games.

Also important is the mental maturity Shanahan showed, improving his work ethic and demonstrating to Coach Jim Schoenfeld that he wanted to improve and would work at it. Should he continue along that path this year, Shanahan could be a revelation for the Devils.

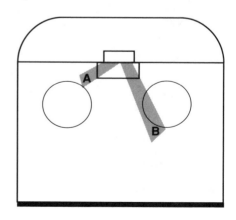

PETER SUNDSTROM

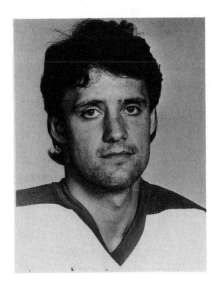

Yrs. of NHL service: 5
Born: Skelleftea, Sweden; December 14, 1961
Position: Left wing
Height: 6-0
Weight: 180
Uniform No.: 12
Shoots: left

Career statistics:

GP	G	A	TP	PIM
317	60	81	141	116

1988-89 statistics:

GP	G	A	TP	+/-	PIM	PP	SH	GW	GT	S	PCT
35	4	2	6	-5	12	0	0	0		1	39	10.3

LAST SEASON

Games played total was a career low (knee injury and benchings).

THE FINESSE GAME

Sundstrom is a well-schooled player with sound fundamental skills. He is a smooth skater who can take off into the openings and carry the puck with him; a player that knows how to use his teammates and can pass well, and a player that sees the ice and can anticipate the play.

But for some reason these qualities don't combine to allow him to score goals. His shot is very weak and not at all difficult for NHL goaltenders to handle. If he's going to score at all it will be by converting the loose pucks sprung free by his checking.

Sundstrom gets scoring opportunities because he's a good checker, using his skating and anticipation to good effect as a defensive player and a forechecker.

THE PHYSICAL GAME

Sundstrom's got a wiry build and is in excellent condition, but he's not physically strong enough for the toll of the NHL's board game. He doesn't usually use his body for hitting, preferring his speed and stick checking to do the work. He's not very strong and is therefore much better in open ice than along the boards.

THE INTANGIBLES

As we said last year, Peter can be an effective role player for Washington, but it is doubtful he'll ever rise above that role. Bounced in an out of the lineup to skate against less physical teams, Peter's diminished role last season may very well foreshadow the rest of his (perhaps ending soon) NHL career.

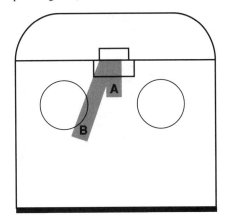

PATRIK SUNDSTROM

Yrs. of NHL service: 7
Born: Skelleftea, Sweden; December 14, 1961
Position: Center/left wing
Height: 6-0
Weight: 200
Uniform no.: 17
Shoots: left

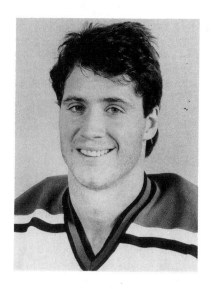

Career statistics:

GP	G	A	TP	PIM
517	176	286	462	259

1988-89 statistics:

GP	G	A	TP	+/-	PIM	PP	SH	GW	GT	S	PCT
65	28	41	69	22	36	12	1	4	1	156	17.9

LAST SEASON

Games played total was career low (recurring back injury), but point total was highest in three seasons. Finished third in scoring, second in power play goals and plus/minus rating.

THE FINESSE GAME

Sundstrom is an excellent skater, because all components of his skating are excellent. He has superb balance and strength, and he complements those assets with exceptional foot speed and agility. He stops and starts well, changes direction on a dime and can outrace all but the fastest NHL players to a loose puck.

His skating dovetails excellently with his puck-handling and play making abilities, which are also of superior calibre. Patrik can not only carry the puck well at top speed, but he can also make any play he sees at that speed.

He controls the puck as if it were nailed to his stick and he uses his excellent touch (whether the puck has to be feathered or fired) to pass well to both sides. He handles the puck just as well in traffic as he does in the open ice.

His anticipation and hockey sense are superb, and he reads the ice easily and clearly; that's why he's a power play and penalty killing regular.

The only finesse skill not at the same level as the others is his shot. Sundstrom has a terrific wrist shot, but he doesn't shoot anywhere near enough despite the opportunities he gets. He looks to pass too much, and should become more selfish.

THE PHYSICAL GAME

Sundstrom has good size and strength, so not only can he take the rough going he can initiate his share as well. That's not to say that he *will* initiate that contact, and his finesse game would certainly expand if he did.

Sundstrom is unafraid of skating into traffic to get the puck, where his excellent balance and strength combine with his excellent hands to make him a very dangerous player in tight to the net.

Good hand and wrist strength propel his shot and allow him to pull the puck out of traffic, and they also make Sundstrom a good faceoff man. He is also willing to sacrifice his body to block shots (doing so with particularly good effect while penalty killing), and is one of the NHL's better shot-blocking forwards.

THE INTANGIBLES

For those who, prior to the 1987-88 season, questioned Sundstrom's talent and refused to accept the Devils playoff run as a testament to his ability consider this:

Two players have come into their own in the last two campaigns: John MacLean and Brendan Shanahan. Know who the common denominator is for those two? Right — Sundstrom.

Patrik is a supremely talented individual who is also supremely courageous; he's played in pain for most of the last two seasons. He also more than upheld his end of the bargain last season by improving his offensive output in an attempt to make the Devils more than just a one-line club.

He's quality goods, and GM Lou Lamoriello should be complimented for acquiring this excellent player.

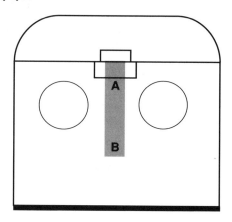

SYLVAIN TURGEON

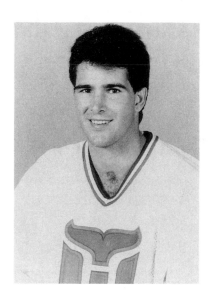

Yrs. of NHL service: 6
Born: Noranda, Quebec, Canada; January 17, 1965
Position: Left wing
Height: 6-0
Weight: 195
Uniform no.: 16
Shoots: left

Career statistics:

GP	G	A	TP	PIM
370	178	150	328	366

1988-89 statistics:

GP	G	A	TP	+/-	PIM	PP	SH	GW	GT	S	PCT
42	16	14	30	-11	40	7	0	1	0	122	13.1

LAST SEASON

Games played total was second lowest of career (shoulder injury). Goal and point totals were career lows.

THE FINESSE GAME

Sylvain is an excellent skater, blessed with excellent speed, one-step quickness, balance and agility. He moves laterally as well as he does forward, making moves with the puck that look like he's pulling it around on a string.

Next in line finesse-wise is his shot. Turgeon has the power to blast the puck past a goaltender from the distances (he'll most often shoot from the top of the faceoff circle), but Sylvain also likes to dip behind the defense and go one-on-one with the goalie, fake him to the ice, and deposit the puck in the far corner. He has a quick release on his shot, but he doesn't maximize it because Turgeon doesn't know how to truly get into scoring position.

He is not very creative and doesn't cut to the holes with his skating. Instead, he's going to decide on a play and make it, and that means a lot of 1-on-1 work versus the defense.

Sylvain thinks shoot before pass, and he'll look to the net before looking to his teammates. He lacks a feeling for creativity, for anticipating the openings and then leading his teammates to those openings.

THE PHYSICAL GAME

There isn't one. Turgeon doesn't get involved in the physical part of the game and he doesn't want to get involved either. While he can take the puck off the boards very quickly and make a play with it, Sylvain won't do even the most elementary body work along the boards — thus rendering his finesse ability ineffective.

THE INTANGIBLES

Turgeon is the kind of player that gets coaches fired and gives general managers ulcers: tremendous talent matched only by his lack of intensity. He is one of the NHL's biggest enigmas.

He's not a bad kid, and he's not a problem discipline wise off-ice; he's not a bad liver. Turgeon is just unmotivated. He's taken a lot of abuse in Hartford (much of it from his own team),and a change of scenery while still young — he's just 24 years old — might help him reclaim what was once a promising career.

By the way, he'll be on a new contract this season.

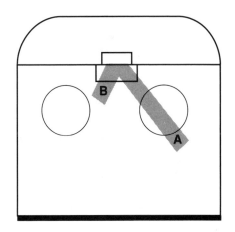

RANDY VELISCHEK

Yrs. of NHL service: 6
Born: Montreal, Quebec, Canada; February 10, 1962
Position: Defenseman
Height: 6-0
Weight: 200
Uniform no.: 27
Shoots: left

Career statistics:

GP	G	A	TP	PIM
330	17	57	74	265

1988-89 statistics:

GP	G	A	TP	+/-	PIM	PP	SH	GW	GT	S	PCT
80	4	14	18	-2	70	0	1	0	0	77	5.2

LAST SEASON

Games played total was career high; goal and point totals match career bests.

THE FINESSE GAME

Velischeck molds smarts with a modicum of finesse skill to become a dependable and valuable player for the Devils. He is a smart, consistent defensive force and that's where his finesse abilities come to the fore.

Though lacking any outstanding skating skills, Randy is nevertheless a good skater both forward and back. He's neither overwhelmingly quick nor exceptionally fast — and he doesn't possess above average agility — but Velischek makes the skills he does have work through brain-work. He plays defense positionally, understanding how to use and exploit his defensive angles to force the opposition wide of the net. Needless to say, his sound defensive thought is bolstered by good understanding of the play as it heads toward him, and good vision to see the ice.

Randy is not offensively gifted and does not usually join the attack inside the opposition's blue line. His shot — which he almost never uses because he is the safety valve (falling back to defense) is no better than average. He won't pinch in to contain the point.

Velischek is generally sound at moving the puck from his end, though that responsibility is usually his partner's (generally Joe Cirella), and will — on rare occasions — carry the puck to center and get rid of it there.

THE PHYSICAL GAME

As he does with his finesse game, Velischek makes his physical game more effective by playing smartly. Randy doesn't have great size, but he more than willingly puts the size and strength he does have to

work against any opponent. He effectively bangs in the corners and clears the front of the net.

He can hold his own against most of the League's stronger forwards, and what makes Velischek's physical work even more valuable is the fact that he executes it without taking penalties.

THE INTANGIBLES

Reliability and smarts are the important elements Randy brings to an all-too mercurial Devils defensive corps. He might even be called an overachiever, because the total of Randy Velischek is better than the sum of his parts. He's a quality player.

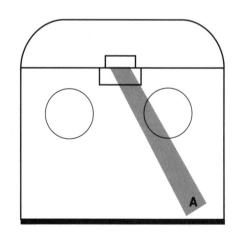

250

CRAIG WOLANIN

Yrs. of NHL service: 4
Born: Grosse Pointe, Mich., USA; July 27, 1967
Position: Defenseman
Height: 6-3
Weight: 205
Uniform no.: 6
Shoots: left

Career statistics:

GP	G	A	TP	PIM
246	15	55	70	422

1988-89 statistics:

GP	G	A	TP	+/-	PIM	PP	SH	GW	GT	S	PCT
56	3	8	11	-9	69	0	0	0	0	70	4.3

LAST SEASON

Games played was second lowest of his career, courtesy of a knee injury. Assist and point totals were lowest of career.

THE FINESSE GAME

Wolanin is at a number of career plateaus, not the least of which come in the finesse skills department. After showing continued improvement in his skating abilities (more quickness and power, better balance and agility) for each of his NHL seasons, he topped (bottomed?) out last season. His injury could take some blame for that, but after four NHL seasons Wolanin should be better than he is.

Craig plays a basic positional style of defense, forcing play wide of the net as often as not. He's helped by the fact that he pivots well and is able to keep pace with the opposition, but must constantly remind himself to rein in his wandering tendencies. He reads the rush toward him fairly well.

As with his skating, his offensive play-reading and making skills have stilled. His puckhandling and movement is below average, and he wavers in making his decisions. Still, he often enough shows the ability to make the right choices. Overall, though, he is less than a sure thing.

He can shoot the puck fairly well from the blue line, but nowhere near often nor hard enough.

THE PHYSICAL GAME

Craig's biggest problem is his size. He's too big for the kind of game he's demonstrated the willingness to play. In other words, he may be 6-3 and 205, but he plays six inches and 20 pounds smaller.

He doesn't have the desire to smash people, and doesn't even use his physical gifts to their fullest extents *without* bashing people.

While tremendously strong and with the ability to be a punishing hitter, Craig does not apply his size consistently in front of the net or along the boards. He consistently fails to complete his checks, pushing and shoving instead of taking the body.

He is willing to sacrifice his body by blocking shots but, essentially, Wolanin has ceased his growth in his physical game as well.

THE INTANGIBLES

We have preached patience with Craig Wolanin for several seasons. He enters his fifth NHL go-round this year, and has not come close to justifying his number one draft choice status. He must now show some kind of above-average ability — something that says he's better than the team's number three defender (*at best*) —or fall into the ranks of the mediocre.

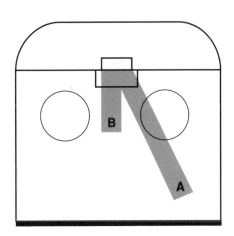

NEW YORK
ISLANDERS

LINE COMBINATIONS
RANDY WOOD-TOM FITZGERALD
PAT FLATLEY
DAVID VOLEK-BRENT SUTTER-DALE HENRY
DEREK KING-PAT LAFONTAINE-ALAN KERR
MIKKO MAKELA-BRYAN TROTTIER
BRAD DALGARNO

DEFENSE PAIRINGS
WAYNE MCBEAN-RICHARD PILON
JEFF NORTON-GERALD DIDUCK
GARY NYLUND-DOUG CROSSMAN

GOALTENDERS
MARK FITZPATRICK
JEFF HACKETT

OTHER PLAYERS
MARC BERGEVIN —Defenseman
BRAD LAUER— Left wing
MICK VUKOTA— Right wing

POWER PLAY

FIRST UNIT:
MIKKO MAKELA-PAT LAFONTAINE
DEREK KING
DOUG CROSSMAN-GERALD DIDUCK

SECOND UNIT:
BRYAN TROTTIER-BRENT SUTTER
BRAD DALGARNO
WAYNE MCBEAN-JEFF NORTON

On the first unit, MAKELA will work the left wing boards, KING will work the right wing corner and behind the net and LAFONTAINE will dodge in and out of the slot. CROSSMAN and DIDUCK will play catch at the points, attempting to isolate MAKELA for a shot from the left faceoffcircle. KING will go to the net, and he and LAFONTAINE will look for rebounds. Shots from the defense are the second option.

On the second unit, DALGARNO will post up in front, with TROTTIER and SUTTER darting in and out of the slot depending upon the puck's rotation around the zone. When MCBEAN or NORTON can get free for a shot, both TROTTIER and SUTTER will join DALGARNO screening the goalie and looking for rebounds.

Last season, the Islanders power play was EXCELLENT, scoring 85 times in 378 opportunities (22.5 percent, fourth overall).

PENALTY KILLING

FIRST UNIT:
BRYAN TROTTIER-BRENT SUTTER
MARC BERGEVIN-GERALD DIDUCK

SECOND UNIT:
RANDY WOOD-TOM FITZGERALD
GARY NYLUND-RICHARD PILON

By the end of last season, both sets of forwards pressured the puck as soon as the opposition crossed the line. One forward would pursue into the offensive zone, with the other sitting up high.Both units played a fairly strict box.

Last season, the Islanders penalty killing was POOR, allowing 103 goals in 390 shorthanded situations (73.6 percent, 20th overall).

CRUCIAL FACEOFFS
SUTTER will get the call for these, with Trottier the back-up.

MARC BERGEVIN

Yrs. of NHL service: 5
Born: Montreal, Quebec, Canada; August 11, 1965
Position: Defenseman
Height: 6-0
Weight: 185
Uniform no.: 39
Shoots: left

Career statistics:

GP	G	A	TP	PIM
324	14	42	56	343

1988-89 statistics:

GP	G	A	TP	+/-	PIM	PP	SH	GW	GT	S	PCT
69	2	13	15	-1	80	1	0	0	0	65	3.1

LAST SEASON

Acquired along with Gary Nylund from Chicago in exchange for Steve Konroyd and Bob Bassen. Games played and PIM totals were second highest of career, assist and point totals career bests.

THE FINESSE GAME

Bergevin's premier finesse skill is his skating, and it is very good. He has strength, quickness and balance — all adding up to speed and agility. When he uses his improving judgment, Marc is able to step up and challenge the puck carrier at the Islander blue line, as well as contain the point and forecheck in the offensive end.

Bergevin can handle the puck too, but is at his best when taking no more than a handful of strides before moving it to a breaking forward. He sees the ice and reads the rush well in both directions, so he can do a little more than just make the simple plays. He'll rush the puck occasionally, but he's far better off when not Bobby Orr-ing the play; that's when he gets into trouble.

He demonstrated some offensive ability last season, getting the puck to the open man in the offensive zone and taking the occasional chance to rush the net (one of his two goals came on a rink-length rush). But generally, Bergevin's offense will come from the point. His shot is average, maybe a little better because it stays low and on net.

THE PHYSICAL GAME

Marc really improved the tenor of his physical play last season, using his skating skill to head off the opposition and then take the man to the boards, as well as using his good size and strength in tandem with his balance to clear the front of the net.

He uses his skill to hit, not just push and shove, and that results in loose pucks the Islanders can take advantage of. Bergevin himself has the ability to make plays after checking, making his physical play more effective.

THE INTANGIBLES

When he first came to the Islanders, there was a real question as to whether Bergevin could play in the NHL. But by season's end Marc had improved tremendously, and the difference was confidence. As he played more, he played better (and don't underestimate the arrival of Coach Al Arbour — a former defenseman — in influencing Bergevin), becoming a good team player who stood up for his teammates. Worth noting, by the way, is that although he finished as a minus player, Marc was a plus player with the Islanders.

Still a youngster, Bergevin has the potential to play even better than he did last season.

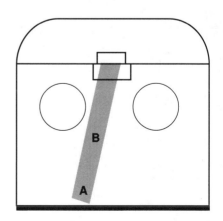

253

DOUG CROSSMAN

Yrs. of NHL service: 8
Born: Peterborough, Ontario, Canada; May 30, 1960
Position: Defenseman
Height: 6-2
Weight: 190
Uniform no.:
Shoots: left

Career statistics:

GP	G	A	TP	PIM
625	70	243	313	380

1988-89 statistics:

GP	G	A	TP	+/-	PIM	PP	SH	GW	GT	S	PCT
74	10	15	25	-11	53	2	0	0	0	137	7.3

LAST SEASON

Traded first from Philadelphia to Los Angeles in exchange for Jay Wells, he was later acquired by the Islanders along with Mark Fitzpatrick and Wayne McBean in exchange for Kelly Hrudey. Games played, assist and point totals were full season career lows. Goal total was six-season high.

THE FINESSE GAME

Crossman's defensive style is influenced by his finesse skills. He is a smooth skater but lacks overall speed, so he's best suited for a stay-at-home role.

Since he is not quick he won't jump into openings, but he is able to rush the puck (and contribute smartly from the offensive blue line) because of his hand skills. Crossman handles the puck well in both the offensive and defensive zone, melding his attacking and defending game better than ever previously.

He operates well on the power play, where the ice opens up for him and gives him more time to think and more space to work in, and he also sees time as a penalty killer because of his surehandedness. He is a good passer to both sides.

Doug's improved his positional play defensively, so that opposing forwards who may have been able to take advantage of his slow turns and less-than-good lateral movement now find themselves forced wide of the net.

THE PHYSICAL GAME

Lack of strength remains Crossman's Waterloo, and any of the League's stronger forwards will overpower him in front of the net or in the corners.

He has a good reach and can pokecheck effectively, but Crossman is in trouble when hit because he'll get bounced off the puck when hit by players like Rick Tocchet.

THE INTANGIBLES

Laid-back may be the most generous way of describing Crossman. He doesn't play with a whole lot of emotion, but that doesn't have to be a bad thing. If Crossman can play the consistent move-the-puck game that got him named to the Canada Cup squad a couple of seasons back, then he'll be doing his job for the Islanders.

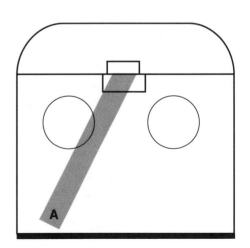

BRAD DALGARNO

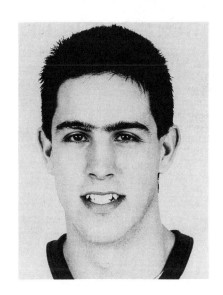

Yrs. of NHL service: 2
Born: Vancouver, B.C., Canada; August 11, 1967
Position: Right wing
Height: 6-3
Weight: 215
Uniform no.: 17
Shoots: right

Career statistics:

GP	G	A	TP	PIM
95	14	18	32	144

1988-89 statistics:

GP	G	A	TP	+/-	PIM	PP	SH	GW	GT	S	PCT
55	11	10	21	-8	86	2	0	1	0	83	13.3

LAST SEASON

Games played, point and PIM totals were career highs. A Februaryeye injury ended his season.

THE FINESSE GAME

Though the strength of Dalgarno's game will always be rooted in the physical area, Brad showed definite signs last season of NHL level finesse skills.

With two exceptions, Dalgarno's skating is unexceptional. He doesn't have great speed or agility, but Brad does have a strong stride and some good balance. Both those traits serve him in his physical game, and they have roles in his finesse game as well.

His hand skills and hockey sense began to flower last season, with Dalgarno showing that he could find a teammate coming into the play,and that he could handle the puck and make the pass to that teammate while in motion.

Brad's hand skills don't extend to his shot. His slap shot is okay, but he still takes too long to get it off. Because of that, his best scoring work will come from grinding in front of the net.

His lack of skating skill betrays him defensively (but not through lack of effort), as he's going to be trapped in a corner when the puck turns over — and Dalgarno's ponderous skating won't get him back into the play.

THE PHYSICAL GAME

The key to Dalgarno's physical game is consistency, and last year — for the first time — he showed the willingness to consistently apply himself in this way. He has great size — exceptional size — and he can really be a dominating boards player if he applies himself.

He's a grinding winger who has to use his body to advantage in order to succeed, and better skating skills would make him a better player by allowing him to catch and check the opposition. He was also showing the ability to not only go to the net and take the abuse, but the ability to make it pay off.

THE INTANGIBLES

Considering how tenuous Dalgarno's hold on a roster spot was at last season's beginning, his improvement is that much more remarkable. The Islanders have to be greatly encouraged by the progress he showed before suffering his season-ending injury. Now all Brad has to do is show he remembers what was making him successful when he returns this season.

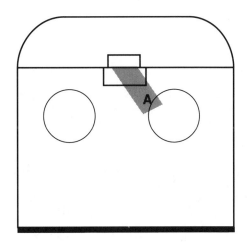

GERALD DIDUCK

Yrs. of NHL service: 4
Born: Edmonton, Alta., Canada; April 6, 1965
Position: Defenseman
Height: 6-2
Weight: 207
Uniform no.: 4
Shoots: right

Career statistics:

GP	G	A	TP	PIM
238	23	46	69	417

1988-89 statistics:

GP	G	A	TP	+/-	PIM	PP	SH	GW	GT	S	PCT
65	11	12	32	9	155	6	0	0	0	132	8.3

LAST SEASON

Goal and point totals were career highs, assist total tied career high. Sidelined near mid-season with a hand injury. He led the club's defense in scoring and plus/minus (second on the club in the latter category). PIM total was club's third highest, second among defensemen.

THE FINESSE GAME

Gerald has a fair degree of finesse skill, and the application of those improving skills has helped improve him as a player. He's a good skater but rigid in his stride, and that rigidity inhibits motion and reduces mobility. Though neither exceptionally fast nor quick, Diduck is fairly mobile laterally. He pinches in and forechecks, and any lapses he suffers in that department are mental.

Getting too involved in the offense is Diduck's biggest problem because — to be blunt — at the best of times his offense wouldn't earn him an NHL contract. He must concentrate on playing strong defensively; when he does so, he can be an above-average player.

Diduck won't usually rush the puck, despite his offensive inclination. He generally moves the puck smartly, finding the open man and getting the puck to him. He'll see some power play duty because of that passing trait, and because of his underrated shot. His slap shot from the point is very strong (and Diduck likes to slide along the blue line to get a better angle on the net), but his shot is underrated because of accuracy problems.

He plays his defense positionally, using his angles to force the play outside and then closing the gap on the forward to take away the puck.

THE PHYSICAL GAME

Diduck's toughness should be *the* strength in his game, but that sometimes slips away as he becomes involved offensively. At his best, Diduck plays an aggressive physical game, putting his excellent size and strength to work along the boards and in front of the net; he's showing the meanness necessary to be an above-average NHL defenseman. He hits whenever possible and makes his hitting more effective by being able to move the puck.

THE INTANGIBLES

If you get the idea that we're down on Diduck, you're wrong; we're not. In fact, by the end of last season he'd shown definite signs that he realized he must concentrate on defense first. Where previously he'd always wanted to work on his offense, Diduck paid more attention to the areas where he can best succeed.

He's working hard to become a much better student of the game. And since he's essentially played only two full NHL seasons, he's showing good maturity in his thought process.

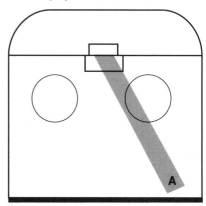

MARK FITZPATRICK

Yrs. of NHL service: 1
Born: Toronto, Ontario, Canada; November 13, 1968
Position: Goaltender
Height: 6-2
Weight: 190
Uniform no.: 29
Catches: left

Career statistics:

GP	MINS	AVG	W	L	T	SO	GA	SA	SAPCT	PIM
28	1,584	3.98	9	12	5	0	105	879	.880	4

LAST SEASON

Acquired along with Doug Crossman and Wayne McBean from Los Angeles in exchange for Kelly Hrudey. First NHL season. He had two assists.

THE PHYSICAL GAME

Fitzpatrick is a standup goaltender, and that style maximizes his good size. He challenges the shooters by moving out on point shots, and Mark also stands up well on plays in close so as to force the opposition into the first move.

He is a good skater with good balance, and he moves well in and out of the net, and from post to post. He does have good reflexes and will close the gap between his legs (the five-hole) fairly quickly, but he falls prey to the problem many tall goalies have and that is low shots to the corners.

Mark clears his rebounds fairly well, but he could improve in his use of the stick for pokechecking. He also needs to improve his puckhandling.

THE MENTAL GAME

Fitzpatrick plays a positional game, and he uses his good vision to see the puck and anticipate the play; he's a thinking goaltender. Mark has good concentration skills and has demonstrated big save capability at the junior level.

THE INTANGIBLES

Fitzpatrick works very hard to stay in shape during the off-season, and that's a manifestation of his intensity and dedication. He wants the responsibility of being the number one goalie, and he badly wants to play.

PAT FLATLEY

Yrs of NHL service: 6
Born: Toronto, Ontario, Canada; October 3, 1963
Position: Right wing
Height: 6-2
Weight: 197
Uniform no.: 26
Shoots: right

Career statistics:

GP	G	A	TP	PIM
311	75	137	212	318

1988-89 statistics:

GP	G	A	TP	+/-	PIM	PP	SH	GW	GT	S	PCT
41	10	15	25	-5	31	2	1	1	0	72	13.9

LAST SEASON

Games played was second lowest full-season total of career (recovery from knee surgery, recurring knee injury and hip injury). Goal and point totals were second lowest of career.

THE FINESSE GAME

Strength on his skates is Flatley's primary finesse quality, and he keys the rest of his game off that trait. While he lacks outstanding speed, quickness or agility, Patrick is the embodiment of the Newton's law of inertia: an object in motion tends to stay in motion. Flatley just goes and goes.

He has more hockey sense than he is given credit for. Pat is smart and he knows where the other players are, making him a strong offensive player in short give-and-go situations.

But one reason why he wouldn't get credit for his smarts is his tendency to over-handle the puck. He tends to hold the puck too long, hoping to make the fancy pass, that spinaround twirl play that looks good on the replays. He doesn't have the skating skill or quickness of foot to do that, to dart between defenders, so he must learn to move the puck more quickly.

His goal scoring will be of the plumber-type, with Flatley filling the front of the net and using his quick shot to net goals from around the front or sides of the net. He also shoots frequently from the corners.

THE PHYSICAL GAME

From the blue line in, Pat is very good at controlling the puck and protecting it with his body. His strength afoot is such that he doesn't care if he gets hit and doesn't care if he hits somebody else, but improved foot speed would give him some greater agility — and another weapon to call on so as not to be so predictable.

Because he is able to use his size and strength to collect the puck, Flatley succeeds in working the corners. The same traits make him a good choice for goalmouth duty on the power play.

THE INTANGIBLES

After six seasons, what you see with Flatley is pretty much what you get. His recent tendency toward injury would indicate that he should avoid some of the contact he craves but, at this point in his career, the chances of Flatley improving his other skills (foot speed, for example) are small. Health will remain a question mark.

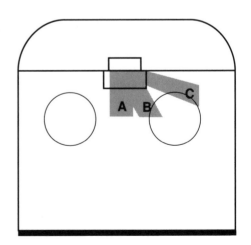

JEFF HACKETT

Yrs. of NHL service: 1
Born: London, Ontario, Canada; June 1, 1968
Position: Goaltender
Height: 6-1
Weight: 175
Uniform no.: 1
Catches: left

Career statistics:

GP	MINS	AVG	W	L	T	SO	GA	SA	SAPCT	PIM
13	662	3.53	4	7	0	0	39	329	.881	2

LAST SEASON

First NHL season. He was New York's second pick in the 1987 Entry Draft.

THE PHYSICAL GAME

Though he has good size, Hackett prefers to play a reflex game. He sits back in his net and uses his reflexes to stop the puck. Jeff likes to use his quick feet to his advantage by playing a butterfly style, and his good balance helps him here.

He regains his stance quickly to establish position for the second shot, and there are going to be a lot of second shots because Jeff leaves a lot of rebounds. His balance extends to his skating, and he moves very well laterally — from post to post. His quickness and that lateral ability make him tough to beat in scrambles near the net.

Hackett has a good glove hand, but he could improve in the use of his stick for pokechecking and puckhandling.

THE MENTAL GAME

Jeff has very good concentration, and he can be mentally tough; he'll hang in there and fight for each goal even when struggling. He tracks the puck fairly well but isn't big in the play-reading or anticipation department.

THE INTANGIBLES

Not yet ready to be a consistent NHL goalie, Jeff nevertheless wants the responsibility of being the Islanders' main man. He's an enthusiastic, likable guy anxious for the challenge of playing in the NHL. He'll have a lot of competition from Mark Fitzpatrick, but that may drive each to play better.

ALAN KERR

Yrs. of NHL service: 3
Born: Hazelton, B.C., Canada; March 28, 1964
Position: Right wing
Height: 5-11
Weight: 195
Uniform no.: 10
Shoots: right

Career statistics:

GP	G	A	TP	PIM
249	54	64	118	557

1988-89 statistics:

GP	G	A	TP	+/-	PIM	PP	SH	GW	GT	S	PCT
71	20	18	38	-5	144	6	0	4	0	147	13.6

LAST SEASON

Games played and PIM totals were full season lows; he was sidelined with a knee injury. Point totals were second highest of career. Finished fourth in PIM total, second among forwards.

THE FINESSE GAME

In terms of speed, quickness, and acceleration ability, Kerr's a pretty good skater. But for a player with Kerr's physical style, his balance is below-average. While he has enough ability to have developed some lateral movement, Alan lacks the degree of balance necessary to be as effective as he can be. Because Kerr doesn't always come out of collisions vertical, he wastes time regaining his position. That lost time makes the difference between making a play and or losing the puck.

Still, Alan's skating and improved vision give him a fair degree of playmaking ability. Kerr can get the puck to his teammates given enough space and time, and he's begun to improve his handling of the puck at a faster speed. Because he doesn't have great hands, Kerr has to make the most of his speed and quickness.

He is not a gifted offensive player so Alan will have to be opportunistic for most of his goals, converting the loose pucks his checking can create.

THE PHYSICAL GAME

He doesn't have great size, but Kerr has pretty good strength. His skating strength drives him through checks to take the opposition off the puck along the boards, and he is relentless in pursuit of the puck. Kerr will fight if need be, regardless of the opponent.

THE INTANGIBLES

Like many plumber-type players who find a scoring touch, Kerr began to believe himself an artist. That's bad, because an artist he ain't. His success is always going to be determined by his physical play. He has to play along the boards and in the corners, banging away, or else he's going to be in trouble.

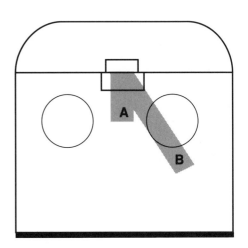

DEREK KING

Yrs. of NHL service: 2
Born: Hamilton, Ontario, Canada; February 11, 1967
Position: Left wing
Height: 6-1
Weight: 203
Uniform no.: 27
Shoots: left

Career statistics:

GP	G	A	TP	PIM
117	26	53	79	44

1988-89 statistics:

GP	G	A	TP	+/-	PIM	PP	SH	GW	GT	S	PCT
60	14	29	43	10	14	4	0	0	0	103	13.6

LAST SEASON

Games played and all point totals were career highs. He was sidelined with hip and shoulder injuries. He led the club in plus/minus.

THE FINESSE GAME

Hand skills are the heart and soul of King's game, particularly in terms of shooting the puck. He has a very quick release on his shot, making him dangerous from near the net, but he also has the shooting ability to convert from further away.

He can handle the puck fairly well when in motion, but his skating undercuts his ability. Derek lacks the NHL level of speed or quickness that would drive him past the defense — or give him the ability to dance past him (King is not agile). Often, then, Derek is easily driven to the boards or the corners and forced to make 40- and 50-foot plays, when shorter passes are always more effective.

He has great hockey sense and smarts, and he's shown throughout his pre-NHL career that he knows how to get into scoring position and how to exploit openings, but King has been unable to demonstrate that skill at the NHL level.

THE PHYSICAL GAME

Despite good size, King is a mild physical presence. He doesn't get involved in the traffic areas, and worse still is satisfied to say, "Okay, I'm stuck here against the boards, I'm out of the play." When he does get involved it's more to push and shove than hit.

THE INTANGIBLES

King is a player the Islanders are counting on very heavily as they head into the latest stage of their development, and in order to be successful he *must* reclaim the scoring touch he boasted in junior. In order to do that, Derek must develop the drive and desire that has been missing from his game since his introduction to the NHL.

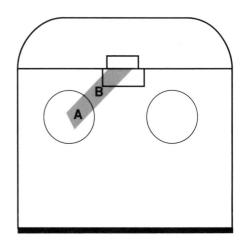

PAT LAFONTAINE

Yrs of NHL service: 6
Born: St. Louis, Missouri, USA; February 22, 1965
Position: Center
Height: 5-10
Weight: 177
Uniform no.: 16
Shoots: right

Career statistics:

GP	G	A	TP	PIM
381	192	184	376	229

1988-89 statistics:

GP	G	A	TP	+/-	PIM	PP	SH	GW	GT	S	PCT
79	45	43	88	-8	26	16	0	4	0	288	15.6

LAST SEASON

Games played and all point totals were second highest of career. He led club in goals, assists, points, SOG total and shooting percentage; was second in power play goals and tied for second in game-winners. He finished fourth in plus/minus among forwards.

THE FINESSE GAME

LaFontaine has all the finesse skills, primary of which is his skating speed. Many of his goals (and many of the Islanders' offensive opportunities) are created by his speed to the outside. He has explosive acceleration capability, and his excellent balance and foot speed provide him with exceptional agility and lateral movement. He can do almost anything with his skating.

LaFontaine can beat a goaltender in many ways; he's not picky. He can deke in tight because of his balance and hands, and he's deadly when left alone in front because of his quick release and his ability to make the puck dance on his stick. He can score from anywhere with any shot.

Pat's hands are super-soft for puck work. He carries the puck excellently at all speeds, but he's also improved in his playmaking by doing less 1-on-1 and by letting the puck do some of the work. While still a scoring center, LaFontaine is looking for his wingers; that opens up the offense.

All his skills make him a specialty teams natural, and LaFontaine has also improved his defense. He's not a Selke Trophy winner, but Pat works at playing a complete game.

THE PHYSICAL GAME

He's not big, but LaFontaine plays big. He and Steve Yzerman are the primary examples of how a physical game opens up a finesse one — especially for smaller players.

LaFontaine plays aggressively, going to the corners for the puck and taking the abuse in the traffic area near the net. Pat initiates contact, and then allows his finesse skills to take over after he's freed the puck.

THE INTANGIBLES

LaFontaine has really become a leader in the last two seasons, and his ability to play in the big games is a reason why. He earned a lot of credibility in the playoff series against the Devils two Aprils back; he played, and a lot of Islanders didn't.

He wants to be a factor in the dressing room, and he wants to improve his leadership role. His work ethic is very high, and his consistency has become unquestionable.

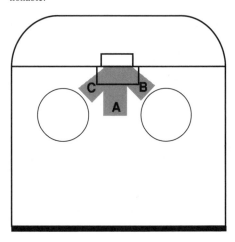

BRAD LAUER

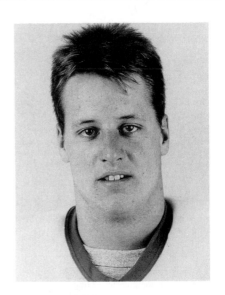

Yrs. of NHL service: 3
Born: Humboldt, Sask., Canada; October 27, 1966
Position: Left wing
Height: 6-0
Weight: 195
Uniform no.: 32
Shoots: left

Career statistics:

GP	G	A	TP	PIM
144	27	34	61	134

1988-89 statistics:

GP	G	A	TP	+/-	PIM	PP	SH	GW	GT	S	PCT
14	3	2	5	-2	2	0	0	0	0	21	14.3

LAST SEASON

Games played total was career low; he was sidelined with a knee injury.

THE FINESSE GAME

Strength is the best asset Lauer brings to his skating; he's incredibly strong on his blades. He is otherwise an up-and-down winger, without exceptional speed or quickness.

He carries the puck no better than fairly when he skates, and his inability to read the play at the NHL level (both in terms of speed and sophistication) mitigates against his being a good playmaker. He must keep his head up when making plays and try to look over the ice before making a play. Thus far he has not demonstrated much flair or creativity in the offensive zone, and broken plays or giveaways are the result.

Brad's outstanding finesse skill is his ability to shoot the puck coming down the wing or off the wall. His slap shot could blow past some goaltenders, but Lauer makes it less effective by taking too long to get it off. He also does not create openings for himself or know how to get into scoring position, so (despite his ability) he will actually have to be at relatively short range to score.

THE PHYSICAL GAME

Lauer has excellent strength that he can put to use, but he hasn't learned how to use his body. Despite his strength and sturdiness afoot, he often gets knocked off (or otherwise relieved) of the puck.

He'd be greatly aided if he kept his feet moving along the boards; that would make him much more difficult to control. Right now, he is far too often content to push and shove.

In all, for a player who needs to be aggressive to be successful, Lauer is surprisingly un-physical.

THE INTANGIBLES

Brad is a big question mark. His mental approach and desire aren't at high enough levels to sustain an NHL career, and he seriously needs to decide if he wants to make the sacrifices necessary to play in the NHL.

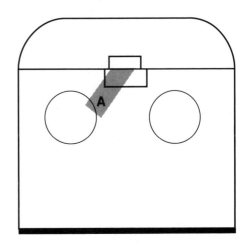

MIKKO MAKELA

Yrs. of NHL service: 4
Born: Tampere, Finland; February 28, 1965
Position: Right wing
Height: 6-2
Weight: 193
Uniform no.: 24
Shoots: left

Career statistics:

GP	G	A	TP	PIM
287	93	121	214	96

1988-89 statistics:

GP	G	A	TP	+/-	PIM	PP	SH	GW	GT	S	PCT
76	17	28	45	-16	22	4	0	0	0	123	13.8

LAST SEASON

All point totals were full-season career lows. He finished fifth on the club in scoring. His plus/minus was fourth worst among fulltime players, second poorest among forwards.

THE FINESSE GAME

Makela has everything needed finesse-wise to be an NHL star. He's an exceptional skater in all aspects of that skill: speed, quickness, agility, balance. He can change speed and direction within a stride, providing him with superior mobility and lateral movement.

Mikko complements his skating skill with brains; his sense tells him where to be, his feet put him there. Makela knows how to get into scoring position, but he also knows how to find and exploit the openings for his teammates. His peripheral vision is excellent and reveals the position of everyone on-ice.

His hand skills are just as good as his other attributes. Makela can carry the puck and make plays with it at any speed. He has great passing touch, and can deliver or accept a pass in full stride.

Makela's shot is the best of his hand skills. While he has the ability to hit the top of the net off a one-time from 10 feet (*that's* touch), he also has the strength to blow the puck past any goaltender from the distances. He's a very dangerous scorer, very creative with the puck.

THE PHYSICAL GAME

Makela's size and strength are just as major-league as his finesse skills — and even if they weren't, he's almost talented enough to make the physical part irrelevant. But nevertheless, Mikko is strong enough to hold off the biggest defensemen in order to make his plays.

He uses his balance and reach excellently in his puckhandling, teasing the defense with the puck. He is willing to take his knocks to make his plays, and his balance and low center of gravity aid him in working for the puck along the boards and in traffic.

THE INTANGIBLES

Instead of going forward, Makela is going backward. Every word written here is true, but predicated on one thing: Makela's desire to make his talent work. His mental outlook and preparation are questionable, to say the least.

Given his almost limitless potential, that's a shame. Makela could do anything if he worked hard enough, and no small part of the Islanders' success — or lack of it — is tied to his contribution.

There's still time for him to turn his career around, but he needs a major maturity lesson.

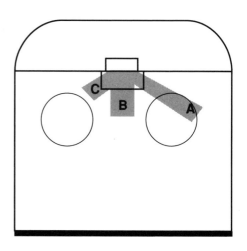

WAYNE MCBEAN

Yrs. of NHL service: 1
Born: Calgary, Alta., Canada; February 21, 1969
Position: Defenseman
Height: 6-2
Weight: 185
Uniform no.: 28
Shoots: left

Career statistics:

GP	G	A	TP	PIM
79	0	7	7	61

1988-89 statistics:

GP	G	A	TP	+/-	PIM	PP	SH	GW	GT	S	PCT
52	0	6	6	-13	35	0	0	0	0	36	0.0

LAST SEASON

Acquired along with Mark Fitzpatrick and Doug Crossman from Los Angeles in exchange for Kelly Hrudey. Games played, assist and point totals were career highs.

THE FINESSE GAME

McBean has finesse potential, but he is a raw prospect, very green. He skates like the wind, which is saying something for a player with his size. He also has exceptional quickness, the kind that lets him cross a specific distance — say two or three strides — very quickly, and then get back to his original position. That helped him as a penalty killer in Los Angeles, where he could get from the net to the far man and back in a snap.

Wayne has a lot of work to do in his own end in terms of learning to see and understand the game, because right now he goes right for the puck every time. The same holds true at the offensive blue line, where he gets sucked in deeper and deeper until the puck is dumped out behind him and he's trapped in the offensive zone.

He has great potential to contribute from the offensive blue line, where he can find the open man and get the puck to him, but Wayne lacks the patience to do so at the NHL level. He panics quickly and unloads the puck when he has time, and the same holds true in his own zone when he moves the puck to the forwards.

He has good scoring skills, but right now any goals he gets will come from the point.

THE PHYSICAL GAME

Wayne has good upper body strength, certainly good enough to handle himself in traffic and checking situations, but he makes his strength look worse by not playing positionally. Instead he forgets all about body position and goes right after the puck carrier, with the result that the puck carrier spins off him — so Wayne looks bad.

That said, there is still room for him to develop better strength. He has good size and willingness, but his physical game is undetermined at the NHL level.

THE INTANGIBLES

Many question marks. Wayne has all the tools but needs time to develop them, and he has to develop and maintain a degree of consistency before he can be counted on to play in the NHL this season.

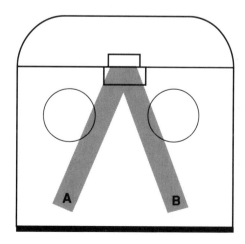

265

JEFF NORTON

Yrs. of NHL service: 2
Born: Cambridge, Mass., USA; November 25, 1965
Position: Defenseman
Height: 6-2
Weight: 195
Uniform no.: 8
Shoots: left

Career statistics:

GP	G	A	TP	PIM
84	2	36	38	88

1988-89 statistics:

GP	G	A	TP	+/-	PIM	PP	SH	GW	GT	S	PCT
69	1	30	31	-24	74	1	0	0	0	126	0.8

LAST SEASON

Norton's first full NHL season. Finished fourth on the club in assists, leading the defense in that category. His plus/minus was the club's worst. He was sidelined with a rib injury.

THE FINESSE GAME

Right now, Norton's got all the tools — he just can't open the tool box. He already possesses excellent skating abilities: speed, strength, quickness and balance. He has exceptional mobility and lateral movement, the kind of talent that will allow him to challenge the puck at both blue lines.

But that's part of the problem. Norton is all over the ice, trying to do everything all the time. Because he carries the puck extremely well, he want to *always* carry the puck. Because he can pinch in and forecheck, he wants to *always* force the play. Because he can make dynamic passes that create offense, he wants to *always* make dynamic passes.

Norton has excellent hockey sense, vision and smarts; what he has to develop now is judgment. His time to be the club's on-ice general will come, but now is not the time.

He plays a defensive style based on his abilities, and because of that he often gets into trouble. While he can step up and close the gap, Jeff should concentrate for now on forcing the play wide of the net and then taking the body and moving the puck if he can.

The story is the same offensively, where Norton's frequent attempts at forcing the play result in turnovers. The best thing he can do for now is to contain the point and not challenge so frequently. He should also use his shot more; it can be a potent weapon — low, hard, quickly released.

THE PHYSICAL GAME

Norton has good size and isn't afraid to use it. He willingly goes to the corners with anyone, and his balance and strength combine to make him a better than even chance to emerge with the puck. His physical play is amplified by his fine ability to make the play after a hit.

He is an aggressive finesse player, and that aggressiveness makes his finesse game that much more effective. Like his other skills, Norton's physical play — while already good — has the ability to improve.

THE INTANGIBLES

Because he made so much of an impact in his short tenure during the spring of 1988 (after joining the club), much was expected of Norton — perhaps unfairly so.

Regardless, he is a highly skilled player who can be a dominating NHL player. What he must do now is concentrate his focus on his own position, and not on trying to do more than he is currently capable of. Norton has to cover his own area and work from a conservative standpoint.

That means developing the mental toughness to control his game (instead of letting his game control him), and staying within himself. Whether he will or not remains to be seen.

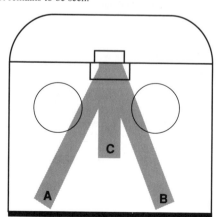

GARY NYLUND

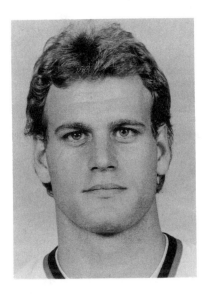

Yrs. of NHL service: 7
Born: Surrey, B.C., Canada; October 23, 1963
Position: Defenseman
Height: 6-3
Weight: 210
Uniform no.: 36
Shoots: left

Career statistics:

GP	G	A	TP	PIM
443	25	95	120	945

1988-89 statistics:

GP	G	A	TP	+/-	PIM	PP	SH	GW	GT	S	PCT
69	7	10	17	-19	137	0	0	0	0	74	9.5

LAST SEASON

Acquired from Chicago along with Marc Bergevin in exchange for Steve Konroyd and Bob Bassen. He was sidelined with chest (two games) and knee injuries. Games played total was five-season low, assist and point totals second lowest of career. PIM total was third among defensemen.

THE FINESSE GAME

Nylund is a stay-at-home defenseman whose skills match his game. He has good balance for a big man but his foot speed is a little slow. Nylund plays his defensive angles fairly well, but his lack of foot speed makes him susceptible in his turns. Improved quickness would also make him more mobile and more able to get to loose pucks. But we're not saying Nylund is immobile, just that he could be more mobile.

He has great strength on his skates and is very difficult to knock off the puck. Nylund generally handles the puck well and he will most usually make the quick, correct pass to his forwards. He is not an exceptional stickhandler when carrying the puck, however, so his only play is going to be straight ahead.

He shoots from the point and one-times the puck on net exceptionally well (which is funny, because he never keeps the puck in at the point on a non-shooting play) but could shoot more frequently, and Gary does have the potential to be effective at the offensive blue line because he does see the ice well. He can find open teammates and get the puck to them, but Nylund's depth of understanding is not such that he will see openings and exploit them.

Defensively he has a tendency toward the giveaway if he is pressured while going back for the puck. Once he's turned and has the play in front of him he's fairly poised and patient, but he's not guaranteed to clear the zone.

THE PHYSICAL GAME

Nylund has exceptional size and strength, and he works hard at improving his already excellent strength. He is always in the weight room and the results can be seen on the ice, though he still has a tendency to be over-aggressive; that hurts the team penalty-wise.

He enjoys hitting and really punishes the opposition along the boards or in front of the net. He sacrifices his body to block shots and, though he is not a fighter per se, Nylund is tough and more than willing to mix it up.

THE INTANGIBLES

Like teammate Marc Bergevin, Nylund improved his game tremendously from the start of the season to the finish, and Gary did it by playing within the boundaries of his game. Nylund played the most consistent hockey of his career by concentrating on his defense.

He's a player who is coachable and has a good attitude, and Coach Al Arbour should be able to to get even more out of him this season, because Nylund still has unfulfilled promise.

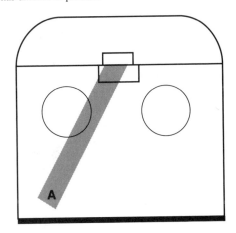

RICHARD PILON

Yrs. of NHL service: 1
Born: Saskatoon, Sask., Canada; April 30, 1968
Position: Defenseman
Height: 6-0
Weight: 202
Uniform no.: 47
Shoots: left

Career statistics:

GP	G	A	TP	+/-	PIM	PP	SH	GW	GT	S	PCT
62	0	14	14	-9	242	0	0	0	0	47	0.0

LAST SEASON

His first in the NHL. He led the club in PIM total. He missed two games with a shoulder injury, and was also sidelined with the flu.

THE FINESSE GAME

Pilon is an underrated finesse player, particularly in the area of his skating. But Pilon could not play the dominating physical game he does play if not for his skating. That skating is marked by a strong stride and some good foot speed, both of which allow Rich to close the gap on the puck carrier. After all, you can't hit what you can't catch.

His finesse game is otherwise limited. Pilon will make the simple play up the boards to get the puck to the forwards, and he will be the last one up ice and the first one to head back to defense. A greater degree of offensive involvement would help the Islanders, because otherwise the team is essentially operating 4-on-5.

He does read the rush toward him very well, and that vision is a big part of his ability to step up and separate the puck carrier from the puck.

Any scoring he does, of which there will not be much, will be done on an average shot from the point.

THE PHYSICAL GAME

There are not many defensemen in the NHL who can hit like Pilon can, and few who attempt it — and fewer still the number who do it as consistently. He's tremendously strong and he can really punish the opposition as they head his way. Pilon uses his good strength in the board and crease battles, and he won't often lose. He is fearless about hitting, and lines up any player.

The one disadvantage to his play is that he is not yet able to consistently make a play after taking the opposition off the puck; that should change with greater NHL experience.

THE INTANGIBLES

Pilon is a throwback to the era of the pure defensive defenseman. His play fell off at the end of the year because of a sore back, and that ailment raised the question of Pilon's continued banging. But such was his impact (pun intended) that the opposition made great attempts to stay away from him. Pilon, in turn, must become more intelligent in his hitting and pick his spots.

He's a very enthusiastic player who just loves to play, and he can be a very important part of the Islanders' next phase. His hitting has made him a marked man, but an indication of his intensity is that he plays better when he knows he's a target.

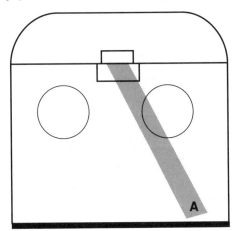

BRENT SUTTER

Yrs of NHL service: 8
Born: Viking, Alberta, Canada; June 10, 1962
Position: Center
Height: 5-11
Weight: 180
Uniform no.: 21
Shoots: left

Career statistics:

GP	G	A	TP	PIM
544	229	250	479	641

1988-89 statistics:

GP	G	A	TP	+/-	PIM	PP	SH	GW	GT	S	PCT
77	29	34	63	-12	77	17	2	2	0	187	15.5

LAST SEASON

Games played total was second highest, point total tied second highest of career. Assist total was third best. Finished second on the club in scoring, first in power play and shorthanded goals, third in SO total.

THE FINESSE GAME

Strength is going to be the strength of any Sutter's game, and Brent is no exception. His skating is marked by balance and power, elements which key his physical game. He lacks exceptional quickness, speed or agility, and plays a style that complements his straight-ahead skating game.

Brent has good hockey sense and the ability to find the open man and get the puck to him, but he's not an especially strong 5-on-5 player in offensive terms. He can carry the puck fairly, but he does have a tendency to over-handle it and to take himself to bad ice because of that. His sense and skills should make him a better playmaker than he's shown himself to be over the last four seasons.

Sutter scores from mucking around the net and preying on loose pucks, particularly on the power play; his strength on his skates helps him here, driving him to those pucks — and Sutter's hands are good enough to do some finessing of the puck in those tight quarters.

He is very solid defensively and a fine positional player in all three zones. His anticipation and sense combine with his strong skating to make him an above-average checker — so forget the plus/minus.

THE PHYSICAL GAME

Sutter takes the body effectively in all three zones, and he is especially successful in forcing opposing defensemen to lose the puck. Brent is strong in the corners and the front of the net, using his balance and skating strength to drive through checks and free the puck; his ability to make plays after checking makes his physical play more valuable.

He is also a very good faceoff man.

THE INTANGIBLES

Sutter's work ethic and hatred of losing make him a leader and his leadership is important to a team like the Islanders, a club embarking on a new phase.

But his on-ice performance has to be labelled disappointing; after all, he scored just 10 even-strength goals last season — just *three* in his last 25 games. That means something; underachievement, perhaps?

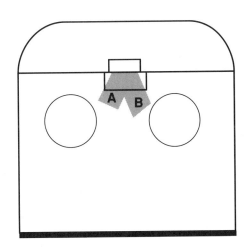

BRYAN TROTTIER:

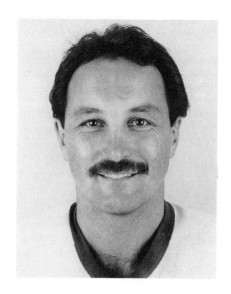

Yrs. of NHL service: 14
Born: Val Marie, Sask., Canada, July 17, 1956
Position: Center
Height: 5-11
Weight: 195
Uniform no.: 19
Shoots: left

Career statistics:

GP	G	A	TP	PIM
1,064	487	842	1,329	769

1988-89 statistics:

GP	G	A	TP	+/-	PIM	PP	SH	GW	GT	S	PCT
73	17	28	45	-7	44	5	0	3	0	163	10.4

LAST SEASON

Games played total was four-season low, all point totals career lows. He finished fourth on the club in scoring. Plus/minus was third best among full-time forwards. He was sidelined late in the season with a back injury.

THE FINESSE GAME

Balance remains the key to Trottier's skating game, giving him a fair degree of agility. He also uses his balance in his physical game to remain vertical and ready to make plays after taking the body. His speed and quickness continue to diminish, but his straight-ahead style disguises those decreasing abilities.

His hockey sense continues to make all his skills better. Bryan is the type of player who will have forgotten more about the game than 99 percent of its players will ever know, and he uses his smarts to reveal a game's patterns. His tremendous understanding of both the offensive and defensive play minimizes — if not completely eliminates — mistakes from his own play.

Trottier still moves the puck well, seeing the openings and getting the puck to his teammates. His own scoring has always been of the grind-it-out type, not the artistic rush or explosive shot, and that remains so today. He'll pick up his goals by working to be in the right place at the right time. He works well in the traffic areas where his great balance allows him to take his knocks but retain control of the puck.

THE PHYSICAL GAME

Strength has always been the— excuse us — strength of Trottier's game, and that remains so today. His skating strength and sense have long made him an outstanding forechecker, and he can still force the opposition to lose the puck — only now, sense plays a bigger role than skating.

He is less of a heavy hitter than he has been, because the foot speed necessary to meet the opposition has decreased, but Trottier is still very strong along the boards in 1-on-1 battles. He willingly takes or makes checks.

Most noticeable in skill fall-off has been his faceoff skill. Trottier lost a lot of faceoffs last year, an indication of decreasing eye/hand coordination and speed (and, to a certain degree, strength as well).

THE INTANGIBLES

Only because his skills were so great to begin with can Trottier's game take the slide it has — and yet he's still a good player. There's nothing wrong with him mentally or physically (except 14 years worth of wear), and he can still go when he wants to.

One important thing worth noting, however, has been his decreasing even-strength production: 15 goals in 1987-88, just 12 last season.

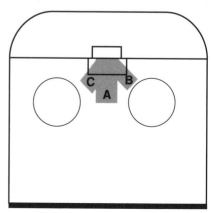

DAVID VOLEK

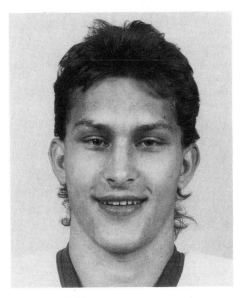

Yrs. of NHL service: 1
Born: Czechoslovakia; June 18, 1966
Position: Left wing
Height: 6-0
Weight: 183
Uniform no.: 25
Shoots: left

Career statistics:

GP	G	A	TP	+/-	PIM	PP	SH	GW	GT	S	PCT
77	25	34	59	-11	24	9	0	7	0	229	10.9

LAST SEASON

First NHL season. Finished sixth in overall rookie scoring (third on the club), fifth in rookie goals (third on club), third in rookie power play goals (and on club), first in rookie game winners (led club) and third in rookie SOG total (second on club). He missed three games with a shoulder injury.

THE FINESSE GAME

The most impressive aspects of Volek's already impressive finesse skills are his hand and foot speed. He's an exceptional skater with terrific quickness — the ability to move short distances in a snap. That quickness gets him to the openings and to loose pucks. He's also got good balance, so his quickness combines with his balance to make him a very agile skater.

David's hands are also extremely quick — which is not to say he has great hands. Rather, the puck will get onto his stick — and off of it (either through a pass or a shot) in the blink of an eye. He'll also do very well at tipping and deflecting pucks because of his hand speed.

Volek has a good shot and he can score from the distances, but he also has the touch to score from in tight. His balance and quickness combine to make him a very effective traffic player — and will make him devastating on the power play.

He is also a smart player, both offensively and defensively — regardless of the plus/minus. He has great understanding of the offensive game and is excellent away from the puck (very creative in finding and forcing openings); he knows how to get into scoring position. David also learned — after a *very* poor start — how to play positional hockey. Though minus-10 by his 40th game, Volek was a much more respectable minus-1 over his last 37 games.

THE PHYSICAL GAME

He doesn't have exceptional size or strength (despite the rumors of his steroid use; in fact, his body is his best defense *against* those charges), but that doesn't mean Volek is shy about contact.

On the contrary, Volek is guaranteeing his future NHL success by integrating physical play into his game from the beginning of his career. What's more, his finesse skills perfectly complement his physical willingness — allowing him to check the opposition and take the body, and then make plays coming away from the boards.

THE INTANGIBLES

Volek has a very strong attitude. He demands a lot from himself and his linemates, and he wants to play in the NHL and play well. He's a worker and a coachable young man who has already adjusted well in the transition from his pre-defection lifestyle. That bodes very well for his continuing — bound to improve — NHL game.

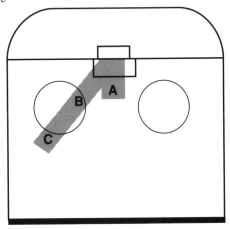

MICK VUKOTA

Yrs. of NHL service: 2
Born: Saskatoon, Sask., Canada; September 14, 1966
Position: Right wing
Height: 6-2
Weight: 195
Uniform no.: 38
Shoots: right

Career statistics:

GP	G	A	TP	PIM
65	3	2	5	319

1988-89 statistics:

GP	G	A	TP	+/-	PIM	PP	SH	GW	GT	S	PCT
48	2	2	4	-17	237	0	0	0	0	19	10.5

LAST SEASON

First "full" NHL season. He was second on the club in PIM total, tops among forwards.

THE FINESSE GAME

Vukota's is a limited finesse game, without exceptional NHL ability — maybe not even average NHL ability. He gets up and down his wing but lacks real speed or quickness, which is fine because he doesn't carry the puck well and really has no idea what to do with it when he's got it.

He has an idea about defensive play, but his propensity for wandering teams with his unexceptional skating to put him almost anywhere but where he has to be to play defense. He must cure himself of that, must relieve himself of his defensive handicaps if he hopes to take a regular shift.

His shot is as unexceptional as the rest of his skills, so any goals he gets are going to have to come from near the goal.

THE PHYSICAL GAME

Vukota may be the smartest tough guy in the League. He's very intelligent when it comes to picking his spots to change the game's tempo, and a good example would be the game against the Flames in Calgary in which Lanny McDonald scored his 500th goal.

After the goal, the crowd is charged and the Flames are pumped, but Mick bumps a couple of guys and suddenly the crowd is out of the excitement and the Flames momentum is stopped.

Otherwise, he's a pretty good fighter — but he's not skilled enough as a skater to play an effective physical game.

THE INTANGIBLES

Vukota is an exceptional team man, and he can be an important player for New York. But in order to gain that position he must improve the level of his skills, particularly defensively.

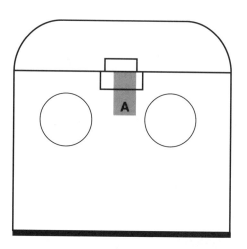

RANDY WOOD

Yrs. of NHL service: 2
Born: Princeton, New Jersey, USA; October 12, 1963
Position: Left wing
Height: 6-0
Weight: 195
Uniform no.: 11
Shoots: left

Career statistics:

GP	G	A	TP	PIM
158	38	29	67	128

1988-89 statistics:

GP	G	A	TP	+/-	PIM	PP	SH	GW	GT	S	PCT
77	15	13	28	-18	44	0	0	0	1	115	13.0

LAST SEASON

Point totals fell in second season. He was demoted to Springfield of the American Hockey League.

THE FINESSE GAME

Wood is an excellent skater with great speed and balance, quickness and agility, strength and acceleration. As they are in every player, these skills are interrelated and Wood uses one to amplify another. His strength powers his acceleration, his balance and foot speed contribute to his quickness and agility.

He complements his speed with the ability to handle the puck well as he carries it — at any speed. That doesn't mean, however, that he can make plays at that speed. While Randy can blow by a defender and cut inside him for a shot, he doesn't have the same ability to move the puck to a teammate in a similar position.

Even after two NHL seasons, Wood continues to work with his head down. Head down means no vision. No vision means no playmaking. No playmaking means blind or ill-conceived passes. Ill-conceived passes mean turnovers and turnovers equal a minus rating. He *must* work on seeing the ice more.

Because Wood shoots the puck fairly well, and because his balance lets him work well in traffic, most of his goals will come from fairly close to the net. He needs great help defensively, particularly in using his skating to make better transitions from offense to defense.

THE PHYSICAL GAME

Randy has excellent upper body strength, and that strength can sometimes work against him by countering his balance. He'll end up over-balance — top-heavy — and he'll lose his footing because of that.

Otherwise, his strength and sturdiness on his feet makes him very effective when digging in the corners. He plays a willing physical game and his hitting creates loose pucks; he can be a punishing hitter because of his strength and skating drive.

Wood would make his physical play more effective if he could improve his ability to see the ice, because he could then make plays off the loose pucks he forces.

THE INTANGIBLES

Randy has an excellent work ethic, and he's obviously very smart; he's a Yale graduate. But he also has a tendency to get down on himself when things don't go well, and that is manifested in his performances.

That's not necessarily negative, because it means Randy cares about how he plays. A happy medium would take some self-induced pressure off of him, and might result in a more relaxed — and, therefore, more effective — performance.

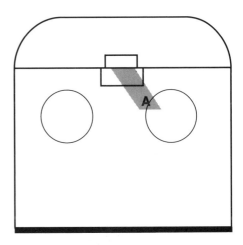

NEW YORK RANGERS

LINE COMBINATIONS
TONY GRANATO-CAREY WILSON
TOMAS SANDSTROM
CHRIS NILAN-LUCIEN DEBLOIS-JAN ERIXON
BRIAN MULLEN-KELLY KISIO-GUY LAFLEUR

DEFENSE PAIRINGS
MARK HARDY-RUDY POESCHEK
BRIAN LEETCH-DAVID SHAW
JAMES PATRICK-MICHEL PETIT

GOALTENDERS
BOB FROESE
JOHN VANBIESBROUCK

OTHER PLAYERS
ULF DAHLEN — Right wing
JOHN OGRODNICK — Left wing
LINDY RUFF — Defenseman/left wing
RON GRESCHNER— Defenseman

POWER PLAY

FIRST UNIT:
CAREY WILSON-TOMAS SANDSTROM
ULF DAHLEN
BRIAN LEETCH-JAMES PATRICK

SECOND UNIT:
BRIAN MULLEN-KELLY KISIO-GUY LAFLEUR

On the first unit, WILSON sets up along the left wing boards, SANDSTROM mirrors him at the right wing and DAHLEN jams the net. WILSON and LEETCH control the play, looking for an open SAND- STROM. Failing that, the second option is a LEETCH shot from the point with SANDSTROM joining DAHLEN in front of the net.

The second set of forwards is led by KISIO around the goal line, with MULLEN and LAFLEUR at their respective circles. MULLEN is the first prefer- ence. DAVID SHAW and MICHEL PETIT will rotate in for LEETCH and PATRICK, but the first unit's duo is the key one.

Last season New York's power play was POOR, scoring 85 goals in 457 attempts (18.6 percent, 19th overall).

PENALTY KILLING

FIRST UNIT:
BRIAN MULLEN-TONY GRANATO
BRIAN LEETCH-DAVID SHAW

SECOND UNIT:
JAN ERIXON-TOMAS SANDSTROM
JAMES PATRICK-MICHEL PETIT

All the forwards are aggressive on the puck, especially ERIXON and GRANATO in the offensive zone. MULLEN is next in terms of aggressiveness outside the defensive zone. All penalty killers hold a standard box but force the puck in their areas.

Last season New York's penalty killing was FAIR, allowing 85 goals in 371 shorthanded situations (77.1 percent, 15th overall).

CRUCIAL FACEOFFS
CAREY WILSON, seconded by KISIO. DEB- LOIS is also fairly strong.

ULF DAHLEN

Yrs. of NHL service: 1
Born: Ostersund, Sweden; January 12, 1967
Position: Right wing
Height: 6-2
Weight: 195
Uniform no.: 9
Shoots: left

Career statistics:

GP	G	A	TP	PIM
126	53	42	95	76

1988-89 statistics:

GP	G	A	TP	+/-	PIM	PP	SH	GW	GT	S	PCT
56	24	19	43	-6	50	8	0	1	1	147	16.3

LAST SEASON

Games played and all point totals fell in second NHL season. He missed 24 games with shoulder bruises and separations.

THE FINESSE GAME

Dahlen is an excellent skater, and it is his exceptional balance that makes him so. While not possessing great speed or quickness (and therefore not having exceptional agility or lateral ability), Dahlen's balance is equal to that of the NHL's best players. That balance excellently complements his willingness to play a physical game and go into traffic, where he is almost impossible to knock down.

He amplifies his ability to maintain body position with the hands, the eyes and the brain to create opportunities. He controls the puck very well when carrying it, and Ulf passes well because he sees the open man and has the hands to get the puck to his teammates. He could improve in his reaction time, because Dahlen has a tendency to hold onto the puck longer than necessary — simply because he can.

Though he's got good hands and controls the puck well at all speeds, Dahlen won't make end-to-end rushes because of his skating; he'll use his hands to make plays away from the boards. He'll get into scoring position, where he'll use his good, quickly released shot — and that makes him a natural for power-play duty.

THE PHYSICAL GAME

Ulf takes a beating because of his complete physical willingness. His balance makes him an extraordinary player against the boards or in the slot, where he has the strength to hold onto the puck despite tough checking and fouling.

He has good size, but he needs greater muscle strength and bulk so as to avoid the injuries he's bound to accumulate as a physical player. He initiates contact in all situations, and certainly accepts hits to make his plays, and Ulf isn't above a scrap or two a season.

Another thing that makes him successful in confrontations is his reach. When that reach is combined with his hand skills, Dahlen is able to not only gain the puck in the corner and then move out to make a play, but he's often able to create an excellent scoring chance for himself.

THE INTANGIBLES

If he can whip the health problems that cropped up last season, Dahlen can be a very important performer for a long time. He can be a presence in front of the net on the power play, and that's something the Rangers have looked for for several seasons.

He's an outgoing and personable player, one who knows how to have fun. He's well-liked among his teammates, and he's also a dedicated and hard-working player. Dahlen should be an NHL success for many seasons.

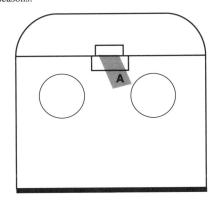

JAN ERIXON

Yrs. of NHL service: 6
Born: Skelleftea, Sweden; July 8, 1962
Position: Right wing
Height: 6-0
Weight: 196
Uniform no.: 20
Shoots: left

Career statistics:

GP	G	A	TP	PIM
354	33	112	145	137

1988-89 statistics:

GP	G	A	TP	+/-	PIM	PP	SH	GW	GT	S	PCT
44	4	11	15	-3	27	0	0	2	0	41	9.8

LAST SEASON

Missed 17 games with a sprained knee, 17 more with back spasms, and one with the flu; games played total was second lowest of career — ditto point totals.

THE FINESSE GAME

Erixon possesses extraordinary — but quiet — skating skills and hockey sense. He is extremely strong on his skates, as well as extremely agile. He has great balance and quickness — which add up to great lateral movement — though he doesn't have rink-length speed.

His hockey sense is exceptional, and it puts him where he is supposed to be remarkably well. He has great anticipation and ice vision, and he uses those traits to relentlessly pursue the puck and actually get into position to score.

He uses his teammates very well and has great hands for passing and accepting passes, and Jan carries the puck very well. In fact, he is almost impossible to separate from the puck by legal means because of his hand skill and balance.

Those skills do not translate into goals, however. Erixon shoots the puck well, but because he's so unaccustomed to thinking offensively, he doesn't shoot the puck at the right moment. He'll hit posts, or force goalies to make great saves, but he lacks a scorer's ability to shoot at the best time — despite frequently getting into position to score.

THE PHYSICAL GAME

We've already talked about balance, but Erixon adds great strength to that balance to make his checking relentless and physically tiring to the opposition. He's not the strongest checking forward in the League (that distinction probably falls to either Derrick Smith or Joel Otto), but because he cannot be slowed down — even illegally — Erixon may very well be the toughest; he takes tremendous punishment from the players he shadows.

He's very smart at using his body to bump the opposition off the puck or to protect the puck himself, and his relentless play forces the opposition into taking penalties to thwart him.

THE INTANGIBLES

The main question is health. Erixon has never played a full season; he's played only 213 of a possible 320 games over the last four seasons.

Any superlative regarding Erixon's defensive ability is completely applicable, and a healthy full season would go a long way toward gaining him the Selke Trophy he deserves as the League's best defensive forward.

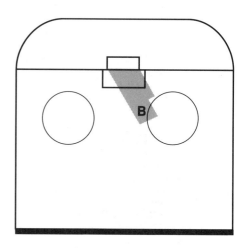

BOB FROESE

Yrs. of NHL service: 7
Born: St. Catharines, Ontario, Canada; June 30, 1958
Position: Goaltender
Height: 6-1
Weight: 178
Uniform no.: 33
Catches: left

Career statistics:

GP	MINS	G	SO	AV	GA	PIM
227	12,639	649	13	3.08	10	90

1988-89 statistics:

GP	MINS	AVG	W	L	T	SO	GA	SA	SAPCT	PIM
30	1,621	3.78	9	14	4	1	102	791	.870	6

LAST SEASON

Posted second consecutive below-.500 season. Missed three games with a hip pointer.

THE PHYSICAL GAME

Bob is an excellent standup goaltender who plays a superior angle game strengthened by strong reflex play. He has good balance and quick feet, and regains his position fairly speedily, but is much better on his feet than off them. Froese will come out of his net to handle the puck, but will only wrap it around the boards, rather than passing it to a teammate.

However, because of the Ranger defense and their less than strict front-of-the-net coverage, Froese must sit a little deeper in his net than he'd prefer, so an incoming forward can't sneak behind him.

He generally prevents rebounds by directing shots to the corners, and Bob moves well in and out of his net, but his lateral movement is not as strong as his movement forward and backward, so he is vulnerable on criss-cross plays across the slot. He's also vulnerable to dekes (particularly to his right) on breakaways.

He sees the puck and anticipates well, and Froese will move out to the top of the screen before butterflying his pads on the ice to cover the lower part of the net.

THE MENTAL GAME

Though his concentration will wander at times, Froese is most always in the game. He prepares well for each contest and has just a small swing in his range of performance. He has the ability to sit for several consecutive games and then play well when he finally appears.

He is apt to lose his temper if he gets fouled too frequently around the crease, but opponents find it pretty tough to knock Froese off his game.

THE INTANGIBLES

Froese is very popular among his teammates, and they enjoy playing for him; he's loose and funny in the locker room. His pairing with John Vanbiesbrouck gives the Rangers one of the best goalie tandems in the NHL, and the advantage of that shows when one needs to bail the other out — as Froese did on the road last season, where Vanbiesbrouck had trouble winning.

TONY GRANATO

Yrs. of NHL service: 1
Born: Hinsdale, Illinois, USA; July 25, 1964
Position: Right wing/left wing
Height: 5-10
Weight: 185
Uniform no.: 18
Shoots: right

Career statistics:

GP	G	A	TP	+/-	PIM	PP	SH	GW	GT	S	PCT
78	36	27	63	17	140	4	4	3		2	234	15.4

LAST SEASON

Granato's first in the NHL. He finished second in scoring, game tying goals and shots on goal among rookies, first in goals and shorthanded goals, third in plus/minus. He led the club in goals, plus/minus, and shorthanded goals, and was third in SOG total. He set a club record for goals by a rookie.

THE FINESSE GAME

Clearly, Granato's best finesse skill is his skating. His speed makes him a breakaway threat (as evidenced by his SHG total), and his quickness combines with his balance to make him a very agile skater. Currently, he uses his skating in a north/south way, in that he's very much a charge up-and-down the ice player. His agility will give him good lateral movement (east/west, as it were) once he begins to think in that dimension.

His skating is made better by the fact that he can handle the puck at his top speed; that may change should he integrate more of a lateral game into his own. Right now, he's going to go right at the defenseman — and then right around him.

Granato's shot is fairly dynamic, in that he gets it away quickly, strongly and accurately. He's got the hands to score on breakaways and to finesse the puck while in traffic, but most of his goals will come from being opportunistic near the net — using his quickness to snare loose pucks.

THE PHYSICAL GAME

Granato plays a very physical game, perhaps even too physical. He certainly doesn't have great size (though Tony is in excellent shape and has good strength for his size), but that doesn't stop Granato from flinging himself at anything he can in true kamikaze fashion.

But that could account for his running out of gas by February of last season. He must learn to better pace himself.

And because his style (and his mouth, and his stick) drives the opposition to distraction, Granato also absorbs a lot of punishment from players anxious to make him pay for his misdeeds.

THE INTANGIBLES

He literally came from nowhere, and his energy boosted the Rangers through the early part of last season. But he is not a 36-goal scorer; Granato is a 25-goal scorer who can kill penalties and check the opposition to death. He scored just five goals in his last 29 games, and one of those was an empty-net tally.

As long as Granato's not expected to duplicate his rookie success, and if he can survive the beatings (he'd benefit from a full season of a healthy Chris Nilan — or some other such type), he'll continue to thrive in the NHL. But those are big ifs.

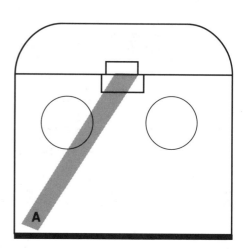

RON GRESCHNER

Yrs. of NHL service: 15
Born: Goodsoil, Sask., Canada; December 22, 1954
Position: Defenseman
Height: 6-2
Weight: 208
Uniform no.: 4
Shoots: left

Career statistics:

GP	G	A	TP	PIM
927	178	422	600	1,173

1988-89 statistics:

GP	G	A	TP	+/-	PIM	PP	SH	GW	GT	S	PCT
58	1	10	11	9	94	0	0	0	0	49	2.0

LAST SEASON

Missed 15 games with assorted injuries (flu, ribs, bruised foot, sore back, concussion) and was otherwise spotted in and out of the lineup. Assist and point totals were third lowest of career. PIM total was three-season high. Plus/minus was second-best among defensemen.

THE FINESSE GAME

Smarts and the intelligent use of the skills he has left are what help Greschner remain successful. Never possessing great speed to begin with, Greschner uses good balance and lateral movement to key his skating game.

His hand skills have eroded as well, but Ron still handles the puck confidently. He makes the most of his puckhandling ability by moving the puck quickly and efficiently, instead of trying to handle it while skating (long a positive, now much less so because of his limited skating skill).

He uses those talents — along with his play reading — to good effect defensively, and he can contribute when necessary as a power play spare.

THE PHYSICAL GAME

Greschner takes the body well along the boards or the front of the net. He's not a punishing hitter, but he has good strength and can hold the opposition out of the play. His puck skills make his physical play more valuable, and his reach helps him get to loose pucks or deflect shots.

He will fight if provoked, and uses his reach to stay away from the opposition in those fights.

THE INTANGIBLES

Though a presence in the locker room, Greschner is essentially a quiet leader. He serves the Rangers now by adding depth and veteran experience, filling in when necessary to plug holes, because he can no longer play every other shift, 80 games a season.

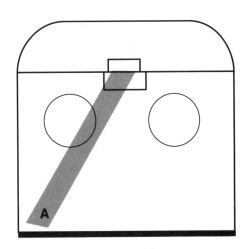

MARK HARDY

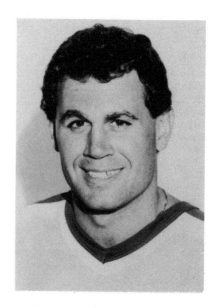

Yrs. of NHL service: 9
Born: Semaden, Switzerland; February 1, 1959
Position: Defenseman
Height: 5-11
Weight: 195
Uniform no.: 14
Shoots: left

Career statistics:

GP	G	A	TP	PIM
668	59	262	321	929

1988-89 statistics:

GP	G	A	TP	+/-	PIM	PP	SH	GW	GT	S	PCT
60	4	16	20	-9	71	0	0	1	0	70	5.7

LAST SEASON

Originally sent to Minnesota in June of 1988, he was reacquired by the Rangers in December. Games played, assist and point totals were all career lows. He missed six games with a wrist injury.

THE FINESSE GAME

Hardy is a strong skater, well balanced on his skates and equipped with a good burst of speed up ice. He is fairly agile while carrying the puck and is able to rush the puck from the defensive zone to relieve forechecking pressure.

Hardy sees the ice well and makes good use of his teammates. He makes a good point man on the power play because of his puckhandling ability, anticipation and shot. He contains the point well and knows when to pinch in and when to fall back. His shot is low and hard from the blue line and is excellent for tip-ins or deflections. Smartly, Hardy shoots often.

Except for the occasional rush he's a fairly conservative defenseman and takes few chances with the puck. He forces the play wide of the net by using his defensive angles, and he is adept at moving the puck quickly from his own end. He is poised with the puck and will generally make the right play.

THE PHYSICAL GAME

Hardy plays a physical game when he can and will dish out checks whenever possible. He has good strength along the boards, but on occasion is guilty of not completely taking the opposing winger out of the play.

He's effective in front of the net, tying up the opposition, but his game is more in hitting and gaining the puck and then starting a play.

THE INTANGIBLES

Hardy's best contribution to the Rangers is his steadiness, his night in-night out stabilizing influence in the defensive zone. His presence adds depth to the blue-line unit, but Mark may find himself fighting for a job this season because of the number of young defensemen the Rangers want to audition. He's a likely candidate to finish the season elsewhere.

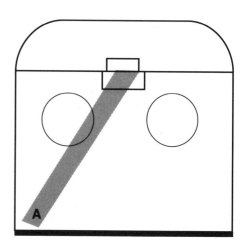

KELLY KISIO

Yrs. of NHL service: 7
Born: Peace River, Alberta, Canada;
September 18, 1959
Position: Center
Height: 5-9
Weight: 180
Uniform no.: 11
Shoots: left

Career statistics:

GP	G	A	TP	PIM
453	141	260	401	427

1988-89 statistics:

GP	G	A	TP	+/-	PIM	PP	SH	GW	GT	S	PCT
70	26	36	62	14	91	2	0	4	0	128	20.3

LAST SEASON

Goal total was career high, despite missing time with flu, fractured hand and back spasms. But assist total was career low, point total lowest in four seasons. Plus/minus tied for team's second highest.

THE FINESSE GAME

Kisio is not overly gifted in the finesse categories, but he definitely makes the most of the skills he has. He doesn't have great speed or agility, but Kelly's strength and balance make him a strong skater who is always on the puck.

His puckhandling ability is such that he can handle the puck at his top speed, and his ice vision and good anticipation skills kick in here to make him a good playmaker. He uses these skills to put teammates in scoring position.

His shot is good, perhaps the best of his finesse skills, and Kisio should take advantage of it by shooting more. He releases it quickly and accurately, important skills because Kisio is usually in traffic when he shoots.

THE PHYSICAL GAME

Kisio's size is no handicap. He pursues the puck relentlessly, fearlessly banging into bigger and stronger opponents. He plays physically at both ends of the rink, and his grinding ability paves the way for his finesse skills.

He is strong and will win many battles, but he can be overpowered by bigger defensemen or opposing centermen who can put their own strength and reach to work for themselves.

THE INTANGIBLES

Kisio succeeds on heart and determination; he's an overachiever whose ability to cash in on consistent hard work makes him a leader by example.

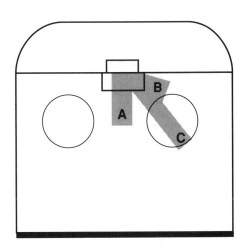

GUY LAFLEUR

Yrs. of NHL service: 15
Born: Thurso, Quebec, Canada; September 20, 1951
Position: Right wing
Height: 6-0
Weight: 185
Uniform no.: 10
Shoots: right

Career statistics:

GP	G	A	TP	PIM
1,028	536	755	1,291	393

1988-89 statistics:

GP	G	A	TP	+/-	PIM	PP	SH	GW	GT	S	PCT
67	18	27	45	1	12	6	0	2	0	122	14.8

LAST SEASON

Returned to NHL after four-year retirement.

THE FINESSE GAME

He doesn't have the speed he once had, but Lafleur is still a very good skater. He retains a portion of his agility and lateral movement, but the fact is he can no longer elude the opposition the way he once did. Still, his skating retains a creativity, a freshness, a lack of mechanical rehearsal that no one in the NHL can match.

Lafleur controls the puck well when he carries it, and he can lug it at his top speed. His hands are good, and he can fake his way through a string of defenders. Once through, his tremendous hockey sense and vision (he's lost nothing in that regard) combine with his hand skills to deliver good passes to his teammates, passes that lead his mates into the clear.

His sense also puts him in good scoring position; without looking, he knows the puck is going to the point — so he heads to the net for a pass or a rebound.

The one thing that would make his skating and puckhandling better would be if he shot more. Guy can create the openings, but too often last season he hesitated in his shooting. It's not that he couldn't get the message from his brain to his hands fast enough; Guy demonstrated frequently enough last year that he could get his shot off. Perhaps he just wanted to be a team player and find a teammate. Nevertheless, he should shoot more.

THE PHYSICAL GAME

Never known as a physical player, Lafleur demonstrated that he can take the rough going despite his age. He still operates best in open ice, more so now that he's lost a degree of the foot speed that used to let him get to the boards for the puck and get away.

He took his lumps last year and held up well (the time he missed was from a broken foot bone after being hit with a shot) and his conditioning was fairly high.

THE INTANGIBLES

Lafleur is a supra-natural (not super-natural) hockey force; he's not in the game, he *is* the game. The team loved him for his freshness and his attitude (first on the ice at practice, the hardest worker, first at the rink for games), and much of the Rangers early-season success can be attributed to the effect Lafleur had on the lesser hockey mortals.

He can still play the game, certainly without hurting the team, and as long as the new management realizes that contributions are measured in class and attitude — and not just points — Lafleur will do just fine here.

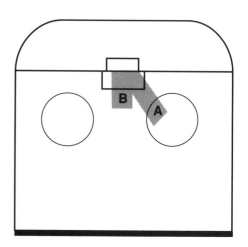

BRIAN LEETCH

Yrs. of NHL service: 2
Born: Corpus Christi, Texas, USA; March 3, 1968
Position: Defenseman
Height: 5-11
Weight: 185
Uniform no.: 2
Shoots: left

Career statistics:

GP	G	A	TP	PIM
85	25	60	85	50

1988-89 statistics:

GP	G	A	TP	+/-	PIM	PP	SH	GW	GT	S	PCT
68	23	48	71	8	50	8	3	1	1	268	8.6

LAST SEASON

Set a rookie defenseman goal scoring mark. Led all rookies in points, assists and SOG totals, was second among rookies in shorthanded goals and fourth in power play goals. Finished third on the club in scoring, second in assists and first in SOG totals. Missed 12 games with a fractured foot and a hip pointer.

THE FINESSE GAME

Already exceptionally talented in the finesse areas, Leetch has the potential to be among the top 10 in the League in skill. He is an excellent skater in every skating category. He has breakaway speed, exceptional one-step quickness, superior balance and tremendous agility and lateral movement. Leetch challenges the opposition at both blue lines — and usually succeeds — knowing his skating will allow him to recover if he makes a mistake.

His skating is made even more impressive by the fact that his hand skills and his hockey sense operate not only at the same high level as his foot skills, but at the same high speeds. Leetch handles the puck exceptionally well and easily goes end-to-end; he handles the puck as if it were nailed to his stick.

But he also passes excellently. He has excellent hands and can put the puck anywhere, and his superior hockey sense tells him when to move the puck to a teammate and when to hold it — and that stands for play at both ends of the ice. Like the NHL's best players, he sees the play earlier than anyone else on the ice.

Maybe the weakest of his skills is his shot, but that's quibbling. His shot is very good, strong, low to the net from the point, and accurate from anywhere. He takes good advantage of it by shooting often. He releases the puck quickly on his wrist shot, coming off the point well to put that loose puck on goal.

THE PHYSICAL GAME

Brian has deceptive strength for his size, and that strength is made better by his smarts. Not that he's going to be confused with Scott Stevens, or even teammate Michel Petit. Rather, Leetch has good strength that is augmented by his ability to make plays in tight and in traffic.

When Leetch goes to the boards with an opponent, chances are good that Brian already knows what play he's going to make — so he's already a step ahead of the opposition. Then, after taking the body, Leetch's finesse skills make the play; thus, he's put his team ahead of the opposition.

And his smarts show in front of the net as well. Trapped with Tim Kerr, Leetch will just wait for the puck to come to the net and simply lift Kerr's stick when necessary, instead of getting into a wrestling match.

That's not to say he shies away from contact or won't take the body; Brian realizes that to be successful, he can't allow himself to get into physical situations where he can be out-muscled. That role is reserved for his defense partner.

THE INTANGIBLES

Leetch does things that are scary. Already he is one of the few players in the League who can grab a game and bend it to his own will. He has tremendous desire to be the best he can be — and that's going to be pretty good. If he's handled right over the next few seasons, Leetch will become one of the game's superstars.

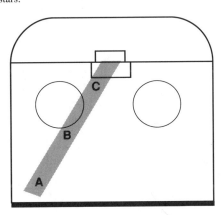

BRIAN MULLEN

Yrs. of NHL service: 7
Born: New York City, NY, USA; March 16, 1962
Position: Left wing
Height: 5-10
Weight: 180
Uniform no.: 19
Shoots: left

Career statistics:

GP	G	A	TP	PIM
524	178	236	414	234

1988-89 statistics:

GP	G	A	TP	+/-	PIM	PP	SH	GW	GT	S	PCT
78	29	35	64	7	60	8	3	5	1	217	13.4

LAST SEASON

Games played total was three-season high, goal total second highest of career, assist and point totals four-season highs. He finished fourth on the club in scoring, tied for first in game winners. He was scratched for two games.

THE FINESSE GAME

Skating and shooting are the hallmarks of Mullen's game. He is very quick (more so than he is fast — but he can turn up the juice) with an explosive first step, and his balance combines with his foot speed to make him a very agile player with excellent lateral movement. Give him the smallest opening and he's in the clear and aiming for the net.

Skill 1A among Mullen's finesse repertoire is Mullen's shot — it is excellent. He wastes few opportunities (meaning that he almost always forces the goaltender to make saves) and he releases his shot quickly. He can hit whatever openings a goalie leaves, and he loves to shoot from weird angles — creating scoring opportunities where none otherwise existed.

Mullen handles the puck well, and he's particularly gifted in that he can do so at top speed. He makes an attempt to use his teammates, but he's really more of a scorer — so he's going to shoot first and ask questions later. He is patient in his puckhandling (sometimes a little too so), but can get the puck to his teammates successfully.

He sees the ice well, and his speed and play recognition allow him to get into openings (one-step quickness is the key here). Importantly, Brian knows how to get into position to score.

THE PHYSICAL GAME

Where previously one didn't exist, Mullen developed a physical game — and that's a big reason for his All-Star status last season. By using his balance, quickness and hand skill, Mullen could bump an opponent off the puck and make a play. His commitment to that game had not previously been a consistent one, but Mullen went to the traffic areas last season and got his nose dirty.

He doesn't have great strength, so Brian has to hit-and-run to avoid prolonged wrestling matches with bigger and stronger opponents.

THE INTANGIBLES

He's the kind of guy who needs (shall we say?) reminding of what it takes for him to be successful, and Mullen did the things necessary for success last season.

Most noticeably, he picked up his intensity — and the results were obvious: 18 of his goals and 35 of his points came on the road; half of his points came against the Patrick Division. Even better, only 16 of those points came on the power play, so Mullen proved his effectiveness at even strength.

Only problem was, his production slowed in the second half — just 11 goals in the last 40 games, just seven of those at even strength. That inequality needs to be addressed, and doing so would answer any final questions about Mullen's ability.

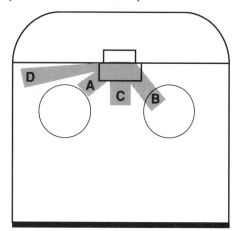

CHRIS NILAN

Yrs. of NHL service: 9
Born: Boston, Mass., USA; February 9, 1958
Position: Right wing
Height: 6-0
Weight: 205
Uniform no.: 30
Shoots: right

Career statistics:

GP	G	A	TP	PIM
566	97	96	193	2,447

1988-89 statistics:

GP	G	A	TP	+/-	PIM	PP	SH	GW	GT	S	PCT
38	7	7	14	-8	177	0	0	1	0	39	17.9

LAST SEASON

Games played was full-season career low (strained pelvic ligament, 42 games). Still finished second on the club in PIM.

THE FINESSE GAME

Though physical performance is why Chris Nilan is in the lineup, he keeps himself there because of often-obscured finesse skills. Though he's no better than average as a skater, Nilan is a good forechecker because of persistence and determination. He also has a small dose of speed that he can use effectively, mostly because it surprises the opposition.

He is disciplined in playing his wing, and he has a pretty good view of the ice and ability to anticipate. He stays with his check fairly deeply into the defensive zone, and his presence in an area often forces the opposition to surrender the puck or pursue it with less vigor.

For a fighter, Chris has good hands, and he can make plays to his teammates and even operate in a little bit of traffic. He'll score by lurking around the net and putting home defensive mistakes.

THE PHYSICAL GAME

If it moves in an opposition uniform, Nilan will hit it. He is an exceptionally hard hitter (made so because he has great strength and fairly good balance, so he remains vertical after collisions) and most difficult to dislodge from his skates.

He's one of the NHL's better fighters (certainly unafraid of any opponent) and he uses his stick liberally.

Chris has good upper body strength and can out-muscle many opponents along the boards, but he can often be guilty of being overaggressive and cancelling his good work out with an extra elbow that loses him the puck he could gain.

THE INTANGIBLES

Much has been said throughout his career about Nilan's leadership quality, and how he'll never let the opposition take advantage of a teammate. That wasn't the case last season; the Rangers got pushed around a lot.

In fairness, the team may have absorbed excess abuse because Nilan was out of the lineup for over half the season; he couldn't defend the Tony Granatos and Brian Leetchs because he wasn't playing. Yet even when he did play, Nilan wasn't the physical force he was supposed to be.

Okay, he was playing hurt. But the question is, if a 31-year old tough guy can't stay in the lineup, what good is he?

There's no questioning his heart, and he can be an excellent team leader — both through word and deed — in the room and on the ice. His play fires up his team. Now, after appearing in just 154 of a possible 240 games in the last three seasons, all Chris has to do is get back on the ice.

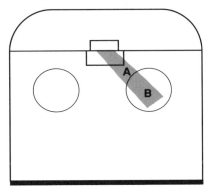

JOHN OGRODNICK

Yrs. of NHL service: 10
Born: Ottawa, Ontario, Canada; June 20, 1959
Position: Left wing
Height: 6-0
Weight: 205
Uniform no.: 25
Shoots: left

Career statistics:

GP	G	A	TP	PIM
695	305	352	657	182

1988-89 statistics:

GP	G	A	TP	+/-	PIM	PP	SH	GW	GT	S	PCT
60	13	29	42	0	14	1	0	1	0	149	8.7

LAST SEASON

Games played and all point totals were full season career lows (games missed were all benchings/demotions to American Hockey League).

THE FINESSE GAME

Ogrodnick is a deceptive skater. He doesn't have great agility or one-step quickness, and he doesn't seem to have rink-length speed either. Yet time and again he'll force the defense backward or out-race an opponent to a loose puck.

He accelerates very well and that ability puts him in the clear to use what used to be his best weapon: his slap shot. Ogrodnick has a boomer from the wing, but he no longer releases it quickly enough to fool NHL goaltending, despite getting openings from the defense, so it sounds and looks better than it is. His wrist and snap shots (also previously superior) have suffered similar fates and, on top of that, he doesn't shoot enough.

He is a scorer first and foremost and will always look to the net before he looks to a teammate. He reads the play well and certainly knows how to get into position to score, but his style is more of a straight ahead, get-a-step-on-the-defenseman-and-blast-at-the-net mode than a dipsy-doodle one.

THE PHYSICAL GAME

Ogrodnick has stepped up the pace of his physical game. He has good size and balance, so he can be successful in battles for loose pucks, and his strength is what propels his shot.

THE INTANGIBLES

Ogrodnick picked up the tempo of his game last year, after former coach Michel Bergeron allowed him back in the lineup. He worked harder than he had in years (and even made the occasional meaningful contribution), but esentially without result.

And when a 30-year-old scorer stops scoring, new surroundings can't be far behind.

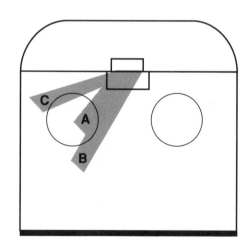

JAMES PATRICK

Yrs. of NHL service: 5
Born: Winnipeg, Man., Canada; June 14, 1963
Position: Defenseman
Height: 6-2
Weight: 195
Uniform no.: 3
Shoots: right

Career statistics:

GP	G	A	TP	PIM
378	61	190	251	316

1988-89 statistics:

GP	G	A	TP	+/-	PIM	PP	SH	GW	GT	S	PCT
68	11	36	47	3	41	6	0	2	1	147	7.5

LAST SEASON

Games played total was full-season low (flu, groin pull, shoulder sprain), point totals were all three-season lows.

THE FINESSE GAME

Patrick is an excellent skater in all areas of those skills, possessing speed, quickness and acceleration skills. He combines those assets with outstanding balance to create outstanding lateral movement and agility — traits that put him near the top of the NHL's best-skater list.

His skating is amplified by his puckhandling ability, and he rushes the puck from his zone as well as any of the NHL's great defensemen. He uses his teammates excellently when they are in front of him, but he is noticeably less successful as a playmaker when he leads a rush himself. If he gets ahead of his teammates, he's going to the net — whether he should or not.

He has a good slap shot from the point, ideal for tips and deflections because it is low and accurate to the net. James also has a superior wrist shot, one that will beat most any goaltender, and he uses it when he cuts to the slot. His hand and foot skills combine to make him good at containing the point and at forechecking.

His skating skill extends to his defensive play, and James closes the gap on the puck carrier to challenge well at the blue line. If his judgment in challenging proves faulty, Patrick's skating easily gets him back into position.

He takes the puck off the boards well, and generally starts the play from his own end efficiently. He still has a tendency to watch the puck, which means an opposing winger can camp in the slot unnoticed.

THE PHYSICAL GAME

Patrick has the tools, but almost refuses to open the tool box. He has good size but his strength is suspect, so he's prone to losing the physical battles on the walls to players who are stronger — but not necessarily bigger — than he is. Ditto, the front of the net.

His skating and balance make him an ideal player for taking the body, and his hand skills give him the ability to make plays out of those collisions, but — even when Patrick does make the attempt — opposing players just drive through his checks. Essentially, Patrick is a finesse player with some size.

THE INTANGIBLES

He has exceptional talent, but Patrick applies it in unexceptional ways (note how 29 of his 47 points came on the power play). He is content to play comfortable, which is not to say that he doesn't care. He just succeeds on what his talent gives him at the moment, with the occasions when he forces more from himself few and far between.

He has not yet reached his potential in the NHL, and may very well never do so. That makes him an underachiever.

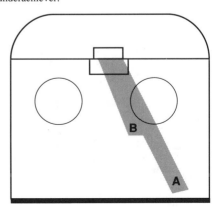

MICHEL PETIT

Yrs. of NHL service: 6
Born: St. Malo, Quebec, Canada; February 12, 1964
Position: Defenseman
Height: 6-1
Weight: 205
Uniform no.: 24
Shoots: right

Career statistics:

GP	G	A	TP	PIM
359	41	106	147	750

1988-89 statistics:

GP	G	A	TP	+/-	PIM	PP	SH	GW	GT	S	PCT
69	8	25	33	-15	154	5	0	1	0	132	6.1

LAST SEASON

Assist and point totals were second highest of his career. He missed 11 games with a fractured collarbone. He finished third in PIM total, and his plus/minus was the club's second-worst.

THE FINESSE GAME

Skating is the best of Petit's finesse assets. He's an excellent skater, equipped with good balance and speed, but what makes him exceptional in this department is his agility. He has good lateral movement and change-of-direction skills for a man with his size and bulk, which could make him an above-average player in all three zones.

But doesn't, because Petit's hockey sense and playmaking abilities are not at the level of his skating. While he's smart enough to keep the play ahead of him, on the whole his play-reading and vision abilities are of the first-play variety. He doesn't get a great look at the ice before making a breakout pass, so Michel will make the first play he sees.

His skating should allow him to step up on the opposition, and Petit will do so to make hits part of the time, but he doesn't make a play after that check. And more likely, Petit will just react to the opposing winger and fall back. In all, his total play without the puck, though already improved, can be better.

He can be a dangerous offensive force, for Petit will rush if given the chance. He handles the puck and shoots it well, but he doesn't shoot anywhere near enough for a guy that gets so many opportunities.

THE PHYSICAL GAME

The physical game is the best plus Petit brings to the Rangers. He's big and has very good strength, which he is not afraid to use against anyone. He can hurt people when he hits them, and Petit hits often — sometimes *too* often.

On penalty killing, for example, where the Rangers need him to clear the front of the net, Petit is often concerned with ramming a puck-carrying opponent into the boards — taking himself out of the play and turning a 5-on-4 into a 4-on-3.

He'll drop the gloves when necessary, and he has also become very liberal in his use of his stick on the opposition. Michel is also talented enough to make a play after taking an opponent off the puck.

THE INTANGIBLES

As long as he stays within his limits, Petit can be a valuable player. But he must concentrate on un-extravagant things: take the body, move the puck, follow the play. The more chances he takes, the more chance he has of making a mistake.

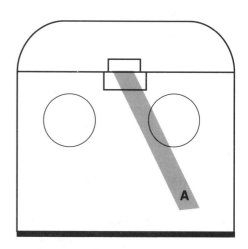

RUDY POESCHEK

Yrs. of NHL service: 1
Born: Kamloops, B.C., Canada; September 29, 1966
Position: Forward/defense
Height: 6-1
Weight: 210
Uniform no.: 29
Shoots: right

Career statistics:

GP	G	A	TP	PIM
53	0	2	2	201

1988-89 statistics:

GP	G	A	TP	+/-	PIM	PP	SH	GW	GT	S	PCT
52	0	2	2	-8	199	0	0	0	0	17	0.0

LAST SEASON

First full NHL season. He led the club in PIM total. He missed two games with a bruised hand, one game with the flu.

THE FINESSE GAME

Rudy doesn't really have one. He showed in his brief stints at defense (he spent most of the year at forward) that he can move the puck from his zone, or that he could handle it while skating, but this is more because he got the time and space he needed to make his plays.

Why? Because people were afraid to go near him. Otherwise, he lacks any real skating ability (increased foot speed would greatly develop his game), and that prohibits any real offensive game. Even his balance — so important to a physical game — is suspect, leaving him in awkward positions (or on the ice) after checks. That means he's unable to continue the play after hits.

THE PHYSICAL GAME

This is where Rudy is going to succeed in the NHL, if he succeeds at all. He'll hit anyone any time, as long as he can catch them, and Poeschek does have good strength to bring to his hitting.

He is also a willing and determined fighter and again, he'll go with anyone.

THE INTANGIBLES

If he's going to contribute, Poeschek has to be in the lineup — and getting ice — every game. For one thing, that will help stop the referees from keying on him when he gets on the ice. For another, it will help

him improve as a player. Finally, his continued presence may help take some of the physical heat off his smaller teammates.

He can give the club a lift with his play — as demonstrated in a January 1989 home game against the Penguins. The Rangers were losing, but Poeschek fired the crowd — and the team — with his seek-and-destroy mission against the Pens' Randy Hillier. Rudy was just looking for anybody to fight, and the fight changed the course of the game — of course, so did Brian Leetch's shorthanded goal while New York killed Poeschek's penalty.

But you get the point. Otherwise, Poeschek isn't even a marginal NHL player. If he wants to stick around, that has to change.

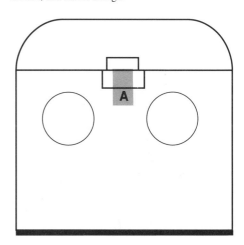

LINDY RUFF

Yrs. of NHL service: 10
Born: Warburg, Alta., Canada; February 17, 1960
Position: Left wing/defense
Height: 6-2
Weight: 200
Uniform no.: 44
Shoots: left

Career statistics:

GP	G	A	TP	PIM
621	102	188	290	1,157

1988-89 statistics:

GP	G	A	TP	+/-	PIM	PP	SH	GW	GT	S	PCT
76	6	16	22	-23	1170	0	0	0	0	88	6.8

LAST SEASON

Acquired from Buffalo in March 1989 in exchange for a draft choice. Games played total was third highest of career, point total third lowest. His plus/minus was the club's worst.

THE FINESSE GAME

As a finesse player, Ruff isn't. He's never been better than average as a skater, and 10 tough seasons and their attendant injuries have slowed Ruff down. He just cruises up and down the ice.

Ruff isn't a good puckhandler but that's all right, because he doesn't know what to do with the puck anyway. He has little vision of the ice or his teammates, and less anticipation for possible plays. If he wins the puck during a foray into the corner, the best Ruff will do with it is the blind pass to the slot.

His shot is consistent with his other finesse skills, and he's unlikely to score from any place other than the edge of the goal crease by shovelling home rebounds and other garbage.

Lindy is a conscientious back checker, very concerned with his defensive play and disciplined enough to stay on his wing and not create any openings by leaving the zone too soon. He is aided in his defensive play by his experience as a defenseman and understands what angles are all about so as to keep his man from the puck.

But when forced to play defense, his lack of skating skill betrays him.

THE PHYSICAL GAME

Ruff is.

He's big and strong and uses that strength to bang around in the corners and jar the puck loose from opposing defensemen. He doesn't have the skills to make a play out of the corner, so his physical game is one-dimensional in that regard.

Ruff also uses his strength to wreak havoc in front of the opposition goal, daring a defenseman to move him from the crease. He is aggressive and will take pokes at people when he has to stand up for the team. Lindy also applies himself physically in the defensive zone, where he will rub out an opposing winger along the boards.

His injury record is a direct result of his play, rather than an indication of any fragility on his part. Ruff counters the injury problem by staying in great condition.

THE INTANGIBLES

Ruff is a great team player, and he knows when it's necessary to assume leadership in the locker room or on the ice so as to produce the best effect for the club. Ruff also helps himself stay around through his versatility, his ability to play either forward or defense as required. Hard work is all he knows.

Given the current uncertainty in the Ranger organization, however, there's a good chance that Ruff will find himself riding the pine or shipped to another club.

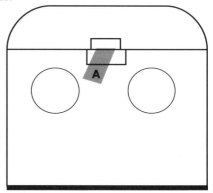

TOMAS SANDSTROM

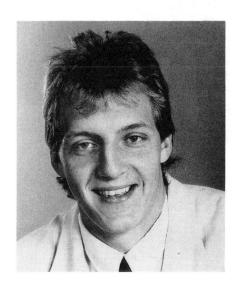

Yrs. of NHL service: 5
Born: Jakobstad, Finland; September 4, 1964
Position: Right wing
Height: 6-2
Weight: 207
Uniform no.: 28
Shoots: left

Career statistics:

GP	G	A	TP	PIM
359	154	188	342	463

1988-89 statistics:

GP	G	A	TP	+/-	PIM	PP	SH	GW	GT	S	PCT
79	32	56	88	5	148	11	2	4	0	240	13.3

LAST SEASON

Led team in assists and points with career in those categories. Goal total was second highest of career, games played total career high (missed one game with flu). Finished second in power play goals and SOG total, fourth in PIM total.

THE FINESSE GAME

Where previously skating and shooting were the hallmarks of Sandstrom's game, he's now added play-making to the list. He's an excellent skater with speed and agility, and has learned to bull defensemen off the blue line with his skating and to then use the extra space created to make a pass and to lead a teammate. Previously, if he got a step he was making the play himself.

His very good hands combine with his balance to make him an ideal traffic player. He maintains body position despite being checked, and he makes plays from all of those contortions.

His great hockey sense shows him the openings, his speed puts him into the holes and his hands power his exceptional shot. His slap shot is among the League's best, and it can beat *any* goalie. He likes the long side of the net, low on the ice, and he gets his shot away in one touch.

Though he still doesn't shoot anywhere near enough, Sandstrom last season mitigated that flaw by getting the puck to his teammates. His overhandling of the puck was held to a minimum, and he allowed his passing skills (he passes and takes a pass extremely well, and he can execute with all of his skills at top speed) to work.

Never a great defensive player, Sandstrom has at least improved to average. He still plays a far more interested game in the neutral and offensive zones, but Sandstrom can be a strong defensive player; his penalty-killing stints showcase his sense and skating to illustrate the point.

THE PHYSICAL GAME

Sandstrom is a very aggressive player, in all manners of the game. He takes the body and checks very well, and he is also among the League's chippiest players with his stick and elbows. The word is out on him now (as evidenced by his career high PIM total), but despite that he still draws penalties by getting under the skin of the opposition; he thrives on their retaliation.

He is not a fighter, but Sandstrom will bump with anyone.

THE INTANGIBLES

It's worth noting that his career-best season came with him in the option year of his contract; let's see how he does now that he's signed a new deal.

But more important is the fact that Tomas played with more intensity — and therefore more consistently — than ever before. When he does that, he's one of the NHL's best players — and he can be better still.

As they head into a huge question-mark season, the Rangers need him to at least maintain — if not improve — on that intensity.

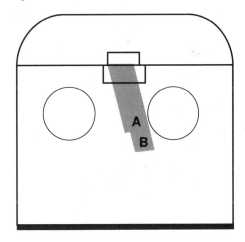

DAVID SHAW

Yrs. of NHL service: 5
Born: St. Thomas, Ontario, Canada; May 25, 1964
Position: Defenseman
Height: 6-2
Weight: 204
Uniform no.: 21
Shoots: right

Career statistics:

GP	G	A	TP	PIM
298	20	74	94	346

1988-89 statistics:

GP	G	A	TP	+/-	PIM	PP	SH	GW	GT	S	PCT
63	6	11	17	14	88	3	1	1	0	85	7.1

LAST SEASON

Games played, assist and point totals were full-season career lows (five games injury: charley horse and shoulder strain; 12-game NHL suspension for slashing Mario Lemieux). His plus/minus was tied for the team's second best, best among defensemen.

THE FINESSE GAME

Smarts are the key to Shaw's game. He plays a conservative defensive game, using his good vision, anticipation and sense to determine his course of action. Dave reads the rush toward him well, and he almost always correctly steers it wide of the net or steps up to challenge the puck carrier.

He doesn't have glamorous skating ability (in terms of speed or agility), but Shaw is a strong skater with good balance and he makes his skating better by using his brains.

The same could be said of Shaw's hand skills. He moves the puck quickly and correctly from his own zone and, though he wouldn't be considered an offensive weapon, Dave also contributes well from the opposing blue line. He moves the puck to his teammates well because of his vision and good hands, and he augments his passing with a howitzer shot from blue line; the shot is his best physical finesse skill.

Shaw would be even more effective from the blue line if he could lose the bad habit of putting his head down once he decides to shoot. Many times he tucks his head in for a slapper, only to drive the puck into a shot-blocking forward who made the challenging move after Shaw looked down. The results are far too many odd-man advantages for breaking opponents, an ironic twist for a conservative defender.

THE PHYSICAL GAME

In his quiet and dependable way, Shaw uses his size and strength very well. Dave isn't a thundering hitter or great fighter — he just forces the opposition from the crease, or ties up the incoming forward along the boards 99 percent of the time. And, he does it smartly — without drawing penalties that harm the team.

He takes the body well and can hit hard, but Shaw is not a punishing hitter. He also puts his reach to work excellently in poking the puck or deflecting shots on goal.

THE INTANGIBLES

Shaw is a vastly under-rated defensive player, and the attention he gained last season for slashing Lemieux was in ironic counterpoint to his usually controlled and effective game. He's a very hard worker (willing to work on improving and coachable), and has potential yet to reach despite the relatively high level of success he's already demonstrated.

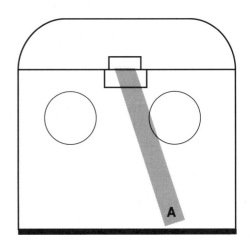

JOHN VANBIESBROUCK

Yrs. of NHL service: 5
Born: Detroit, Mich., USA; September 4, 1963
Position: Goaltender
Height: 5-9
Weight: 179
Uniform no.: 34
Catches: left

Career statistics:

GP	MINS	G	SO	AVG	A	PIM
269	15,106	816	6	3.24	16	129

1988-89 statistics:

GP	MINS	AVG	W	L	T	SO	GA	SA	SAPCT	PIM
56	3,207	3.69	28	21	4	0	197	1,666	.881	30

LAST SEASON

He finished fourth in the League in wins and games played. Win total was second highest of career, but so was goals-against-average. He missed one game with the flu.

THE PHYSICAL GAME

The strength of John's game comes from his ability to stand up and square himself to the puck. He can be an excellent angle goaltender, but he struggles when he lets the puck play him. Unfortunately for Vanbiesbrouck and the Rangers — though it wasn't solely his fault — he did too much struggling last season.

He is an excellent skater with exceptional balance, which usually puts him in good position for the second save. But Vanbiesbrouck's style has changed some, in that he now plants himself so solidly on his inside edges (in order to butterfly his pads and then get up from that maneuver) that he cannot take advantage of his feet. He can move well from the net to cut the angle, but again, not with his weight on his inside edges. And too, that weight distribution harms his lateral movement — a weakness previously improved that has resurfaced.

He has very good hand skills, in that his glove is one of the NHL's best — certainly top five and maybe top three — and he also handles his stick well. There are, however, exceptions. He still needs to improve his judgment passing the puck in his defensive zone, and he has a tendency to accumulate penalties by tossing the puck over the glass (he finished fifth among goalies in PIM total).

He has good foot speed, better to his left side than his right.

THE MENTAL GAME

Regardless of outcome, Vanbiesbrouck is usually ready to play every game. He certainly has big save capability, as he has shown throughout his career, and is one of the few goalies in the League who can actually win games by himself — but he cannot turn it on and off. Vanbiesbrouck must play a stretch of games to bring his concentration and confidence to its best level.

He is strong when a game is within a goal either way, but can become disinterested if he falls behind by a couple.

THE INTANGIBLES

The best insight we can give into Vanbiesbrouck's character is the fact that he was ready for opening night last season, despite a wrist injury (and surgery) that was supposed to shelve him until December at the earliest. He's a proud and very driven athlete, confident on the verge of being cocky, but he can back up his words with action when given the chance.

His inconsistency last season was a big reason for the Rangers' ultimately disappointing season, but former coach Michel Bergeron never got John the coaching he needed to help him regain his consistency and reclaim his game. That will be a priority for the new Ranger coach.

Unless Vanbiesbrouck spends the season elsewhere, a possibility because he is a valued commodity around the League. In which case it is a priority for his new team.

CAREY WILSON

Yrs. of NHL service: 5
Born: Winnipeg, Man., Canada; May 19, 1962
Position: Center
Height: 6-2
Weight: 205
Uniform no.: 17
Shoots: right

Career statistics:

GP	G	A	TP	PIM
390	134	204	338	194

1988-89 statistics:

GP	G	A	TP	+/-	PIM	PP	SH	GW	GT	S	PCT
75	32	45	77	-11	59	14	0	5	0	164	19.5

LAST SEASON

Acquired from Hartford in exchange for Brian Lawton, Don Maloney and Norm Maciver in December, 1988. Goal and point totals were career highs. He missed three games with a wrist injury after joining New York. He finished second on the club in scoring, first in power play goals, tied for first in game winners.

THE FINESSE GAME

Wilson is loaded with upper level finesse skills. To begin with, he is an excellent skater with speed, quickness and agility. He can move laterally or change directions at will.

He has exceptional hands and hockey sense and he can be an excellent playmaker because of those skills. He has the ability to give the soft pass and knows where to send that pass, leading his teammates to the opening if he doesn't take advantage of them himself. Wilson also likes to carry the puck (especially across the opposing blue line) and beat people 1-on-1 (he is an excellent 1-on-1 player), so he won't always make those passes.

Wilson has good sense around the net and is dangerous if left unguarded. He has an accurate and quick wrist shot that is effective both in close and from a distance.

He combines all his skills to be an excellent defensive player as well, and he's also a very smart one — as his PIM total indicates. He does the defensive job without taking penalties — he was a plus player for New York.

THE PHYSICAL GAME

Carey is not a physical hockey player in terms of bashing people into the boards, but he has outstanding physical skills. He has terrific eye/hand coordination (which makes him an excellent faceoff man) and his balance makes him a superior player in traffic — both along the boards and when checked in front of the net.

He'll maintain his puck control through most all physical situations.

That balance also serves Wilson when he initiates the checking game. He is very strong and will outmuscle many opponents along the boards, and stay vertical and ready to make plays after those collisions.

He is a remarkably conditioned athlete and works very hard at staying in shape year round.

THE INTANGIBLES

The questions around Wilson have always centered on his concentration and intensity, his desire to always play at his best level. He addressed that question after coming to New York — the longest he went without a point was two games.

If he gets someone to clear the way for him, a tough guy to open up space and keep Wilson unmolested, he can put up a 100-point season.

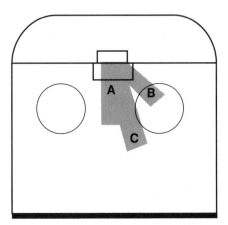

PHILADELPHIA
FLYERS

LINE COMBINATIONS
BRIAN PROPP-RON SUTTER-RICK TOCCHET
SCOTT MELLANBY-DAVE POULIN-TIM KERR
DERRICK SMITH-PELLE EKLUND
DOUG SULLIMAN

DEFENSE PAIRINGS
MARK HOWE-GORD MURPHY
TERRY CARKNER-JEFF CHYCHRUN
KJELL SAMUELSSON

GOALTENDERS
RON HEXTALL
KEN WREGGET

OTHER PLAYERS
KEITH ACTON — Center
MIKE BULLARD — Center
MURRAY CRAVEN — Left wing
ILKKA SINISALO — Right wing
JAY WELLS — Defenseman

POWER PLAY

FIRST UNIT:
BRIAN PROPP-PELLE EKLUND-TIM KERR
MARK HOWE-GORD MURPHY

SECOND UNIT:
SCOTT MELLANBY-MIKE BULLARD
RICK TOCCHET-TERRY CARKNER

KERR is the main man on the first, with everything aimed at getting him the puck. EKLUND works the left wing boards and PROPP rotates around the net to the right side. If the Flyers can't get the puck to KERR, point shots are the second option, with PROPP moving to the front of the net for rebounds.

On the second unit, MELLANBY and TOCCHET rotate in and out of the slot to jam the net as the puck moves to their opposite sides. BULLARD does the distribution, with CARKNER shooting.

Last season Philadelphia's power play was EXCELLENT, collecting 98 goals in 367 opportunities (26.7 percent, first overall).

PENALTY KILLING

FIRST UNIT:
BRIAN PROPP-DAVE POULIN
MARK HOWE-KJELL SAMUELSSON

The Flyer penalty killers are ultra-aggressive, forcing the puck all over the ice. They want to force the opposition to dump it in, so goaltender RON HEXTALL can snare it and fire it out. The Flyers will also play the puck back to him soccer-style to kill time.

Other players seeing penalty killing time include EKLUND, TOCCHET, KEITH ACTON and CARKNER.

Last season PHILADELPHIA's penalty killing was EXCELLENT, allowing 80 goals in 432 shorthanded situations (81.5 percent, fifth overall).

CRUCIAL FACEOFFS
DAVE POULIN and RON SUTTER.

KEITH ACTON

Yrs. of NHL service: 10
Born: Newmarket, Ontario, Canada; April 15, 1958
Position: Center
Height: 5-10
Weight: 167
Uniform no.: 25
Shoots: left

Career statistics:

GP	G	A	TP	PIM
668	182	289	471	741

1988-89 statistics:

GP	G	A	TP	+/-	PIM	PP	SH	GW	GT	S	PCT
71	14	25	39	10	111	0	2	1	0	112	12.5

LAST SEASON

Acton was acquired from Edmonton at the All-Star break in exchange for Dave Brown. Games played total tied second lowest of his career, but PIM total was career high. Plus/minus was third best among forwards.

THE FINESSE GAME

Acton skates well, applying some good foot speed and agility, strength and acceleration in his role as a checking forward. He combines those assets effectively with good anticipation and hockey sense. He likes to use his speed to jump into openings and he loves to dive to draw a call from the referee.

Those finesse skills make him persistent in his pursuit of the puck and also make him effective on the specialty team units, particularly the penalty killing squad where he is a definite threat for a shorthanded goal.

Acton has a good feel for the play and its implications and he sees the ice well, allowing him to close the openings the opposition was planning to exploit. He is conscientious defensively, working hard at both ends of the ice.

Keith has good hands and he controls the puck well and is able to use his teammates well because of his hand skills and anticipation. He is fairly creative away from the puck when he is on offense, but lacks the dynamic shot that would make him an offensive force. He must be within medium range of the net to score.

THE PHYSICAL GAME

Acton plays a physical game and is aggressive, certainly more so than his size would indicate. He will hit and bump and take the rough going up and down the ice. He is also very liberal in the use of his stick, and that use (constantly jabbing the opposition in the back of the knee, for example) works for him as a checker by distracting the opposition.

He will not, however, extend his physical play toward fighting, which is the common result of his own belligerence. Once he's instigated a commotion, Acton retires to the outer edges of the fray.

THE INTANGIBLES

Acton is a hard worker and an honest hockey player. He is feisty and also yaps incessantly to drive the other team to distraction. He is well-liked by his teammates and is a leader through his work ethic.

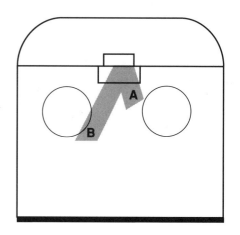

MIKE BULLARD

Yrs. of NHL service: 9
Born: Ottawa, Ontario, Canada; March 10, 1961
Position: Center
Height: 5-10
Weight: 183
Uniform no.: 10
Shoots: left

Career statistics:

GP	G	A	TP	PIM
592	288	294	582	596

1988-89 statistics:

GP	G	A	TP	+/-	PIM	PP	SH	GW	GT	S	PCT
74	27	38	65	2	106	10	0	3	0	189	14.3

LAST SEASON

Traded to St. Louis from Calgary in the summer of 1988, Bullard was sent to Philadelphia in exchange for Peter Zezel near the season's quarter-pole. Goal total was second lowest of career.

THE FINESSE GAME

Speed and acceleration mark Bullard's game, and they power him as a finesse player. He'll beat many opponents with his speed to the outside, and his balance helps him make his cuts around those defenders. Bullard is a very agile player, possessing great foot speed and lateral movement.

Mike's hockey sense and scorer's anticipation complement his skating skill, showing him the openings his speed takes him to. These skills make him a natural for specialty teams play.

Bullard is also a good passer, though his proficiency here is not always converted by his less skilled Flyer teammates. Mike applies his sense and sensitive hands to his passing, leading teammates with accuracy and good timing. His puckhandling is good, certainly good enough to keep up with his skating, but his goal scoring ability — his ability to get into scoring position — is excellent.

Mike shoots off the pass very well, especially on his off wing. Both his slap shot and wrist shot are effective weapons.

Defensively, Bullard has learned to play positional hockey and will stay with his check into the Flyer zone.

THE PHYSICAL GAME

He is not a physical guy himself, but Bullard will take his punishment to make his plays. He has good strength and uses it to shrug off defenders along the boards, and he also uses his body very well to shield the puck. Mike is also taking the body more — at both ends — than he has previously, but he is not a crushing hitter.

THE INTANGIBLES

We told you last year that falloff in his production was inevitable, but in Bullard's favor much of the responsibility for that must be laid at the trading doorstep. Two moves in a year would affect most any player's production, and Bullard was no exception. Still, he scored just 13 goals in his last 36 games. Those are bad numbers for a goal scorer, but he is probably the most talented finesse player on a team of bangers.

Bullard also suffers in that he has less talented teammates in Philly than he did in Calgary; there are no Mullens and Nieuwendyks to flank him with the Flyers, and that will continue to mark his production.

Positively, his work ethic remains good (something he learned in Calgary) and that should continue.

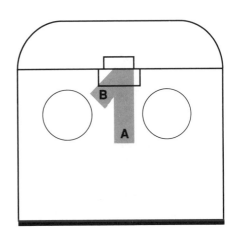

TERRY CARKNER

Yrs. of NHL service: 3
Born: Smith Falls, Ontario, Canada; March 7, 1966
Position: Defenseman
Height: 6-3
Weight: 210
Uniform no.: 29
Shoots: left

Career statistics:

GP	G	A	TP	PIM
193	16	69	85	326

1988-89 statistics:

GP	G	A	TP	+/-	PIM	PP	SH	GW	GT	S	PCT
78	11	32	43	-6	149	2	1	1	0	84	13.1

LAST SEASON

Acquired by Flyers in off-season deal with Quebec. Games played total was career high (missed one game with ankle injury), as were all point totals. He led the Flyers defensemen in scoring, but his plus/minus was worst among Philly defenders.

THE FINESSE GAME

Carkner has improved his skating since his entrance into the NHL, though he could still use improvement in his foot speed (thus giving him better turning ability, agility and lateral movement, as well as quickness, so as to keep pace with the NHL's fleeter forwards; this is where his plus/minus comes from). He has improved his transition game in both directions, exhibiting better decision making regarding pinching in and falling back.

Though he plays a generally conservative defensive game, Terry has fairly good offensive skills. He reads the offensive blue line fairly well (he ran the power play as a junior in Peterborough) and he has the skill to move the puck to the open man.

He demonstrates that same skill to a large degree in the defensive zone, where he generally moves the puck efficiently. He rarely rushes the puck from danger, but his puckhandling continues to improve at the major league level.

He'll score some goals from the point but, strangely, his good strength doesn't translate into a threatening NHL shot. He's more likely to make a pass for an assist.

THE PHYSICAL GAME

Carkner is a very physical player, certainly getting the most from his size and strength. He will take the puck away from most players along the boards, just as he will thwart most players in front of the net. When Terry hits you, you know it.

His physical play has been made more effective by his growing ability to make a play following a hit. Carkner is a very tough player who willingly fights the League's toughest players. And holds his own, we might add.

THE INTANGIBLES

Tremendous heart and desire, seconded by a superb work ethic, are the foundations for Carkner's NHL success. He is an excellent team player who is willing to sacrifice himself to win. As his confidence grows, Carkner's play will improve correspondingly. And remember, he's still only 23 years old.

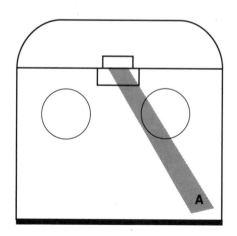

JEFF CHYCHRUN

Yrs. of NHL service: 1
Born: Nepean, Ontario, Canada; May 3, 1966
Position: Defenseman
Height: 6-4
Weight: 200
Uniform no.: 6
Shoots: right

Career statistics:

GP	G	A	TP	PIM
84	1	4	5	253

1988-89 statistics:

GP	G	A	TP	+/-	PIM	PP	SH	GW	GT	S	PCT
80	1	4	5	11	245	0	0	1	0	53	1.9

LAST SEASON

Chychrun's first full NHL season (he was the only Flyer to play all 80 games). He was second among defensemen in plus/minus and he led the club in PIM.

THE FINESSE GAME

Chychrun is not an overly talented finesse player, but don't let his penalty minutes fool you. He's no better than average at the NHL as a skater (and maybe even below average), but Jeff plays smartly and doesn't leave his position foolishly (thus avoiding getting caught up-ice).

He'll have trouble catching many of the League's forwards, but Chychrun minimizes the chasing he has to do by forcing the play wide when possible, and then taking the opposition to the boards.

He doesn't have great hands and really can't make plays from the boards, nor will he carry the puck from the defensive zone, but Jeff can make the one pass to get the puck from the Flyers end — just don't ask him to make a Mark Howe-type read of the ice.

Chychrun's pretty much a one-play player now but, again, he plays with discipline and makes that one play stand up.

As an offensive threat, he isn't. He rarely shoots the puck (and, in fact, rarely contributes at all offensively — he's the safety valve at falling back from the point) and doesn't have a great shot anyway. Any goals he gets will come on squibs from the point.

THE PHYSICAL GAME

Chychrun is a very physical player, as his PIM total indicates. He's a punishing player in front of the net, and is a willing fighter against all challengers.

He'll fistically defend his goalie or his smaller teammates without a thought, and he more than holds his own there, but Chychrun isn't one of the NHL's heavyweights.

THE INTANGIBLES

Observers looking just at Jeff's PIM numbers will see a tough guy — and that's all. And Chychrun is a tough guy, but he can also play competent NHL defense. He needs to make improvements in his skating to raise himself from fifth or sixth defenseman status (paired — obviously — with the more gifted finesse defenseman on the club), but Chychrun's already shown he can contribute at the NHL level.

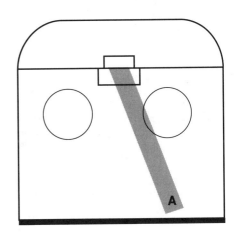

MURRAY CRAVEN

Yrs. of NHL service: 6
Born: Medicine Hat, Alta., Canada; July 20, 1964
Position: Left wing/center
Height: 6-2
Weight: 175
Uniform no.: 32
Shoots: left

Career statistics:

GP	G	A	TP	PIM
404	109	183	292	224

1988-89 statistics:

GP	G	A	TP	+/-	PIM	PP	SH	GW	GT	S	PCT
51	9	28	37	4	52	0	0	2	0	89	10.1

LAST SEASON

Games played total was five season low (eye, knee and wrist injuries).

THE FINESSE GAME

Just as he was beginning to learn how to most effectively use his finesse skills (coming off a 30-goal 1987-88 season) Craven was halted in that progress by an injury-filled campaign last season.

Craven's an above-average skater with good speed and acceleration, and he complements that speed with good lateral movement and agility — perhaps more than could be expected in a bigger man.

He handles the puck well at top speed and makes the most of his reach, but his tendency to be a one-on-one player slows him in his development as a playmaker. He finds the openings in the offensive zone, and considers shooting before passing. He fires his quick wrist shot from any opening, and his hands are good enough to put him above .500 on breakaways.

For all his offensive tendencies, Craven is a dependable defensive player, conscientious in the neutral and defensive zones.

THE PHYSICAL GAME

Murray is not an overly strong player, but one of the things he was learning to do was to use his body smartly. he has good size (if not great strength), and he's begun to use that size to shield the puck from the opposition — both when carrying it and when protecting it along the boards defensively.

Craven is not a player to initiate a lot of contact, and he certainly won't be found in the traffic areas in the corners or the front of the net. He is essentially an open-ice player.

THE INTANGIBLES

We told you last year that Craven would have difficulty retaining a spot at center-ice for the Flyers, and he was shifted to left wing last season. His problem there is that he is not a corner-and-boards player and, of course, the Flyers have always stressed that style of play.

What also doesn't help his case is the fact that he doesn't score like Brian Propp, and he doesn't hit like Derrick Smith or Scott Mellanby — the latter, it should be noted, converted from right wing to left wing.

That adds up to a precipitous hold on a left wing spot, and perhaps a precipitous hold on a job with the Flyers.

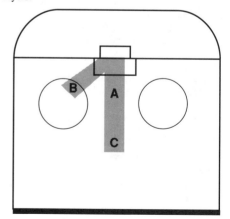

PER-ERIK EKLUND

Yrs. of NHL service: 4
Born: Stockholm, Sweden; March 22, 1963
Position: Center
Height: 5-10
Weight: 170
Uniform no.: 9
Shoots: left

Career statistics:

GP	G	A	TP	PIM
292	57	175	232	49

1988-89 statistics:

GP	G	A	TP	+/-	PIM	PP	SH	GW	GT	S	PCT
79	18	51	69	5	23	8	1	2	0	121	14.9

LAST SEASON

Games played, goal and point totals were career highs. Assist total tied career high. Finished fourth in scoring and first in assists.

THE FINESSE GAME

Hand and stick skills are the hallmarks of Eklund's game, closely followed by vision and anticipation.

He passes the puck excellently, regardless of time or obstruction, and Eklund also carries the puck well when skating. Eklund complements those hand skills with excellent ice vision (particularly peripherally) and superb anticipation. He has great hockey sense and understanding of the offensive play, and uses both that sense and those hand/stick skills to great effect on the Flyers power play.

Just underneath those abilities is Eklund's skating skill. His is not a dynamic, exciting style of skating; rather, he's a smooth and fluid skater with excellent agility and lateral movement.

He still subjugates his shooting to his passing, and we still say Eklund should shoot more, if only to loosen up the opposing defense.

THE PHYSICAL GAME

Eklund is not a physical player by any means, which is just as well because his size mitigates against him. He works best in open ice, not in the traffic areas.

THE INTANGIBLES

A bit of a renewal year for Eklund, who clearly enjoys working with Tim Kerr on the power play. He saw some more ice time under Paul Holmgren than he did under Mike Keenans, but was still generally regulated to fourth-line status because of the need to put two big wings with him.

That situation is unlikely to change, because of the Flyers' style of play. That style will see Ron Sutter and Dave Poulin as the club's top two pivots, and former 100-point scorer Mike Bullard as the top finesse center.

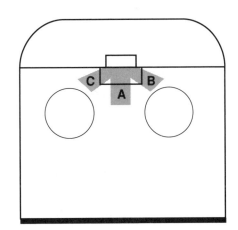

RON HEXTALL

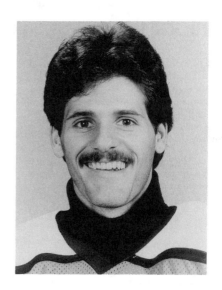

Yrs. of NHL service: 3
Born: Brandon, Manitoba, Canada; May 3, 1964
Position: Goaltender
Height: 6-3
Weight: 190
Uniform no.: 27
Catchs: left

Career statistics:

GP	MINS	G	SO	AVG	A	PIM
192	11,115	600	1	3.24	20	321

1988-89 statistics:

GP	MINS	AVG	W	L	T	SO	GA	SA	SAPCT	PIM
64	3,756	3.23	30	28	6	0	202	1,860	.891	113

LAST SEASON

Games and minutes played totals were second highest of career. He won 30 games for the third straight season. He led the League in games and minutes played, finishing third in wins. He led all goalies in scoring and PIM.

THE PHYSICAL GAME

Hextall is a standup goaltender who mixes that challenging style with excellent reflexes. He comes out of the net well to cut the shooter's angles, thus using his size to mask much of the cage.

He is an outstanding skater, maybe the best among the NHL's goalies, and he displays outstanding foot speed as he moves across the net and around his crease. His great balance allows him to easily regain his stance after going to the ice, and his foot speed renders useless the conventional wisdom of shooting to a big man's feet.

His skating readily complements his stickhandling game, clearly the best among NHL goalies. He'll get to most every loose puck and make a play, and Hextall remains the only goalie in the League who has to be forechecked. Though he prefers his forehand, Hextall is equally adept at using either side for stickhandling. He is an active part of the Flyers' penalty killing effort.

His hand speed is good, but nowhere near his foot speed. He's good to his glove side, and his main window of weakness is high to the stickside.

THE MENTAL GAME

Hextall has tremendous mental toughness and big save capacity. He focusses and concentrates extremely well, complementing his intensity with great vision and anticipation; rare are the goals that beat him that Hextall hasn't gotten a piece of.

He's also improved his control of his temper and high-strung nature (bad news for the NHL), so that he's less likely to be distracted into mistakes during games. He comes back tougher after bad outings and bad goals.

THE INTANGIBLES

No other current NHL goaltender has posted three 30-win seasons in his first three NHL seasons, and only one other goalie (Mike Vernon) has accomplished that feat at all. That gives you some indication of Hextall's value.

He is a superb player and competitor, and he is the cornerstone of any successes the Flyers accumulate.

302

MARK HOWE

Yrs. of NHL service: 10
Born: Detroit, Mich., USA; May 28, 1955
Position: Defenseman
Height: 5-11
Weight: 180
Uniform no.: 2
Shoots: left

Career statistics:

GP	G	A	TP	PIM
706	175	440	615	367

1988-89 statistics:

GP	G	A	TP	+/-	PIM	PP	SH	GW	GT	S	PCT
52	9	29	38	7	45	5	1	1	0	95	9.5

LAST SEASON

Courtesy of groin and knee injuries, games played total was lowest of NHL career, with assist and point totals correspondingly low (goal total was second lowest). He was second in plus/minus among Flyer defensemen.

THE FINESSE GAME

Though gradually succumbing to age, Howe remains an excellent skater, certainly still among the best of the NHL's defensemen. He combines agility with excellent hand skills to become very dangerous with the puck, and — as such — remains the key man for developing Philly's offense.

Mark rushes the puck excellently, and he'll stay as a fourth attacker even after he's forced to dish it off because his speed gets him back into the defensive play.

He combines his hand skills with excellent vision and anticipation to become an excellent passer, especially (and this is his greatest value) in getting the puck from the Flyers' defensive zone. He's Philadelphia's most consistent player in that area.

Offensively, he has a low and accurate shot from the left point (perfect for deflections), and he'll sneak into the slot if he can. Mark also likes to tail away to the right wing boards for a shot, because he'll get a better angle at the net.

His finesse skills make him a specialty teams natural.

THE PHYSICAL GAME

Not known as a physical player, Howe nevertheless applies himself physically. He won't crush anyone with a hit, but Mark takes the body along the boards (and he's aided here by his ability to remain balanced and in position to make a play from the boards). Because he's just average at clearing the front of the net, Mark can be overpowered by stronger forwards. He can also be worn down by constant physical abuse.

By pairing him with a stronger, more physical defense partner (first Brad McCrimmon and now Kjell Samuelsson), Howe is free to play the game he knows best — that of starting plays, rather than stopping them.

THE INTANGIBLES

Probably the best defenseman never to have won the Norris Trophy, Howe's consistency, willingness to play through pain, character and dedication make him the Flyers' most valuable player, probably the most irreplaceable. His intensity and desire make him a leader both on the ice and in the dressing room.

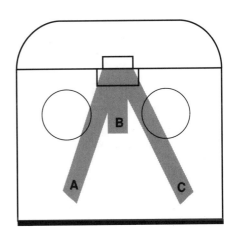

TIM KERR

Yrs. of NHL service: 9
Born: Windsor, Ontario, Canada; January 5, 1960
Position: Right wing/center
Height: 6-3
Weight: 215
Uniform no.: 12
Shoots: right

Career statistics:

GP	G	A	TP	PIM
534	329	249	578	535

1988-89 statistics:

GP	G	A	TP	+/-	PIM	PP	SH	GW	GT	S	PCT
69	48	40	88	-4	73	25	0	2	1	236	20.3

LAST SEASON

Kerr was sidelined throughout the year with a recurring shoulder injury. He led the club in points, goals and power play goals.

THE FINESSE GAME

Tim Kerr lives and dies by his shot, which is probably released faster than any other in the NHL. The puck is beyond a blur when it leaves his stick and heads for the net some 15-20 feet away, and that shot is almost impossible to defend against.

Otherwise, Kerr is not much of a finesse player. He's no better than average as an NHL skater, lumbering up and down the ice with neither great speed nor agility. His skating strength, however, makes him like a runaway locomotive as he steamrolls to the net; nothing is going to stop him.

His non-shooting stick skills are also average. He uses his reach and his body to protect the puck well, but Kerr doesn't use his teammates well. In his defense, that's often because he's in a better shooting position than they are.

He has learned to move out from the net and not get trapped close, and he'll convert on any defensive miscue around the goal. He's also a power play natural, but remains a defensive disaster.

THE PHYSICAL GAME

His hand and arm strength are demonstrated in his shot, and we've already mentioned his skating strength. Kerr has excellent size but is not an overly physical player; he is generally unwilling to impose himself physically upon anyone, and Kerr certainly does not use his size well in checking.

His strong hands and arms also allow the Flyers to use him on offensive zone faceoffs, especially on the power play.

THE INTANGIBLES

Despite setbacks during the season, Kerr showed that he can still play effectively in the NHL. He surely would have scored 50 goals had he played a full season, and his return invigorated the Flyers' power play.

Still, he remains essentially a one-dimensional player. And what do you think of the fact that he scored just 23 even-strength goals?

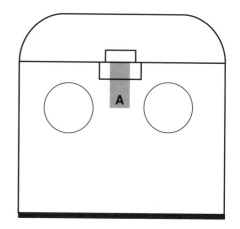

SCOTT MELLANBY

Yrs. of NHL service: 3
Born: Montreal, Quebec, Canada; June 11, 1966
Position: Right wing
Height: 6-1
Weight: 205
Uniform no.: 19
Shoots: right

Career statistics:

GP	G	A	TP	PIM
224	57	76	133	462

1988-89 statistics:

GP	G	A	TP	+/-	PIM	PP	SH	GW	GT	S	PCT
76	21	29	50	-13	183	11	0	3	0	202	10.4

LAST SEASON

Games played total was a career high. His plus/minus rating was the team's third worst.

THE FINESSE GAME

Mellanby's more of a strong than fluid skater. He's got good rink length speed but little quickness or balance, so his agility and lateral movement aren't great. Right now he's a straight-ahead player, much to the detriment of his game (because he's predictable; all the defense has to do is force him wide).

He still has yet to fully acclimate to the speed of the NHL game in terms of play reading and puck movement, but he continues to show the understanding of a play's implications and he does get into scoring position — eventually. Scott's hockey sense allows him to use his teammates fairly well, and his hands are definitely his best finesse asset.

Mellanby has a good-to-very-good shot, released quickly with a great deal of power. His hands are soft enough to manipulate the puck in small space and to score from in tight, and he certainly has the strength to drive his shot from longer range. As with his other finesse skills, he must work on releasing his shot still quicker. His fake shot down the right wing doesn't fool anybody.

His lack of NHL understanding comes to the fore in his defensive game, which remains a mess. He has yet to understand the importance of positional play — especially coming back through the neutral zone — and he must also learn to make the certain plays at his blue line. Scott also positions himself too high on breakouts, leaving the opposition a clear route to forecheck the Flyer defenseman with the puck.

THE PHYSICAL GAME

Mellanby's size and strength, in typical Flyer fashion, are his strong points. He uses his good upper body strength and strong skating to drive to the net, and that's how he'll score most of his goals. Scott also has the arm and hand strength to get off a quality shot even when being checked.

He's a good bet to out-muscle the opposition for the puck because of his string boards and corners game, and Mellanby plays the physical game with gusto. He has a tendency to go one step too far, as his PIM total dictates, and he doesn't pad that total by fighting.

THE INTANGIBLES

Mellanby has all the tools to be an exceptional NHLer, and this season is a critical one for him. Where the Flyers were looking for him to take a step forward last year (his nemesis, Mike Keenan was gone and Mellanby enjoyed a fine relationshoip with Paul Holmgren), and even moved him to the left side to get him more ice-time, Mellanby instead stepped backward.

This year, he must demonstrate the will and dedication to cash in on his considerable talents. So far in his NHL career, Mellanby hasn't shown the willingness to do so.

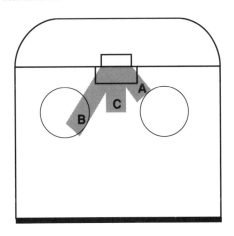

GORD MURPHY

Yrs. of NHL service: 1
Born: Willowdale, Ontario, Canada; March 23, 1967
Position: Defenseman
Height: 6-1
Weight: 185
Uniform no.: 3
Shoots: right

Career statistics:

GP	G	A	TP	+/-	PIM	PP	SH	GW	GT	S	PCT
75	4	31	35	-3	68	3	0	1	0	116	3.4

LAST SEASON

Murphy's first in the NHL. He led the defense in shots on goal.

THE FINESSE GAME

Murphy's a good skater in an efficient way. He won't explode up-ice or dazzle with his agility, but he has a solid, balanced stride that moves him quickly to and fro. He's also fairly strong on his feet, and that helps him in his battles in front of the net.

He reads the ice fairly well, maybe surprisingly so for a player with just 75 games of NHL experience, but Gord must still acclimate completely to the NHL's speed of execution. In that regard, increased foot speed would help.

Murphy is smart enough to play a positional style of game, and he generally won't gamble with the puck. He's shown the ability to make the quick and correct decisions in getting the puck from his zone, and that increased foot speed would get him to the puck faster and give him more time to make the play.

Gord puts that hockey sense and passing ability to some degree of work offensively, because he can find the open man and get the puck to him. His shot is okay from the point and won't yet fool NHL goaltending consistently, but Murphy makes his offense effective by not forcing plays at the offensive blue line. If given the chance, he'll sneak to the faceoff circle for a shot — but he's smart enough to just put it one net when in doubt.

THE PHYSICAL GAME

Murphy has rangy, good size. He's tall and has good reach, and he uses that reach to tie men up in the corners and the front of the net. He is not a hitter, and added strength would aid him in his blue line duties against the League's bigger forwards.

Again, though not overwhelmingly strong, Murphy is unafraid of the opposition and will go into the corners with anyone.

THE INTANGIBLES

Gord made the Flyers off an impressive training camp, and the thing that was most impressive about him was his poise. He's a smart, heady player who plays a consistently steady game, and his eager attitude and work ethic indicate that he'll do the things necessary to improve as an NHLer.

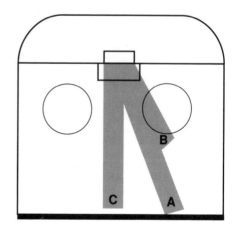

PETE PEETERS

Yrs. of NHL service: 10
Born: Edmonton, Alta., Canada; August 1, 1957
Position: Goaltender
Height: 6-0
Weight: 180
Uniform No.: 1
Catchs: left

Career statistics:

GP	MINS	G	SO	AVG	A	PIM
439	25,289	1,291	19	3. 06	12	188

1988-89 statistics:

GP	MINS	AVG	W	L	T	SO	GA	SA	SAPCT	PIM
33	1,854	2. 85	20	7	3	4	88	790	. 889	8

LAST SEASON

Games played total was full-season career low (recurring groin injury); ditto minutes played. Win total was three-season high. He finished third in GAA, second in shutouts (second-highest career total).

THE PHYSICAL GAME

Standup is the name of Peeters' game and he plays that style religiously. His pure angle game succeeds because of Washington's attention to defense, so Peeters is free to make the first save and leave the rebounds for the defense.

His good hand quickness and solid upper body positioning is in direct counterpoint to his woeful leg and foot play; Peeters has no mobility — just get his feet moving and you'll have an open net to shoot at.

Because he is so set and inflexible on his inner skate edges, he gives away shots between his legs far too frequently. Peeters doesn't handle the puck well at all when it is shot at his feet, and he allows rebounds by failing to clear the puck to the corner. His lack of foot speed and lateral movement across his crease make low shots to the net's corners — and scrambles in front — almost sure scoring plays.

Peeters handles the puck well and has cut down on the roaming and poor judgement that had rendered his puckhandling less effective. And, he's improved his vision when he does handle the puck, making better passes and fewer giveaways.

THE MENTAL GAME

Peeters' long-time problems have been his concentration and consistency, both within games and from contest to contest. That difficulty in maintaining his concentration is the key to his consistency problems.

At *best*, his ability to make big saves and to win crucial games is questionable.

THE INTANGIBLES

We're getting bored repeating the same old thing about Peeters. He can take a team to a certain level and provide credible enough goaltending during the regular season, but during the playoffs he's the great equalizer — for the Caps' opposition.

He consistently fails to deliver in the clutch, and one can't help but feel that this is why the Caps fail in the same way.

DAVE POULIN

Yrs. of NHL service: 6
Born: Mississauga, Ontario, Canada;
December 17, 1958
Position: Center
Height: 5-11
Weight: 175
Uniform no.: 20
Shoots: left

Career statistics:

GP	G	A	TP	PIM
439	152	225	377	291

1988-89 statistics:

GP	G	A	TP	+/-	PIM	PP	SH	GW	GT	S	PCT
69	18	17	35	4	49	1	5	4	0	81	22.2

LAST SEASON

Games played total was second lowest of career (concussion, shoulder, hand injuries). All point totals were career lows. He led the team in shorthanded goals.

THE FINESSE GAME

Poulin's best finesse asset is one that can't be measured, and that's his hockey sense and smarts. He reads plays excellently, both offensively and defensively. Poulin is an excellent checker and defensive player because of his speed and instincts, and those same attributes make him one of the NHL's premier penalty killers.

Physically, Poulin is a very strong skater with good speed and excellent acceleration. Dave is smart enough to read the ice and give up his good shot for a teammate's better one. He's got good hands (soft enough to send a pass over a defenseman's stick and onto a teammate's), and they're strong enough to strip an opposing player of the puck.

He can score from a distance with a powerful wrist shot, but Poulin is more likely to score from within 15 feet or so (converting on opposing miscues). He should shoot more, in order to take advantage of the openings his speed and brains afford him.

He prefers to go to his backhand when he is one-on-one with the goalie.

THE PHYSICAL GAME

Strength plays a large part in Poulin's skating game. His balance allows him to drive the net (which is why that's his most effective scoring area), but also keeps him vertical and positioned to make a play after a hit; he's very difficult to knock down. That's an important trait for a physical forward.

Dave initiates contact in all three zones, taking men out of the play intelligently. His great arm, hand and wrist strength makes him an excellent faceoff man.

He willingly sacrifices his body to block shots, but the evidence suggests that Poulin's all-around physical play takes its toll in injuries.

THE INTANGIBLES

His is the quiet type of game that doesn't gain immediate fan appreciation or newspaper headlines, but 20 other NHL teams would take Dave Poulin in a minute. Poulin characterizes everything a team captain should: intensity, determination, heart and willingness to sacrifice. He is the Flyers' leader both on the ice and in the locker room.

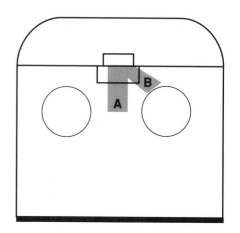

BRIAN PROPP

Yrs. of NHL service: 10
Born: Lanigan, Sask., Canada; February 15, 1959
Position: Left wing
Height: 5-9
Weight: 185
Uniform no.: 26
Shoots: left

Career statistics:

GP	G	A	TP	PIM
750	356	465	821	638

1988-89 statistics:

GP	G	A	TP	+/-	PIM	PP	SH	GW	GT	S	PCT
77	32	46	78	16	37	13	2	5	1	245	13.1

LAST SEASON

Games played total was five-season high, point total three-season best. Finished third on club in scoring, second in assists and plus/minus. He led the club in SOG total.

THE FINESSE GAME

Propp has always succeeded as a finesse player by finding the openings and exploiting them with excellent anticipation and hockey sense complemented by fine skills. Once he sees the openings and gains them (because of his good speed and acceleration — his balance and lateral movement are excellent also) Propp can either make a play for a teammate or — more likely — himself.

He has outstanding stick skills, taking and giving passes smoothly at all speeds, but Brian is a scorer first (as his SOG total indicates) and will take a bad shot even though a teammate is in better position.

Propp can score with an assortment of shots from all over the offensive zone, but his agility and one-step quickness make him a menace around the opposing goal, allowing him to easily convert loose pucks into points.

He remains a solid defensive player by playing his position well throughout all three zones. His anticipation and finesse skills also make him a regular in all specialty team situations.

THE PHYSICAL GAME

Brian is not big on physical contact, though he'll initiate some every once in a while (knowing his teammates will back him up). His balance, agility and hand skills allow him to control the puck in traffic, but Propp is not likely to be in the high-traffic areas.

THE INTANGIBLES

We spoke last year of Propp's consistency, and this year he once again broached the point-per-game plateau. Though age and wear-and-tear are taking their tolls (he's no longer as fast as he once was, for example), Propp remains an important part of the Flyers, as his game-winning goal total (tied for the team lead) shows.

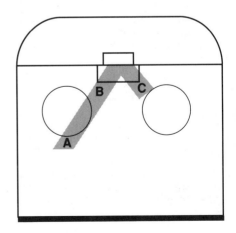

KJELL SAMUELSSON

Yrs. of NHL service: 4
Born: Tingsryd, Sweden; October 18, 1956
Position: Defenseman
Height: 6-6
Weight: 235
Uniform no.: 28
Shoots: right

Career statistics:

GP	G	A	TP	PIM
228	12	50	62	470

1988-89 statistics:

GP	G	A	TP	+/-	PIM	PP	SH	GW	GT	S	PCT
69	3	14	17	13	140	0	1	0	0	60	5.0

LAST SEASON

A foot injury sidelined Samuelsson for part of the year, forcing him to his lowest full-season games played total. He led the defense in plus/minus rating.

THE FINESSE GAME

Finesse is not exactly the name of Samuelsson's game. He's a better skater than given credit for (if you play in the NHL, your skating better improve), but he is far from being fleet-footed. A modicum of foot speed and a huge stride keep Samuelsson near both the puck and opposing forwards. Otherwise, he has little agility, quickness or lateral movement.

His hand skills are as limited as his foot skills, but Samuelsson makes them work by not over-stepping his bounds. Kjell won't carry the puck, but will make the correct pass to an open winger. He'll get power play time because of that, but more to act as the safety valve than as an offensive force.

He will score a handful of goals on an average slap shot.

THE PHYSICAL GAME

Playing against Samuelsson must be tremendously frustrating, because the guy is *always* there; you can't get away from him. His great size allows him to forever poke pucks away and force the opposition wide, and he has probably usurped Brad Marsh's title as the best holder in the NHL.

He's stepped up the tempo of his own hitting game and is more aggressive, and Samuelsson will take any rough stuff anybody dishes out.

THE INTANGIBLES

Samuelsson is undoubtedly Philadelphia's steadiest and most dependable defenseman behind his own blue line, with the emphasis on defense. He is a simple player who stays within his limits, and therein lies his value.

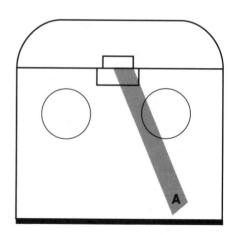

310

ILKKA SINISALO

Yrs. of NHL service: 8
Born: Helsinki, Finland; July 10, 1958
Position: Left wing
Height: 6-1
Weight: 190
Uniform no.: 23
Shoots: left

Career statistics:

GP	G	A	TP	PIM
467	176	187	363	154

1988-89 statistics:

GP	G	A	TP	+/-	PIM	PP	SH	GW	GT	S	PCT
13	1	6	7	6	2	0	0	0	0	15	6.7

LAST SEASON

Arm and ankle injuries kept Sinisalo on the shelf for much of the season. Games played total was career low.

THE FINESSE GAME

Sinisalo is a finesse player with the typical European skills. He's a superior skater, and is also an effective scorer. He's fast from his first stride and has good acceleration. He also varies his speed to make it more effective. His balance gives him good agility and allows him to make some nice "inside" moves.

He's pretty adept at using his teammates, and that's because he ably combines his stick skills with vision and anticipation. He looks to make the best possible plays in the offensive zone (and Sinisalo passes well to both sides), but he also knows when it's time to stop playing with the puck and shoot.

His shot is very good, quickly released and accurate, as his shooting percentage attests. He's deadly from 15 feet and loves the upper right hand corner of the net. He can also take advantage of the tight area around the net because of his hands, and is always a threat to convert rebounds into goals.

Because of his shooting ability and ice vision, Sinisalo can be a valuable power play performer. He keeps the passing lanes open with one-step quickness and forces the defense to spread itself thin in attempts to guard both him and Tim Kerr.

THE PHYSICAL GAME

Though orginally labelled an aggressive player, Sinisalo is not a physical forward. He much prefers pulling the puck from an opponent's feet to banging the opposition off the puck, so he hits neither hard nor often.

Ilkka is fairly strong on his skates (balance is the key here), making him more than a little difficult to dislodge from the puck, if you can catch him at all.

THE INTANGIBLES

Clearly, Sinisalo has shown an injury problem over the last three seasons. His health, therefore, remains his biggest intangible (his report this season remains unchanged from his last one because of his injuries and time missed).

A second strike against him is his age — he turned 31 during the summer. Still, his skills are good enough to keep the scales balanced in his favor, if he can remain healthy.

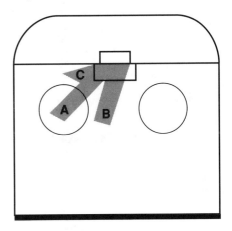

DERRICK SMITH

Yrs. of NHL service: 5
Born: Scarborough, Ontario, Canada; January 22, 1965
Position: Left wing
Height: 6-2
Weight: 210
Uniform no.: 24
Shoots: left

Career statistics:

GP	G	A	TP	PIM
367	66	71	137	269

1988-89 statistics:

GP	G	A	TP	+/-	PIM	PP	SH	GW	GT	S	PCT
74	16	14	30	-4	43	0	1	3	0	115	13.9

LAST SEASON

Smith tied his second-highest goal total.

THE FINESSE GAME

Smith's entire game is predicated on strength, so it's no surprise that his best finesse skill is his strength on his skates. That strength gives him excellent checking ability away from the puck, and makes him very difficult to out-run or out-muscle. His good balance helps here as well.

His skating ability is complimented by his hockey sense and anticipation defensively, where he forces the play well (Smith is one of the NHL's better forecheckers), but those qualities don't translate into offensive success.

Derrick's hand skills don't come anywhere near his foot skills, which means he — by and large — is unable to take advantage of the offensive opportunities his checking creates. He lacks the confidence that would breed the patience necessary for scoring success.

Accordingly, Smith neither handles nor shoots the puck well. While his strength allows him to retain control of the puck by straight-arming the opposition, Smith is unable to cash in on that advantage. Instead, he'll collect any goals he gets from in close to the net, though he does possess the strength to drive the puck from a distance.

THE PHYSICAL GAME

As we've said, strength is the hallmark of Smith's game. His great upper body strength makes him very hard to handle in the corners — like Rick Tocchet — though he lacks the hands to make effective offensive plays out of the corner.

Similar to Tocchet, Smith takes the body and hits hard enough to hurt. He puts that strength to work excellently on the boards and against his opponents, whom he routinely out-muscles.

The key to his physical game is his balance, which allows Smith to apply his strength and hitting ability and yet remain vertical and still in the play after collisions. He's at his best in a physical contest.

THE INTANGIBLES

Through five NHL seasons, Smith's skills — superbly though he applies them — have kept him essentially a role-playing forward. He's a pretty smart player, playing a physical game without taking the penalties that would hurt the club, but he seems to have reached his level as an NHL player.

That's not to say he couldn't play for any other NHL club, but an increased offensive ability would move him from role-player to all-around contributor status.

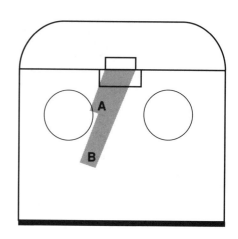

RON SUTTER

Yrs. of NHL service: 6
Born: Viking, Alta., Canada; December 2, 1963
Position: Center
Height: 6-0
Weight: 180
Uniform no.: 14
Shoots: right

Career statistics:

GP	G	A	TP	PIM
400	98	169	267	658

1988-89 statistics:

GP	G	A	TP	+/-	PIM	PP	SH	GW	GT	S	PCT
55	26	22	48	25	80	4	1	2	0	106	24.5

LAST SEASON

Games played total was second lowest full season total of career (broken jaw), but goal total was a career high. He led the team in plus/minus.

THE FINESSE GAME

More than any other finesse skill, Sutter's hockey sense makes him the player he is. In fact, that sense makes up for the other deficiencies he has. He has a great read of the ice and situations, and he's able to apply that read to a degree offensively and exceptionally defensively.

His play without the puck is very good (as his plus/minus indicates), and last year that play left him more and more in position to score some goals. Sutter's goals will generally come from directly in front of the net, where he'll be in position to convert loose pucks his checking creates. His shot isn't going to beat any NHL goalie from long distance, so he has to be opportunistic.

He doesn't have the hand skills to be an exceptional puckhandler, and he's best off not carrying the puck over the blue line because neither his hands nor his feet will carry him past a defender.

His short, choppy skating stride doesn't afford him much balance, and he has neither great speed nor much quickness. Because of his lack of balance, his turns are a little wide and his pivoting could improve. However, the chances of their improving after six NHL seasons is slim.

THE PHYSICAL GAME

Sutter is an extremely physical forward, hitting at every opportunity. He fearlessly goes into the corners with players 40 pounds heavier than himself, and he frequently out-muscles those opponents once there. However, his ability after the hit is suspect because of his aforementioned balance problem. Ron is not often left in a playmaking position after a collision.

He is very strong on faceoffs, one of the game's best. Sutter's hands are very fast and he gets down almost to the blade on his stick when he positions himself for faceoffs. The wide stance of his skates gives him even more power.

THE INTANGIBLES

One clear question is Sutter's inability to play a full NHL season; he's missed 77 games — almost a full season — over the last three seasons because of injuries.

His checking ability and work ethic make him a player any team would want, although he retains the Sutter characteristic of getting down on himself if things aren't going well.

He is a dedicated team man, and a valuable commodity. The Flyers would love for him to hold onto the scoring touch he found last year (doubtful), because it elevates Sutter from the role-player role. That goal-scoring touch combines with his checking ability and intensity to make him a valuable commodity — and a valuable trading commodity too.

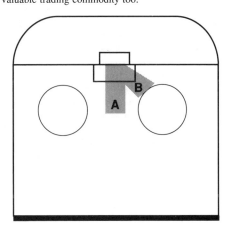

RICK TOCCHET

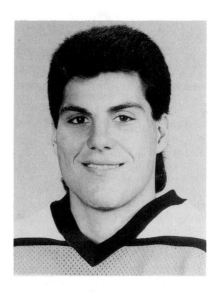

Yrs. of NHL service: 5
Born: Scarborough, Ontario, Canada; April 9, 1964
Position: Right wing
Height: 6-0
Weight: 195
Uniform no.: 22
Shoots: right

Career statistics:

GP	G	A	TP	PIM
344	125	141	266	1,235

1988-89 statistics:

GP	G	A	TP	+/-	PIM	PP	SH	GW	GT	S	PCT
66	45	36	81	-1	183	16	1	5	3	220	20.5

LAST SEASON

Games played total was second lowest of career (in part because of a 10-game suspension), but all point totals were career highs. PIM total was second lowest of career. Second on the team in goals, points, power play goals; third in shots on goal.

THE FINESSE GAME

Tocchet's physical skills belie his finesse abilities. He's a very strong skater with pretty good speed up-ice. He has a good degree of agility for a player with his size and strength, but he's more likely to operate in a confined space by knocking everyone else down instead of skating through them.

His increasing confidence continues to power his developing offensive game. Tocchet is taking the time to look up for a play, and that improved vision is more and more putting him into excellent scoring position. He's also more and more willing to hold the puck to make a play, rather than his previous style of throwing it away and charging after it.

Rick's shot is undoubtedly his best finesse asset. His wrist shot is fast, hard and accurate, and Tocchet has made it more dangerous by releasing it more quickly; he's become adept at shooting on the fly, a la Tim Kerr. He's also shooting more frequently — almost 20 percent more often last season than in 1987-88.

THE PHYSICAL GAME

Tocchet is in the elite NHL category of true power forward. He is a fearsome hitter and fighter, so much so that he remains essentially unchallenged by the rest of the League. He is one of the NHL's most punishing hitters, taking the body relentlessly, and his strength will almost always jar the puck free.

That strength allows him to excel in the traffic areas of the corners and the front of the net, and only the NHL's most powerful defensemen will contain him.

THE INTANGIBLES

We told you last year that Tocchet could easily score 40 goals. This year, we tell you he could score 50. He's learned how to control his temper and stay out of the penalty box without sacrificing his outstanding physical play.

He remains one of our favorites, and his character, work ethic and dedication contribute to his development into one of the NHL's best players.

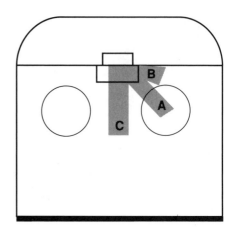

JAY WELLS

Yrs. of NHL service: 10
Born: Paris, Ontario, Canada; May 18, 1959
Position: Defenseman
Height: 6-1
Weight: 210
Uniform no.: 7
Shoots: left

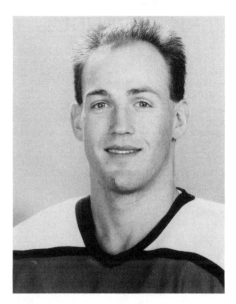

Career statistics:

GP	G	A	TP	PIM
671	36	162	198	1,630

1988-89 statistics:

GP	G	A	TP	+/-	PIM	PP	SH	GW	GT	S	PCT
67	2	19	21	-3	184	0	0	0	0	67	3.0

LAST SEASON

Acquired by the Flyers from Los Angeles in exchange for Doug Crossman. Point total was four-season low. He was second in PIM among defensemen. He was sidelined by shoulder and finger injuries.

THE FINESSE GAME

Jay is one of those players for whom simple play is best. He grades out to average in all of his finesse abilities but Wells isn't a bad skater. He can contribute some speed and has some agility, and he can combine that agility with a degree of puckhandling talent so as to play more than just a defensive game.

But Wells runs into problems when he believes his skills to be better than they are. When he gets the puck it should be moved off his stick, preferably up the boards — because he is a capable puckhandler — to force himself into situations where the puck gets pokechecked away while trying a 1-on-1 deke at his own blue line. More often than not the result of that poor play is a cheap goal against.

Wells reads the rush toward him well and is very difficult to beat one-on-one because of both his size and his positional play. He will follow the rush up-ice but doesn't jump into the play often, preferring to throw the puck around at the point to pinching into the zone. Once the puck is turned over, Wells is the first man back.

THE PHYSICAL GAME

Wells is very, very tough and very underrated in his toughness because he hasn't had to show it off for several seasons.

He is one of the best in the league at clearing the front of the net. And Wells doesn't care who's planted there, he'll take them on. He hits often and hard and is an excellent — and punishing — body checker. Wells will jar the puck loose with his hits and he's mean enough to add a little something extra if he can.

Wells will also sacrifice his body to block some shots and he can, by the way, throw 'em pretty good too.

THE INTANGIBLES

Jay's reputation has brought him that extra yard of room so he can function, but he's not always consistent in his output. Wells has to be constantly reminded to keep the play simple, to move the puck quickly and to take the body consistently.

When he does those things he's a force defensively. When he doesn't do them he's a very average defenseman.

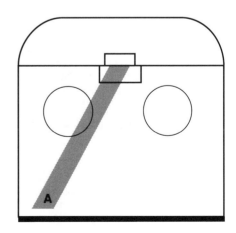

KEN WREGGET

Yrs. of NHL service: 5
Born: Brandon, Man., Canada; March 25, 1964
Position: Goaltender
Height: 6-1
Weight: 180
Uniform no.: 35
Catches: left

Career statistics:

GP	MINS	G	SO	AVG	A	PIM
203	11,053	804	3	4.36	13	106

1987-88 statistics:

GP	MINS	AVG	W	L	T	SO	GA	SA	SAPCT	PIM
35	2,018	4.52	10	21	2	1	152	1,110	.844	20

LAST SEASON

Acquired by the Flyers from Toronto for draft choices on March 6. Games played total was three-year low.

THE PHYSICAL GAME

Wregget's style of goaltending is a challenging, standup one. He is at his best when he squares himself to the puck and allows it to hit him. He follows that same pattern on screen shots, coming out to the top of the screen to prevent deflections. It's important for Wregget to play this style because he's not a great skater and he tends to become scrambly when forced to move his feet. When he starts flopping around on the ice (or when he has to move his feet to make a skate save), you know he's in trouble.

When he doesn't go to the ice Wregget has fairly good balance, meaning he'll generally regain his stance for a second shot. He has good peripheral vision and sees the play at the side of the net or moving across his body well. That helps him cover the posts and move across the net well.

He has good hands in terms of reflex speed, but he doesn't control the puck well with his glove. He'll get his hand in the way of a shot but won't catch it, so when the puck falls to the ice he has to make another save on the rebound. Wregget also doesn't handle the puck well, and that leads to a lot of defensive confusion. As such, he can be said to be a poor communicator with his defensemen.

THE MENTAL GAME

Wregget uses great anticipation to complement his positional play, and when he's on the combination this makes him tough to beat. He has big save capability, but he can be his own worst enemy in terms of his mental outlook.

He goes beyond concentration to worry and puts too much pressure on himself. He'll burn up energy in one game that another goalie needs three or four games to disperse. Sometimes he'll burn up so much energy in pregame fidgeting and worrying that he'll be completely out of gas within the game's opening minutes and has to get pulled because he has nothing left.

THE INTANGIBLES

He's got the capability to be a front-line goalie, though Wregget's chances of getting that opportunity in Philadelphia (behind Ron Hextall) are slim indeed. He's also a better playoff goalie than one would think at first; his playoff GAA is better than (for example) Mike Vernon's or Grant Fuhr's.

So there's talent here. The only question is, when will Wregget get to show it?

PITTSBURGH
PENGUINS

LINE COMBINATIONS
PHIL BOURQUE-JOHN CULLEN-TROY LONEY
RANDY CUNNEYWORTH-DAN QUINN
DAVE HANNAN
BOB ERREY-MARIO LEMIEUX-ROB BROWN

DEFENSE PAIRINGS
PAUL COFFEY-RANDY HILLIER
STEVE DYKSTRA-JIM JOHNSON
ZARLEY ZALAPSKI-ROD BUSKAS

GOALTENDERS
TOM BARRASSO
WENDELL YOUNG

OTHER PLAYERS
KEVIN STEVENS — Left wing
JOCK CALLANDER — Center
JAY CAUFIELD — Right wing
GORD DINEEN — Defenseman

POWER PLAY

FIRST UNIT:
DAN QUINN-MARIO LEMIEUX-ROB BROWN
PHIL BOURQUE-PAUL COFFEY

SECOND UNIT:
JOHN CULLEN-MARIO LEMIEUX
RANDY CUNNEYWORTH
ZARLEY ZALAPSKI

LEMIEUX sits in the left faceoff circle waiting to one-time the puck home. BROWN is off the right wing post and QUINN is in the slot. BOURQUE and COFFEY (and ZALAPSKI will also see first unit time) play catch until LEMIEUX gets open, usually with QUINN and BROWN sliding to the right side to overload that wing.

On the second unit CULLEN works behind the net on the left wing side and CUNNEYWORTH is in front, but the LEMIEUX plan is the same. CULLEN will cut to the net on any shot.

Last season Pittsburgh's power play was EXCELLENT, scoring 119 goals in 491 opportunities (24.2 percent, third overall).

PENALTY KILLING

FIRST UNIT:
MARIO LEMIEUX-DAVE HANNAN
JIM JOHNSON-RANDY HILLIER

SECOND UNIT:
TROY LONEY-(HANNAN or LEMIEUX)
PHIL BOURQUE

Pittsburgh's penalty killing is very aggressive, particularly LEMIEUX, who will pressure the puck at all times in search of a shorthanded break. In order to maximize LEMIEUX's presence, HANNAN will take the faceoffs, leaving LEMIEUX free to break for an opening.

Last season Pittsburgh's penalty killing was POOR, allowing 111 goals in 482 shorthanded situations (77.0 percent, 16th overall).

CRUCIAL FACEOFFS
CULLEN gets the call for a lot of these, but the Pens lack a consistent faceoff winner.

TOM BARRASSO

Yrs. of NHL service: 6
Born: Boston, Mass., USA; March 31, 1965
Position: Goaltender
Height: 6-3
Weight: 206
Uniform no.: 35
Catches: right

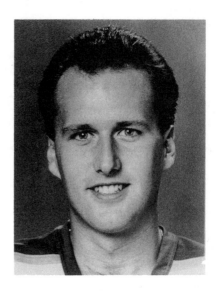

Career statistics:

GP	MINS	G	SO	AVG	A	PIM
310	17,869	1,007	13	3.38	22	231

1988-89 statistics:

GP	MINS	AVG	W	L	T	SO	GA	SA	SAPCT	PIM
54	2,951	3.29	20	22	7	0	207	1,730	.880	70

LAST SEASON

Acquired by the Penguins from Buffalo in exchange for Doug Bodger and Darrin Shannon on Nov. 12. Finished sixth in the NHL in games played, third in shots against, second in PIM total. Win total was the second lowest of his career. He failed to record a shutout for the first time in his career. Sidelined with leg and groin injuries.

THE PHYSICAL GAME

Barrasso is an excellent skater in his movement in and out of his net. His lateral movement is less good, and he's very vulnerable to crossing plays — mostly because he spends so much time on his butt. He plays a reflex and butterfly style game, and Barrasso — though he has the reflexes — is sometimes very slow to get off the ice. He does have exceptional foot speed, so Barrasso is less vulnerable to low shots than many tall goaltenders.

Tom also uses his size excellently when he butterflies to the ice, covering a lot of net with his long legs. He could use his size better by playing a stronger challenging game.

He handles the puck pretty well and will come out of his net to play it to a teammate, but Barrasso is weak in controlling rebounds. He is very prone to rebounds on saves that are off his stick and upper body, and has yet to learn what to do with the puck after making a pad save. He must either cover the rebounds off his pads or kick them to the corners.

Barrasso is betrayed by his inconsistent angle game when he loses his position on the ice and doesn't mark his short post. This makes him susceptible to shots on the short side, especially shots low to the ice.

THE MENTAL GAME

Barrasso has good concentration and anticipates well too. He'll fight you after a bad goal and, since Barrasso is confident in his abilities, he's able to bounce back after a bad outing as well.

THE INTANGIBLES

Tom responds to the responsibility of being the number one goalie, and he's gone quite some way to dispel the notion (to which, we confess, we subscribe) that he can't win a big game via his performance with the Pens last season.

He's improved his all-around effort and works harder in practice than ever before, and that maturity sends messages to his teammates — especially important because of the prima donna attitude Barrasso has been accused of carrying since entering the NHL.

PHIL BOURQUE

Yrs. of NHL service: 2
Born: Chelmsford, Mass., USA: June 8, 1962
Position: Left wing/defense
Height: 6-1
Weight: 206
Uniform no.: 29
Shoots: left

Career statistics:

GP	G	A	TP	PIM
132	23	42	65	73

1988-89 statistics:

GP	G	A	TP	+/-	PIM	PP	SH	GW	GT	S	PCT
80	17	26	43	-22	97	5	2	3	0	153	11.1

LAST SEASON

First full NHL campaign. He was the only Penguin to play all 80 games. Point totals were all career highs.

THE FINESSE GAME

Bourque is a good skater with a lot of speed and skating strength. He uses those assets when he's checking as a good forechecker, and they meld well with his good puckhandling skills.

A former defenseman (and he still sees some time on the blue line), Bourque is very comfortable rushing the puck. He carries it from his zone well, but he's not tremendously creative with it once he gains the offensive zone. One reason is because he doesn't have a lot of agility; he'll cut outside and swoop around a defender instead of stutter-stepping or skipping past him. But because he stays outside, Phil can be easily defended against.

He looks to use his teammates, but because he can be forced to bad ice his playmaking skills can be minimized. He's not a great passer besides, lacking true NHL touch, but through application of his other skills Bourque makes the most of his opportunities.

Phil shoots fairly often, but his shot is no better than average at the NHL level (lacking the quick release, strength and accuracy necessary for it to be a truly dangerous weapon).

He works at playing a solid defensive game (recognizing when to stay high in the offensive zone, for example), but his lack of NHL experience (in terms of speed of the play and recognizing its implications) sometimes mitigates against him.

THE PHYSICAL GAME

Bourque has good size and strength and he willingly uses both. He works the boards and corners by taking the body whenever he can, and he also goes to the front of the net and gets his nose dirty.

His skating strength helps him drive through checks when hitting, and it also carries him through checks when being hit. He uses his body smartly when checking, keeping himself out of the penalty box.

THE INTANGIBLES

This guy works like nobody's business. He has a great attitude, and he did everything he could to make the most of his first real NHL chance — proving Coach Gene Ubriaco right to have confidence in him.

Bourque is also a versatile player, in that he can be shifted back to defense. He'll see a lot of time there on the Penguin power play, subbing for Paul Coffey or Zarley Zalapski.

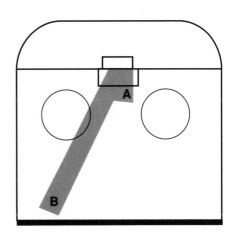

ROB BROWN

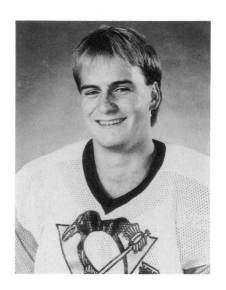

Yrs. of NHL service: 2
Born: Kingston, Ontario, Canada; April 10, 1968
Position: Right wing
Height: 5-11
Weight: 185
Uniform no.: 44
Shoots: left

Career statistics:

GP	G	A	TP	PIM
119	73	86	159	174

1988-89 statistics:

GP	G	A	TP	+/-	PIM	PP	SH	GW	GT	S	PCT
68	49	66	115	27	118	24	0	6	0	169	29.0

LAST SEASON

Games played, all point and PIM totals were career highs. Finished second on the club in goals, points (fifth in NHL), power play goals (third in NHL) and game winners, first in shooting percentage (led NHL) and third in plus/minus. He missed time with post All-Star Game shoulder injury.

THE FINESSE GAME

This guy is a scoring machine. Brown's got exceptional — truly superior — hand skills, best manifested in his shot. Because he operates so well in traffic, Brown is going to get the puck in close to the net a lot. All he needs to cash in is the slightest opening because of his hand speed and his touch. He's got a lightening release that makes him deadly on the power play, but Rob can score most anywhere, most any time.

He gets into position to score excellently, and if he can't get to a hole he'll skim the puck to a teammate (again, his sense reveals the ice to him). Brown controls the puck very well when skating, and he's certainly not afraid to work with it while under pressure. He can also handle the puck while in an awkward position or while he seems to be falling and that's where his balance comes into play.

His skating is the weakest of his finesse skills (and the reason many felt he would fail at the NHL level), but that doesn't mean he's a poor skater. He lacks rink-length speed and outstanding quickness or agility, but Rob has the ability to turn up the juice a notch or two (as well as down when necessary). He also has the superb balance that powers his traffic game.

He is a fairly conscientious checker, and will stay with his man deep into the defensive zone. Brown also makes the transition from offense to defense well.

THE PHYSICAL GAME

Rob has tremendous eye/hand coordination, which makes him excellent at tipping and deflecting the puck.

He's also going to take many faceoffs (relieving linemate Mario Lemieux of this duty) because of that skill.

Brown plays a fairly good physical game for his size. He takes and give hits, and his balance really comes to the fore along the boards — where he can take the puck and make a play in one motion — and the front of the net (where he takes a pounding). He's not a fighter, but he won't back down from a confrontation.

THE INTANGIBLES

He's cocky, he mouths off, he's a hot dog, he runs goalies — Rob Brown is giving Claude Lemieux a run for his money as the NHL's most hated opponent.

But who cares? He's a great player with tremendous drive, great confidence and desire. He works hard and he's fun to watch. Now, watch him score 50 goals a season, playing Jari Kurri to Lemieux's Wayne Gretzky.

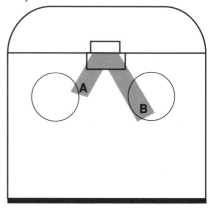

ROD BUSKAS

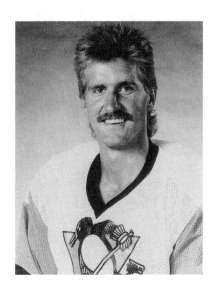

Yrs. of NHL service: 7
Born: Wetaskiwin, Alberta, Canada; January 7, 1961
Position: Defenseman
Height: 6-1
Weight: 206
Uniform no.: 7
Shoots: right

Career statistics:

GP	G	A	TP	PIM
425	16	48	64	946

1988-89 statistics:

GP	G	A	TP	+/-	PIM	PP	SH	GW	GT	S	PCT
52	1	5	6	-2	105	0	0	0	0	15	6.7

LAST SEASON

Games played was a five season low (benchings, knee injury); ditto all point and PIM totals.

THE FINESSE GAME

Buskas is not an exceptional finesse player, probably not even good in this category. He's no better than an average skater, without great agility, quickness or strength on his skates. His passing and puckhandling are also weak, but he has improved his ability to make the right pass under pressure. Buskas is smart enough, though, to not over-extend his game, and he won't attempt the rushes that teammates Paul Coffey and Zarley Zalapski successfully complete.

Improved anticipation and understanding of the NHL game have helped Buskas become a solid defenseman. He reads the play coming toward him fairly well, and he uses his defensive angles to force it wide of the net. He also has better understanding of the lateral play around the goal — the cross-ice centering pass, for example — and he dependably covers the front of the net by concentrating on the oppposing forward instead of the puck.

His offense will come almost completely from the point, but it is practically non-existent. Once in a very great while he'll sneak into the faceoff circle for a shot.

THE PHYSICAL GAME

Buskas is good along the boards and the corner, but he is more of a pusher and shover than he is a hitter. He doesn't have great strength, but he can generally hold his own against the opposition in the traffic areas. He gets by in front of the net more by holding than by levelling the enemy.

THE INTANGIBLES

Buskas succeeds by making the most of what he has, but he is a marginal NHL player. He's fairly sound defensively, but he's not like a Brad McCrimmon, whose outstanding defense allows his partners to practise their own offensive play. In fact, Buskas must be placed with someone who can move the puck and skate so as to relieve pressure on Buskas, rather than the other way around. That makes him a liability.

He's a hard worker and willing to work to improve, and he has his teammates' respect because of that.

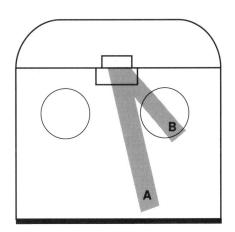

JOCK CALLANDER

Yrs. of NHL service: 1
Born: Regina, Sask., Canada; April 23, 1961
Position: Center
Height: 6-1
Weight: 187
Uniform no.: 14
Shoots: right

Career statistics:

GP	G	A	TP	PIM
71	17	21	38	65

1988-89 statistics:

GP	G	A	TP	+/-	PIM	PP	SH	GW	GT	S	PCT
30	6	5	11	-3	20	2	0	0	0	35	17.1

LAST SEASON

Callander's second go-round with the Penguins.

THE FINESSE GAME

Callander's best finesse play rests in his hockey sense and playmaking ability, followed close after by his shot.

He's not a great skater at the NHL level, lacking the foot speed necessary to be outstanding, but Jock's anticipation skill and hockey sense can put him in the right place at the right time. He is handicapped in that department, however, by his lack of NHL experience and understanding, therefore, of the speed of the NHL play.

He gives and takes the pass well as he's moving, and Callander has an excellent release of his shot — he almost one-times his wrist shot off the pass.

He backchecks well and stays with his man in all three zones but, again, he suffers in his game because of his skating.

THE PHYSICAL GAME

Callander has okay size and less than impressive strength, but takes the body fairly well. He holds frequently in the defensive zone, because after taking the man he isn't strong enough to hold him out of the play. Greater overall strength would help his game.

THE INTANGIBLES

Callander has gone about as far as he can go in the minors, but he's on the tail-end of time for making it in the NHL. Already 28 years old, he'll need at least another season to make a dent in his NHL weaknesses. He could probably contribute 17-20 goals to the Pens this season, but to do so he has to be in the lineup every day — and whether that will happen is extremely iffy.

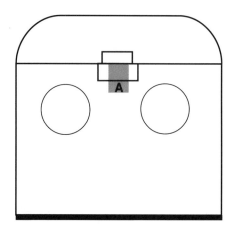

JAY CAUFIELD

Yrs. of NHL service: 1
Born: Philadelphia, PA., USA; July 17, 1960
Position: Right wing
Height: 6-4
Weight: 240
Uniform no.: 16
Shoots: right

Career statistics:

GP	G	A	TP	PIM
72	3	5	8	330

1988-89 statistics:

GP	G	A	TP	+/-	PIM	PP	SH	GW	GT	S	PCT
58	1	4	5	-4	285	0	0	0	0	10	10.0

LAST SEASON

Games played, assist, point and PIM totals were career highs. Led club in PIM.

THE FINESSE GAME

There isn't one. By default, Caufield's best skill is his skating — and that's not saying a lot. He doesn't have the balance, the quickness or the agility to skate at the NHL level. About all Jay can do is get up and down the ice — and at 28 years of age, that's not going to get much better.

He can't handle the puck while skating, and he has almost no passing skill or sense of the ice. If he scores, it's going to be from in front of the net on a loose puck with the goalie out of position.

THE PHYSICAL GAME

This is why Jay is in the NHL. He doesn't check particularly well (because he has neither the mobility nor the smarts to do so), but if he happens to catch someone that check will hurt. He's tremendously strong and in excellent muscular condition — not surprising considering that he was a linebacker in college.

Caufield is Pittsburgh's designated tough guy, but while he's willing to assume that role he's less than the NHL's worst nightmare. For one thing, he doesn't have the balance to be a good fighter (disagreeable though it may be, there's a skill in throwing a punch while on skates). Because of that, Jay can't get all of his strength behind his punches, and his fights become wrestling matches.

THE INTANGIBLES

Quiet and personable off the ice, Caufield knows what his job is on the ice. He accepts that role willingly, and it is that acceptance that keeps him in the NHL. But his lack of skill means he can't be used in skating games — or in close ones — and Caufield will always be vulnerable to replacement because of that.

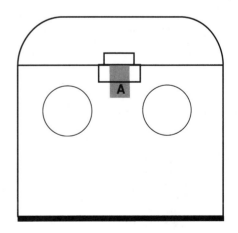

JOHN CULLEN

Yrs. of NHL service: 1
Born: Puslinch, Ontario, Canada; August 2, 1964
Position: Center
Height: 5-10
Weight: 187
Uniform no.: 11
Shoots: right

Career statistics:

GP	G	A	TP	+/-	PIM	PP	SH	GW	GT	S	PCT
79	12	37	49	-25	112	8	0	0	0	121	9.9

LAST SEASON

First in the NHL. His plus/minus was the club's second worst.

THE FINESSE GAME

Cullen has many finesse skills, but he has yet to prove that he can bring them to bear successfully at the NHL level. He's a good skater with more agility and quickness than speed, so he's a darter on the ice rather than a rocket.

He uses his one-step quickness and good lateral movement to get to loose pucks and into the openings, but his playreading ability is not yet completely acclimated to the NHL speed. That slowness affects his passing and playmaking, but Cullen has shown that he has the right sense of the play — greater experience will help him make those plays in time.

John's more of a playmaker than he is a scorer. He looks for his teammates and he has the hands to make good passes. Again, greater understanding of the NHL game will manifest itself in his point totals. Like the rest of his skills, Cullen's shot needs improvement if it is to consistently fool NHL goaltending — as the fact that he had only four even-strength goals attests. He'll have to be opportunistic and score from near the net.

While his skills are of the offensive bent (and particularly suitable for the power play), Cullen spent much of last year centering a checking line of Phil Bourque and Troy Loney. His skating helped here, and his poor defensive rating is not solely attributable to poor effort. Rather, the combination of being out against the opposition's best players — along with his adapting to the NHL and playing with less-than-greatly talented linemates — helped him to that minus-25.

THE PHYSICAL GAME

Cullen's a fairly aggressive little guy, with the emphasis here on little. He's not going to bowl anyone over with his size or strength, though he will benefit in traffic because of his balance and hand skills.

But in order to be successful in the long term, John is going to have to find a way to get out of the congested areas. If he sticks around where the big guys are, he's going to find himself out-muscled and overwhelmed. That, by the way, also applies to his checking

game. He can't go one-on-one against a Mike Ridley or Carey Wilson — he's going to have to check those guys by closing their skating and passing, not by knocking them off the puck.

His eye/hand coordination is very good, so Cullen will more than hold his own on faceoffs.

THE INTANGIBLES

Cullen's presence is one reason Dan Quinn found himself out of the picture — especially on the power play — so frequently. Cullen has developable skills, and the desire to develop them — but the fact that he's already 25 years old limits the amount of time he has to A) learn and B) contribute to the Pens.

While not necessarily so, he must be considered vulnerable to replacement three — or even two — seasons down the road.

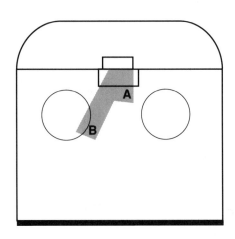

324

PAUL COFFEY

Yrs. of NHL service: 9
Born: Weston, Ontario, Canada; June 1, 1961
Position: Defenseman
Height: 6-0
Weight: 200
Uniform no.: 77
Shoots: left

Career statistics:

GP	G	A	TP	PIM
653	254	595	849	979

1988-89 statistics:

GP	G	A	TP	+/-	PIM	PP	SH	GW	GT	S	PCT
75	30	83	113	-10	193	11	0	2	0	342	8.8

LAST SEASON

Games played and all point totals were three-season highs, PIM total career high. Led NHL defensemen in goals, assists and points (sixth in NHL). Finished fourth in NHL in assists, third in shots on goal. Second on Pens in PIM total, third in scoring, first in SOG total. He missed time with a shoulder injury.

THE FINESSE GAME

Coffey is an excellent skater (maybe — just maybe — the NHL's best pure skater) with excellent acceleration, explosive foot speed, lateral movement and change of direction skills, all based on great balance. He has the tightest turning radius of any NHL player. He plays his defense through his skating, rather than through positional play. He challenges the play at both blue lines — and generally gets away with it — because he can skate himself back into the play.

Paul complements his skating skill with excellent vision and hockey sense, and his great stick skills amplify both of these aforementioned skills. He carries the puck better than any defenseman in the NHL, is an excellent one-touch passer and always looks for a breaking winger or open teammate at the blue line when distributing the puck.

He can score any way from anywhere, and he must shoot the puck to be effective. He'll go to the net with the puck and use his hard, accurate wrist shot, but his laser-precise slap shot is just as effective.

His skills make him a natural special teams player.

THE PHYSICAL GAME

Coffey will play a physical style of defense, pushing and shoving along the boards and in the corners, but he is not a hitter and never will be. He is fairly strong in the upper body, but it is the strength in his

thighs that powers his fantastic skating or allows him to take the opposition off the puck.

THE INTANGIBLES

Coffey took a lot of penalties last year; he could play a little smarter in defending his zone. And his plus/minus — he'd have had to score 123 points to just be *even*. That's a little too porous.

But there's no questioning his talent, or his leadership. Pittsburgh's defensive corps looks to him for leadership in tight situations, and he knows how to play big games.

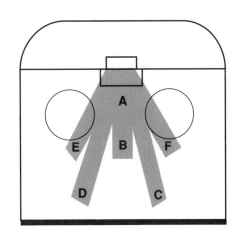

GORD DINEEN

Yrs. of NHL service: 6
Born: Toronto, Ontario, Canada; September 21, 1962
Position: Defenseman
Height: 6-0
Weight: 195
Uniform no.: 5
Shoots: right

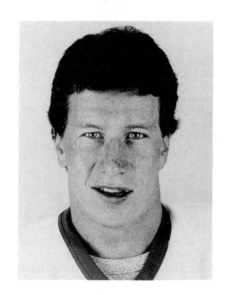

Career statistics:

GP	G	A	TP	PIM
331	13	57	70	443

1988-89 statistics:

GP	G	A	TP	+/-	PIM	PP	SH	GW	GT	S	PCT
40	1	3	4	-9	44	0	0	0		32	3.1

LAST SEASON

Traded from Minnesota to Pittsburgh in exchange for Ville Siren. Games played total was full-season low.

THE FINESSE GAME

Dineen has modest finesse skills at the NHL level. He moves forward and backward as well as a defenseman should be expected to, and he turns well, but he lacks acceleration. He doesn't have tremendous agility, so he's more likely to back in from the blue line than he is to challenge the puckhandler. He will, occasionally, pinch in at the offensive blue line.

Once he gets his shot off, Dineen has a good shot from the right point — low and hard for deflections and tip-ins; he must improve his release in terms of quickness. Gordie must also pick up his head when he shoots, as he often has his shot blocked by an unseen (by him) defender. He must shoot more frequently.

Dineen's hand skills are average. Gord can take advantage of his teammates, but he's going to need some time and space to make the correct pass. He can handle the puck in the open while in his own end but has difficulty carrying it through traffic.

THE PHYSICAL GAME

Dineen takes people off the puck with fairly good consistency, and he completes his checks along the boards to eliminate the opposition from the play.

Gord has good strength and makes good use of it in front of the net, where he is also mean. He plays a generally aggressive game.

THE INTANGIBLES

Confidence remains the biggest factor in Dineen's play. He plays with a lot of fire and with tremendous intensity, but he wants to play so badly that sometimes that hurts him, because he tries to do too much and gets into trouble.

All his finesse skills are based on his having good confidence, for when he doesn't he makes bad decisions and mistakes. He has a great work ethic and plays in pain, and his attitude will be good for the club. Gord is driven by the knowledge that he has to work in each practise and every game to be successful at the NHL level.

Given all of that, there's still a good chance he won't be protected in the waiver draft.

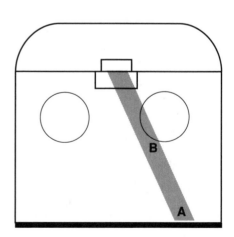

STEVE DYKSTRA

Yrs. of NHL service: 4
Born: Edmonton, Alta., Canada; December 1, 1962
Position: Defenseman
Height: 6-2
Weight: 210
Uniform no.: 22
Shoots: left

Career statistics:

GP	G	A	TP	PIM
208	8	32	40	543

1988-89 statistics:

GP	G	A	TP	+/-	PIM	PP	SH	GW	GT	S	PCT
65	1	6	7	-12	126	0	0	0	0	38	2.6

LAST SEASON
Games played total was career high.

THE FINESSE GAME
Dykstra is an average skater with no real speed, so he can't jump into the play as a fourth attacker, nor can he really skate the puck from his zone. His skating is at the same level forward and back and his pivots are a little slow and could use some work. His skating isn't good enough to allow him to challenge the play at either blue line.

Steve doesn't have a real good idea of the play around him. He's one-dimensional in that he'll have to deal with the play or player in front of him, because he lacks the play reading or anticipation skill necessary to see a second option. If he's going to succeed, he'll have to do so by playing good, positional hockey.

He doesn't have good hands, which means that both taking the puck off the boards and getting it out of the zone quickly are going to be problems for him. That puck work is best left for his partner. He is not likely to score many goals, so any offense he will generate will come from the point.

THE PHYSICAL GAME
Dykstra is big and strong and he throws his weight around in front of the net. He'll knock opposing forwards off the puck and can be a tough hitter at times. He does have room to bulk up his upper body, so he may be able to carry a little more muscle, but Steve is already very strong and can knock opponents dizzy if he catches them squarely. Catching them is the big problem.

THE INTANGIBLES
Dykstra's skill level is questionable, and he'll be spotted in and out of the lineup because of that. He's a useful addition against the tougher teams in the League, but he's rendered obsolete in a skating game. He will probably be on the outside looking in.

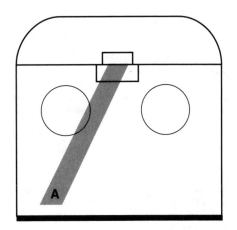

BOB ERREY

Yrs. of NHL service: 6
Born: Montreal, Quebec, Canada; September 21, 1964
Position: Left wing
Height: 5-10
Weight: 177
Uniform no.: 12
Shoots: left

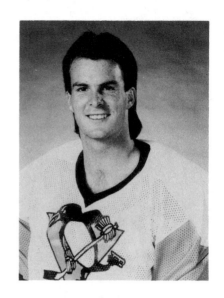

Career statistics:

GP	G	A	TP	PIM
283	65	77	142	232

1988-89 statistics:

GP	G	A	TP	+/-	PIM	PP	SH	GW	GT	S	PCT
76	26	32	58	40	124	0	3	5	0	130	20.0

LAST SEASON

Games played and all point totals were all career highs; ditto PIM total. Finished fifth on the club in scoring, second in shorthanded goals and plus/minus.

THE FINESSE GAME

The key to Errey's success as a finesse player last season is based on two things: A) his physical willingness and B) his improved grasp of the NHL's speed.

Not that he couldn't keep up skating-wise; Errey is an exceptional skater with speed, agility, balance and quickness. But where previously he had no idea of what to do once he got where he was going — if he even knew where he was going — now Bob has a good handle on playreading. He's looking for a man to pass to after he gains the puck, and he's being patient; he's not making the first play he sees.

He's also able to use that ice vision in tandem with his skating to be a good checker and penalty killer. He's also very determined defensively, and he plays well positionally in all three zones.

As for scoring, Bob is going to have to be relatively opportunistic. His shot isn't great, but his quickness will get him to a lot of loose pucks near the net. He'll have to cash those in for goals.

THE PHYSICAL GAME

Errey doesn't have great size, but he certainly plays as if he does. He's always involved in the play along the boards, terrier-like in his pursuit for the puck, and he isn't above doing more than a little disturbing with his elbows and his stick. He's the kind of player that runs goalies.

It is his physical play that keys his finesse game, as he works to dig the puck out of the corners for his linemates. But he also has the hands — and has developed the brains — to make those battles pay off point-wise. That makes him a two-pronged threat.

THE INTANGIBLES

We wondered how this first-round draft choice could contribute in the NHL, and last season — after five tries — we got our answer. Now we're not foolish enough to say that his success is all his own (after all, he does play with Mario Lemieux and Rob Brown), but we'd be liars if we didn't say Errey manufactures his own success.

He works extremely hard to succeed on the ice, and he deserves every credit for making the most of his opportunities last season. And he plays an important role on that line, doing the dirty work at both ends of the ice.

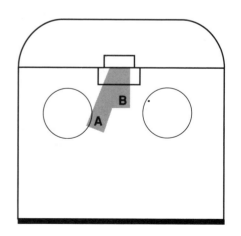

RANDY GILHEN

Yrs. of NHL service: 2
Born: Zweibrucken, West Germany; June 13, 1963
Position: Left wing
Height: 5-10
Weight: 190
Uniform no.: 39
Shoots: left

Career Statistics:

GP	G	A	TP	PIM
81	8	6	14	53

1988-89 statistics:

GP	G	A	TP	+/-	PIM	PP	SH	GW	GT	S	PCT
64	5	3	8	-24	38	0	1	1	0	76	6.6

LAST SEASON

Games played, point totals and PIM mark were all career highs. He was sidelined with a shoulder injury. Plus/minus was the club's fourth worst, third among forwards.

THE FINESSE GAME

Gilhen has some finesse skills he can bring to bear. He's primarily a fourth-line checking type with a strong skating stride that helps make him relentless in pursuit of the puck. He's can deliver some speed if given enough room to take off, but he is otherwise a heavy skater.

He gets a fairly good read of the ice when the play is ahead of him, so he can be a good forechecker and penalty killer. He lacks exceptional hand skills, so he'll have to be an opportunistic scorer —preying on loose pucks near the goal.

Randy does have a heavy slap shot, but he takes too long getting it off.

THE PHYSICAL GAME

As indicated by his skating, strength and a degree of power are what Gilhen brings to the rink. He can't be said to be a physical force, because he lacks the skill to consistently check physically, but he'll take the body along the boards. He also has the strength to get his shot away while being checked.

THE INTANGIBLES

He's strictly a penalty killer and fourth line player. He adds some versatility (and helps his own cause) by playing all three forward positions, but Gilhen is not very effective because he lacks the ability to produce.

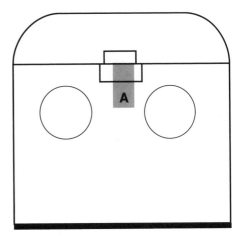

DAVE HANNAN

Yrs. of NHL service: 5
Born: Sudbury, Ontario, Canada; November 26, 1961
Position: Center
Height: 5-10
Weight: 185
Uniform no.: 32
Shoots: left

Career statistics:

GP	G	A	TP	PIM
406	69	99	168	573

1988-89 statistics:

GP	G	A	TP	+/-	PIM	PP	SH	GW	GT	S	PCT
72	10	20	30	-12	157	2	1	3	0	72	13.9

LAST SEASON

Point total was three-season high. Re-acquired by Pittsburgh in Waiver Draft. Suffered early season hip injury.

THE FINESSE GAME

Hannan is an average skater, meaning that he possesses neither outstandingly good or outstandingly poor speed, agility or quickness. He succeeds more by effort than by skill, but he can fill a role as a fourth-line forward or checker.

He's not very skilled in playmaking, lacking both the hand skills and the hockey sense to make this part of the game work. He is reading the play a little better, but Hannan's foot skills aren't developed enough for him to take real advantage of what his modest ice vision shows him.

He doesn't handle the puck real well, so Hannan will have to have time and space to make his plays. His checking can create some loose pucks, but his shot lacks the quick release that might gain him some goals.

Because of his eye/hand coordination, Hannan is good on faceoffs. When he's in the lineup, he'll take the majority of defensive zone draws.

THE PHYSICAL GAME

Hannan can dig the puck out of the corners and he has no fear about bumping people, which is the strongest aspect of his game. Hannan will use his body to make the play and is unafraid to hit or be hit. He plays bigger than his size, making the most of what he has.

THE INTANGIBLES

Dave doesn't have the natural ability to score, but because of his attitude and work ethic, the players have a lot of respect for him. More of a leader than a follower, he's an extremely hard worker. His attitude has kept him in the NHL, but his modest skills may very well have him finishing the season — perhaps even starting it — in some place other than Pittsburgh.

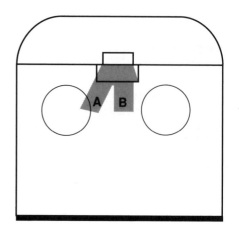

330

RANDY HILLIER

Yrs. of NHL service: 8
Born: Toronto, Ontario, Canada; March 30, 1960
Position: Defenseman
Height: 6-1
Weight: 186
Uniform no.: 23
Shoots: right

Career statistics:

GP	G	A	TP	PIM
415	11	95	106	744

1988-89 statistics:

GP	G	A	TP	+/-	PIM	PP	SH	GW	GT	S	PCT
68	1	23	24	-4	141	0	1	0	0	37	2.7

LAST SEASON

Games played total was five season high, despite being sidelined with groin and rib injuries.

THE FINESSE GAME

There isn't a lot of skill Randy brings to his finesse game, mostly because the NHL game still moves too fast for him — even after 400 games. His hockey sense and anticipation are no better than fair on his best days, which means Hillier is handicapped in both his defense and his offense.

Defensively, he is forced to react to the opposition instead of forcing the opposition to react to him (and Hillier's sub-par skating doesn't help either). For Hillier, a successful defensive play means a forward steered wide of the net.

In making the transition to offense, Hillier must have time and space. His passing — when divorced from the pressure of forechecking — isn't bad; he does have some touch. But once under game pressure, Randy's lack of vision and anticipation means his passes have to be rushed; that's where turnovers result.

He doesn't carry the puck much, which is smart because he doesn't have great puckhandling skill. He contributes very little from the offensive blue line, and he shoots the puck almost never.

THE PHYSICAL GAME

Hillier makes the most of his size and strength, working the corners and clearing the net with fairly good effectiveness. He's a little mean (as his PIM total indicates), but he is a one-dimensional player in that he won't make plays after taking out the man.

THE INTANGIBLES

He's got a good attitude, he's coachable and he works hard, but what you see with Hillier is what you get. He's no better than a sixth defenseman, and that status — along with his propensity toward injury — make him dispensable.

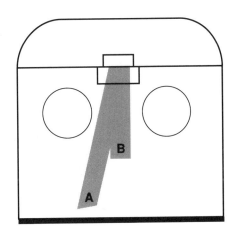

JIM JOHNSON

Yrs. of NHL service: 4
Born: New Hope, Minn., USA; August 9, 1962
Position: Defenseman
Height: 6-1
Weight: 190
Uniform no.: 6
Shoots: left

Career statistics:

GP	G	A	TP	PIM
291	11	77	88	483

1988-89 statistics:

GP	G	A	TP	+/-	PIM	PP	SH	GW	GT	S	PCT
76	2	14	16	7	163	1	0	0	0	70	2.9

LAST SEASON

Games played and all point totals second lowest of career. PIM total was career high. Plus/minus was second best among defensemen, fifth best overall.

THE FINESSE GAME

Johnson has improved his skills so that he is above what might be considered the NHL's average. His skating is good and Jim has the mobility necessary to play a challenging type of defense. While not tremendously agile, Johnson does have the foot speed and lateral ability to step up and force the puck carrier. He won't take chances in challenging, so Johnson will primarily play a defensive angle game (forcing the play wide).

Johnson won't contribute much from the offensive blue line because of his defensive posture, and that includes even shots on goal. His shot isn't bad (Johnson gets it to the net low and with power — ideal for tip-ins), but because Jim is always falling back to defense he averages less than a single shot per game. He doesn't forecheck at the offensive line, and he won't generally join the play as a fourth attacker. He remains almost totally defensively oriented, so he won't contribute much from the blue line. His shot is improved — more accurate and more powerful — but he still doesn't shoot enough, so much so that he can actually take away from the Pens' offense and not just not add to it.

His puckhandling ability is probably the weakest of his finesse skills, but Johnson makes the most of it by not taking chances. He gets rid of the puck as soon as possible, and only once in a very great while will he be forced into turnovers.

THE PHYSICAL GAME

Johnson has the size and strength necessary to play an effective physical game, and Jim enjoys doing so. He's generally aggressive without being stupid, though he did spend far more time in the box this year

than in previous seasons, and that smart play makes his physical play more valuable.

Johnson willingly sacrifices his body by blocking shots, but he also does the less spectacular grunt work by taking out opposing forwards in front of the net and on the boards. His strength and reach allow him to move forwards off the puck, or keep the puck himself to make the play.

THE INTANGIBLES

Johnson is Pittsburgh's best defensive defenseman, so there's no need to complain about his lack of offense. He's got an excellent work ethic, powered by his positive attitude, determination and heart. He brings these things to bear in his all-out performances in practise and in games.

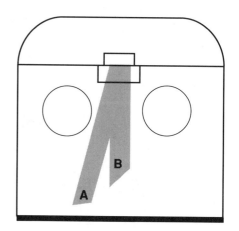

JIM KYTE

Yrs. of NHL service: 6
Born: Ottawa, Ontario, Canada; March 21, 1964
Position: Defenseman
Height: 6-5
Weight: 210
Uniform no.: 6
Shoots: left

Career Statistics:

GP	G	A	TP	PIM
399	11	25	36	772

1988-89 statistics:

GP	G	A	TP	+/-	PIM	PP	SH	GW	GT	S	PCT
74	3	9	12	-25	190	0	0	0	0	56	5.4

LAST SEASON

Games played, assist and point totals were career highs. PIM total was third highest on club, second among defensemen and a career high. Plus/minus was club's third worst.

THE FINESSE GAME

There really isn't one — and that's not meant in disrespect to the work Kyte's put in to improve his abilities. He has improved his skating speed and balance to become more mobile, but Jim can do little else but keep up with his teammates or the opposition.

He doesn't handle the puck all that well, so his play is going to have to be the simple one off the boards and out of the zone — as quickly as possible. He is little of a factor offensively, rarely becoming an attacker and rarely even following the play in an offensive mode, though he does have a good slap shot from the point. He'll be the first defenseman to fall back.

THE PHYSICAL GAME

Kyte must play a physical game to be effective, and we'll go one step further — he must fight in order to stay in the NHL, because he isn't skilled enough to survive just on banging bodies along the boards (if he can catch them to begin with).

He makes good use of his size and strength in front of his own net. He's mean defending the crease, especially while penalty killing. As a fighter, he can be one of the League's better pugilists.

BUT ...

THE INTANGIBLES

Jim is a big, big question mark because he doesn't want to fight any more. And without discussing the moral or ethical value of that stance *outside* the NHL, *inside* the NHL he doesn't have enough talent to play — and not for lack of trying.

He's worked very hard to improve his skills but, at age 25, they're not going to get any better. What got him to the NHL is his toughness and that's what will keep him here, but Jim has lost the mental edge necessary to succeed as a fighter. He may very well end the season outside a Jets uniform.

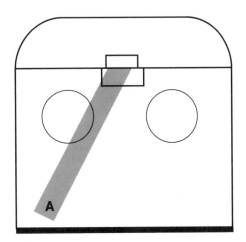

MARIO LEMIEUX

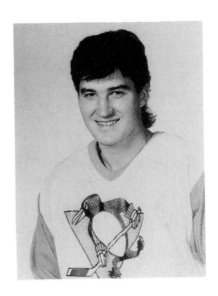

Yrs. of NHL service: 5
Born: Montreal, Quebec, Canada; October 5, 1965
Position: Center
Height: 6-4
Weight: 210
Uniform no.: 66
Shoots: right

Career statistics:

GP	G	A	TP	PIM
368	300	415	715	346

1988-89 statistics:

GP	G	A	TP	+/-	PIM	PP	SH	GW	GT	S	PCT
76	85	114	199	41	100	31	13	8	1	313	27.2

LAST SEASON

Led NHL in goals, assists, points, power play goals, shorthanded goals and first goals. Was sixth in NHL in game winners, fourth in shots on goal. All point and PIM totals were career highs. He led club in plus/minus. Was sidelined early in season with wrist/fore-arm injury.

THE FINESSE GAME

There is nothing Mario cannot do better, finesse-wise, than almost every player on the planet. His puck handling ability is probably the best of his skills, and he is undoubtedly the NHL's best one-on-one player. While his size and reach are responsible for great parts of all his stick skills, to lay his success solely at their doors is to de-emphasize his touch and pure hand skill.

Lemieux teases defenders with the puck, with his soft hands cradling the puck on the end of his stick. But his hand and arm strength are such that he can do anything with the puck regardless of traffic or his own body position. He does all this at any speed.

His phenomenal passing ability puts the puck anywhere at any time, in any way necessary — that's what we mean by touch. But his hands don't operate on their own; Lemieux's incredible hockey sense is the key to his playmaking ability. His anticipation, vision and superb feel for the game and its opportunities are second only to Wayne Gretzky.

Overall, he's a better finisher than Wayne. Mario is a remarkable scorer who will beat you in any way possible, shooting and scoring from anywhere, with any shot — regardless of traffic, or opening. He's excellent around the net because of his reach and hand skills and also likes to take the bad angle shot for the far corner. He's deadly on breakaways.

His skating often takes a beating from critics, but mistakenly so. He has exceptional — superior — balance, and his fluid skating stride takes him away from the opposition — and toward loose pucks — excellently.

THE PHYSICAL GAME

The end boards are 10 feet from the goal-line. With his feet touching the end boards, Mario can still wrap the puck into the net; what does that say for physical ability?

He uses his body extremely well against his opponents, using his hips and long, thin torso to squirt free from the opposition along the boards or to avoid a hit. Lemieux is not strong in terms of pure muscular strength, but put him on the boards and he'll move people through balance. Even if he can't, his hand and arm strength is enough for him to make plays.

On the negative side, Lemieux is far more liberal with his stick than a player of his talent — than a player of *any* talent — should be. In particular, he slashes and hacks with impunity when he's being checked closely or is otherwise frustrated.

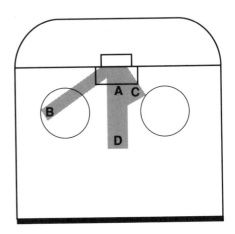

THE INTANGIBLES

A paradox: You can't score 199 points without working, but Lemieux back-slid last season from the work ethic and intensity he'd developed in 1987-88. He shied away not only from some of the physical play he'd done two seasons ago (which greatly loosened up his finesse game), but also from the demonstration of work that convinced some of his critics of his maturity (us included). In the meantime, it's worth noting that in this past season — his best ever in all point categories — Mario's goal total would be third-best on the Gretzky list, his assist total seventh best and his point total fifth best.

He's also shown that — especially in the third period — if he's having a tough game, Mario will just throw in the towel. When he got slashed by David Shaw? Third period and Lemieux was gone from the game — but he wasn't too hurt to challenge some of the Madison Square Garden fans as he left the ice. In Game Four of the Patrick Division Final against Philadelphia, Lemieux got pounded all night and finally left the game — in the third period — after running into teammate Randy Cunneyworth. How hurt was Mario? So much so that he scored eight points in Game Five.

Finally, no one dives like Lemieux — especially at home. Needless to say, that acting by the man acclaimed as the League's best player gains him no respect from officials or the opposition. Put the diving together with the stickwork and the question many in the NHL ask is, "If he's the best, he wouldn't need to do all that other stuff, would he?"

The point is this: Mario Lemieux is the NHL's most talented player, a man who can do anything he wants to on the ice. If he wanted to, he could score 250 points. But because he is satisfied to accept what his prodigious talent produces — rather than working to be his best at all times — we find ourselves forced to say that Mario has a way to go before his total package approaches — let alone surpasses — that of Wayne Gretzky.

TROY LONEY

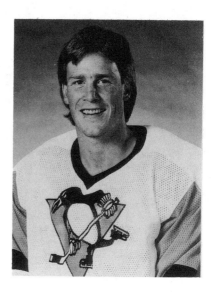

Yrs. of NHL service: 4
Born: Bow Island, Alberta, Canada;
September 21, 1963
Position: Left wing
Height: 6-3
Weight: 205
Uniform no.: 24
Shoots: left

Career statistics:

GP	G	A	TP	PIM
263	36	43	79	503

1988-89 statistics:

GP	G	A	TP	+/-	PIM	PP	SH	GW	GT	S	PCT
69	10	6	16	-5	165	0	0	1	1	90	11.1

LAST SEASON

Games played and PIM totals were career highs; goal total tied career best. His PIM total was second-highest among forwards.

THE FINESSE GAME

Troy is not a gifted finesse player, probably topping out as average — at best — in this area. He has no real mobility to speak, lacking the quickness and agility to skate with anyone of average NHL ability.

Because he possesses neither the instincts nor the hands, Loney is no better than fair at passing the puck and using his teammates. On top of that, he generally makes his plays with his head down. That lack of skill extends to his puckhandling ability.

Troy is simply not a scorer. He doesn't get into scoring position, doesn't have the hands to finesse the puck in traffic and doesn't shoot quickly enough. He launches a lot of shots *at* the net, but very few on the net.

THE PHYSICAL GAME

This is the part of the game where Loney makes his — uh — impact. He's got great size and pretty good strength, and he'll use both anywhere on the ice. He's particularly effective when grinding along the boards, although that effectiveness is mitigated by his lack of hand skills.

He willingly sacrifices his body, and that's best articulated when he kills penalties — where Troy blocks shots with abandon.

Despite what the PIM total might indicate, Loney is not primarily a fighter.

THE INTANGIBLES

Troy is one of those "if wishing could make it so" players. He gets a lot of responsibility from Coach Gene Ubriaco, and Loney rewards that faith and confidence with 100 percent effort all the time; that makes Troy a leader on and off the ice — despite the fact that his talent dictates he won't rise above third-line NHL duty.

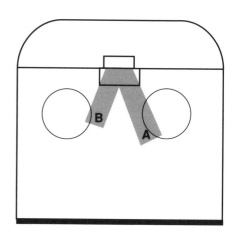

ANDREW MCBAIN

Yrs. of NHL service: 6
Born: Toronto, Ontario, Canada; February 18, 1965
Position: Right wing
Height: 6-1
Weight: 195
Uniform no.: 20
Shoots: right

Career Statistics:

GP	G	A	TP	PIM
408	101	129	230	421

1988-89 statistics:

GP	G	A	TP	+/-	PIM	PP	SH	GW	GT	S	PCT
80	37	40	77	-35	71	20	1	3	2	180	20.6

LAST SEASON

Games played and all point totals were career highs. He finished first on the club in power play goals (sixth in the NHL), second in goals and third in points. His plus/minus was the club's worst, fourth worst in the NHL.

THE FINESSE GAME

The greatest portion of McBain's NHL success has come on the power play: 40 of the 69 goals he's scored over the last two seasons have come on the power play and just 28 at even strength. There are two reasons for that: his skating and his shot.

Andy's skating is no better than good, marked more by strength on his skates than it is by quickness or agility. His strength has given him some degree of speed off the wing, and his ability to move with the puck at that speed does force the defense to back up. But, for the most part, McBain's skating doesn't strike fear into the opposition — and it certainly doesn't get him into the clear in 5-on-5 situations.

But when the ice opens up on the power play Andy uses his strength afoot to plant himself near the net, where he exploits loose pucks with his quick shot.

Because he's not a creative player, McBain isn't much of a playmaker. He's improved his ability to see and react at the NHL level, but the bulk of his assists are going to come on the power play.

His defense is, obviously, atrocious. His skating and playreading are part of that, but McBain doesn't try awful hard either.

THE PHYSICAL GAME

In order to succeed, McBain must use his good size and strength consistently. He has to play aggressively, but he's reluctant to do so. For a straight-ahead player with size, that's a grievous flaw. He is a one-play player, making a hit if he can but having very little idea what to do afterward.

THE INTANGIBLES

Consistency of scoring is a factor here: McBain scored the less-than-awesome total of 17 even-strength goals, just five of those in his last 38 games. He has the potential to be a well-rounded player, but he must improve his flaws to do so. Given the fact that he's entering his seventh season, one is inclined to believe that what one sees is what one gets.

He's a streaky player, but his attitude has come a long way in the last four years (when it was the club's poorest). A better work ethic would make him a better player.

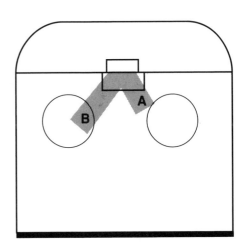

DAN QUINN

Yrs. of NHL service: 6
Born: Ottawa, Ontario, Canada; June 1, 1965
Position: Center
Height: 5-11
Weight: 180
Uniform no.: 10
Shoots: left

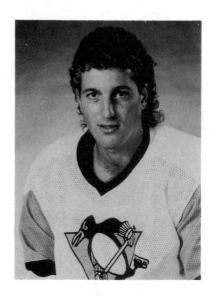

Career statistics:

GP	G	A	TP	PIM
435	174	261	435	292

1988-89 statistics:

GP	G	A	TP	+/-	PIM	PP	SH	GW	GT	S	PCT
79	34	60	94	-37	102	16	0	4	0	200	17.0

LAST SEASON

Games played total was second highest of career; ditto goal total. Assist and point totals were career bests. Finished third on the Pens in goals, power play goals and shots on goal, fourth in assists and points. His plus/minus was the club's worst, second worst in the NHL.

THE FINESSE GAME

Dan is a very good finesse player, with his skating and hockey sense tops among his finesse skills. His skating is excellent in all areas, especially those that comprise mobility: balance and quickness. He's got great foot speed and can make moves in any direction — and at any speed — within a stride. That gives him great lateral movement and, while he also has the strength needed for breakaway speed, Dan is more a darter than a rocket.

His hockey sense makes his skating more effective, as his anticipation and vision allow him to lead his teammates into openings or to exploit those openings (courtesy of his quickness) himself.

Of course, his hand skills are largely responsible for his ability to make plays. Quinn has great hands with a real soft touch and he's able to make his plays — weathering feathering passes or carrying the puck himself — at full speed.

Because his skills get him into the open quickly, Quinn is an opportunist at goal scoring. He'll get those loose pucks because of his quickness, and that skill combines with his sense to put him in the clear on the power play. He gets his shot away quickly, and shoots frequently.

THE PHYSICAL GAME

Quinn has incorporated a willingness to accept contact into his game, and that has helped him succeed (his finesse skills let him work favorably in traffic — especially his balance). He does not, however, initiate a great deal of contact, so Quinn will most likely be when the puck squirts free. If he is caught in traffic, the opposition will most likely take the puck from him, because he is not overwhelmingly strong.

THE INTANGIBLES

Quinn didn't have a great deal of consistency in his game last season: just six goals in his final 26 games — and just four of those at even strength. His defense continues to be woeful and, while he made a great show of attempting to go after David Shaw after the latter slashed Mario Lemieux, Quinn isn't a great (or greatly liked — he cuts up his teammates while on the ice, in full view and hearing of the opposition) team guy.

His 94-point season is far from out of character, but of what value is it when his minus-37 rating turns 94 points into 57 points; that's a pretty average total for an essentially one-way player, especially since he's not even facing the opposition's best checkers.

Something's got to give here, and it just may be Quinn out of a Pittsburgh uniform.

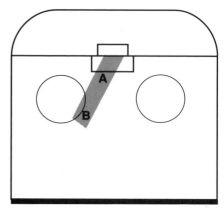

KEVIN STEVENS

Yrs. of NHL service: 1
Born: Brockton, Mass., USA; April 15, 1965
Position: Left wing
Height: 6-3
Weight: 220
Uniform no.: 25
Shoots: left

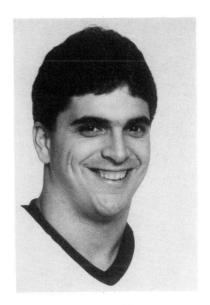

Career statistics:

GP	G	A	TP	PIM
40	17	5	22	27

1988-89 statistics:

GP	G	A	TP	+/-	PIM	PP	SH	GW	GT	S	PCT
24	12	3	15	-8	19	4	0	3	0	52	23.1

LAST SEASON

Joined club from International Hockey League in January.

THE FINESSE GAME

Stevens is a talented finesse player whose game is — if you'll excuse the expression — powered by his all-around strength. He's not a fluid skater with great agility. Rather, Stevens succeeds because of his great skating strength. He's very difficult to slow down once he gets moving, and his leg strength makes him very effective in physical circumstances.

He's not tremendously talented in puckhandling, partly because his skating lacks the agility that good puckhandling needs for success, but Kevin minimizes that flaw by handling the puck only when necessary — like after bouncing someone off it in the corner.

Then Stevens will look to make a pass and head to the net, where he has the hand skills (very quick shot) to cash in from the crease. He'll get a lot of tip in and deflected goals.

His defense could use some help, and his entire all-around game will improve as he improves his ability to think and react at NHL speed.

THE PHYSICAL GAME

Stevens has tremendous physical potential — if he can keep himself in shape. He has great size and strength, but he ballooned to about 240 pounds before sticking with Pittsburgh last season, and he can't play at that weight.

His strength — both upper and lower body — makes him a good (with potential to be excellent) traffic player, and he's more likely than not to come out of a confrontation with the puck. He uses his good strength and balance to best effect by plugging the front of the net, especially on the power play. He can get shots off while being checked, and that's a credit to his arm, wrist and shoulder strength.

While he hits willingly, Kevin is not a fighter.

THE INTANGIBLES

Stevens came into his own with a fine playoff effort last season. He's one of those players who hasn't gotten a big buildup but, if he continues his progress (and we think he will), he'll be critical to Pittsburgh's future success.

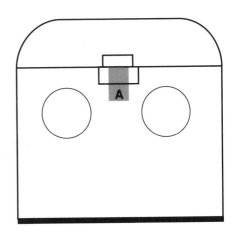

WENDELL YOUNG

Yrs. of NHL service: 2
Born: Halifax, N.S., Canada; August 1, 1963
Position: Goaltender
Height: 5-8
Weight: 185
Uniform no.: 1
Catches: left

Career statistics:

GP	MINS	G	SO	AVG	A	PIM
58	2,913	208	13	4.28	3	4

1988-89 statistics:

GP	MINS	AVG	W	L	T	SO	GA	SA	SAPCT	PIM
22	1,150	4.80	12	9	0	0	92	673	.863	4

LAST SEASON

Games played total tied career high, minutes played set career high. Missed time with early season leg injury.

THE PHYSICAL GAME

Young is a standup goaltender. He plays his angles well, but he has difficulty with clearing rebounds.

He is also weak when he is off his feet and flopping around. He does not move particularly well yet, but Wendell does have quick feet and a deceptive glove hand.

He handles the puck well when he is out of the net and can move it to his defensemen, but his lack of skating skill and balance shows up when he is unable to regain his stance quickly for a second save.

THE MENTAL GAME

Young has got a mental toughness that allows him to bounce back from bad goals or games. He holds his concentration well and has demonstrated good anticipation, making him difficult to beat in the bang-bang plays around the net.

Young has the ability to respond to presure and make the big save and nothing gets him down. If he keeps that attitude, he'll flourish.

THE INTANGIBLES

Young is a good, young goaltender, and he seems to have settled in behind Tom Barrasso. He's shown well at his previous levels, but he is 26 years old. That's old to — essentially — start an NHL career, so Young may very well be consigned to backup duty for the remainder of his career.

ZARLEY ZALAPSKI

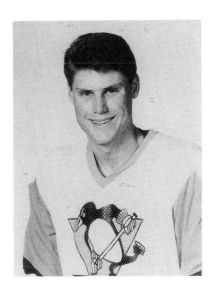

Yrs. of NHL service: 2
Born: Edmonton, Alberta, Canada; April 22, 1968
Position: Defenseman
Height: 6-1
Weight: 204
Uniform no.: 33
Shoots: left

Career statistics:

GP	G	A	TP	PIM
73	15	41	56	64

1988-89 statistics:

GP	G	A	TP	+/-	PIM	PP	SH	GW	GT	S	PCT
58	12	33	45	9	57	5	1	2	1	95	12.6

LAST SEASON

First full NHL season. Plus-9 was best among Pens' defensemen. Missed 20 games with a knee injury.

THE FINESSE GAME

Zalapski has many finesse skills, all of which point toward the excellent end of the scale. His skating is the best of his skills, powered by his strength and balance — both of which are exceptional. His strength gives him excellent speed and acceleration, and his balance gives him great agility. Together with his foot speed, they combine to make Zalapski an extremely mobile defenseman. He makes his speed more effective by moderating it, and he uses his quickness and lateral movement to get to the loose pucks or into the openings.

His hockey sense — both defensively and offensively — is excellent. He cuts off or re-directs many opposition passes once the play is established in the Pittsburgh zone, but Zalapski also challenges well at his blue line.

His transition game is excellent, and he'll turn the play around very quickly with a rush himself or the appropriate breakout pass. He moves well with the puck at all speeds, controlling it well in traffic. He joins the play as a fourth attacker (going as far as the opposing net when he can). He passes extremely well to both sides, and Zalapski excels at finding the open man.

Though forechecking and containing the puck well at the offensive blue line, Zalapski could do better by being a little more selfish. He has a — not great — shot from the blue line, low and on net, so it's good for deflections and rebound goals.

THE PHYSICAL GAME

Zalapski holds his own in the trenches, but he's not a banging type of defender. He has good strength and size (both of which should improve as his body matures), and his balance and hand skills will help him win many crease and corner wars.

But because he's going to provide a finesse game, it's not necessary for Zarley to overwhelm people — only to overpower them and take the puck.

THE INTANGIBLES

Zalapski is a game breaker and a franchise player, with all the talent necessary to become one of the NHL's top defensemen. He's dedicated and intense, and he'll benefit from the presence of Paul Coffey (in that Zalapski won't be expected — as Ranger rival Brian Leetch is — to provide offense for an entire team).

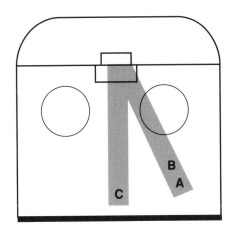

QUEBEC
NORDIQUES

LINE COMBINATIONS
ALAIN COTE-WALT PODDUBNY
GAETAN DUCHESNE-JOE SAKIC-IIRO JARVI
MICHEL GOULET-PETER STASTNY
JEFF JACKSON-PAUL GILLIS

DEFENSE PAIRINGS
STEVEN FINN-JEFF BROWN
JARI GRONSTRAND-RANDY MOLLER
ROBERT PICARD-CURTIS LESCHYSHYN

GOALTENDERS
MARIO GOSSELIN
RON TUGNUTT

OTHER PLAYERS
MARC FORTIER — Center
LANE LAMBERT — Right wing

SECOND UNIT:
MARIO MAROIS — Defenseman

POWER PLAY

FIRST UNIT:
MICHEL GOULET-JOE SAKIC-IIRO JARVI
JEFF BROWN-RANDY MOLLER

GOULET takes the left faceoff circle, JARVI the right circle. BROWN is at the left boards and MOLLER at the right side with SAKIC at the blue line. BROWN and GOULET shots are the primary objectives, but SAKIC will shoot to have the forwards get the rebounds.

A second formation has PETER STASTNY working behind the net and SAKIC on the left point. The left wing will plug the net and the right wing (most usually the now-departed ANTON STASTNY) poised for a shot at the right circle. WALT PODDUBNY also sees extensive power play time, usually camped to the right of the goalie, working the left wing side. ROBERT PICARD fills in defensively.

Last season Quebec's power play was GOOD, scoring 85 goals in 392 opportunities (21.7 percent, sixth overall).

PENALTY KILLING

FIRST UNIT:
PAUL GILLIS-JOE SAKIC
ROBERT PICARD-CURTIS LESCHYSHYN

SECOND UNIT:
GAETAN DUCHESNE-JEFF JACKSON

The penalty killers are generally unaggressive in the offensive and neutral zones, though they will force the puck carrier at the blue line. Otherwise, a fairly strict box predominates.

Last season Quebec's penalty killing was FAIR, allowing 82 goals in 385 shorthanded situations (78.7 percent, 13th overall).

CRUCIAL FACEOFFS
PAUL GILLIS

JEFF BROWN

Yrs. of NHL service: 3
Born: Ottawa, Ontario, Canada; April 30, 1966
Position: Defenseman
Height: 6-1
Weight: 202
Uniform no.: 22
Shoots: right

Career statistics:

GP	G	A	TP	PIM
208	47	107	154	148

1988-89 statistics:

GP	G	A	TP	+/-	PIM	PP	SH	GW	GT	S	PCT
78	21	47	68	-22	62	13	1	1	0	276	7.6

LAST SEASON

Games played tied and all point totals set career highs. He finished third on the club in scoring (seventh among all NHL defenders), second in assists and tied for second in power play goals, and first in SOG total. His plus/minus rating was the club's fifth worst.

THE FINESSE GAME

Jeff's combination of power, quickness and strength give him speed, acceleration and outstanding lateral ability — all combine to make him an excellent skater. He can jump into an opening or change direction within a stride, and his lateral movement is especially pronounced when he's skating backward and controlling the puck at the offensive blue line.

He's an excellent puckhandler, and Brown loves to carry the puck from the Quebec zone and lead a Nordiques attack, charging to — and then blasting a shot from — the offensive right faceoff circle.

Brown sees the play well when it is ahead of him, so he can get the puck to an open teammate in any zone. He uses his outstanding skating ability to control play in the offensive zone (though he could improve his judgement on pinching in), and combines his containment ability with his vision and anticipation to lead a teammate into an as-yet-unopen opening.

Brown has a good shot from the blue line, low and hard, and he also likes to charge the net on give-and-gos.

Jeff's defense is still questionable, in that he succeeds more on talent than he does on sense — forcing plays by charging at puck carriers to create turnovers — instead of making the safe defensive play. Jeff also has a concentration flaw, becoming hypnotized by the puck rather than covering his side of the net.

THE PHYSICAL GAME

Brown doesn't really have a physical game. His skills would allow him to take the body well, but Jeff sometimes just kinda gets in the way. Of course, any degree of physical play is amplified by his terrific ability to make a play out of a confrontation. Otherwise, his play in the corners and the front of the net is no better (and could be worse) than average.

He is able to use his body to protect the puck from the opposition, particularly at the offensive blue line where Brown is very good at keeping the puck away from defenders.

THE INTANGIBLES

As previously in his Quebec career, Brown ran into some differences of opinion with management regarding his attitude. He needs some more maturity (not surprising; he's only been in the League three seasons), and he especially needs to learn to work hard each shift —even though he can get by on talent.

Jeff made his NHL debut under Michel Bergeron, but played just 44 games that season (1986-87). How he deals with Bergeron, and Bergeron with him, is worth watching.

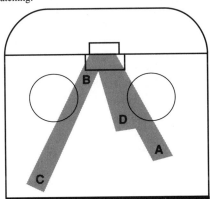

JOE CIRELLA

Yrs. of NHL service: 7
Born: Hamilton, Ontario, Canada; May 9, 1963
Position: Defenseman
Height: 6-2
Weight: 205
Uniform no.: 2
Shoots: right

Career statistics:

GP	G	A	TP	PIM
503	50	159	209	938

1988-89 statistics:

GP	G	A	TP	+/-	PIM	PP	SH	GW	GT	S	PCT
80	3	19	22	-14	155	0	1	1	0	84	3.6

LAST SEASON

Played all 80 games for second consecutive season. Goal and point totals were all full-season career lows. His plus/minus was second worst among defensemen.

THE FINESSE GAME

Cirella stands middle-of-the-road in his abilities and their applications. He is a limited skater with some agility and forward quickness that is offset by lesser abilities backward — especially in his pivots to his right. His skating is further limited by his high center-of-gravity. Joe's extremely top heavy, and when he gets hit in the shoulders he'll be knocked off his feet — certainly out of his skating stance — more often than not.

Cirella can carry the puck well but, because his vision and playmaking abilities are limited, he's better off moving the puck from his zone with a breakout pass than he is in becoming part of the attack. He doesn't read the play coming at him particularly well, and a strong forechecking effort makes him hurry his passes.

He's talented enough to take passes well in the offensive zone, and Cirella shoots the puck well while in motion. That makes his shot more effective, with his wrist shot more of a threat than his slap shot.

THE PHYSICAL GAME

Cirella has decent size and strength and is willing to use them (though far more so against smaller opponents), but his lack of balance can sometimes undermine his physical intentions.

He has the ability to do fairly well in front of his own net, and he can out-muscle his share of forwards in the corners. He's not especially aggressive, but Joe is not intimidated by the League's tough guys. He'll fight for himself or a teammate when necessary.

THE INTANGIBLES

What you see is pretty much what you get with Joe Cirella. He'll pick up a few points, lead a few rushes and take some dumb penalties. Middle-of-the-road, as we said.

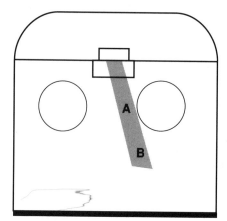

ALAIN COTE

Yrs. of NHL service: 9
Born: Matane, Quebec, Canada; May 3, 1957
Position: Left wing
Height: 5-10
Weight: 200
Uniform no.: 19
Shoots: left

Career statistics:

GP	G	A	TP	PIM
696	156	190	346	383

1988-89 statistics:

GP	G	A	TP	+/-	PIM	PP	SH	GW	GT	S	PCT
55	2	8	10	-1	14	0	1	0	0	31	6.5

LAST SEASON

Games played total was eight season low, all point totals were career lows. Plus/minus was second best among forwards, third best on the club.

THE FINESSE GAME

Where skating and hockey sense once commanded Cote's game, only the hockey sense remains. Alain is still a good skater, but a dozen years of pro hockey have taken their toll. What remains of his once-speedy style is skating strength and balance; he never had much agility.

But his sense, vision and anticipation are strong enough to counter Cote's diminished skating — sometimes. He gets an exceptional read of the opponent's play and can combine his mental skills with his skating to be a good penalty killer and checking forward. In essence, though, the game has become too fast for him.

When turning to offense Alain handles the puck fairly well, and he uses his stickhandling ability especially well to rag the puck as a penalty killer. He combines his decent hand skills with his sense to be a good passer, but his role as a checker and mucker minimizes that skill.

He isn't a big goal scorer, so any goals he gets will have to be of the opportunistic, loose-puck-around-the-net variety. He does keep the opposition honest by shooting from farther out, but to little effect.

THE PHYSICAL GAME

Cote has always been a physical player, and his insistent pounding has made him an old 32. Though he was never a thunderous hitter Alain's balance always worked in his favor, keeping him vertical and ready to continue the play after checking. He makes his physical play better by not taking penalties.

He is also one of the few forwards in the League willing to give up his body to block shots.

THE INTANGIBLES

Long the best unknown defensive forward, Cote may well be beyond the twilight of his career. His drive, work ethic and professionalism make him an example to the younger players and, should he retire, the Nords will lose a fine, character player.

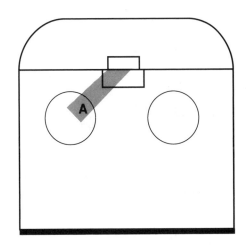

LUCIEN DEBLOIS

Yrs. of NHL service: 12
Born: Joliette, Quebec, Canada; June 21, 1957
Position: Center
Height: 5-11
Weight: 204
Uniform no.: 23
Shoots: right

Career statistics:

GP	G	A	TP	PIM
806	219	241	460	685

1988-89 statistics:

GP	G	A	TP	+/-	PIM	PP	SH	GW	GT	S	PCT
73	9	24	33	-6	107	0	0	2	0	117	7.7

LAST SEASON

Assist and point totals were five-season highs. He missed seven games with a bicep muscle tear.

THE FINESSE GAME

Strength and balance, rather than speed and fluidity, mark Deblois's skating game. His ability to recognize plays and his willingness to get where he has to be (as opposed to speed) serve to make him a pretty effective checking center.

Offensively, Deblois's game is almost non-existent. Because he generally mucks up and down, he will almost never beat a defender one-on-one. Lucien can control the puck fairly well, but he's neither exceedingly intelligent nor creative in the offensive zone Deblois doesn't know how to continue a play after he's gotten rid of the puck, so he'll make the first play he can see.

He doesn't have a great offensive touch around the net and will need to be in close proximity of the goal to score. He's got a hard shot that he fires from close in, and he'll get most of his goals on second efforts and rebounds.

THE PHYSICAL GAME

Deblois plays hard but clean, and he takes his man out well along the boards. He's also strong enough to hold his man out of the play when necessary, and he complements his physical play with a small degree of ability in making plays off the boards.

He is successful because of good upper body strength and balance on his skates, and can hit hard enough to hurt.

THE INTANGIBLES

As with last season, Deblois will be operating on a new contract — if he operates in the NHL at all. Despite the plus/minus, he was a positive defensive player, and he filled in excellently when Jan Erixon was injured.

But the Rangers have a lot of players to audition at the center spot, and that surplus may spell the end of Lucien's stay in New York. Of note, by the way — the Rangers won every game in which Deblois scored a goal.

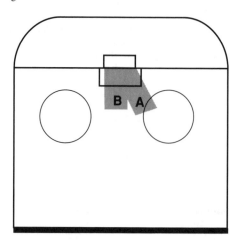

346

STEVEN FINN

Yrs. of NHL service: 3
Born: Laval, Quebec, Canada; August 20, 1966
Position: Defenseman
Height: 6-0
Weight: 198
Uniform no.: 29
Shoots: left

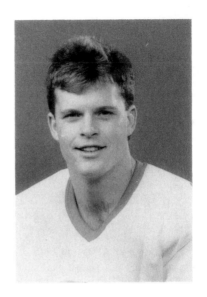

Career statistics:

GP	G	A	TP	PIM
205	7	19	26	501

1988-89 statistics:

GP	G	A	TP	+/-	PIM	PP	SH	GW	GT	S	PCT
77	2	6	8	-21	235	0	1	0	0	86	2.3

LAST SEASON

Games played and PIM marks were career highs, leading the club in the latter category.

THE FINESSE GAME

Finn is an average skater at the NHL level, not showing exceptional — or even above average — talent in any particular area of his skating. Right now, he'd be best described as competent. Still, he'll rush the puck when necessary — nothing fast or fancy but he does recognize the openings. He's also challenging the puck better in the neutral zone.

His growing NHL experience has helped him improve his puck movement skills in open ice, and he'll make that correct pass much of the time, but he has difficulty taking the puck off the boards when being checked and will turn over the puck at that time.

He's not an offensive player and won't contribute much at the blue line. His shot strength is average but his release knocks that down to less than average. Finn takes a long time getting it off because he likes to move to the center of the blue line for the shot.

In order to succeed defensively, Finn must not stray from his position — because he may not get back in time to thwart an opposing offensive thrust.

THE PHYSICAL GAME

Steven is a very aggressive player, and he does his best work in front of the Nordiques goal by punishing any opposing forward camped there. He takes the body well along the boards and he hits hard, but he doesn't follow through on his takeouts — with the result that the opposition sneaks back into the play.

He is also a more than willing fighter who backs down from no one.

THE INTANGIBLES

Finn has made some progress during his three seasons with Quebec, almost surprising considering now difficult it is to improve with a bad team. He brings some intelligence and determination to his game and he should continue to improve. He'll need to if he wants to remain in Quebec.

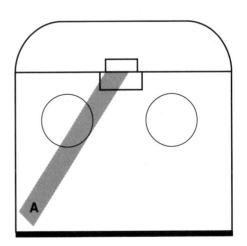

MARC FORTIER

Yrs. of NHL service: 2
Born: Sherbrooke, Quebec, Canada; February 26, 1966
Position: Center
Height: 6-0
Weight: 192
Uniform no.: 9
Shoots: right

Career statistics:

GP	G	A	TP	PIM
84	24	29	53	57

1988-89 statistics:

GP	G	A	TP	+/-	PIM	PP	SH	GW	GT	S	PCT
57	20	19	39	-18	45	2	2	2	1	90	22.2

LAST SEASON

Games played, all point and PIM totals were career highs. He missed three games with a shoulder injury. He led the club in shooting percentage.

THE FINESSE GAME

Hockey sense is what Fortier best offers in his game. He has puck smarts and knows how to do the simple yet effective offensive things, like keeping the puck and the rest of the ice on his forehand so he can give and take passes more easily. He keeps his head up in the offensive zone and sees the play around him (as well as avoiding hits because he sees the enemy coming), and his ability to react at NHL speed is improving.

The same high marks can't yet be applied to his skating, which must improve if he is to be a solid NHLer. Marc needs to improve his foot speed, and doing so would allow him to better use his sense (both offensively and defensively — that plus/minus rating is no accident) and his hand skills — that extra quickness would gain him an extra moment in which to make his play.

He has good hands, and his soft touch means he can work from around the net in a better than opportunistic way; he doesn't have to wait for a loose puck and a lost goalie to score. Right now, he won't beat NHL goaltending from the distances.

THE PHYSICAL GAME

He has good size and is unafraid of contact, but Fortier does not play what would be considered a physical game. He hasn't gained any space for himself by banging bodies — but, of course, if his skating isn't good enough to get him near those bodies he can't hit them, now can he?

He has a fair degree of balance and strength on his feet, and those qualities are what allow him to function near the net.

THE INTANGIBLES

Marc has good potential, and he certainly proved offensive ability as a junior (201 points for Chicoutimi in 1986-87). Those are points the Nordiques could use, but Fortier's possible NHL improvement cannot have been helped by the instability behind the Quebec bench over the last year.

Add the fact that new coach Michel Bergeron is notoriously tough on young players, and Fortier may have another up-and-down season.

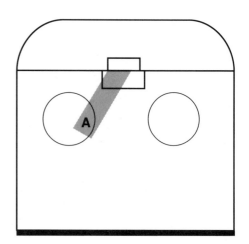

PAUL GILLIS

Yrs. of NHL service: 6
Born: Toronto, Ontario, Canada; December 31, 1963
Position: Center/right wing
Height: 5-11
Weight: 198
Uniform no.: 23
Shoots: left

Career statistics:

GP	G	A	TP	PIM
456	76	124	200	1,026

1988-89 statistics:

GP	G	A	TP	+/-	PIM	PP	SH	GW	GT	S	PCT
79	15	25	40	-14	163	5	0	1	0	97	15.5

LAST SEASON

Games played and goal totals were second highest of career. He finished second on the club in PIM total, first among forwards.

THE FINESSE GAME

Gillis's skating game reflects his game in general. He's a strong skater with a good pace (almost tireless), and he combines that strength with a dose of foot speed to become a good forechecker, defensive forward and penalty killer.

He augments his skating (and powers his game) with his anticipation, but Paul can't convert those two ingredients into a successful offensive game because he lacks the hand skills to do so.

Paul doesn't carry the puck exceptionally well, nor does he read the ice well in an offensive mode. His skating and checking will create a lot of opportunities because of the loose pucks he forces, but Gillis will have to be an opportunistic — and not artistic — scorer.

THE PHYSICAL GAME

He doesn't have great size, but don't tell Gillis size determines a successful physical game. Paul is very aggressive and hits everything he can get his body into, making him a very good corner and boards player (though he lacks the hand skills to capitalize totally on his efforts).

Because he forechecks and closes gaps so well, Gillis puts himself into position to use his good upper body strength and skating power to hit and drive through his bodychecks.

He has good eye/hand coordination, and is the team's primary faceoff man.

THE INTANGIBLES

Paul is an excellent team man, demonstrating his desire through his work ethic and intensity to be a leader for Quebec. His physical play sets a tone for the game and forces the Nords' opponents to back track — coach Michel Bergeron likes that, and he'll use Gillis in the way he once used Dale Hunter.

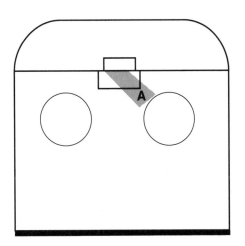

MICHEL GOULET

Yrs. of NHL service: 10
Born: Peribonqua, Quebec, Canada; April 21, 1960
Position: Left wing
Height: 6-1
Weight: 195
Uniform no.: 16
Shoots: left

Career statistics:

GP	G	A	TP	PIM
756	440	460	900	571

1988-89 statistics:

GP	G	A	TP	+/-	PIM	PP	SH	GW	GT	S	PCT
69	26	38	64	-20	67	11	0	2	0	162	16.0

LAST SEASON

Games played total tied career low. Goal, assist and point totals were second lowest of career. He missed 11 games with a knee injury and finished fourth in scoring and SOG total.

THE FINESSE GAME

Michel has always used his skating to key the rest of his finesse game, but his skating is — only naturally, after a decade of pro hockey — losing some of its snap. Where once his foot speed and balance gave him exceptional agility and lateral movement, Goulet has lost some of that ability — making him eminently catchable. And, since he'd really been more of a straight-ahead player than a shifty one, the loss of a step or two of speed is really telling.

Naturally then, because he doesn't get open as well as previously, his scoring totals diminish — his goal totals have fallen for seven seasons (and last season's knee injury isn't the sole reason for that). When delivered, his shots are still good. His wrist shot is as dangerous as his slap shot and he will charge the net for second effort goals. He shoots often and accurately, forcing the goaltender to make saves and is especially devastating on the power play.

Michel has always demonstrated unselfishness despite his goal-scoring ability. His soft hands control the puck well, and he'll make the pass to a free teammate instead of gambling against a defender himself. The anticipation that gets him in position to score helps him make those passes.

His defense has always mirrored his offense, and now more than ever he needs a linemate with the speed and desire to play defense.

THE PHYSICAL GAME

Michel has never played a physical game — the occasional bump inthe corner or charge through the traffic in the slot is the extent of his involvement with contact. His skating strength powers his drives to the net — and he'll accept the abuse while going there — but that's it.

He also has a temper and can sometimes be a little mean with his stick.

THE INTANGIBLES

His consistent performance over a half-dozen seasons made Goulet among the best — if not *the* best — left wingers in the business. But, as for many of his teammates, time and wear and tear are taking their tolls. He can continue to be important to the Nordiques but, in order to be a role model for the younger players, he must work at making consistent contributions — he scored just six goals in his last 24 games (only four at even strength).

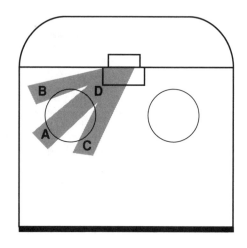

JARI GRONSTAND

Yrs. of NHL service: 3
Born: Tampere, Finland; November 14, 1962
Position: Defenseman
Height: 6-3
Weight: 197
Uniform no.: 5
Shoots: left

Career statistics:

GP	G	A	TP	PIM
134	5	20	25	104

1988-89 statistics:

GP	G	A	TP	+/-	PIM	PP	SH	GW	GT	S	PCT
25	1	3	4	-9	14	0	0	0	0	18	5.6

LAST SEASON

Acquired from New York (along with Walt Poddubny and Bruce Bell) in August 1988 in exchange for Norm Rochefort and Jason Lafreniere.He missed time with a broken cheekbone. Games played, assist and point totals were career lows.

THE FINESSE GAME

Gronstrand's finesse skills are good and improving, but are still not at a consistent NHL level. He skates well forward and has fairly good agility moving toward the offensive zone, but his backskating and turns are weak and need improvement.

Jari moves the puck well from the defensive zone because he has good hands and good vision, but he's not a real threat to rush the puck himself. He can handle the puck well enough when he skates, but Gronstrand is going to get the puck to the open man and then fall back defensively. He won't force an offensive play.

He does, however, follow the play up-ice and will contribute to a small degree at the offensive blue line but — as his shot and point totals indicate — Gronstrand is not a big offensive player.

He understands defensive angles well and uses them to his advantage in angling off the opposition. He forces the play wide and can start the play up-ice after gaining a loose puck.

THE PHYSICAL GAME

Gronstrand has height and reach, but he's not a very strong defender. He uses his reach well in poke-checking and in tying up an opponent's stick, but he will be out-muscled in front of the net and along the boards.

That said, Gronstrand isn't afraid to suffer physical abuse. He'll take whatever hits are necessary to make his plays, and he'll certainly initiate contact regardless of the opponent.

THE INTANGIBLES

Gronstrand's persistence has fooled a lot of people, especially his willingness to play physically and to not back down in a confrontation. He can continue to progress in the NHL, but age mitigates against him.He'll probably continue to shuttle in and out of the lineup, and may even finish the season for a different team.

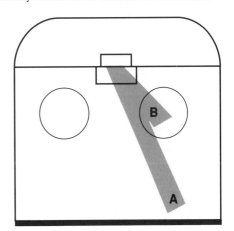

JEFF JACKSON

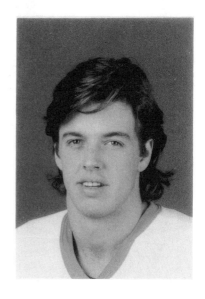

Yrs. of NHL service: 3
Born: Chatham, Ontario, Canada; April 24, 1965
Position: Left wing
Height: 6-1
Weight: 195
Uniform no.: 25
Shoots: left

Career statistics:

GP	G	A	TP	PIM
187	27	35	62	236

1988-89 statistics:

GP	G	A	TP	+/-	PIM	PP	SH	GW	GT	S	PCT
33	4	6	10	-15	28	0	1	2	0	40	10.0

LAST SEASON

Games played was a full-season career low (he missed three games with a back injury and seven games with a knee injury before succumbing to the knee problem).

THE FINESSE GAME

Before his recurring knee injuries, Jeff was a good skater. He had strength in his stride, and that gave him good speed. He also had some foot speed and balance, which resulted in a fair degree of agility.

His hand skills had not yet developed — in terms of functioning at the NHL — to the level of his skating skill, so despite his ability to motor past defensemen, Jackson's puckhandling ability would be ranked as no better than fair.

His playmaking and passing are included in that assessment, as Jackson has the intelligence to look the ice over but does not yet have the ability to read the play at NHL speed. He must learn to move the puck quicker, just as he must learn to examine all his options and show patience instead of making the first play he sees (but given that lack of ability, it's easy to see why he makes the first play).

Jackson has a good slap shot from the left circle, but needs to shoot it more instead of driving past the defenseman and into the corner with the puck.

THE PHYSICAL GAME

Jackson is a very physical hockey player and he consistently uses his size and strength. He puts that size and strength into action along the boards by constantly bodying the opposition, and because his legs are always moving the opposition has to take penalties to stop him.

Jeff has good strength and can take the puck in those battles and he also has the strength and balance to operate successfully in traffic. Because of that, he can be used to jam the net on the power play.

Jackson has also shown that he can be mean, in that he'll hit opponents from behind with his stick. Shots like that usually force him into fights, where he holds his own but doesn't terrorize anyone.

THE INTANGIBLES

Jackson has the finesse and physical tools necessary to be a good NHLer. He must stay healthy, something he's had trouble doing over the last two seasons, particularly since he has anything but a roster spot nailed down.

Of note is the fact that he's essentially played just one real NHL season (a season minimally interrupted) — that was the 1987-88 campaign. His plus/minus was Quebec's second best that season.

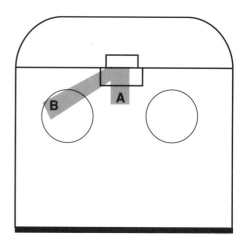

IIRO JARVI

Yrs. of NHL service: 1
Born: Helsinki, Finland; March 23, 1965
Position: Left wing/right wing
Height: 6-1
Weight: 198
Uniform no.: 11
Shoots: left

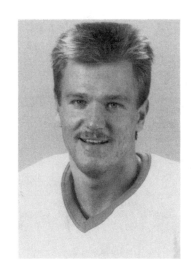

Career statistics:

GP	G	A	TP	+/-	PIM	PP	SH	GW	GT	S	PCT
75	11	30	41	-13	40	1	0	1	0	109	10.1

LAST SEASON

Jarvi's first in the NHL; he was a third round choice in the 1983 entry draft.

THE FINESSE GAME

Jarvi has the typical European skills of skating and puckhandling. He has good speed and quickness, and a nice touch of balance, making him an agile forward with good lateral movement.

He handles the puck well when he carries it and has the ability to make use of his teammates, but Jarvi is not quite acclimated to the speed of the NHL game; greater experience should help alleviate that problem.

Jarvi can handle the puck in tighter circumstances because of his good hands and his balance, and his hockey sense puts him in scoring position near the net.

He uses that anticipation well in specialty team situations, where he is a regular.

THE PHYSICAL GAME

Jarvi isn't much of a physical forward, in terms of imposing himself on the opposition, but he has no fear of the congested areas. He willingly goes to the traffic area near the front of the net to convert loose pucks, and he'll take his knocks to make his plays.

Just don't expect him to smack anyone into the cheap seats.

THE INTANGIBLES

Jarvi is a very talented player, and he has the skills and determination to improve. He can be a big part of any Nordiques resurgence.

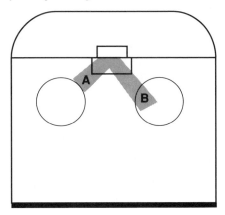

LANE LAMBERT

Yrs. of NHL service: 6
Born: Melfort, Sask., Canada; November 18, 1964
Position: Right wing
Height: 6-0
Weight: 185
Uniform no.: 7
Shoots: right

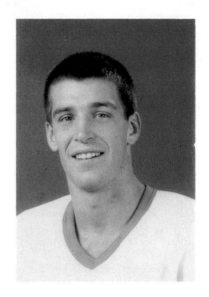

Career statistics:

GP	G	A	TP	PIM
283	58	67	125	521

1988-89 statistics:

GP	G	A	TP	+/-	PIM	PP	SH	GW	GT	S	PCT
13	2	2	4	-2	23	0	0	0	0	19	10.5

LAST SEASON

Games played and all point totals were career lows.

THE FINESSE GAME

Lane is a straight-ahead player and his finesse skills are suited for that style of game. He has a strong stride and can get some good acceleration and rink-length speed out of it, but he is neither exceptionally agile nor quick. He does have good balance and that aids his physical game.

Lambert gets a pretty good read of the ice and he checks well in all three zones because of that vision, but that skill doesn't translate into offensive success. He is a little tough with the puck and has a tendency to make his plays with his head down, so he'll need time and space to complete his playmaking.

Also handicapping his offense is his straight-ahead thinking. Lambert isn't a creative player in the offensive zone, and he plays more by reacting than acting upon the opposition. His lack of foot speed also hinders him, preventing him from cashing in on loose pucks.

Lambert has a decent shot from the faceoff circles, but will have to do most of his scoring from in close.

THE PHYSICAL GAME

Lambert not only succeeds when playing a physical game, but he *must* play a physical game to succeed: he isn't good enough otherwise. His problem is that he doesn't take advantage of his excellent upper body strength and physical ability (note we didn't say size) consistently enough. His strength and good balance should add up to an unbeatable physical game; he can be a punishing hitter.

But those parts don't add up to a greater whole. He can play a strong — if not dominating — boards and corners game, but he is just as apt to avoid the corners and the physical play as he is to look for it.

He must initiate more contact.

THE INTANGIBLES

We told you last season that Lambert would find himself out if Iiro Jarvi cracked the lineup. We include Lane now only because of the possibility Coach Michel Bergeron may want his sometimes-physical presence in the lineup.

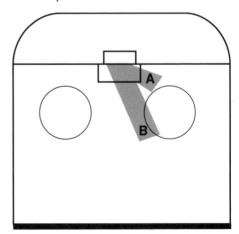

CURTIS LESCHYSHYN

Yrs. of NHL service: 1
Born: Thompson, Man., Canada; September 21, 1969
Position: Defenseman
Height: 6-1
Weight: 205
Uniform no.: 46
Shoots: left

Career statistics:

GP	G	A	TP	+/-	PIM	PP	SH	GW	GT	S	PCT
71	4	9	13	-32	71	1	1	0	0	58	6.9

LAST SEASON

Leschyshyn's first in the NHL; he was Quebec's first choice in the 1988 entry draft. His plus/minus was the club's second worst, worst among defensemen.

THE FINESSE GAME

Curtis is a talented finesse player, belying his size. He has good skating ability and mobility, using his strong stride to accelerate and gain good speed. He also has good foot speed and balance, so his turns and pivots are strong in all directions. His mobility is surprising for a player with his size.

He has good offensive instincts and finds the open man very well in the offensive zone, but his puck movement in the defensive zone could use some help; Curtis needs to be better acclimated to the speed of NHL checking. He does pass well, and he can take advantage of players on both his forehand and backhand sides.

Leschyshyn's good hands extend to his shooting ability, and his hands are soft enough for him to score from near the net; he'll charge the slot when given the opportunity. But he also has a good slap shot, and all of his shots are accurate and quickly released.

Curtis currently plays his defense reactively, making his mobility less valuable. He drifts back to keep the play wide of the net, but he's not getting a good idea of the rush or its possibilities. He's also too concerned with the puck, and not concerned enough about the man. This should improve.

THE PHYSICAL GAME

He has size and strength, but Leschyshyn is not a tough guy. He can take care of the front of the net, and also takes out the man fairly well in the corner (and he has the finesse skills to take advantage of his size and strength), but he's not going to bounce anyone into next week.

A little extra meanness wouldn't hurt him.

THE INTANGIBLES

He's already accepted a lot of on-ice responsibility, playing a regular shift plus power play and penalty killing. And Leschyshyn is going to improve; he has tremendous potential. His big problem will be dealing with Coach Michel Bergeron, who has a tendency to be impatient with younger players.

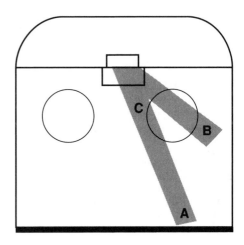

CLAUDE LOISELLE

Yrs. of NHL service: 7
Born: Ottawa, Ont., Canada; May 29, 1963
Position: Center
Height: 5-11
Weight: 190
Uniform no.: 19
Shoots: left

Career statistics:

GP	G	A	TP	PIM
345	62	78	140	703

1988-89 statistics:

GP	G	A	TP	+/-	PIM	PP	SH	GW	GT	S	PCT
74	7	14	21	-10	209	0	1	1	0	92	7.6

LAST SEASON

Games played total was second highest of his career, but all point totals were full-season lows. He missed time with a first-quarter shoulder injury. PIM total was a career high.

THE FINESSE GAME

Loiselle's skating game — and thus his value as a checking forward — is based on strength and balance. His wide stance allows him to generate a great deal of power (and that power helps when he hits), and tends to keep him vertical, but that stance also undermines Loiselle's agility and lateral movement. There are no quick feet here.

While he shows good-to-excellent anticipation defensively, Claude is generally unable to convert that anticipation into offensive output. He needs time and space to find his teammates, and his anticipation will net him some scoring opportunities, but Loiselle is essentially a one-dimensional player.

Loiselle doesn't handle the puck well, and he demonstrates his lack of offensive understanding by consistently taking himself to his backhand. What goals he does collect will have to come on miscues in the opponent's zone.

THE PHYSICAL GAME

If he's a teammate, you call Loiselle "feisty." If he's the opposition, the *best* you call him is "chippy," because Loiselle is a bit cavalier with his stick. He plays a crash-and-bang game that generally belies his not-great size, and Claude also puts the lumber to work in his cause — hence his penalty minutes. Loiselle doesn't fight the battles he stirs up.

None of this changes the fact that Loiselle's persistent checking can wear down an opponent. He goes to the traffic areas willingly and he takes the body well in all three zones. His balance helps him in his physical style, keeping him vertical and ready to move again after collisions.

Because of his good hand and arm strength, as well as eye/hand coordination, Loiselle excels at faceoffs; he's the Devils' number one man in that department.

THE INTANGIBLES

On a team of third and fourth line players, Loiselle is a fine enough checker to deserve special recognition. He's not a defensive player by default, and he also excels at penalty killing. He will not, however, develop into anything other than a role player.

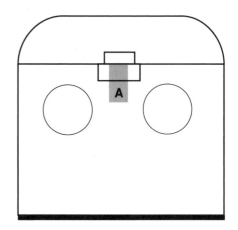

MARIO MAROIS

Yrs. of NHL service: 10
Born: Ancienne Lorette, Quebec, Canada;
December 15, 1957
Position: Defenseman
Height: 5-11
Weight: 190
Uniform no.: 44
Shoots: right

Career statistics:

GP	G	A	TP	PIM
773	70	324	394	1,489

1988-89 statistics:

GP	G	A	TP	+/-	PIM	PP	SH	GW	GT	S	PCT
49	3	12	15	-21	118	1	0	0	0	71	4.2

LAST SEASON

Acquired from Winnipeg in exchange for Gord Donnelly. Games played total was second lowest full-season total of career; he missed time with a shoulder injury.

THE FINESSE GAME

Even after a decade in the NHL, Marois remains a good skater. He is fairly agile on his skates and has a good burst of speed up-ice, and is also a good skater backward. His turns are a touch slow, making him a little weak in one-on-one situations, but he can still rush the puck from the defensive zone when he chooses to.

The key to his current success is that Mario is choosing *not* to rush the puck. He's playing smartly and patiently, only creating plays if there is an opportunity and not forcing situations. He handles the puck well while skating (always has) and will follow the play up-ice to become an offensive force at the opposition blue line.

He moves the puck well at both ends of the ice because he sees the zone well and can certainly find the open man; that's why he plays the point on the power play.

Those same high levels of vision and puck movement skills are present in the defensive zone. Marois also plays the man fairly well, staying in position and sticking with his check. These are recent improvements.

THE PHYSICAL GAME

Marois will hit whenever he can and has a mean streak that makes him difficult for opposing forwards to ignore. He will slash or elbow in front of the net and will do the same while fighting for the puck in the corners or along the boards.

He hits the opposition, rather than just pushing and shoving in the corners, and the hitting jars the puck free. Marois has the ability to take advantage of those loose pucks, making his hits more effective.

THE INTANGIBLES

Marois is a leader, in that he's matured and has gotten his emotionalism under control; he's no longer an easy mark because of his temper. Management has great confidence in him and they should, because he remains dedicated and committed to the game.

By the way, we were wrong last year when we said he was an important part of the Jets. Obviously, he wasn't important enough to not get traded.

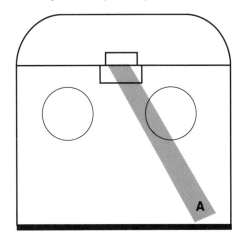

RANDY MOLLER

Yrs. of NHL service: 7
Born: Red Deer, Alta., Canada; August 23, 1963
Position: Defenseman
Height: 6-2
Weight: 205
Uniform no.: 21
Shoots: right

Career statistics:

GP	G	A	TP	PIM
508	33	119	152	1,002

1988-89 statistics:

GP	G	A	TP	+/-	PIM	PP	SH	GW	GT	S	PCT
74	7	22	29	2	136	2	0	0	0	117	6.0

LAST SEASON

All point totals tied career highs; PIM total was second lowest of career (and second among defensemen). He was sidelined late in the season with hip and foot injuries. He led the club in plus/minus.

THE FINESSE GAME

Skating and play reading ability are the traits that make Moller Quebec's most dependable defenseman. He has good speed, quickness and balance, and those traits combine to make Randy an extremely mobile defender. His acceleration and lateral movement serve him at both blue lines, where he will successfully challenge the puck more often than not. He forechecks and contains the point smartly and well, and also steps up to force the puck carrier at his own blue line.

He is not generally a rushing defenseman, but — when necessary — he can avail himself of good puck-carrying skills to relieve pressure on the Nordique forwards. His sense and vision allow him to find the open man in both zones but, unlike teammate Jeff Brown, Moller's passes are safe ones more than they are designed to create offense.

Randy has a strong slap shot and will score his goals from the point, but he should shoot more frequently.

All of his skills make him a specialty teams natural, and they also combine to give him a very effective transition game.

THE PHYSICAL GAME

Moller plays a quiet but effective physical game. He covers the front of the net well and makes the opposition pay for its shots(thus the majority of his penalty minutes). His strength allows him to rub out the opposition along the boards, and his balance and finesse skills make his physical play more effective by keeping him vertical and ready to continue the play after hits.

THE INTANGIBLES

Night in and night out, Moller is Quebec's best and most consistent defenseman. He's a leader through his discipline and hard work, and those are traits he can pass along to the younger Quebec defdensemen — traits that would be particularly important for Bryan Fogarty to emulate as he makes his transition to the NHL.

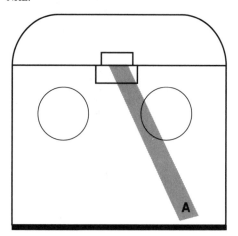

ROBERT PICARD

Yrs. of NHL service: 12
Born: Montreal, Quebec, Canada; May 25, 1957
Position: Defenseman
Height: 6-2
Weight: 207
Uniform no.: 24
Shoots: left

Career statistics:

GP	G	A	TP	PIM
855	104	311	415	977

1988-89 statistics:

GP	G	A	TP	+/-	PIM	PP	SH	GW	GT	S	PCT
74	7	14	21	-28	61	2	1	1	1	102	6.9

LAST SEASON

Assist and point totals were second lowest of career. His plus/minus rating was the club's third worst, second poorest among defensemen.

THE FINESSE GAME

Picard is a good skater, both forward and backward, though he needs work on his pivots. He has good acceleration up-ice and will carry the puck if the opportunity presents itself. Because of his weakness in turning, however, he is a good target for forecheckers. When forced, he throws blind passes around the boards.

Offensively, Picard is a good passer and can spot the open man, though he has no better than average anticipation skills. Still, he sees the ice and can make use of it by jumping into the openings himself or by leading a teammate with a pass.

Picard has a fairly good shot from the point and will see time on the power play because of his passing and shooting skills. He also likes to charge the net when he can.

Defensively, Picard still shows a tendency to gamble too frequently, pinching into the offensive zone too often and too deeply. Though he has the speed to recover, Picard doesn't hustle back and will also wander from his position in the defensive zone, making things difficult for his partners.

THE PHYSICAL GAME

Picard can be a pretty good hitter. He has a mean streak and that makes a good defenseman, but he doesn't hit consistently. He can hurt you when he hits, but sometimes is left checking air because he is so unsubtle.

He has good, not great, strength and can be muscled off the puck by the opposition. Though he hits hard, Picard also does a lot of pushing and shoving and he would be better served by increased upper body strength.

THE INTANGIBLES

After a dozen NHL seasons, what you see with Picard is probably more than you're going to consistently get. Because he plays comfortable and isn't driven to succeed, Picard's consistency is questionable at best. And because of age and his limited contributions, his time with Quebec may be coming to an end.

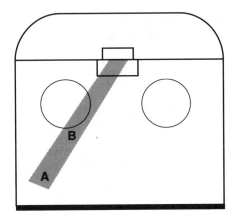

JOE SAKIC

Yrs. of NHL service: 1
Born: Burnaby, B.C., Canada; July 7, 1969
Position: Center
Height: 5-11
Weight: 185
Uniform no.: 88
Shoots: left

Career statistics:

GP	G	A	TP	+/-	PIM	PP	SH	GW	GT	S	PCT
70	23	39	62	-36	24	10	0	2	1	148	15.5

LAST SEASON

Sakic's NHL debut (he was Quebec's second choice — 15th overall — in the 1987 draft). He finished third in overall rookie scoring, first in rookie power-play goals and fourth in rookie assists. He was fifth on the club in points, and his plus/minus rating was the club's worst (third worst in the NHL). Missed time with an ankle injury.

THE FINESSE GAME

Sakic is already solid at the NHL level in terms of finesse skills, and he's got potential for great improvement. His skating is very good, marked by speed and exceptional balance. Joe is very strong on his skates, very difficult to knock down in traffic, and tough to stop as he drives the net.

His puckhandling matches his skating ability, so that Sakic can handle the puck well at his best speed. He has very soft hands, so he can control the puck in tight quarters and while being checked. Joe is also a very good passer, strong moving the puck to both sides.

Sakic's hockey sense is very strong. He knows how to get into scoring position himself (his speed and quickness help here), but he also reads the ice and anticipates well and then uses his passing skills to sew up his teammates. He is very creative and very strong in his play without the puck, and he already shows exceptional patience and poise around the net.

He has an excellent selection of shots, all of which are outstanding. He delivers his shots quickly to the net, and his accurate touch forces the goalie to make saves. Joe also has a great backhand, which he uses frequently.

Joe is just as strong defensively as he is offensively. He is a good positional player who understands his defensive responsibilities, his poor plus/minus to the contrary.

THE PHYSICAL GAME

Sakic doesn't have great size, but that doesn't stop him from playing big. He works well in the traffic areas (and won't be intimidated), and his balance and hand skills make his plays along the boards even more effective.

He works to keep himself in excellent condition.

THE INTANGIBLES

Sakic is extraordinarily talented, and his spark and leadership (he's very mature for his age — this is a guy who could have entered the League the year he was drafted but sent *himself* back to junior because he didn't think he was ready for the NHL; this is a guy who said he won't have anything to do with rookie hazing practices) are just what the Nordiques need as they attempt to retool for the 1990s.

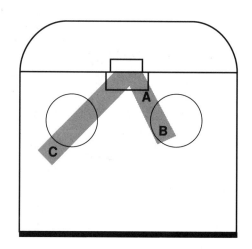

PETER STASTNY

Yrs. of NHL service: 8
Born: Bratislava, Czechoslovakia; September 18, 1956
Position: Center
Height: 6-1
Weight: 200
Uniform no.: 26
Shoots: left

Career statistics:

GP	G	A	TP	PIM
675	356	630	986	663

1988-89 statistics:

GP	G	A	TP	+/-	PIM	PP	SH	GW	GT	S	PCT
72	35	50	85	-23	117	13	0	5	0	195	17.9

LAST SEASON

Games played and point totals were second lowest of career. Goal total was third lowest and assist total career low, while PIM total was career high. He led team in assists, points and game winners, tied for second in power play goals and was third in SOG total. He missed six games with a knee injury. His plus/minus rating was the team's fourth worst, second among forwards.

THE FINESSE GAME

Even factoring in age and NHL wear and tear, Peter remains an elite level player. His hockey sense and anticipation are the keys to his game. His vision reveals the entire ice surface, and his anticipation and sense show him the soon-to-be-openings. He is excellent at using his teammates because of these skills.

He complements his sense with his skating, even though time has eroded some of his ability. While he has never been a rink-length speed demon, Stastny's skating is still marked by balance and agility; he has great lateral movement and one-step quickness, allowing him to swoop into openings and snare loose pucks. Peter's balance allows him to make plays while being checked.

Stastny combines his head and foot skills with his hand skills to become a superior playmaker. He skims passes through the openings to his teammates, but can also stickhandle his way into the opening for a shot himself; he is one of the NHL's best puckhandlers on the backhand.

Like most Europeans, Peter uses an accurate wrist shot almost exclusively, and he's going to get as near to the net as he can before shooting.

He's never been keenly interested in defense, so — despite his club's poor defensive orientation — Stastny's plus/minus rating isn't completely unjustified.

THE PHYSICAL GAME

While he accepts hits, Stastny doesn't like a hitting game. He's more likely to be found in mid-ice than he is near the congested board areas. He doesn't initiate contact (unless he's found a smaller player), and he's very liberal with his stick: he carries it way too high way too often, and will slash and hook with abandon.

THE INTANGIBLES

The departure of brother Anton may work on Peter's psyche, and his intensity and dedication have never been rock-solid anyway — so he's not a leader in that regard. His heart and desire don't match up to his offensive talents, and there's little reason to expect a change after nearly a decade in the NHL.

But he is a world class player, and there's little doubt that he's been Quebec's most important player since the team joined the NHL.

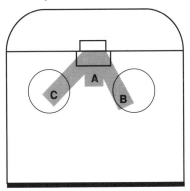

RON TUGNUTT

Yrs. of NHL service: 1
Born: Quebec, Canada; January 25, 1967
Position: Goaltender
Height: 6-3
Weight: 180
Uniform no.: 30
Catches: left

Career statistics:

GP	MINS	G	SO	AVG	A	PIM
34	1,651	98	0	3.56	4	2

1988-89 statistics:

GP	MINS	AVG	W	L	T	SO	GA	SA	SAPCT	PIM
26	1,367	3.60	10	10	3	0	82	756	.891	2

LAST SEASON

First full NHL season. He was a fourth-round pick in the 1986 Entry Draft. He led rookie goalies in save percentage. He joined club from American Hockey League in January.

THE PHYSICAL GAME

Tugnutt is a well-balanced goaltender and, considering his reflex style, that's good. He's a good skater with good to very good lateral movement, and he moves well across the net as well as out and back. His balance gets him back into his stance quickly after he extends himself or leaves his feet.

Ron has excellent reflexes. His quick feet block the shots toward the corner, and his glove matches his feet for speed. Because of his speed, he'll get a piece of many of the pucks that beat him for goals.

He handles the puck behind the net, but right now Tugnutt concentrates on first things first and doesn't dally out of the net.

THE MENTAL GAME

Tugnutt is always prepared to play, and he has the ability to maintain his concentration within games and from contest to contest. He's a confident player, and isn't easily shaken by goals or games.

THE INTANGIBLES

Quebec feels that Tugnutt can be their number one goalie, and the Nords are going to give him that chance this season.

ST. LOUIS
BLUES

LINE COMBINATIONS
GINO CAVALLINI-BERNIE FEDERKO
GREG PASLAWSKI
CLIFF RONNING-TODD EWEN
SERGIO MOMESSO-PETER ZEZEL
BRETT HULL
RICK MEAGHER-HERB RAGLAN

DEFENSE PAIRINGS
BRIAN BENNING-DAVE RICHTER
MIKE LALOR-PAUL CAVALLINI
GORDIE ROBERTS-TOM TILLEY

GOALTENDERS
GREG MILLEN
VINCENT RIENDEAU

OTHER PLAYERS
TONY HRKAC — Center
TONY MCKEGNEY — Left wing
STEVE TUTTLE — Right wing

POWER PLAY

FIRST UNIT:
SERGIO MOMESSO-PETER ZEZEL-CLIFF RON-
NING
BRIAN BENNING-BRETT HULL

SECOND UNIT:
GREG PASLAWSKI-TONY HRKAC-GINO
CAVALLINI
(GASTON GINGRAS)-TOM TILLEY

The first unit looks for any excuse to feed HULL at the point for blue line blasts. RONNING takes the right side of the net and MOMESSO the left wing corner, with ZEZEL the back of the net and the side boards.

On the second unit, CAVALLINI plugs the front of the net, PASLAWSKI is in the right faceoff circle and HRKAC controls. This unit wants a PASLAWSKI shot, and the defense (GINGRAS, now departed) will play catch with HRKAC to free up PASLAWSKI. BERNIE FEDERKO and TONY MCKEGNEY will also see time, with FEDERKO controlling play behind the net and MCKEGNEY stationed in the left faceoff circle.

Last season St. Louis's power play was FAIR, scoring 74 goals in 370 opportunities (20.0 percent, 14th overall).

PENALTY KILLING

FIRST UNIT:
RICK MEAGHER-STEVE TUTTLE
MIKE LALOR-PAUL CAVALLINI

SECOND UNIT:
GREG PASLAWSKI-
GORDIE ROBERTS-TOM TILLEY

Neither of these units is aggressive in any part of the ice, with MEAGHER and PASLAWSKI most likely to pressure the puck. PETER ZEZEL will also see penalty-killing time.

Last season St. Louis's penalty killing was POOR, allowing 83 goals in 356 shorthanded situations (76.7 percent, 17th overall).

CRUCIAL FACEOFFS
ZEZEL is the one for these, with FEDERKO and MEAGHER backing him up.

BRIAN BENNING

Yrs. of NHL service: 3
Born: Edmonton, Alta., Canada; June 10, 1966
Position: Defenseman
Height: 6-1
Weight: 185
Uniform no.: 2
Shoots: left

Career statistics:

GP	G	A	TP	PIM
225	29	93	122	319

1988-89 statistics:

GP	G	A	TP	+/-	PIM	PP	SH	GW	GT	S	PCT
66	8	26	34	-23	102	3	0	0	0	91	8.8

LAST SEASON

Games played, assist and point marks were all career lows. He led Blues defenders in scoring and his plus/minus was the team's worst.

THE FINESSE GAME

Brian has a whole package of finesse skills, and his skating is primary among them. His excellent balance and foot speed make him a very agile skater and give him excellent lateral ability. That allows him to force the opposition at the Blues blue line, to be active instead of reactive. He also has good speed and acceleration, enough to back the defense off the opposing blue line.

Benning carries the puck very well and likes to rush from the Blues zone. He stickhandles well and his hockey sense shows him the openings; Brian looks to use his teammates and he jumps into the offense himself as a fourth attacker.

While he can be a good scorer, he doesn't have exceptional goal scoring ability. Most of his goals will come from the point, but he'll cheat to the faceoff circle if there's an opening.

His skating allows him to cheat defensively, and he takes a lot of chances (many of which demonstrate poor judgement). While he can turn the play around quickly, Benning needs to play better positionally in his own zone and not try to run down every loose puck.

THE PHYSICAL GAME

Brian has good size and strength and he's not afraid to combine a physical game with his finesse one. He gets into the corner and mucks around, but his taking the body is more like pushing and shoving than it is hitting.

Importantly, he'll initiate contact. His balance and hand skills make that contact more effective because they allow him to make plays away from the boards after hitting. The best part of his physical game is that he not only takes his hits to make plays, but he makes the plays after taking hits.

THE INTANGIBLES

The 1987-88 season could be explained by a sophomore jinx, but last season demonstrates that Benning is going backward — not forward — in his NHL development. He has trouble fitting into the Blues style of play, and he hasn't necessarily demonstrated the greatest dedication to trying to either.

He can be a dominating player (and he is only 23 years old) but Brian must demonstrate not only the ability to improve his game, but the desire as well.

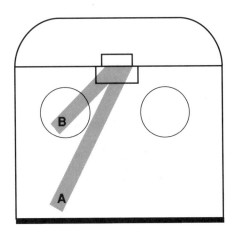

GINO CAVALLINI

Yrs. of NHL service: 5
Born: Toronto, Ontario, Canada; November 24, 1962
Position: Left wing
Height: 6-1
Weight: 215
Uniform No.: 17
Shoots: left

Career statistics:

GP	G	A	TP	PIM
302	72	88	160	271

1988-89 statistics:

GP	G	A	TP	+/-	PIM	PP	SH	GW	GT	S	PCT
74	20	23	43	2	79	1	0	4		1	153	13. 1

LAST SEASON

Games played total was three-season high, goal and PIM totals career highs. He missed time with shoulder and knee injuries.

THE FINESSE GAME

Gino's finesse skills are often overshadowed by his physical abilities, which are high. His skating has improved tremendously since the start of his NHL career, and his foot speed and agility allow him to put his physical strength to work (by getting him to the opposition) as an excellent forechecker.

His hand skills haven't caught up with his improved foot skills, but Gino will carve out enough room for himself that he'll take advantage of the loose pucks his forechecking creates. He'll pot 17-20 goals a season on loose pucks, but his playmaking isn't going to make anyone forget Denis Savard.

Cavallini lacks the soft hands for effective passing and stickhandling, and the imagination necessary for creative playmaking. He'll be a one-play player (making the first play he sees, in other words), but with enough success to put some points on the board.

He plays well positionally in all three zones, and is conscientious defensively.

THE PHYSICAL GAME

Gino has excellent physical capabilities, but he must concentrate on using them all the time; they are his bread and butter, his reasons for NHL success and the reasons he is here.

He's got great size and is very strong and, when he hits you, you stay hit. No one on the Blues hits harder than he does, and Gino keys the Blues attack by bashing the enemy defensemen. Cavallini's punishing checks also take the enemy forwards off the puck along the boards, setting the stage for a teammate to make a play with the loose puck.

He makes his checking more effective by hitting smartly and not taking penalties.

THE INTANGIBLES

Cavallini is the kind of player who will often be unsung and unknown — except to his teammates. But he must dedicate himself to playing his bruising style all the time. Injuries may have played a part in tentativeness last season, but Gino must return to his old game if he is to remain valuable to St. Louis.

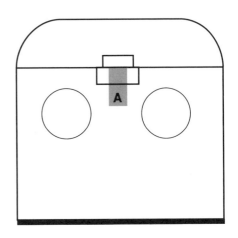

PAUL CAVALLINI

Yrs. of NHL service: 2
Born: Toronto, Ontario, Canada; October 13, 1965
Position: Defenseman
Height: 6-2
Weight: 200
Uniform No.: 14
Shoots: left

Career statistics:

GP	G	A	TP	PIM
143	10	32	42	288

1988-89 statistics:

GP	G	A	TP	+/-	PIM	PP	SH	GW	GT	S	PCT
65	4	20	24	25	128	0	0	0	0	93	4.3

LAST SEASON

Suffered a late season shoulder injury, but still recorded career marks in assists and points. He led defense in PIM, and his plus/minus was the team's best.

THE FINESSE GAME

Paul is a gifted finesse player, with his skating his primary asset. He uses his skating well in both his offensive and defensive games. Paul has very good acceleration and speed, and he uses those abilities to rush the puck from the Blues' zone when necessary. Defensively, plays a steady game in forcing the enemy wide of the St. Louis goal. He also has the agility to step up and force the play at the blue line, making him an active — rather than re-active — defenseman.

Cavallini shows good instincts in his puck movement, moving the puck up ice smoothly and efficiently. Paul sees the play well in both directions, and he contributes from the offensive blue line by containing the point well. He shows intelligence in his forechecking by not taking chances from which he cannot recover.

His shot is good — not great — and he'll get most of his goals from the blue line. When opportunity permits, Cavallini will cut closer to the net.

THE PHYSICAL GAME

Unlike brother Gino, Paul is not an overwhelming physical player. But he is, nevertheless, blessed with good strength and size and the ability to use both intelligently and effectively.

Paul takes the body well in the defensive zone, and he's very involved in the traffic areas; he just doesn't hit as hard as his brother does.

THE INTANGIBLES

Paul has made tremendous strides after just two full seasons. He's a solid all-around defenseman who plays with great enthusiasm for the game and is well-liked by his teammates.

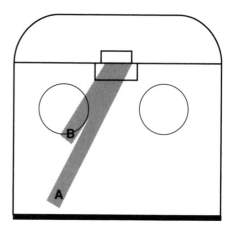

TODD EWEN

Yrs. of NHL service: 2
Born: Saskatoon, Sask., Canada; March 26, 1966
Position: Right wing
Height: 6-2
Weight: 215
Uniform No.: 21
Shoots: right

Career statistics:

GP	G	A	TP	PIM
121	10	7	17	482

1988-89 statistics:

GP	G	A	TP	+/-	PIM	PP	SH	GW	GT	S	PCT
34	4	5	9	4	171	0	0	0	0	22	18. 2

LAST SEASON

Ewen led the club in PIM, despite missing large chunks of time to injury (eye and shoulder).

THE FINESSE GAME

Not a whole lot here. Ewen doesn't have a lot of skating skill, though he is fast and strong on his feet. He's tough to move off the puck should he have it, which makes him effective in front of the net, but he's only effective in front of the net if the goaltender's having coffee and the defensemen are discussing the weather.

Like an Einstein equation, Ewen needs plenty of time and space to make any kind of play; he certainly won't finesse the puck into a small opening. Anything he gets will have to be because of brute strength.

He wanders from his position, but that's not surprising because he needs the whole rink to make a turn. His speed, however, indicates that he might — *might* — have some NHL success as a checker.

THE PHYSICAL GAME

When he catches anybody, Ewen's a pretty tough player. He's got great strength and uses it well when checking and along the boards, but he can't make the strength pay off in points because he has no hands — at least not at the NHL level.

He's also a pretty good fighter, evidence by the fact that he's the only man to beat Bob Probert (now suspended from the Red Wings) in a fight.

THE INTANGIBLES

For one, he'll be serving a 10-game suspension when the season opens. For another, as the atmosphere around the League becomes more and more charged with anti-fighting fever, Todd may just have to learn to play another style of game, a style his skills don't favor.

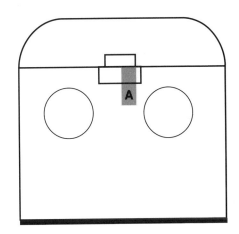

TONY HRKAC

Yrs. of NHL service: 2
Born: Thunder Bay, Ontario, Canada; July 7, 1966
Position: Center
Height: 5-11
Weight: 165
Uniform No.: 18
Shoots: left

Career statistics:

GP	G	A	TP	PIM
137	28	65	93	30

1988-89 statistics:

GP	G	A	TP	+/-	PIM	PP	SH	GW	GT	S	PCT
70	17	28	45	-10	8	5	0	1	0	133	12.8

LAST SEASON

Games played and goal totals were career highs.

THE FINESSE GAME

Hrkac's potential is in the areas of skating and playmaking. He's an excellent skater with both speed and quickness, and his skating is complemented by his anticipation and hockey sense. He uses these two skills to both exploit and create openings.

He reads the ice very well and can excel at setting up his wingers, and he's shown that he can read and execute plays at the NHL level. He's a creative player who knows how to use all of the offensive zone. He has the hand skills to be an above average NHL playmaker, but he should also learn to balance his selflessness with selfishness and take greater advantage of his speed by going to the net when he can.

Tony generally puts himself at a shooting disadvantage by setting up teammates closer to the net. Then, when they kick the puck back to him, he has to shoot through traffic. He does, however, dart around the goal, so he'll pick up some points on loose pucks.

THE PHYSICAL GAME

Hrkac's size is always going to be a concern. While he has shown, on occasion, the willingness to get involved along the boards, Hrkac doesn't have the strength to succeed in this style of play. What's more, without discussing muscling for the puck, bigger forwards are just going to reach around him or over.

THE INTANGIBLES

Hrkac definitely has the finesse skills to counter the size negative. He has tremendous potential, but he

didn't show the work ethic necessary to capitalize on those skills last season.

As such, his time was limited. and now, with the arrival of Rod Brind' Amour, Hrkac has found himself *at least* fourth on the depth chart (behind Bernie Federko, Peter Zezel and Rick Meagher). He's facing a tremendous challenge to remain with the Blues.

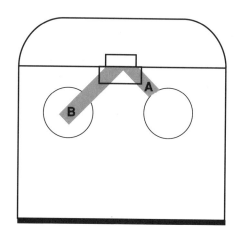

BRETT HULL

Yrs. of NHL service: 1
Born: Bellevile, Ontario, Canada; August 9, 1964
Position: Right wing
Height: 5-11
Weight: 190
Uniform No.: 16
Shoots: right

Career statistics:

GP	G	A	TP	PIM
148	74	75	149	49

1988-89 statistics:

GP	G	A	TP	+/-	PIM	PP	SH	GW	GT	S	PCT
78	41	43	84	-17	33	16	0	6	1	305	13. 4

LAST SEASON

Hull led the Blues in goals, points, power play goals, game winners (tied for first) and shots on goal (fifth in NHL). His plus/minus was club's fourth worst (second worst among forwards).

THE FINESSE GAME

Undoubtedly, Brett's best finesse asset is his shot — or shots, to be more accurate. While the first thing you see about him is the big slapper from the wing, Hull also has excellent snap and wrist shots. In close, when he can't get the big blast off, he cocks his wrists and delivers a hard and fast shot. Though predictable in his shooting (he's going high stick-side *every* time with the slap shot — and the goalies know it; they just can't stop it), Brett would be better served by taking some of the tremendous velocity off his shot and aiming elsewhere.

His skating doesn't approach his shooting, though it is improving through simple concentration. Hull is more constantly keeping his feet moving than ever before; that movement delivers him to the open spaces where he can get his shot off. The added benfit of that movement is that it drives the defense back, thus creating more room.

He's primarily a shooter and scorer, and he'll get many of his assists on rebounds of his point shots. He could improve in his playmaking from the point, which in turn might help his scoring. We all know he's the main man on the power play, but if moves the puck around the defense won't be able to key on him — then he might get more opportunities.

His defense is awful, and he has a long way to go to become a well-rounded player because of that flaw.

THE PHYSICAL GAME

Hull isn't a very physical player in terms of board work, but one thing he did do last year was drive the net a little more. Brett moved in tighter for some shots, but that doesn't mean he's imposing himself on the opposition.

He's also working through checks better than he did in his rookie season.

THE INTANGIBLES

When you see a talent like Hull, the tendency is to forget his relative youth and NHL inexperience. Happily, Brett showed last season that he can and will do the things necessary to improve his game. He's a dynamic player who led the Blues in scoring from opening to closing, and he'll be counted on heavily as the Blues try to make the transition from middle-of-the-road to elite club.

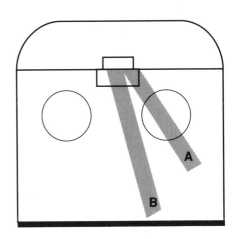

MIKE LALOR

Yrs. of NHL service: 4
Born: Buffalo, N.Y., USA ; March 8, 1963
Position: Defenseman
Height: 6-0
Weight: 193
Uniform No.: 26
Shoots: left

Career statistics:

GP	G	A	TP	PIM
233	6	43	49	285

1988-89 statistics:

GP	G	A	TP	+/-	PIM	PP	SH	GW	GT	S	PCT
48	2	18	20	14	69	0	0	2	0	52	3.8

LAST SEASON

Games played total was career low. Acquired from Montreal in mid-season.

THE FINESSE GAME

Skating is the hallmark of Lalor's game. He skates equally well forward and back and has good agility and lateral movement ability (though he is a little weak on his turns to the left). He also has a good touch of speed and acceleration.

Lalor uses his skating skill defensively and is not inclined to rush the puck. He passes the puck quickly and efficiently to the forwards to get the play started from the Blues zone. He's also learned to react more quickly to the play at the NHL level and that's made Mike less vulnerable to forechecking pressure. Otherwise Lalor does not frequently handle the puck.

Lalor plays his defensive angles well, better from the right side than the left (his left pivots can be exploited to the outside when he plays the port side). He reads the incoming rush well and he combines that skill with his skating to see some penalty killing time.

Lalor is not a goal scorer, so any goals he does get will come from the points.

THE PHYSICAL GAME

Lalor has good size and can generally handle himself against the big forwards who camp in the crease. He certainly works at moving them out, but his takeouts along the boards could improve (as the opposition sometimes sneaks back into the play).

He has a good reach and can poke check effectively or deflect the puck.

THE INTANGIBLES

Lalor is an up and coming player with size, strength, smarts and a good work ethic. That combination makes him a sound defenseman, already one of St. Louis' most dependable, and he should continue to improve with regular playing time.

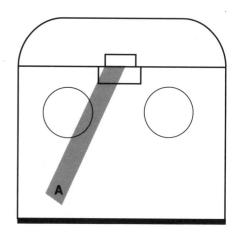

PAUL MACLEAN

Yrs. of NHL service: 8
Born: Grostenquin, France; March 9, 1958
Position: Right wing
Height: 6-2
Weight: 205
Uniform no.: 15
Shoots: right

Career statistics:

GP	G	A	TP	PIM
604	284	305	589	844

1988-89 statistics:

GP	G	A	TP	+/-	PIM	PP	SH	GW	GT	S	PCT
76	36	35	71	7	118	16	0	5	1	148	24.3

LAST SEASON

MacLean finished fourth on the club in scoring, third in goals, second in power play goals and game winners. He led the team in shooting percentage.

THE FINESSE GAME

Paul's hand skills and his smarts are his outstanding finesse assets. His excellent hands allow him to take the puck off the boards smoothly, and he has the ability to skim a pass to a teammate or to step away from the boards with the puck and make a play himself. He handles the puck well in traffic and gets rid of it when necessary; MacLean rarely overhandles the puck.

His hand skills are made important because of MacLean's hockey sense. He sees the play very well and has excellent anticipation, and Paul doesn't look for fancy plays. He just gets the job done. His shot is excellent from in close, very powerful because of his wrists and hands, and he can also blow the puck past a goaltender from a distance. He excels on the power play.

MacLean's skating skill meshes well with his other finesse assets, and it is his excellent balance and strength on his skates that allow him to succeed in the traffic areas in front of the net and in the corners. He doesn't have a whole lot of speed, but he's a little quicker than might be expected for someone his size. That quickness combines with his balance to give him a fair amount of agility for close quarters work.

THE PHYSICAL GAME

MacLean uses his size and strength to his best advantage as a superior mucker and grinder, digging the puck out of the corner and then charging the net for a return pass. His size and strength work in tandem to make MacLean difficult to control in front of the net or to out-muscle along the boards. He hits hard and well and is an aggressive though clean hockey player.

THE INTANGIBLES

He can score goals, but last season MacLean failed to do so consistently (just seven goals in his last 23 games — just four of those at even strength). Paul also angered coach Jacques Demers with some lackadaisical defensive efforts late in the season, and MacLean even found himself benched during the playoffs.

What Paul needs to do now is demonstrate his career-long character and rebound from what essentially became a disappointing season.

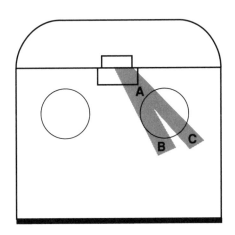

RICK MEAGHER

Yrs. of NHL service: 9
Born: Belleville, Ontario, Canada; November 4, 1953
Position: Center
Height: 5-8
Weight: 175
Uniform No.: 22
Shoots: left

Career statistics:

GP	G	A	TP	PIM
592	133	147	280	330

1988-89 statistics:

GP	G	A	TP	+/-	PIM	PP	SH	GW	GT	S	PCT
78	15	14	29	9	53	0	1	1	0	109	13.8

LAST SEASON

Point total was full-season low. His plus/minus was the team's third best, best among forwards.

THE FINESSE GAME

Meagher is an excellent skater with superior one-step quickness and agility, as well as rink-length speed. He uses that speed — and his ability to anticipate and read the plays — as an excellent penalty killer and all-around defensive forward. Meagher is a very aggressive penalty killer and the pressure he applies causes turnovers.

His smarts make him an excellent positional player who plays well at both ends of the ice; His plus/minus rating is evidence enough of that. That a defensive center should be plus 9, while his team was minus 10 is testament to his checking ability.

Meagher is the man the Blues send out for the clutch, defensive zone faceoffs. He is not really a goal-scorer, but Meagher has a good touch around the net from the slot area. He doesn't have the power to blow the puck past a goaltender from farther out, but because his speed presents him with opportunities he's going to shoot after getting a step on the defense at the left faceoff circle.

THE PHYSICAL GAME

Meagher is a remarkably well conditioned athlete, and that he is able to function at the level he does despite his age (he will be 36 in November) is a testament to his physical ability.

And he doesn't take any easy ways out. Rick uses his body well, willing and able to play a grinding game that will surprise bigger forwards and jar the puck loose — and he's not afraid of doing a little disturbing by putting his stick into the opposition after the whistle.

THE INTANGIBLES

Without pointing fingers at Lou Lamoriello (since it wasn't his fault), Meagher is one player the Devils should never have traded away. He's a leader by example, both on-ice and off, because he's a super-hard worker, a tremendous leader and a great influence on the club. He's one of hockey's best defensive forwards — and one of the game's most unknown, but best, players.

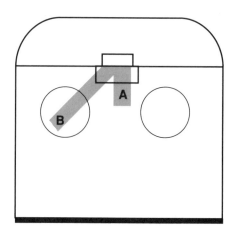

GREG MILLEN

Yrs. of NHL service: 11
Born: Toronto, Ontario, Canada; June 25, 1957
Position: Goaltender
Height: 5-9
Weight: 175
Uniform No.: 29
Catches: right

Career statistics:

GP	MINS	G	SO	AVG	A	PIM
542	31,932	2,067	16	3. 88	18	72

1988-89 statistics:

GP	MINS	AVG	W	L	T	SO	GA	SA	SAPCT	PIM
52	3,019	3. 38	22	20	7	6	170	1,411	. 879	4

LAST SEASON

Games played total was highest in four seasons, tied for sixth League-wide. Shutout total was career best (he led the NHL in that category). Win total was second best of career; ditto GAA.

THE PHYSICAL GAME

As he's matured, Millen has more and more utilized a standup style. That's not to say he isn't using his reflexes (he still works from deep in his net), but Greg is playing a more relaxed, energy-conservation game that allows the puck to just hit him than he ever has before. He's squaring himself to the puck excellently.

He's still a flamboyant, acrobatic goalie, popping up and down quickly and regaining his stance well (though he is likely to lose his angles after those acrobatics). He doesn't, however, have great balance (Millen keeps his weight on his inside edges excesively) and that means his movement across the crease is flawed. His lack of superior lateral movement — as well as his habit of hanging back in the net — are why he gives up goals inside the posts.

He skates out to snare loose pucks, but Millen prefers to leave them for his defense. His glove hand is good when he stands up, but since he goes to the ice on play around the net a lot of pucks elude him up high. He also hangs back on screens, another reason for pucks to fly over his hand and into the net.

Millen doesn't control rebounds off his chest protector well, leaving loose pucks floating around the front of the net.

THE MENTAL GAME

After a decade in the NHL, Greg knows how to prepare himself mentally. He has good concentration and above-average anticipation, and he's a tough competitor mentally. However, his concentration can wander from period to period and game to game (it means something that Millen was 16-20 last season, without counting his six shutouts). The fact that he can play excellent games merely underlines the fact that he can keep himself playing at a higher level, yet, after playing one game by standing on his head, his next game will be as if he has two left feet.

Still, he has a good attitude and approaches each game with confidence. That bolsters the team's confidence in him.

THE INTANGIBLES

Greg is the kind of goalie who makes the kind of saves that inspire a team — the dramatic, acrobatic kind of stops that a team draws strength from. He rewarded the Blues' faith in him last season with an excellent overall performance, but it's worth noting that he enters this season with more minutes-played behind him than all but two goalies (Mike Liut and Bill Smith).

That means we must question how much longer he can continue to perform at his best.

SERGIO MOMESSO

Yrs. of NHL service: 3
Born: Montreal, Quebec, Canada; September 4, 1965
Position: Left wing
Height: 6-3
Weight: 200
Uniform No.: 27
Shoots: left

Career statistics:

GP	G	A	TP	PIM
190	38	55	93	372

1988-89 statistics:

GP	G	A	TP	+/-	PIM	PP	SH	GW	GT	S	PCT
53	9	17	26	-1	139	0	0	0	0	81	11. 1

LAST SEASON

Acquired from Montreal (along with Vincent Riendeau) in exchange for Darrell May and Jocelyn Lemieux in June, 1988. PIM total was career high. He missed time with an early-season ankle injury.

THE FINESSE GAME

Momesso is a swooping kind of skater, the kind that swings wide of the defenseman and then cuts back in. He has some agility and foot speed, but not a lot of speed overall.

He handles the puck well and can use his teammates because of good hockey sense and vision. He has a nice touch around the net and is opportunistic in getting to loose pucks, but he can also score with a wrist shot from a little further out. His slap shot is powerful and delivered low on the ice, but Momesso takes a long time to get it off.

Sergio is not much defensively, mostly through lack of effort. He doesn't pay close attention to his check and he has a tendency to wander out of position in the defensive zone.

THE PHYSICAL GAME

Momesso is strong, the kind of player who succeeds by bulling his way around the corners and the boards, and by using his strength in the front of the net. He does drive to the net and, because of his size, can work effectively there.

He is not a tough guy, but he'll take the rough going to make his plays. Right now though, Momesso is not guaranteed to make plays after taking the hits and that renders his physical play less than effective.

THE INTANGIBLES

As we've said, intensity is the key to Momesso, from night to night, and shift to shift. He's the kind of guy who could score 30 goals a year but he needs to work at doing so. He seems to be the kind of guy who was a star at the junior level because he was so far above the competition and didn't have to work to succeed. Obviously, that doesn't work in the NHL.

He showed in the playoffs (seven points in 10 games) that he can succeed. Now all Sergio has to do is want to.

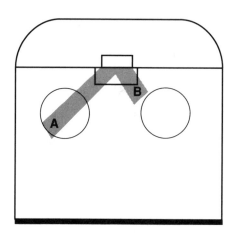

ADAM OATES

Yrs. of NHL service: 4
Born: Weston, Ontario, Canada; August 27, 1962
Position: Center
Height: 5-11
Weight: 185
Uniform no.: 21
Shoots: right

Career statistics:

GP	G	A	TP	PIM
246	54	145	199	65

1988-89 statistics:

GP	G	A	TP	+/-	PIM	PP	SH	GW	GT	S	PCT
69	16	62	78	-1	14	2	0	1	1	127	12.6

LAST SEASON

All point totals were career highs. Oates finished third on the team in scoring, second in assists.

THE FINESSE GAME

Playmaking is the highlight of Adam's game, and that skill showcases his hands and smarts. He is very good puckhandler when he skates up-ice, takes the puck off the boards easily and passes to both the forehand and backhand sides with precision.

Complementing his hand skills are his anticipation and vision skills. Adam sees the ice well and recognizes the plays, and he can get the puck to his teammates either when they are in the clear or by leading them to the openings. He's made the transition to the speed of the NHL, and that's the reason for his improvement.

Oates's skating is no better than average at the NHL level, lacking exceptional quickness, speed and agility. He does have good balance, so he can make plays when being checked or in close quarters.

His hockey sense and his hands will often get him into position to score, but he needs a quicker release and better strength on his shot and he needs to shoot more often.

THE PHYSICAL GAME

Oates doesn't have great size or strength, but he's not afraid to use what he does have. More and more in his NHL career he's putting his hand skills to work in the traffic areas, and he's improving at taking the body along the boards.

His hand speed also makes him good on faceoffs.

THE INTANGIBLES

We said last year that Oates could improve but that he'd have a hard time getting time because of the three centers ahead of him. What Adam did was simply take one of them — John Chabot — out of the equation; Oates's playmaking saw to that.

He may be challenged this season by Adam Graves (who may be moved to wing), but Oates has shown that he can succeed at the NHL level. His attitude and work ethic speak in his favor.

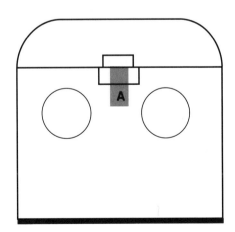

GREG PASLAWSKI

Yrs. of NHL service: 5
Born: Kindersley, Sask., Canada; August 25, 1961
Position: Right wing
Height: 5-11
Weight: 190
Uniform No.: 28
Shoots: right

Career statistics:

GP	G	A	TP	PIM
356	110	103	213	109

1988-89 statistics:

GP	G	A	TP	+/-	PIM	PP	SH	GW	GT	S	PCT
75	26	26	52	8	18	8	0	3	0	179	14.5

LAST SEASON

Games played and all point totals were second highest of career. He finished second on the club in goals and shots on goal, and his plus/minus was second best among forwards.

THE FINESSE GAME

Paslawski is a kind of "good news/bad news" player, in that he has NHL skills but doesn't always bring them to bear. He's a good skater and he has good movement and speed in his skating, but he doesn't always use his skating to his best ability by forcing the defense to retreat or by jumping into holes.

He's shown that he has good vision and anticipation, that he can see the openings, but — again — he doesn't always exploit them. When he does he's successful, but Paslawski also shows a tendency to delay moving to openings.

Greg can be a sniper and definitely has talent that could be further developed. The problem is, Paslawski waits for the holes to open, rather than forcing them open with his speed and better-than-average puck sense. That shows in his power play goal total, where the open ice is created for him; almost 33 percent of his goals came on this specialty team — making him a less than dynamic even strength player.

He's fairly good with the puck and does look for his teammates, but don't look for him to thread any needles with his passes. Paslawski is fairly conscientious defensively and will come back into his own zone.

THE PHYSICAL GAME

One area that Paslawski shored up was his physical game. He was more involved along the boards last season, taking the body alertly and putting his hand skills to work from the traffic areas. He's still not a corners and boards player — and isn't built for success in that style — but his game is more well-rounded.

THE INTANGIBLES

Overall, Paslawski is a well-balanced player. He's effective in all three zones and pushed himself more last year than he ever has before. The Blues would like him to show more offense, as that would help pick up the slack left by the departure of Mark Hunter, as well as ease some of the checking on Brett Hull.

But whether Greg will be able to do that — well, let's just say history isn't on his side.

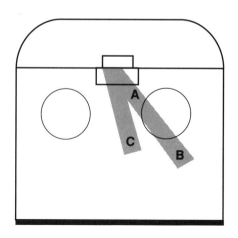

HERB RAGLAN

Yrs. of NHL service: 3
Born: Peterborough, Ontario, Canada; August 5, 1967
Position: Right wing
Height: 6-0
Weight: 200
Uniform No.: 25
Shoots: right

Career statistics:

GP	G	A	TP	PIM
192	23	35	58	498

1988-89 statistics:

GP	G	A	TP	+/-	PIM	PP	SH	GW	GT	S	PCT
50	7	10	17	-8	144	0	0	1	0	86	8.1

LAST SEASON

Shoulder (six games) and groin (16 games) injuries shortened his season. Games played and PIM totals were career lows. He was second on the club in PIM.

THE FINESSE GAME

Raglan is a strong skater and he gets up and down the ice well because of that strength, but there isn't a lot of finesse in his play. He lacks real NHL speed or agility (and he's got the turning radius of a battleship), but his strength makes him a relentless skater. He's very difficult to get away from, which in turn makes him a good checker and a tremendous player without the puck.

His hand skills approximate the level of his foot skills finesse-wise. He neither carries nor passes the puck especially well, and doesn't shoot exceptionally either. He'll shoot from the faceoff circle, and from the left wing circle too (remember his bad turns) because he rotates around the net and stays deep on the left wing side, but he'll have to do his scoring from in close.

THE PHYSICAL GAME

Raglan's strength makes it difficult to dislodge him from the puck, so he's a good player for the front of the net and in traffic (but he doesn't have the hands to score in tight; he'll just cause commotion).

Raglan hits hard, really punishing the opposition with his checks, and Herb eagerly uses his size and strength in the corners and along the boards. His physical effectiveness is somewhat tempered by the fact that he won't make the play out of the corner, but his points are all going to come via his physical style.

THE INTANGIBLES

His physical style betrays him with injury, so that's the biggest question mark: How often will he be in the lineup to contribute? Otherwise, Herb has a great attitude. He's a very hard worker on the ice, always focused on doing the things he does best. He's a good team guy who stands up for his teammates.

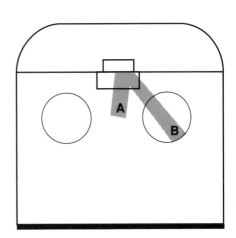

DAVE RICHTER

Yrs. of NHL service: 5
Born: Winnipeg, Man., Canada; April 8, 1960
Position: Defenseman
Height: 6-5
Weight: 220
Uniform No.: 5
Shoots: right

Career statistics:

GP	G	A	TP	PIM
363	9	40	49	1,030

1988-89 statistics:

GP	G	A	TP	+/-	PIM	PP	SH	GW	GT	S	PCT
66	1	5	6	-21	99	0	0	0	0	23	4.3

LAST SEASON

Plus/minus was club's second worst.

THE FINESSE GAME

Richter is not talented in the finesse areas of the game. He sees the play poorly at both ends of the ice, meaning he cannot help sustain an attack in the offensive zone, nor help thwart one in the defensive zone.

He has little foot speed or agility, so he can't close the gap between himself and a forward, and he can't turn well enough to go after them as they pass him. He is easily confused in his own end, wandering from position and leaving openings.

He will give the puck away if forechecked, and is not likely to make good passes if left alone because he doesn't understand a play and his hands aren't good enough to move the puck quickly and efficiently. He will score only rarely, and then on shots from the point.

THE PHYSICAL GAME

Richter has been obtained by Minnesota, Philadelphia, Vancouver, and St. Louis for one thing: physical play. He has been traded by Minnesota, Philadelphia, and Vancouver because of a lack of one thing: physical play.

Richter will coast if the game is not mean, and he doesn't like to be pushed to be aggressive. He'll use his size to knock people off the puck (though he can't do much of anything after that) but he could certainly be more aggressive in normal game situations.

He would have to be judged as playing smaller than he is.

THE INTANGIBLES

To have put this guy in a leadership role (as Coach Brian Sutter did) is laughable, because Richter isn't exactly a character player. He has a poor work ethic and doesn't wish to apply himself.

With the emergence of players like Tom Tilley and Glen Featherstone — and the presence of players like Todd Ewen and Herb Raglan — Richter's St. Louis days have to be numbered.

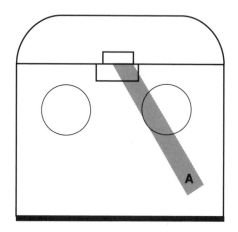

VINCENT RIENDEAU

Yrs. of NHL service: 1
Born: St. Hyacinthe, Quebec, Canada; April 20, 1966
Position: Goaltender
Height: 5-10
Weight: 185
Uniform No.: 30
Catches: left

Career statistics:

GP	MINS	G	SO	AVG	A	PIM
33	1,878	113	0	3.61	1	4

1988-89 statistics:

GP	MINS	AVG	W	L	T	SO	GA	SA	SAPCT	PIM
32	1,842	3.52	11	15	5	0	108	836	.870	4

LAST SEASON

His first full NHL season. He was acquired from Montreal (along with Sergio Momesso) in exchange for Darrell May and Jocelyn Lemieux in summer, 1988.

THE PHYSICAL GAME

Riendeau plays somewhere between a standup and reflex game. He's generally at his best when challenging the opposition, but he has a tendency to hang back in the net (particularly on point shots with screens in front — that's a reflex move), and NHL shooters will beat him to the corners with shots in those instances.

That's also evident on shots from the slot, where Vincent is too deep in his net to possibly hope to get a piece of shots to the corners. He must move out and cut the angle in those circumstances, and — instead of going down — he must stay on his feet and be mobile.

Problem is, he doesn't move his feet real well and is a little slow going from post to post on play around the net, nor does he see the puck as well as he could in those circumstances. His lack of mobility also makes him vulnerable to dekes, but his skating is good enough for him to leave the net and handle pucks behind the goal.

He does stand up well on stick-side shots, perhaps because Riendeau knows he has a weakness there; he has a tendency to allow goals to sneak between his body and his stick arm. He leaves stick rebounds in front.

THE MENTAL GAME

Riendeau's anticipation of the play at the NHL level is no better than average — if that. That's something experience can change. His history indicates that he prepares for games fairly well, and that he can step into a game cold and get his concentration working.

He can get up for some big games, but has yet to show he can do that on a consistent basis within the NHL.

THE INTANGIBLES

Riendeau showed himself to be an adequate backup last season to Greg Millen. Vincent has been an all-star at the previous levels he's played, and he's young enough to develop into a dependable NHL goalie; only time will tell.

GORDIE ROBERTS

Yrs. of NHL service: 10
Born: Detroit, Mich., USA: October 2, 1957
Position: Defenseman
Height: 6-1
Weight: 195
Uniform No.: 4
Shoots: left

Career statistics:

GP	G	A	TP	PIM
761	47	292	339	1,132

1986-87 statistics:

GP	G	A	TP	+/-	PIM	PP	SH	GW	GT	S	PCT
77	2	24	26	7	90	0	0	0	0	52	3.8

LAST SEASON

Games played total was four-season high; ditto assist and point totals.

THE FINESSE GAME

Despite his time around the League (and four WHA seasons), Roberts retains a good degree of finesse ability — which he complements with generous doses of smarts. Gordie is a good skater, probably underestimated in that regard. He's got speed both forward and backward, though his agility is weak (his pivot to the left while skating backwards particularly so). Still, he can rush the puck when need be.

He reads the rush coming back very well and plays good positional defense (the smarts), forcing the opposition wide of the net. He has the ability to break up the play and turn it back up-ice quickly, taking the puck of the boards and sending it to a teammate in one motion. Roberts throws a good pass to either side because he sees the ice well, and that ability helps him in his offense too.

He's not much of a goal scorer, but he does have a good slap shot from the point that he gets away quickly and on target, and that makes it good for rebounds or deflections. Roberts will also charge the net for a return pass on a give and go.

THE PHYSICAL GAME

Roberts plays a good physical game, willingly bringing the best of his less-than-exceptional size and strength to play at all times. He has the strength to keep the front of his net clean and he can also steer the opposition wide of the net and hold them out of the play for as long as necessary.

Roberts can also hit hard and he does, but his game is best when he takes the body and moves the puck. For a guy without the greatest size, Roberts plays an extremely effective physical game. He is very tough.

THE INTANGIBLES

His work ethic (especially in light of his experience) is a fine example to the younger Blues, and his steady play has made him one of St. Louis's most dependable players — forward or defenseman.

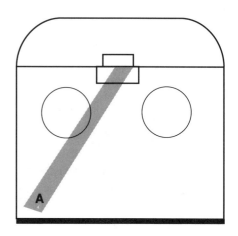

CLIFF RONNING

Yrs. of NHL service: 2
Born: Vancouver, B.C., Canada; October 1, 1965
Position: Center
Height: 5-8
Weight: 175
Uniform No.: 7
Shoots: left

Career statistics:

GP	G	A	TP	PIM
132	40	53	93	36

1988-89 statistics:

GP	G	A	TP	+/-	PIM	PP	SH	GW	GT	S	PCT
64	24	31	55	3	18	16	0	1	0	150	16.0

LAST SEASON

Ronning's first full NHL campaign. All point totals were career highs. He tied for team lead in power play goals.

THE FINESSE GAME

Ronning is a neat little package of finesse skills. He's an excellent skater with superior quickness and agility; those are his best assets and are particularly valuable on the power play — where Ronning excels.

He also has outstanding playmaking smarts. His hockey sense, his understanding of the game's flow and his ability to not just see but to find openings is excellent. Cliff can make the most of those openings himself (with his skating) or by using his teammates. He passes well because of his soft hands.

Ronning has a good shot, not extremely powerful but very quickly released (thus making his ability to jump into an opening even better). He's also accurate with his shot, forcing goaltenders to make saves. He'll score best from near the net, where he can use his good hands in tight.

His defense is conscientious, and Cliff plays a fairly good positional game in all three zones.

THE PHYSICAL GAME

There really isn't one. Not that he isn't willing, but Cliff doesn't have a lot of strength to bring to bear, certainly not a lot of size. He's not afraid (Ronning will cover the Jim Korns of this world when they go to the Blues net), but so what? Once caught, Ronning is going to be out-muscled and out-reached by bigger and stronger opponents.

He must stay away from crowds to succeed.

THE INTANGIBLES

The thing with Ronning is, you have to decide how many small players to have on the ice at one time— hence his frequent centering for bookend behemoths Craig Coxe and Todd Ewen. Of course, teaming him with players of that calibre guarantees he has to do all the work; linemates like that do nothing but open up the ice — they can't convert playmaking.

Ronning's power play success demonstrates how dominant he can be, but he must demonstrate that ability at even-strength; the gap between his extra-man and even-strength production is just too big.

The fact that he made the most of his opportunities once presented (Cliff could have made the club out of training camp) speaks well for his drive and work ethic.

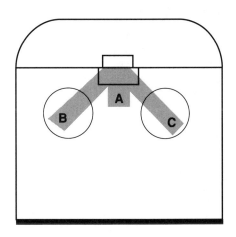

TOM TILLEY

Yrs. of NHL service: 1
Born: Trenton, Ontario, Canada; March 28, 1965
Position: Defenseman
Height: 6-0
Weight: 180
Uniform No.: 20
Shoots: right

Career statistics:

GP	G	A	TP	+/-	PIM	PP	SH	GW	GT	S	PCT
70	1	22	23	1	47	0	0	0	0	77	1.3

LAST SEASON

First NHL campaign. Games played total was second highest among defense.

THE FINESSE GAME

Tilley is a good skater in both directions, with NHL-level (and improvable) speed and agility. Right now, he uses his defensive angles to force the play wide of the net (and he's smart and poised enough to not double-team an opponent in the corner and thus leave the front of the net clear), but he's demonstrated the smarts and the agility that will allow him to step up on the puck carrier and challenge the play at the blue line.

He continues his smart play by making smart plays; he won't force a pass or a rush. Tilley looks the ice over and makes correct decisions, then he follows the play up ice — but without putting himself at a defensive disadvantage.

He does pinch in sensibly at the opposing blue line, and most of his goals and points will come on plays from there. He can shoot the puck in stride, but his shot won't give NHL goaltenders nightmares.

THE PHYSICAL GAME

Tilley succeeds in his crease and corner confrontations because of good balance. He applies fairly good strength (despite less than overwhelming size) and handles himself well in these battles, and he makes his physical play (more bumping than smashing) effective by making plays after the puck is loose.

THE INTANGIBLES

One indication of Tilley's potential is that he led the Blues in plus/minus through the playoffs. Another is that he worked hard to make the team in training camp and kept that determination and work ethic intact throughout the season.

He's already one of the Blues most consistent players.

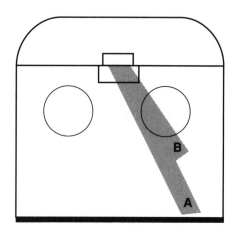

STEVE TUTTLE

Yrs. of NHL service: 1
Born: Vancouver, B.C., Canada; January 5, 1966
Position: Right wing
Height: 6-1
Weight: 180
Uniform No.: 35
Shoots: right

Career statistics:

GP	G	A	TP	+/-	PIM	PP	SH	GW	GT	S	PCT
53	13	12	25	3	6	0	1	3	0	82	15.9

LAST SEASON

Tuttle's first NHL season. He missed time with knee and shoulder injuries.

THE FINESSE GAME

Tuttle demonstrates finesse skills that are average and improvable. Probably first among his skills are his smarts on-ice. He's the kind of player who knows to come down the wing with the puck and then open up to middle of the ice so as to see the action and make a play.

Steve demonstrates those smarts in another way, as a good penalty killer. He anticipates and reads the play well, and he uses his skating ability (good balance and quickness, making for good agility) to pressure the points on the power play.

Those smarts combine with Tuttle's hands to make him a fairly good passer, but he needs more experience to bring that skill to the point where he's a consistent NHL threat — especially in understanding the speed of the play.

He gets into position to score to a fair degree (again, improved ability at recognizing openings at NHL speed is essential), and Tuttle's shot — like his other skills — is at a level no better than average (quicker release and better strength would help).

He is a fairly consistent defensive player.

THE PHYSICAL GAME

Improved strength for the NHL grind would help Tuttle in a number of ways. It would allow him to better compete against the League's defensemen, and would also help him in terms of conditioning and injury prevention. a s such, his ability to succeed in traffic is limited.

THE INTANGIBLES

Steve has developable NHL skills, but his concern must be the depth chart; he has *at least* Brett Hull and Greg Paslawski (scorers) ahead of him, followed by players like Herb Raglan and Todd Ewen (bangers). Where Tuttle fits in is a big question mark.

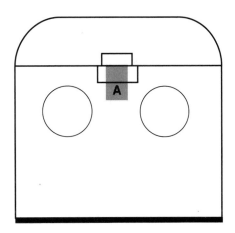

PETER ZEZEL

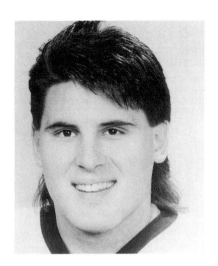

Yrs. of NHL service: 5
Born: Toronto, Ontario, Canada; April 22, 1965
Position: Center
Height: 5-10
Weight: 195
Uniform No.: 9
Shoots: left

Career statistics:

GP	G	A	TP	PIM
362	108	206	314	257

1988-89 statistics:

GP	G	A	TP	+/-	PIM	PP	SH	GW	GT	S	PCT
78	21	49	70	-14	42	5	1	4	0	149	14. 1

LAST SEASON

Acquired from the Flyers in exchange for Mike Bullard. Missed three games with a shoulder injury, but games played total was second highest of career; ditto point total. Assist total was career high and led club. Finished second in scoring. Plus/minus was third worst among forwards.

THE FINESSE GAME

Zezel is an excellent skater, fast on his feet, agile and strong. He can stop, start and turn on a dime. He's the League's best at controlling the puck with his feet, allowing him another dimension of control when he takes the puck off the boards. It also makes him dangerous when the puck seems to have gotten away from him.

Peter's playmaking ability has improved because of patience and confidence. Already possessing good hockey sense, ice vision, and stick skills, Zezel's improved playmaking ability comes from seeing patience pay off, and knowing that looking the ice over — and not just making the first play he sees — makes for scoring opportunities.

His anticipation, vision and sense (together with his skating ability) also make him a fine defensive center, as long as he maintains his concentration toward that task.

Zezel has a good selection of shots. His wrist shot is quickly released and generally accurate, forcing the goaltender to make a save. He also has the power to score from a distance and is good at getting defensemen to set screens.

His finesse talents alone are enough to force the opposition into taking penalties, but Zezel augments that penalty-drawing ability with some of the League's best dives.

THE PHYSICAL GAME

Zezel carries a lot of muscle on his frame and he hits hard. His size, strength and — above all — balance allow him to plant himself to the side of the opponent's net and stick his butt into the defenseman covering him, thus not allowing the opposing player to get at the puck, or even to hold Zezel's arms.

He plays a very physical game at both ends of the rink, and is not above putting his stick into the opposition. He does not back up that stickwork by fighting.

THE INTANGIBLES

Zezel's lack of concentration has been concern for several seasons. It's not that Peter isn't a hard worker, because he is — he just needs to maintain his focus from night to night and shift to shift. As he does so, he'll mature into an above-average NHL player.

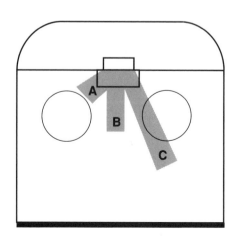

TORONTO
MAPLE LEAFS

LINE COMBINATIONS
MARK OSBORNE-ED OLCZYK
GARY LEEMAN
WENDEL CLARK-TOM FERGUS
VINCENT DAMPHOUSSE-PETER
IHNACAKDAN MAROIS
TODD GILL-DAVE REID-JOHN KORDIC

DEFENSE PAIRINGS
BRAD MARSH-AL IAFRATE
LUKE RICHARDSON-DARRYL SHANNON

GOALTENDERS
ALLAN BESTER

OTHER PLAYERS
CRAIG LAUGHLIN — Right wing
DAN DAOUST — Center

POWER PLAY

FIRST UNIT:
WENDEL CLARK-TOM FERGUS-ED OLCZYK
(CHRIS KOTSOPOULOS)-GARY LEEMAN

SECOND UNIT:
VINCENT DAMPHOUSSE-PETER IHNACAK-
DAN MAROIS
DARRYL SHANNON-AL IAFRATE

The first unit posts CLARK in the right wing corner and OLCZYK in the left wing corner. Toronto overloads the right wing, stationing FERGUS at the faceoff circle. He dishes the puck between CLARK and LEEMAN at the point (the since-departed KOTSO-POULOS was the safety valve) to set up LEEMAN for a shot. CLARK and OLCZYK crash the net for rebounds.

On the second unit, IHNACAK runs the play from the left wing corner, with the overload on this side; DAMPHOUSSE at the faceoff circle and SHANNON on that point. MAROIS will flit in and out of the slot from the right side, but the play is DAMPHOUSSE for the shot and MAROIS the poke or tip in.

Last season Toronto's power play was POOR, scoring just 56 goals in 334 opportunities (16.8 percent, 21st overall).

PENALTY KILLING

FIRST UNIT:
ED OLCZYK-GARY LEEMAN
DARRYL SHANNON-(CHRIS KOTSOPOULOS)

SECOND UNIT:
MARK OSBORNE-DAVE REID
BRAD MARSH-AL IAFRATE

The entire first unit is very aggressive (KOTSO-POULOS was not) because of its collective mobility. They'll force the puck all over and look for the break. The second unit is more conservative (a standard box) except for IAFRATE, who will skate the puck in search of a shorthanded goal.

Last season Toronto's penalty killing was POOR, allowing 98 goals in 359 shorthanded situations (72.7 percent, 21st overall).

CRUCIAL FACEOFFS
FERGUS gets the call for these, with OLCZYK second.

ALLAN BESTER

Yrs. of NHL service: 5
Born: Hamilton, Ontario, Canada; March 26, 1964
Position: Goaltender
Height: 5-7
Weight: 155
Uniform no.: 30
Catches: left

Career statistics:

GP	MINS	G	SO	AVG	A	PIM
157	8,510	558	7	3.93	6	26

1988-89 statistics:

GP	MINS	AVG	W	L	T	SO	G	SA	SAPCT	PIM
43	2,460	3.80	17	20	3	2	156	1,420	.890	2

LAST SEASON

Games and minutes played totals were career highs. He missed two games with a leg injury.

THE PHYSICAL GAME

Though his frequent flailings and floppings may seem to belie it, Bester is a standup goalie. He challenges the shooters well, which is smart considering he's only 5-foot-7; after all, if he was to hang back in the net and depend solely on reflexes to stop the puck, he'd develop a terrible case of whiplash from watching pucks sail over his shoulders.

That doesn't mean Bester squares himself to the puck as well as he could, so he'll frequently react to shots that are nowhere near the net.

He moves to the top of the screen — again, playing the percentages — and generally forces the opposition to make the first move. Bester is well balanced on his skates and that's important, because he often needs to regain his stance quickly after leaving rebounds from his pad and glove saves.

He has a quick glove hand and will block the puck, but not catch it, frequently juggling it till it falls to the ice. He'll leave rebounds in front from his pad saves too, but is otherwise good about clearing the puck.

He holds the post well and has a quick left foot, but Bester is just average in his lateral movement from post to post. He doesn't handle the puck well and that creates all kinds of defensive confusion.

THE MENTAL GAME

Bester is a worrier, always fidgeting about doing his best and sometimes that mitigates against him. He has a tendency to lose his concentration because he's worrying about how he's playing instead of stopping the puck, and then he allows goals.

One sign that his concentration is good is his vision of the puck. When his concentration is on he sees it well, following the play all through the offensive zone. That allows him to make saves based on anticipation.

THE INTANGIBLES

Being Toronto's number one goalie may or may not alter Bester's temperament; we doubt it. But he did play well for Toronto after his elevation to number one status, frequently showing why he was among the league's leaders in save percentage.

He's not a great team guy, because of his arrogant and cocky attitude, and his stand-offishness sets him apart from other Leafs.

WENDEL CLARK

Yrs. of NHL service: 4
Born: Kelvington, Sask., Canada; October 25, 1966
Position: Left wing
Height: 5-11
Weight: 194
Uniform no.: 17
Shoots: left

Career statistics:

GP	G	A	TP	PIM
189	90	49	139	644

1988-89 statistics:

GP	G	A	TP	+/-	PIM	PP	SH	GW	GT	S	PCT
15	7	4	11	-3	66	3	0	1	0	30	23.3

LAST SEASON

Clark returned late in the season from a year's absence due to back injury.

THE FINESSE GAME

Clark's whole game is power, so it should come as no surprise that his best finesse assets are powered by his strength. His skating is marked by explosive acceleration and strength (so he has great speed and the ability to drive through his checks), but Wendel's balance and agility rank below the two former traits. He moves fairly well laterally, but his is a battering ram style.

Because of his relative NHL inexperience, his vision and anticipation remain no better than average. Clark needs time and space to pass well, and he continues to overhandle the puck; he needs to lose his 1-on-1 tendencies.

If he can improve that aspect of his game, his offense would improve, because moving the puck better would draw the defense away from him. Then he could get into the open to use his excellent wrist shot, which might be the League's best in terms of heaviness, release and accuracy. He does shoot a lot, and Clark does have the hand skills, strength and speed to drive the net.

His backchecking and general defense could use work, as Wendel lacks patience in his defensive end and takes himself out of the play by trying to do too much (like pound an opposing player). He does, however, apply himself — so he is making errors of commission rather than omission.

THE PHYSICAL GAME

Clark has the ability to smash people, to really hurt them with his checks. He has the ability to work the corners excellently because of his superior upper body strength and foot balance. He has the ability to beat people up. He has the ability to take the body in the corner and come out with the puck.

That's because Wendel is very strong, very tough, very aggressive. And very inconsistent. He has yet to demonstrate the ability to do all those things consistently — both within games and from game to game.

THE INTANGIBLES

Assuming that his back injury is behind him, Clark can resume his path toward becoming one of the NHL's premier players. He is still, in many ways, a *very* inexperienced NHLer, but he has fabulous potential.

He's a tremendous team player, and the Leafs benefit greatly from his spirit and enthusiasm. He's a born leader, and he can be the franchise player the Leafs sorely need.

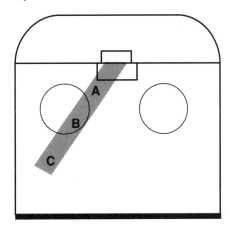

VINCENT DAMPHOUSSE

Yrs. of NHL service: 3
Born: Montreal, Quebec, Canada; December 17, 1967
Position: Center/left wing
Height: 6-1
Weight: 195
Uniform no.: 10
Shoots: left

Career statistics:

GP	G	A	TP	PIM
235	59	103	162	141

1988-89 statistics:

GP	G	A	TP	+/-	PIM	PP	SH	GW	GT	S	PCT
80	26	42	68	-8	75	6	0	4	0	190	13.7

LAST SEASON

Played 80 games for second time in three seasons. All point totals were career highs. He finished third in team scoring and shots on goal.

THE FINESSE GAME

And in his third year, Vincent Damphousse began to show some return on his promise. His skating demonstrates both quickness and rink-length speed, and his improving balance has given him greater — not great — agility and lateral movement.

Vincent has an excellent shot, and he's shown improvement in his shooting positioning by moving more to the center of the rink. We said last year that he needed to shoot more, and last season Damphousse did: 190 SOG versus just 111 in 1987-88.

His hand skills extend to his puck control ability. Damphousse has the ability to stickhandle and make plays at full speed. Last season, Vincent used his patience to improve his playmaking. By cutting down on his overhandling of the puck, Damphousse was able to make better use of his teammates, though he wasn't a really a selfish player to begin with.

His defensive game isn't bad, but he needs to pay more consistent attention to it.

THE PHYSICAL GAME

Damphousse plays the body fairly well, though by no stretch of the imagination are we saying he's a terror of physical force. Rather, he knows that just getting his body in the opposition's way will pay benefits — and that's what Vincent does.

He bumps along the boards, not really smacking guys but leaning on them enough to put his hand skills to work. He also has pretty good size and he uses his body well to protect the puck.

THE INTANGIBLES

We told you last year that the 1987-88 season would be a crucial one for Damphousse, and he responded relatively well to that challenge. Like many of the Leafs he still needs to apply his talent consistently from shift to shift and game to game; his success last season should point him the right way this season.

What he must avoid is a stretch like last season's where he scored seven goals in his first 10 games, and then just eight in the next 30. That's crucial — for both his success, and for any success the Leafs are to have.

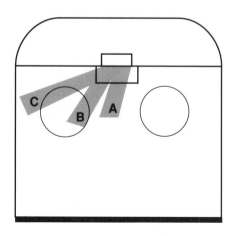

DAN DAOUST

Yrs. of NHL service: 7
Born: Montreal, Quebec, Canada; February 29, 1960
Position: Center
Height: 5-11
Weight: 170
Uniform no.: 24
Shoots: left

Career statistics:

GP	G	A	TP	PIM
457	80	156	236	455

1988-89 statistics:

GP	G	A	TP	+/-	PIM	PP	SH	GW	GT	S	PCT
68	7	5	12	-20	54	0	2	1	0	66	10.6

LAST SEASON

Games played total was three season high. Plus/minus total was team's third worst.

THE FINESSE GAME

Daoust is a good skater, equipped with speed and balance on his skates, giving him good lateral movement. He changes direction quickly and that is a big help to him as a defensive forward.

He sees the ice very well (another defensive plus), has good anticipation skills and reads the play excellently. Those skills also make him an excellent penalty killer.

Dan has good stick skills and can use his teammates excellently when he has the opportunity. His scoring, what little he does of it now, will come from the slot, as his shot doesn't measure up to his other skills.

THE PHYSICAL GAME

Daoust, despite his small stature, will play a fearless physical game against any team. As a defensive forward Daoust bumps his man up and down the ice, playing tough but clean. He has deceptive strength for his size and will play with anyone against the boards.

That style, however, takes its toll in terms of injury.

THE INTANGIBLES

Daoust's value lies in his ability to play effectively despite limited ice time (don't let the plus/minus fool you — he's on-ice against some of the NHL's best centers).

He's an enthusiastic player on the ice and he dedicates his energy now to a good defensive game. He gives what he has and is always ready to play, despite his role player status.

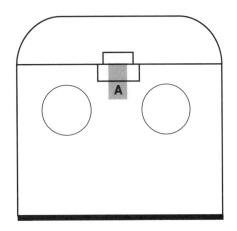

TOM FERGUS

Yrs. of NHL service: 8
Born: Chicago, Ill., USA; June 16, 1962
Position: Center
Height: 6-3
Weight: 210
Uniform no.: 19
Shoots: left

Career statistics:

GP	G	A	TP	PIM
567	191	284	475	340

1988-89 statistics:

GP	G	A	TP	+/-	PIM	PP	SH	GW	GT	S	PCT
80	22	45	67	-38	48	10	1	3	0	151	14.6

LAST SEASON

Played 80 games for second time in career. Point totals were three-year highs. He finished second on the club in assists and power play goals, fourth in points. His plus/minus rating was the NHL's worst.

THE FINESSE GAME

Hand skills are the hallmark of Fergus's game, and that's both good news and bad news. He has an excellent wrist shot, one of the NHL's best, but he doesn't use it anywhere near enough. One reason is his distaste for the game's traffic areas. Tom's sensitive hands are perfect for working tight to the goal, scooping up loose pucks, but he won't be seen in this neighborhood.

He handles the puck well and makes good use of his wingers by moving it quickly and accurately — when he avails himself of that talent. Tom, however, tends to make that one extra move, the one that closes a passing lane or puts him in bad ice. Simple plays — like give and goes with the points — would benefit his play.

Fergus skates well, given his size, with surprising acceleration though not a lot of foot speed. That lack of quickness affects his agility and lateral movement, but what he does possess in those categories is above average for a player his size.

Tom certainly has the ability to be a good checker, but more and more his defensive play has slipped. Strange, for a player who spent the early part of his career more concerned with his play in his defensive end than he was in the offensive zone.

THE PHYSICAL GAME

Fergus has great size and he does absolutely nothing with it. He is not at all interested in a physical game, preferring to wait on the outside of scrambles for the puck. He does have excellent reach, which he uses to a good degree in his puckhandling, but Fergus has difficulty using his body to shield the puck.

He doesn't have great strength, so Tom is apt to lose any battle he happens to get into while accidentally strolling through a traffic area and, as already mentioned, he avoids contact when he can.

THE INTANGIBLES

What you see is what you get with Fergus. After eight years in the NHL, and despite his great innate ability, he remains essentially unmotivated. He plays comfortable and certainly doesn't work anywhere near hard enough.

And as for his plus/minus, we told you last year about his lackluster defensive play.

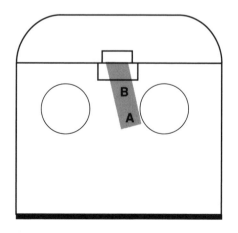

TODD GILL

Yrs. of NHL service: 3
Born: Brockville, Ontario, Canada; November 9, 1965
Position: Defenseman/left wing
Height: 6-1
Weight: 185
Uniform no.: 23
Shoots: left

Career statistics:

GP	G	A	TP	PIM
210	25	60	85	336

1988-89 statistics:

GP	G	A	TP	+/-	PIM	PP	SH	GW	GT	S	PCT
59	11	14	25	-3	72	0	0	1	0	92	12.0

LAST SEASON

Games played total was a full-season career low, but goal total was a career high and point total tied career high.

THE FINESSE GAME

Gill's finesse potential continued to show through the cracks of his game last season. Todd skates well and with good speed, but he must improve his foot speed and balance so as to A) develop some much-needed agility and B) improve his backskating and pivots for when he plays defense.

He can control the puck at his best speed, though he remains essentially a straight-ahead player. His good vision and reading ability is mitigated by his overhandling of the puck but, because he keeps his head up, he can make good breakout decisions. That tendency to overhandle the puck is worse when he plays left wing. Gill's vision and speed also allow him — when he plays defense — to join the play effectively as a fourth attacker.

As an offensive threat, he'll score from the blue line, but will cheat to the faceoff circle when he can. He'll also crash the net after one of his forays into the corner, and his hands are good enough for him to score in tight.

THE PHYSICAL GAME

Gill's physical play is a double-edged sword. While he has good strength and uses it more than willingly (Todd loves to hit and works the boards and crease well, over-powering many of the League's forwards) his lack of balance leaves him stumbling and out of the play.

He makes his physical game effective by having the hand skill to make plays after the checks — except,

again, for that big if of balance. Todd is also a good fighter, and willingly mixes it up.

THE INTANGIBLES

This guy's got talent, though not without flaws. His concentration is a big question mark, and he must bring a more consistent attitude to the rink in that regard. Which isn't to say Gill is a malingerer. On the contrary, he's very competitive and coachable. What he needs most now is a season without being shuttled between the wing and defense — and a season of regular ice-time above all.

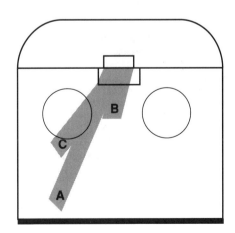

AL IAFRATE

Yrs. of NHL service: 5
Born: Dearborn, Mich., USA; March 21, 1966
Position: Defenseman
Height: 6-3
Weight: 215
Uniform no.: 33
Shoots: left

Career statistics:

GP	G	A	TP	PIM
355	57	112	169	298

1988-89 statistics:

GP	G	A	TP	+/-	PIM	PP	SH	GW	GT	S	PCT
65	13	20	33	3	72	1	2	3	1	105	12.4

LAST SEASON

Games played total tied career low (finger injury and off-ice problems). He led Leafs defensemen in scoring.

THE FINESSE GAME

Though his size would say otherwise, Iafrate is a finesse player. He skates well — probably his best finese skill — but he isn't outstandingly mobile. He has some rink-length speed and a fair degree of agility, and he uses his puckhandling ability to make his skating more effective.

Al carries the puck very well, though he does have a tendency (and it is one that he should have lost after five NHL seasons) to overhandle the puck and force a play. He rushes the puck extremely well, and it is on those rushes that most of his goals will come.

Iafrate is aided in his rushes by his playreading ability. He reads the play in front of him — and moves the puck to the forwards — well. He'll join the play as a fourth attacker and follow it to the net. His shot is excellent, but Iafrate hesitates to use it to its best advantage, just putting the puck on net instead of shooting to score.

His defensive game has matured and he plays a basically sound positional game, fairly consistently steering the opposition wide of the net.

THE PHYSICAL GAME

To damn with faint praise, Iafrate is a finesse player with size despite size conducive to some kind of efficient physical game. He plays a clutch-and-grab game and will initiate *some* contact on his own, but he doesn't do that anywhere near consistently enough. Perhaps that's just as well, because his strength is no better than average.

THE INTANGIBLES

Iafrate is probably the League's biggest enigma, because the gap between his talent and the application of same is huge. His concentration is erratic at best, and his dedication to playing to his potential is somewhere beneath that.

That said, perhaps we should consider the idea that maybe Iafrate just isn't as talented as he has been made out to be — and may never fulfill the notices his innate talent suggests.

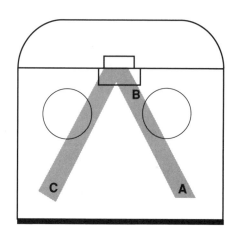

PETER IHNACAK

Yrs. of NHL service: 7
Born: Poprad, Czechoslovakia; May 3, 1957
Position: Center
Height: 6-1
Weight: 200
Uniform no.: 15
Shoots: right

Career statistics:

GP	G	A	TP	PIM
412	102	163	265	175

1988-89 statistics:

GP	G	A	TP	+/-	PIM	PP	SH	GW	GT	S	PCT
26	2	16	18	3	10	0	0	0	0	30	6.7

LAST SEASON

Games played and all point totals were career lows. Ihnacak bounced between the American Hockey League and the NHL.

THE FINESSE GAME

At this point in his career, what Ihnacak best brings to the game is his hockey sense. He reads the ice well and can anticipate openings (that's why he'll play on the power play), and Peter uses his patience and poise to make good decisions.

He has good hand skills and can lead his teammates into those openings with good passes (sometimes to his own detriment — he could be more selfish) on both the forehand and backhand sides. He also carries the puck well (he likes to carry it over the blue line rather than dump it in) and he can dangle the puck.

Ihnacak is a good skater in terms of strength and balance (along with a degree of speed), and those qualities help him in his physical and defensive games. He's a sound positional player.

He has a good shot, but he doesn't shoot enough.

THE PHYSICAL GAME

What makes Peter's finesse game work (in its modest way) is his willingness *and* ability to play in the corners and along the boards, and this is where his strength on his skates and his great balance help him. They allow him to take the body along the walls without losing his vertical stance, and thus he remains able to make a play.

Along with that "un-European" trait of physical play (which, by the way, greatly aids his defensive game), Ihnacak is also unintimidated by the League's tougher, stronger players.

He also handles the puck very well with his skates.

THE INTANGIBLES

Another in the Leafs long line of role players, Ihnacak may very well continue to float in and out of the lineup. He had some success late last season centering for youngsters Vincent Damphousse and Daniel Marois (and his work ethic may also rub off on the pair), but Ihnacak's NHL road is clearly heading downward.

Don't be surprised is he's with another team by season's end.

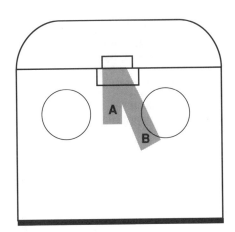

JOHN KORDIC

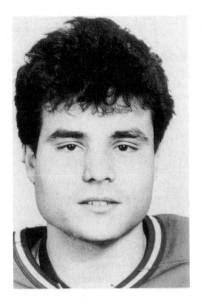

Yrs. of NHL service: 3
Born: Edmonton, Alta., Canada; March 22, 1965
Position: Left wing
Height: 6-0
Weight: 200
Uniform no.: 27
Shoots: left

Career statistics:

GP	G	A	TP	PIM
161	8	12	20	520

1988-89 statistics:

GP	G	A	TP	+/-	PIM	PP	SH	GW	GT	S	PCT
52	1	2	3	-14	198	0	0	0	0	35	2.9

LAST SEASON

Kordic was acquired from Montreal in exchange for Russ Courtnall. He led the team in PIM.

THE FINESSE GAME

There ain't much here. Kordic is no better than fair as an NHL skater. He doesn't have the speed and quickness to keep up with the NHL play, and he doesn't have the hockey sense or anticipation skills to compensate for that lack of skating ability.

John has little playmaking ability, both in terms of vision and understanding of the play and in his hand skills. That lack of skill also applies to his shot, which is almost non-existent.

He is a fair defensive player in that he plays positionally. He doesn't understand the intricacies of the game, so a creative winger can do a lot of damage opposite him.

THE PHYSICAL GAME

Kordic is big and strong, but that doesn't make him an effective physical player. He can hit well when he catches somebody, but he's not a real good hitter because he often isn't near enough the puck carrier to make a check.

He is a fighter of some ability, and it's for that ability that Kordic is in the NHL.

THE INTANGIBLES

Kordic is with Toronto as a policeman, his job being to go against the division's heavyweights — the McRaes, Kocurs and Ewens. Should the need for a policeman disappear, or should the Leafs gain a player (Tai Domi?) who brings both some kind of finesse game and a physical presence, then Kordic becomes obsolete.

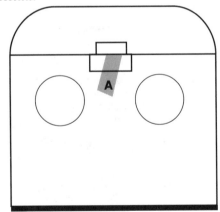

CHRIS KOTSOPOULOS

Yrs. of NHL service: 9
Born: Toronto, Ontario, Canada; November 27, 1958
Position: Defenseman
Height: 6-3
Weight: 210
Uniform no.: 26
Shoots: right

Career statistics:

GP	G	A	TP	PIM
477	44	109	153	817

1988-89 statistics:

GP	G	A	TP	+/-	PIM	PP	SH	GW	GT	S	PCT
57	1	14	15	-4	44	0	0	0	0	66	1.5

LAST SEASON

Games played total was highest in three seasons, despite rotating in and out of the lineup (an ankle injury explains part of that). Goal total was a career low.

THE FINESSE GAME

Kotsopoulos is not gifted in the finesse aspects of the game. His skating is ponderous, and his lack of speed and agility leaves him with little else to do but lumber up and down the ice.

He can handle the puck if unpressured, but forechecking will force him into mistakes. Given time and space he'll find a play to make, but otherwise Kotsopoulos will make hurried, blind passes that result in turnovers. He almost never rushes the puck, and the only offense he'll add to the Leafs is on his hard slap shot from the point. But Chris is so infrequently involved in the offensive zone — and he shoots the puck more infrequently still — that he cannot be considered any kind of offensive threat.

Kotsopoulos counters these seeming negatives by playing a fairly steady defensive game. He's learned to reduce his game to simple tasks, and he succeeds — and knows he succeeds — by staying within that simple game.

THE PHYSICAL GAME

Almost as a mirror to his mental game, Chris has learned to consistently apply his good strength to his defensive tasks. He's tough in front of the net and along the boards, and Chris has a mean streak within him that allows for an extra elbow here or there.

His strength powers his slap shot and also allows him to clear the front of the net or outmuscle the opposition in the corners, though he is not very good with the puck after gaining control of it.

He's also gotten his weight under control.

THE INTANGIBLES

Kotsopoulos is a simple player who can succeed on an understaffed team like Toronto. His role as the Leafs' most consistently effective physical defenseman will be challenged by the developing Luke Richardson, and it should be no surprise if Chris continues to rotate in and out of the lineup.

What will help him is his lately-developed work ethic and willingness to apply himself game in and game out. He's also valuable in another way — he drives the opposition crazy through his constant yapping.

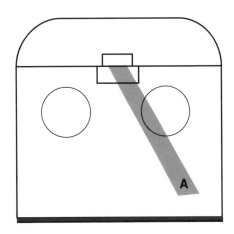

CRAIG LAUGHLIN

Yrs. of NHL service: 8
Born: Toronto, Ontario, Canada; September 19, 1957
Position: Center/right wing
Height: 6-0
Weight: 190
Uniform no.: 18
Shoots: right

Career statistics:

GP	G	A	TP	PIM
549	136	162	298	364

1988-89 statistics:

GP	G	A	TP	+/-	PIM	PP	SH	GW	GT	S	PCT
66	10	13	23	-22	41	0	0	0	0	87	11.5

LAST SEASON

Laughlin was signed as a free agent during the summer of 1988. Games played total was second-lowest for full season during his career. His plus/minus rating was team's second worst.

THE FINESSE SKILLS

Laughlin is a good skater, strong on his skates and difficult to dislodge from the puck. He handles the puck well, laying passes for his teammates fairly well off of his work in the corners.

He has some scoring touch, but Craig will have to be in fairly close proximity of the net to score. He'll generally pick up pucks in the crease, but will also net a few on snapshots from the dot in the left faceoff circle. Laughlin is also a good defensive player (good vision and anticipation) despite what his plus/minus rating says.

THE PHYSICAL GAME

This is where Laughlin shines. He is a grinder, pure hustle and hard work. He'll win those battles in the corners by just digging and digging until he can fight the puck free.

The same holds true in his defensive zone. Laughlin takes pride in being a two-way hockey player and has always taken care of his own end first.

He is not a fighter, but will mix it up if he has to. He has good strength, particularly in the upper body, and that's what wins him the one-on-one battles. This serves him around the net too.

THE INTANGIBLES

Laughlin has a tremendously positive attitude and a will to win, held over no doubt from his days with the Canadiens. Laughlin is pure heart and guts. He's a mucker and could play at the NHL level for another few years.

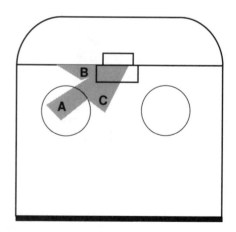

GARY LEEMAN

Yrs. of NHL service: 6
Born: Toronto, Ontario, Canada; February 19, 1964
Position: Right wing/defense
Height: 5-11
Weight: 175
Uniform no.: 11
Shoots: right

Career statistics:

GP	G	A	TP	PIM
379	101	162	263	317

1988-89 statistics:

GP	G	A	TP	+/-	PIM	PP	SH	GW	GT	S	PCT
61	32	43	75	5	66	7	1	3	0	195	16.4

LAST SEASON

Games played total was three-season low (back and ear injuries), but all point totals were career highs. He finished second in team scoring, shots on goal, and plus/minus among forwards.

THE FINESSE GAME

Primary among Leeman's good (and still growing) finesse skills are his skating and puckhandling skills. Leeman's tremendous speed, quickness and agility make him an excellent skater. His explosive quickness and ability to change directions and speeds within a step easily drives defenders backward and draws penalties.

Gary's skating is augmented by his hand skill, because he can do anything with the puck at even his fastest speed. He also has excellent touch with his passes (complemented by his good ice vision), and for the first time made better use of his teammates by cutting down on his one-on-one maneuvers.

Leeman's accurate and quickly released shot reflects his superior hand skill. He can score from anywhere because of his shot, one-times the puck exceptionally well and makes his excellent shot better by practicing patience and forcing the opposition (both defense and goaltender) to commit itself. He'll be moved to a defensive position on offensive zone faceoffs so that the Leafs can take advantage of that shot.

THE PHYSICAL GAME

Leeman plays bigger than his size, but that's not to say he plays a Wendel Clark-type game. He has deceptive strength for his build, and will surprise the opposition by muscling through checks to get his shot off. A more active physical game — and not just the

acceptance of hits — would benefit him greatly, as it would open up more ice in which to work.

Leeman is also a surprisingly good fighter, but — again — that is not his style of game.

THE INTANGIBLES

There's still plenty of room left in Leeman's game for improvement; he could be a 40-goal scorer. He's already Toronto's most talented player, one to whom the game comes easily, but he does need the ocassional kick in the butt to get motivated.

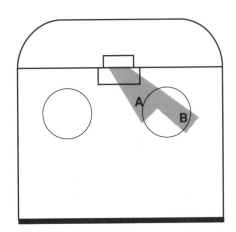

DAN MAROIS

Yrs. of NHL service: 1
Born: Montreal, Quebec, Canada; October 3, 1968
Position: Right wing
Height: 6-1
Weight: 180
Uniform no.: 32
Shoots: right

Career statistics:

GP	G	A	TP	+/-	PIM	PP	SH	GW	GT	S	PCT
76	31	23	54	-4	76	7	0	4	1	146	21.2

LAST SEASON

Marois's first in the NHL (he played three playoff games in 1987-88). He finished third on the club in goals (second among the NHL's rookies).

THE FINESSE GAME

Marois is a pretty good package of finesse skills, the explosive kind that can be readily seen. He skates well with good quickness and agility and some pull-away NHL speed, and he uses that skill to get into the open for passes and into scoring position for his shooting.

He is a very creative offensive player and creates his own openings through skating and hockey sense. He displays rookie tendencies, however, by failing to do those things on a consistent shift-to-shift and game-to-game basis.

Daniel has good-to-very-good hands (good enough to handle the puck in traffic when it must be close to his body, and good enough to take passes in stride) and he can use those hands to pass the puck well, but he is primarily a finisher and will shoot the puck when given the opportunity. He shoots well from both the short ranges and the distances, with his excellent release the highlight of those shots.

Like his offense, his defense tends to be erratic at best. But, to be a rookie goal-scorer and to be *only* minus-4 on a team that was an overall *minus-83* — well, that's not too bad.

THE PHYSICAL GAME

Marois has good — not great — size, but he's willing to put it to use when necessary. He won't belt anyone into the cheap seats, but he'll do the bumping along the boards and in traffic that will free the puck and let his hand skills do their thing.

He takes checks to make plays, and he'll cut to the net for goals. He won't be intimidated, and he uses his body well to protect the puck.

THE INTANGIBLES

Not a bad rookie year, considering the surroundings. Marois go a little stronger as the year progressed (13 goals in his first 40 games, 18 in his last 36), and that bodes well for his future progress. He's one of the youngsters who must develop if the Leafs are to break their cycle of mediocrity.

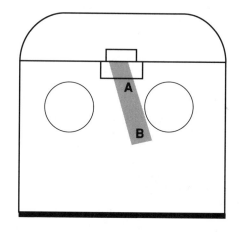

BRAD MARSH

Yrs. of NHL service: 11
Born: London, Ontario, Canada; March 31, 1958
Position: Defenseman
Height: 6-2
Weight: 215
Uniform no.: 8
Shoots: left

Career statistics:

GP	G	A	TP	PIM
851	18	152	170	1,032

1988-89 statistics:

GP	G	A	TP	+/-	PIM	PP	SH	GW	GT	S	PCT
80	1	15	16	-16	79	0	0	0	0	69	1.4

LAST SEASON

Marsh played 80 games for the first time in eight seasons, the only Toronto defenseman to play the full season. His point total was a four-season high.

THE FINESSE GAME

Never known as   — and never to be mistaken for —a finesse player, Marsh showed a real decline last year. Though still a better skater than he's often credited, Marsh's foot speed has noticeably decreased. The improvement he'd shown in moving up and down the ice over the last few seasons was nowhere to be found last year, so he more and more must atone for his skating deficiencies with positional play.

He uses his defensive angles very well, reads the rush approaching him excellently. Because he's so determined to help out, Marsh often gets out of position around the net, falling here to block a shot, diving there to stop a pass. Appreciated though this determination may be, it also serves to make Marsh's partner and the goaltender crazy.

Though his role is not that of puckhandling defeseman, Marsh will get it out of his end quickly and well.

THE PHYSICAL GAME

Marsh is a strong, physical player. He clears the front of the net well and probably keeps the oppositon out of the play as well as anyone in the League. He's no doubt helped in that last aspect by the fact that he's also an excellent holder, one of the League's best. He willingly sacrifices his body to block shots.

He will muscle the opposition off the puck along the boards — *if* he can catch anyone — and has a good reach that helps him to pokecheck the puck away from incoming forwards.

THE INTANGIBLES

Despite his diminishing skating skill, Marsh still puts out all the time. Because of that he remains a leader through his work ethic and dedication, and as such can continue to have a positive effect on the Leafs despite his limited on-ice contributions. It is the arrival of players like Darryl Shannon, by the way, that may be forcing the limitations on Marsh's ice time.

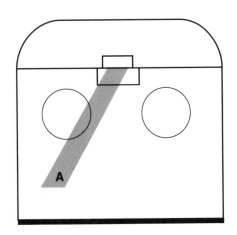

ED OLCZYK

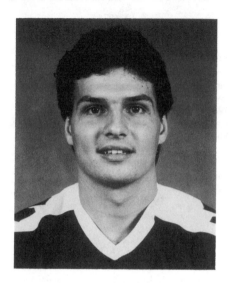

Yrs. of NHL service: 5
Born: Chicago, Illinois, USA; August 16, 1966
Position: Center/right wing
Height: 6-1
Weight: 200
Uniform no.: 16
Shoots: left

Career statistics:

GP	G	A	TP	PIM
388	145	200	345	363

1988-89 statistics:

GP	G	A	TP	+/-	PIM	PP	SH	GW	GT	S	PCT
80	38	52	90	0	75	11	2	4	1	249	15.3

LAST SEASON

Olczyk led the club in scoring, goals, power play goals, and shots on goal. Assist and point totals were career highs. He played 80 games for the second consecutive season.

THE FINESSE GAME

Poise and patience are the watermarks of Olczyk's game, and they combine with his anticipation to give him good-to-very-good hockey sense — so much so that Olczyk can be counted on to make the right play almost 100 percent of the time. He's almost completely unaffected by pressure from the opposition because of those assets, so he'll not only make correct decisions but good ones.

Though those abilities last season allowed him to use his teammates better than he ever has before, Olczyk remains a scorer first and a playmaker second — as his SOG total indicates. Of course, since his hockey sense is also likely to put him into scoring position, that's just fine.

His excellent snap shot is his best weapon: strong, accurate, quickly released. Olczyk also loves to pick the top corners for his goals, and his scoring and mental abilities make him a specialty teams natural.

Ed is a good skater, equipped with speed and quickness not usually found in bigger men. He can out-race an opponent in the long haul, but his quickness will also get him to a lot of loose pucks. That quickness gives him agility, and also allows him to force offense from a broken play.

He's not a defensive star, but Olczyk is far from inept in that category. While he makes the occasional positional mistake, Ed's plus/minus rating is remarkable considering his tremendous ice time and the fact that his team was an astonishing *minus-83*.

THE PHYSICAL GAME

As much as he maximizes his finesse skills, Olczyk minimizes his physical ones. He has great size, but has done almost nothing to improve his strength. In fact, he does little with the strength he already has, assiduously avoiding contact. He prefers the open ice to the traffic areas and that's surprising, because with his skills he could be a tremendous presence on the ice.

That lack of attention also demonstrates itself in his conditioning, or lack thereof; he comes off the ice after 30 seconds as if he were half-dead.

THE INTANGIBLES

He can be a better player than currently (and Olczyk is already a pretty good one), but Ed is one of those players who plays comfortable. He takes what his talent alone provides and he doesn't work at becoming a better player. We're not saying he doesn't work during games, or that he doesn't honestly care. What it means is that he isn't motivated enough to work at improving.

Desire will be the key to his career. If he wants to, he can join the League's elite.

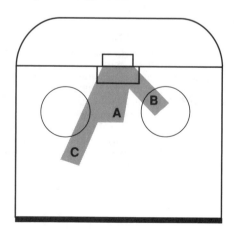

MARK OSBORNE

Yrs. of NHL service: 8
Born: Toronto, Ontario, Canada; August 13, 1961
Position: Left wing
Height: 6-2
Weight: 205
Uniform no.: 12
Shoots: left

Career statistics:

GP	G	A	TP	PIM
546	149	213	362	672

1988-89 statistics:

GP	G	A	TP	+/-	PIM	PP	SH	GW	GT	S	PCT
75	16	30	46	-5	112	5	0	1	0	118	13.6

LAST SEASON

Goal total tied full-season career low. PIM total was team's third highest, first among forwards.

THE FINESSE GAME

Though primarily a physical, grinding player, Osborne boasts two good finesse skills. He's a surprisingly good skater for a guy with his size and bulk, using the strength in his stride to power his rink-length speed. He doesn't have good balance, though, so Mark lacks the agility that would give him good lateral movement. He also is lacking in foot speed.

Mark's shot is his other notable finesse ability. He delivers it to the net with great power but, because Mark is neither exceptionally accurate nor especially quick with his release, the shot is not the weapon it could be.

Mark's other hand skills generally mirror the negatives of his shot. He's not a gifted puck carrier, especially when in full flight, and his hockey smarts don't make up for his tough hands. Osborne doesn't see the ice particularly well, so he's reduced to one-dimensional play — charging ahead himself or tossing the puck around the boards. If he could learn to keep his head up, his play would improve.

THE PHYSICAL GAME

Though his skating is his best finesse asset, it tends to betray Osborne in his willing and strong physical game. Because he has a higher center of gravity, Mark has a tendency to end up on the ice after checks. That leaves him unable to rejoin the play immediately.

He's got good size and strength and uses those tools to bang around in the corners and along the boards, though his inability to make a play coming out of the corner lends dubious value to that physicality.

Mark's also in excellent condition, and that allows him to finish his checks all over the ice throughout the game.

THE INTANGIBLES

We questioned whether Osborne could continue the success he discovered in 1987-88. Osborne isn't talented enough to succeed on talent alone, so if he works hard he can raise himself out of the role player class. If not, then he's just another body on a team full of bodies.

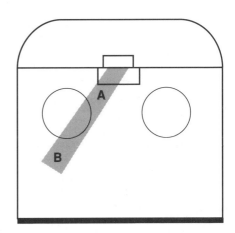

ROB RAMAGE

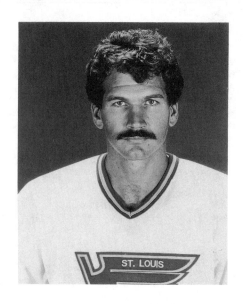

Yrs. of NHL service: 10
Born: Byron, Ontario, Canada; January 11, 1959
Position: Defenseman
Height: 6-2
Weight: 195
Uniform no.: 55
Shoots: right

Career statistics:

GP	G	A	TP	PIM
755	112	339	451	1,620

1988-89 statistics:

GP	G	A	TP	+/-	PIM	PP	SH	GW	GT	S	PCT
68	3	13	16	26	156	2	0	0	0	91	3.3

LAST SEASON

Games played total was second lowest of career, goal, assist and point totals career lows. PIM total was three-season high, second highest among defensemen.

THE FINESSE GAME

Ramage is an excellent skater, more so considering his size and bulk. He moves well backward and forward, and his good foot speed and lateral movement allow him to challenge the puck at both blue lines. Rob moves up into the play as a fourth attacker well, but with Calgary's array of talent from the blue line he doesn't need to challenge much.

He will grab the puck and rush with it, alleviating pressure on the forwards, but Ramage is more likely to gain the puck and whisk it up-ice to the forwards. He has good anticipation for the openings at both ends of the ice and will get the puck to his teammates in those openings; he's a good passer.

He's more likely to act as a defensive anchor for the Flames because of their potent blue line talent, and Ramage fits easily into that role by reading rushes well and playing good positional hockey.

Offensively, he has a good hard slap shot from the point, and will sneak to the slot if he can.

THE PHYSICAL GAME

Ramage is a very strong player, and he plays a physical game befitting his strength. He hits frequently along the boards and does an excellent job eliminating the opposition. Ramage makes his physical game better by having the finesse skills to make a play after gaining the puck.

Rob is just as effective in front of the net (and mean too), where only the NHL's strongest forwards will win a 1-on-1 battle against him.

THE INTANGIBLES

Though a well-rounded performer, Ramage sacrificed his offensive opportunities for the good of the team, so that he could concentrate on the defensive work the Flames needed to balance out their blue line corps.

Rob is — even after 11 seasons of professional hockey — an above average player with great maturity and a positive work ethic.

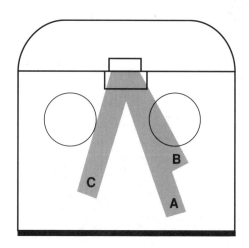

DAVE REID

Yrs. of NHL service: 3
Born: Toronto, Ontario, Canada; May 15, 1964
Position: Left wing
Height: 6-1
Weight: 205
Uniform no.: 14
Shoots: left

Career statistics:

GP	G	A	TP	PIM
172	37	47	84	61

1988-89 statistics:

GP	G	A	TP	+/-	PIM	PP	SH	GW	GT	S	PCT
77	9	21	30	12	22	1	1	0	0	87	10.3

LAST SEASON

Games played total was career high.

THE FINESSE GAME

Reid is no better than average as a skater, doing more plodding up and down the ice than anything else. He has no real speed or quickness to speak of, and his agility and lateral movement are at the same levels.

His hand skills also fall into the average (and probably below average) categories. He doesn't handle the puck well at all and that's reflected in his scoring ability, which is minimal. If he doesn't have the goaltender down and out and is just a step from the net, he doesn't have much chance of scoring. Likewise, his playmaking ability is limited as well.

Reid is willing to play defense and is fairly good at it. He sticks to his position in the defensive zone (and the offensive zone too, where he demonstrates neither anticipation nor imagination) and stays in the way of his check.

THE PHYSICAL GAME

Reid knows how to obstruct the opposition with his body, but he's not really a hitter. He'll accept contact as he goes to make his plays and he'll impose himself to a degree, but he doesn't bring a great physical value to his game.

THE INTANGIBLES

Reid succeeded last season by doing a lot of grunt work, frequently absorbing the defensive responsibilities while playing between Vincent Damphousse and Daniel Marois.

He is otherwise little more than a utility, fourth-line player whose best asset is the work ethic and desire he brings.

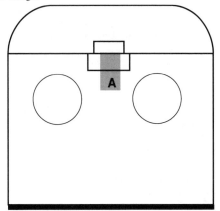

LUKE RICHARDSON

Yrs. of NHL service: 2
Born: Ottawa, Ontario, Canada; March 26, 1969
Position: Defenseman
Height: 6-3
Weight: 210
Uniform no.: 2
Shoots: left

Career statistics:

GP	G	A	TP	PIM
133	6	13	19	196

1988-1989 statistics:

GP	G	A	TP	+/-	PIM	PP	SH	GW	GT	S	PCT
55	2	7	9	-15	106	0	0	0	0	59	3.4

LAST SEASON

PIM total was second highest among defensemen.

THE FINESSE GAME

Richardson is an outstanding skater, made even more so by virtue of the bulk he carries around the rink. He skates excellently both back and forth, and he also has good mobility and lateral movement to close the gaps and force the play. Good acceleration skills help him here, and right now Richardson uses his skating skill defensively. He won't challenge at the blue line, preferring to fall back and defend.

He plays defense smartly by not putting himself in bad situations. Luke protects his area of the ice as well as any player on the Leafs, but he also possesses the ability to recover if he becomes trapped. He closes the skating lane down and takes the man out of the play.

When he does play offensively, Richardson moves the puck from his end well. He has a good slap shot from the blue line and he's using it more frequently, but it will need to improve if it is to consistently fool NHL goaltending.

THE PHYSICAL GAME

Richardson has excellent size and strength and he brings them to bear as the team's best 1-on-1 defensive bodychecker — the mid-season hit he laid on New York's Tony Granato essentially ended the Ranger rookie's season.

Luke is exceptionally strong in front of the net and his strength allows him to out-muscle most other players along the boards or in the corners. And he'll only improve in these areas, as his body continues to mature and fill out.

THE INTANGIBLES

Richardson would be better served as he serves his NHL apprenticeship if he played for a more consistent — and better — team. That way he'd get some positive reinforcement from the team's positive situation, and there'd be less defensive chaos to force him into mistakes.

But even with that he has an excellent attitude and will work on anything the coach asks. He'll develop into a leader for Toronto because of his desire and work ethic.

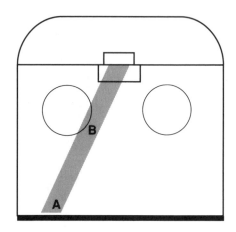

DARRYL SHANNON

Yrs. of NHL service: 1
Born: Barrie, Ontario, Canada; June 21, 1968
Position: Defenseman
Height: 6-2
Weight: 190
Uniform no.: 34
Shoots: left

Career statistics:

GP	G	A	TP	+/-	PIM	PP	SH	GW	GT	S	PCT
14	1	3	4	5	6	0	0	0	0	16	6.3

LAST SEASON

Shannon joined the Leafs late in the season, otherwise playing for Newmarket of the AHL.

THE FINESSE GAME

Shannon is a good skater both forward and backward, demonstrating good NHL speed, acceleration and agility in both directions. That allows him to be more active as a defender, stepping up to close the gap between himself and puck carrier instead of just backing in on his goaltender and trying to force the play wide. He turns well to both sides, and Darryl has enough confidence in his skating that he'll carry the puck from the zone when he can.

He can also do that because he handles the puck well when carrying it, and Darryl makes this skill more effective by not forcing himself into the offense when there are no openings. He'll look for the open forward once he's gained the neutral zone and then make the pass. In short, Shannon has the vision and sense necessary, and he stays within his game.

He's aggressive in the offensive zone and will cut to the slot for a shot if he can (his sense and skating get him back into position after he challenges). Again, his skills allow him to contain the point fairly well.

THE PHYSICAL GAME

Shannon has good size and strength and isn't afraid to use those assets in front of his net. But unlike teammate Luke Richardson, whose hits are eye-openers, Shannon is more efficient than he is spectacular. He knows how to use his size and strength to gain the puck, especially along the boards, and his hand skills allow him to make plays coming out of those confrontations.

He is willing to sacrifice his body (he plays in pain), and his good physical game should improve with further NHL experience.

THE INTANGIBLES

Shannon has an excellent work ethic, and his desire and attitude will carry him a long way on his road to NHL success. They are particularly important traits because they indicate maturity, and that ability to keep focused is a necessary ingredient for success in the sometimes chaotic world of the Leafs.

He too is one of the youngsters Toronto is hoping hard about.

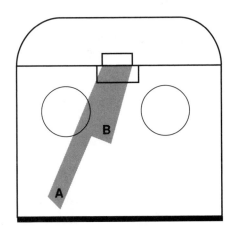

VANCOUVER
CANUCKS

FORWARDS

LEFT WING
MEL BRIDGMAN-PETRI SKRIKOBRIAN
RICH SUTTER-GREG C. ADAMS

CENTER
TREVOR LINDEN-BRIAN BRADLEY
GREG ADAMS-STEVE BOZEK

RIGHT WING
JIM SANDLAK-STAN SMYL
TONY TANTI

DEFENSEMEN

LEFT DEFENSE
LARRY MELNYK-HAROLD SNEPSTS
JIM BENNING-PAUL REINHART

RIGHT DEFENSE
DOUG LIDSTER-ROBERT NORDMARK
GARTH BUTCHER

GOALTENDERS
KIRK MCLEAN
STEVE WEEKS

OTHER PLAYERS
DAVID BRUCE — Right wing
BARRY PEDERSON — Center

POWER PLAY

PETTRI SKRIKO and TONY TANTI work from their respective faceoff circles (TANTI sliding closer to the net), while TREVOR LINDEN works from the hashmarks and in the slot. JIM SANDLAK plugs the front of the net and snares rebounds, GREG ADAMS darts into the slot for shots off defensive passes.

PAUL REINHART and ROBERT NORD-MARK, along with DOUG LIDSTER run the blue line.

Last season Vancouver's power play was POOR, scoring 78 goals in 410 opportunities (19.0 percent, 18th overall).

FIRST UNIT:
Vancouver's penalty killing was not very aggressive. RICH SUTTER, STEVE BOZEK, TREVOR LINDEN and BARRY PEDERSON are the main forwards, and they'll pressure the puck at the blue line but not the other zones. Defensemen will be JIM BENNING, GARTH BUTCHER, LARRY MELNYK and HAROLD SNEPSTS. Only BENNING will be aggressive; the rest watch the front of the net.

Last season Vancouver's penalty killing was GOOD, allowing 66 goals in 341 shorthanded situations (80.6 percent, ninth overall).

CRUCIAL FACEOFFS
BARRY PEDERSON and TREVOR LINDEN.

GREG ADAMS

Yrs. of NHL service: 4
Born: Nelson, B.C., Canada; August 1, 1963
Position: Center
Height: 6-3
Weight: 185
Uniform no.: 8
Shoots: left

Career statistics:

GP	G	A	TP	PIM
327	122	132	254	117

1988-89 statistics:

GP	G	A	TP	+/-	PIM	PP	SH	GW	GT	S	PCT
61	19	14	33	-21	24	9	0	2	0	144	13.2

LAST SEASON

Games played and all point totals were full-season lows. His plus/minus was the club's worst. He was sidelined with a twisted knee.

THE FINESSE GAME

Greg succeeds as a scorer because of his ability to get into scoring position. The key to that ability is his sense and anticipation, which reveal the openings to him — after that, the rest is up to his physical finesse skills.

He's an unexceptional skater, but he does have very good balance. He uses that skill to lean in on the defense en route to the goal, and also to lean away from the defense to protect the puck. He's neither fast nor quick, but his long stride will carry him past the opposition. Improved foot speed would help him in his play around the net by providing him with the ability to get to loose pucks. As it is, he is almost completely an up-and-down player because he lacks lateral ability.

Greg carries the puck well when he moves up-ice but again, because he lacks the requisite agility he could not be considered a puckhandling threat; he'll succeed by keeping the puck away from the defense because of his reach.

His shot is good, hard to the net and quickly released, and he also has the strength to score from a distance. He'll be a power play regular because of his shot and ability to get open.

THE PHYSICAL GAME

Adams has exceptional reach, as we've already discussed, but his great size is contradicted by his lack of strength. He has no real bulk, so he can be taken off the puck by smaller and/or stronger forwards. He does use his body to protect the puck extremely well; his wingspan is almost unmatched (only Mario Lemieux and Joel Otto comes to mind) in the League.

THE INTANGIBLES

Adams does this good-year-bad-year thing, so this season is supposed to be a good year. He has certain exceptional skills, but Greg hasn't shown any signs of doing the things necessary to improve his game and raise it to a consistent level.

And his defense is so poor, he practically renders his offense useless.

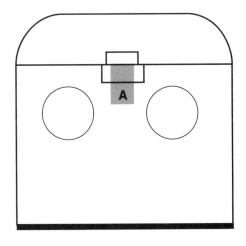

GREG C. ADAMS

Yrs. of NHL service: 6
Born: Duncan, B.C., Canada; May 31, 1960
Position: Left wing
Height: 6-2
Weight: 200
Uniform no.: 22
Shoots: left

Career statistics:

GP	G	A	TP	PIM
510	80	133	213	1,140

1988-89 statistics:

GP	G	A	TP	+/-	PIM	PP	SH	GW	GT	S	PCT
61	8	7	15	3	117	2	0	1	0	71	11.3

LAST SEASON

Acquired from Edmonton after mid-season. Games played, all point and PIM totals were full-season career lows.

THE FINESSE GAME

Though not a great skater, Adams has fairly good mobility for a bigger man. He does need some room for his turns and is wanting in the foot speed department, but Adams is a strong skater with fairly good balance and a little acceleration because of that leg strength. He uses his skating in his defensive play, going deep into his zone.

Greg is not a playmaker of any great note, but he does make the attempt to keep his head up and use his teammates when he can. He doesn't have NHL level hands in terms of sensitivity for making or receiving passes, and the play has to be slowed down for Adams to be successful at moving the puck. It is his checking (and particularly his hitting) that frees up pucks and creates scoring opportunities.

His shot is average, a slapper blasted from just inside the blue line or the top of the circle that catches the goaltender by surprise. If he shot more, and gave himself some tighter angles, Adams could score more goals, but that argument comes back to smarts and understanding of the game — combined with ice vision — and those are not the strengths of Greg's game.

THE PHYSICAL GAME

Adams enjoys a physical game and that's good, because that's where he's most effective. He hits anything in an opposing jersey with abandon, and that forces the opposition to worry about his hitting and takes their minds off making their own plays.

He'll also plug the front of the net on the power play every once in a while, and he can succeed there because he pesters goaltenders beyond belief with little pokes and shoves and elbows.

Adams uses his size to tie up the opposition as he backchecks and is effective at taking his check out of the play. He can duke it out too.

THE INTANGIBLES

Greg Adams is the kind of guy that would probably be called an honest player. He sticks to what he does best and doesn't try to do what is beyond his abilities. He works to succeed within the framework of his game, and is a tough, hard-nosed player who will sacrifice himself for the good of the team.

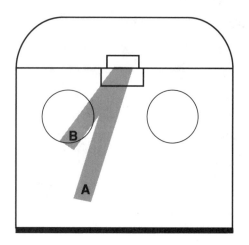

JIM BENNING

Yrs. of NHL service: 8
Born: Edmonton, Alta., Canada; April 29, 1963
Position: Defenseman
Height: 6-0
Weight: 185
Uniform no.: 4
Shoots: left

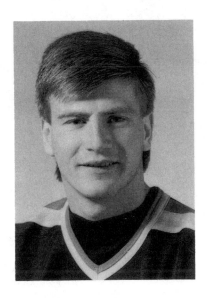

Career statistics:

GP	G	A	TP	PIM
560	49	182	231	435

1988-89 statistics:

GP	G	A	TP	+/-	PIM	PP	SH	GW	GT	S	PCT
65	3	9	12	-4	48	1	0	0	0	55	5.5

LAST SEASON

Assist and point totals were career lows. He was sidelined at mid-season with a back injury.

THE FINESSE GAME

Benning is an above-average skater with excellent mobility, the kind of skating skill that allows him to challenge the puck at both blue lines. His excellent acceleration and lateral movement abilities allow him to pinch in and forecheck offensively (as well as contain the point on the power play), and those same skills help him step up and close the gap on the puck carrier to be an active (as opposed to *re*-active) defenseman.

He tends to show good judgment in his pursuit of the puck, but he can still miscalculate in his wandering toward the play and thus leave openings behind him. His ability to read the rush going away from him is fairly strong, so Jim will most usually get the puck efficiently to the forwards. He can, however, be forced to make blind passes around the boards by strong forechecking.

Jim follows the play up-ice (he also has the ability to rush the puck) but seldom does more than take up position at the blue line. He can find the open man there, and he has a good shot from the point.

THE PHYSICAL GAME

Jim is a finesse player with size. He'll tie men up along the boards or in front of the net, but he won't knock anyone into the nickel seats. And since he always has his attention on the puck and not the man, it's no surprise he could play the body better than he does.

THE INTANGIBLES

He's a fairly well-rounded player, able to contribute offensively and defensively, and Benning plays at a fairly consistent level most every night. His dependability is important to the Canucks.

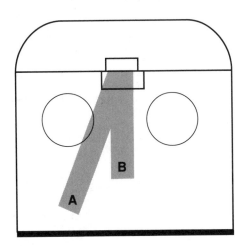

STEVE BOZEK

Yrs. of NHL service: 7
Born: Kelowna, B.C., Canada; November 26, 1960
Position: Left wing
Height: 5-11
Weight: 180
Uniform no.: 14
Shoots: left

Career statistics:

GP	G	A	TP	PIM
463	127	133	260	228

1988-89 statistics:

GP	G	A	TP	+/-	PIM	PP	SH	GW	GT	S	PCT
71	17	18	35	1	64	0	2	2	0	138	12.3

LAST SEASON

Acquired with Paul Reinhart from Calgary for future considerations. Games played total tied career high. PIM total was second highest of career. Was sidelined by a knee injury.

THE FINESSE GAME

Bozek is a very quick skater with exceptional speed. He accelerates well and is also very quick in any direction and has good balance on his skates, allowing him to change direction and move laterally well.

He uses that skill when on the penalty-killing unit, where he is a definite threat for the short-handed goal. Additionally, that speed and quickness is a staple of Bozek's role-playing defensive game, a role that he fills very well.

As a goal scorer, Bozek isn't. He plays the game at 100 miles per hour, gets 100 scoring chances and can't score because his hands are terrible. Steve's not very clever around the net and doesn't have the strength to blow the puck past anyone from a distance. He will pick up rebound and junk goals to the tune of 20 goals a year and he'll have to be in close proximity of the net to do so. One reason why Bozek doesn't score more — excepting his defensive role — is that he puts himself at bad shooting angles.

Bozek can be a good passer, but he doesn't see the ice very well and makes many of his plays with his head down, so he can't be said to use his teammates any better than averagely. Another thing to remember is that Bozek's hands aren't as skilled as his feet, and his hands become less effective the faster he goes.

He does, however, use his smarts as a defensive forward and is able to check not only because of his speed, but also because of his understanding of the action around him.

THE PHYSICAL GAME

Though not predominantly a physical player, Bozek is very strong for his size (which isn't 5-11

either). This helps him in his checking role when fighting for the puck, but he won't knock anyone into the middle of next week.

Steve is also an exceptionally conditioned athlete, and he works on some phase of conditioning everyday.

THE INTANGIBLES

Steve is a cut above regular role player status because of his modicum of offensive ability and his attitude. He's a very positive person, demonstrated by the fact that he doesn't complain when he doesn't play, and he performs well when given the chance. He has the skills to check even the most talented players to a standstill.

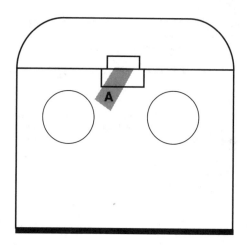

BRIAN BRADLEY

Yrs. of NHL service: 2
Born: Kitchener, Ontario, Canada; January 21, 1965
Position: Center
Height: 5-10
Weight: 170
Uniform no.: 10
Shoots: right

Career statistics:

GP	G	A	TP	PIM
127	31	51	82	64

1988-89 statistics:

GP	G	A	TP	+/-	PIM	PP	SH	GW	GT	S	PCT
71	18	27	45	-5	42	6	0	3	0	151	11.9

LAST SEASON

Games played, all point and PIM totals were career highs. Finished fifth on the club in points.

THE FINESSE GAME

Bradley has primarily been a playmaking center throughout his career, and he's continued that trend in the NHL during his first full season. Brian uses his quickness and agility to get into the open and to snare loose pucks, and his sense and anticipation help him in that regard.

He gets a fairly good view of the ice and can get the puck to his teammates, but he needs a better grasp of the NHL's tempo. He has good hand skills and should be able to adjust to that tempo (in terms of recognizing a play and then making it) with greater NHL experience.

His skating will kick in for his goal scoring, getting him to the net for loose pucks and allowing him to get a step on a defenseman for a cut-in shot. Bradley's ability to get open and get his shot away explain why he's on the power play.

He needs better positional play and understanding of the transitional game between offense and defense in order to become a better two-way player.

THE PHYSICAL GAME

Bradley is a finesse player, not a physical one. Which is fine, because there isn't a lot he can bring to a physical game. He'll succeed physically by engineering hit-and-run missions that bump the opposition off the puck and then carry him away before the opponent can recover.

His size is going to be a concern, especially in a division where many of the centers are bigger than he.

THE INTANGIBLES

In all, not a bad rookie year — which is essentially what 1988-89 was for Brian. Now he has to show the ability and determination to correct his flaws.

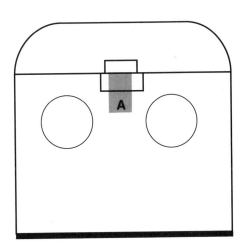

MEL BRIDGMAN

Yrs. of NHL service: 13
Born: Trenton, Ontario, Canada; April 28, 1955
Position: Center
Height: 6-0
Weight: 190
Uniform no.: 28
Shoots: left

Career statistics:

GP	G	A	TP	PIM
977	252	449	701	1,625

1988-89 statistics:

GP	G	A	TP	+/-	PIM	PP	SH	GW	GT	S	PCT
15	4	3	7	-4	10	2	0	0	0	17	23.5

LAST SEASON

Signed as a free agent late in the season. Games played was career low.

THE FINESSE GAME

Bridgman is a fair skater, losing a step or two as age creeps into his game. But he counters that with smarts and good hockey sense. Bridgman is always aware of where he is on the ice and what his play will be after he has the puck. That's what anticipation is all about.

He's a good shooter with strong hands and he'll do the dirty work in the crease. Mel is not much of a puck handler; those strong hands betray him when softness is needed and he doesn't take or give a pass with much touch.

Bridgman's an average goal scorer — in the 20-25 goal range over a full season — but he also contributes with his defensive play. He uses anticipation well in the defensive zone and comes back to help out the defensemen.

THE PHYSICAL GAME

Bridgman is aggressive. He uses his size to advantage all over the ice and likes to hit because it wakes up both him and the team and keeps him in the game.

THE INTANGIBLES

Brought in as a late-season addition to fill a hole caused by injuries, Bridgman showed well. His attitude is terrific, a team leader who gets his nose dirty and leads by example, a guy who takes coaching despite his decade-plus of NHL experience.

Given that, whether or not he'll return to Vancouver once their centers are healthy is a big question mark.

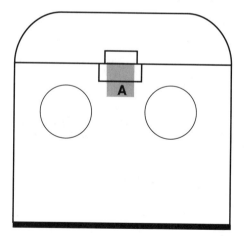

DAVID BRUCE

Yrs. of NHL service: 3
Born: Thunder Bay, Ontario, Canada; October 7, 1964
Position: Right wing
Height: 5-11
Weight: 187
Uniform no.: 25
Shoots: right

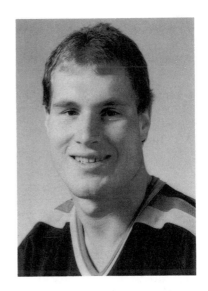

Career statistics:

GP	G	A	TP	PIM
143	23	18	41	245

1988-89 statistics:

GP	G	A	TP	+/-	PIM	PP	SH	GW	GT	S	PCT
53	7	7	14	-16	65	1	0	2	0	86	8.1

LAST SEASON

Games played total was career high, even after being sidelined with surgery to an injured finger. Plus/minus was the club's second worst.

THE FINESSE GAME

Bruce is no better than average in the finesse department. His improved stride and foot speed have made him a halfway decent NHL skater, good enough that he can function as a checking forward. He's added mobility to his game as well, and the ability to stop, start and change direction abruptly are important skills for a checker to have.

David has a fair dose of hockey smarts, possessing a good idea of how a play will develop and how he can either help it or prevent. He is not tremendously creative in open ice, but his vision is good enough that he will recognize openings and get to them. Bruce concentrates on using those skills defensively, but his history shows he can contribute offensively.

He has a hard wrist shot but doesn't shoot enough (again, the defensive role taking priority), but because he's not going to blow any slap shots past NHL goaltending Bruce will have to be in close proximity of the net to score.

THE PHYSICAL GAME

Bruce's balance and physical strength help him in his checking game, but he's not an exceptionally gifted physical player. He remains vertical after collisions, so he can continue his plays.

THE INTANGIBLES

Health is the big factor here, especially considering that Bruce is a 25-year-old role player. If he can't stay in the lineup, he might not get back into the lineup. In his favor is the fact that he has great desire, as epitomized by his work toward improvement.

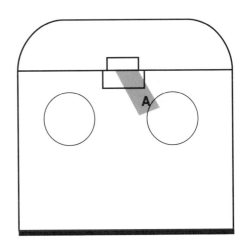

GARTH BUTCHER

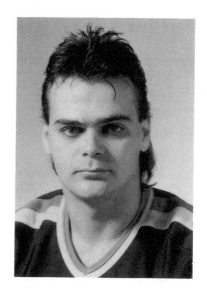

Yrs. of NHL service: 7
Born: Regina, Sask., Canada; January 8, 1963
Position: Defenseman
Height: 6-0
Weight: 200
Uniform no.: 5
Shoots: right

Career statistics:

GP	G	A	TP	PIM
461	21	81	102	1,206

1988-89 statistics:

GP	G	A	TP	+/-	PIM	PP	SH	GW	GT	S	PCT
78	0	20	20	4	227	0	0	0	0	101	0.0

LAST SEASON

Games played total was second highest of career, assist total career high. He led club in PIM total and was third in plus/minus, first among defensemen.

THE FINESSE GAME

Though limited in the offensive area of the game, Butcher plays to the limits of his finesse ability. His skating has improved to the point where he can keep pace with most any player in the league in any direction. Butcher's improved foot speed and balance have given him a fair degree of mobility, so now Garth can play an active — as opposed to *re*-active — defensive game. He can step up on the puck carrier to force the play, and Butcher makes the most of his limited skill by staying within his capabilities.

Though he rarely does so (especially being paired with Paul Reinhart), Garth has the ability to rush the puck and create offensive chances at the opposition's blue line. His improved foot speed has gained him extra time to make plays, and that helps the Canucks — no longer are they (essentially) playing 4-on-5 when Garth is at the blue line; he does not, as a rule, pinch in or challenge the puck at the offensive blue line.

Butcher also moves the puck well to the forwards for breakout passes, using his poise to look for the right play.

THE PHYSICAL GAME

Butcher plays a tough, aggressive game. He takes the body well in the corners and along the boards (though he is really one-dimensional, in that he won't make a play after the hit), and makes the opposition pay for every chance they get in front of his net.

He's Vancouver's policeman and tough guy, taking on the League's heavyweights to protect his teammates.

THE INTANGIBLES

An honest, dedicated player and a good team man, Butcher plays an important role for the Canucks by being their most consistent defensive force.

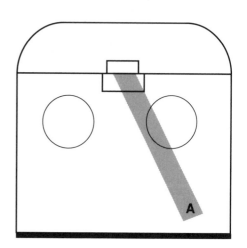

DOUG LIDSTER

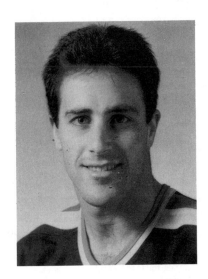

Yrs. of NHL service: 5
Born: Kamloops, B.C., Canada; October 18, 1960
Position: Defenseman
Height: 6-1
Weight: 200
Uniform no.: 3
Shoots: right

Career statistics:

GP	G	A	TP	PIM
371	39	140	179	338

1988-89 statistics:

GP	G	A	TP	+/-	PIM	PP	SH	GW	GT	S	PCT
63	5	17	22	-4	78	3	0	0	0	116	4.3

LAST SEASON

Games played total was full-season career low (hand injury, fractured cheekbone); ditto point total. Assist total was second lowest of career.

THE FINESSE GAME

Skating is the best of Lidster's finesse skills, and he is exceptionally gifted in that area. He has excellent mobility and agility — especially laterally — and the ability to move in any direction within a step. His foot speed and balance are the keys. He lacks truly explosive acceleration, but Doug can get to nearby loose pucks because of his foot speed.

He uses his skating to challenge the puck at both bluelines, forechecking and pinching in offensively and stepping up to close the gap defensively.

He rushes the puck very well because of his skating and his puckhandling; Lidster manipulates the puck excellently with his soft hands. He tempers his offensive bent with good judgment, but Doug is also going to join the play as a fourth attacker whenever possible.

He finds the open man well at both ends, and Lidster can certainly make the pass up the middle consistently. He does, however, have a tendency toward the fancy play and can be guilty of turnovers because of that. He passes well off the stickhandle and his vision and hockey sense make him a regular in all situations.

The one thing he lacks finesse-wise is an exceptional point shot, and he doesn't use the one he has enough anyway, but his wrist shot from the faceoff circle is a good weapon.

THE PHYSICAL GAME

Lidster is primarily a finesse player with size. His skating certainly lets him take the body, but he'll be out-muscled along the boards and in front of the net by stronger forwards. When he does get involved in those wrestling matches, Lidster does more pushing and shoving than hitting.

THE INTANGIBLES

Lidster is a hard worker and an enthusiastic player, but his game is going backward instead of forward — and at 29 years old that's the wrong way to go. Injury can take some blame for that, but it seems to be becoming more and more clear that the outstanding offensive season he enjoyed in 1986-87 (12-51-63) was the exception and not the rule.

He has to show the desire and intensity necessary to force himself to raise his game.

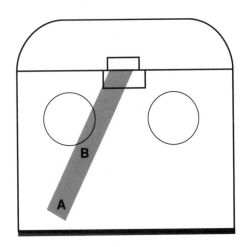

TREVOR LINDEN

Yrs. of NHL service: 1
Born: Medicine Hat, Alta., Canada; April 11, 1970
Position: Center/right wing
Height: 6-4
Weight: 200
Uniform no.: 16
Shoots: right

Career statistics:

GP	G	A	TP	+/-	PIM	PP	SH	GW	GT	S	PCT
80	30	29	59	-10	41	10	1	2	0	186	16.1

LAST SEASON

First in the NHL after being selected as Vancouver's number one pick in the 1988 Entry Draft. He finished second on the club in scoring (fifth among rookies), tied for first in goals (third among rookies) and led the club in power play goals (second among rookies). He was third in SOG total and was one of only two Canucks to play all 80 games (Robert Nordmark was the either). His plus/minus was tied for third worst among regulars.

THE FINESSE GAME

Linden's greatest skills are in his physical game, but that's not to say he isn't talented in the finesse areas — not by a longshot.

He's an exceptional skater in a powerful way, using his strength to create speed and acceleration. But he is also a mobile player courtesy of his balance, and he combines that skill with his foot speed to be more agile than a player his size would be given credit for.

His hand skills are as developed — and developable — as his skating skills. Trevor can accept or dish out passes on the move, and he uses both his forehand and backhand sides equally well. He also has good touch, so his passes are as strong or as soft as they need to be. He handles the puck well when moving, as his hands and feet combine to make him a good stickhandler.

Trevor is extremely gifted in the hockey sense department, and his anticipation skills key both his offensive and defensive play. He knows how to get to the scoring areas (or to lead his teammates there), and he also gets a very good read of the ice when forechecking.

He's dangerous as a scorer from 25-feet and in, especially as his skills allow him to operate in traffic. Linden is also a regular in all situations, and is a very strong positional player.

THE PHYSICAL GAME

Linden has excellent size and strength and he not only knows how to use them, he uses them. His skating strength allows him to drive the net, just as it allows him to drive through his checks in the corners to take the opposition off the puck.

He can get his shots away while being checked, and Trevor also plays a smart physical game by avoiding wandering and foolish penalties. He knows how to establish position along the boards, and makes his play more effective by having the skills to make plays away from the boards.

THE INTANGIBLES

This is the franchise player the Canucks have been looking for. His poise, intensity, work ethic and maturity — both on ice and off — make you forget that Linden is just 19 years old. Which is a scary thought for Vancouver's opponents, because this kid is just going to get better and better.

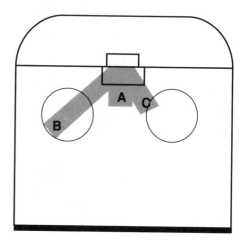

KIRK MCLEAN

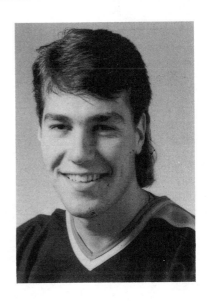

Yrs. of NHL service: 2
Born: Willowdale, Ontario, Canada; June 26, 1966
Position: Goaltender
Height: 6-0
Weight: 195
Uniform no.: 1
Catches: left

Career statistics:

GP	MINS	G	SO	AVG	A	PIM
89	5,128	295	5	3.45	3	14

1988-89 statistics:

GP	MINS	AVG	W	L	T	SO	GA	SA	SAPCT	PIM
42	2,477	3.08	20	17	3	4	127	1,169	.891	6

LAST SEASON

Games and minutes played totals were career highs. Shutout total was seasonal best (third in the NHL).

THE PHYSICAL GAME

Kirk is a standup goaltender who maximizes his good size. He plays his best when squaring to the puck and challenging the shooter. His good skating makes him a better goaltender by helping him move out of the net to challenge, or to move across the net on lateral plays.

His balance is good and improving, helping him regain his stance quickly after going to the ice. That puts him back in position to make the second save. McLean knows he is much better on his feet than off (you can tell he's not playing with confidence when he goes down too frequently).

Kirk is fairly quick with his hands, and faster with his feet than many of the NHL's taller goaltenders; no doubt his lower playing weight added a touch of quickness. As an angle goaltender, he's going to give away the far corners — that's the nature of the business — but Kirk is quick enough to reclaim those corners and stop the puck. His long legs cover the bottom of the net well.

McLean generally controls his rebounds well, and he leaves his net to snare the puck and wrap it around the boards.

THE MENTAL GAME

Though he has the tendency to get down on himself when things aren't going well, McLean has developed good mental toughness. While he is susceptible to lapses in concentration that result in bad goals, Kirk also showed that he can put strings of excellent games together. He's becoming more and more prepared to play each game, and his playoff performance is evidence of that.

THE INTANGIBLES

McLean showed very well in the playoffs against Calgary, playing almost even with Mike Vernon in the last game of the series — not bad for an NHL sophomore (even added an OT win in Game One for good measure).

He has great potential, and Kirk will improve as the team around him improves. Almost needless to say, he's a critical part of any Vancouver success.

LARRY MELNYK

Yrs. of NHL service: 7
Born: Saskatoon, Sask., Canada; February 21, 1960
Position: Defenseman
Height: 6-0
Weight: 195
Uniform no.: 24
Shoots: left

Career statistics:

GP	G	A	TP	PIM
365	11	61	72	595

1988-89 statistics:

GP	G	A	TP	+/-	PIM	PP	SH	GW	GT	S	PCT
74	3	11	14	3	82	0	1	1	0	59	5.1

LAST SEASON

Games played total was career best, goal total tied career best. He was second in plus/minus among defensemen.

THE FINESSE GAME

Because he has limited finesse skills, Melnyk has to operate on smarts. And his smarts tell him to stay within his limited finesse skills.

He's not exceptionally mobile, and that's because of his skating stance — all his weight is on his heels, cutting down the speed and lateral movement he can generate.

Larry counters that seeming flaw by playing a solid defensive angle game. He forces the opposition wide of the net and is tough to get around because of his positional play.

He is not at all offensive-minded and will pinch into the offensive zone only on the rarest of occasions. He does not have an exceptional shot and he hardly shoots at all for that matter.

THE PHYSICAL GAME

Larry has good size and strength, and he marshals them both to succeed in the corners and the front of the net. He can be out-maneuvered in front of the net because of his less-than-exceptional balance, but he uses his strength to counter that.

He willingly sacrifices his body to block shots and is aggressive in a non-fighting way.

THE INTANGIBLES

Larry can be a steady player as long as he stays within his abilities and concentrates for the game's entire stretch. That's how he gets the best from his modest talent.

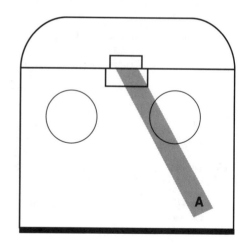

ROBERT NORDMARK

Yrs. of NHL service: 2
Born: Lulea, Sweden; August 20, 1962
Position: Defenseman
Height: 6-1
Weight: 200
Uniform no.: 6
Shoots: right

Career statistics:

GP	G	A	TP	PIM
147	9	53	62	157

1988-89 statistics:

GP	G	A	TP	+/-	PIM	PP	SH	GW	GT	S	PCT
80	6	35	41	-4	97	5	0	1	0	156	3.8

LAST SEASON

Acquired from St. Louis during summer 1988 in exchange for Dave Richter. One of only two Canucks to play all 80 games (Trevor Linden was the other). Point and PIM totals were career highs; he finished second among defensemen in second category.

THE FINESSE GAME

Nordmark is a finesse player who also has physical abilities. He is a an excellent skater, really world class because of his mobility. He has good speed and quickness up and back and he's very agile and balanced in his turns. He has good to very good lateral movement.

His anticipation and play-reading abilities are also high, and that goes for both ends of the ice. Nordmark moves the puck extremely well from his own end of the ice because his hand skills mesh with his smarts. He makes good decisions in getting the puck to his wingers. He'll also carry the puck if given the chance, and he does that smartly too. Robert won't force a play that isn't there.

He reads the offensive blue line well and can get the puck to the open man. His shot is good, but like most Europeans Nordmark is going to pass to a player in better position.

His defensive play is fairly solid, as he forces the play wide of the net with regularity.

THE PHYSICAL GAME

Nordmark is big enough, strong enough and willing enough to be a mucker in the corners, but that style is going to take its toll on him because he is unused to the pace of the NHL game. That means he'll tire both within individual contests and over the course of the season.

He sacrifices his body by blocking shots.

THE INTANGIBLES

Robert was acquired in one of those quiet deals that works out to be a steal. Think St. Louis wouldn't want him back? After all, he'd have led their defense in scoring. He's a quality player who has shown his intensity and desire through his ability to immediately contribute at the NHL level, despite the adjustment problems inherent in jumping from the European to North American games.

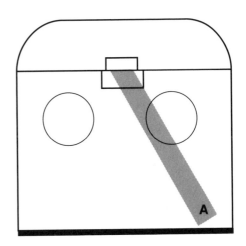

BARRY PEDERSON

Yrs. of NHL service: 9
Born: Big River, Sask., Canada; March 13, 1961
Position: Center
Height: 5-11
Weight: 185
Uniform no.: 7
Shoots: right

Career statistics:

GP	G	A	TP	PIM
564	221	375	596	404

1988-89 statistics:

GP	G	A	TP	+/-	PIM	PP	SH	GW	GT	S	PCT
62	15	26	41	5	22	7	1	0	0	98	15.3

LAST SEASON

Games played and all point totals were second lowest of career (shoulder injury, broken nose, broken collarbone). Plus/minus was the club's second best.

THE FINESSE GAME

Hockey sense has always been the strength of Pederson's game. He has excellent anticipation and vision, and those assets reveal the whole ice surface to him both offensively and defensively.

Barry puts his mental prowess to work in league with his physical finesse skills. He's a very good skater with strength, balance and quickness. Though not exceptionally fast, Barry's combination of quickness and balance makes him a very agile player — one who is difficult to trap defensively.

His skating is complemented by his puckhandling, and the opposition is forced to respect his ability to take the puck into the openings himself or to lead his teammates into those openings with excellent passes.

For a guy with his shot, Pederson doesn't shoot anywhere near enough. He's dangerous from the slot with a hard wrist shot, and also has long-range scoring capability.

His skills make him valuable in all situations, and Barry is also a complete player, very strong in the positional and defensive aspects of the game.

THE PHYSICAL GAME

Pederson plays a physical game, despite his less-than-exceptional size. His balance and sturdiness afoot help him greatly in this, keeping him vertical and ready to make plays after collisions. His hitting is also made more effective by his ability to make plays off the boards. He'll always initiate contact to knock an opponent off the puck and will take a hit to make his own plays.

Strong forearms and wrists power his shots, just as they power his hands for faceoffs, an area where he does well.

THE INTANGIBLES

Pederson is a character player, the kind of heart and soul player a developing team like Vancouver needs. He's a leader for the Canucks.

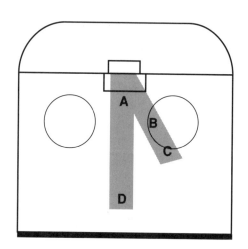

PAUL REINHART

Yrs. of NHL service: 10
Born: Kitchener, Ontario, Canada; January 6, 1960
Position: Defenseman
Height: 5-11
Weight: 205
Uniform no.: 23
Shoots: left

Career statistics:

GP	G	A	TP	PIM
581	116	386	502	247

1988-89 statistics:

GP	G	A	TP	+/-	PIM	PP	SH	GW	GT	S	PCT
64	7	50	57	-4	44	3	0	1	0	133	5.3

LAST SEASON

Acquired along with Steve Bozek from Calgary during the summer of 1988 in exchange for future considerations. Led club in assists with third highest total of career. Finished third on club in points, tops among defenders. He was sidelined with hip and rib injuries.

THE FINESSE GAME

When he's healthy, Reinhart's finesse skills show no signs of wear. He remains an excellent skater in both directions, with exceptional balance and agility. He has a low center of gravity and is very strong in the thighs, so he is very difficult to take off the puck.

Reinhart uses his skating skill to carry the puck from the zone, relieving pressure on the forwards. He likes to carry the puck on the power play, where his skill makes him a natural.

Paul uses his excellent anticipation and uncanny vision to great result at even strength as well. He finds the open man excellently and passes very well, either through traffic or into an opening to lead a teammate. Reinhart controls the point well, able to keep the puck in the zone and heading toward a teammate.

Reinhart has a strong, low slap shot from the point, but he will move to the deep slot if he can.

He uses his skating and vision to play his position well defensively. Reinhart is rarely beaten one-on-one because he is good at forcing the opposition wide of the net. Once he gains the puck it's gone from the Vancouver zone, courtesy of a smart breakout pass to a forward.

THE PHYSICAL GAME

Reinhart's skating strength is his biggest physical plus. He can play a physical style, though his best game is clearly in the open ice. He can turn a play up-ice after either making a hit or being hit because his strength on his skates means he is balanced and almost always vertical.

Paul is, however, generally weak in his coverage in front of his own net. While he has the size and strength to be effective in front of the opposition's net, Reinhart is less than consistently effective in front of his own goaltender.

THE INTANGIBLES

Probably 50 percent of Vancouver's success can be attributed to the acquisition of Reinhart. After all, his 25 minutes on-ice are 25 minutes Vancouver doesn't have to worry about getting the puck from its zone. And his presence makes all the other Canucks better players.

Health will always be a concern (and we told you that it would drive him from Calgary), but he's Vancouver's best defenseman and, as Coach Bob McCammon says, if he's not in traction Paul will be in the lineup.

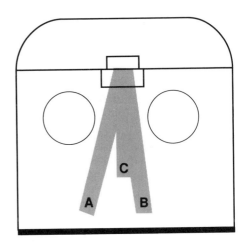

JIM SANDLAK

Yrs. of NHL service: 4
Born: Kitchener, Ontario, Canada; December 12, 1966
Position: Right wing
Height: 6-4
Weight: 219
Uniform no.: 19
Shoots: right

Career statistics:

GP	G	A	TP	PIM
222	52	59	111	256

1988-89 statistics:

GP	G	A	TP	+/-	PIM	PP	SH	GW	GT	S	PCT
72	20	20	40	8	99	9	0	4	1	164	12.2

LAST SEASON

Games played and assist totals were second highest of career, but goal and point totals were career bests. PIM total was career high, and plus/minus was club's best.

THE FINESSE GAME

The attributes of a power forward are the attributes Sandlak brings to the rink. His skating is unexceptional, marked — as would be expected — by a strong stride that carries him through checks along the boards and toward the net. He lacks the two speed elements that would most improve his game: explosive acceleration and quickness. He neither pulls away from the opposition nor gets to the loose pucks as well as he could — the latter quality especially bad for a player who will plug the net and needs to snare loose pucks. That lack of foot speed also inhibits his agility; he's not a very agile skater.

Jim best finesse quality is his shot. The shot itself is excellent: heavy, fast and powerful both wrist and slap shots. But Sandlak must work on his release; he takes too long getting those shots away. And again, if he had the skating skill to get open more consistently, he'd be a better scorer.

He is below average in his use of his teammates. While his game is a straight-ahead and non-creative one to begin with, Sandlak has developed little feel for the tempo of the NHL game. And like his feet, his hands and eyes don't respond at major league speed.

THE PHYSICAL GAME

The potential is scary, and so is Sandlak's use of his talent. He has excellent size and strength, the type only a handful of NHL players could claim, yet Jim is exceptionally inconsistent in his application of his talents.

Sandlak *must* hit to be effective, but he does so on infrequent occasions and backs away from the confrontations that follow his banging around. Sandlak has trouble even doing simple things, like fighting through checks, consistently.

He is, therefore, essentially a finesse player with size, and he generally plays smaller than he is.

THE INTANGIBLES

The Canucks think that Sandlak could be the first 50-goal scorer in franchise history, and they're right — Sandlak *could* be. He is the classic case of the mishandled 18-year-old, a first round draft choice who was neither physically nor mentally ready for the NHL, and the Canucks are trying to bring him around.

He certainly showed good signs last season, but he still has just a tenuous grip on a spot with the Canucks; Vancouver will listen to trade offers. But having already given away Cam Neely, the Canucks want to be sure Jim won't blossom.

Jim can do anything he wants to; he just has to want to. This coming season will give a good demonstration of Sandlak one way or another.

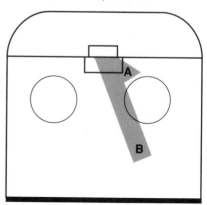

PETRI SKRIKO

Yrs. of NHL service: 5
Born: Laapeenranta, Finland; March 13, 1962
Position: Right wing
Height: 5-10
Weight: 175
Uniform no.: 26
Shoots: right

Career statistics:

GP	G	A	TP	PIM
375	152	165	317	177

1988-89 statistics:

GP	G	A	TP	+/-	PIM	PP	SH	GW	GT	S	PCT
74	30	36	66	-3	57	9	0	5	0	204	14.7

LAST SEASON

Led club in scoring (tied for first in goals) and game winners, was second in assists and SOG total. Sidelined with a knee injury.

THE FINESSE GAME

Speed, acceleration and exceptional balance make Skriko an excellent skater. His balance combines with his quickness to give him excellent mobility and lateral movement, and Petri uses his skating to force the defense off the blue line — thus creating space for his teammates.

He works at being a good team player and at using his teammates, but Skriko has some difficulty fulfilling his playmaking role for several reasons. He likes to go 1-on-1 a lot (restricting his playmaking to begin with), and Skriko does a lot of his rushing with his head down — so he misses openings. He has his head up for passing and can lead a teammate with a soft pass, or Petri will exploit an opening with his quickness.

Skriko shoots the puck very well, quick and accurate with his wrist shot so as to make the most of opportunities around the net. Because he is a right-handed shot playing his off-wing, Skriko will circle to his forehand for most of his scoring opportunities.

His sense and anticipation combine with his one-step quickness to make him a natural on specialty teams.

THE PHYSICAL GAME

Petri tries to make the most of his less-than-exceptional size by playing the body in all three zones. He accepts hits to make his plays but he is neither strong enough nor aggressive enough to play a truly effective physical game.

His lack of strength also hurts him defensively, as he cannot restrain some of the league's bigger forwards; if he can't make a defensive play by finesse, he's in trouble. His conditioning and strength are not great enough to sustain him throughout the year and he goes through periods of fatigue that limit his effectiveness.

THE INTANGIBLES

Petri has excellent on-ice work habits, but is a streaky player; nothing will change that. He's good for 30-goals a season and could be better, but his age puts him out of synch with the Canucks' development as an improving team — he's already 27 years old.

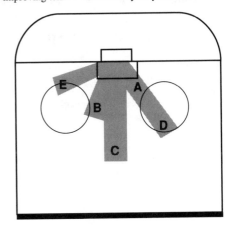

STAN SMYL

Yrs. of NHL service: 11
Born: Glendon, Alta., Canada; January 28, 1958
Position: Right wing
Height: 5-8
Weight: 185
Uniform no.: 12
Shoots: right

Career statistics:

GP	G	A	TP	PIM
804	259	384	643	1,398

1988-89 statistics:

GP	G	A	TP	+/-	PIM	PP	SH	GW	GT	S	PCT
75	7	18	25	0	102	1	0	0	0	89	7.9

LAST SEASON

Games played total was four-season high (missed two games with a shoulder injury). All point totals were career lows.

THE FINESSE GAME

Not much left here finesse-wise. Stan's skating strength and balance power him in his physical play, but he lacks exceptional quickness or agility.

His hockey sense is still high, and Smyl uses his ability to check and play well defensively. The anticipation, good vision and understanding he used when he was an offensive threat continue to serve him in his defensive game.

Stan can still dig the puck out of the corner and make a play with it, but the chances of his getting to the net in time to complete the give and go are now remote. He will need to be opportunistic for his goals from now on.

THE PHYSICAL GAME

Smyl plays a robust physical game — always has, always will. He's a very aggressive player, and his balance and strength allow him to keep playing that style. He barrels around in the corners and along the boards, and he remains very strong and very difficult to knock down.

THE INTANGIBLES

Intangibles are the keys to what Smyl delivers for the Canucks, and the consistent physical play he delivers. He has tremendous heart and dedication, and his hate-to-lose attitude makes him a good leader for the Canucks. Age and health remain considerations, as both have served to limit his game tremendously.

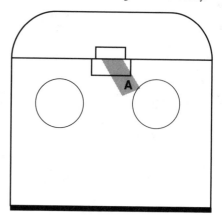

HAROLD SNEPSTS

Yrs. of NHL service: 14
Born: Edmonton, Alta., Canada; October 24, 1954
Position: Defenseman
Height: 6-3
Weight: 210
Uniform no.: 27
Shoots: left

Career statistics:

GP	G	A	TP	PIM
933	36	187	223	1,923

1988-89 statistics:

GP	G	A	TP	+/-	PIM	PP	SH	GW	GT	S	PCT
59	0	8	8	-3	69	0	0	0	0	27	0.0

LAST SEASON

Signed as a free agent during summer 1988. He missed time with a viral infection (eight games), as well as throat and back injuries. Games played total was four-season high.

THE FINESSE GAME

The finesse game has never been Harold's game, and it is less so today than ever before. He was never a great skater and has almost no speed to speak of. In fact, he can not keep up with the play as it moves around him, either by skating forward or backward, and he is apt to be beaten one-on-one by opposition forwards who go around him as if he didn't exist.

He is very weak at handling the puck in his own end and frequently has his back to the play, meaning that he'll make bad, blind passes around the boards or up the middle.

But Snepsts makes his play effective by staying away from his weaknesses; he doesn't, regularly, for example, handle the puck.

He has almost no mobility — and absolutely no interest — in playing within the offensive zone. He will not pinch in to the play and has an impotent shot from the point.

THE PHYSICAL GAME

Harold puts fear into the opposition and makes them pay for camping in front of the Canucks' net. Snepsts loves to hit and can do so with authority, and he has learned to temper that desire with common sense.

Snepsts doesn't run around the defensive zone in search of prey, but waits for the opposition to come to him. And then he lets them have it. He clears men from the slot well because he is big and strong. He adds size to the defense and keeps things honest in his zone.

THE INTANGIBLES

The key to Harold is his play in front of the net, and he played very well last year. He is also a great team guy and has a good sense of humor, so he's important in the locker room too.

He showed better than anyone could have hoped for in Vancouver, and he'd like to play at least one more season. If he does he'll be on a new contract, as he signed a one-year deal with the Canucks for 1988-89.

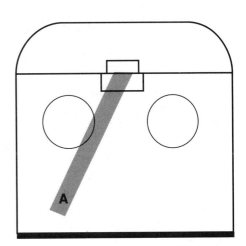

RICH SUTTER

Yrs. of NHL service: 6
Born: Viking, Alta., Canada; December 2, 1963
Position: Right wing
Height: 5-11
Weight: 185
Uniform no.: 15
Shoots: right

Career statistics:

GP	G	A	TP	PIM
442	87	99	186	761

1988-89 statistics:

GP	G	A	TP	+/-	PIM	PP	SH	GW	GT	S	PCT
75	17	15	32	3	122	1	3	4	0	125	13.6

LAST SEASON

Games played total was four-season low. Goal total was second best of career. PIM total was club's second highest, tops among forwards, and plus/minus fourth best (third among forwards). He led the club in shorthanded goals.

THE FINESSE GAME

Finesse has never been big in any of the Sutters and Rich is no exception. He is just average as an NHL skater in terms of his balance and agility, but he has power in his stride and can accelerate well. For a straight-ahead guy, that's about par for the course.

Sutter has difficulty handling the puck, especially as he skates up-ice and cutting to his right. He has a sense of the game and can read its ebbs and flows (and that's why he succeeds as a checking forward) but he can't do much offensively.

He'll never score more than 25 goals a year and many times won't even come near that mark. His shot is undistinguished and won't often fool NHL goaltending, so he'll have to be opportunistic and score off scrambles and loose pucks created by his checking.

THE PHYSICAL GAME

As with every Sutter, Rich is a physical player. His own style begins at chippy and moves swiftly to dirty, as he hits anyone in an enemy uniform and finishes the check with his stick. Naturally he refuses to fight after stirring up all kinds of troubles, and that just frustrates the opposition more.

Rich is good on the boards and will run at anyone, but is no good after hitting because he's unlikely — for two reasons — to make a play: First, he lacks the requisite hand skills. Second, his balance isn't good enough for him to stay vertical after all those collisions. Those flaws make his physical play one-dimensional.

THE INTANGIBLES

He took his licks last season, first clipped in the mouth by Mark Messier's stick and then (later in the season) run from behind by Craig Berube. As with all Sutters, his work ethic is unassailable. He's an honest hockey player, but he'll never approach the heights hit by any of his five brothers.

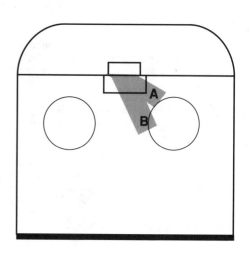

TONY TANTI

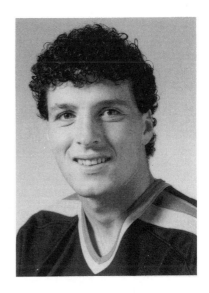

Yrs. of NHL service: 7
Born: Toronto, Ontario, Canada; September 7, 1963
Position: Right wing
Height: 5-9
Weight: 185
Uniform no.: 9
Shoots: left

Career statistics:

GP	G	A	TP	PIM
493	237	202	439	439

1988-89 statistics:

GP	G	A	TP	+/-	PIM	PP	SH	GW	GT	S	PCT
77	24	25	49	-10	69	8	0	3	1	211	11.4

LAST SEASON

Goal and point totals were full-season career lows, assist total second lowest full season mark of career. Finished fourth on the club in points, third in goals. Plus/minus tied for third worst among team's regulars. Led team in SOG total.

THE FINESSE GAME

Primary among Tanti's fairly considerable finesse skills is his shot, which is very under-rated. Tony's release is exceptionally quick,maybe the best in the NHL; that's why he can score goals. The puck is gone as soon as it touches his stick and he always forces the goalie to make a save. He shoots off the pass very well, and he needs only the slightest opening; T a n t i loves to go upstairs on goalies. He is also very good on tip-ins because of his eye/hand coordination, and he augments that skill by using a big blade on his stick.

Tony uses his excellent skating ability to get into scoring position and to create openings. His great balance, speed and agility make him extremely difficult to contain, and his one-step quickness and ability to change direction within a stride will snare him most any loose puck.

His anticipation keys his ability to get into scoring position, but he can also use that ability to make plays. But make no mistake: Tanti is a finisher, not a playmaker.

THE PHYSICAL GAME

His leg strength powers his skating game, giving him the explosive acceleration he needs to drive past defenders. Tanti isn't a physical player, but he's fairly willing to get involved by taking hits to make his plays — as he must when crashing the crease for loose pucks.

He's pretty sturdy on his feet, so Tony can be effective in hit-and-run missions for the puck against the boards but will be overwhelmed if trapped in the traffic areas.

THE INTANGIBLES

Where did Mr. Tanti's goal scoring go last season? He suffered through some pretty bad dry spells: just seven goals in his first 23 games, just four goals in his last 26 games. And, he had just 47 shots-on-goal in those last 26 games — an average of fewer than two SOG per game. Oh — and no goals in the playoffs.

That could be a symptom of any numbers of things, but the point is last season was a very un-Tanti like performance. He's always been a consistent goal scorer, so it's reasonable to assume he'll rebound. His continued output is very important to Vancouver, a club which cannot afford to not have all its players playing their best.

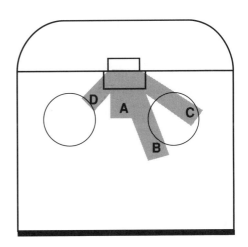

STEVE WEEKS

Yrs. of NHL service: 8
Born: Scarborough, Ontario, Canada; June 30, 1958
Position: Goaltender
Height: 5-11
Weight: 165
Uniform no.: 31
Catches: left

Career statistics:

GP	MINS	G	SO	AVG	A	PIM
232	13,209	796	5	3.62	2	14

1988-89 statistics:

GP	MINS	AVG	W	L	T	SO	GA	SA	SAPCT	PIM
35	2,056	2.98	11	19	5	0	102	953	.892	4

LAST SEASON

Games and minutes played totals were second highest of career. Goals-against-average was career best, and he finished fifth in the League save percentage.

THE PHYSICAL GAME

Steve is a good skater. He has learned to rein in his forays around the ice and that has made him a better goaltender. In previous seasons he roamed all over the ice to pick up loose pucks and, because his puck handling isn't good, would turn the puck over and have to scramble back to the net.

Steve is a good angle goaltender and he is particularly good at shots at his feet because he keeps his entire skate blade on the ice as he kicks his foot out, rather than raising the toe as he moves, so he'll get that shot headed for the far post.

He is good on screen shots because he moves to the top of the screen. Weeks has a good glove hand above his waist, but it is suspect below his waist. He directs pucks to the corners well but fails to control rebounds from high off his chest protector.

Steve is also weak on the short side and that indicates a failure to cut the angle completely and a failure to be completely squared to the puck. He is not very quick to regain his feet after going down. That's because he usually winds up on his butt rather than his knees, and there's no way to be mobile in that position.

THE MENTAL GAME

Weeks starts a game with tremendous concentration and he can maintain it for the full 60 minutes unless — and this is a big unless — he gives up a bad goal.

Bad goals devastate him, and he won't recover if he allows one. He doesn't have the mental toughness to put that goal out of his mind, and that's a big flaw for a goalie.

He is otherwise consistent from night to night, and that concentration gives him something of a big save capability.

THE INTANGIBLES

Vancouver's new attention to defense is one reason why Steve showed so well last season. Weeks's game is to stop the first shot and leave the rebounds to others, and the Canucks took care of those rebounds last season. This season, he'll have to contend with Troy Gamble, who'll be looking to crack the Canucks' lineup.

428

WASHINGTON
CAPITALS

LINE COMBINATIONS
KELLY MILLER-MIKE RIDLEY-STEVE LEACH
GEOFF COURTNALL-DALE HUNTER-DAVE
CHRISTIAN
LOU FRANCESCHETTI-PETER SUNDSTROM-
BOB GOULD

DEFENSE PAIRINGS
ROD LANGWAY-KEVIN HATCHER
SCOTT STEVENS-NEIL SHEEHY

GOALTENDERS
PETE PEETERS
DON BEAUPRE

OTHER PLAYERS
DINO CICCARELLI — Right wing
CALLE JOHANSSON — Defenseman
MICHAL PIVONKA — Center
BOB ROUSE — Defenseman

POWER PLAY

The acquisitions of DINO CICCARELLI and CALLE JOHANSSON change the texture of the Capitals power play. The power play would be a mix of GEOFF COURTNALL at the left faceoff circle if CICCARELLI is on-ice (because CICCARELLI will work from the right faceoff circle in to the slot), with DALE HUNTER or MIKE RIDLEY in the slot and SCOTT STEVENS and KEVIN HATCHER on the points.

With both COURTNALL AND CICCARELLI on-ice, STEVENS and HATCHER play catch at the blue line hoping to isolate one or the other. If COURTNALL gets open, CICCARELLI joins HUNTER or RIDLEY in the slot for rebounds. COURTNALL doesn't move if CICCARELLI gets the shot. If CICCARELLI is not out, COURTNALL flips to the right wing circle, and *both* HUNTER and RIDLEY jam the net.

JOHANSSON and DAVE CHRISTIAN (CHRISTIAN posted off the net for one-timers) will also see power-play time, and the CAPITALS wants STEVENS out for the full two minutes.

Last season the Washington power play was GOOD, collecting 96 goals in 443 opportunities (21.7 percent, seventh overall).

PENALTY KILLING

FIRST UNIT:
BOB GOULD-PETER SUNDSTROM
ROD LANGWAY-KEVIN HATCHER

SECOND UNIT:
KELLY MILLER-MIKE RIDLEY
SCOTT STEVENS-NEIL SHEEHY

The Capital forwards are aggressive penalty killers, dogging the puck throughout the offensive zone to break up the attack before it starts. GOULD and SUNDSTROM pressure the puck more than MILLER and RIDLEY, making the first unit less of a strict box. STEVENS and HATCHER pressure the puck in their corners.

Last season Washington's penalty killing was FAIR, allowing 73 goals in 362 shorthanded situations (79.8 percent, 11th overall).

CRUCIAL FACEOFFS
DALE HUNTER gets the call, with MIKE RIDLEY the second choice.

DON BEAUPRE

Yrs. of NHL service: 8
Born: Kitchener, Ontario, Canada; September 19, 1961
Position: Goaltender
Height: 5-8
Weight: 155
Uniform No.: 33
Catches: left

Career statistics:

GP	MINS	G	SO	AVG	A	PIM
327	18,411	1,139	4	3. 71	3	134

1988-89 statistics:

GP	MINS	AVG	W	L	T	SO	GA	SA	SAPCT	PIM
12	637	2. 92	5	5	0	1	31	295	. 890	6

LAST SEASON

Games played total was lowest of career. He was acquired from Minnesota on Nov. 1 and spent much of the season in the American Hockey League.

THE PHYSICAL GAME

The hallmarks of Beaupre's game are his hand and foot speed and his tremendous balance. He plays his angles fairly well, but lives and dies by his reflexes.

His exceptional balance makes him a fine skater and allows him to move in and out of the net very well. His balance comes to the forefront of his game by allowing him to regain his stance very quickly after a save, and then get into position to stop the next shot.

Don's hands are also very quick. He has an excellent glove hand and is also strong high on his stick side, an area many goaltenders find hardest to defend. He is so successful with his hands and feet because he sees the puck well and is able to track its flight toward the goal.

He would profit by playing a better angle game and would reduce at least one area of weakness — low stick side on the short side — by doing so.

Beaupre is aggressive in his crease, becoming phsically involved in keeping it clear, whether that means pushing or slashing an opposing player.

THE MENTAL GAME

Beaupre is going to give up that one bad goal per game; that's just the way he is. Don has a great deal of difficulty maintaining his concentration within a game and from contest to contest. He's very streaky; he can get hot but he won't stay hot and will in fact go through many cold outings.

Don does not get over bad goals or games, and he stays rattled for a period of time after the event; he'll give up goals in bunches. Those performances prompt criticism of his work and that just makes the problem worse, because Beaupre is very sensitive to criticism and is unnerved by it.

He needs a pat on the back and not a kick in the ass in order to succeed.

THE INTANGIBLES

He's a good guy and well liked by his teammates but consistency is going to remain Beaupre's problem. In his favor now is the fact that he's playing with a sound defensive club; Beaupre should draw strength from their ability to clean up his mistakes. Also, he'll be working with Warren Strelow, maybe the NHL's best goaltending coach.

And, with Pete Peeters having performed his annual playoff swan dive last April, Beaupre may just find himself installed as the team's no. 1 goaltender.

DAVE CHRISTIAN

Yrs. of NHL service: 9
Born: Warroad, Minn., USA; May 12, 1959
Position: Right wing/center
Height: 5-11
Weight: 180
Uniform No.: 27
Shoots: right

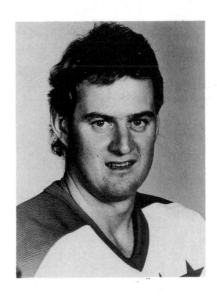

Career statistics:

GP	G	A	TP	PIM
706	269	346	615	178

1988-89 statistics:

GP	G	A	TP	+/-	PIM	PP	SH	GW	GT	S	PCT
80	34	31	65	2	12	16	1	1	2	177	19. 2

LAST SEASON

Christian played all 80 games for the seventh time in nine seasons. He finished fourth on the club in goal scoring with his second consecutive 30-plus goals season. His PIM total was the second lowest of his career, and lowest among all Capital regulars. He tied for the club lead in power play goals.

THE FINESSE GAME

Goal scorers need two things: good hands and the ability to get into scoring position. Though lacking great speed or quickness, Christian knows how to get into position to score (he does kick up the juice a little when coming to the net from the outside on the backhand — down the left wing). He exploits defensive breakdowns regularly because of his excellent anticipation. He also possesses a scorer's patience and poise, and Dave waits as long as necessary for the defense or goaltender to commit before making his own play.

Christian's best asset is his shooting, and he is a deadly accurate one from around the net. He one-times shots with the NHL's best, and he likes to work between the crease and the lower edge of the right faceoff circle. On two-on-one breaks he wants the puck at the crease's edge for a shot upstairs.

His sensitive hands and excellent release — as well as his ability to get open — make him especially valuable on the power play, where last year he scored almost half of his goals.

Dave moves well with the puck when he carries it and, when he does pass, gets the puck efficiently to open teammates. His defense, however, is often no better than perfunctory, and he needs to be teamed with a more defensively conscious teammate.

THE PHYSICAL GAME

Christian is a finesse player, and his physical game reflects that. Because of the balance he has on his skates, Christian avoids most hits, and he doesn't really go out of his way to instigate contact either. Most of the time he'll be on the outside of the scrum looking in.

He does, though, use his body well to protect the puck.

THE INTANGIBLES

Given Christian's skills, his decreasing goal totals (41 in 1985-86, 37 in 1987-88, 34 last season) must be of concern to the Caps. He should continue as a 30-goal scorer, and the Caps do have firepwoer elsewhere, but those declining totals indicate something.

Harder work at even-strength is also something that should be of concern to Christian and Washington. Despite his power play success, Christian was less than dominant at even-strength, scoring just 17 goals. But we have the feeling that what you see with Dave Christian is what you get, and that there'll be little change in his play.

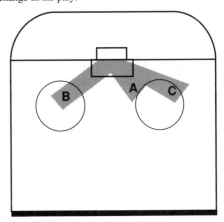

DINO CICCARELLI

Yrs. of NHL service: 9
Born: Sarnia, Ontario, Canada; February 8, 1960
Position: Right wing
Height: 5-10
Weight: 180
Uniform No.: 22
Shoots: right

Career statistics:

GP	G	A	TP	PIM
613	344	322	666	654

1988-89 statistics:

GP	G	A	TP	+/-	PIM	PP	SH	GW	GT	S	PCT
76	44	30	74	-6	76	16	0	8	1	247	17.8

LAST SEASON

Ciccarelli was acquired at the trading deadline, along with Bob Rouse, from Minnesota in exchange for Mike Gartner and Larry Murphy. Dino's point total was a four-year low. He finished third on the Caps in scoring, first in goals, power play goals and shots on goal. He was second in game winners.

THE FINESSE GAME

Dino's an excellent skater with terrific speed and agility, excellent balance and lateral movement. His balance keeps him in possession of the puck and allows him to get his shot away from all body angles and while being punished by the opposition.

His quickness and agility let him snare loose pucks and his speed carries him past the defense for a shot on goal. Dino makes his skating more effective by taking dives, getting calls that later serve to intimidate the opposition into not touching him — for fear of another penalty.

He has a goal scorer's anticipation, reading the ice and finding the openings; he excels at stepping in front of a defender to cut the puck off along the boards. Ciccarelli takes passes very well and delivers the puck to the net with a quick, hard wrist shot. He also has an excellent slap shot that will blow by goaltenders; he can put the puck anywhere he wants. He has very good hands and can pass the puck, but Ciccarelli is a scorer first and a passer second.

He excels on the power play, where his one-step quickness gets him to that crossing puck to one-time it home. He works especially well from the left side.

His defensive game has improved steadily over the course of his career so that Dino is no longer a liability when he is on the ice. He plays his position well and doesn't wander in the defensive zone.

THE PHYSICAL GAME

Ciccarelli is successful because he goes to the areas where he knows he's going to get beat up. And then he scores. He has great physical courage in that regard and in that respect is very similar to Calgary's Joe Mullen. This is where his balance serves him best.

Dino definitely initiates contact and likes to dish out the bodywork that creates more space for him in which to work. He has good strength and can apply it along the boards to muscle the opposition off the puck, but he is most effective in the open ice.

THE INTANGIBLES

Here's a classic case where a change of scenery should do some good. Out from under the pressure of his on- and off-ice behavior while in Minnesota, Ciccarelli should thrive for the Caps. Here he has players who will protect him from some of the abuse he has taken over the years, and he should continue to succeed offensively because he has always worked in the game's toughest place — the front of the net.

As for his plus/minus, by the way: Dino was a plus-10 in his 11 games with the Caps. He knows how to play both ends of the rink, and his hellbent style should sufficiently energize his Washington teammates.

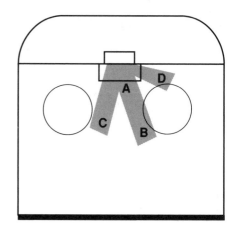

GEOFF COURTNALL

Yrs. of NHL service: 5
Born: Victoria, B.C., Canada; August 18, 1962
Position: Left wing
Height: 6-1
Weight: 195
Uniform No.: 14
Shoots: left

Career statistics:

GP	G	A	TP	PIM
350	124	123	247	495

1988-89 statistics:

GP	G	A	TP	+/-	PIM	PP	SH	GW	GT	S	PCT
79	42	38	80	11	112	16	0	6	0	239	17.6

LAST SEASON

Courtnall was acquired from Edmonton during the summer of 1988 in exchange for Greg Adams. Games played and all point totals were career highs. He finished second on the team in goals, points and shots on goal, and tied for first in power play goals.

THE FINESSE GAME

Courtnall is an excellent skater, strong on his feet and with good acceleration for breakaway speed.

By learning to moderate his speed (he used to be all out, all the time), Courtnall has become a powerful offensive force. Where previously he always charged full throttle at the defense, now Courtnall keeps the play in front of him instead of out-racing it. Because of that, his on-ice vision has improved and he makes plays to get the puck to his teammates.

And, because they no longer had to keep up with his feet, Geoff's hand skills also improved. After his dynamic speed gets him into the open, Courtnall has time to shoot the puck (his shot is very good, hard and very quick to the net). But he only gets open now because he's no longer so straight-line predictable.

Because of his shot and ability to get open, Courtnall has become a power play mainstay. His defensive play has also improved, with Courtnall showing better understanding of the opposition attack and then using his great speed to break it up.

THE PHYSICAL GAME

Courtnall's other great asset is his physical game. He is in great shape and has strength to match his conditioning, and Courtnall hits hard when he checks — his leg power gives his checks extra oomph.

He eagerly hits in the corner and doesn't back down from a challenge. He also takes hits to make plays.

THE INTANGIBLES

We told you last year that last season was the most important one of Courtnall's career, and he came through with flying colors. His scoring consistency had been questionable, but Geoff showed well in that area last season.

The main thing in his improvement is ice-time and confidence from the coaching staff. He got time but no confidence in Boston, and none of either in Edmonton, but Geoff rewarded the Caps' faith in him.

He does all the things right to succeed in the NHL, and we think he'll continue to do so.

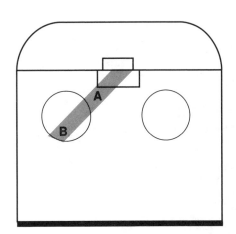

LOU FRANCESCHETTI

Yrs. of NHL service: 5
Born: Toronto, Ontario, Canada; March 28, 1958
Position: Left wing
Height: 6-0
Weight: 190
Uniform No.: 25
Shoots: left

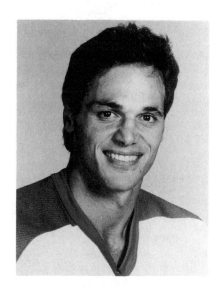

Career statistics:

GP	G	A	TP	PIM
327	36	58	94	562

1988-89 statistics:

GP	G	A	TP	+/-	PIM	PP	SH	GW	GT	S	PCT
63	7	10	17	-4	123	0	0	0	0	55	12.7

LAST SEASON

Split season between American Hockey League and Washington. Games played and point totals were second highest of career. Plus/minus was second worst among full-time forwards.

THE FINESSE GAME

Franceschetti is a below average finesse player. He gets up and down his wing without a great deal of speed, doesn't handle the puck particularly well (especially not when coming away from the boards), won't terrorize enemy goaltenders with his shot and probably won't score when he shoots anyway.

He's never been and never will be a scorer, because his hockey sense and anticipation are poor at the NHL level. He stays to the outside of any offensive play and shows no ability to think on the ice.

THE PHYSICAL GAME

Lou plays a grinding, physical game — the kind that wears down the opposition physically and mentally. If it moves in an opposition jersey, Franceschetti will hit it. Contact is his game at both ends of the ice and Franceschetti, well muscled, makes anyone he hits pay a price. He does suffer when absorbing hits, however, as his balance is a little awkward — therefore, he's frequently in a bad body position after a check and needs time to regain his stance.

Franceschetti is a fairly disciplined player — in terms of using his body — and he hits purposefully rather than recklessly. He will also back up his actions with his fists, if need be, something he is not frequently called upon to do because he does fight well and no one wants a piece of him.

THE INTANGIBLES

He's a grinder, a role player and an aging one at that. Franceschetti will probably continue bopping between the minors and the big league, though his determination and willingness to sacrifice are impressive.

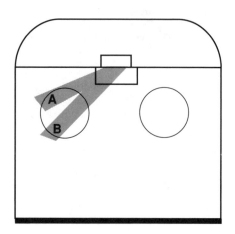

BOB GOULD

Yrs. of NHL service: 8
Born: Petrolia, Ontario, Canada; September 2, 1957
Position: Center/right wing
Height: 5-11
Weight: 195
Uniform No.: 23
Shoots: right

Career statistics:

GP	G	A	TP	PIM
620	137	142	279	480

1988-89 statistics:

GP	G	A	TP	+/-	PIM	PP	SH	GW	GT	S	PCT
75	5	13	18	-2	65	0	1	0	0	91	5.5

LAST SEASON

Games played total was second lowest of his career. Goal and point totals were full season lows.

THE FINESSE GAME

A good skater with a strong, steady pace, Gould uses that pace well in his role as a defensive forward, staying with his check up and down the ice. He has neither great speed nor outstanding agility.

His anticipation and vision — his superior hockey sense — helps him excel in his defensive work. He counters the opposition's offense either by shadowing his check or by protecting a certain zone of the ice and cutting off passing lanes.

Though he doesn't show great offensive creativity, he can handle the puck fairly well, sometimes working a little give and go from the right corner. His goals will come from in close to the net, and he is a threat for the short-handed goal, using his anticipation to read the power play and find an opening.

THE PHYSICAL GAME

Intelligence rather than overt strength is the key to Gould's physical game. Though not unwilling to become involved, Bob is not the kind of player that throws his weight around. He uses his body intelligently, holding his man out of the play for the extra second necessary to make a good defensive play.

Gould does not run from contact and is not a thumper, but will certainly hit or be hit if the play dictates. He can't be intimidated.

THE INTANGIBLES

Gould is an excellent team man, working hard all the time for the team first and himself second. He is a role player and a fine defensive forward, so ignore the bad plus/minus. His durability, however, must be questioned, as he has played a complete NHL season just once in his career.

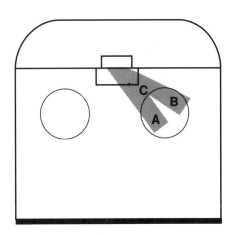

BENGT GUSTAFSSON

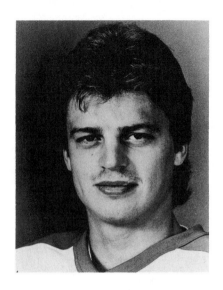

Yrs. of NHL service: 9
Born: Kariskoga, Sweden; March 23, 1958
Position: Center
Height: 6-0
Weight: 185
Uniform No.: 16
Shoots: left

Career statistics:

GP	G	A	TP	PIM
629	196	359	555	196

1988-89 statistics:

GP	G	A	TP	+/-	PIM	PP	SH	GW	GT	S	PCT
72	18	51	69	13	18	5	4	6	0	107	16.8

LAST SEASON

Point total was second highest of career. Led club in shorthanded goals and finished third in plus/minus.

THE FINESSE GAME

Gustafsson is a package of superb finesse abilities. He's a fine skater with excellent speed (a long, fluid stride with great balance), outstanding acceleration and one-step quickness. He uses that ability when killing penalties to "jump" the power play unit and soar in for a short-handed score, and Gustafsson keeps Washington's power play passing lanes open because he moves so quickly, even within his first stride.

He has great hands (he likes to carry the puck across the opposing blue line) and can get the puck to his teammates on sheer quickness, and he has the ability to do everything at high speed. The vision and anticipation abilities that make him a specialty teams natural combine with his skating to make him a solid defensive player.

He has a good, quickly released snapshot which he should use more often; he's too unselfish. He is deadly from 10-feet and in and loves to stand at the base of the faceoff circles, especially on the power play, and hammer home the pass from behind the net. He also has an excellent backhand. Because of his package of playmaking abilities, Bengt will also see some time on the point of the power play.

THE PHYSICAL GAME

Gustafsson could be said to play bigger than his size. His balance and strength on his skates allow him to hit effectively and to bounce many opponents off the puck. He's not afraid to initiate contact and he'll go to the traffic areas (where, once again, he'll benefit because of his balance and hand skills).

THE INTANGIBLES

We questioned Bengt's intensity and commitment after 1987-88's lackluster performance, but he was a far better player last season. He has tremendous ability — all he has to do is want to play to that ability. Mitigating against him is Mike Ridley's development as a 40-goal scorer and the need to have Dale Hunter in the lineup each night. That makes Gustafsson no better than the third center, so he may be moved to the wings to keep his ice-time regular.

If, that is, he stays in the NHL and doesn't return to Sweden — amost probable possibility.

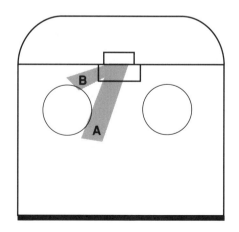

KEVIN HATCHER

Yrs. of NHL service: 4
Born: Detroit, Mich., USA; September 9, 1966
Position: Defenseman
Height: 6-4
Weight: 215
Uniform No.: 4
Shoots: right

Career statistics:

GP	G	A	TP	PIM
292	45	80	125	503

1988-89 statistics:

GP	G	A	TP	+/-	PIM	PP	SH	GW	GT	S	PCT
62	13	27	40	19	101	3	0	2	0	148	8.8

LAST SEASON

Games played total was career low (three games groin, 15 games foot injuries). Matched career high for assists and set second-highest marks for goals and points. He led the team in plus/minus.

THE FINESSE GAME

Injuries put a crimp in Hatcher's developing finesse skills. Though he doesn't have great speed, Kevin continues to demonstrate improved skating ability, particularly in agility and foot speed. He turns well in all directions and changes direction fairly quickly — impressive skills for a player his size.

He reads the play very well at the NHL level at both blue lines (as his plus/minus attests). Hatcher will make good-to-very good decisions in getting the puck from his own end in both passing and carrying it, and he mirrors those decisions at the offensive blue line — where he moves the puck skillfully to an open teammate. This is where his NHL experience has combined with his improved footwork to make his hand skills better. For example, Hatcher has no problem pulling the puck from his skates to get a shot off.

He has a good shot from the blue line, and Hatcher is smart enough to just wrist a quick shot on net when he's pressured. He'll also sneak to the slot if there's an opening (just as he'll step up from his own zone to create a 3-on-2), but he doesn't take chances to create openings by cutting to the slot.

Because of his mental and physical finesse abilities, Hatcher has become a specialty teams natural.

THE PHYSICAL GAME

Hatcher has excellent size, and he uses it very well. He hits hard and punishes he opposition, and he does so in smart fashion — without taking penalties that hurt his team.

His improved balance and hand skills make Kevin's physical game all the more effective, because he can now make plays after gaining the puck along the boards. His strength means he can handle any player along the boards or in front of the net.

THE INTANGIBLES

Conventional wisdom says a young defenseman needs five NHL seasons to mature; Hatcher is entering his fifth now. Great things were expected of him last season (off his 1988 playoff success), but his injuries hampered his development.

Injuries are another question. He has never played all 80 games of the regular season, and now that his body is near its physical maturity that is another plateau Hatcher must gain.

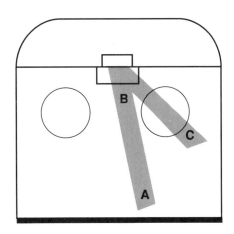

DALE HUNTER

Yrs. of NHL service: 9
Born: Petrolia, Ontario, Canada; July 31, 1960
Position: Center
Height: 5-10
Weight: 190
Uniform No.: 32
Shoots: left

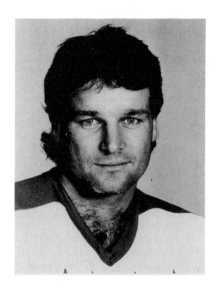

Career statistics:

GP	G	A	TP	PIM
682	182	392	574	2,004

1988-89 statistics:

GP	G	A	TP	+/-	PIM	PP	SH	GW	GT	S	PCT
80	20	37	57	-3	219	9	0	3	0	138	14.5

LAST SEASON

Hunter played 80 games for the sixth time in his career and first time in three seasons. He finished second on the club in PIM, first among forwards. Point total was full season career low.

THE FINESSE GAME

Dale is a smart player, and his sense of the game and ice vision make him a good forechecker and power play Man.

He's a good — not great — skater, with good speed and very good balance and strength on his skates. Look for him to use that strength in front of the net, especially as a screen on the power play.

Hunter uses his good skating ability when checking, and he can complement that skill with his hockey sense to contribute offensively. He can be a good playmaker, mostly because his physical game earns him time and space to get the puck to his teammates.

His hands are a little tough, though, so don't expect him to feather passes through traffic or to stickhandle around the entire opposing team. Hunter will get where he is going in one straight line.

THE PHYSICAL GAME

Dale's strength and willingness to take abuse are evident in the goals he scores. He can work around the net because of his upper body and arm strength, as well as his strength on his skates to stay upright after collisions.

Hunter is a very physical player. He hits a lot and that willingness — and a few well-placed elbows — opens up ice for Dale and his teammates. Hunter also sacrifices his body by frequently blocking shots.

He's a prototypical disturber, willing to dish it out with anyone at any time — regardless of size or reputation. But Hunter is more likely to use his abrasive style to goad the opposing player into dropping his gloves first.

THE INTANGIBLES

Hunter is a gutsy, determined leader, playing with tons of heart and character. He's an excellent team man, willing to do whatever is necesary to win.

He's an instigator of the first order, but he's also the kind of player every team would like to have.

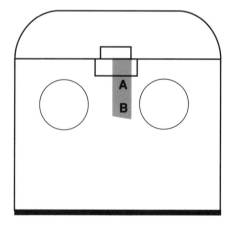

CALLE JOHANSSON

Yrs. of NHL service: 2
Born: Goteborg, Sweden; February 14, 1967
Position: Defenseman
Height: 5-11
Weight: 198
Uniform No.: 6

Career statistics:

GP	G	A	TP	PIM
130	7	56	63	74

1988-89 statistics:

GP	G	A	TP	+/-	PIM	PP	SH	GW	GT	S	PCT
59	3	18	21	-6	37	1	0	1	0	75	4.0

LAST SEASON

Johansson was traded to Washington from Buffalo in exchange for Grant Ledyard and Clint Malarchuk. He was sidelined early in the season with a thumb injury.

THE FINESSE GAME

Johansson's poise is the best of his finesse skills, as he shows good patience and decision making in the defensive zone. He's strong and quick, which is a not-always-usual combination. He has good speed and quickness on his feet, and that speed allows him to get the puck and look over his options before making a play.

Calle passes very well, and he does so because of his good hands and ice vision. He shoots well from the point, but not as frequently as he should. He contains the offensive play well and is especially effective on the power play, where he easily finds the open man and gets the puck to him.

His defensive game is marked by the same smarts. Johansson closes the gap well on the puck carrier and turns the play up-ice well. Though finishing the season as a minus player, Calle was plus-1 in his 12 games with Washington.

THE PHYSICAL GAME

Calle has good strength and he uses that strength well defensively. He's good in the corners and takes the body well when he can. As with most Europeans, his skating demonstrates the fundamental of balance, and that aids him greatly in his physical game. And, he's not afraid to get his nose dirty.

He covers the front of the net fairly well, but this is not his game. He'll succeed by being the outlet man, not the front-of-net punisher.

THE INTANGIBLES

Johansson has the skills and the smarts to be an above-average NHLer. The Caps will count on him to replace some of the offense they were supposed to get from Larry Murphy.

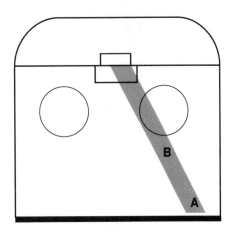

ROD LANGWAY

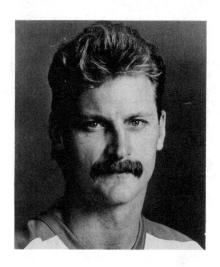

Yrs. of NHL service: 11
Born: Formosa, Taiwan; May 3, 1957
Position: Defenseman
Height: 6-3
Weight: 215
Uniform No.: 5
Shoots: left

Career statistics:

GP	G	A	TP	PIM
795	50	250	300	744

1988-89 statistics:

GP	G	A	TP	+/-	PIM	PP	SH	GW	GT	S	PCT
76	2	19	21	12	65	0	0	0	0	80	2.5

LAST SEASON

Langway failed to play 80 games for the fifth consecutive season. His plus/minus was second-highest among defensemen, fifth best on the club.

THE FINESSE GAME

Where skating and brains had been the hallmarks of Langway's game, only smarts remain. That's not to say that Rod can't skate any more, but last season showed that time and wear have taken their tolls on his wheels.

Though he still moves well forward and back, Langway's foot speed (and the inherent agility that made him so superior) has slowed. That makes him slower in turning, slower in getting to the puck or the Man. What saves him are his playreading and hockey sense — his defensive anticipation.

Rod still sees the defensive play with superb clarity, and he's using that ability to compensate for his slowing skating. His knowledge of the League's forwards and their abilities aids him in making his defensive plays, and he still moves the puck from his own zone alertly.

He's never been a scorer and will take even fewer forechecking and pinching chances now, but Langway keeps the opposition honest with a good shot from the left point or with the *very* ocassional rush to the slot.

THE PHYSICAL GAME

If anything, Langway (always tough, strong, and mean) has gotten more so in his old age. Much of that is through necessity; if he can't hit what he can't catch, he'll at least punish what he *can* track down.

He still uses his body intelligently to thwart the opposition, and he has never taken penalties that hurt the team. But where he previously could win any board battle, Langway is now less sure a victor — particularly against the League's stronger forwards. As a result, he holds and interferes more than he ever did to maintain an advantage.

THE INTANGIBLES

What Langway does best now is clean up the Caps zone while defensive partner Kevin Hatcher improves his all-around game and his offense.

Langway was playing poorly and looked his age (he needed 61 games to haul himself from a negative plus/minus rating), and there was much talk about his being in the way in Washington. But his last quarter of the season was very strong, and Rod continues to play with heart and determination.

He is just no longer the heart of the Capitals, and right now no one has stepped forward to fill that vacuum.

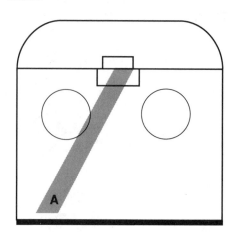

STEPHEN LEACH

Yrs. of NHL service: 2
Born: Cambridge, Mass., USA: January 16, 1966
Position: Right wing
Height: 5-11
Weight: 180
Uniform No.: 21
Shoots: right

Career statistics:

GP	G	A	TP	PIM
108	14	21	35	119

1988-89 statistics:

GP	G	A	TP	+/-	PIM	PP	SH	GW	GT	S	PCT
74	11	19	30	-4	94	4	0	0	0	145	7.6

LAST SEASON

First complete NHL season, with resulting career highs in points and PIM.

THE FINESSE GAME

In a lot of ways, Leach is a mirror image of frequent linemate Kelly Miller. Leach is a good skater with a lot of speed (and he always keeps his feet moving), but that speed is often rendered useless by Stephen's predictable, straight-ahead approach. He doesn't have a great deal of agility (not yet anyway), and while he goes a mile a minute his hands and smarts struggle to catch up.

He has demonstrated some ability to get the puck to his teammates, but not with any great frequency. That's because Leach cannot yet read and react at the NHL level of play; only experience can change that.

Stephen also needs work on his understanding of positional play, especially defensively. He has a tendency to wander all over the offensive zone (one reason he played frequently with defensive stalwarts Miller and Mike Ridley), and to release too quickly from the defensive zone.

His shot is not yet at NHL calibre, so Leach will have to go to the slot and crease for his goals.

THE PHYSICAL GAME

Despite not having great size — and again, like Miller — Leach has no problem barreling into the opposition in his shot-from-a-gun style. He's built with a low center of gravity, so he'll remain vertical and in the play after hitting somebody — the only problem is, right now he doesn't know what to do after that collision. His strong skating keeps him strong on the puck.

He'll have to develop greater strength to counteract his size if he wants to succeed in the NHL.

THE INTANGIBLES

All told, an average NHL debut for what is so far an average player. Leach has shown the ability to score at the collegiate and international levels, and now he must show the ability to adapt and improve his game to the NHL.

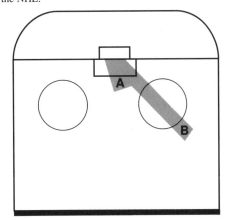

KELLY MILLER

Yrs. of NHL service: 4
Born: Lansing, Mich., USA; March 3, 1963
Position: Left wing
Height: 5-11
Weight: 185
Uniform No.: 10
Shoots: left

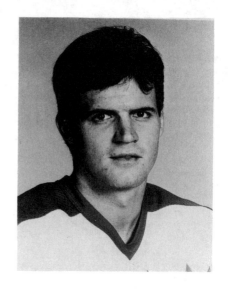

Career statistics:

GP	G	A	TP	PIM
314	57	92	149	182

1988-89 statistics:

GP	G	A	TP	+/-	PIM	PP	SH	GW	GT	S	PCT
78	19	21	40	13	45	2	1	3	0	121	15.7

LAST SEASON

Games played total was second highest of career (knee and leg injuries), with goal and point totals career bests. His plus/minus was the club's fourth-best, third among forwards.

THE FINESSE GAME

Skating is clearly the best of Miller's finesse assets, and speed is what makes that so. Kelly can blow by defensemen because of his tremendous speed, though he doesn't possess great one-step quickness, or great lateral movement and agility.

What makes his speed increasingly valuable is his ability to moderate it and to avoid the predictability his game once showed. Miller used to just gun past defenders; now he'll fake a move and go the other way. He still isn't Denis Savard, but he's better than the Kelly Miller that entered the NHL four seasons ago.

Kelly carries the puck fairly well, with his hands and brain catching up to his feet. He's learning to look for his teammates, but Miller still primarily goes right to the net.

His speed makes Miller an excellent checker. And, because he keeps his head up when he doesn't have the puck, Miller augments his speed in checking with vision and brains. He anticipates the play fairly well and is a natural penalty killer.

If his hand skills were better, he'd be an overwhelming threat for short-handed goals. Miller will net most of his 17-22 goals a year from 25-feet and in on a fair-to-good wrist shot.

THE PHYSICAL GAME

He doesn't have good size, but Kelly puts what he does have to its best use. He has increased his strength dramatically in the last few seasons, and that added power compensates somewhat for his lack of natural bulk; it even puts him on better footing against some of the League's stronger but less intelligent (hockey-wise) players.

Miller's improved strength makes his willing board work more effective, and he'll always pursue the puck regardless of physical price. However, he will be out-muscled by bigger and stronger players if caught against the boards. The only question is, will those players know what to do with the puck after they get it? That is where Kelly's advantage is.

THE INTANGIBLES

Just as he worked to gain NHL strength, Miller worked to improve the mix of his foot speed and hand skills. He is a tremendously hard worker both on and off the ice, and his excellent character and work habits make him more valuable than just his skills would allow.

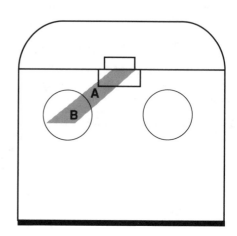

MICHAL PIVONKA

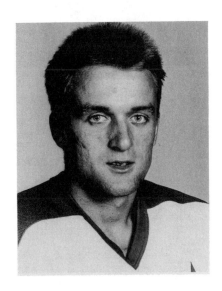

Yrs. of NHL service: 3
Born: Kladno, Czechoslovakia; January 28, 1966
Position: Center/left wing
Height: 6-2
Weight: 200
Uniform No.: 20
Shoots: left

Career statistics:

GP	G	A	TP	PIM
196	37	67	104	99

1988-89 statistics:

GP	G	A	TP	+/-	PIM	PP	SH	GW	GT	S	PCT
52	8	19	27	9	30	1	0	1	0	73	11.0

LAST SEASON

Games played was a career low, as were all point totals.

THE FINESSE GAME

Pivonka is an excellent open-ice skater, combining balance and quickness for good lateral movement and agility. He also has a strong, powerful stride that helps him accelerate away from the opposition.

He carries the puck extremely well, but remains unable to convert his puck-carrying into successful NHL playmaking. Even after three seasons, Michal neither understands nor reacts to the play at NHL speed. Though he has excellent hands, Pivonka often finds himself a second behind. So, his passes skitter past teammates or into their skates instead of finding their sticks.

Pivonka has great hockey sense and knows how to get into position to score, but again is handicapped by his less-than-NHL-level playreading ability. His shot is good — not great — and is released quickly. He rarely uses a slap shot.

Pivonka has improved his defense by staying in his lane. He has also worked harder at integrating a defensive ethic into his game.

THE PHYSICAL GAME

When we say Pivonka is an open-ice skater, that doesn't mean he lacks the components necessary to succeed in close quarters. Rather, he has fine balance and skate strength, but Pivonka doesn't play the type of game that allows those attributes to come to the fore.

He's a finesse player with size who won't initiate contact to gain the puck. He will willingly go to the high traffic areas to score, but his great balance — and his ability to make a play off the boards — could be put to good use in tussles along the boards. He must learn — as Pat LaFontaine and Steve Yzerman (two *smaller*

players) learned — that an element of physical play opens up a finesse game.

THE INTANGIBLES

We said that last year was Pivonka's put-up-or-shut-up year, but that judgement must be carried forward to this season. The Caps have enough role players to score eight goals a year; what they need is a capable finesse player.

Pivonka, now 23 and with three NHL seasons under his belt, must show that he is valuable NHL material — and good playoff performances alone don't do that. He must make determined and conscious effort to play to his potential this season.

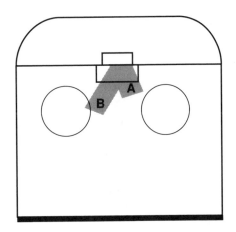

MIKE RIDLEY

Yrs. of NHL service: 4
Born: Winnipeg, Man., Canada; July 8, 1963
Position: Center
Height: 6-1
Weight: 190
Uniform No.: 17
Shoots: right

Career statistics:

GP	G	A	TP	PIM
308	122	161	283	180

1988-89 statistics:

GP	G	A	TP	+/-	PIM	PP	SH	GW	GT	S	PCT
80	41	48	89	17	49	16	0	9	0	187	21.9

LAST SEASON

Ridley led the team in scoring and tied for first in power play goals. He was third in goals and assists, second in plus/minus and first in game winners (third in NHL). Point totals were all career highs, and he played 80 games for second time in career.

THE FINESSE GAME

Balance is the finesse quality that powers Mike's game, seconded by his hockey sense. Ridley is not a great skater in terms of quickness or speed, but his exceptional balance allows him to work excellently in crowded areas and while being checked. That balance also gives him excellent agility and lateral movement.

Ridley's hockey sense reveals where he is in relation to his teammates and to the net. His anticipation and excellent peripheral vision complement his hand skills and make him a good passer by showing him openings.

He has good touch on his passes, and he'll lead a teammate to an opening. Mike also carries the puck well, and his accurate wrist (delivered from anywhere) forces the goaltender to make saves.

He uses his finesse skills on both specialty team units, and defensively too. He excels at getting the puck from his own zone.

THE PHYSICAL GAME

Because Mike's low center of gravity makes him very difficult to knock down, he can play a physical game and not suffer for it. That means he'll control the puck in traffic despite being checked, and it also means he'll come out of collisions vertical and ready to go. He amplifies his physical ability with his playmaking ability out of the corner.

He is not overwhelmingly strong along the boards but is aggressive and stays involved in the action at all times. Ridley will bump anyone he has to in order to make his plays and he is impossible to brutalize, ignoring the abuse to concentrate on his assigned task.

THE INTANGIBLES

Heart, character, dedication. Those words describe Ridley's attitude toward the game. He is eminently coachable and is a very hard worker in practice and during games, making him a quality individual and hockey player. He will always turn in a solid performance, and he still has the potential to improve his game.

Ridley had to overcome a poor start to finish as he did, particularly in his plus/minus. By game 30, he was 18g-10a-28pt and minus-11. Thirteen games (and seven goals and 21 points) later, he was plus-5, a 16-point turnaround.

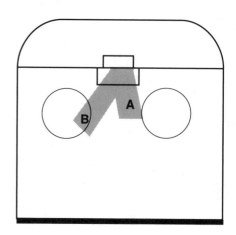

BOB ROUSE

Yrs. of NHL service: 5
Born: Surrey, B.C., Canada; June 18, 1964
Position: Defenseman
Height: 6-1
Weight: 210
Uniform No.: 8
Shoots: right

Career statistics:

GP	G	A	TP	PIM
364	9	60	69	771

1988-89 statistics:

GP	G	A	TP	+/-	PIM	PP	SH	GW	GT	S	PCT
79	4	15	19	-3	160	0	1	0	0	85	4.7

LAST SEASON

Rouse was acquired at the trading deadline, along with Dino Ciccarelli, from Minnesota in exchange for Mike Gartner and Larry Murphy. Games played and all point totals were career highs.

THE FINESSE GAME

Rouse is just slightly better than average as a skater (both forward and backward) and, because his foot speed is weak, his agility is too. His turning and pivoting ability should be improved.

Because of his skating Rouse is no threat to carry the puck, and he will do so only on the rarest of occasions — and then never carrying over the opposing blue line. If he gets that far, Bob will dump the puck into the corner. His play is to move it up to the forwards to get it out of the zone.

His lack of foot speed leaves him susceptible to forechecking and turnovers. If he can turn back up-ice with the puck he'll usually move the puck efficiently. He reads the play defensively, as he sees and understands the rush coming at him well and he steers the opposition to the boards smartly.

As could be expected, Rouse rarely joins the play in the offensive zone; his responsibility is that of the fallback defenseman. It is when he plays outside his skills that Rouse gets into trouble, and those occasions are when his performances are inconsistent and downright poor.

Rouse has an average shot from the point and he doesn't shoot frequently. Any goals he gets will come from there and they will be few and far between.

THE PHYSICAL GAME

Though blessed with good physical tools, Rouse is erratic in their application. He can be one mean and miserable son of a gun, but he doesn't get the most out of his physical skills — doesn't even come close.

Why? Because he's very inconsistent in the use of his size. He's big and strong and when he plays that way his value to the team rises. He can clear the front of the net very well because of his strength and meanness. He hits well and hard — rather than just pushing and shoving along the boards — and can muscle the opposition off the puck.

He is a very tough player and plays that way. Sometimes.

THE INTANGIBLES

Rouse has got to play with more fire in his game, and that is tough for him because he's a low-key guy. And when he plays low-key his value to the team plummets. He is a hard worker and should improve with continued experience, particularly because — unlike in Minnesota — in Washington he doesn't have to be the big hitter.

Still, he can be better than a fourth or fifth defenseman.

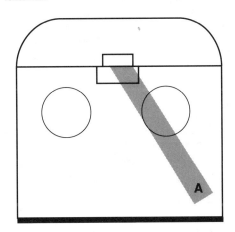

NEIL SHEEHY

Yrs. of NHL service: 5
Born: International Falls, Minn., USA;
February 9, 1960
Position: Defenseman
Height: 6-2
Weight: 215
Uniform No.: 15
Shoots: right

Career statistics:

GP	G	A	TP	PIM
285	16	40	56	901

1988-89 statistics:

GP	G	A	TP	+/-	PIM	PP	SH	GW	GT	S	PCT
72	3	4	7	-1	179	0	0	0	0	22	13.6

LAST SEASON

Sheehy was acquired by the Caps in the summer of 1988 (along with Mike Millar) from Hartford in exchange for Grant Jennings and Ed Kastelic. Games played was a career high. He was the Caps' lowest scoring regular.

THE FINESSE GAME

Sheehy is a far better finesse player than he is given credit for. He is a good skater though not especially fast or agile, but he is strong on his skates and improving in the areas of balance (he took ballet lessons for that) and foot speed. He moves fairly well forward and backward and maintains his position well when checking in his own zone.

In puck handling, Sheehy again is more than adequate and improving. He sees the open man and makes the smart plays, and Neil can also handle the puck and rush it when necessary, though he prefers to move the puck rather than skate it.

He will not frequently become a fourth attacker in the offensive zone, but Sheehy can move into the play and control the point — which is where his goals will come from — though he will rarely pinch in. He is smart enough to know his limitations and not force his offensive game beyond its boundaries.

THE PHYSICAL GAME

Sheehy is as tough as they come and he hits hard and often. He is a very strong presence in front of his own net (though not as strong as he could be when killing penalties) and he is also mean with his stick.

He will outmuscle almost anyone along the boards and is a very good fighter — as would be expected of a guy who was on his university's boxing team.

THE INTANGIBLES

Sheehy is a very intelligent player (as demonstrated by his staying within his limits as a player) and he is also a prime disturber on the ice.

He is a good player and may make some small improvements in his play over the next few seasons, but at 29 years old what you see is basically what you get. His value is in toughness, and his ability to successfully spell players like Scott Stevens and Kevin Hatcher.

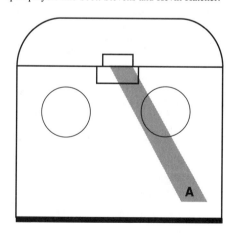

SCOTT STEVENS

Yrs. Of NHL service: 7
Born: Kitchener, Ontario, Canada; April 1, 1964
Position: Defenseman
Height: 6-1
Weight: 215
Uniform No.: 3
Shoots: left

Career statistics:

GP	G	A	TP	PIM
545	87	302	389	1,476

1988-89 statistics:

GP	G	A	TP	+/-	PIM	PP	SH	GW	GT	S	PCT
80	7	61	68	1	225	6	0	3	0	195	3.6

LAST SEASON

Stevens played all 80 games for the second consecutive season. His assist total was a career high (he led the team in this category — second best among NHL defensemen), and his point total second highest. He finished eighth in League-wide defensive scoring, leading the team's defense. He also led the Caps in PIM.

THE FINESSE GAME

Scott is an excellent skater, combining balance, speed and strength in that skill. He has excellent foot speed for quickness and rink length speed to accelerate away from the opposition. His combination of balance and foot speed gives him excellent agility and lateral movement, and his ability is made even more impressive because of his excellent size.

His excellent vision and anticipation make him a force in both the offensive and defensive zones. He finds the open man excellently at both ends, and his passing is more effective by virtue of his patience; he generally can't be forced to make mistakes.

Stevens handles the puck especially well in traffic because of his strength and balance. He carries it well and makes his plays with his head up. He'll charge the net when the opportunity arises, but his offensive forays don't harm his defense because he is fast enough to get back into position.

His slap shot is hard and accurate from the point, but because he doesn't have a quick release many of his shots get blocked (strange, because he can one-time a shot on net off a pass). He didn't shoot the puck enough last season, and his SOG total of 195 was almost 20 percent less than in 1987-88 (when he had 231 SOG). Only one of his goals came at even-strength.

THE PHYSICAL GAME

Stevens may be the League's strongest physical player, and maybe its best too. His superior upper *and* lower body strength put him at the elite level, allowing him to control any area of ice easily. His upper body power allows him to out-muscle anyone, and his leg strength allows him to drive through his checks and make them truly punishing.

That leg strength and balance power his great skating and make his physical game that much more effective, because he is always on the vertical side of his collisions. He's also an excellent fighter.

THE INTANGIBLES

A great team player with tremendous heart and character (Play with pain? A given.), Stevens overcame a poor start (23 points and an incredible *minus-21* in the first 30 games) to finish strongly.

He's quality goods, and a solid season will return him to Norris Memorial Trophy-contending status.

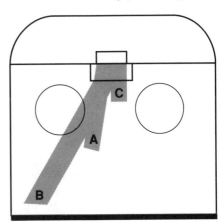

WINNIPEG JETS

LINE COMBINATIONS
IAIN DUNCAN-DALE HAWERCHUK
ANDY MCBAIN
PAUL FENTON-LAURIE BOSCHMAN
GORD DONNELLY
BRENT ASHTON-THOMAS STEEN
PAT ELYNUIK

DEFENSE PAIRINGS
RANDY CARLYLE-PETER TAGLIANETTI
DAVE ELLETT-FREDRIK OLAUSSON
JIM KYTE-TEPPO NUMMINEN

GOALTENDERS
ELDON REDDICK
DANIEL BERTHIAUME

OTHER PLAYERS
BRAD BERRY — Defenseman
RANDY GILHEN — Left wing
HANNU JARVENPAA — Right wing
BRAD JONES — Left wing
DOUG SMAIL —Left wing

POWER PLAY

FIRST UNIT:
ANDY MCBAIN-DALE HAWERCHUK-IAIN DUNCAN
DAVE ELLETT-FREDRIK OLAUSSON

SECOND UNIT:
BRENT ASHTON-THOMAS STEEN-PAT ELYNUIK
RANDY CARLYLE-TEPPO NUMMINEN

On the first unit, MCBAIN patrols the left wing corner to the faceoff circle, HAWERCHUK works the right side and MCBAIN posts upin front of the net. ELLETT and OLAUSSON will play catch to free space for MCBAIN at faceoff spot, then try to isolate him for shot; HAWERCHUK will move to slot for rebound. Shots from both ELLETT and OLAUSSON are also in the game plan if the power play cannot break the penalty killers, in which case MCBAIN moves to the net for junk goals.

The second unit posts ASHTON at the left circle, with ELYNUIK his mirror image at the right circle. STEEN works behind the net and the slot, and the JETS will try to keep ELLETT out for all two minutes (otherwise NUMMINEN makes his appearance). Shots from the faceoff circles are the plan, with STEEN going to the front for tips, screens and rebounds.

Last season Winnipeg's power play was GOOD, scoring 79 goals in 357 opportunities (22.1 percent, sixth overall).

PENALTY KILLING

FIRST UNIT:
RANDY GILHEN-ANDY MCBAIN
JIM KYTE-PETER TAGLIANETTI

SECOND UNIT:
THOMAS STEEN-DOUG SMAIL
DAVE ELLETT-TEPPO NUMMINEN

Both units have the forwards very aggressive on the puck, jumping the opposition as it crosses the blue line. KYTE and TAGLIANETTI are very conservative and serve to punish any opposition player in front of the net, while ELLETT and NUMMINEN pressure the puck in the corners and try to create offense. BRENT ASHTON and BRAD JONES will also see penalty-killing time.

Last season Winnipeg's penalty killing was FAIR, allowing 82 goals in 374 shorthanded situations (78.1 percent, 14th overall).

CRUCIAL FACEOFFS
This is THOMAS STEEN territory, as he's taken over from LAURIE BOSCHMAN.

BRENT ASHTON

Yrs. of NHL service: 10
Born: Saskatoon, Sask., Canada; May 18, 1960
Position: Left wing
Height: 6-1
Weight: 210
Uniform no.: 7
Shoots: left

Career Statistics:

GP	G	A	TP	PIM
714	222	252	474	437

1988-89 statistics:

GP	G	A	TP	+/-	PIM	PP	SH	GW	GT	S	PCT
75	31	37	68	-5	36	7	1	1	0	180	17.2

LAST SEASON

Goal total ties second best of career, point total was second best and assist total was career high. Finished fourth on the club in scoring and in plus/minus among forwards. He was sidelined with a late-season knee injury.

THE FINESSE GAME

Brent is a solid balance of finesse and physical skills. He's a very good skater with speed, quickness and agility. His good foot speed and powerful stride combine to give him explosive acceleration, and he has the ability to shift gears up and down within two strides. He also has a surprising degree of agility for a bigger man, and he can change direction as well as he changes speed.

Ashton keeps his head up when making plays, but he does have a tendency to be a selfish player; he wants the puck and wants to shoot it — which is good — but that causes him to overhandle the puck and turn it over instead of moving it when needed — which is not good.

He carries the puck well, better now that he's moderated his speed and his feet aren't outracing his hands, and his agility and quickness can get him around defensemen. Brent's shot is exemplary. Though not hard, it is quick and very accurate.

Ashton isn't Bob Gainey reincarnate, but he's a good positional player who plays conscientious defense. So ignore the plus/minus.

THE PHYSICAL GAME

Brent has good size and strength and he uses those attributes in a non-spectacular way. He won't drive the opposition through the boards with his hits, but Ashton's strength, balance and quickness allow him to take the body well and to drive through his checks. Those checks force loose pucks, and he certainly has the hand skills to make a play coming away from the boards.

His excellent balance helps him get goals in tight, and his willingness to play in the traffic area in front of the net keys much of his scoring success.

THE INTANGIBLES

He's the kind of player that will score everywhere he goes, and Ashton is also the kind of player who can help most any club. He works hard and is coachable. He's also versatile, in that he can play either wing, and he shows up ready to play every day. All these factors make him an important part of Winninpeg's lineup.

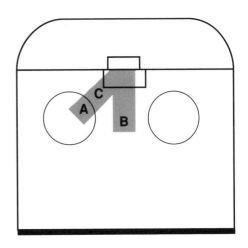

BRAD BERRY

Yrs. of NHL service: 3
Born: Bashaw, Alta., Canada; April 1, 1965
Position: Defenseman
Height: 6-2
Weight: 190
Uniform no.: 29
Shoots: left

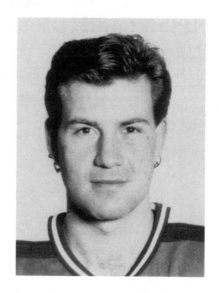

Career Statistics:

GP	G	A	TP	PIM
151	3	23	26	190

1988-89 statistics:

GP	G	A	TP	+/-	PIM	PP	SH	GW	GT	S	PCT
38	0	9	9	-8	45	0	0	0	0	21	0.0

LAST SEASON

Games played was three-season low, but assist total was career high. He shuttled back and forth between Winnipeg and Moncton of the American Hockey League.

THE FINESSE GAME

Berry is not a very skilled player, but he's skilled enough to play in the NHL. His skating is unexceptional, but it is his balance that really hinders his play. Because of his lack of balance, Brad loses far too many 1-on-1 battles for the puck in the corner and the front of the net.

He is otherwise an unremarkable player who will succeed by making the simple, up the boards plays. He's not apt to join the offense at the opposition blue line, and Brad has little to add there anyway.

He reads the play in a linear way, in that he reacts to what he sees in front of him without anticipating any further action.

THE PHYSICAL GAME

Berry plays a fairly strong game in the traffic areas (balance problem excepted). He can handle the front of the net but is in trouble when matched against the League stronger forwards, because he lacks the leverage to move them.

THE INTANGIBLES

The Jets wanted Berry to improve his physical strength, and he did that. But you can lift weight all day and get nowhere without balance, and that's why Brad will continue being a part-time NHLer.

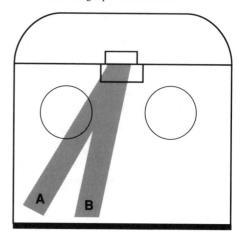

DANIEL BERTHIAUME

Yrs. of NHL service: 3
Born: Longeuil, Quebec, Canada; January 26, 1966
Position: Goaltender
Height: 5-9
Weight: 150
Uniform no.: 30
Catches: left

Career Statistics:

GP	MINS	G	SO	AVG	A	PIM
96	5,211	313	4	3.60	2	14

1988-89 statistics:

GP	MINS	AVG	W	L	T	SO	GA	SA	SAPCT	PIM
9	443	5.96	0	8	0	0	44	255	.826	0

LAST SEASON

Games played total was career low, GAA career high. He was demoted to the American Hockey League, and suspended by the Jets when he did not report.

THE PHYSICAL GAME

Daniel is a hybrid as a goalie, one who combines the best aspects of both the reflex and stand-up games. He uses his skating to play a challenging game, moving in and out of his net well and demonstrating good lateral movement post to post (but better going left than right). Daniel doesn't skate from his net to flag down loose pucks, nor is he the type to even cut the puck off around the net; he rarely handles the puck at all.

He stands up well on bad angle shots and doesn't often allow the bad short side goal, but Berthiaume butterflies to cover the lower part of the net. His quick legs and feet — and the balance he maintains in his stance — enable him to regain his position quickly after making a save.

Berthiaume covers or deflects his rebounds well, particularly off pad saves. He does less well (but only marginally so) above his waist. His quickness extends to his hands and he'll intercept passes across the crease or pokecheck the puck when it's in reach. He plays the first bounce on high, bouncing shots and that prevents him from handling the puck safely after the save.

THE MENTAL GAME

Two separate issues: He maintains his concentration and intensity throughout the game, using his good anticipation and vision skills to make his reflexes work better. He can also keep his concentration high from game to game, shaking off bad goals or games. He'll make the big save to keep the Jets in the game.

That's the first issue.

THE INTANGIBLES

The second issue is his attitude away from the game. He believes the game will just come to him and he did nothing during the summer of 1988 to prepare for the 1988-89 season — no skating, no running, no nothing. He came to training camp out of shape and was shipped out.

Berthiaume has NHL skills, but he must learn to work at using his skills.

LAURIE BOSCHMAN

Yrs. of NHL service: 10
Born: Major, Sask., Canada; June 4, 1960
Position: Center
Height: 6-0
Weight: 185
Uniform no.: 16
Shoots: left

Career Statistics:

GP	G	A	TP	PIM
720	191	295	486	1,861

1988-89 statistics:

GP	G	A	TP	+/-	PIM	PP	SH	GW	GT	S	PCT
70	10	26	36	-17	163	3	0	1	0	113	8.8

LAST SEASON

Games played and point totals were six-season lows (leg injury). Goal total was career low. PIM total was club's fourth highest, second among forwards.

THE FINESSE GAME

Age and wear and tear have taken their tolls on Boschman. Though previously a strong finesse player, Boschman's skating skill has diminished — so much so that his ability is questionable at the NHL level. The quickness and agility he counted on as a two-way player have decreased, leaving Laurie to work from his smarts.

But his skating has affected his smarts, in that he's no longer getting the time to make good reads of the ice. He's not seeing plays offensively (and his hands aren't fast enough to work often enough in the smaller periods of time he's getting), so his work is pretty much confined to defensive play. He can be a very heady player and good defensive forward.

For what goals he'll get, Boschman will be most effective in front of the net, where he is more than willing to take his lumps and where he can cash in on the turnovers his checking has forced.

THE PHYSICAL GAME

Boschman has always been a physical, chippy player — and all his success has been based on that. His willingness to hit anything in an opposition sweater made him the team's spark plug. Boschman would win many board battles because of his strength and his willingness to apply it.

But there's a reason this is written in the past tense.

THE INTANGIBLES

Laurie has always thrived because of his attitude, that mental edge that allowed him to play aggressively against any one at any time. But he lost that edge last season, and without it he's a fourth-line player. He wasn't even winning key faceoffs — a crucial part of his importance.

If he can regain that edge, that willingness to be aggressive at all times, he can probably regain some portion of his previously fine two-way game. Right now, he looks very much like a fourth-line hockey player.

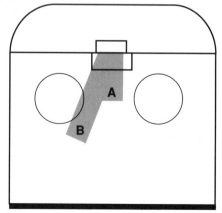

RANDY CARLYLE

Yrs. of NHL service: 13
Born: Sudbury, Ontario, Canada; April 19, 1956
Position: Defenseman
Height: 5-10
Weight: 200
Uniform no.: 8
Shoots: left

Career Statistics:

GP	G	A	TP	PIM
862	134	455	589	1,238

1988-89 statistics:

GP	G	A	TP	+/-	PIM	PP	SH	GW	GT	S	PCT
78	6	38	44	-19	78	2	0	2	0	124	4.8

LAST SEASON

Games played total tied career high, PIM total nine-season low.

THE FINESSE GAME

Carlyle's physical finesse skills continue to diminish, his skating in particular. Once gifted with excellent wheels, Randy no longer has the skating speed, quickness or agility he previously possessed. He can still rush the puck, but those offensive forays are going to be fewer and further between.

But while his skating skill has fallen, Randy's smarts have risen; that's why he'll still succeed at the NHL level. Carlyle knows how to complement his skating with positional play and smart puck movement, so he'll make the correct play — and a good play — more often than not. Exception: strong forechecking which takes advantage of his diminished skating can force Carlyle to make blind, panicky passes around the boards.

His vision (particularly peripherally) and anticipation show him the ice, and he complements those assets with good hand skills. He'll lead his teammates with good passes, find the open man, and contain the point at the opposition blue line.

He's still strong on the power play, but he's ceded his first unit role to Dave Ellett. Not primarily a goal scorer, Randy will earn his points on a low and accurate point slap shot; he'll cheat to the faceoff circle if he can.

THE PHYSICAL GAME

Carlyle can take the body fairly well against the boards (liberal stick use to hook, and some proficiency at holding help here), but stronger forwards who continue to drive their legs will either get free or draw penalties.

He does more pushing and shoving than hitting, so the corner and crease work will more likely fall to his tougher defensive partner.

THE INTANGIBLES

Carlyle is a character player on a team not known for character — that makes him tremendously important. He no longer has 80 games a season in him,and he accepts that, so the Jets shouldn't try to force those games out of him. He's got tons of heart, but he just doesn't have the skills at his command that he did earlier in his career.

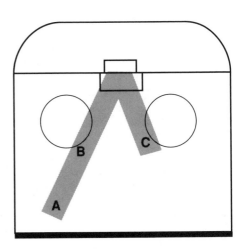

RANDY CUNNEYWORTH

Yrs. of NHL service: 5
Born: Etobicoke, Ontario, Canada; May 10, 1961
Position: Center/left wing
Height: 5-11
Weight: 190
Uniform no.: 15
Shoots: left

Career statistics:

GP	G	A	TP	PIM
316	103	119	222	562

1988-89 statistics:

GP	G	A	TP	+/-	PIM	PP	SH	GW	GT	S	PCT
70	25	19	44	-22	156	10	0	1	0	163	15.3

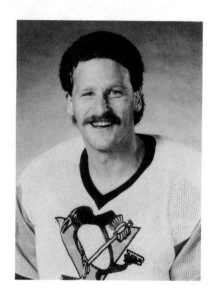

LAST SEASON

Games played total was four-season low; ditto assist and point totals. Goal total was three-season low. PIM total was career high. Was sidelined with mid-season foot injury, and missed one game with a late-season back injury. Plus/minus tied for team's third worst, second worst among forwards.

THE FINESSE GAME

Balance and strength are the keys to Cunneyworth's game, both physically and finesse-wise. His balance keeps Randy upright through collisions and that's important, given his play-the-body style. His skating strength allows him to both drive through his own checks and to drive to the net against opposing checking. He also uses that balance to key a fairly agile skating style, one that provides him with some speed and quickness.

His hockey sense is at a fairly high level, though Cunneyworth did tend to out-think himself last season in the pressure to repeat his 35-goal success of 1987-88. Still, he acts and reacts well at NHL speed, looking over the ice before making a play.

His hand skills are good, but Cunneyworth will not usually try to stickhandle through a team to score. He'll give the puck to an open teammate and charge the net.

His balance and strength render him impervious to the traffic close to the net, and it is those assets that let him deliver a good wrist shot while being checked, or while off-balance.

THE PHYSICAL GAME

Cunneyworth is a very tough, aggressive player — despite the fact that he has less than intimidating size — and he uses his body in all three zones. He likes to hit (sometimes he's too aggressive), and his style is powered by the balance and strength mentioned earlier. His physical play is more valuable because of his ability to make plays out of traffic.

He also sacrifices his body to block shots.

THE INTANGIBLES

We mentioned in last year's book how Randy's increased point totals were tied to his increased SOG totals: 169 SOG in 1986-87 for 26 goals, but 229 SOG in 1987-88 for 35 goals. But last year (and this is where the out-thinking part comes in) just 163 SOG, and only 25 goals.

Cunneyworth has to remember what got him where he is — and artistic playmaking isn't it. He's got to remember to crash the net, and to leave the art work to others.

In fairness, he played a lot last season with Dan Quinn, who struggled through much of the season (despite a career-best point mark). Randy's plus/minus is a good indication of how his season went, because he's a much better defensive player than minus-22 says.

To reclaim his success of two seasons back, all he needs to do is reclaim that style. His work ethic says he should be able to do so.

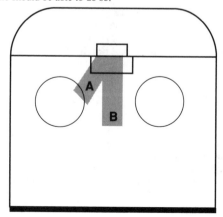

GORD DONNELLY

Yrs. of NHL service: 4
Born: Montreal, Quebec, Canada; April 5, 1962
Position: Right wing
Height: 6-1
Weight: 202
Uniform no.: 22
Shoots: right

Career Statistics:

GP	G	A	TP	PIM
270	16	22	38	896

1988-89 statistics:

GP	G	A	TP	+/-	PIM	PP	SH	GW	GT	S	PCT
73	10	10	20	-20	274	1	0	0	0	67	14.9

LAST SEASON

Acquired from Quebec in exchange for Mario Marois. All point totals were career highs. PIM total led club, and was second highest of career.

THE FINESSE GAME

Let's just say Gord isn't a finesse player. He needs a big lead to do anything creative — like pass or shoot — in the offensive zone and he isn't real mobile on his feet for turns and pivots in the traffic areas.

Donnelly doesn't handle the puck well and he does the smart thing of not handling it frequently. He won't rush the puck up-ice but he will get into the action often enough for a shot or two a game. He'll get his goals from the front of the net.

He has a linear understanding of the game, meaning he can see the play in front of him and counter that (or make an attempt to counter it) but he doesn't anticipate secondary options.

THE PHYSICAL GAME

He doesn't have the skill to play a physical game, in that Gord cannot close the gap on the opposition to check them. What he is, is a fighter. He's one of the NHL's toughest players, is in excellent condition and has great strength, and he puts that strength to work as one of the NHL's top enforcers.

THE INTANGIBLES

Gord's role is pretty straightforward, and he accepts. He steps into any mix up and is a good team guy, but he'll never be more than a fourth-line winger at best. He should not play a lot.

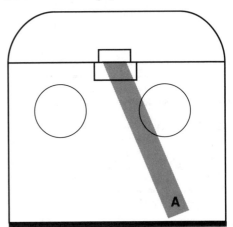

455

IAIN DUNCAN

Yrs. of NHL service: 1
Born: Toronto, Ontario, Canada; August 4, 1963
Position: Left wing
Height: 6-1
Weight: 200
Uniform no.: 19
Shoots: left

Career Statistics:

GP	G	A	TP	PIM
125	34	55	89	147

1988-89 statistics:

GP	G	A	TP	+/-	PIM	PP	SH	GW	GT	S	PCT
57	14	30	44	-17	74	1	0	0	0	91	15.4

LAST SEASON

Games played and goal total fell in second NHL season (rib injury, four games; elbow injury), but assist and PIM totals were career highs.

THE FINESSE GAME

Since strength is the name of Duncan's game, it's fitting that strength — ahem — power his skating game. He's not a fancy skater by any means, but he is a very strong skater with good acceleration and speed, and the balance necessary for a successful physical game. His skating strength serves him in his physical game by driving him through checks along the boards.

His sense of the game is good, and it powers his offensive ability. He knows to go the front of the net and Iain *must* do so, because his shooting is not exceptional at the NHL level — it lacks the quickness of release necessary to consistently defeat NHL goaltending.

Duncan has fairly good hands and a good view of the ice, so he can use his teammates well, and he's beginning to understand the tempo of the NHL game and speed his reactions accordingly.

He is a fairly good player positionally, but his lack of foot speed and corners game combine to leave him trapped deep in the offensive zone and unable to recover when the puck turns over.

THE PHYSICAL GAME

Duncan has all the tools for success in the NHL's physical style: size, strength and a fair degree of skating balance. What he does not have, however, is the ability to use his tools consistently.

He is generally not a tough player on the road, and anytime the opposition responds to his hits with runs of their own against him, Duncan's own physical game vanishes.

When playing well (and he *must* crash and bang to play well), he uses his body and strength to gain the puck along the boards — or he uses his strength by going to the front of the net and out-wrestling the defense there.

THE INTANGIBLES

He has the ability, no question, to succeed at the NHL level. But physical consistency is the key — and so far, only Duncan's inconsistency has been consistent. And too, he still hasn't shown that he's physically prepared for the NHL season, missing substantial parts of both of his NHL seasons.

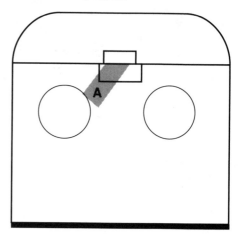

DAVE ELLETT

Yrs. of NHL service: 5
Born: Cleveland, Ohio, USA; March 30, 1964
Position: Defenseman
Height: 6-1
Weight: 200
Uniform no.: 2
Shoots: left

Career Statistics:

GP	G	A	TP	PIM
328	74	168	242	402

1988-89 statistics:

GP	G	A	TP	+/-	PIM	PP	SH	GW	GT	S	PCT
75	22	34	56	-18	62	9	2	5	0	209	10.5

LAST SEASON

Goal total was career high, assist and point totals second highest of career. He was second on the club in game winners, and led the Jets defense in goals. He was sidelined with an ankle injury.

THE FINESSE GAME

Dave is a very talented player, strong in all areas of the finesse game. He's an excellent skater because of his speed, quickness and agility, and he uses his skating to challenge the puck at both blue lines. He closes the gap to the puck carrier quickly, and turns the play around rapidly by carrying the puck.

Ellett rushes the puck very well and becomes an offensive force as a fourth attacker. He combines his exceptional hand skills with good hockey sense to see both openings and teammates, and Ellett will exploit both. He can find the open man, but he can also lead the man to the hole with a good pass. Or, he'll jump into that opening himself courtesy of his foot speed — and then let his puckhandling bedevil the opposition.

His shot is also exceptional, low and hard to the net; it creates all kinds of opportunities for rebounds and deflections.

Dave's lateral movement is best shown on the power play, where he commands the offensive blue line. He contains the point very well and is a good forechecker, and he can afford to challenge because his skating will get him out of any trouble he gets into.

In fact, his ability to manipulate the open space makes him better on the power play (probably 60 percent of points come there) than he is at even strength.

THE PHYSICAL GAME

Ellett is a big, strong defender (that strength powers his speed and shot) who uses those assets well. He's not real tough (in terms of punishing people) in front of the net or in the corners, so his game could stand some improvement there, but bashing people isn't his job. He can clear the front of the net and be effective along the boards and in the corners, holding the opposition out of the play and out-muscling opposing wingers off the puck in traffic situations.

He takes the body well in all three zones, and his size and skating ability make him very difficult to get around at the blue lines.

THE INTANGIBLES

Dave can do it all; we're looking at a solid All-Star contender. If the team can become a winning one, that's where we'd see how good Ellett is; in that regard, he could provide a bit more leadership. But we're not questioning his character. He's got good work habits and is a good team guy who doesn't give anyone a problem.

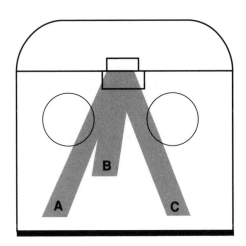

PAT ELYNUIK

Yrs. of NHL service: 1
Born: Foam Lake, Sask., Canada; October 30, 1967
Position: Right wing
Height: 6-0
Weight: 185
Uniform no.: 15
Shoots: right

Career Statistics:

GP	G	A	TP	PIM
69	27	28	55	41

1988-89 statistics:

GP	G	A	TP	+/-	PIM	PP	SH	GW	GT	S	PCT
56	26	25	51	5	29	5	0	6	0	100	26.0

LAST SEASON

First full NHL season. Finished fifth in goals (fourth overall among rookies), 10th in rookie scoring, second in rookie game winners (first on the club) and first in rookie shooting percentage (fourth in NHL and first on club). Was sidelined by a late season shoulder injury.

THE FINESSE GAME

Elynuik has all the components necessary for NHL success. His speed and quickness make him a good skater, and added strength on his skates would make him that much better.

He uses his skating in conjunction with his hockey sense to get into scoring position and to drive the net, and his hand skills will net him goals from the tight quarters around the goal. He has soft hands and gets his shot off excellently — hard, accurate and quick. Those are the marks of a scorer. He also has the ability to score from further away; he's dangerous anywhere from the top of the circles in.

He handles the puck well, and he is a creative player without. His skating and sense have given him some good moves, and he knows how to get open — even if he's not in good scoring position. Pat moves the puck effectively, and he passes fairly well to both sides.

Elynuik is also a good defensive player (he's a good forechecker too). He plays his position well in all three zones (credit his sense and skating). He takes his man all the way back to the Jets goal.

THE PHYSICAL GAME

Pat needs help in this part of his game. He doesn't have great strength, and since he's going to drive the net and go to the traffic areas, Elynuik needs strength to shrug off defenders. He also needs the upper body strength to get off his shot when checked.

THE INTANGIBLES

Pat is a good, honest kid, a hard worker who wants to play hockey, is coachable and willing to work hard and learn. He'll need to recuperate from off-season shoulder surgery, and that will be a roadblock to his strength improvement program.

But, now that he knows what he's up against in the NHL, expect Elynuik to do all he can to improve. He has the potential to be a regular 35-40 goal scorer, and he's a key player in the next phase of the Jets' growth.

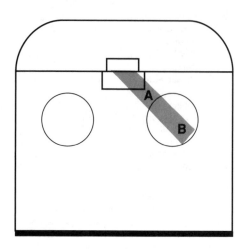

PAUL FENTON

Yrs. of NHL service: 3
Born: Springfield, Mass., USA; December 22, 1959
Position: Left wing
Height: 5-11
Weight: 180
Uniform no.: 11
Shoots: left

Career Statistics:

GP	G	A	TP	PIM
193	43	40	83	97

1988-89 statistics:

GP	G	A	TP	+/-	PIM	PP	SH	GW	GT	S	PCT
80	16	12	28	-16	39	1	0	0	0	135	11.9

LAST SEASON

Acquired from Los Angeles in exchange for Gilles Hamel. Games played total was career high, point totals second highest.

THE FINESSE GAME

Paul succeeds more on brains and determination than anything else. He does have some foot speed, but his rink-length speed and his balance are not exceptional at the NHL level.

His quickness combines with his vision and anticipation to make him a good forechecker, and he can exploit some openings near the net because of that. He'll force some loose pucks around the net through his angle play and quickness, and his hands are good enough to score from in close — which he'll have to do, because he otherwise does not shoot the puck well.

He's not a gifted puckhandler, but he does pursue the puck well. He's very aggressive at getting to the puck but is not as strong when he is on it as you'd like.

THE PHYSICAL GAME

Fenton doesn't have a great deal of size or strength to bring to his physical game, but he packs enough willingness to achieve some success. He goes to the net and takes his lumps there, but Paul isn't strong enough to out-muscle the defense to get his hands free if he's checked, and he's not skilled enough physically to force the defense to lose the puck when checking them.

THE INTANGIBLES

Paul is not a gifted player by any means, but he is a work horse. But he cannot physically contain the opposition and his lack of toughness will always counterbalance his offensive contributions. He would not play regularly on a good team.

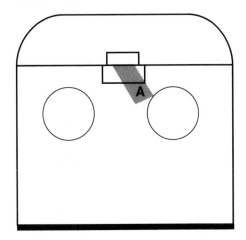

DALE HAWERCHUK

Yrs. of NHL service: 8
Born: Toronto, Ontario, Canada; April 4, 1963
Position: Center
Height: 5-11
Weight: 185
Uniform no.: 10
Shoots: left

Career Statistics:

GP	G	A	TP	PIM
634	353	495	848	408

1988-89 statistics:

GP	G	A	TP	+/-	PIM	PP	SH	GW	GT	S	PCT
75	41	55	96	-30	28	14	3	4	1	239	17.2

LAST SEASON

Led team in goals, points (11th in NHL), shorthanded goals and SOG total. Games played total was career low, goal and assist total third lowest, point total second lowest of career. Plus/minus was club's second worst.

THE FINESSE GAME

There is nothing Dale cannot do finesse-wise. He is a deceptive skater in that he doesn't seem fast, but his long stride gives him power for acceleration and break away speed. Hawerchuk also has excellent one-step quickness which, combined with his exceptional balance, give him exceptional agility and lateral movement. He can move in any direction within a step.

Hawerchuk's superior hockey sense complements his skating, pointing out the openings his quickness can gain. His sense and anticipation are the keys to his playmaking skills, but his excellent hands deserve equal credit. Dale can put the puck anywhere at any time (though he's historically used his right wingers better than his left wingers because the RW is on his forehand). He leads his teammates into the clear excellently.

Hawerchuk can also tantalize the opposition with his stickhandling, but his ability can also be a curse. Dale tends to over-handle the puck and work himself into predicaments that lead to turnovers (one reason for his plus/minus), and his 1-on-1 work often leaves his teammates standing trapped deep in the zone.

He scores from most everywhere in the offensive zone. His great hands give him the ability to control the puck regardless of traffic, proximity to the goal or angle. He's deadly around the net, especially because his excellent eye/hand coordination makes him expert at deflecting the puck.

Simply, his defense stinks. He's a defensive liability, largely because he has a tough time playing within a structured system.

THE PHYSICAL GAME

Dale is not really a physical player, but he does play in the traffic areas. He will initiate some contact in the offensive zone, but just because he's giving and taking hits doesn't mean he likes them. Hawerchuk has a short fuse and he'll lose his temper over close checking, frequently taking stupid retaliatory penalties in the offensive zone.

THE INTANGIBLES

We were wrong last year when we said Hawerchuk's consistency of attendance and effort over his career shows just how much of a character player he is. His attitude is awful and he's a terrible leader, as demonstrated by the way he cut up the organization and his teammates throughout last season.

Hawerchuk believes that everyone else is at fault in Winnipeg and that he's blameless for the club's performance, and that's a strange attitude for a player who coasted through the season (but still got 96 points!) — and to say so publicly and humiliate the organization is certainly a curious thing for a captain to do.

The Jets need to deal with the Hawerchuk situation, because no coach can create a winning atmosphere until it is; remember, by the way, that in our first book three years ago we told you Hawerchuk would get Dan Maloney fired?

If Dale wants to make Winnipeg a winner, fine. If not, it's time to move him.

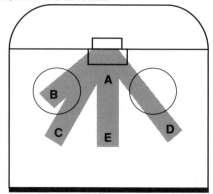

HANNU JARVENPAA

Yrs. of NHL service: 3
Born: Ilves, Finland; May 19, 1963
Position: Right wing
Height: 6-0
Weight: 193
Uniform no.: 23
Shoots: left

Career Statistics:

GP	G	A	TP	PIM
114	11	26	37	83

1988-89 statistics:

GP	G	A	TP	+/-	PIM	PP	SH	GW	GT	S	PCT
53	4	7	11	-14	41	1	0	0	0	27	14.8

LAST SEASON

Games played total was career high, but point totals were career lows.

THE FINESSE GAME

Though Hannu is gifted in the typically European skills of skating (he has good speed and quickness) and puckhandling (he can carry it up the wing), his skills are still marginal at the NHL level. His balance is particularly suspect, and he's apt to fall down a lot when battling for the puck in the corner.

He has good hockey sense and the ability to one-time the puck (valuable on the power play), but his lack of NHL speed prevents him from getting into scoring position or from exploiting the holes.

THE PHYSICAL GAME

Jarvenpaa goes to the corners to fetch the puck, but he can't initiate meaningful contact because he lacks the balance and foot speed to do so. He accepts the physical part of the game, even if he doesn't initiate any part of it himself, and he goes to the front of the net without complaint.

THE INTANGIBLES

He's a worker, but overall Jarvenpaa's skills may just be too marginal for the NHL. And at age 26, he's not going to get any better.

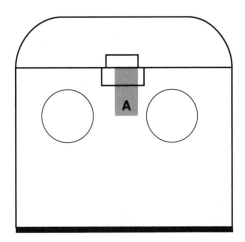

461

BRAD JONES

Yrs. of NHL service: 2
Born: Sterling Heights, Mich., USA; June 26, 1965
Position: Left wing
Height: 6-0
Weight: 180
Uniform no.: 38
Shoots: left

Career Statistics:

GP	G	A	TP	PIM
45	9	10	19	21

1988-89 statistics:

GP	G	A	TP	+/-	PIM	PP	SH	GW	GT	S	PCT
22	6	5	11	0	6	0	1	0	1	25	24.0

LAST SEASON

Games played, goal and point totals were career highs. He shuttled between Winnipeg and Moncton of the American Hockey League.

THE FINESSE GAME

Jones has tremendous skills, with a big if. He could be among the top five fastest skaters in the League — just explosive speed and quickness. He's got the ability to move into openings and to create them as well, driving defensemen off the blue line. He's also a pretty agile player.

Brad also has a tremendous wrist shot, laser-sharp, fast to the net. But what's the if?

If, we're just talking about drills, where Jones can look like the best player on the club. But in games, where he has to think and read, he has a few shortcomings. He's been largely unable to capitalize at the NHL level, losing himself in the pace and tempo of the contest.

THE PHYSICAL GAME

Brad doesn't have the tools for a physical game, and he's not tremendously gifted in this area. His balance and strong stride aid him in collisions by keeping him vertical, and greater upper body strength would help him in battles along the boards and in front of the net.

THE INTANGIBLES

At this stage, Jones doesn't know the NHL game real well. He's okay until he has to demonstrate some guts and drive in game situations, and his desire to address his flaws — and become a better player — is questionable. But the Jets can't afford to give up on a kid who skates like Brad does.

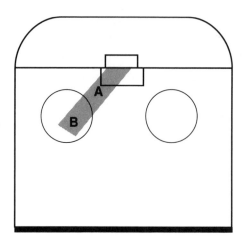

TEPPO NUMMINEN

Yrs. of NHL service: 1
Born: Tampere, Finland; July 3, 1968
Position: Defenseman
Height: 6-1
Weight: 190
Uniform no.: 27
Shoots: right

Career Statistics:

GP	G	A	TP	+/-	PIM	PP	SH	GW	GT	S	PCT
69	1	14	15	-11	36	0	1	0	1	85	1.2

LAST SEASON

First full NHL season. His plus/minus was second best among defensive regulars. He missed eight games with a shoulder injury.

THE FINESSE GAME

Numminen has a fine complement of finesse skills. He's a very good skater, possessing speed, quickness and agility. He's a very mobile player, able to challenge the puck at both blue lines, and he also has the ability to change gears up and down within a stride.

His hockey sense is good and will improve as he continues to become acclimated to the NHL tempo. He passes the puck very well and he can rush with it too, making him a threat to become an attacker — though so far he plays a conservative game.

Teppo can find the open man and make not just the correct play but a great one if given the time. He shoots the puck in stride well.

THE PHYSICAL GAME

As with many first-season Europeans, the physical game last season proved Numminen's Waterloo. He's not developed physically, and he can be knocked off the puck in the corner. He must improve his physical strength in order to improve his NHL play.

THE INTANGIBLES

The first season is an adjustment season for Europeans. Now let's see if Teppo has the mental toughness and desire to do the things necessary for improvement at the NHL level. He's got all the skills; now let's see if he has the guts.

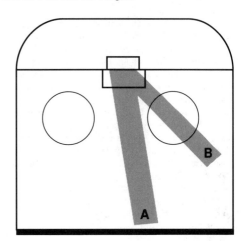

FREDRICK OLAUSSON

Yrs. of NHL service: 3
Born: Vaxsjo, Sweden; October 5, 1966
Position: Defenseman
Height: 6-2
Weight: 200
Uniform no.: 4
Shoots: right

Career statistics:

GP	G	A	T	PIM
185	27	86	113	74

1988-89 statistics:

GP	G	A	TP	+/-	PIM	PP	SH	GW	GT	S	PCT
75	15	47	62	6	32	4	0	1	0	178	8.4

LAST SEASON

Games played, all point totals and PIM marks were career highs. He led Jet defensemen in points (11th overall in NHL), was third on the club in assists and plus/minus (tops on defense in last category).

THE FINESSE GAME

In terms of innate, natural ability Olausson might — *might* — be among the top five players in the League — *that's* how talented he is. He's an exceptional — superior — skater in every area: speed, power, quickness, balance. He meets the play at the Jets blue line to force the puck carrier, and he contains the point at the offensive blue line with his quickness and lateral ability. His skating is so good, that when the Jets want to pick up the tempo of a game they often put Olausson on the wing.

His sense and hand skills are at the same high level. Fredrick is great at getting the puck out of his zone by either passing it or rushing it, and he joins or leads the attack excellently. He easily finds the open man in any situation, and his ability to see the ice is a key to his success in 5-on-5 situations (where he is a better player than teammate Dave Ellett).

Of course, Olausson is also excellent on the power play (where he puts his excellent shot — A 1 MacInnis-hard, fast, low and accurate) because of the extra time and space. He's a penalty-killing natural because of his quickness and sense.

His positional play and transition game are both excellent. All Fredrick needs to improve in his finesse game is his shots-on-goal total — it's way too low for someone with the type of weapon Olausson fires.

THE PHYSICAL GAME

Olausson has the size and strength — and, in general, the willingness — to play a physical game. But he's not consistent in this area, because he's not used to jamming in the corners all the time. The flaw is a mental one of concentration.

Because he doesn't impose himself (and is, instead, imposed upon) Olausson has difficulty bringing his skills to bear in grinding, physical games. He can be taken advantage of because of his lack of aggressiveness.

THE INTANGIBLES

He could become one of the NHL's elite players, but Olausson may not be sticking around. He intends to return to Sweden (perhaps as early as this season if a contract dispute between the Jets and the Swedish Ice Hockey Federation goes in the SIHF's favor). Olausson can't be accused of not being tough enough mentally or emotionally — last fall, he and his wife suffered through the death of a stillborn daughter. But Fredrick (after a brief return home) rejoined the NHL and played his best hockey ever.

His presence, therefore, is the only intangible. His absence, however, would be devastating for the Jets.

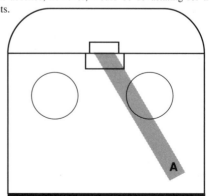

ELDON "POKEY" REDDICK

Yrs. of NHL service: 3
Born: Halifax, N.S., Canada; October 6, 1964
Position: Goaltender
Height: 5-8
Weight: 170
Uniform no.: 33
Catches: left

Career Statistics:

GP	MINS	G	SO	AVG	A	PIM
117	6,358	395	1	3.73	1	20

1988-89 statistics:

GP	MINS	AVG	W	L	T	SO	GA	SA	SAPCT	PIM
41	2,109	4.10	11	17	7	0	144	1,132	.872	6

LAST SEASON

Games played total was second highest of three seasons. He led all Winnipeg goalies in games and minutes played.

THE PHYSICAL GAME

Reddick is by and large a standup goaltender, though he does not challenge the shooter as often as one might expect from a standup goalie. He plays his angles fairly well but is rarely further out of the net than the top of his crease.

He works from a deep crouch, in order to see around players rather than over them, and he picks up the flight of the puck fairly well. He complements his standup play with very quick feet, and he is also quick to regain his feet after going to the ice, though he is not always balanced and back in his stance as quickly.

Reddick has had some trouble with his style because smart shooters go right over his shoulders and past his feet due to his depth in the net. He is also weak at controlling rebounds from his blocker saves.

He leaves the net to retrieve the puck stopping the puck and handing it off to the defensemen, but he doesn't handle or move it especially well. Reddick does, however, communicate well with his defensemen, so they aren't flying blind.

THE MENTAL GAME

Reddick is a very cool customer, akin to — but not in the same class as — Edmonton's Grant Fuhr. He just stands in the net and does his job, regardless of circumstance or goals previously allowed — good or bad.

He can perhaps be too nonchalant, but generally he seems to be poised and confident, concentration intact.

THE INTANGIBLES

Consistency of effort remains the big question mark. Reddick played well at the start of 1988-89, played poorly from December until the end of March, and then played very well in his last two games. But he hasn't improved his game at the NHL level, and he just might not be talented enough to do so.

DOUG SMAIL

Yrs. of NHL service: 9
Born: Moose Jaw, Sask., Canada; September 2, 1957
Position: Left wing
Height: 5-9
Weight: 175
Uniform no.: 9
Shoots: left

Career Statistics:

GP	G	A	TP	PIM
597	163	182	345	393

1988-89 statistics:

GP	G	A	TP	+/-	PIM	PP	SH	GW	GT	S	PCT
47	14	15	29	12	52	0	2	0	0	68	20.6

LAST SEASON

Games played total was second lowest of career, lowest since rookie season (leg injury, seven games; broken cheekbone). Plus/minus was club's second best.

THE FINESSE GAME

Smail is a phenomenally quick skater, maybe the quickest in the NHL. Doug makes that skill more important by also having rink-length speed and good hockey sense, (and he makes his speed and quickness more effective by always showing speeds other than "Full" — that makes him unpredictable, a particular advantage when killing penalties) so that he can be a checker, an excellent penalty killer, and an offensive contributor.

His anticipation and quickness will get him the loose pucks that his checking helps create, and he can convert those loose pucks to the tune of 20 goals a season.

His hand skills are otherwise not at the level of his skating skill. He's not a great puckhandler, but Smail controls the puck while in motion and can get the puck to his teammates if given ample opportunity — but he won't thread needles with his passes. He likes to stutter-step just over the blue line to get the defense committed, and then jump in another direction, when he carries the puck.

THE PHYSICAL GAME

Doug plays bigger than his size, courtesy of his surprising strength. He can take the body against bigger opponents along the boards and gain the puck, and then his quickness gets him away from the boards before the opposition can recover. He's very successful with those hit-and-run missions and has to be, because he'll get out-muscled if trapped.

Doug shows a proficiency in using his stick to punish the opposition.

THE INTANGIBLES

The team misses Smail when he's out of the lineup, because his skating could tilt many games in favor of the Jets. He's a very dedicated athlete (working hard to always be in great condition), and he makes the most of everything his skill has to offer.

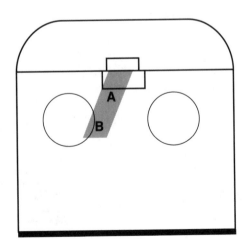

THOMAS STEEN

Yrs. of NHL service: 8
Born: Tocksmark, Sweden; June 8, 1960
Position: Center
Height: 5-10
Weight: 195
Uniform no.: 25
Shoots: left

Career Statistics:

GP	G	A	TP	PIM
614	168	340	508	519

1988-89 statistics:

GP	G	A	TP	+/-	PIM	PP	SH	GW	GT	S	PCT
80	27	61	88	14	80	9	1	2	1	173	15.6

LAST SEASON

Played 80 games for first time in career. All point totals were career highs. Finished second on the club in points, first in assists and tops in plus/minus.

THE FINESSE GAME

Thomas is a greatly skilled player. He's an excellent skater with speed, quickness and balance, and those assets turn him into an exceptionally agile player; he has great one-step quickness and lateral movement, and those traits are big reasons why he's a dynamic two-way center.

Steen's hockey sense matches his skating ability. He reads the play very well both defensively and offensively. As a checker, he sees the openings and cuts for them to close them, while he has the ability offensively to lead his teammates to those openings.

Steen is a talented puckhandler, and his sense and patience are the reasons why; he uses this skill creatively, opening space for his teammates. He also passes well to both sides, and Steen has a very good shot — which he doesn't use often enough.

His skills — especially his quickness and sense — make him dangerous near the net and in both specialty team situations. He is also an excellent and conscientious two-way player. To be plus-14 on a club that was minus-55 is a tremendous show of ability.

THE PHYSICAL GAME

Steen excels in the physical part of the game, more through desire and determination than through sheer size and strength. He does have good strength and can wear down an opponent with his persistent hitting. Though breaking down one European stereotype through his willing physicality, Steen reinforces another by being very mean with his stick.

THE INTANGIBLES

If he had a good set of wingers, Thomas could chase 100 points and be a plus player all the time. He's Winnipeg's best all-around player, bar none, and he can be used in any situation in any position (including defense). The Jets would be in real trouble without Steen, who is a true team leader.

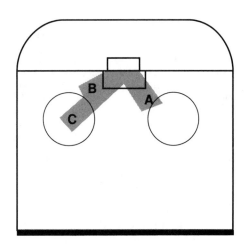

467

PETER TAGLIANETTI

Yrs. of NHL service: 3
Born: Framingham, Mass., USA; August 15, 1963
Position: Defenseman
Height: 6-2
Weight: 200
Uniform no.: 32
Shoots: left

Career Statistics:

GP	G	A	TP	PIM
158	7	31	38	468

1988-89 statistics:

GP	G	A	TP	+/-	PIM	PP	SH	GW	GT	S	PCT
66	1	14	15	-23	226	1	0	0	0	72	1.4

LAST SEASON

Games played and all point totals fell in second full NHL season, but PIM total was career high (second highest on club, tops among defensemen). His plus/minus was the defense's second worst.

THE FINESSE GAME

Taglianetti is not a tremendously gifted finesse player, but that's okay because his physical play makes up for that. He's an average skater forward and back, but he's not quick or balanced enough to have the lateral movement necessary to challenge the puck at either blue line. He's going to have to play positional defense and force the puck wide of the net. Otherwise, a speedy forward can get him turned and out-race him to the net.

He can make a breakout pass, but his plays are going to have to strictly be of the up-the-boards-and-out variety. Anything fancy, any extra time taken in making plays, and Peter is going to be in trouble. Taglianetti can carry the puck ahead of him, but he's not a rushing defenseman. He tends to hold the puck too long when he does carry it and misses the opportunity to take advantage of open teammates.

He is not an offensive force, but will join the play at the offensive blue line and score some goals from the point with a good low slap shot (he'll see occasional power-play time because of that shot).

He's a lefthanded shot playing right defense, so Peter might be better off on the left side — that way, the entire ice surface would be on his forehand and he could take the puck off the boards better. Right now he has to take the puck off the boards on his backhand, and that gives him a little trouble.

THE PHYSICAL GAME

Peter is a very strong physical player, and his toughness in front of the net and in the corners makes up for the lack of same by teammates Dave Ellett and Fredrick Olausson. Taglianetti enjoys a physical game and is very aggressive (as his PIM total indicates). He hits hard along the boards (but can sometimes be knocked off the puck because of his high center of gravity) and certainly isn't afraid to back up his physical play with his fists if need be.

THE INTANGIBLES

He's a tough competitor who plays hard. Peter is a great worker and team guy who doesn't have great skills but plays solid defense. He's important to the Jets for that reason.

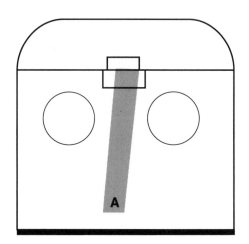

INDEX OF
PLAYERS

Acton, Keith, 296
Adams, Greg C., 408
Adams, Greg, 407
Allison, Mike, 170
Anderson, Glenn, 124
Anderson, John, 147
Anderson, Perry, 223
Andreychuk, Dave, 34
Archibald, David, 192
Arniel, Scott, 35
Ashton, Brent, 449

Babych, Dave, 148
Barber, Don, 193
Barr, Dave, 100
Barrasso, Tom, 318
Bassen, Bob, 78
Baumgartner, Ken, 171
Beaupre, Don , 430
Bellows, Brian, 194
Benning, Brian,364
Benning, Jim, 409
Berezan, Perry, 195
Bergevin, Marc, 253
Berry, Brad, 450
Berthiaume, Daniel, 451
Bester, Allan, 386
Beukeboom, Jeff, 125
Bodger, Doug, 36
Boschman, Laurie,452
Bourque, Phil, 319
Bourque, Ray, 13
Bozek, Steve, 410
Bradley, Brian, 411
Brickley, Andy, 14

Bridgman, Mel, 412
Brooke, Bob, 196
Broten, Aaron, 234
Broten, Neal, 197
Brown, Dave, 126
Brown, Doug, 235
Brown, Jeff, 343
Brown, Keith, 79
Brown, Rob, 320
Bruce, David,413
Buchberger, Kelly, 127
Bullard, Mike, 297
Burke, Sean, 236
Burr, Shawn, 102
Burridge, Randy, 15
Buskas, Rod, 321
Butcher, Garth, 414
Byers, Lyndon, 16

Callander, Jock, 322
Carbonneau, Guy, 213
Carkner, Terry, 298
Carlyle, Randy, 453
Carpenter, Bobby, 17
Carson, Jimmy, 128
Casey, Jon, 198
Caulfield, Jay, 323
Cavallini, Gino, 365
Cavallini, Paul, 366
Chabot, John, 103
Chambers, Shawn, 199
Chelios, Chris, 214
Chevrier, Alain, 80
Chiasson, Steve, 104
Christian, Dave, 431

Chychrun, Jeff, 299
Ciccarelli, Dino, 432
Cirella, Joe, 344
Clark, Wendel, 387
Cloutier, Jacques, 37
Coffey, Paul, 325
Corson, Shayne, 215
Cote, Alain, 345
Cote, Sylvain, 149
Courtnall, Geoff, 433
Courtnall, Russ, 216
Craven, Murray, 300
Creighton, Adam, 81
Crossman, Doug, 254
Crowder , Keith, 18
Cullen, John, 324
Cunneyworth, Randy, 454

Dahlen, Ulf, 275
Dalgarno, Brad, 255
Damphousse, Vincent, 388
Daneyko, Ken, 237
Daoust, Dan, 389
Deblois, Lucien, 346
Degray, Dale, 172
Diduck, Gerald, 256
Dineen, Gord, 326
Dineen, Kevin, 150
Donnelly, Gord, 455
Driver, Bruce, 238
Duchesne, Gaitan, 200
Duchesne, Steve, 173
Duguay, Ron, 174
Duncan, Iain, 456
Dykstra, Steve, 327

Eklund, Per-Erik, 301
Ellett, Dave, 457
Elynuik, Pat, 458
Erixon, Jan, 276
Errey, Bob, 328
Evason, Dean, 151
Ewen, Todd, 367

Federko, Bernie, 101
Fenton, Paul, 459
Fergus, Tom, 390
Ferraro, Ray, 152
Finn, Steven, 347
Fitzpatrick, Mark, 257
Flatley, Pat, 258
Fleury, Theoren, 57
Foligno, Mike, 38
Fortier, Marc, 348
Fox, Jim, 175
Franceschetti, Lou, 434
Francis, Ron, 153
Fraser, Curt, 201
Froese, Bob, 277
Frycer, Miroslav, 129
Fuhr, Grant, 130

Gagner, Dave, 202
Gainey, Bob, 217
Gallant, Gerard, 105
Galley, Garry, 19
Gartner, Mike, 203
Gavin, Stewart, 204
Gilbert, Greg, 82
Giles, Curt, 205
Gilhen, Randy, 329
Gill, Todd, 391
Gillis, Paul, 349
Gilmour, Doug, 58
Gosselin, Mario, 176
Gould, Bob, 435
Goulet, Michel, 350
Graham, Dirk, 83
Granato, Tony, 278
Graves, Adam, 106
Green, Rick, 218
Gregg, Randy, 131
Greschner, Ron, 279
Gretzky, Wayne, 177
Gronstand, Jari, 351
Gustafsson, Bengt, 436

Habscheid, Marc, 107
Hackett, Jeff, 259
Hanlon, Glen, 108
Hannan, Dave, 330
Hardy, Mark, 280
Hartman, Mike, 39
Hatcher, Kevin, 437
Hawerchuk, Dale, 460
Hawgood, Greg, 20
Hayward, Brian, 219
Healy, Glen, 178
Hextall, Ron, 302
Higgins, Tim, 109
Hillier, Randy, 331
Hogue, Benoit, 40
Houda, Doug, 110
Housley, Phil, 41
Howe, Mark, 303
Hrkac, Tony, 368
Hrudy, Kelly, 179
Huddy, Charlie, 132
Hull, Brett, 369
Hull, Jody, 154
Hunter, Dale, 438
Hunter, Dave, 133
Hunter, Mark, 59
Hunter, Tim, 60

Iafrate, Al, 392
Ihnacak, Peter, 393

Jackson, Jeff, 352
Janney, Craig, 21
Jarvenpaa, Hannu, 461
Jarvi, Irro, 353
Jennings, Grant, 155
Johansson, Calle, 439
Johnson, Jim, 322
Johnson, Mark, 239
Johnston, Greg, 22
Jones, Brad, 462
Jonsson, Tomas, 134
Joyce, Bob, 23

Kasper, Steve, 180
Keane, Mike, 220
Kennedy, Dean, 181
Kerr, Alan, 260
Kerr, Tim, 304
King, Derek, 261

Kisio, Kelly, 281
Klima, Petr, 111
Kocur, Joe, 112
Konroyd, Steve, 84
Kordic, John, 394
Korn, Jim, 240
Kotsopoulos, Chris, 395
Krupp, Uwe, 42
Krushelnyski, Mike, 182
Kurri, Jari, 135
Kurvers, Tom, 241
Kyte, Jim, 333

Lacombe, Norm, 136
Ladoceur, Randy, 156
LaFleur, Guy, 282
Lafontaine, Pat, 262
Laidlaw, Tom, 183
Lalor, Mike, 370
Lambert, Lane, 354
Langway, Rod, 440
Larmer, Steve, 85
Larson, Reed, 206
Lauer, Brad, 263
Laughlin, Craig, 396
Lawton, Brian, 157
Leach, Stephen, 441
Ledyard, Grant, 43
Leeman, Gary, 397
Leetch, Brian, 283
Lemelin, Reggie, 24
Lemieux, Claude, 221
Lemieux, Mario, 334
Leschyshyn, Curtis, 355
Lidster, Doug, 415
Linden, Trevor, 416
Linseman, Ken, 25
Liut, Mike, 158
Loiselle, Claude, 356
Loney, Troy, 336
Lowe, Kevin, 137
Ludwig, Craig, 222

MacDermid, Paul, 159
MacInnis, Al, 61
MacIver, Norm, 160
MacLean, John, 242
MacLean, Paul, 371
MacLellan, Brian, 62
Macoun, Jamie, 63

MacTavish, Craig, 138
Maguire, Kevin, 44
Makela, Mikko, 264
Malarchuk, Clint, 45
Maloney, Don, 161
Manson, Dave, 86
Marois, Dan, 398
Marois, Mario, 357
Marsh, Brad, 399
McBain, Andrew, 337
McBean, Wayne, 265
McClelland, Kevin, 139
McCrimmon, Brad, 64
McDonald, Lanny, 65
McGill, Bob, 87
McKegney, Tony, 113
McLean, Kirk, 417
McPhee, Mike, 223
McRae, Basil, 207
McSorley, Marty, 184
Meagher, Rick, 372
Mellanby, Scott, 305
Melnyk, Larry, 418
Messier, Mark, 140
Millen, Greg, 373
Miller, Jay, 185
Miller, Kelly, 442
Moller, Randy, 358
Momessa, Sergio, 374
Moog, Andy, 26
Mullen, Brian, 284
Mullen, Joe, 66
Muller, Kirk, 243
Muni, Craig, 141
Murphy, Gord, 306
Murphy, Larry, 208
Murray, Bob, 88
Murray, Troy, 89
Murzyn, Dana, 67
Musil, Frantisek, 209

Napier, Mark, 46
Naslund, Mats, 224
Natress, Ric, 68
Neely, Cam, 27
Neufeld, Ray, 28
Nicholls, Bernie, 186
Nieuwendyk, Joe, 69
Nilan, Chris, 285
Nill, Jim, 114

Nordmark, Robert, 419
Norton, Jeff, 266
Norwood, Lee, 115
Numminen, Teppo, 463
Nylund, Gary, 267

O'Callahan, Jack, 244
O'Connell, Mike, 116
Oates, Adam, 375
Ogrodnick, John, 286
Olausson, Fredrick, 464
Olczyk, Ed, 400
Osborne, Mark, 401
Otto, Joel, 70

Pang, Darren, 90
Parker, Jeff, 47
Paslawski, Greg, 376
Patrick, James, 287
Patterson, Colin, 71
Pedersen, Allen, 29
Pederson, Barry, 420
Peeters, Pete, 307
Peplinski, Jim, 72
Peterson, Brent, 162
Petit, Michel, 288
Picard, Robert, 359
Pilon, Richard, 268
Pivonka, Michal, 443
Playfair, Larry, 48
Poddubny, Walt, 245
Poeschek, Rudy, 289
Poulin, Dave, 308
Presley, Wayne, 91
Propp, Brian, 309
Puppa, Daren, 49

Qenneville, Joel, 163
Quinn, Dan, 338

Raglan, Herb, 377
Ramage, Rob, 402
Ramsey, Mike, 50
Ranford, Bill, 142
Reddick, Eldon "Pokey", 465
Reid, Dave, 403
Reinhart, Paul, 421
Richardson, Luke, 404
Richer, Stephane, 225
Richter, Dave, 378

Ridley, Mike, 444
Riendeau, Vincent, 379
Roberts, Gary, 73
Roberts, Gordie, 380
Robertson, Torrie, 117
Robinson, Larry, 226
Robitaille, Luc, 187
Roenick, Jeremy, 92
Ronning, Cliff, 381
Rouse, Bob, 445
Roy, Patrick, 227
Ruff, Lindy, 290
Ruutu, Christian, 51

Sakic, Joe, 360
Salming, Borje, 118
Samuelsson, Kjell, 310
Samuelsson, Ulf, 164
Sandlak, Jim, 422
Sandstrom, Tomas, 291
Savard, Denis, 93
Shanahan, Brendan, 246
Shannon, Darryl, 405
Sharples, Jeff, 119
Shaw, David, 292
Sheehy, Neil, 446
Sheppard, Ray, 52
Sidorkiewicz, Peter, 165
Simpson, Craig, 143
Sinisalo, Ilkka, 311
Siren, Ville, 210
Skriko, Petri, 423
Skrudland, Brian, 228
Smail, Doug, 466
Smith, Bobby, 229
Smith, Derrick, 312
Smith, Steve, 144
Smyl, Stan, 424
Snepsts, Harold, 425
Stastny, Peter, 361
Steen, Thomas, 467
Stefan, Greg, 120
Stevens, Kevin, 339
Stevens, Scott, 447
Sundstrom, Patrick, 248
Sundstrom, Peter, 247
Suter, Gary, 74
Sutter, Brent, 269
Sutter, Duane, 94
Sutter, Rich, 426

Sutter, Ron, 313
Svoboda, Petr, 230
Sweeney, Bob, 30

Taglianetti, Peter, 468
Takko, Kari, 211
Tanti, Tony, 427
Taylor, Dave, 188
Thelven, Michael, 31
Thomas, Steve, 95
Tikkanen, Esa, 145
Tilley, Tom, 382
Tippett, Dave, 166
Tocchet, Rick, 314
Tonelli, John, 189
Trottier, Bryan, 270
Tucker, John, 53

Tugnutt, Ron, 362
Turgeon, Pierre, 54
Turgeon, Sylvain, 249
Tuttle, Steve, 383

Vaive, Rick, 55
Vanbiesbrouck, John, 293
Velischek, Randy, 250
Verbeek, Pat, 167
Vernon, Mike, 75
Vincelette, Dan, 96
Volek, David, 271
Vukota, Mick, 272

Walter, Ryan, 231
Wamsley, Rick, 76
Watters, Tim, 190

Weeks, Steve, 428
Wells, Jay, 315
Wesley, Glen, 32
Wilson, Carey, 294
Wilson, Doug, 97
Wolanin, Craig, 251
Wood, Randy, 273
Wregget, Ken, 316

Yawney, Trent, 98
Young, Scott, 168
Young, Wendell, 340
Yzerman, Steve, 121

Zalapski, Zarley, 341
Zezel, Peter, 384
Zombo, Rick, 122